Multimedia Technology
and Applications

Springer

Berlin
Heidelberg
New York
Barcelona
Budapest
Hong Kong
London
Milan
Paris
Santa Clara
Singapore
Tokyo

Multimedia Technology
and Applications

Vincent W. S. Chow (Ed.)

Springer

Vincent W.S. Chow
School of Business
Hong Kong Baptist University
Kowloon Tong
Hong Kong

ISBN 981-3083-16-6

© Springer-Verlag Singapore Pte. Ltd. 1997
Printed in Singapore

The publisher makes no representation, express or implied, with regard to the accuracy of the information contained in this book and cannot accept any legal responsibility or liability for any errors or omissions that may be made.

Typesetting: Camera-ready by editor
5 4 3 2 1 0

Preface

With the help of technological advancement and IT innovation, the development of multimedia technology has evolved from an experimental stage to practical applications in industry. Although multimedia research and applications are well established, its revolution has changed in such a rapid pace that yesterday's multimedia technology is obsolete/outdated. The objective of this book is to serve as a bridge to update our knowledge in this area. Most, if not all, of the papers in this book are addressing the applications of multimedia in business.

A total of 61 papers selected from 22 countries are included in this book, all of these papers were presented at the *International Conference on Multimedia Technology and Management* that was held in Dec 11-14, 1996 at the Hong Kong Baptist University, Hong Kong. These papers covered a widely range of multimedia applications. In this book, we clustered these papers in according to the nature of their area, and are hosted in one the following 8 topics: hypertext/hypermedia, distributed multimedia, synchronization & image synthesis, system development, multimedia education, multimedia training, telecommunications & technology, and business applications. In order to make it more easy reading for all readers, an introductory paper entitled "Multimedia at work" is further added at the beginning of this book. I hope that this book would enrich the knowledge of all readers in the use of multimedia technology.

Acknowledgements
I am grateful to each of the parties involved in organizing and participating the *International Conference on Multimedia Technology and Management*, especially to Mrs Vivienne WM Luk, Director of The Wing Lung Bank International Institute for Business Development (IIBD) of Hong Kong Baptist University. Finally, my thanks to the two of my graduate students, Ms Kin Y. Choi and Mr King H. Lui, and Ms Cindy ML Leung for their patience and valuable time invested in preparing the conference and the book. Resource allocation from the School of Business at the HKBU is also highly appreciated.

Wing S. Chow
Hong Kong Baptist University, 1996

Contents

PART 4:   SYNCHRONIZATION & IMAGE SYNTHESIS

PART 5:   SYSTEMS DEVELOPMENT

PART 7:   MULTIMEDIA TRAINING

PART 8: TELECOMMUNICATIONS & TECHNOLOGY

PART 9:   BUSINESS APPLICATIONS

PART 1

INTRODUCTION

1.1

MULTIMEDIA AT WORK

Wing S. Chow, Kin Y. Choi and King H. Lui
Hong Kong Baptist University, Hong Kong

This paper presents the general concept of multimedia in term of its development, technology and assembling a MPC system. A conclusive remark on the impact of multimedia to our future life style is also provided.

1.0   Introduction

The ways of using personal computers (PC) have changed significantly since the IBM introduced it in early eighties. With the rapid growth of computer technology, the effective use of PCs is no longer a single component issue. It is now a general trend that PCs are used in conjunction with a number of different media. The effective use of these media altered the facet of PC in terms of their visual display, secondary data storage and retrieval, and data interchange with our trading partners. A PC that composed of a number of different media may refer as an Multimedia PC (MPC) system.

The term 'Multimedia' is not strictly delineated within a single definition. A board sense of its definition may refer as the integration of different communication media in a PC which generates the effect of animation, text, graphics, videos and audio within a computer platform. These media are highly interactive. Users gain a total control in retrieving, displaying and exchanging information in an MPC. The applications of MPC are now widely adopted in the business arena such as desktop publishing, animation production, audio and video production.

This book provides an extensive collection of multimedia applications in businesses. The objective of this paper is thus not to further review another application; instead we offer readers a different prospectus of MPC by reviewing the concept of its development, technology and "making it work". In the next section, the development of multimedia is first reviewed, followed by its technology and MPC-at-work in the subsequent sections. A conclusion is also provided in the last section.

2.0   Multimedia development

Historically, there was a little or even no standardization among the early stage of multimedia applications. This phenomenon poses a threat to software development in a way that the issues of compatibility and interchangeability of information and data between systems cannot be achieved. It was not until in 1990 that this issue was addressed by the Multimedia Marketing Council, which formed by a group of commercial companies, and proposed the first MPC system configuration which known as MPC Level 1 system (Jeffcoate, 1995).

The general idea of the first MPC configuration ensures that the specification works and conforms to the Application Programming Interfaces (API) that described in the programmers reference of Microsoft Windows Software Development Kit (SDK). Any system configuration which matches to this specification is then qualified to earn a label of an MPC logo. The developmental stage of MPC is now progressed to the level 3. Table 1 reviews the configuration of MPC Level 1 to MPC Level 3.

Table 1: The development stage of MPC standards

System/	MPC Level 1	MPC Level 2	MPC Level 3
PC systems	386	486	Pentinum 75 MHz
RAM	2MB	4MB	8 MB
CD ROM	150K	3000K	540 MB
Data retrieval	1000 ms	400 ms	250 ms
Audio	CD-Audio	CD-Audio, CD	CD-I
Sound card	8-bit	Multisession	16-bit
Video	Video	16-bit sound	MPEG1

The MPC technology is not only popularly adopted in different business settings such as in the area of administrative work, staff training, and conducting meeting, it further extends to the entertainment such as video games, listening to music and even watching video or TV programs. In the next section, we will review the distinctive features of MPC that makes it overwhelmingly to all users.

3.0   Multimedia technology

The revolution on the use of computers has changed from the only text-based input/output source to a more innovative features. Below we offer readers some of extra technology that appeared in an MPC system.

Images. An MPC enables to handle images of art works that inputted from either the clip art work or scanned images. Further refinement work can be carried out to these art works by the use of conjunctive software such as Adobe, Photoshop, and CorelDraw. Recently, these images can further be obtained by the use of a digital camera. Since the storage of these images requires a lot of bytes of space, a compressed format is usually adopted. Some of the most common compressed format includes TIFF (Tagged Image File Format), JPEG (Joint Photographic Experts Group), and GIF (Graphics Interchange Format).

Audio. Another feature of an MPC is to process the audio effect as an input or output source. To produce digital sound, you should have a sound card with microphone, sound recorder, and/or media player software. You also need to have a sound card and speakers to hear the sound. The input source can then be converted into digital signal and stored onto the secondary storage such as harddisk or compact disk (CD). With multimedia technology, an MPC system can produce musical sound like piano and guitar. Musical Instrument Digital Interface (MIDI) is generally regarded as industry standard for computer-based music generation.

Video. One of the important features of an MPC is its capability to produce video effect. However, the use of video effect requires a large storage space. Accordingly, the development of compression standards is again essential. The most widely adopted industry standard in video is called Moving Picture Experts Group (MPEG), developed in 1988, defined the standards of compression and decompression of motion video with digital audio. Now, numerous manufacturers adhere to this standard.

4.0   MPC at work

To put an MPC system at work, essential media include a motherboard, memory, floppy, secondary storage devices, controller, case, power supply, keyboard, monitor, and adapters. Constructing an MPC system is not a simple task, some additional hardware may be needed. As suggested by Pilgrim (1994) that these additional media may include modems, FAX boards, scanners, input/out boards, CD-ROM, sound boards, video camera, loudspeakers, video camera and microphones are the common ones. Readers who interested in learning the functions of these media can refer to

Pilgrim (1994) for further details. In this section, we attempt to offer a set of procedures for organizing and acquiring a proper set of MPC system. Since some of basic configurations of an MPC system were already reviewed in Table 1, we also intent that no duplication afford is made here.

Step 1. Getting a basic computer system. Users are advised to follow an acquisition of PC configuration from Table 1. At present, it is likely that a Pentinum system is acquired.

Step 2. Adding expansion boards. Some expansion boards like sound board, a SCSI-2 board, a video capture board could be chosen if your MPC system intends to include these functions. For a high-performance, a 16-bit board is preferred.

Step 3. Checking board compatibility. You are strongly recommended to ensure that all media attached to your MPC are compatible, which including the new boards and the computer itself, external/internal devices like microphones, speakers, video sources, fax/modem, scanner, printer, CD-ROM etc., and together with the application/system software. Configuring each media well before integrating all of them altogether is highly recommended.

Step 4. Designing a work area of MPC. Ergonomics is an important issue relates to a success MPC. The location of furniture, the design of lighting, or the condition of air will impact to the long hours of use of an MPC system. A layout plan for the multimedia workstation is extremely crucial element prior to a vast capital investment.

Step 5. Guaranteeing reliable power. When finishing the integration of hardware, other items such as power source should not be neglected.

Step 6. Installing software. Software installation could be explained in details in each program's documentation. Special attention should be paid to programs on modifying CONFIG.SYS and AUTOEXEC.BAT files as it may cause previously installed software to stop working. Making a backup for all programs is a most useful and preventive method.

Step 7. Testing the final assembly. When the hardware and software are installed, test it out as thoroughly as possible. Bugs and programming mistakes are commonly encountered from software side. Thus, confirmation of a clear signal from the main application program is a must.

Step 8. Getting help when needed. First, manuals are the good sources of help. If the documentation cannot render the solution of your problems, then look at the README or READ.ME file supplied with the program. If the problems cannot be solved, it is time to get help from company's help line.

5.0   Conclusion

Gaining a full understanding on the use and development of Multimedia technology is a relative important issue to general publics and also to the Information Systems practitioners. For the latter case, the reason is being that an MPC produces a great impact to the way in which information systems are used at work in the future. Most of the features which described in MPC are generally found in a type of information systems known as Executive Information System. It is, therefore, our believe that the future development of information systems would definitely greatly involve with the use of multimedia in, particularly, the system development phase. With the help of multimedia, the future information systems become even more end-user friendliness. Migrating the use of multimedia to our daily life should not be underestimated. We will see that more multimedia functions would enter our home shortly, good examples of such applications are the use of Internet and the launching of Video-on-demand service in our society. Therefore, we recommend that everyone should get involve with the use and development of multimedia. Like it or not, our future life style cannot be voided on the use of multimedia technology.

References:

1. Jeffcoate, Judith (1995), Multimedia in Practice: Technology and Applications, Prentice Hall, U.S.A.
2. Pilgrim, Aubrey (1994), *Build Your Own Multimedia PC*, McGraw-Hill, USA.

PART 2

HYPERTEXT/HYPERMEDIA

2.1

HYPERMEDIA DOCUMENTS: A JOURNEY THROUGH WORKING MODELS

Peter Ward and Roger Browne
University of Leeds, UK

This paper will look at an evolutionary sequence of experimental prototypes of workstation-based hypermedia systems leading to a working model of a Windows-based multimedia document browser. The browser provides a mechanism for bridging the gap between on-line web access on the internet, and the off-line viewing and distribution of multimedia documents on Floppy Disk and CD-ROM.

1.0   Introduction

The extraordinary development of the World-Wide-Web is highlighting a number of basic issues which are recognised as requirements for "hypermedia-in-the large" systems ie multiuser, browsable and linkable documents, distributed on the network.   These include "getting lost in hyperspace" and the need for better mechanisms for navigation and querying in large, richly-linked and loosely organised multimedia resources. The "distributed digital multimedia document" has a variety of potential applications - including computer-supported cooperative working, publishing, marketing, on-line product support, and teaching and learning.   Its development can be regarded as a generic component of any computer-based information system, and brings together research from the arenas of hypertext, databases, hypermedia, interfaces and HCI, operating systems and telematics.

In the first part of the paper ideas about hypertext, hypermedia and the digital distributed multimedia document will be introduced. In the second part, there is an account of a series of experimental models on Unix workstations and the features of a new multimedia browser for the Windows PC.   This will be followed in the third part by a discussion of the trends in hypermedia systems development, and an approach to the evolution of a new generation of software - designed to meet user needs, including for distributed multimedia documents. Finally, the current state of evolution of the multimedia document browser will be placed into the context of bridging the gap between on-line internet and off-line user access. The evaluation of this multimedia browser is part of a programme of applied research being conducted by the IMP Unit at the University of Leeds. Conceptually, this research is concerned with the design of information modelling tools, user-driven rapid application development, and the evolution of working models of hypermedia systems employing object-oriented technology. The applied research element has focused on interface design and strategies for developing mechanisms for the organisation, the distribution and the enabling of access to distributed multimedia information resources. A series of experimental prototypes have been tested in a programme of user-driven case studies in a variety of domains.

We believe that there is a need for simpler interfaces and the facilitation of information access, modelling and communication mechanisms for non-technical "end-users". Many users find access to the internet frustrating because of the complexity of the available technology and tools, and because in fact very high bandwidth is necessary for satisfactory access and delivery of high quality materials and for the support of the required interactivity. There are opportunities for the exploitation of alternative and parallel mechanisms of distribution, including CD-ROM, which provide smaller more contained hypermedia environments. The simple idea is that components can be developed that can bridge the gap between internet and off-line multimedia materials distributed in a document format - both in terms of complexity and efficiency - providing for alternative and perhaps simpler means for access and organisation.

The bigger idea is that these components can be developed within a larger digital multimedia delivery and interaction framework - which is a distributed object-oriented model; which has a generic hypermedia and electronic document model, which can be incrementally enhanced through evolutionary user-driven development; and which can accomodate other best-of-breed components providing specilaised services.

2.0 A series of experimental models on UNIX and a new multimedia browser for the Windows PC

2.1 Applied research - the IMP series of prototypes

A series of experimental prototype hypermedia tools have been deployed in a programme of applied research by the IMP Unit at the University of Leeds. These include the Media Language (Parrott and Ward 1993) and The Garden Framework and models of delivering multimedia information have been evaluated in a series of case studies in a range of domains (see Ward 1996a). The work has focused on the user-driven development of working models of information modelling tools and applications, the employment of object-oriented technology in rapid application development, and the evolution of the "distributed digital multimedia document"

(Ward 1995). The technical strategy was open systems, client-server multiuser computing on the network, employing the Unix/X11 operating system and distributed display model. Object-oriented technology (including the Eiffel object-oriented programming language; Meyer 1992) was employed for portability and evolution of application code. These developments have been essentially concerned with "authoring"/"organising" and "publishing"/"distributing", but application to marketing and education has been explored.

2.2   A New Example : Paris Multimedia Browser

We have been taking part in the development and testing of a new, windows-based multimedia browser (called "Paris"), which is focused on non-computer literate users wanting simple, high quality access to the new generation of electronic multimedia documents on the desk-top and portable PC's, and which provides a simple mechanism for distributing documents on Floppy Disk and CD-ROM. It employs the HTML-standard for document mark-up and distribution. It has been designed with a simple user interface - borrowing features from the experimental workstation prototypes Media Language and the Garden Framework - focusing on the more immediate needs of novice end-users wanting easy access to information who are concerned with the content not the the process.

The idea is to 'bridge the gap' between more the more sophisticated on-line telematic access and distribution of multimedia documents, and a simpler off-line mechanisms. As an alternative to richer interfaces and slower and less reliable access - the multimedia browser aims to exploit a need of non-technical users for simple-to-use attractive access to multimedia materials and to accomodate rich high quality images and embedded audiovisual elements and provide high levels of interactivity.

In keeping with an appeal to non-technical novice users, no installation as such of the Paris browser is required. It doesn't need or touch the hard disk. The browser program is distributed with the document materials and with no installation necessary, the end-user is just one click away from content. The browser can be integrated with other applications eg launching standard Windows applications such as a Calculator, Word Processor, or Spreadsheet, Special Animations etc. and the browser can be called up from within other applications eg to provide a hypertext help, glossary or any detailed documentation extension. This feature is facilitated by a simple macro script which can be embedded in the host application to call up a Paris document display or any embedded multimedia resource including sound and video files.

14

2.3   The User Interface

The Paris user interface consists of a Page (for information display with page-turning and text-control buttons), a Background (a graphic, which can be a simple colour, textured image or picture), and Framework Buttons (situated on the Background, on the left-side of the Page).

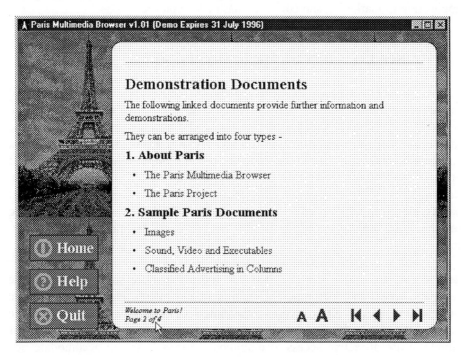

Figure. 1: The Paris user interface

User interaction is with three types of buttons: Page Turning Buttons and Text Scaling Buttons on the bottom of the page, and the Framework Buttons outside the page, on the left, including Document Thumbnails which facilitate navigation, providing a serial history list of visited documents. Hyperlinks include coloured text (hypertext) and images with a coloured border.   As in standard HTML, Hyperlinks are selected to navigate to a linked page.

Four of the buttons at the bottom-right of the screen are used to move forward or backward through the pages of the current document. To move from page to page, the user clicks on the buttons (arrows) at the bottom right of the page. To move from document to document, the user clicks the mouse on coloured text, or on images that are highlighted with a coloured border.

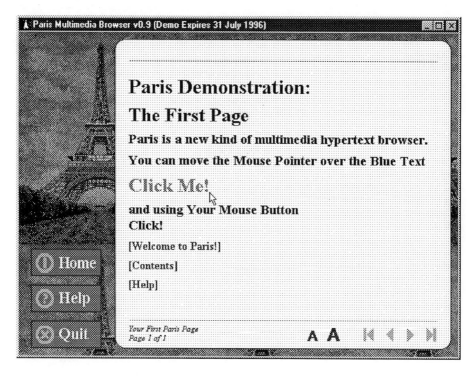

Figure. 2: Document thumbnail icons

A default three-phase "selectable behaviour" is provided. When the user locates a selectable button or hyperlink - the selected entity is highlighted (eg hypertext changes colour). When the user clicks-on the entity it changes colour again - indicating that the link is being made and this results in the display of the linked material. Images included in the document page can be marked up as links and will provide this user feedback. The page-turning and text-scaling buttons, and the document thumbnail and standard framework buttons also provide this visual feedback to user interaction.

Text can be made bigger or smaller. Headings can also have big and small text, just as they can have any other kind of character formatting. This includes superscripts and subscripts and special effects such as word undeerlining and word strikethrough.

A set of content display heuristics and the treatment of textual content as a displayable object means that Paris can adjust the page display continously - in response to available screen area and user modification of window size. All of the screen is used for information presentation and navigation. The user may have made their Paris window very small, or may have maximized it to full screen size without any border. Multi-column page layouts are available for ease of reading.

16

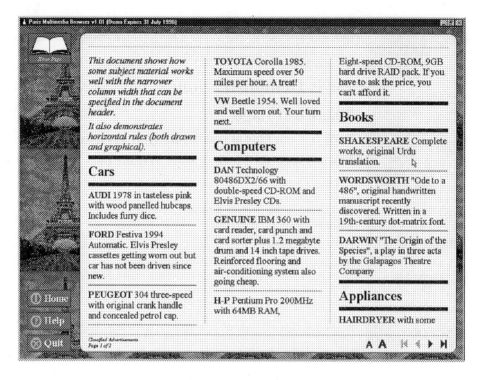

Figure. 3: Multi-column layout

A variety of text-handling is enabled - including, preformatted text with wide columns, non-monospace, monospace, and program source code.

2.4   Document title & document section

The title of the current document appears at the bottom left of the page. Information about what page you are on, and how many pages are in the currently displayed document, is given in the bottom left-hand corner of the page. The title of the current document section is displayed on the top right of the page.

The paper is the area behind the text and graphics of documents. It also holds the navigation buttons. By default, the paper is a very light cream colour; it can be specified. By default, the paper outline is shown as a thin black line. The colour of this outline can be changed. By default, the corners of the paper are square. Rounded corners can be specified.

It is possible to customise many aspects of the behaviour and appearance of the document browser in a "paris.ini" file.

The document border is the area around the edges of the displayed page, and around the command buttons and thumbnails. By default, this border is a uniform light grey colour; it can be specified, alternatively, a graphical image can be specified to be used for the default border. It will be tiled (repeated) if necessary. The image must be stored in the directory from which the program is started, as a bitmap file named "_border.bmp".

Figure. 4: Dynamic paging model

2.5   Thumbnails

These are the miniatures displayed to the left of the document page, which can be clicked-on to return to the corresponding page. Thumbnails may be displayed either as miniature pictures of the corresponding page ("miniatures"), or as specific graphical images ("icons"). The default is to display an icon. If a file "_thumb.bmp" is found in the current directory, it will be used as the icon. Otherwise, a standard icon will be used. A custom icon (representing the document or page in any required fashion) can be stored in "_thumb.bmp". A caption (showing as much of the document title as will fit) is normally displayed towards the bottom of the icon. The icon can be displayed with a custom caption, by including the following line in the "[thumbnail]" section of the "paris.ini" file: caption=n.

A miniature image of the actual document page can be displayed instead of an icon, by including the following line in the "[thumbnail]" section of the "paris.ini" file:type=miniature. Good-quality miniatures can be produced, but the process is very slow (many seconds per image). They can be computed by including the following line in the "[thumbnail]" section of the "paris.ini" file:method=computed.

2.6 Comparison of the interface models : media language, garden framework and Paris

In the Media Language model - users interact with buttons and hypertext (default colour-coded red) - both providing a three-phase visual feedback. Information is displayed as chunks and is essentially a fix-framed display model as in KMS (Ascyn et al 1988). The Garden Framework model supports a top-down hierarchical document model with hyperlinks between documents through simple menus or graphical browsers external to the content. This is essentially an unfixed-canvas display model as in Augment (Englebart 1984). The page display is dynamic and page size is a simple function of the current window-size. Hypertext links to an Index - represented by a card-index metaphor, provide glossary definitions. This Index mechanism provides a simple global reference point for hypertext links from content. An extension enables reference links to be made between cards and from the index to any point in any content file.

The Paris document model is based on the emerging HTML-standard on the WWW and borrows features from both Media Language and Garden. The browser employs the idea of pages for the display of content, with accompanying (application framework) buttons. As in Garden, there is a dynamic multi-column paging of contents according to the destination window size and user-alterations in window size. As in Media Language, there is a selectable list of thumbnails of previously visited material (pages). In the Garden Framework model, the end-user had no access to altering the display window. Similarily, the Paris browser can be set to display, omitting the Windows control border.

3.0 Future research: smarter interactivity better productivity : user- driven development

It is difficult to conceive of the perfect design for the perfect hypermedia system or application - it all depends and requirements evolve with awareness and experience of benefits. That the perfect is the enemy of the good has been learnt in a programme of applied research and the development of a series of working prototypes - leading to Paris document browser.

The user knows best. In the absence of a solution, we believe that one approach is to provide a small, general-purpose, working model as a starting point and to place this in a real world ('concrete') scenario and test it. By doing this - better ideas generate better designs for enhancements - and these can be clustered and prioritised and incrementally developed to meet real user needs.

Better mechanisms for querying and support for the efficient location of information are needed and this issue is being addressed in the new generation of commercial applications. Beyond simple text-string and boolean-text searching, smarter mechanisms will need to be developed to monitor user-interaction and to provide adaptive feedback to querying e.g. matching preliminary or loosely structured querying with existing browsers organised with clustered nodes to provide access to related subject material. A hypermedia system might be incremented with computational features (e.g. employing genetic algorithm and neural network techniques of optimisation) and be capable of dynamically transforming information structures as a result of user-interaction.

Object-oriented technology enables engineering and the construction of generic components (Coad and Yourdon 1991). The object oriented approach encourages modular design and new modular flexible systems - in contrast to old monolithic, multiunit systems, where adhoc enhancements create a complexity and few people if anyone can really understand the system. It facilitates the scaling up of systems and the possibility of reusing formal design components and even object code. In theory - and in our practical experience - it enables "rapid application development" (Ward 1994b). The object oriented approach encourages modular design and modular systems. With relatively short cycles of user-driven development and system flexibility, and development to meet chaning requirements, the system can evolve.

4.0   Bridging the gap between on-line internet and off-line access with a multimedia document browser

The development of standard mechanisms for distributing and viewing electronic documents has taken off, beyond the SGML standard and emerging mechanisms such as Adobe Acrobat, with the development of the internet. In the meantime, the HTML standard been developed and it has promoted the development of the WWW and a variety of web browsers and viewers for multimedia materials linked together by hyperlinks and presented as documents.

While the Media Language and Garden Framework models provided mechanisms on Unix workstations, the Paris document browser has been developed to take advantage of the emerging HTML-standard, and with a focus on non-computer literate users wanting simple, high quality access, on the Windows PC. In its current state of evolution, the Paris multimedia document browser can be viewed within the context of bridging the gap between on-line internet and off-line user access. It is small (less than 300kbyte binary) and simple to use. It sits easily with the content on a floppy disk or CD-ROM and doesn't require installation on a host machine. The ideas has been to keep the interface as simple as possible - easy to use for the reader. Its simplicity and ease of use provides an example of a component bridging the gap between more sophisticated applications and on-line access to multimedia information and alternatives. It can be used by editors and authors as a simple means to distribute multimedia information marked up in HTML - with off-line access to information and interactivity orders of magnitude faster and more efficient. A strategy of automating presentation might provide a pragmatic alternative to individual hand-crafted interfaces, especially useful for distributing large amounts of material.

It is being used in a number of case studies - with a focus on the requirement for the modelling and distribution of multimedia materials among members of working groups. It is being employed in a healthcare project involving the development of a multimedia electronic patient record; in a project involving the synthesis and distribution of information in an agricultural research dissemination and extension context; and in a project to develop small packets of browsable learning and training materials which need to be distributed by floppy disk.

The facility of the browser to link with other Windows applications, has led to its use as a hypertext help facility in one project. In another project the browser is being used as a browsable shell, access and distribution mechanism for a large collection of documents already constructed in Adobe Acrobat format - Paris is able to launch the Acrobat viewer program so that the documents can be viewed. It is also being employed as a mechanism for the organisation and publication of a hyperbook version of a forthcoming book about building object-oriented models of hypermedia systems (Ward & Browne 1996).

References:

1. Arshad FN, Kelleher G and Ward PS (1995) "Creating Interactive Learning Environments : delivering effective computer-based advice" Book LEA: Immediate Publishers
2. Ascyn, R, McCracken, D, and Yoder, E (1988) "KMS: a distributed hypermedia system for managing knowledge in organisations" Communications of the ACM ACM 31 (7) 820-835
3. Bush, V (1945) "As We May Think" : Atlantic Monthly August

4. Coad P and E Yourdon (1991) "Object-Oriented Design" 2nd Edition, Prentice Hall, Englewood Cliffs, NJ

5. Cotton B and Oliver R (1993) "Understanding Hypermedia" Phaidon Press, London

6. Conklin J (1987) "Hypertext: An introduction and survey". IEEE Computer 17-40

7. Englebart D C (1984) "Collaboration support provisions in Augment" In OAC Digest: Proc. AFIPS Office Automation Conference Los Angeles 51-58 Feb

8. Gronbaek K, Hem J A, Madsen O L and Sloth L (1994) "Hypermedia Systems: A Dexter-based architecture" Communications of the ACM Special Section: Hypermedia 37 (2) 65-74

9. Halasz FG (1988) "Reflections on Notecards: Seven Issues for the next generation of Hypermedia Systems". Communications of the ACM 31 (7) 836-852

10. Halasz F and M Schwartz (1990) "The Dexter hypertext reference model" In Proc. Hypertext Standardisation Workshop (Gaithersburg, Md) 95-133

11. Harrison H and Minsky M (1993) "The Turing Option" Warner Books Inc. 1992; ROC Penguin Books

12. Hunter L , Beetham M, Fuller, Arshad FN, Ward, P and Parrott C (1994) "Hypertext for Research and Learning about 19th Century Periodicals". Monograph to be published by CTI Centre for Textual Studies.

13. Johnson L, Jellnick H, Klotz H, Rao R, and Card S (1993) "Bridging the paper and electronic worlds: the Paper User Interface" Proceedings of INTERCHI'93, Amsterdam (New York: ACM) 507-512

14. Meyer B (1992) "Eiffel: The Language" New York Prentice Hall

15. Neilson J "Hypertext and Hypermedia" Boston: Academic Press (1990)

16. Nelson T H "Getting It Out of Our System" In, Information Retrieval: A Critical Review, edited by George Schecter. Philadelphia, Penn. Frankford Arsenal 1967.

17. Parrott C and Ward PS (1993) "Media Language: an Object-Oriented Approach to Generic Application Development". Proc. Tools USA'93 11th International Conference on the Technology of Object-Oriented Languages and Systems. Santa Barbara, USA, August.

18. Seyer PC (1991) "Understanding Hypertext : Concepts and Applications" Windcrest Mcgraw-Hill Inc.

19. Ward PS (1990) Guest Editor for Current Psychology: Research and Reviews (Special Edition) "Hypermedia and Artificial Intelligence" 9 (2) Summer.

20. Ward P S and Collins AMK (1991) "An Interactive Multimedia Guidance System for Libraries : Improving Access and Adding Value to Information Spaces for People". Presentation at Online '91 Information : 15th International Online Information Meeting Olympia London, December.

21. Ward, PS (1992a) "Collected Conclusions: the application of multimedia in education" in Kjelldahl, L (ed) Multimedia: Systems, Interaction and Application: Eurographics Seminars. Springer-Verlag
22. Ward PS (1994a) "Distributed Digital Multimedia Materials : towards new document centred user interfaces?" in Interactive Media International September
23. Ward PS (1994b) "The role of objects in multimedia" Objects in Europe 1 (3) Summer
24. Ward PS (1995) "Building Models of Multimedia Systems" Tutorial TOOLS Europe'95 International Conference 'The Technology of Object-Oriented Languages and Systems' Versailles Paris March 6-10 Proceedings: Prentice Hall
25. Ward PS (1996a) "Information Modelling Tools and Frameworks for the Delivery, Distribution and Management of Digital Multimedia Materials". Chapter 10 pp 121-142 In 'Digital Media and Electronic Publishing' eds by Earnshaw, Jones and Vince, Academic Press Inc (London)
26. Ward PS (projected 1997) "Building Object-Oriented Multimedia Systems" forthcoming book commissioned : Advances in Object-Oriented Software Engineering Series, Prentice-Hall

2.2

A TOOL FOR VISUALIZING HIERARCHICAL RELATIONS

W. Lai
University of Southern Queensland, Australia

Visualization is an efficient and powerful tool for expressing, understanding and manipulating various objects, relations, or other information. Tree structure diagrams allow visualisation of hierarchical relations. However, different applications may need different tree structure diagrams. This paper presents a tool for supporting the user in selecting a preferred tree diagram interface.

1.0   Introduction

Visualization is an efficient and powerful tool for expressing, understanding and manipulating various objects, relations, or other information. Visualization has find wide applications in various information processing areas nowadays. Tree structure diagrams can be used to visualise hierarchical relations. However, different applications may need different tree structure diagrams. In Figure 1, there are five layout forms of a tree. Which one is the "nice" layout? This should be decided by the user. Although there are some tree drawing algorithms (Wetherell and Shannon, 1979; Vaucher, 1980; Reingold and Tilford, 1981; Supowit and Reingold, 1983), one of problems is that they lack flexibility. These algorithms try to produce layouts by optimizing specific fixed aesthetics which are prescribed by the designer. For example, one of aesthetics defined in (Wetherell and Shannon, 1979; Vaucher, 1980; Reingold and Tilford, 1981; Supowit and Reingold, 1983) is that *a parent (node) should be centered over its children.* In applications specific users may need to vary aesthetics for specific tree layouts.

In this paper we present a tool for assisting the user to select a tree structure diagram interface that he/she wants. The tool provides the advantages of graphical interaction so that the user can select a tree structure diagram by way of direct manipulation. The tool integrates some facilities for drawing various tree diagrams. A facility we developed for drawing various inclusion tree diagrams has proved to be quite successful in practice.

24

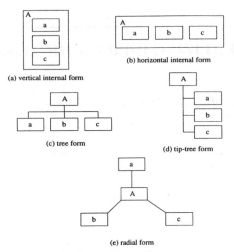

(a) vertical internal form

(b) horizontal internal form

(c) tree form

(d) tip-tree form

(e) radial form

Figure 1: Five layout forms of a tree structure

The main point is that the user (or the application program) can choose from a variety of shapes and layout algorithms for each subtree. The design and implementation of this tool are introduced as follows.

2.0   Representation

Structure relations appear in many application areas, such as data structures, organisation's reporting structures, software design structures, and so on.

We define a node x in a tree diagram has attributes (x, *shape*, Ix, Lx).

The shape is chosen from a fixed set of predefined shapes, such as *box*, or *circle*, or *diamond*.

Ix is the set of nodes which are direct children of x. If $Ix = \varnothing$, then x is a *primitive* node; otherwise Ix is a finite set of child nodes and x is called a compound node.

Lx means the   *layout form*, specifying a layout function to operate on x. For example, Figure 1 shows five layout forms of an compound node A whose $IA = \{a, b, c\}$, and its layout forms (LA) are *inclusive-v*, *inclusive-h*, *tree*, *tip-tree* and *radial* respectively.

For each y in Ix, there is a *structural* relation (parent-child) between x and y (see Figure 1). In some layout forms, structure relations are represented by the node and its child nodes themselves (such as Figure 1 (a), (b)), while in others these relations are represented by adding some lines and the node is over its child nodes or is in the centre of its child nodes (see Figure 1 (c), (d), (e)).

We have developed a textual language DNode based on (Eades, Lai and Carrington, 1991) to define a node and its attributes. With DNode, a tree diagram can be defined hierarchically. For example, an organisation's reporting structure is a tree with the chief executive as its root (shown in Figure 2 (a)), that can be described in DNode. First define the primitive nodes (*Per-a, Per-b*, ..., *Per-i*). Next define the four compound nodes (*Sal-M, Act-M, Per-M* and *Res-M*) in terms of these primitive nodes. An example is shown in Figure 2 (b). Finally define the compound nodes *Gen-M* to complete the DNode definition of this, as in Figure 2 (c).

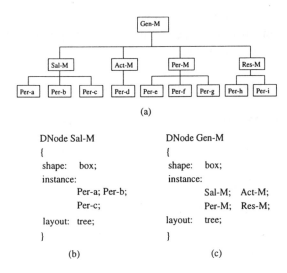

(a)

DNode Sal-M
{
shape: box;
instance:
            Per-a; Per-b;
            Per-c;
layout: tree;
}

(b)

DNode Gen-M
{
shape: box;
instance:
            Sal-M;   Act-M;
            Per-M;   Res-M;
layout: tree;
}

(c)

Figure 2: An organisation chart and Dnode

A different layout can be obtained by changing the definition of layout forms of some compound nodes. For example, changing the definition of layout forms of the four compound nodes (*Sal-M, Act-M, Per-M* and *Res-M*) to **tip-tree**, produce another layout shown in Figure 3.

26

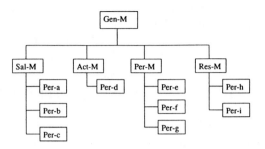

Figure 3: Another layout version of Figure 3 (a)

3.0   A layout toolbox

As well as using DNode as a textual specification language, the user can use the *layout toolbox* in our tool to operate just on the graphical appearance of a node. The layout toolbox is defined as

layout = {S-toolbox, L-toolbox}

The **S-toolbox** contains a selection of shape forms. The **L-toolbox** contains a selection of layout forms.

The user can choose any one of the shape (or layout) forms in the layout toolbox and instantiate a node name to change that node's graphic appearance dynamically. For example, if we choose **circle** in the **S-toolbox** to operate on the nodes *Gen-M, Sal-M, Act-M, Per-M and Res-M* in Figure 2 (a) respectively, and choose **tip-tree** in the **L-toolbox** to operate on the node *Gen-M*, we get the diagram in Figure 4.

The layout toolbox gives the user a choice of aesthetics and drawing conventions. Figure 1 is an example of five different layout forms available with the layout toolbox for the same graph. The layout toolbox allows the user to experiment interactively in order to achieve a satisfactory result.

The layout toolbox retains the advantages of graphical interaction. It can provide the user with a multiple view environment for tree structure diagrams.

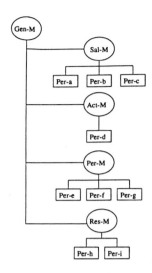

Figure 4: another layout version of Figure 3 (a)

4.0   Tree drawings

The layout form defines a tree layout. For each layout form, we should provide a layout function for drawing the corresponding tree diagram in the implementation.

In this section we introduce some methods of drawing tree structure diagrams used in our tool.

To draw classical trees (for example, see Figure 1 (c)), many algorithms have been developed (Wetherell and Shannon, 1979; Vaucher, 1980; Reingold and Tilford, 1981; Supowit and Reingold, 1983; Moen, 1990, Bliesch, 1993). In our tool, we draw a classical tree by putting every sub-tree in a rectangle (see Figure 5 (a)). We use the same approach to tip-over tree drawing (see Figure 5 (b)) which is a slight variation of the classical tree. Although this approach cannot produce a tree drawing as compact as those approaches in (Reingold and Tilford, 1981; Moen, 1990; Bliesch, 1993), it is more flexible for changing a sub-tree from one form to another. For example, we can change the sub-tree in Figure 5 (a) to Figure 5 (b).

28

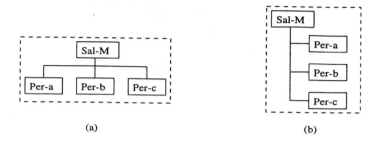

(a)   (b)

Figure 5: Drawing a sub tree in a rectangle

The methods for radial tree drawings (for example, see Figure 1 (c)) are introduced in (Eades, 1991).

We have developed a method for drawing inclusion trees. It focuses on the creation of various inclusion trees by changing the gaps between a node and its inside nodes, and the gap amongst inside nodes.

Before introducing our method for drawing inclusion trees, we should first describe the tree structure used in our tool. In the tree structure, we assign some attributes for the spaces and positions of nodes. The attributes w and h represent the size of the node, that is, the width and height of the bounding box of the node. The *offcorner* and *offcentre* represent the relative coordinates of the corner and centre of the node with respect to its parent's top-left corner, respectively. This is illustrated in Figure 6 (we assume a coordinate system where the value of x increases from left to right, and the value of y from top to bottom). Based on the *offcorner* and *offcentre*, it is easy to compute the absolute coordinates of the centre and top-left corner of the node.

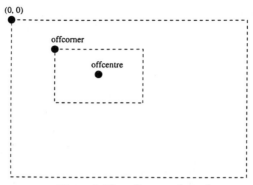

Figure 6: The *offcentre* of a node

The **inside_gaps** defines a set of gaps for a node. It includes: *g_gap*, *l_gap*, *r_gap*, *u_gap* and *b_gap*. The parameter *g_gap* defines the minimal gap between two inside nodes. The parameters l_gap, r_gap, u_gap and b_gap represent the minimal gaps between the inside nodes and left side, right side, up side, and bottom side of the node, respectively. Figure 7 illustrates these gaps.

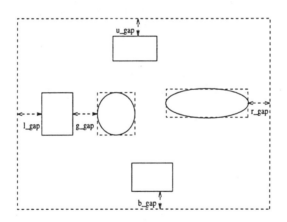

Figure 7: The inside gaps

For example, the diagram on the left in Figure 8 is the result of applying a layout function for drawing vertical internal form tree. That is to draw the nodes in a vertical arrangement with the definition of that: all gaps are a default value (a fixed size). The diagram on the right in Figure 8 is the result of changing the definition of gaps for the diagram on the left in Figure 8: gaps between inside nodes are zero (ie. *g_gap* is 0), gaps between right side of the node and its inside nodes are zero (ie. *r_gap* is 0), and the others are a default fixed value.

By defining all gaps (except *u_gap*) to be zero for a horizontal internal tree, we can get a *form* diagram. An example is shown in Figure 9.

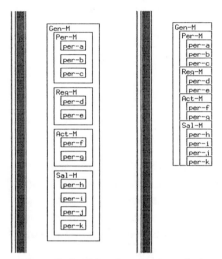

Figure 8: Applying function recursively

Gen-M								
Sal-M			Act-M	Per-M			Res-M	
Per-a	Per-b	Per-c	Per-d	Per-e	Per-f	Per-g	Per-h	Per-i

Figure 9: A tree based form drawing

5.0   Implementation

Based on the ideas above, a tool for selecting various tree diagram has been implemented. Some different layout examples are shown in Figures 10-12. The tool includes a menu area and a display area. The display area is used to display a tree diagram. The menu area provides some operations for the user to interact with tree diagrams. The operation **Exit** is used to quit this tool. The operation **Erase** means to clear the display area. The operation **Parse File** supports to parse a DNode file and displays the correspond tree diagram. The pop-down menu **Layout** is the layout toolbox which includes **S-toolbox** and **L-toolbox** (see last section). When the user click **Gap** in the menu area, a dialogue box is popped up (see Figure 13). This dialogue box supports the user to define the gaps for an inclusion tree diagram (General means *g_gap*, Left *l_gap*, Right *r_gap*, Top *u_gap*, Bottom *b_gap*).

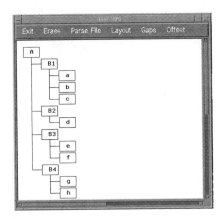

Figure 10: A layout in tip-tree form

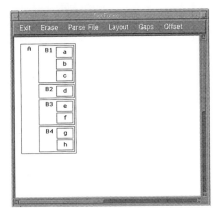

Figure 11: A layout in vertical internal form

Figure 12: A layout in horizontal internal form

Figure 13: A dialogue box for defining gaps

Figure 14: A layout by changing gaps

Figure 15: Another layout by changing gaps

6.0   Conclusion

Designing tree structure diagrams is an application dependent task. In this paper a tool is presented that can support the user to select a preferred tree structure diagram according to the requirement of his/her application. A textual description language DNode is developed to specify tree diagrams. It retains the advantages of textual interaction. The tool provides layout facilities for the user to interactive select a tree diagram visually.

Some tree drawing algorithms have been incorporated and developed. A method for drawing various inclusion trees has been introduced. This tool can also be used to develop tree drawing algorithms. More layout forms need to be added into DNode and the layout toolbox. Of course, the corresponding layout functions should be developed.

References:

1. Wetherell, C. and Shannon, A. (1979), "Tidy drawing of the trees", *IEEE Transaction on Software Engineering*, 5(5):514--520.
2. Vaucher, J. G. (1980), "Pretty-printing of trees", *Software-Practice and Experience*, 10(7):553--561.
3. Reingold, E. and Tilford, J. (1981), "Tidier drawings of trees", *IEEE Transactions on Software Engineering*, 7(2):223--228.
4. Supowit, K and Reingold, E. (1983), "The complexity of drawing trees nicely", *Acta Informatica*, 18:377 -- 392.
5. Eades, P., Lai, W. and Carrington, D (1991), "Dion: A visual language for representing abstract relational in formation", *Proceedings of the 14th Australian Computer Science Conference*, Sydney, Pages 270-279.
6. Moen, S (1990), "Drawing dynamic trees", *IEEE Software*, pages 21--28, July.
7. Bliesch, A. (1993), "Aesthetic layout of generalized trees", *Software-Practice and Experience*, 23(8):817--827.
8. Eades, P. (1991), "Drawing free trees", *Technical Report IIAS-RR-91-17E*, International Institute for Advance Study of Social Information Science, Fujitsu Limited.

2.3

ARCHITECTURAL FOUNDATIONS OF HYPERMEDIA-ENABLED EXPERT SYSTEMS

Y. Alex Tung, Ram D. Gopal & James R. Marsden
University of Connecticut, USA

*The purpose of this research is to develop a standardized set of techniques and an architectural blueprint for the construction of hypermedia-enabled expert systems. We propose an architecture termed **HYPES** for the development of media-rich expert systems. We then develop a knowledge-based taxonomy of various media types and a set of **KNOWME** tools which enable these objects to directly manipulate knowledge in native or near-native formats. Following the design guidelines of **HYPES**, we propose a prototype expert system that provides a rich variety of media types and **KNOWME** methods.*

1.0   Introduction

Information technology has evolved significantly since its inception a few decades ago and has provided the impetus for transforming industrialized countries into knowledge and information based economies (Laudon and Laudon, 1996). According to the U.S. Department of Commerce, knowledge and information work account for 75% of the U.S. gross national product and nearly 70% of the labor force. As a result, investments in information technology have experienced a rapid growth and by 1989 over 70% of all capital investment in U.S. was in the area of information technology (Laudon and Laudon, 1996). As the industrial nations become increasingly information-based, technologies to manage information products are becoming vital. Expert systems and hypermedia constitute two important technologies used by organizations for the creation, storage and overall management of information products.

Traditional expert systems rely directly on the users to translate diagrams of problem structures and characteristics into text form and then convert them back when interpreting the recommendations from the expert system (Sipior and Garrity, 1992). A number of applications rely on expertise that is based on visual reasoning (Carbonell, et. al., 1987), acoustic analysis (Oxman, 1991), and temporal and spatial reasoning involving complex interactions among related components (Fischer and Richards, 1995) that are not inherently textual in nature. Current expert system applications approximate such knowledge by converting it into a textual format.   This transformation might lead to inconsistencies, potential misrepresentation, and loss of important knowledge

(Suetens and Oosterlinck, 1987; Leonard-Barton and Sviokla, 1988). This is due to the lack of a one-to-one correspondence between nontextual information and its text-based equivalent.

The potential use of hypermedia technology within the framework of expert systems is recently being recognized. According to Ragusa (1994), the use of hypermedia can offer significant benefits in certain expert system applications. The multimedia technologies have been utilized for the presentation of expertise to the users (Bielawski and Lewand, 1991). The potential exists for the use of hypermedia technology in major facets of expert systems, including user interface, knowledge acquisition, and explanation of expertise (Fuerst, et. al. 1995). The inherent appeal of hypermedia is that it permits the management of expertise in its native or near-native format, without the need to resort to conversion to text-based formats.

The purpose of this research is to develop a standardized set of techniques and an architectural blueprint for the construction of hypermedia-enabled expert systems. We propose an architecture termed **HYPES** (Hypermedia-enabled Expert System) for the development of media-rich expert systems. We then propose a knowledge-based taxonomy of various media types and a set of **KNOWME** (Knowledge Method) tools which enable these objects to directly manipulate knowledge in native or near-native formats. The **KNOWME** tools can be employed to enable the hypermedia objects to perform a variety of tasks, ranging from enhanced communication with end users to embedding knowledge directly into the media objects. Following the design guidelines of **HYPES**, we develop a prototype expert system shell that provides a rich variety of media types and **KNOWME** methods. The prototype is extensively evaluated through an application for circuitry quality control. An experimental study that contrasts the human processing of text-based and hypermedia information for input and output purposes illustrates the potential benefits of the use of hypermedia technologies within the expert system framework.

The remainder of the paper is organized as follows. Section II provides the proposed approach that includes the development of **HYPES** architecture and **KNOWME** tools. Section III outlines the prototype shell and the empirical study that underscores the potential practical benefits. Finally, concluding remarks are presented in Section IV.

2.0   Architecture and toolset development

In this section we develop the architectural foundations for the development of hypermedia-enabled expert systems. **HYPES** is designed to employ multiple media

36

for knowledge acquisition, storage and user interface activities. **HYPES** is equipped with a set of **KNOWME** tools that aid in the management of media objects for knowledge purposes.

2.1 HYPES architecture

HYPES is designed to extend the functionality of expert systems beyond the realm of text-based environments. While **HYPES** is clearly not a panacea for all expert system applications, it significantly widens the application domain of expert systems. Fuerst et. al. (1995) identify numerous applications areas that benefit from the use of such integrated environments.

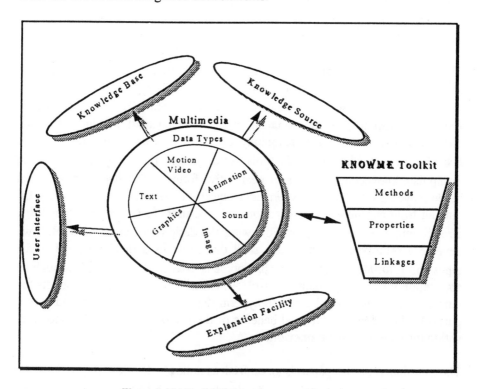

Figure 1: HypEs Architecture - a component view

Turban (1995) identifies four components of an expert system - **knowledge source, knowledge base, user interface** and **explanation facility**. Figure 1 illustrates the component view of the **HYPES** architecture. The media objects depicted in Figure 1 have associated with them *linkages, methods* and *properties* that operate on these objects. The four components of the expert system employ these multimedia objects and the operators. The operators are made functional through **KNOWME** tools and their detailed development is presented later in the section. Below we describe the expert system components and their interface with the multiple media.

Knowledge Source: The typical knowledge sources for expertise are experts and documentation. In a number of applications, the knowledge sources reside on documents which in their natural formats are available as multimedia objects. These include, for example, angiograms and aerial views of locations that are image-based (Suetens and Oosterlinck, 1987), sounds from malfunctioning high-pressure air supply system (Oxman, 1991), system diagrams of complex engine parts, and time-based animated views of complex, inter-related systems such as automobiles and manufacturing systems (Fischer and Richards, 1995). In the case of expert system that performs diagnostic analysis of angiograms, the typical experts are radiologists and cardiologists (Long, et. al. 1991). Angiograms are x-ray photographs of the heart taken by a rapid-exposure cine cinema immediately after radiographic contrast is injected into the coronary arteries. These experts use perceptual reasoning and are often unable to give unambiguous verbal description or to explain reasoning involved in the interpretation of the angiogram (Suetens and Oosterlinck, 1987). An expert system that permits knowledge acquisition directly through the angiograms would significantly enhance the effectiveness of the diagnosis.

When documentation is naturally available in multiple media formats, **HYPES** can directly access these sources and provide an interface to the experts to manipulate these objects for knowledge extraction. This allows experts to function in their natural environments and utilize their perceptual, visual, acoustic reasoning abilities and thus overcome ambiguities and inaccuracies associated with verbalizing such knowledge to create text-based systems. The experts interact with **HYPES** through the **KNOWME** toolkit that incorporates pattern recognition and segmentation, feature extraction, object description and comparison, and other algorithms that are embedded in the object operators. This permits the expert to focus explicitly on the knowledge domain and ignore the algorithmic details on how efficiently and effectively to translate the domain knowledge into computer-understandable formats.

Knowledge Base: The knowledge base stores the knowledge that is acquired from the knowledge source. The acquired knowledge is typically stored in a rule-based or frame-based formats. **HYPES** can incorporate media objects in the knowledge base and embed knowledge directly in the stored media objects. The media-rich knowledge base incorporates expert heuristics through the **KNOWME** toolkit. For example, production rules might operate on existence of certain patterns in the media objects, or characteristics of a media object, or a comparison of an object under study with a reference object. An example of a possible production rule that features image analysis is shown in Figure 2.

User Interface: The user interface in most traditional expert systems is centered around the keyboard and the computer screen. The consulting session typically involves textual dialogue between the system and the user. Input information that naturally exists in non-textual formats has to be processed and translated to text format by the user. As a result the advice or the results provided by the expert system are critically dependent on the efficacy with which the user can process and translate non-textual information. Inaccuracies, ambiguities and inconsistencies that tend to arise in such translations potentially hinder the practicality of expert systems in some application domains. Leonard-Barton and Sviokla (1988) describe a failed prototype expert system to diagnose problems in soldering of computer components. The crucial deficiency of the prototype was that the operators who consulted with the expert system often missed the subtle irregularities in the components and thus failed to provide correct information to the expert system.

IF

The following pattern is present in the input image

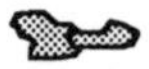

AND

The color contrast between the pattern and its immediate neighborhood exceeds the predefined threshold

AND

The acoustic frequency resulting from the object sound test is above 50MHz

AND

The amplitude articulation resulting from the object sound test is equivalent to object #7

THEN

The diagnosis indicates early stages of benign tumor with CF=90

Figure 2: Sample production rule in HYPEs's knowledge base

HYPEs is designed to provide input facilities in a variety of media formats. For example, an image of an external object or audio recording can be directly read and processed by the system. Further more, **HYPEs** allows for multimodal input and preprocessing of information. For example, various images of the same object from different view points and in different environments, and augmenting images with associated acoustic properties or with textual descriptions are accepted by **HYPEs**. While redundant, the multimodal input can take advantage of the unique features of the individual media objects (in that each media object can better capture certain types of information than others), can perform data error checks, account for and eliminate "noise" and other extraneous and misleading data. Thus, **HYPEs** provides features that ensure the completeness and accuracy of the information communication between the user and the system.

Explanation Facility: Explanation of the expert advice can be more effective if conducted in multimodal formats (Fuerst, et. al. 1995). Media such as graphics, animation and sound are more effective at conveying information that involves two and three dimensional spatial relationships, and behavior and evolution of complex systems (Fisher, et. al., 1992). Awad (1996) describes an expert system that utilizes virtual reality to help the user experience the advice or solution in a realistic environment via visualization and sensing. Further examples include explanations of statistical information through graphs, computer animation of the solution offered if the problem involves temporal patterns such as growth of a tumor or formation of weather patterns. **HYPEs** provides a media-rich environment within which a plethora of multisensory capabilities can be augmented to the solutions offered by the expert system.

Figure 3 provides a process view of **HYPEs**. As illustrated in the figure, the proposed architecture provides valuable services to both the experts and the users in their interactions with the expert system. **HYPEs** is designed to work with multiple media objects to garner the advantages they offer to increase the effectiveness of expert systems and the scope of the application domain. This is accomplished through a toolkit that is equipped with a set of **KNOWME** tools that manage the media objects and are specifically tailored for expert system development. The toolkit is based on the principles of object orientation and is modular in nature. The modular design enables the toolkit to add new operators and as a result the scope of **KNOWME** can be expanded to incorporate advanced features such as more complex reasoning abilities, detection of subtler visual, audio or spatial cues, and more powerful explanatory capabilities to iteratively improve its functionality.

2.2   KNOWME toolkit

KNOWME toolkit provides for the management of media objects utilized in the **HYPEs** architecture. The toolkit is designed to provide services to both the experts and the non-expert users. We begin our discussion with a description of media taxonomy.
The media objects can be classified along two dimensions: **Reality** dimension and **Complexity** dimension. The media objects on the reality dimension are either

real and/or **abstract**. The distinction is based on a mapping of the media object with the external world. If every element of the media object corresponds to an element on the representative object in the external world, the media object is termed **real**. Otherwise, it is termed **abstract**. Complexity of a media object is determined based on the effort expended in the computer storage and manipulation for knowledge activities.

The commonly used media types are **text, sound, image, graphics, animation** and **motion video**. A brief description of the objects along with the above classification is provided below.

  • **Text**: It is most commonly used data type and it exhibits the least levels of complexity for computer manipulation. Text can be real or abstract depending on the context. For example, the textual representation of height of individuals is real and musical talent is abstract.

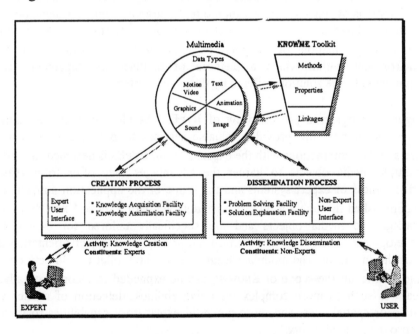

Figure 3: HYPEs architecture - a process view

  • **Sound:** This data object consumes more computer resources than the text object. Sound can also be real or abstract depending on the context. Noise from an automobile engine and heartbeat heard through a stethoscope are example of real sound and computer simulated voice is an example of abstract sound.

• **Image:** Images are pictures which result from a mechanical mapping of the external world into two dimensions (Clark, 1995). This data object is real and consumes more computer resources than the text object.

• **Graphics**: Simply defined, graphics are pictures that are not images (Clark, 1995). By definition they are abstract. Two forms of graphics **Charts** and **Diagrams** are of particular interest in the expert system context. Charts are based on numerical data (for example, a bar chart) and diagrams (for example, data flow diagrams) are graphics constructed based on a limited set of two dimensional shapes that prescribe to preset diagrammatic conventions (Fischer and Richards, 1995). The general graphic data type assumes a complexity level similar to an image. Some elements of charts and diagrams can be represented textually and thus they require lesser computing resources.

• **Animation:** Animation brings static objects to life. It can be used to add realism to artificial objects or surrealism to images of real objects (Harrison, 1995). We adopt the definition that animation is a collection images, graphics and sound where *at least* one object is abstract. Therefore, animation is abstract and more complex than its individual constituents.

• **Motion Video:** Motion Video refers to pictures of an event captured and recorded over a period of time (Harrison, 1995). It can be viewed as a collection of images and real sound that is temporally sequenced. Therefore, motion video is real and complex as it consumes significant computing resources.

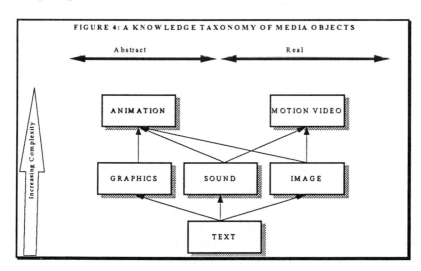

Figure 4: A knowledge taxonomy of media objects

Figure 4 provides a graphical illustration of the media objects on the two classification dimensions and the interrelationships among the objects. KNOWME toolkit provides three types of operators for knowledge manipulation of the media objects: **Properties, Methods** and **Linkages**. Properties are attributes of the media objects. Examples include frequency and amplitude of a sound object and colors and brightness of an image object. Methods act on the objects to produce another object. The resultant object can be the same object with different properties, or a different object of the same data type, or a completely different data type. Linkages are relationships among the media objects.

The operators facilitate the development of hypermedia-enabled expert systems. They allow the experts to reason and analyze directly through the media objects such as images and sound. This obviates the need for the experts to deal with textual translations of higher level objects. The operators also process input information in native or near-native formats, thus relieving the user of the burden to translate input information to textual equivalents. They also provide better interface and explanation facilities through the use of multiple media. The following section outlines our proposed prototype development and empirical study.

3.0   Prototype development and experimential analysis

Our current efforts in prototype development center around expert systems that incorporate textual and image objects for knowledge purposes. The prototype is equipped with the KNOWME tools that operate on these two media types. It is being implemented on a microcomputer equipped with a 166 MHz pentium processor and a digital camera. The software component of the system utilizes Visual Basic 4.0 and Microsoft Access 2.0 on Windows 95 platform for code development. The expert system application of the prototype involves detection of defects on analog circuit boards utilized in radios. The KNOWME tools utilized for identification of defects will be operationalized through neural network techniques for pattern detection.

The experimental study provides a limited validation of the proposed architecture. Two sets of experiments will be conducted to highlight the superiority of hypermedia-enabled systems over their textual counterparts for informational input and output. A comparative analysis of information in text and image formats by non-expert users will provide the basis for the potential benefits of hypermedia technologies in developing expert systems.

4.0 Conclusion

This research addresses the incorporation of hypermedia technologies into expert systems. Hypermedia technologies extend the functionality of expert systems beyond the realm of text-based environments and thus improve the effectiveness and widen the domain of expert system applications. We propose an architecture termed **HYPES** that is designed to employ multiple media for knowledge acquisition, storage and user interface activities of expert systems. We then propose a knowledge-based taxonomy of various media types and a set of **KNOWME** (**Know**ledge **Me**thod) tools which enable these objects to directly manipulate knowledge in native or near-native formats. Our current efforts are aimed at prototype development and experimental validation of the superiority of hypermedia-enabled expert systems over their textual counterparts.

References:

1. Adie, C. (1993), "Distributed Multimedia Information Systems," *Computer Networks and ISDN Systems*, 25(S2), S49-S57.
2. Awad, E.M. (1996), Building Expert Systems, St. Paul, Minnesota, West.
3. Bielawski, L. and R. Lewand (1991), Intelligent Systems Design: Integrating Expert Systems, Hypermedia, and Database Technologies, New York, Wiley.
4. Carbonell, N., D. Fohr, and J. Haton (1987), "Aphodex, An Acoustic-Phonetic Decoding Expert System," in *Proceedings of IEEE Workshop on Expert Systems and Pattern Analysis*, edited by C.H. Chen, Paris, France, World Scientific, 31-44.
5. Clark, D.R. (1995), "Defining the Multimedia Engine," in Multimedia Systems & Applications, edited by R.A. Earnshaw and J.A. Vince, San Diego, Academic Press Inc., 3-20.
6. Fischer, D. and C. Richards (1995), "The Presentation of Time in Interactive Animated Systems Diagrams," in Multimedia Systems & Applications, edited by R.A. Earnshaw and J.A. Vince, San Diego, Academic Press Inc., 141-159.
7. Fisher, G., J. Grudin, A. Lemke, R. McCall, J. Ostwald, B. Reeves, and F. Shipman (1992), "Supporting Indirect Collaborative Design with Integrated Knowledge-Based Design Environment," *Human-Computer Interaction*, 7(1), 281-314.
8. Fuerst, W.L., J.M. Ragusa, and E. Turban (1995), "Expert Systems and Multimedia: Examining the Potential for Integration," *Journal of Management Information Systems*, 11(3), 155-179.
9. Harrison, M.A. (1995), "The Essential Elements of Hypermedia," in Multimedia Systems & Applications, edited by R.A. Earnshaw and J.A. Vince, San Diego, Academic Press Inc., 79-99.

44

10. Hatcher, M. (1995), "A Tool Kit for Multimedia Supported Group/Organizational Decision Systems (MSGDS)," *Decision Support Systems*, 15(1), 211-217.
11. Leonard-Barton, D. and J.J. Sviokla (1988), "Putting Expert Systems to Work," Harvard Business Review, March-April, 91-98.
12. Long, J.M., J.R. Slagle, E.A. Irani, M.R. Wick, J.W. Johnson, and J.P. Matts (1991), "Two Expert Systems Applied to Clinical Trails," in Operational Expert System Applications in the United States, edited by J. Liebowitz, New York, Pergamon Press Inc., 52-66.
13. Oxman, S.W. (1991), "The Development of the AIRAID Expert System: A Case Study," in Operational Expert System Applications in the United States, edited by J. Liebowitz, New York, Pergamon Press Inc., 130-143.
14. Parkinson, E.L., M.L. Hailey, C.F. Lo, B.A. Whitehead, G.Z. Shi, and G.W. Garrison (1994), "Integration Architecture of Expert Systems, Neural Networks, Hypertext, and Multimedia can Provide Competitive Opportunities for Industrial Applications," *Computers and Industrial Engineering*, 27(1), 269-272.
15. Ragusa, J.M. (1994), "Models and Applications of Multimedia, Hypermedia, and Intellimedia Integration with Expert Systems," *Expert Systems with Applications*, 7(1), 7-13.
16. Ragusa, J.M. and G.W. Orwig (1991), "Attacking the Information Access Problem with Expert Systems," *Expert Systems: Planning, Implementation, Integration*, 2(4), 26-32.
17. Ramesh, B. and K. Sengupta (1995), "Multimedia in a design rationale decision support system," *Decision Support Systems*, 15(1), 181-196.
18. Sipior, J.C. and E.J. Garrity (1992), "Merging Expert Systems with Multimedia Technology," *Data Base*, 21(4), 45-49.
19. Suetens, P. and A. Oosterlinck (1987), "Using Expert Systems for Image Understanding," in *Proceedings of IEEE Workshop on Expert Systems and Pattern Analysis*, edited by C.H. Chen, Paris, France, World Scientific, 61-74.
20. Turban, E. (1993), Decision Support and Expert Systems, 2nd Ed., New York, Macmillan.
21. Wagner, C. (1995), "Facilitating space-time differences, group heterogeneity and multi-sensory task work through a multimedia supported group decision system," *Decision Support Systems*, 15(1), 197-210.

2.4

THE IMPLEMENTATION OF A HYPERMEDIA DATABASE MANAGEMENT SYSTEM

Shyu, Shyong Jian
Ming Chuan University, Taiwan

In this paper a prototype of a hypermedia data base management system (HDBMS) is designed and implemented on a client/server architecture. This HDBMS combines the linkage relation among hypermedia objects and the management functionality of database systems for various kinds of media objects. Not only can multimedia data objects be maintained and queried but also can the presentations be organized as hypermedia forms by using a single software. The consistent integration and communicative effectiveness of information could be improved by the advantages of the database management systems and the active participation and self-pace control for users' navigation on the hypermedia.

1.0   Introduction

With the rapid advancement of computer technologies such as networks, database management systems (DBMS) ..., information technology becomes a very critical resource in persuading the successfulness for almost every kind of organizations. It is rare nowadays for, say, a business to enter the market and claim its success without the help of the computer and information technologies. More on that, the everlasting growth of computer technology nerve stops its step in influencing the management and control of the information resource. With the maturity of multimedia and hypermedia, the computer mediated communications (CMC) improve the reading style and reasoning effect of information for human beings [Tomek 1991, Nielsen 1990, Jonassen 1990, Lanza and Roselli 1991, Gronbaek and Trigg 1994]. Hypermedia makes possible the users to navigate the information-space at their own choice and pace [Jonassen 1991, Gronbaek and Trigg 1994, Kappe, Maurer and Sherbakov 1993]. This kind of users' nonlinear visiting of information seems more alike the thinking style of human beings [Jonassen 1990, Nielsen 1990]. It becomes an effective way to organize the increasingly growing information [Gronbaek and Trigg, 1994, Macher, Cadish, Clerc and Pretsch 1995]. Research areas and applications related to CMC can be found in computer assisted learning (CAL), group decision support systems (GDSS), computer conferencing systems and so on [Hornung, Jager, Santos and Tritsch 1993, Hiltz 1994, Marchionini and Crane 1995, Bieber 1995].

Let us take a glimpse at some successful software tools related with DBMS or hypermedia. Some practical general-purpose DBMS are emerged and wildly used in the last decade such as, Sybase, Oracle, Informix, DBMaker, ..., etc. With the help of these DBMS, information including multimedia data objects can be easily maintained or queried as databases in computers. As to the hypermedia, it is utilized in authoring tools such as, Authorware, ToolBook, Director, Media Works, ... etc., to produce various kinds of CD titles. While combining with network, the most influential hypermedia application would be the World-Wide Web on the Internet. Its speedy growing makes the communication of information more rapid and more easy through the design of the hyperlinks among the information-space on the networks. These tools improve the effectiveness of managing and presenting human knowledge.

The author would like to propose a prototype of a hypermedia database management system (HDBMS) on a client/server architecture in this paper. The object is to combine the capability of controlling data of various media forms via database management systems and the effectiveness of CMC via hypermedia for presenting and managing information. Besides data types in a traditional DBMS, multimedia objects such as texture, audio, image, animation are manageable in our HDBMS. Hyperlinks can further be constructed to connect the logical relationships among these media objects for users to navigate at his own choosing. It is suggested to use our system to build up necessary data in various media as database systems which can be updated and queried, and to generate hypermedia presentations which ease users' navigation by simply clicking on the linked objects. As a way, the multimedia objects can be organized and managed by the functionality of DBMS and the cognition of the presented information can be improved by the users' active participation via hypermedia. Applications of our HDBMS can be expected in a variety of areas such as courseware preparation in the CAL, knowledge database in GDSS, fine art works arrangement in an art gallery, enterprise information management, tour-guidance systems, music, videos or photos exhibitions of specific purposes for public or private usages, ..., and so on.

This rest of this paper is organized as follows. The functional description of our HDBMS prototype is proposed in Section 2. Our implementation results are illustrated in Section 3. Section 4 gives the concluding remarks and some possible future extensions.

2.0   The functional description of our HDBMS prototype

Our HDBMS is built upon the database engine of DBMaker which is developed by SYSCOM in Taiwan. It is an *extended* relational database management system for its ability in handling the binary data objects which might be images, audio, or video and so on in its relation database system. The software cost is more economical as compared to the other DBMS mentioned above. It also supports the network communication as a client/server architecture. Thus in our system it is the DBMaker engine who actually operates the data manipulations like insertion, deletion, updating, locking on concurrent accessing, ..., etc.

The elementary item in our HDBMS is the *object* which might be a traditional data object (i.e. *normal data*) like integer, character, date, ...etc., or a multimedia object such as a *texture* (which might be a *label* for a short sequence of words or a *text* for an article,) *image, audio,* or *animation.* A logical collection of objects can form a *database.* Related objects in or outside the database can comprise a *slide* which is a multimedia presentation itself. A group of related slides can further form an *album* which could be used to present information or knowledge for a certain specific purpose. Linking objects including *buttons, images* and *labels* on a slide can be deliberately designed to connect with other slides, albums or even databases whenever needed. Therefore the album itself becomes a hypermedia presentation and the users (or audiences, visitors) can determine by their own choices to find out the knowledge or information provided in the album. Figure 1 illustrates the relation among the objects, slides and the album.

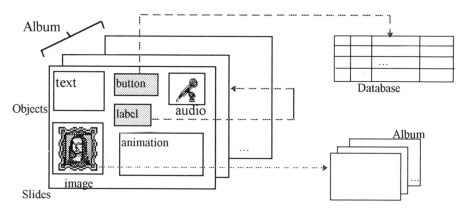

Figure 1: Objects, slides, album and the hyperlinks

To meet the requirements that might be encountered in the real-world applications, we decompose our HDBMS in this stage into three subsystems: *multimedia database (MDB) manager, album manager* and *query/navigation (QN) manager.* The MDB manager takes charge of the data manipulation and management of normal data and multimedia objects in the databases based upon DBMaker. Thus the designers can create, delete and modify the databases by using our MDB manager. The album manager can be used to generate slides by collecting objects from the databases (or external media files) and create albums for specific purposes. Layout tools are supported in both the MDB manager and the album manager which could be used to arrange the layout of these multimedia objects on the screen and set up the link structure among databases, slides and albums for further query or navigation.

The QN manager can be applied to query the databases or to navigate those already-made albums. When a database is opened by the user's choice under the QN manager, a query form comes out first for the user's request. The queried results are shown according to the predefined layout set by designers in the MDB manager. These records can be browsed one by one. Because some links might be attached to linking objects in the MDB manager, some albums or other databases might be activated and referenced by the user's clicking on the corresponding objects. The hyperlinks enrich the presentation of the selected records by the support of a set of related albums or databases. Correspondingly when an album is opened under the QN manager, the user can navigate the album by following the guidance of the hyperlinks. Likewise, some linking objects might also be arranged on the slides. Thus the information on the databases or other albums might be exposed as the corresponding link objects are activated by the users.

As a result, the designer possesses the flexibility in combining the databases and the albums together by hyperlinks to present the information. Whenever there is a need of a link from an object to a database, album or slide, the designer can easily connect this linkage by our HDBMS. The visual effects provided in our system also refine the multimedia effects of these slides. Therefore an improved interaction among the information and the users can be designed in this way.

3.0   The implementation of our HDBMS

Our HDBMS is implemented as a client/server architecture via the network for multi-users. A SUN Sparc machine running UNIX is used as the server which contains the MDB, album and QN managers and awaits the requests from a number of clients. We choose the DBMaker by SYSCOM in Taiwan as our database engine. The communication between the server program and the database engine is achieved by the open database communication (ODBC). The platforms of the clients are personal computers running Windows 3.1/Windows 95 and the client interface of our HDBMS is designed with Visual Basic. The communication between the server and the clients are fulfilled by the socket programming and the TCP/IP protocol. The client/server architecture of our HDBMS is illustrated in Figure 2. The screen outlooks will be shown in the following to illustrate the implementation of our HDBMS prototype.

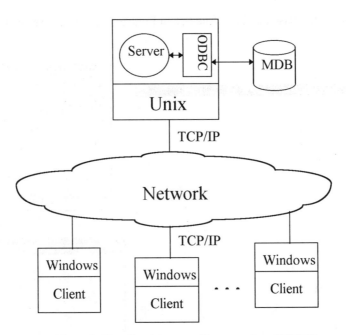

Figure 2: The client/server architecture of our HDBMS.

The window format of our HDBMS is shown in the client's interface as Figure 3 where three icons are there for representing the MDB manager, album manager and QN manager respectively.

Figure 3. The screen outlook of our HDBMS prototype

Let us start with the database subsystem, that is, the MDB manager. Once the icon of the database manager is clicked, the window as Figure 4 (a) will show up. There are two icons for two already-made databases and a specific icon named 'NEW' which is specifically for creating new databases. Legal users and fields of a newly created database can be defined as in Figure 4 (b) and (c) respectively.

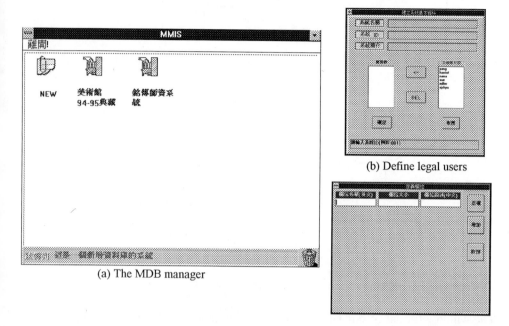

(a) The MDB manager

(b) Define legal users

(c) Define fields

Figure 4. The MDB manager and its operations

As for the layout design of displaying items in the database, our HDBMS provides tools shown as the toolbox in the left of Figure 5 (a). Selected media objects can be relocated by drag-and-drops of the mouse to obtain a better display-layout on the screen. The designer could insert new records as in the Figure 5 (b) and after finishing it would be displayed on the screen according to the predefined layout as in Figure 5 (c). In the left of Figure 5 (c), there are some transition effects to be chosen to decorate the presentation of this record. Note that the image and the label objects can be attached with hyperlinks to some albums or databases. Suppose that a certain already-made database icon instead of "NEW" is clicked in the database manager, the modification of that database could be further accomplished.

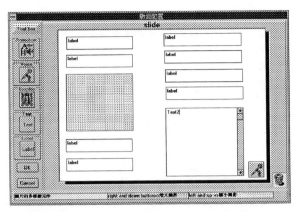

(a) The interface for the layout design in the MDB manager

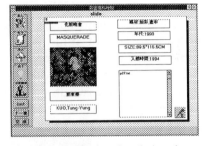

(b) Inserting a new record   (c) The record is displayed as designed.

Figure 5: Insertion and layout formatting in the MDB manager

The screen format of the album manager is quite common to the MDB manager. A window as Figure 4 (a) would come out once the album manager was triggered. An icon named "NEW" also exists with other icons for those already-made albums. The user group of a newly created album could be defined just like Figure 4 (b). The layout-design interface in the album manager is illustrated in Figure 6.

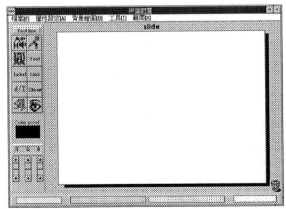

Figure 6. The interface for the layout design in the album manager

More tool buttons are provided here than in the database manager to enrich the visual effects of the presentation of the slides in the album. Media objects such as animation, audio, image, text and label, and the link object (e.g., button) are provided in the toolbox with additional text input and the background template setting. A color palette makes the designer to adjust the color of the inputted text or the background. The media objects can be imported from the existed databases or form some media files. Each media object has its own property-setting box to describe its own features.

Note that the linkage information between objects is recorded right here as link-property in some object which provides the hyperlink ability. The hyperlink can connect to some database or album or even the slide inside the album. A dialog box comes first once the link button (shown in Figure 6) is clicked. If the designer would like to link 'outside the album', a window with icons of all the databases and albums will show up. A single click to the icon could construct this hyperlink's connection. If the choice is 'inside the album', a windows with icons of the existing slides will appear.

Figure 7 shows the window of the QN manager. The user can click the corresponding icon to query a database or to navigate an album.

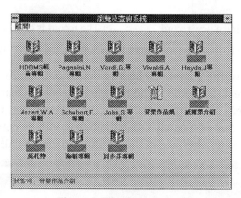

Figure 7. The QN manager

The databases and the albums together in our HDBMS offer an affluent mechanism to maintain and represent the information. Whenever necessary, a link can be arranged to connect a certain object in a database (or slide) with some album or other databases which can offer explanation in more detail about that object. The user might follow such links to query a database or to navigate an album for more related information. The flexibility of presenting information has been broadened as compared to a traditional database system or a typical multimedia presentation/authoring tool. For example, the stuff in a art gallery can construct some databases for the works of some painting masters while some albums are also constructed to describe their life histories, some albums (databases) for the description of the current exhibition, some albums (databases) for the introduction of the gallery, even some albums for the traffic guidance to the gallery. After the link relations are connected, all of these albums and databases might be referenced by simply activating these hyperlinks. Figure 8 illustrates an example where a database "音樂作品集" is queried by the form in Figure 8 (a). The result is shown in Figure 8 (b). A link can be attached with an object in Figure 8 (b), say a label "莫札特" (Mozart) to an album for Mozart as in Figure 8 (c).

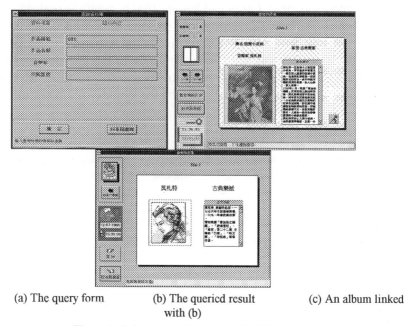

(a) The query form   (b) The queried result   (c) An album linked
with (b)

Figure 8. A database and an album for Mozart

4.0   Concluding marks and possible further extensions

We propose our idea and implementation of a prototype of HDBMS in a client/server paradigm in this paper. The quality of this prototype undoubtedly requires more criticisms. Nevertheless the essential object of our design is to integrate the advantages of the database management systems and the effectiveness of hypermedia presentations. Ideally users can query by conditions or follow predefined links to explore the information. The philosophies of these two ways are quite distinct in exploring information. In our HDBMS the designers possess not only the ability to arrange the information in the databases

54

but also the hyperlink structure in the albums/databases. The user has an extensive flexibility in finding the information he wants. The hypermedia also encourages the users' active participation and self-pace control when navigation. These features help to improve the user's control of information and his comprehension of knowledge. Our prototype could be customized into more effective tools that meet a wide range of applications such as CAL, strategic planning, GDSS, tour-guidance, ..., etc.

Our idea can be improved and extended in many aspects. The navigation control should be seriously concerned to prevent from users' disorientation and cognition overhead [Jonassen 1990, Lanza and Roselli 1991]. Auxiliary tools like global or local linkage maps, historic recording or bookmarks will be established. In the near feature a time-line table will be provided in the layout design interface of the album manager for defining the temporal relation of the included media objects. More visual effects will be augmented also. As a long-term goal, we shall try to make connections between our HDBMS and the World-Wide Webs on Internet.

Acknowledgement: The author would like to give his appreciation to SYSCOM for supporting the DBMaker engine in the design and implementation of this prototype. Thankfulness from the author should also be sent to Yang, C. C. and Lin, U. F. for their help in writing critical programs.

References:

1. Bieber, Michael (1995), On integrating hypermedia into decision support and other information systems, *Decision Support Systems*, 14, 251-267.
2. Gronbaek, K. and Trigg, R. H. (1994), Hypermedia systems: A Dexter-based architecture, *Communications of the CAM*, 37(2), 65-74.
3. Hiltz, S. R. (1994), *The Virtual Classroom: Learning without Limits via Computer Networks*, Norwood, NJ: Ablex Publishing Corporation.
4. Hornung, C., Jager, M., Santos, A. and Tritsch, B. (1993), Cooperative hypermedia: an enabling paradigm for cooperative work, *The Visual Computer International Journal of Computer Graphics*, 9(6).
5. Jonassen, D. (1990), Problems and issues in designing hypertext/hypermedia for learning, in *Designing Hypermedia for learning* edited by Jonassen, D. and Mandl, H., Berlin, German: Springer-Verlag, 3-25.
6. Jonassen, D. H, (1991), Evaluating constructivistic learning, *Educational Technology*, 31(9), 28-33.

7. Kappe, F., Maurer, H. and Sherbakov, N. (1993), Hyper-G: A universal hypermedia systems, *Journal of Educational Multimedia and Hypermedia,* 2(1), 39-66.

8. Lanza, A. and Roselli, T. (1991), Effects of the hypertextual approach versus the structured approach on student's achievement, *Journal of Computer-Based Instruction,* 18(2), 48-50.

9. Macher, Christian L., Cadish Marc, Clerc Jean-Thomas and Pretsch Erno. (1995), Hypermedia — a new concept for information management, *Chemometrics and Intelligent Laboratory Systems,* 28, 213-228.

10. Marchionini, Gary and Crane, Gregory. (1995), Evaluating hypermedia and learning: methods and results from the Perseus project, *ACM Transactions on Information Systems,* 12(1), 5-34.

11. Nielsen, J. (1990), *Hypertext and Hypermedia,* San Diego, CA: Academic Press.

12. Tomek, I. (1991), Hypermedia bibliography, *Journal of Microcomputer Applications,* 14, 63-103.

2.5

INTERACTIVE MATRIX - A BUILDING MAINTENANCE MANAGEMENT INFORMATION SYSTEM UTILIZING AN INTERACTIVE HYPERMEDIA PARADIGM

B.F. Will & Matchy J.M. Ma
University of Hong Kong, Hong Kong

The ever increasing complexity and scale of Hong Kong buildings has driven a greater demand for sophisticated building maintenance control systems. As the traditional approaches are usually responsive rather than predictive, coordination of the interactive determinants, operations, and building systems are usually poor. Thus preventive maintenance is a haphazard process and often financially difficult to rationalize. The Interactive Matrix facilitates the generation of comprehensive building maintenance management systems by the use of hypermedia technology. Instead of traditional multiple-independent filing systems, it organizes the information in an hierarchical and logical manner, where the general principles are represented in a multi-dimensional interactive grid, and related information are extensively linked to supplement one another. With the help that computer assisted intelligence provides, accurate control of preventive maintenance becomes realizable.

1.0   Introduction

For the past four years, the Department of Architecture, University of Hong Kong has been developing interactive multimedia with real-time 3D modeling as the pivotal element of its computer reset. This paper is an exploration of a management information system (MIS) of this multimedia research applied to building maintenance in Hong Kong. The core construct of the system is a three dimensional matrix embedded with hyper-linked information for navigation, comparison, and analysis. The original system has reached an advanced stage of development and it is now being used for teaching, research, and practice.

2.0   Building maintenance management in Hong Kong

Maintenance is generally a balanced operation of two complimentary and interacting systems, namely the schedule system and the contingency system. The schedule system covers items which tend to deteriorate at a more or less uniform rate and which do not have a high degree of urgency. Aspects included are:-
• preventive maintenance, e.g. painting at fixed intervals

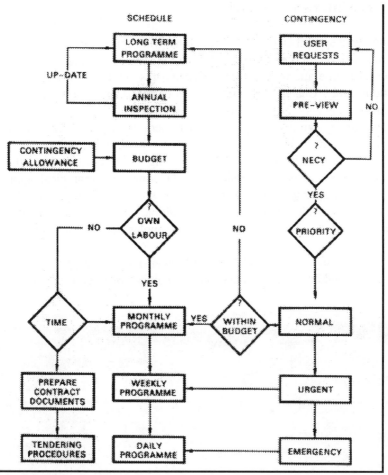

Figure 1: Schematic flowchart showing the interaction between the schedule and the contingency systems (lee, 1986: p.111)

- inspections to detect failures or the imminence of failure, and to determine the extent of works

The contingency system entails a policy of waiting until a complaint is received from the user before taking action. It is describe as casual maintenance. (Fig. 1)

In Hong Kong, building maintenance management systems generally are operated by different companies, and most commonly these are derived from the availability of a maintenance budget by the owners and the availability of skilled labor while the actual needs of building maintenance may require a much more comprehensive approach. Current methods of maintenance programming lack an overall relationship among the determinants, operations, and the building systems.

58

3.0   The interactive matrix

This modeling system is a multi-dimensional grid representing a range of related attributes in a vector space. It relates building systems to their set of associated maintenance operations and the determinants that determine when such operations apply. Changes in the attributes of determinants and the occurrences of determinate events trigger concomitant operations in other layers of the matrix and these effects can be viewed at either a theoretical or applied level. Because the operation on building systems is not a discrete or monolithic process, considerable complexity is involved in modeling the system. To keep the matrix to a manageable level of complexity, a layering or hierarchical approach is adopted and thus only requested relationships are normally displayed. However, this does not preclude the ability to have multiple databases open simultaneously but the default display opts for the lowest or simplest level of the hierarchy.

The matrix is infinitely expandable in all dimensions but in practice this is not necessary as building systems have a finite number of operations in which they operate. (Fig. 2)

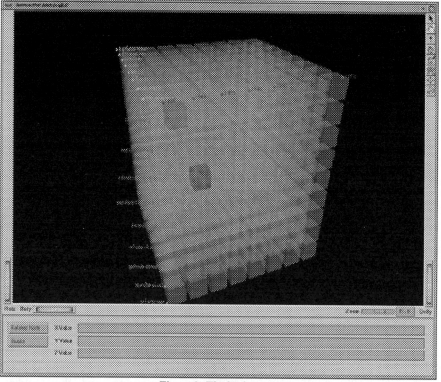

Figure 2: The basic matrix

The Matrix acts as a structured navigation tool and presents the manager with a summary view of the relevant building systems and their associated operations, the current state of the systems and the determinants that will trigger operations on the corresponding building systems.

4.0   Information organization in the matrix

The Matrix defines an N-dimension vector space $V = R_1 \times R_2 \times ... \times R_n$, where $R_1, R_2, ..., R_n$ are sets of principles or entities. For a vector $v = (r_1, r_2, ..., r_n) \in V$, such that $r_i \in R_i$, for $i = 1, 2, ..., n$, it represents a relationship among the n attributes $r_1, r_2, ..., r_n$. In our Building Maintenance Management Information System, the Matrix is a 3 dimensional grid which relates building systems, their associated operations and the corresponding determinants as described in the last section. Each relationship is represented by a voxel cell in the 3D grid, the cell is hyper-linked to information describing the relationship. The system is capable of displaying information in various media types; text descriptions, spread sheets, images, animation, audio, 2D vector drawings, and 3D models. To support cross referencing, information contained in a cell can be further linked to other information or voxel cells. This is vital for the establishment of a comprehensive information system as cross referencing enables representation of inter-related vectors, as in the case of building maintenance, changes in the attributes of determinants can trigger concomitant operations in other layers of the Matrix.

The construction of inter-linked information is facilitated by the use of standard markup languages, which provide portability and readability. HTML is employed for describing text documentation and images, HyTime for describing continuous media such as audio and animation, VRML for describing the 2D vector drawings and 3D Models, and finally SGML with a carefully designed document type definition (DTD) for describing the Matrix itself. (Fig. 3)

```
<!-- Document Type Definition (DTD) for the IrMatrix file format -->
<!doctype IrMatrix [
    <!element IrMatrix - - (body)>
    <!-- matrix body is compose of axes attributes and instances>
    <!element body - - (xLabel, yLabel, zLabel, (instance)*)>
    <!-- each axis has at least one label attribute>
    <!element (xLabel; yLabel; zLabel) - - (label+)>
    <!-- labels are string of text>
    <!element (label) - - (#PCDATA)>
    <!element instance - - ((cmd|rel)*)>
    <!-- cmd is the shell command to be executed when instance is invoked>
    <!element cmd - - (#PCDATA)>
    <!-- rel is another instance which is closely related to the one defining>
    <!element rel - - (#PCDATA)>
    <!-- 3D coordinate and medium type of the instance>
    <!attlist instance
    x NUMBER #REQUIRED
    y NUMBER #REQUIRED
    z NUMBER #REQUIRED
    t NUMBER 0>
    <!-- 3D coordinate of the related instance>
    <!attlist rel
    x NUMBER #REQUIRED
    y NUMBER #REQUIRED
    z NUMBER #REQUIRED>
]>
```

Figure 3: Document type definition (dtd) for the interactive matrix

Instead of a flat structural organization, a hierarchical layering approach has been adopted to organize the attributes within a given principle such that the number of attributes contained in a layer is kept to a minimum to keep the Matrix manageable by users. As a result, a number of sub-Matrices then follow this hierarchical approach. These sub-matrices remain hidden until the relevant subset is activated and once this happens the main matrix retreats to a non-visible layer. (Fig. 4)

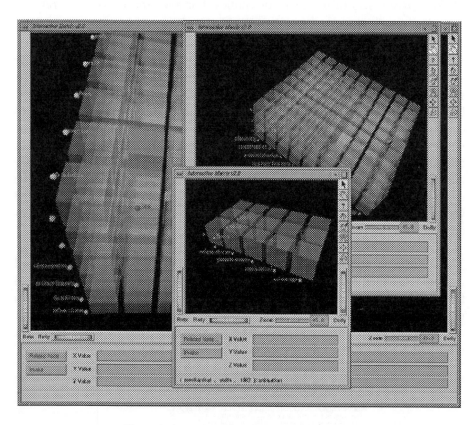

Figure 4: A number of overlapping sub-matrices

5.0   Information space navigation

The Matrix is presented as a cubic array of voxel cells, hyper-linked cells are highlighted with specific colors that indicate what type of media information are contained in the cells, while the rest of the cells are semi-transparent. Users can freely navigate in the information space in all directions; however, rotation of the

Matrix is disabled as experiments with previous prototypes show that users can lose their orientation in the information space easily when they have rotated the Matrix. Instead, a number of preset viewing positions are available for users to familiarize themselves.

A user can extract a 2D plane of information out of the 3D Matrix by specifying a value for one of the three axes. For example, if a manager discovers there is a leakage problem in the drainage system, and wishes to learn what remedy action to take. He would specify "drainage system" as the attribute value for the Building Systems axis, the system will return him a 2D Matrix containing all the associated operations that are applicable to the drainage system and the determinate events that would trigger such operations.

To go further, a user can reduce the 2D matrix to a 1D linear list by specifying one more value for one of the remaining two axes. For example, if the manager now selects the "leakage" attribute in the Determinant axis, a linear list shows all the associated operations that have to be taken for this situation and the operations are arranged in the order of increasing priorities.

When the manager selects one of the operations in the list, he invokes the hyper-linked information attached to this cell. For example, this can be a detailed description of the action needed to be taken, such as steps for shutting down the drainage system, date of the last such action took, and photo images of the problematic part of the drainage system of the last leakage. Subsequently the manager is also be able to update the database about the current status of the drainage system.

6.0   Navigational aids

A user can zoom-in, zoom-out, and move the Matrix to adjust the view. The text labels on the axes and the cells automatically adjust themselves so that they always face towards the viewing plane of the user, no matter how the user changes the Matrix's orientation. Also the level of detail of these labels increases[decreases] as the user zooms in[out].

Tools such as link previewer, history list, and search engine are available to assist navigation. For example, when the cursor enters the pick region of a cell a preview window automatically shows the associated order triple for the cell. To track a user's path a history list is kept showing all the visited cells and these cells can be revisited directly by selecting the corresponding entry in the list.

62

7.0   Conclusion

The Interactive Matrix is a three-dimensional grid relating various building systems with the associated operations and the determinants. To keep the Matrix to a manageable level of complexity, a layering or hierarchical process is employed and thus only the requested information is displayed. This does not preclude the ability to have multiple database open simultaneously but the default display opts for the lowest or simplest level of the hierarchy.

This Interactive Matrix permits free comparisons of information from various aspects of the total building maintenance program. Hence, an optimization of resources can be achieved to increase the efficiency of the maintenance management. An office building, in Central District, Hong Kong, is taken as an example to illustrate the application of the interactive system.

ACKNOWLEDGMENT This research was supported by a grant from the Committee on Research and Conference Grant, University of Hong Kong. The original source for the diagrammatic representation is a report prepared by Vincent K.T. Kwong, Wayne K.Y. Mak, and Shereen S.L. Mon, Forth Year students in the Department of Architecture, University of Hong Kong.

References:

1. Bradford J.W., Hart I.E., Will B.F., (1995) "Cognitive Construction in Architectural Education", paper presented to the First International Cognitive Technology Conference, Hong Kong.
2. Bradford J.W., Will B.F. (1994) "The Temple Tutor Teaching System", paper presented to the Design Decision Support Systems '94 Conference, Vaals, The Netherlands.
3. Wong W.C.H., Yau C.Y.P., Bradford J.W., Will B.F. (1994) "Authoring and Delivering in a Hypermedia System for Architectural Education", paper presented to the Design Decision Support Systems '94 Conference, Vaals, The Netherlands.
4. Will B.F., Bradford J.W., Ng F.F. (1993) "Architectural Education Objectives and the Use of Multimedia", paper presented to the ECAADE '93 Conference, Eindhoven.
5. Bradford J.W., Ng F.F., Will B.F. (1992) "3D Models and Hypermedia for Architectural Education", paper presented to the ECAADE '92 Conference, Barcelona.
6. Bradford J.W., Ng F.F., Will B.F. (1992) "Multimedia CIA in Architectural Education", paper presented to the Design & Decision Support Systems in Architecture and Urban Planning Conference, Eindhoven.
7. Lee, R. (1986), Building Maintenance Management, Granada Publishing.

2.6

USING HYPERTEXT TECHNIQUE IN SOFTWARE TESTING

Pantovic, V[1]. & D. Velasevic[2]
[1]Energoprojekt Holding, [2]University of Belgrade, Yugoslavia

The purpose of this paper is to present a development of the software system intended to support non-computer-based testing (human testing techniques) through the use of hypertext. This is a new approach in this kind of testing: namely, we use the computer for non-computer-based testing. Because this testing technique requires team work, we establish a model of PCs in a local network. Both approaches - code inspections and walkthroughs - will be included. This Hypersource technique is also very useful for documenting the applications.

1.0   Introduction

Testing is a very important phase in the software development because it verifies the correctness of software and its readiness for implementation in operational mode (Velasevic, 1990). In a typical programming project, approximately 50% of the elapsed time and over 50% of the total cost are expended in testing the program or system being developed (Myers, 1979; Stucki, 1976). That these propositions from relatively dated references are still valid is provided by the statement of Bill Gates (Chairman and CEO, Microsoft Corporation): "The costs of software development are much more in testing than in development. In a way you can say Microsoft is a software testing organization."

For many years, the majority of the programming community worked under the assumptions that programs are written solely for machine execution and are not intended to be read by people, and that the only way to test a program is by executing it on a machine. This attitude began to change in the early 1970s, largely as a result of Weinberg's *"The Psychology of Computer Programming"*. Experience has shown that these human testing techniques are quite effective in finding errors, so much so that one or more of these should be employed in every programming project. Practice with these methods has found them to be effective in finding from 30% to 70% of the logic design and coding errors in typical programs.

Automation of the testing process is important on account of economical reasons. Several systems automating the testing phase are available (Velasevic, 1996). We have studied the use of hypertext as the way in which the classical non-computer-testing process (NCBTST) can be improved. Some kind of interaction with program at source code level is used in debuggers, but this is only upon program compilation, and driven by program execution. It is very important to remove as many defects as possible early in the development process (Mosklin, 1996). There are two principal reasons for testing. They are to produce a more reliable product and to reduce costs (Bronecke, 1985). Fixing a defect early in the software development cycle is less costly than correcting that same error later in the cycle.

The text is further organized in such a way that the next Section presents the concept of human testing techniques (non-computer-based testing), based on Myers' book *"The Art of Software Testing"*. The third Section presents the proposed hypersource concept, i.e. the possibility of organizing source code in the form of hypertext. The fourth Section presents the concept of implementing the NCBTST software system in conferencing model of PCs in local network and highlights the plans for further development of the NCBTST software. The Conclusion points out the advantages of such approach in application testing over the classical implementation of human testing techniques.

2.0 Non-computer-based testing

2.1 Human testing techniques

Experience has shown that non-computer-based testing (human testing) is quite effective in finding errors. The methods presented in this Section are intended to be applied between the time that the program is coded and the time that computer based testing begins. Earlier errors are found, the costs of correcting the errors are lower and the probability of correcting the errors correctly is higher. Code inspections and walkthroughs are two primary "human testing" methods.

Inspections and walkthroughs involve the reading or visual inspection of a program by a team of people. The objective of the meeting is to find errors, but not to find solutions to the errors (to test but not to debug). The process is performed by a group of people (optimally three or four), only one whom is the author of the program. People occasionally state that an inspection or walkthrough is simply a new name for the older "desk-checking" process (the process of a programmer reading his or her own program before testing it), but inspections and walkthroughs have been found to be far more effective, because people other than the program's author are involved in the process.

2.2   Code inspections

A code inspection is a set of procedures and error-detection techniques for group code reading. An inspection team usually consists of four people. One of the four people plays the role of moderator. The moderator is expected to be a competent programmer, but he or she is not the author of the program and not acquainted with the details of the program. The duties of the moderator include distributing materials, scheduling the inspection session, leading the session, recording all errors found, and ensuring that the errors are subsequently corrected. Hence the moderator can be likened to a quality-control engineer. The second team member is the programmer. The remaining team members usually consist of the program's designer (if different from the programmer) and a test specialist.

2.3   Walkthroughs

Like the inspection, the walkthrough is an uninterrupted meeting of one to two hours in duration. The walkthrough team consists of three to five people. One of these people plays a role similar to that of the moderator in the inspection process, another person plays the role of a secretary (a person who records all errors found), and a third person plays the role of a "tester". The initial procedure is identical to that of the inspection process: the participants are given the materials several days in advance to allow them to "bone up" on the program. However the procedure in the meeting is different. Rather than simply reading the program or using error checklists, the participants "play computer". The person designated as the tester comes to the meeting armed with a small set of paper test cases-representative sets of inputs (and expected outputs) for the program or module. During the meeting, each test case is mentally executed. That is the test data are walked through the logic of the program.

2.4   Desk checking

A third human error-detection process is the older practice of desk checking. A desk check can be viewed as a one-person inspection or walkthrough; a person reads a program, checks it with respect to an error list, and/or walks test data through it.

3.0   Hypersource

3.1   Hypersource concept

Hypertext interconnects related pieces of information in a computer so that the user can move to new locations in the information space by following links.

Tools for creating hypertext documents and hypertext viewers have lowered the cost of creating documentation and shortened the time needed to deliver it. The most obvious hypertext application is probably on-line manuals. World Wide Web is also a kind of hypertext (hypermedia).

Hypersource is a kind of hypertext which interconnect related pieces of source code text of a application. The application source code is normally divided into units (modules, programs, subprograms, procedures). These source units in a hypertext information space forms a graph structure (Fig. 1). Source code is transformed into structured hypertext documents. Hypersource interconnects source units so that user can navigate through source code text.

Good documentation is a basis from which program improving and upgrading can proceed. Through program testing (at least at the current level of program validation methods) it is not possible prove that a program is without errors. However, in the course of its operation there may appear errors which have to be removed. An exhaustive and quality documentation supports easier application developing, reading, understanding, testing, using, and reengineering.

3.2   Hypersource as a Windows Help Style application

We have made first NCBTST environment as Windows Style Help application. In the next few sentences we are going to explain some basic concepts and steps for making that kind of application.

Hypersource consists of one or more Hypersource files that contain text needed to communicate on-line the information about the application source code. Each Hypersource file contains one or more topics a member of a team can select. The primary unit of information in a Hypersource file is a topic, i.e., a subroutine in the source code. A topic is a self-contained body of text which contains one routine. Some topics contain hot spots (links) that can be used to get a source of another subroutine. Jumps are cross-references to related topics. When the user clicks a jump, the Hypersource window switches to a screen displaying source code of another topic. During the testing session of the team, the secretary of the team can insert, at the proper places, the remarks of all members, as comments, and updates, if necessary, the inspection error-checklist. Annotation is solved with standard Annotate function in Windows Help application.

To create Hypersource system for an application under test, it is necessary to perform a series of actions: enter all required links into the Source Code files which must be saved in RTF (Rich Text Format), build the Hypersource Project File, and use the Help Compiler to convert Source files into the Hypersource file.

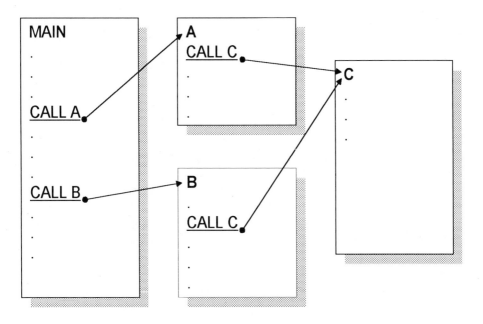

Figure 1: Hypersource structure

3.3 Hypersource in HTML Form

Computer communications is changing the way that we work and do business. As the popularity and importance of the Internet and intranets applications grow (Pantovic, 1996) we have decided to develop NCBTST in intranet (Web) environment.

It is well known that Home pages and other Internet hypertext documents created by developers should conform to hypertext markup language specifications. HTML files are special form of ISO 8879, widely known as the standard generalized markup language (SGML).

The main part of NCBTST system is HTML Translator (Fig. 2) which can insert some HTML links automatically in the source and generate Hypersource. Programmer can also add another HTML tags "manually" with standard HTML authoring tools.

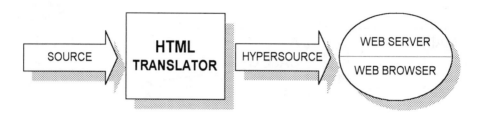

Figure 2: Hypersource Generation

3.4 Psychology of Computer Programming and Testing

Although one can discuss the subject of testing from several technical points of view, it appears that the most important considerations in software testing are the issues of economics and human psychology. Very important testing principle is: A programmer should avoid attempting to test his or her own program (Myers, 1979).

Testing is the destructive process. It is extremely difficult, after a programmer has been constructive while designing and coding a program, to suddenly, overnight, change his or her perspective and attempt to form a completely destructive frame of mind toward the program. Most programmers cannot effectively test their own programs because they cannot bring themselves to form the necessary mental attitude: the attitude of wanting to expose errors.

In addition to this psychological problem, there is a second significant problem: the program may contain errors due to the programmer's misunderstanding of the problem statement or specification. If this is the case, it is likely that the programmer will have the same misunderstanding when attempting to test his or her own program.

Testing is more effective and successful if performed by another party. Hypersource is a way for efficient supporting that team process. Debugging (correcting known errors) is more efficiently performed by the original programmer.

3.5 Testing With Hypersource in Groupware and Intranet environment

People pay more attention to a system when they know other people are paying attention to it (Ackerman, 1996). Group members working on a common problem communicate to one another a sense of urgency that tends to heighten their mobilization of energy, and thus their motivation. We are working to provide constructions facilities for multi- user discussion.

Groupware systems explicitly support groups of users working together. Also called computer-supported cooperative work systems, groupware system differ from single-user systems in their emphasis on collaboration and joint work.

The Internet is also an alternative to groupware applications. Enterprise-wide intranets use the Internet as an access medium to corporate databases, but instead of being global and open to all users only authorized have access privileges. A typical intranet scenario includes several servers that connect to the Internet over leased lines. In-house users can connect over a LAN to these resources. Other corporate sites as well as individual customers access the servers over the Internet for the price of a local call. In that environment distributed usage of hypersource for testing purposes is possible all around the world.

3.6   NCBTST/Hypersource Benefits

Typically, testing and debugging is done at the end of the development process just before final release. When errors are found at this point, the time and money to fix them can devastate a product-release schedule. To avoid this situation, every development organization should follow two rules. First, remove as many defects as possible early in the development process. Second, remove as many defects as possible before the product ships.

The cost of finding defects is only one part of the cost equation, the other is the cost of fixing them. Fixing a defect early in the product development cycle is less costly than correcting that same error later in the cycle. The longer a bug remains in the software, the more expensive it becomes to remove. An error-detection tool that finds the error earlier lowers the cost of error fixing significantly. Developers who adopt the "paradigm shift" of "check early, check often" will find that both the cost of correcting errors and the time spent developing drop sharply.

NCBTST/Hypersource is tool for testing and locating errors, analyses of source code, investigation of program structure and module connections at the beginning of development process. With Hypersource system NCBTST, the user can navigate through application and perform very efficient non-computer-based testing (30-40% more efficient in time domain when all activities are accounted for than in the classical approach). Hypersource (NCBTST) supports: distribution without paper, annotates, white box testing, incremental testing, module testing, team work, parallel activities of several test teams, distributed teams, etc.

NCBTST is very good tool (support) for human finding (locating) errors. NCBTST supports mental execution of program. It is an improvement of the already proved good techniques.

Savings in printer operation and paper consumption. One of moderator's duties is to distribute materials to the members of the testing team. In this approved approach it is enough to tell URL (Universal Resource Locator) where Hypersource of the application is.

Hypersource supports white box testing in which test cases exercise or cover the logic (source code) of the program. Hypersource also supports module testing (or unit testing) as a process of testing the individual subprograms, subroutines, or procedures in a program.

As it is recommended that testing is not carried out by those who wrote the program, it substantially facilitates walk through the source. The participants can easier familiarize themselves with the application prior the session.

In a large project (many modules and people) it is possible with Hypersource to parallel activities of several test teams.

Test techniques concern not only the accuracy of measurement but also how quickly a test can be accomplished without significantly sacrificing coverage. Hypersource is very user-friendly and it is very easy to include it in software development process. It provides an excellent insight into the program documentation. Hypersource makes program easier to read and understand, and it can be an efficient way in the process of learning programming languages.

3.7   Further Improvement of NCBTST

To understand program execution, it is very important to visualize it (Shimomura, 1991; Ball, 1996). The invisible nature of software hides system complexity, particularly for large team-oriented projects. Visual representations of code help to solve this problem. We plan to use some visual representations of the source code to improve NCBTST, like using different colours of text and background. We shall also include version and history of source text, and multimedia annotates (speech comments, pictures, even a movie). NCBTST will facilitate multi user discussion through the use of video-conferencing. For example, the possibility of using telephone over Internet will allow joint testing by people located in remote places. We are intending to make detail specifications for the roles for all the members of the testing team and especially the rules for making annotates.

4.0 Conclusion

It is generally recognized that the earlier errors are found, the lower are the costs of correcting the errors and the higher is the probability of correcting the errors correctly. Hypersource is the way in which the testing process can be automated at the beginning.

With Hypersource significant advances have been made in automation of the testing process (code inspections and walkthroughs). With Hypersource system NCBTST, the user can navigate through the application and perform very efficient non-computer-based testing (30-40% more efficient in time domain when all activities are accounted for than in the classical approach). Hypersource (NCBTST) supports: distribution without paper, annotates, white box testing, incremental testing, module testing, team work, parallel activities of several test teams, distributed teams, etc.

The Hypersource also has several side effects in addition to its main effect of finding errors. The Hypersource technique is also very useful for documenting the applications. Hypersource makes program easier to read and understand, and it can be an efficient way in the process of learning programming languages.

We have used Web as a tool improving testing but ever increasing usage of Internet/intranet applications indicates that Web applications will also be the object of testing to ensure the quality and integrity of Web sites.

References:

1. Ackerman, M.S., Starr, B. (1996), "Social Activity Indicators for Groupware", IEEE Computer, 29(6), 37-42.
2. Ball, T., Eick S.G. (1996), "Software Visualization in the Large", IEEE Computer, 29(4),33-43.
3. Bronecke, P. (1985), "The Economics of Test", IEEE Design&Test, June 1985, 18-19.
4. Mosklin, J. (1996), "Improving software quality requires a 'check early, check often' approach", IEEE Spectrum, January 1996, 63.
5. Myers, G.J. (1979), "The Art of Software Testing", New York, John Wiley & Sons.
6. Pantovic, V., Dinic, S., Vuckovic, M. (1996), "Energoprojekt's Info-Center", Proc. InfoTeh '96, YURIT, Donji Milanovac, 228-232.
7. Shiomura T., Isoda, S. (1991), "Linked-List Visualization for Debugging", IEEE Software, May 1991, 44-51.

72

8. Stucky, L.G. (1976), "A Case for Software Testing", IEEE Trans. on Software Engineering, 2(3), 194.
9. Velasevic, D. (1990), "Introduction to Systems Programming", (in Serbian), Beograd, Naucna knjiga.
10. Velasevic, D. (1995), "Testgraph: Software for Automatic Generation of Test Case Patterns", Proc. InfoTeh '95, YURIT, Donji Milanovac, 1-9.

PART 3

DISTRIBUTED MULTIMEDIA

3.1

HANURI: A FRAMEWORK FOR DISTRIBUTED MULTIMEDIA APPLICATIONS

Han Namgoong & In-Won Yoo
Electronics and Telecommunications Research Institute, Korea

This paper explores an experimental approach to distributed multimedia applications requires many features: distributed services, management of systems and interoperability with legacy applications. We tried an experimental approach, which resulted in a new framework, HANURI. HANURI is in middleware layer and based on client/server model. HANURI provides one top service, management of distributed systems and interoperability with legacy data through HANURI's three components: HANURI/C, HANURI/M and HANURI/T respectively. For this we show one typical example, Travel Reservation Service(TRS), where HANURI provides and efficient approach to legacy data. One of weaknesses of HANURI is that it needs different backgrounds, transaction and system management, and a little poor performance compared with non-HANURI approach.

1.0   Introduction

Distributed multimedia applications need many different kinds of features such as security, distributed time, file service, naming service, multimedia service, multimedia I/O, interoperability with existing legacy data and so on. Furthermore from end user point of view it is necessary to have single service point, one stop service, for the access of all services in the network. The service point may be agent or unified graphical user interface, which accepts all requests and does necessary works. In distributed multimedia applications environment it is very important to know others' status such as failure, network traffic and time-out etc. to handle both network and system management. There are still many legacy applications which acts as one of resources in distributed environment. For example personal bank account is expected to be under current legacy applications quite a long time. Of course user interface may be changed in a short time but its operational state will not be changed. In user point of view exactly once execution is good for applications programming in the complex and distributed multimedia applications environment. Such a concept is a transaction service, which provides automatic failure recovery in a fashion of all or nothing. Many applications in distributed systems need interoperability with legacy applications as a last step(ex. payment of VoD service) and usually it works on data(bank account etc.) in a transactional mode. To be a good platform for distributed multimedia applications application we have to provide an efficient solution of three requirements as follows: integration of distributed application(one stop service provision), management of distributed systems and interoperability with legacy application.

This paper is organized as follows. Section 2 and 3 describe HANURI Model and architecture. In section 4 we present one example of HANURI application, Travel Reservation Service(TRS). Finally, section 5 offers some conclusions.

2.0   HANURI model

There are three basic models of distributed processes: filter, Peer-to-Peer and Client/Server. Filter processes do a prefixed operation on a stream of data and passing the results to next process. Peer-to-Peer model uses identical process each other and interacts in a cooperative fashion for a work. Client/Server model contains two independent processes, client process sends requests to a server process which responds with result. One model widely used in distributed systems is the Client/Server model. A program, the client, requests an service to another program, server, which provides. Upon receiving request from client server do prefixed operation and returns the result. Client/Server model can be thought three different types depending on how to manage service requests and necessary information such as where and how to get a specific service. Three operational types are described in Figure 1[10]. Broker frees clients from maintaining information on where and how to obtain necessary services. The necessary information includes naming, data format, connection interface and specific information of implementations. A forwarding broker relays a client's request to the relevant server, retrieves reply, and relays it back to the client. A handle-driven broker returns a service "handle" back to the client and the client uses this handle to issue request directly to the server. The handle provides necessary steps like connection, request format and so on.

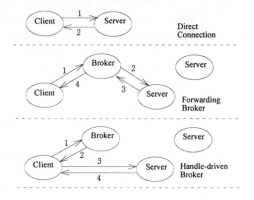

Figure 1. Three Operational Types of Client/Server Model

3.0   HANURI architecture

Figure 2 shows overall structure and components of HANURI which uses Distributed Computing Environment(DCE)[1] as a basic distributed processing environment. HANURI resides in middleware layer between system services and user applications. First component of HANURI is Distributed Transaction Processing module, called HANURI/T, which has Transaction Processing Monitor with Objected-oriented interface. System management module, called HANURI/M, is the second and it provides the management of network and distributed systems. Another one is for client/server application development tool, called HANURI/C.

HANURI provides user interfaces through HANURI/C and supports a combination model, called Hybrid Broker Model, of all three operational types depending on requested services. The handle provides necessary steps like connection, request format and so on. Client can connect directly to server or request to some specific services to dedicated server like HANURI/Y or HANURI/M and later receives replies from those servers. Sometimes client receives handle from other servers and request service to server using returned handle. HANURI/T follows X/Open DTP[2] model and interfaces, XA, TX and TxRPC. HANURI/M supports network management using management in DCE environment. HANURI/M and HANURI/C have another path, direct connection to TCP/IP not through DCE RPC, for current wide usage of TCP/IP protocol. In end users view points architecture has to play a role of service pool which contains many services as middlewares and the services be cooked by user interact with computer system via graphical interface and it is enough to give users singleservice point in distributed environment.

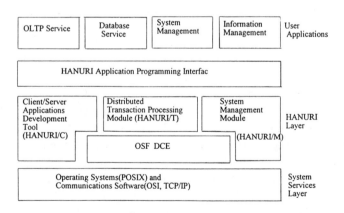

Figure 2: Structure of HANURI

78

3.1 Interoperability with legacy system

Typical transactions share the resources in the local area. In the distributed environment, however, multiple servers on different machine jon one global transaction. To handle such a situation we need distributed transaction processing which coordinates many local transactions as one global transaction. Distributed processing is the next-generation information processing technology that will change the traditional information processing infrastructure in the mid 1990's

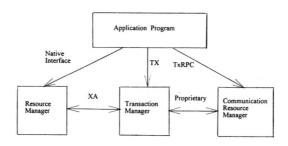

Figure 3: Inside of HANURI/T

HANURI/T, as shown Figure 3, follows X/Open DTP model and adopts three interfaces: XA,TX,TxRPC.
The interface between manager is proprietary for XA+is now snapshot and the scenario is not clear yet.

3.2 Management of distributed systems

To manage distributed environment efficiently there must be a consistent view of the environment, so we designed our own management architecture called HANURIM[4]. Initially, we referred to OSF Distributed Management Environment(DME) model because DME was one of reasonable models based on DCE. Figure 4 shows our own management architecture and it consists of network and systems management modules. In Network Management Module users can manage configuration, fault and performance of the networks. Network Monitoring is also accomplished by the basic functions of SNMP and Managers can get information using SNMP Management Information Base value. Network Management applications are shown via graphical user interfaces. System Management Module includes the management of DCE control services and distributed applications. When distributed environment is configured using DCE the management of DCE is the key function of the systems management. DCE is a set services that together make up a high-level, coherent environment for developing and running distributed applications.

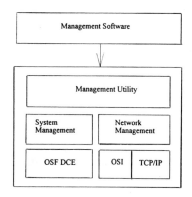

Figure 4: Inside of HANURI/M

These services provide a set of tools that support DCE management tasks[5] but DCE control program is too complex to program. We designed the administration tools for the easy use of DCE control program and it supports various types of service managements depending on management purposes. In the design of the DCE tool we only focuses on the help for administrators of DCE environment. The tool shows management status with graphical user interface.

3.3   One stop service provision

HANURI/C[3], shown in Figure 5, has two layer. The userware layer has the presentation interface functions for the end user programs and the middleware layer for control integration of services. the HANURI/C API is a common interface path to HANURI/C interface, ODBC interface, DCE interface and the HANURI/T interface module. A user can access database server consistently and transparently without checking the status of the interface and communication network protocols using the HANURI/C Application Programming Interface(APIs). In HANURI/C application a form is a collection of screen of several pages and each page contains more than one object. Form Processing Module generates, modifies, organizes and shows object(s) to user, where object can be any data item like numeric data, video data, audio data and complex data. In addition to simple text users can add buttons, menus, tables, and multimedia windows.

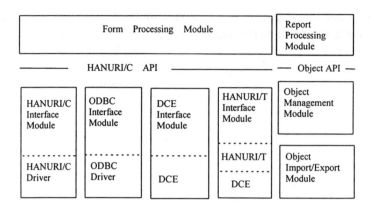

Figure 5: Inside of HANURI/C

HANURI/C has a connection to Transaction Processing via HANURI/T interface. Typical transactions share the resources in the local area. In distributed environment, however, multiple servers on different machine jon one global transaction. To handle such a situation we need distributed transaction processing which coordinates many local transactions as one global transaction. Distributed processing is the next-generation information processing technology that will change the traditional information processing infrastructure in the mid 1990's. Two types of reports can be generated by report Processing Module. One is a simple report which shows SQL statement result, another is a user-defined report. User-defined report includes table, multi-colimn, matrix and list. Usually ODBC of Microsoft is used for the access DBMS and if no interface in DBMS then HANURI/C interface is adopted. HANURI/C has a function for cut-paste of object which is any data type using Object Linking and Embedding and Dynamic Data Exchange, where object handling is done through our own script interface language. In HANURI distributed services are provided by DCE interfaces and HANURI/T interface gives transaction service.

The HANURI/C API is a common interface path to HANUIR/C, ODBC, DCE and HANURI/T interface modules. The APIs is categorized as follows:
- ✓ Service Source Connection/Administration
- ✓ Query Edit/Execution
- ✓ DBMS Scema/Catalog Information Retrieval
- ✓ Error Handling

The service source is a logical item necessary for administration and has three fields: Host Name, DBMS and Description.

4.0   Example of HANURI

Figure 6 shows Travel Reservation Service workflow and it contains many multimedia data: video, audio, graphics and text. User receives Travel Reservation Service through transaction operation, distributed services on several services of different platforms via TCP/IP and DCE environment(in figure 7 and 8). The related module is interface and corresponding operations are done by separate modules in local or remote machines. HANURI/C gives user one stop service using graphical user interface, which is similar to windows display, and keeps consistent view of different services. We can think Travel Reservation Service workflow as 7 steps and each step needs different communication mode with different reasons. The communication model of each step is explained as follows:

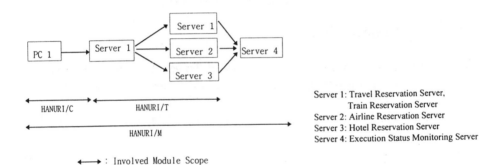

Figure 6: Travel reservation service flow

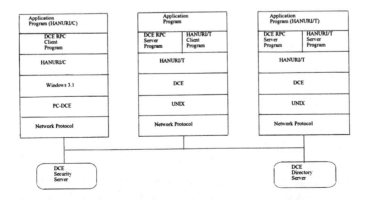

Figure 7. HANURI/T and HANURI/C Connection

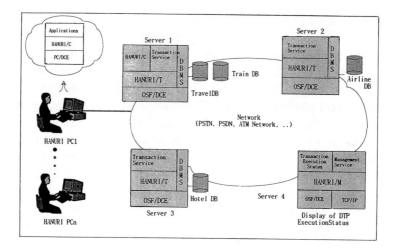

Figure 8: Travel Reservation Service Environment

4.1   Initial display and reservation

After power on users see initial display play of Travel Reservation Service and select product catalog display. In this step users connect to Train, Hotel and Airline DB server in connection-oriented way(TCP/IP) for catalogue contains many multimedia data(means big size of transmission data) and does not need to show data in atomic operation.

There will be many concurrent to order after catalog display and order information contains very short packet data like customer name and product number. To handle many concurrent users in a given time efficiently connectionless(UDP/IP, for short data) and at-most0once style operation is proper in this step. TCP/IP based connection is another candidate but it holds communication time to send small data. At-most-once style operation is enough to cover simple communication errors.

4.2   Cancel/confirm reservation

Both steps also contain very small data, cancel or confirm and payment, so it will be better to connect Travel DB server in connection less with at-most-once operation.

4.3   Payment (bank and credit card)

In these steps all data should be kept first into secure storage for the communication and server failure. To guarantee data and operation consistency we use transaction processing module, HANURI/T, and communication method based on SUN RPC, and DCE RPC. Figure 8 shows the integration of HANURI/C and HANURI/T. HANURI/C does not call distributed transaction service client program calls client program of HANURI/T. Upon receipt of the request of transaction service client program calls Transaction Processing Server. Client program can be located in the machine of HANURI/T and HANURI/C uses DCE RPC to communicate with transaction processing server.

5.0 Conclusion

Many multimedia applications need interoperability with legacy data(ex. bank account) as a last step and we prototyped a new platform, which provides distributed services, interoperability with legacy data and management facility of distributed systems. There have been many proposals, framework, for distributed multimedia applications and have got considerable results. Unfortunately they do not cover all the aspects of real environmental factors: management of distributed systems in the failure of service, one stop service provision and a guarantee of persistent result to legacy data(example, payment of purchase). Several frameworks(or platforms) are available on the market today. Common Point[4] has many good features such as objected-oriented system base(Operating system), domain functions and support functions but lacks for transaction services and transaction service. HANURI provides object manipulation and transaction service, which are considered very important functions to applications in distributed multimedia applications. We have a little poor performance(30% down) compared with Non-HANURI approach and will do performance enhancement.

References:

1. Open Software Foundation(1992), DCE Administration Guide, Cambridge, Open Software Foundation
2. X/Open Company Limited(1993), Distributed Transaction Processing Reference Model, Berkshire U.K., X/Open Company Limited
3. Soran Ine et al.(1994), "Database Server Client Tool in Client-Server Model", *Korea Database Journal, kDBs*, Vol.1, No., August
4. Taligent(1993), building Object-Oriented Frameworks, Taligent, CA.
5. Object Management Group(1992), The Common Object Request Broker: Architecture and Specification, Object Management Group
6. Richard Adler(1995), "Distributed Coordination Models for Client/Server Computing", *Computer*, Vol.28, No.4, April

7. Dimitrios Georgakopoulos et al.(1993), "An Extended Transaction Environment for Workflows in Distributed Object Computing", *IEEE Bulletin of the Technical Committee on Data Engineering*, Vol.16, No.2
8. Jim Gray and Andreas Reuter(1993), transaction Processing: Concept and Techniques, Morgan Kaufmann, San Mateo, CA

3.2

MODELING DISTRIBUTED MULTIMEDIA APPLICATIONS

Hans Scholten, Pierre G. Jansen, Andrej Koelewijn,
Marc T.M.J. Rissewijck & Jan D. Zijlstra
University of Twente, The Netherlands

To gain experience in designing and modeling distributed multimedia applications a general multimedia toolkit is designed and implemented. It allows for rapid prototyping and contains many ideas as can be found in SUMO, MMS, The Touring Machine and MASI. The multimedia toolkit takes care synchronisation of multiple media streams within a heterogeneous distributed system, and provides a straightforward way of handling different media servers. It allows applications to specify quality of service and offers network transparent services, temporal access commands for continuous media, quality of service management, synchronisation management and dynamic management of the application's topology.

1.0   Introduction

Emphasis of our research lies on the application of multimedia technology: teleteaching, teleconferencing and collaborative work. To support this research we need an environment that supports rapid prototyping of distributed multimedia applications. Because other systems did not offer what we wanted, we decided to build our own environment, rather then using one of the available ones and extending it. Key are: dynamically configurable, heterogeneous, system synchronization, actors and flows.

2.0   Related work

Substantial work is and has been done on distributed multimedia systems. Examples are found in SUMO [CBPS9], MMS [HIS93, HIS94], The Touring Machine [AKR92, Bel93] and MASI [BDFT94].

2.1   SUMO

In the SUMO project at Lancaster University a distributed multimedia system is designed by extending the Chorus micro-kernel.

- The abstractions provided by the Chorus API are a good starting point, but insufficient for distributed multimedia applications. That is why the Chorus API is extended with new low level calls and abstractions.

The programming model is also extended with the two following compound abstractions:

- invocation - a request/reply service composed of multiple message flows, and
- pipeline - concatenations of QoS controlled stream flows containing intermediary processing stages.

2.2 Touring machine

The Touring Machine is a research project at Bellcore The touring machine is designed from a communication providers point of view. This means that things like billing, robustness and availability have been looked at. Version three of the Touring machine makes use of DCE. Some extensions have been build on top of it, mainly for sharing information among users. The other facilities are implemented as applications. This results in greater extensibility and scalability.

The system is designed as a client-server system. Trading is used for the registration and discovery of useful system services. The Touring Machine model consists of two layers, the session control layer and the transport control layer. The session control layer provides logical control of communication, the transport control layer takes care of the physical resource allocation and provides network transparency.

2.3 Middleware System Services

Middleware Systems Services, MSS, is designed as a layer between the operating system and applications. It uses DCE and the DCE-extension CORBA. CORBA provides distributed objects. This means that the interface of an object is visible both local and remote.

There are three types of MSS objects: virtual resources, format and stream objects. Virtual devices, virtual clocks, groups and virtual connections are subclasses of the virtual resource class. A virtual resource is an abstraction of a physical resource that provides a consistent programming model, independent of the details of the implementation. Before a resource can acquire its underlying physical resources, the desired QoS should be specified. The acquisition of resources is handled by resource managers. These can supervise resource sharing between virtual resources. A user can influence the way these resource managers work through resource policy agents.

A virtual device is a data-processing object. It has one or more ports which abstract the input or output mechanism. To encapsulate the medium specific information, every port has a format object. Every virtual device also has a stream object. This object provides the user with an interface to observe media stream position. It can also provide interfaces for stream flow control and synchronisation.

Virtual connections provide interfaces to connections between ports. A virtual connection also has a stream object to enable observation of the stream position. The virtual connections are based on the media stream protocol. This protocol supports media-independent transport and synchronisation. A virtual connection will have to determine if ports can be connected. This depends on the format and QoS of the ports. Internally the connection is implemented with a virtual connection adapter object. This object decides what transport method is needed. If two ports are located on the same machine this can be, e.g., memory sharing, if the ports are not on the same machine the transport will use the media stream protocol.

The combination of virtual devices and the virtual connections can be described by data flow graphs. A whole graph can be handled using a group object. This object provides a mechanism for resource allocation and specification of quality of service for a group of connection- and device-objects. It can also be used to control the stream flow of the graph as a whole.

A registration and retrieval service is available to find and instantiate objects whose capabilities satisfy a list of constraints. One might, e.g., want a virtual device giving MPEG data from camera A. Objects are instantiated using a factory

The MSS-system does not provide special session or collaboration functionality. This has to be implemented using a group sub-class.

2.4 MASI laboratory

In [BDFT94] the basic principles of a general architecture for distributed multimedia support over ATM based networks are presented. The goal of this distributed multimedia communication architecture is to provide an environment which allows an easy design and support of multimedia applications. The architecture is based on the quality of service and communication management functions associated to the services it provides.

This architecture differs from other existing multimedia architectures in that it provides a way to compute a path, from the application level down to the communication subsystem level. Such a path is given to a connection manager entity. It is computed according to a communication profile by a QoS manager. This way, it is possible to bypass some communication services if they are not relevant for the application.

2.5 Conclusion

In all existing systems quality of service is an important issue. In the MASI project where everything depends on quality of service. In the SUMO project all objects of the system have a quality of service specification.

To provide transparent distributed multimedia most systems use an objects abstraction. Objects can be run anywhere on a network, and location dependent issues are handled by a name and location server.

Grouping of objects is important to offer a consistent interface to a group of related objects. SUMO has flows to abstract a group of sequential-related connections, MSS has a group object to to group virtual connections. These groups can be used both for parallel and serial grouping of objects.

Where appropriate, we will indicate simularities and differences between our model and the above described systems in the following sections.

3.0 TMT model

The TMT (Twente Multimedia Toolkit) toolkit consists of three types of objects:

- Actors
- End points on actors
- Methods at end points

An example of an actor with end points and methods is shown in figure 1.

3.1 Actors

An actor is the basic entity of activity. An actor is the only distributed object which actually does something. All other (user) objects in the system that are not actors cannot do anything. Producing, consuming, processing, controlling, generating, etc. must be done by actors. Actors processing media can be compared with SUMO's devices [CBPS94] or with MSS's virtual devices [HIS94, HP93].

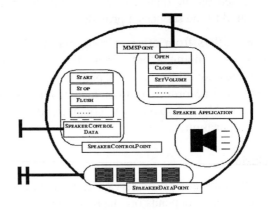

Figure 1: A speaker actor

3.2   End points:

Actors must be able to communicate with other actors. This communication is done by means of end point to end point(s) communication in a location independent way. An end point is the only way for an actor to communicate with other actors. Here we can identify two kinds of communication: control communication and data communication. This duality results directly in two kinds of end points.

- control points, which are used to control some object. For example to control a medium stream or to control the behaviour of another actor. Like figure 1 shows, a set of methods and a context part are attached to each control point. This set of methods contains all methods which can be issued to this end point. The context part is used as private data of the control point, for example to hold status.
- Data points are used to transport bulk data between two data points. In this context, bulk data means several data(units) of one medium type. These data units are called media units. A natural way to control such a transport between data points is to associate one control end point with one data point (both end points belong to the same actor). This can also be seen in figure 1.
  The actual transport of media units between data points is done using a protocol called the media transport protocol (MTP), most probably realised using an unreliable protocol like UDP or IP.
  Data points resemble rtports in SUMO, ports in MSS or ports in the Touring Machine.

An actor can have several control points and several data points. Actors which actually produce or consume media data are called media drivers; they drive or process at least one medium stream. Here we can distinguish three kinds of media drivers, namely source media drivers which produce data, sink media drivers which consume data and filter media drivers which consume, process and produce data.

3.3   Methods

In order to make an actor do something one has to issue a command to this actor. Issuing commands is done by calling a method of a particular control point of the actor. This resembles the object oriented way of message passing, as can, for example, be seen in MSS's —CORBA's— distributed objects. In some way methods also resemble handlers in SUMO —Chorus—.

Methods must be seen as dynamic primitives offered by a control point. Here, dynamic means that an actor, or an application for that matter, can attach at run time a (internal, C) primitive to a control point, thereby making it a method.

After this, other actors can execute this remote primitive by issuing the corresponding method. Of course, a method can also be detached by the actor who owns it. Methods are means to execute primitives which are not necessarily fixed or known at compile time or startup time of both client and server.

4.0   Architecture

4.1   Introduction

Actors, end points and methods together form the basic building blocks of our toolkit. With these we can make a general framework for distributed multimedia handling. To provide the desired multimedia functionality several system actors are defined.

These basic multimedia capabilities include default temporal access control (TAC) [LG93] and QoS control via default methods of control points.

4.2   Media drivers

A media driver is a logical device driver which processes data of one or more media. They are abstractions for devices like cameras, speakers or media storage drives. This functionality is also seen in SUMO's devices and MSS's virtual devices.

Applications can request media driver services by issuing appropriate methods, after which control points, data points and connections are created. A media driver can get commands, like Start or SetQoS, and use other media drivers to realize the correct behaviour of these commands. A media driver can also give feedback to other actors to monitor its behaviour. Because media drivers actually are the objects which have to be synchronised with each other, they must be capable of synchronising.

The MTP realizes the actual transport of bulk data by using network protocols, e.g., UDP or IP, shared buffers, or direct access of hardware, like DMA.

A media driver must have the following features in order to handle the actual multimedia.

- MMSPoint. A standard control point attached with many standard methods in order to offer a default and standard control over an actor. For example, methods like Open, Close, ReportOn, GetCPointList and Destroy can be issued here. This end point is very important, especially during the initialisation phase of an application, because then initialisation, configuration and tuning of different actors is needed. The MMSPoint also offers methods for getting all kinds of information about the actor, e.g., about methods, control points, data points, feedback, etc.

- Application. A media driver is an application on its own, consisting of two parts: a basic actor part which causes the application to live in the toolkit's world; and an application specific part which has to realize the specific behaviour of the application. The latter part is called the application.

  A clear and straightforward interface between those two parts is essential for flexible and complex behaviour needed for multimedia. There are two types of interfaces.

  One type is found at the control points by the direct translation of method calls to function calls —internal C function calls—.

  The other type is characterised by the interaction between data points, the basic part, and the internal C functions of the application part. These interactions are specified by mapping all possible interaction types to corresponding functions. This mapping is shared by both data point and application specific part.

  When, for example, data units received at the data point are scheduled, the end point will, at schedule time, forward this data by calling the application specific function found in the GetMediumData entry in the mapping. When the application wants to put medium data, it should call the data points function referenced by the PutMediumData entry in the mapping.

- Interface. A control point/data point pair, shortly denoted as end point pair, is the bridge between its application and other actors transporting data or controlling this transportation. Control is possible via the control point of this end point pair by issuing default control methods attached to it. These default control methods, the majority of them typically needed for multimedia systems, can be categorised as follows:

  - TAC. TAC is handled by the following methods: Start, Stop, Shoot, Prime, Flush, Goto, Where, SetSpeed and GetSpeed
  - QoS. For QoS control two methods are needed: GetQoS and SetQoS.
  - Others. Methods to make an end point capable of handling state information requests, agreement between two connected data points, event based and periodic feedback.

With this multimedia package an actor is capable of generating, transporting and presenting media units in a way that abstracts from QoS – transportation, buffering and timing – and basic multimedia control like TAC.

4.3   System services

A media driver capable of handling multimedia does not make an application. Most multimedia applications consist of several actors all acting according a specific role and all interacting with each other. In order to abstract from these roles and interactions, and to control and synchronise actors —or group them—, TMT offers several system services.

92

These system services include a name server, essential for making TMT distributed, and a synchronisation server responsible for good media synchronisation between actors.

System services themselves are actors providing a predefined function. They are: Name server, Clock server, Connection server, Flow server, Synchronization server and Session server.

TMT architecture consists of two parts. The first part can be found in the application actors itself. Media drivers are part of the application and are responsible for the actual producing, consuming and processing of media units. Transfer of this media data is done by the data points according the media transport protocol. The second part is the system part which offers system services: a name server, a connection server, a flow server, a synchronisation server and a session server. The system part gives adequate means to handle important multimedia features like QoS behaviour, grouping facilities and general multimedia handling.

5.0 Applications

This chapter an applications is described that is implemented with TMT. It is used to outline the capabilities of TMT , the way to use them and to test the functionality of the system. This excercise has shown that a consistent API is created, transparent distribution is provided, and multimedia transport and synchronised presentation are possible.

5.1 General information

Before anything will run, the name server Delphi has to be started.

```
dasboot@cs:spavo% delphi  s &
```

Now the actors needed to run the application should be started. Once they are running, an application is created by connecting the actors, using a script file, shell commands or by running executable code.

Four phases can be distinguished when building an application. First a data transport topology is necessary. This is done by opening end point combinations at media drivers. These end point should be connected using a connection. Second, the required system services must be added to the application, i.e., logical and parallel grouping of connections and data streams, by using flows and synchronisers. Third, the required quality of service should be specified. This can be done at the highest level of an application, as the quality of service specifications will automaticly be distributed through the application. And, fourth, the generation and presentation of media is controlled by using temporal access commands.

Currently a command line interface is provided for controlling applications at runtime. This may be completed with graphical interfaces in the future. The following commands are available:

- `issue ActorName CPointID MethodName ArgFmt ResFmt Arg`
  Issue can be used to issue a method. The caller specifies the name of the actor, the control point identifier, the name of the method, argument format of the method, result format of the method, and the arguments. Issue is a C programm executable. All other commands described below are script files using the issue executable.
- `destroy ActorName`
  Destroys an actor. The actor is unregistered at the name server.
- `killem [ActorName ... ]`
  Destroys a number of actors.
- `setqos ActorName CPointID QoSString`
  Set the quality of service for a specified control point.
- `getqos ActorName CPointID`
  Get the quality of service of some specified control point.
- `start ActorName CPointID`
  Issue start on a specified end point.
- `stop ActorName CPointID`
  Issue stop on a specified end point.
- `debugon [ActorName ...]`
  Switch debug reporting for specified actors on.
- `debugoff`
  Switch debug reporting for specified actors off.

The following section will describe an audio application.

5.2 Audio application

The first example shows an application that uses a tracker and a speaker actor. A tracker actor generates music with up to four different voices, i.e. four different instruments can be played at the same time. One datapoint transmits one music channel which carries one of these four voices. A speaker actor receives audio samples at its data points, one channel per data point. The contents of the channels are mixed and played together on a local loadspeaker. The application expects all actors to be running. This means that a user has to start all actors if they are not running. A future feature of the name server should be that if actors aren't running the name server will start them. The media drivers are started as follows:

```
dasboot@cs:spavo% md_tracker  n tracker1  L  f
mod.lotus &
rainman@cs:spavo% md_tracker  n tracker2  L  f
mod.lotus &
psycho@cs:spavo% md_speaker  n speaker1 &
bladerunner@cs:spavo% md_speaker  n speaker2 &
```

Then system service actors are started, in this case a synchroniser actor and a connection actor:

```
dracula@cs:spavo% syncact synchroniser &
critters@cs:spavo% connactor connection &
```

Now all required actors are running and the application can be created. The audio application opens four source end point pairs and four sink end point pairs. Each tracker sends two channels of music out of four channels. Tracker 1 sends channels 1 and 3, tracker 2 sends channels 2 and 4. Each speaker actor receives one channel from tracker 1 and one from tracker 2. Music played at speaker 1 must be synchronized with music played at speaker 2. Figure 2 shows the data transmission topology for this application.

The following script constructs the application.

```
#!zsh
# Open two end-point pairs at tracker1 and two at
tracker2
issue tracker1 1 Open
issue tracker1 1 Open
issue tracker2 1 Open
issue tracker2 1 Open

# Open two end-point pairs at speaker1 and two at
speaker2
issue speaker1 1 Open
issue speaker1 1 Open
issue speaker2 1 Open
issue speaker2 1 Open
# Create four connections at a connection actor named
connection
issue connection 1 Open "con1 tracker1 2 speaker1 2"
issue connection 1 Open "con2 tracker1 3 speaker2 2"
issue connection 1 Open "con3 tracker2 2 speaker1 3"
issue connection 1 Open "con4 tracker2 3 speaker2 3"
# Open a synchroniser at a synchronisation actor named
synchroniser
issue synchroniser 1 Open "sync1"
```

```
# Add the four connections to the bundle synchronised
by
# control-point 2 of the synchronisation actor
issue synchroniser 2 AddSyncObj "connection 2 3"
issue synchroniser 2 AddSyncObj "connection 3 3"
issue synchroniser 2 AddSyncObj "connection 4 3"
issue synchroniser 2 AddSyncObj "connection 5 3"
# Set the quality of service for the application
issue synchroniser 2 SetQoS \
```
"MNDLY 0 MXDLY 65536 SKEW 4096 PRD 4195 MXJTR 256000"

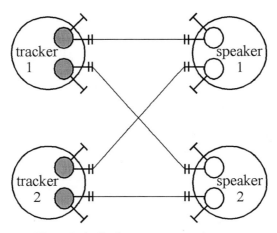

Figure 2: Audio data transport topology

First the end point pairs at the media drivers are opened. Then the connections between the data points are created. Then a synchroniser is opened and the four connections are added to the synchroniser. Finally, the quality of service is set at the synchroniser.

Now the application is created and data can be presented at the speaker media drivers. For example, to start all connections, issue a start at control point 2 of the synchroniser:

```
casablanca@cs:spavo% start synchroniser 2
```

And to stop all connections issue a stop at the synchroniser:

```
casablanca@cs:spavo% stop synchroniser 2
```
One more example, which changes the skew between the connections, stops one connection and changes the voice of a data point of tracker1:

```
casablanca@cs:spavo% setqos synchroniser 2 "0.0 SKEW
```

```
16384"
casablanca@cs.spavo% stop connection 4 "0.0"
casavlanca@cs.spavo% issue tracker1 4 SetSoundChannel
"%d" "%d" "0"
```

Tests with this application have shown that synchronisation based on global clocks results in acceptable skew values. Depending on the network load and cpu load stereo sound can be achieved. Currently we have been testing with up to 16 connections and 4 distributed sources and 4 distributed sinks. These tests also show that it may be advisable to integrate the flow actor, synchronisation actor and connection actor into one system services actor, thus causing less network load.

6.0   Conclusion

We started this project to gain experience in designing and specifying distributed multimedia applications. Based on a extensive literature study a multimedia extension to a standard operating system is designed and built, thus offering a distributed multimedia platform for our experiments.

TMT has the following features:

- Network transparent multimedia services,
- Temporal access commands for continuous media,
- Quality of service management for all services,
- Low level inter media and spatial synchronisation,
- Dynamic management of application topology.

We found these features adequate for specifying, modeling and implementing distributed multimedia applications. Anomalies, like a rather large latency from source to destination were due to heavy network load caused by other users of our network string. Allthough only initial tests are executed, we expect TMT to perform better with our new ATM based network.

Building a topology and starting actors involves a multitude of runtime arguments, which is a little bit awkward. Research on a, hopefully better, graphics based modeling tool will start in the second half of this year.

References:

1. [AKR92] Mauricio Arango, Michael Kramer, and Steven L. Rohall: "Enhancing the touring machine api to support integrated digital transport", Network and Operating System Support for Digital Audio and Video, 176-

182, Springer Verlag, Berlin Heidelberg, 1992

2. [BDFT94] Besse L. et al, "Towards an architecture for distributed multimedia applications support, in IEEE Multimedia, 1994.

3. [Bel93] Bellcore: "Touring machine system", Communications of the ACM, 36(1), January 1993

4. [CBPS94] G. Coulson, G.S. Blair, P.Robin, and D. Shepherd: "Supporting continuous media applications in a microkernel environment", Technical Report MPG 94 16, University of Lancaster: Multimedia Projects Group, 1994, ftp://ftp.comp.lancs.ac.uk/pub/mpg/MPG 94 16.ps.Z

5. [CGHea] B.A. Coan, G. Gopal, G. Herman, and et al: "The Touring Machine System (Ver. 3): An Open Distributed Platform for Information Networking Applications", Bellcore

6. [GHV92] G. Gopal, G. Herman, and M. Vecchi: "The touring machine project: Toward a public network platform for multimedia applications", Proceedings of the 8th International Conference on Software Engineering for Telecommunications Systems and Services, March 1992

7. [HIS94] HP, IBM, and Sunsoft: "Multimedia Systems, chapter 9: Middleware Systems Services Architecture", 1994

8. [HIS93] HP, IBM and Sunsoft: "Multimedia System Services Version 1.0", 1993

9. [LG93] T.D.C. Little and A. Ghafoor: "Interval Based Conceptual Models for Time Dependent Multimedia Data", 1993

10. [MAH93] V. Mak, M. Arango, and T. Hickey: "The Applications Programming Interface to the Touring Machine", Bellcore, 1993

11. [Mil89a] David L. Mills: "Internet time synchronization: the Network Time Protocol", October 1989.

12. [Mil89b] David L. Mills: "Network Time Protocol (Version 2), Specification and implementation", September 1989

3.3

A WORLD WIDE WEB MULTIPLE CHOICE AUTHORING TOOL FOR NON-TECHNICAL TUTORS

Ian Rainey[1] & Peter Nicholl[2]
[1]GSS Development Ltd. and [2]University of Ulster, UK

In the past, the use of multiple choice questionnaires has been limited to the mark sense test papers used by some postal-based universities or used on stand-alone computers for quick quizzes. Distance learning is becoming a more viable option in the age of the Information Super Highway. The tool developed by this project creates Web pages and allows for instant feedback to the students using the multiple choice questionnaires. Various statistics are recorded for the tutor so that easy evaluation of the results is possible. It allows the generation of topic specific questionnaires by non-advanced computer literate users.

1.0   Introduction

Before there was ever a notion of a World Wide Web (WWW), computer users began to navigate cyberspace on the world's largest computer network, the Internet. A global lattice of national, regional and local computer networks, the Internet was rapidly gaining in popularity outside of the scientific community (largely due to a preponderance of college students wanting access to electronic mail). But beyond the basic capability of e-mail and several other network services, the Internet was incomprehensible to the vast majority of users. Based on a series of complex protocols, the Internet required an intimate knowledge of computers and network operating systems, a knowledge that most users neither had the time or the interest to gather. Clearly, the Internet had the technical capacity to handle a variety of complex applications (downloading files from distant computers, transferring digitised photos and sounds, etc.), but because it was by no means a user-friendly network, its uses were limited. In order to give Internet publishers the necessary tools to design complex on-line multimedia documents, an entirely new protocol would have to be formulated. In 1989 at the European Particle Physics Laboratory (CERN) in Geneva, British computer scientist Tim Berners-Lee developed a protocol which he called the World Wide Web. As the name suggests, the Web allows Internet publishers to intertwine information in multiple directions and layers. Though a similar lattice structure certainly applied to the Gopher protocol, the Web offered some fascinating new features.

First of all, text and links to other information could now be presented on the same screen by highlighting certain words within a paragraph. By selecting these words with either a mouse or by moving a cursor, you can link to any other document on the Internet. These pages, in turn, can offer additional links to even more specific information. Beyond its general ease of navigation, the Web also allows for a publisher to present information in a multimedia context. In other words, while a Web page may offer segments of text, it may also include graphics, audio, even video. Essentially, a Web site can easily look like a page of information of a multimedia CD-ROM. Unlike such a device, the Web interconnects with computers around the world, creating a new dimension to cyberspace, full of images, sounds and ideas.

At first, the Web remained an experimental method of organising Internet information, and only a handful of research sites around the world were capable of presenting it. In 1993, though, programmers at the University of Illinois at Urbana/Champaign released Mosaic [HREF 1], an easy to use Web browser which was freely distributed over the Internet. Eventually, other browsers such as Netscape[HREF 2] began to proliferate, making the Web more accessible to casual users than ever. By the autumn of 1994, it was estimated that there were anywhere between 7,000 and 10,000 Web sites around the world, with upwards of 10 million users. In one week alone, August 96, more than 1 million copies of the latest Microsoft Web Browser were downloaded [HREF 3]. This site, http://microsoft.com, recorded 45 million hits in a single day, during this week. The World Wide Web, originally envisioned to allow researchers and computer enthusiasts better access to each other's information, has now turned into a powerful force on the Information Highway.

The most basic element of using the Web as a pedagogical instrument is found in its ability to present information clearly, attractively and practically. Hypertext Markup Language standards dictate how a Web site is to be interpreted by a Web browser, so when a document is converted from text into a Web document, its appearance as a user-friendly HTML document can be predicted with ease. Additionally, one can use hypertext to organise enormous amounts of data in a relatively lucid fashion, using menus, key word searches, even clickable graphics as a means to link the user to more and more information.

From a curricular point of view, the Web can be used to design tutorials and on-line lessons for a variety of subjects. For example, Roger Blumberg of the Institute for Brain and Neural Systems at Brown University has created an on-line tutorial on basic genetics known as MendelWeb [HREF 4]. With Mendel Web, students are introduced to basic genetics and the writings of scientist/monk Gregor Mendel by reading a hypertext version of his seminal treatise, Experiments in Plant Hybridisation (available in both English and in German). The hypertext version of Mendel's writings contain links to a dictionary of terms,

100

as well as annotated comments from other readers that can be added to by any user. In a sense, an automatic tutor is already built into the Web site; discussion and questions are presented as they would be in a live introduction to biology course, yet because the coursework is built into the Web, each student may dissect the subject (and thus progress there comprehension of it) at there own rate.

The World Wide Web provides an excellent tool in which to design on-line curricula. Yet the potential of Web tutorials has yet to be realised largely because most Web textbooks have been technically oriented, and in order for this technology to reach the mainstream, Web tutorials must also be designed for history, music, language arts, and other less technically-minded disciplines.

At present educators and technologists can seem polarised and therefore there is a great need for an easy to use World Wide Web authoring tool that enhances learning for large and diverse groups such as those found on the Internet. Using the Internet/Intranets to provide such training material would be beneficial to multi-campus institutions and also permit teaching resources to be shared among different organisations.

2.0   Multiple choice questions

Methods of assessment in Higher Education are currently the subject of considerable attention. Initiatives on assessing teaching quality and Enterprise in Higher Education (EHE), a learning outcomes approach to course and syllabus design, and coping with the assessment of large numbers of students in a semester system are some of the factors that have contributed to a re-examination of assessment practices [1].

Ellington, Percival and Race [2] state that a good assessment procedure should be able to demonstrate that it is valid, reliable, practicable and that it should be fair and useful to students. They also state that because multiple choice questions (MCQs) look easy to construct, this often results in amateurish questions with poor validity and it is these questions that give MCQ tests a poor reputation.

In 1994 just before the University of Ulster introduced modularisation and a semester system, the introductory module for the Marketing Faculty was redesigned. The new module was designed to be common across all courses and levels of study. This included a common syllabus, teaching plan, core text and where possible, given the different modes and levels of study, common assignments and examinations.

Last year, 1995, one of the coursework assignments, and in the case of some undergraduate courses the sole assignment, was an MCQ test consisting of 90 questions to be completed in a one hour lecture period. The MCQ test was administered to students during week 7 of the 12 week semester and test questions covered the first 6 weeks work. Some 500 students took the test including students on 12 different courses of study, undergraduates and postgraduates (on the first year of taught programmes), full and part time students at both levels of study and students on 3 of the University's 4 geographically remote campuses.

Originally, it was intended to administer the test to students by computer. The number of computers in any one laboratory (or more if more than one member of staff is available to supervise the test) determines the number of students that can sit the test at any one time. For larger classes (80 - 100 students), a number of test sittings would have been required. Due to the lack of suitable software and network facilities, it was more efficient in respect of staff time to administer a pen and paper test to each class. The test was designed in such a way that as the students marked their replies they were in fact completing a pre-coded 'questionnaire' whose data was later entered by data preparation staff. Results were available to students within one week of completing the test, and staff had detailed breakdowns of class averages and information on potential 'problem areas' for their students a week later.

Information was also provided on the quality of the test items. For example, on 12 of the 90 multiple choice test questions, less than 30% of students identified the correct answer and, given their poor contribution to the test, they should be replaced or rewritten to be less ambiguous.

3.0   Lack of current authoring tools

Until recently computers have had a limited use in structured teaching of varied curriculum activities, they were usually reserved for the practice of computing subjects. To enable the use of computers in assisting teaching across many subject areas, the encoding of tutoring expertise and delivery of tools intended to facilitate such learning must be simplified. Simplification would provide a vehicle for experts who are not in the information technology arena to easily convey material to their prospective students. Delivery of learning material using knowledge-based tutors will be a bridge between those worlds of individual face to face scenes and one to many approaches. This project permits the individual nature of the training to be retained and to permit the students to work at their own pace and in their own time. It also identifies to the tutor any areas of student difficulty by indicating the questions which students frequently answer incorrectly.

The main aim of the project was to
- Develop a WWW authoring tool to assist non-technical tutors to generate multiple choice, self-assessment exercises for students.

Which in turn would
- Enhance student learning by providing self-assessment on demand in a non-threatening manner.
- Assist the tutor to identify any topics which require further clarification.
- Reduce time to collate the results and produce the final output.

The current emphasis being placed on modular courses is leading to increasing class sizes. This in turn, makes it difficult for tutors to supply regular and individual feedback on students' progress. A WWW based multiple choice assessment provides a mechanism for this feedback without placing undue burden on the tutors or other resources. This project facilitates tutors to easily construct these exercises.

Individual feedback aids the student to more accurately gauge their own level of performance and since exercises are easy to create and require no further maintenance by the tutor, it is possible to construct different exercises for students of various abilities. Using the WWW permits these resources to be used across multiple campuses or even shared between different organisations, enhancing the prospects of distance and remote learning [HREF 5]. This project simplifies accessing of information from different hardware platforms by using a common medium, the World Wide Web. By abstracting the tutor from the technical details of establishing a WWW application, it makes the technology available to a wider community of tutors. Students gain access to a wider variety of training materials which provide immediate and individual feedback.

4.0   Question authoring tool

The software produced to provide the above functionality is called QATool, and runs under Microsoft Windows. Essentially QATool consists of two interfaces, a lecturer interface used to author Web questions, and a student interface, used by people attempting to answer questions, accessible using any Web browser.

The first screen the lecturer is shown is used to enter details about who the questionnaire is intended for, such as title, module name, etc.. Guidance notes can also be entered as a means of providing extra information for students. The ability to restrict student access to answers before a given date is also catered for, by the option to enter a date before which correct answers will not be available. This option is vital if tests as opposed to tutorials are to be designed using QATool.

Once all the title details have been entered, the user is presented with the data entry screen, Figure 1. Text can be entered for each question, together with an optional hint. Up to five answers can be input per question, again additional text(option) can be entered to give the student some feedback on their chosen answer. This additional information is especially useful in tutorial situations as it provides the student with a reason for selecting an incorrect answer. Questions and answer text can be enhanced by the addition of multimedia, such as sounds, pictures and video clips.

When all the question and answer data is entered, the user can select to create the Web page. Once created the Web page can be viewed locally before being sent to the Web Server. The task of downloading the Web page together with any multimedia clips is abstracted from the user, who need only enter host address and account details to initiate file transfer. If the tool is to be used in an organisation that has individual accounts for each of its staff then it will only place the appropriate files in the user's directories; saving space and allowing the use of CGI facilities in a safe and secure way by not giving root status to potentially rogue scripts. Once all the requisite files are in place, file permissions are set-up to facilitate immediate use of the Web document by students.

Students can access the questions using any Web browser, although to view the multimedia clips, a graphical browser is recommended. To identify students, personal details are entered, without which they are not permitted to submit answers for marking. Results are available as soon as the Server can mark them, with copies of the results being collated in files for the lecturer to view at leisure. The format of the results files is such that they may be imported into any popular spreadsheet package.

5.0 Conclusion

The idea for this project was first conceived in September 1995 at a time when the Internet had approximately just over 100,000 Web sites, this figure has since grown to approximately 269,000 sites in May 1996 [HREF 6]. The enormous growth in WWW usage is testimony to the need for tools which provide easy authoring of HTML pages used for educational purposes.

A great deal of enthusiasm for QATool was shown by all users who evaluated it. The simple and intuitive interface meant that using QATool did not require in depth analysis of user documentation. Abstracting the details of how and where the Web Document goes to on the server computer was welcomed from the non-technical users who openly admitted, that prior to using QATool they would not have even contemplated WWW authorship.

The output of results from the server was in an easily accessible format. Two files are created, one containing a detailed breakdown on a question by question basis, and the other file containing a summary for the complete class of students. This enables the lecturer to quickly identify any potential areas of difficulty.

Distance learning based around printed paper has been available for a number of years. As communications technologies have developed they have been incorporated into distance learning. The use of tools such as QATool to create material for distance learning should not be used in isolation, but combined with other methods and media to offer an enhanced learning environment.

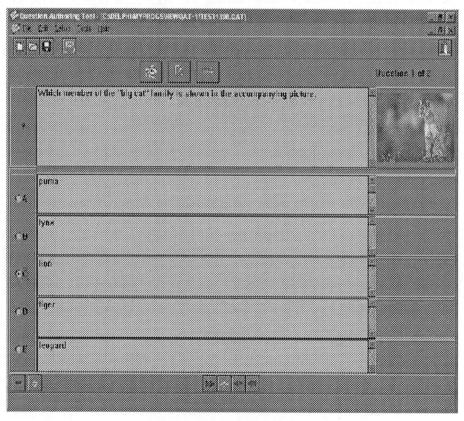

Figure 1: Lecturer data entry screen

References:

Books:

1. Brown, S., and Knight, P., (1994), Assessing Learners in Higher Education, Kogan Page.
2. Ellington, H., and Race, P., (1993), Producing Teaching Materials, 2nd Edition, Kogan Page.

Hypertext:

[HREF 1] Mosaic
    http://www.mosaic.com/
[HREF 2] Netscape
    http://www.netscape.com/
[HREF 3] Microsoft press release
    http://www.microsoft.com/corpinfo/press/1996/aug96/1MILLPR.htm
[HREF 4] Mendel Web
    http://netscape.students.brown.edu/MendelWeb/
[HREF 5] Mindweave: Communication, Computers and Distance Education
    http://acacia.open.ac.uk/Mindweave/Mindweave.html
[HREF 6] Netree Internet Statistics
    http://www.internetsol.com/netbin/internetstats

PART 4

SYNCHRONIZATION & IMAGE SYNTHESIS

4.1

COMPRESSING AND RESTORING MULTIPLE IMAGES USING VARIABLE THRESHOLD VALUES

R.C.H. Law and K.F. Wong
The Hong Kong Polytechnic University, Hong Kong

This article proposes a technique called Variable Threshold Values (VTV) to compress and restore multiple graphical pictures. Polylines are used to demonstrate the operation of VTV. The image compression and restoration techniques which are used, so far, mostly concentrate on single images. VTV extends the original data compression and restoration for a single image into a set of multiple images, that we always find in the multimedia environment. Most of the previous research and development efforts on image synthesis failed to provide sufficient insight of handling multiple images in multimedia and in multiple images transmission on Internet.

1.0   Introduction

Image information reduction has long been a major research area in computer science and engineering fields. Researchers have attempted to reduce the storage space of an image at the expense of a minimal distortion between the original image and the restored image. Data compression can be performed before storing the image data, in order to reduce the required memory and storage space (Bret, 1992; Marion, 1991). Alternatively, images can be compressed before transmitting the images to the receiving end. Major image compression techniques consist of predictive coding in the spatial domain and mappings of data in a transform domain. Also, there are other approaches for image compression such as the Noncausal Autoregressive Model (Mohamed & Law, 1989) and Polylines (Pham & Abdollahi, 1988).

In spite of the abundant supply of image compression and restoring techniques, not much previous work has been attempted to incorporate the image compression techniques into the multimedia and Internet domains. This paper introduces an approach which adopts Variable Threshold Values (VTV) for compressing and restoring multiple images. A consistent value of *root mean square error* is used to control the iterative procedures for different images. This is to ensure that the quality of the restored image is comparable to the original image with a minimal amount of information loss. Two natural application areas for VTV would be the storage of images in multimedia and the transmission of images on Internet (Harris, 1993; Harris & West, 1993).

The following sections will provide a discussion of the VTV approach. The image compression procedure is utilized to demonstrate the operation of VTV. Finally, a concluding section will summarize the research and provide insight for future research possibilities.

2.0   The variable threshold value model

In recent years, much work has been performed to obtain reasonable models for image compression and restoring. An example of this is the polylines model which facilitates rapid image compression and restoration. Polylines, however, deals with a single image. On the basis of polylines, VTV approach adopts the *root mean square error* to maintain an overall consistent quality of the compressed and reconstructed images. The following paragraphs depict the operation of multiple images compression using VTV.

$$\textit{Root mean square error (RMSE)} = \sqrt{\frac{1}{X}\sum_{x=0}^{x=X-1}\left[F(x,y)-Fr(x,y)\right]^2}$$

Where F(x,y) and Fr(x,y) represent the grey levels of the original and reconstructed pixels at spatial location (x,y). X is the total number of rows and Y is the total number of columns.

Algorithm to compress multiple images (for a row with 512 pixels)

1. Assign an arbitrary number to threshold value.
2. Record the grey level of pixel at x-coordinate 0.
3. Let Xbegin = 0 (left-most pixel), Xend = Xbegin + 2.
    If sum of variances ≤ threshold value (limit) then
        Xend = Xend + 1 and repeat the above procedure until
            either Xend = 511 (last element of a row) or sum of deviation >
    threshold   value.
4. If sum of deviation > threshold value then
        Record the coordinate of Xend - 1 and the grey level
            of the pixel at x-coordinate Xend - 1. (Finished building a straight
    line)
        Let Xbegin = Xend - 1, Xend = Xbegin + 2 and start to build another
    straight line.
5. If Xend = 511, record 511, and the grey level of pixel at x-coordinate of 511.
    (Finished a row)
6. If RMSE ≥ ∝(a constant value) then
        adjust threshold value and repeat steps 3 to 5.

7. Repeat the above procedures for other rows of the image.
8. Repeat steps 1 to 7 for other images.

Restoring an image can simply follow the original polylines method. An iterative restoring procedure can be performed for multiple images.

3.0   Discussion

The threshold value determines the performance of a compression algorithm. A large threshold value creates a small number of polylines but the reconstructed image will have a large distortion. On the other hand, a low threshold value yields a better reconstructed image but with more polylines.

So, selecting the most appropriate threshold value becomes a compromise of the number of polylines and quality of the reconstructed image. In the original polylines image compression approach, a fixed value of threshold is used. However, in the VTV approach, threshold values vary with different images. Since RMSE is used to determine the overall compressed images, variable threshold values are thus employed for multiple images. VTV technique thus allows for all images to be handled for a uniform quality of compression result. The constant value $\propto$, chosen by the user, judges the speed and quality of the entire process. A large $\propto$ value allows for a faster compression speed at the expense of lower quality of compression result. A smaller value of $\propto$ will produce a lower distortion between the original image and the reconstructed image. The drawback for a smaller value of $\propto$ is that it takes a longer time complete the iterative compression procedures.

4.0   Conclusion

The increasing popularity of multimedia stimulates the research and development activities of multiple images handling. Another similar stimulation is the frequent transmission of multiple images on Internet. The necessity for a smaller storage space and rapid transmission of multiple images is urgently needed to be fulfilled. The shortcoming of this multiple images compression is the minimal amount of information loss. The VTV technique proposed in this paper surely benefits the multiple images handling activities in multimedia.

A future research possibility is to incorporate VTV technique into other compression approaches like the transform coding and predictive coding methods. In such a future research activity, a direct mapping of the internal compression technique can be adopted to replace the polylines method as shown in section 2. The top level concept of VTV can remain the same as it can be applied to other compression approaches as well. However, a future investigation needs to be performed to confirm this.

References:

1. Bret, M. (1992) Image Synthesis, Doedrecht: Kluwer Academic Publishers.
2. Harris, K.J. (1993) "Interactive Video: The Instructional Tool of the '90s", Hospitality Journal, Vol. 16, No. 2, pp. 75-92.
3. Harris, K.J. and West, J.W. (1993, Aug) "Using Multimedia in Hospitality Training", The Cornell H.R.A. Quarterly, pp. 75-82.
4. Marion, A. (1991), An Introduction to Image Processing, London: Chapman and Hall.
5. Mohamed, A.S.A. and Law, R.C.H. (1989, Oct), "A Noncausal AR Model for Breast Tissue Image Compression", Proceedings of the International Symposium on Computer Architecture and Digital Signal Processing, Hong Kong, pp. 590-594.
6. Pham, D.T. and Abdollahi, M. (1988), "Image Compression Using Polylines", Pattern Recognition, Vol. 21, No. 6, pp. 631-637.

4.2

A HUMAN FACE DETECTION AND TRACKING SYSTEM FOR COMPLEX BACKGROUNDS

Mingbao Liu and Wen Gao
Harbin Institute of Technology, PRC

Detecting and tracking human faces in a complex background is one of the most important multimodal human-machine interface . This paper presents a human face detection and tracking system which based on eigen-subface . We establish a standard human face template and use the method of template matching as the first step . We then propose the concept of eigen-subface and design a set of effective basis of human face's organ space . The eigen-subface's resolution measure and the strategy of human face detection and tracking are also presented. Experimental results show that this system could detect and track human faces satisfactorily in various unconstrained backgrounds.

1.0   Introduction

Effective Human-to-Human communication involves natural language and body language.   Recent worldwide efforts are aimed at providing such multimodal capabilities for Human-Machine communication as well as by introducing expression, lipreading, eye tracking and gesture.   Most of them require a located face (Sung 1994).

Face detection has direct relevance to the face recognition problem, for it is the first important step of a fully automatic human face recognition system . But so far , most face recognition system had avoided this work(Brunelli 1993, Turk 1991).

From an academic standpoint, human face detection is a significant problem in the area of pattern recognition. Human face detection is to identify human face patterns from enormous non-face patterns (Sung 1994) .

In recent years,human face detection and tracking has attracted considerable worldwide attention. There have been five main approaches for this problem : Fixed templates (Brunelli 1993), Deformable templates(Yuille 1992), Image invariants(Sinha 1994), Learning from examples (Sung 1994) and Color based method(Hunke 1994) .

114

Face detection and tracking is difficult for three main reasons. (1) There can be a large component of non-rigidity and textual differences among faces, not only presented by different person's face, but also by the different state of the same person's face , such as various expressions. (2) Certain common but significant features, such as glasses or a mustache, destroy the features of human faces to some degree . (3) Face detection and tracking can be further complicated by unpredictable imaging conditions in an unconstrained environment (Hunke 1994)

The system presented in this paper uses template-matching as a pre-detection , where the template is based on grey distribution . Then we propose the concept of sub-face and corresponding detection strategy. The system can fulfill human face detection and tracking in various unconstrained backgrounds with high precision and fast speed.

2 .0   System   overview

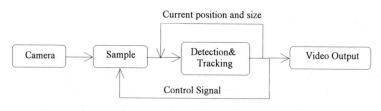

Figure 1   System structure

System structure is shown in figure 1. The camera used in   this system is JVC TK″ 1070E, the image sampling card is VC32 and the video output is SONY TRINITION .

Human face detection and human face tracking have the same main task that is to verify whether a window image's pattern in an object image belongs to   human faces or not . When system start , it has different detection route from when system is in the course of work,   just as figure 2 .

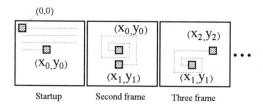

Figure 2   Detection route

Suppose that training samples are n $\%$n, and object image is N $\%$N, N > n. The range of face's size that can be detected is n$\%$n ~ N $\%$N. Practically face's size that need detecting is set to be $n_1\%n_1$ ~ $n_2\%n_2$, n $\doteq n_1$, $n_2 \doteq$ N. When detecting faces of n' $\%$n' ($n_1 \doteq$ n' $\doteq n_2$), rescale the object image by ratio n'/n, then scan the shrinked object image pixel by pixel. Pick a n $\%$n window image at (i , j), and send it into detection module after masking (Figure 3). In this system we set : n=19, N=128 , n_1= 19 , n_2 = 40.

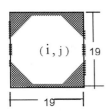

Figure 3   Figure 4

3 .0   Detection   method

3.1   Template-Matching

There are some spatial image relationships common to all face pattern. We design a face template shown in figure 4. Divide a face image into 14 regions, $\tau_0, \tau_1, \cdots, \tau_{13}$, to represent eyebrows } eyes } mouth } cheek, etc. Compute the average grey value of all pixels included in each region as the description of that region. Normalized by the average grey value of whole face, we get a 14-D feature vector , { g_0, g_1 # , g_{13} } ⊔

$$g_i = \frac{1}{f_a} \cdot \frac{1}{N_i} \cdot \sum_{(j,k)\in \tau_i} f(j,k) \tag{1}$$

where f_a is the mean grey value of the whole face, N_i is the number of pixels in τ_i.

Calculate the average vector of all samples' in the training set as the standard template. Matching a window image's feature vector with the standard template, if the distance less then threshold 汛, feed the detection image into next detection module. Otherwise, discard it as a non-face image and pick the next window image. Euclidean distance is utilized as matching measurement.

116

$$d = \frac{1}{14} \sum_{j=0}^{13} (g_j - \overline{g}_j)^2 \qquad (2)$$

The maximum distance and the minimum distance between all samples' vectors and the standard template define a interval $^{---}$, 汎∈ $^{---}$. We define $P = N_p / N$ ԩ N_p is the number of samples which has a less matching distance than 汎, and N is the number of all samples . Testing all 300 samples contained in face set , relationship of P and 汎 is shown in figure 5. Thus, let 汎= 0.08.

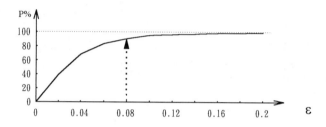

Figure 5   Relationship of P and 汎

3.2   Eigen sub-face

A human face is a configuration of organs . As to a front human face, we could divide it into three regions of eyes, cheek and jaw. Just like figure 6, swap eyes image of (a)'s and (b)'s, they are also faces respectively, like (c) and (d) . In terms of a certain organ in human faces, there exist some principle organ images, and the organ image in a human face in the training set can be represented by a linear combination of them(Bichsel,94). Let M to be the number of principle organ images, and N to be the number of all samples in the training set. Pratically, we can set 1<M<N. Those principle organ images are the basic vectors of human face organ space, called eyes space, cheek space and jaw space. The basic vectors are also called eigen eyes, eigen cheek and eigen jaw, in general, eigen sub-face.

Figure 6

Suppose a training set (eyes set, cheek set or jaw set) is $\{P_1, P_2, \cdots, P_N\}$. With every sample being normalized with its own mean grey value, we have $\{\Gamma_1, \Gamma_2, \cdots, \Gamma_N\}$. The average sample is defined by $\Psi = \frac{1}{N}\sum_{i=1}^{N}\Gamma_i$. Each face differs from the average by $\Phi_i = \Gamma_i - \Psi$. The covariance matrix is :

$$C = \frac{1}{N}\sum_{i=1}^{N}\Phi_i\Phi_i^T \qquad (3)$$

Calculate matrix C's eigen vectors and eigenvalues. The best M eigenvectors, $\{\mu_1, \mu_2, \cdots, \mu_M\}$, which have the largest M eigenvalues, span a sub-space, where $M \le N$. When a new test image is projected into this sub-space, its projection coordinates, $\Omega^T = [\omega_1, \omega_2, \cdots, \omega_M]$, can be used as a feature vector for human face detection, where

$$\omega_k = \mu_k(\Gamma - \Psi) \qquad k = 1, \# , M \qquad (4)$$

Projection of sample 样 can be computed by :

$$\Phi' = \sum_{k=1}^{M}\mu_k \cdot \omega_k \qquad k = 1, \# , M \qquad (5)$$

Projection distance d is defined as :

$$d = \frac{1}{N_\Phi}|\Phi - \Phi'| \qquad (6)$$

where N_Φ is the number of pixels .

d indicates effectiveness of the projection, smaller d, information lost less. Figure 7 shows the comparison of projection into the same sub-space from human face images and non-face images. Notice that human face images have closer projection distance than non-face images.

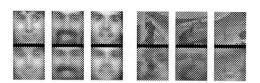

Figure 7: Upper - original   lower - projection

Execute template matching on two complex images which contain no human face and collect the error detected window images to construct the negative set , Sn, which contains 600 non-face samples. Human face images construct positive set , Sp, which contains 300 front face samples. Use the method described in the above to calculate the basic vectors of sub-face space ,

118

$\{\mu_{pe}^{(k)}\}, \{\mu_{pc}^{(k)}\}, \{\mu_{pm}^{(k)}\}, k = 1, \cdots, M_p$ and $\{\mu_{ne}^{(k)}\}, \{\mu_{nc}^{(k)}\}, \{\mu_{nm}^{(k)}\}, k = 1, \cdots, M_n$. Mp and Mn will be determined with experiments. Projection distances from sample 忙 to eyes space) cheek space and mouth space of Sp and Sn are d_{pe}) d_{pc}) d_{pm} and d_{ne}) d_{nc}) d_{nm} . Detection consists two sequential steps : (1)If $d_{pe} \le \theta_e \& d_{pc} \le \theta_c \& d_{pm} \le \theta_m$ て忙 is passed ; otherwise, 忙is not a face .

(2)If $d_{pe} \le d_{ne} \& d_{pc} \le d_{nc} \& d_{pm} \le d_{nm}$ て忙 is a face ; otherwise, 忙 is not a face . $\theta_e, \theta_c, \theta_m$ will be determined with experiments .

Let $M_p \in \{5,10,15,20,25,30,35\}$, $M_n \in \{5,10,15,20,25,30,35\}$, detect all samples in positive set and negative set by the second step described above . With all combinations of Mp and Mn , error detection rate reaches to the smallest when $M_p = 25$ and $M_n = 30$. Considering the time complexity , Mp and Mn should not be too large. Method of determination of $\theta_e, \theta_c, \theta_m$ is similar to 汎, even the curve shapes are similar.

4.0   Experimental results

4.1   Static detection

Choose 20 images with complex backgrounds as test images . There are 22 faces included altogether (none included in the training set) and the system detected 21 ones therein. 2 background window images were error detected to be faces. Some examples are shown in figure 8 .

Figure 8   Static detection examples

4.2 Dynamic detection and tracking

Let 10 persons (their faces are not included in the training set) sit in front of a camera and move their heads. In the course of detection and tracking, the background was also changed sometimes. The system worked very well in all cases. 3 person's test image series are shown in figure 9.

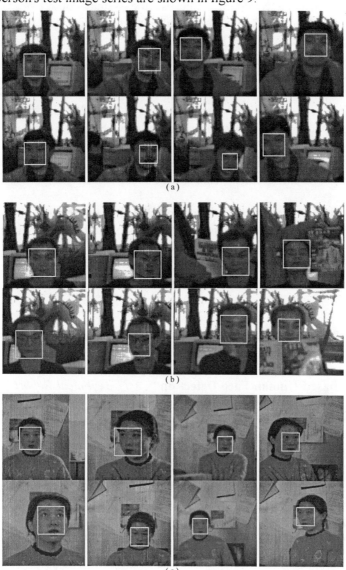

Figure 9: Dynamic detection and tracking

5. 0   Conclusion

The system presented in this paper is a background-free human face detection and tracking system.   It can work under various unconstrained complex backgrounds.   The system has a strong robustness to object images.   It permits some attachments on the face, such as glasses, and demands no very strict limitation of imaging condition.   Because the system doesn't need long time training, its performance can be improved esaily by adding new training samples into the training set.

We utilize PENTIUM 586 / 133 as the system platform and the system can reach to a near real time detection and tracking. For static detection (128%128), average time cost is 3 s. For dynamic tracking (128%128), the speed is faster to some degree and reach to 1s. The reason why dynamic is faster than static detection is that the system is a mono-face tracking system. In the course of tracking, when the face is located, the system stop to sample the next frame of input image. The background is simpler, the speed is faster.

Because that only front face images are included in positive set, the system can only detect front faces, although slight turning permitted. If   multi-posed face detection demanded, the face set must be rebuilt to include faces under various pose. However, system time complexity increased simultaneously.   How to solve this problem is the next step of research.

References:

1.   Kah-Kay Sung , Tomaso Poggio (1994) , **"Example-based Learning for View-based Human Face Detection"** , *MIT Technical Report* , A.I.Memo No.1521.
2.   R.Brunelli , T.Poggio (1993) , **"Face Recognition : Feature versus Templates"** , *IEEE Transactions on   Pattern Analysis   and   Machine Intelligence* , 15(10):1042-1052 .
3.   Matthew A.Turk (1991) , **"Face Recognition Using Eigenfaces"** , *Proc.IEEE Computer   Soc. Conf. on   Computer Vision   and Pattern Recognition* , pp.586-591 .
4.   A.Yuille , P.Hallinan , D.Cohen (1992) , **"Feature Extraction from Faces Using Deformable Templates"** , *International Journal of Computer Vision* , 8(2):99-111 .

5. P.Sinha (1994) , **"Object Recognition via Image Invariants : A Case Study"** , *Investigative Ophthalmology and Visual Science*, Vol.35, pp.1735-1740 , Sarasota , Florida .

6. H.Martin Hunke (1994) , **"Locating and Tracking of Human Faces with Neural Networks"** , *CMU Technical Report* , CMU-CS-94-155 .

7. M.Bichsel, A.P.Pentland (1994) , **"Human Face Recognition and the Face Image Set's Topology"** , *CVGIP: IMAGE UNDERSTANDING*, Vol.59, No.2, pp.254-261.

8. A.Pentland, B.Moghaddam, T.Starner (1994) , **"View-based and Modular Eigenspace for Face Recognition"**, *Proc.IEEE Conf. on Computer Vision and Pattern Recognition*, pp.84-91.

9. G.Yang, T.S.huang (1993) , **"Human Face Detection in a Scene"**, *IEEE Computer Society Conference on Computer Vision and Pattern Recognition*.

4.3

DIFFERENTIAL POLYLINES IN MULTI-IMAGE TRANSMISSION

R.C.H. Law
The Hong Kong Polytechnic University, Hong Kong

Image compression by polylines was introduced by Pham and Abdollahi (Pham & Abdollahi, 1988). Utilizing polylines, image compression is achieved by storing the x-coordinates and grey levels of end point pixels of straight line segments. This paper presents an approach, named differential polylines, to enhance the image compression ability of polylines. In differential polylines, differences between x-coordinates are stored but not the actual value of x-coordinates. The x-coordinate differences are always smaller in value than the actual x-coordinates. Hence, further image compression is attained as information of an image can now be represented using less bits.

1.0   Introduction

An inherent yet important aspect of image processing is the large amount of data carried. This problem gets more complicated as image size increases. During the transmission of images (a common form in multimedia) on Internet, it would be beneficial to have a way of reducing the size of an image. In addition to the smaller chance of getting inference from unwanted noise, image compression could also lessen the transmission time and storage space. In other words, we can represent the information of an image with fewer numbers or bits. Thus, image compression is achieved. The opportunity cost for this image compression is the small sacrifice of image quality. Image compression can be successfully applied to various industrial areas such as telecommunications (Bret, 1992), medical treatment (Mohamed & Law, 1989; Pham & Abdollahi, 1988), and engineering (Marion, 1991).

Common image compression techniques basically follow two approaches (Mohamed & Law, 1989). These are the predicative coding in the spatial domain and the transform coding which maps data of an image in a transformed domain and then successfully selects the most suitable data. Sometimes, a combination of the predictive coding and the transform coding is used. Unfortunately, the aforementioned approaches have computational drawbacks. In predictive coding, values of element in the current scan line and/or previous line(s) or frames are utilized to form a prediction for the value of the current element. Albeit predictive coding is simple and easy to implement, it is sensitive to variation in input data statistics and to transmission channel errors. In case of transmission channel errors, the errors could influence to neighboring pixels. Hence, an undesirable effect may be created in the reconstructed image. Transform coding produces coefficient sequences which are approximately uncorrelated with most of the redundancy in the input signal being removed. Nevertheless, transform coding is relatively complex which requires a large amount of calculation. The applicability of transform coding is therefore limited if the available space is restricted or when fast coding is required.

The polylines image compression approach was introduced in 1989 (Pham & Abdollahi, 1989). A polyline is simply a series of interconnected straight line segments. Polylines are constructed using straight lines and can be reconstructed by knowing the coordinates of end points of each line. Image compression is accomplished by recording the coordinates and grey levels of end points of straight lines instead of all grey levels in a row. It was demonstrated that using polylines for image compression is simple to implement and the amount of calculation to obtain polylines and to reconstruct an image is relatively small. On the basis of polylines, this paper presents the approach of differential polylines which stores the differences between x-coordinates at end points. Similar to Differential Pulse Code Modulation (Pham & Abdollahi, 1989), fewer bits are required to store the differences between x-coordinates at end points. Hence, further image compression is achieved.

The next section of this paper will provide a discussion on the algorithm of building a differential polyline. Next, there will be a section to depict the procedure of restoring the pixels from a differential polyline. Finally, concluding comments will be provided for the application of differential polylines in the multiple images transmission context. Multiple images handling is an essential part of the multimedia environment.

2.0   The differential polylines model

Image compression algorithm (For a 512 x 512 image):

1. Record the grey level of pixel at x-coordinate 0.
2. Let Xbegin = 0 (left-most pixel), Xend = Xbegin + 2.
    If sum of variances ≤ threshold value (limit) then
        Xend = Xend + 1 and repeat the above procedure until
            either Xend = 511 (last element of a row) or sum of
            deviation > threshold value.
3. If sum of deviation > threshold value then
        Record the coordinate of Xend - 1 and the grey level

of the pixel at x-coordinate Xend - 1.
(Finished building a straight line)
Let Xbegin = Xend - 1, Xend = Xbegin + 2 and start
to build another straight line.
4. If Xend = 511, record 511, and the grey level of pixel
at x-coordinate of 511. (Finished a row)
5. Compute and store the variances of adjacent end point
x-coordinates obtained in step 3 until 511
(for a row with 512 elements) is reached.
6. Repeat the above procedures for other rows of the image.

Where

$$slope = \frac{F(Xend,y) - F(Xbegin,y)}{Xend - Xbegin}$$

$$Fr(x,y) = slope * (x - Xbegin) + F(Xbegin,y)$$

$$\text{Sum of variances} = \sum_{x=Xbegin}^{Xend} |F(x,y) - Fr(x,y)|$$

Xend = x-coordinate of end point.
Xbegin = x-coordinate of beginning point.
F(x,y) = original grey level at location (x,y).
Fr(x,y) = grey level at location (x,y) obtained from the reconstructed image.

Example:

A specific row of the image can be recorded as (bold italic numbers represent the variances between end point x-coordinates) :

4 **36** *21* **65** *20* *19* *33* *12* *24* *56* 21 233 12 10 87 255 7 10 40

21 100

The running time complexity of the algorithm to construct a differential polyline is $O(n^2)$. In other words, there is no increase in computational complexity as compared to the original polylines approach.

3.0   Image rebuilding from a differential polyline

Reproducing the differential polylines can reconstruct an image.

Image rebuilding algorithm:

1. Rebuild the original x-coordinate end points by adding adjacent numbers.
2. Read x-coordinates until 511 is met, then read the rest
   of a line for grey levels of end point pixels.
   THE NUMBER OF STRAIGHT LINES IS THEN KNOWN
   (NUMBER   OF X-COORDINATES). THE FIRST IS THE END
   POINT'S X-   COORDINATE   OF   THE   FIRST   LINE.
   (STARTING POINT OF THE   SECOND LINE)
3. Reconstruct pixel grey levels for a row by:
   $Fr(x) = m' * (x - Xi) + Fs(Xi) \quad Xi \le x \le Xi+1$

$$m' = \frac{F s (X i + 1) - F s (X i)}{(X i + 1) - (X i)}$$

Where $Xi = i^{th}$ x-coordinate read.
   $Fr(x)$ = grey level at location x along the current row obtained from the
                              reconstructed image.
   $Fs(Xi)$ = grey level at location Xi along the current row.

Similar to the revised algorithm in depicted in section 2, the running time for the algorithm to rebuild a row of an image from differential polyline data is $O(n^2)$. That is, there is no sacrifice of increasing computational complexity.

4.0   Conclusion

In the previous sections, the concepts of image compression and image compression by polylines are examined. On top of polylines, a differential polylines model is developed in this research. Inheriting the simplicity of polylines, differential polylines are easy to implement and requires a small amount of computational effort compared to the predictive coding and transform coding approaches. Most importantly, less bits are required to stored the compressed image as only the variances of end point x-coordinates are stored. Consequently, further information reduction is achieved.

A feasible application of differential polylines to the hotel and tourism industry is for image transmission on Internet. With the advances in computer hardware technology, differential polylines can be efficiently applied to increase the transmission speed of hotel and tourism related images. This makes it easier to disseminate tourism information of a particular region, promoting the local hospitality and tourism activities.

126

References:

1. Bret, M. (1992), Image Synthesis, Doedrecht: Kluwer Academic Publishers.
2. Marion, A. (1991), An Introduction to Image Processing, London: Chapman and Hall.
3. Mohamed, A.S.A. and Law, R.C.H. (1989, Oct), "A Noncausal AR Model for Breast Tissue Image Compression", Proceedings of the International Symposium on Computer Architecture and Digital Signal Processing, Hong Kong, pp. 590-594.
4. Pham, D.T. and Abdollahi, M. (1988), "Image Compression Using Polylines", Pattern Recognition, Vol. 21, No. 6, pp. 631-637.

4.4

CONTENT BASED IMAGE RETRIEVAL

R. Srivaths and S. Srinivasan
Indian Institute of Technology,Madras, India

Color, shape and dominant edges of image objects and regions form important attributes to an image. Image content therefore offers possible means for developing methods of image retrieval from image databases. More importantly, pre-computing image features that typify these attributes greatly reduces the time required to traverse through the search space. This paper presents a model for efficient retrieval of images, which provides a framework for developing methods of content based image retrieval.

1.0   Introduction

Multimedia information systems are increasingly being employed in the many realms of human activities. They include medicine, education and training, fashion, art, architecture, tourism etc. One important issue in this regard concerns accessing and retrieving images. Traditional image retrieval systems employ access methods based on captions or keywords. This approach is prone to failure due to the inadequacy of distinct textual descriptions and the high dependence on the vocabulary of the user. Human beings perceive most of the information about their environment through their visual sense. Hence, it becomes imperative that modern retrieval systems utilise the visual content of the images for retrieval. In the proposed model, image content is used to develop search mechanisms for effective and efficient retrieval. The two main aspects of the proposed model are image feature pre-computation and feature matching. The methods of retrieval were implemented on databases consisting of still images and frames of video sequences. The simplicity of this technique makes it amenable for adaptation in the design of multimedia information systems.

2.0   Image retrieval model

Multimedia databases are characterized by the large size of their constituents, especially images . In many cases, such as CD-ROM image collections or image archives, updates are rare. Database changes are at most append operations. These characteristics suggest that image features, which are attributes that characterize an image, can be pre-computed thereby avoiding the problem of analysing large volumes of data on-line.The image retrieval model is shown in Figure 1. First, all the database images are processed. Then, the features are pre-

128

computed and stored for all the images in the database. Whenever a query is submitted, the query image is processed and its features are computed. These features are then matched against the stored features of the database images. This ensures that bulk of the processing is done prior to query handling, so that feature computation is restricted just to the query image at the time of the query. This arrangement improves the speed of retrieval and calls for evolution of matching schemes with the underlying notion of features.

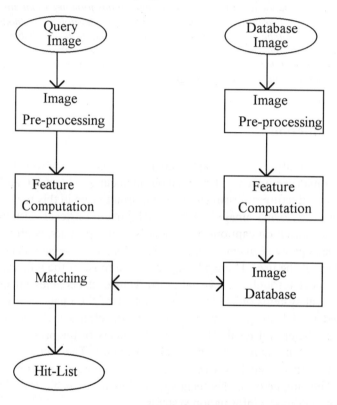

Figure 1: The image retrieval model

3.0 Image features and matching

Color, shape and edges are features significant to an image. Matching procedures developed for these features are explained in the following sub-sections.

3.1 Color

Color matching can be implemented in many ways. The Reference Color Table method proposed by (Mehtre,Kankanhalli,Narasimhalu,Man,1995) has been modified for this purpose. The gray scale histograms (normalized by the image size) are first pre-computed for all the color images in the database . A pre-defined set of colors is used that range broadly over the entire gray scale spectrum. For every image, the histogram is sampled at these colors to yield the resultant feature vector,

$$f = (p_1, p_2, p_3....p_n),$$

where p_i is the normalized pixel frequency at the ith color. The Euclidean distance between the query image feature vector f_q and the stored feature vector of a database image f_i forms the matching score.

3.2   Shape

Shape based retrieval typically handles queries of the form : *Is the query object present in one of the database images ?* Retrieval based on shape imposes the task of pre-computing geometric properties of object(s) in an image. First, the binary images were generated for the entire database by thresholding. Region identification (Sonka,Hlavac,Boyle,1993) was then done by using 8-connectivity masks and the output was then separated into distinct object images. The object border representation was done using chain codes (Jahne,1993) to facilitate storage as well as algorithmic computation of geometric properties. Circularity and Eccentricity were chosen as size-invariant and size-indicative properties to form the C-E shape feature vector of the object. A weighted Euclidean distance measure between the C-E feature vectors of the query and database object images yields the matching score, with the weights pre-settable.

3.3   Edges

Edge based retrieval is highly favored when the user is searching for frames best resembling the query frame when the database consists of frames of video sequences.The feature needed to support *Frame Search* consists of the edge map of each image. Edge maps were pre-computed for all the database images using the Sobel operator (Sonka,Hlavac,Boyle,1993). An added requirement is that the edge maps of the database and query images are of the same size or are reducible to the same size (128 x 128 was the size adopted). The query edge map is first partitioned into 8 x 8 sized blocks or local blocks. For each image in the database, each local block is correlated with a corresponding search area of 16 x 16 in the database image. The overall matching score is merely the sum of the correlation scores of each local block. The advantage of having a larger search area for each local block lies in the fact that a certain amount of spatial warping is allowed.

4.0 Retrieval accuracy

The Success Rate of retrieval is measured in terms of the capacity of a method to return all similar images in the hit-list. The issue of importance is not whether false hits are generated but whether similar images are not missed. The databases consisting of images collected from different sources as well as frames of video sequences were tested using query images for different hit-list sizes. Typical average success rates (possible range being from 0 to 1) for the different methods are indicated in Table 1. It must be noted that the success rate of a method based on ,say, shape can not be compared with that based on color because of the nature of the query handled.

Table 1: Average success rates of the methods of retrieval

Method	Average Success Rate
Modified Reference Color Table	0.75 - 0.85
C-E feature based Retrieval	0.75 - 0.80
Frame Search	1.0

5.0 Conclusion

An image retrieval model has been outlined for tackling the issue of retrieving images from image collections. The characteristic identified as most important to the model was pre-computation of the feature vectors.The main advantage of the proposed scheme is its capability to exploit the inherent properties of an image to provide fast and efficient retrieval.

References:

1. Jahne, B. (1993), Digital Image Processing, Springer Verlag.
2. Mehtre, B.M., Kankanhalli, M.S., Narasimhalu, A.D., Man, G.C. (1995), "Color Matching for image retrieval", *Pattern Recognition Letters*, Vol. 16, pp. 325-331.
3. Sonka, M., Hlavac, V., Boyle, R. (1993), Image Processing, Analysis and Machine Vision, London, Chapman and Hall.

4.5

TRAVERSE FEATURES AND STRUCTURAL FEATURES IN HANDWRITTEN CHINESE CHARACTER RECOGNITION

Daming Shi, Jianglong Tang, and Wenhao Shu
Harbin Institute of Technology, PRC

While recognizing a Chinese character, people usually regard it as an image and also relate it to structural information. From this point of view, we extract the statistical features from the Rapid transformation of the horizontal and vertical traverse numbers and the structural features from contour components in this paper. The statistical features are insensitive to translation and slight revolution, and considering there is plenty of contour information in a Chinese character, we also propose an approach to components extraction by sub-structure detector. The result of our experiment on 40,000 Chinese character samples shows that this approach is useful and suitable for a practical Chinese character recognition system.

1.0   Introduction

Since the manuscripts of Chinese character information are usually handwritten, it is especially important to recognize handwritten Chinese characters in daily use. The characteristics of   handwritten Chinese characters may be listed as follows:
1). great distortion of strokes, which is different for each person
2). connection of strokes and components
3). Instability of the stroke width and the relative length

To obtain stable features, which is easy to be extracted and stored, we select recognition features as follows:
1). **statistical features:** The Rapid transformation of the horizontal and vertical traverse numbers of Chinese characters. From each Chinese character, we extract 256 primary features, then through the Rapid Transformation, we select 48 features from the result of the transformation as the rough classification features.
2). **structural features:** The contour components of Chinese characters. We select 200 contour components to describe the contour structures of Chinese characters, and each component is recognized by its correspondent sub-structure detector. To tolerate the unstable relationship in handwritten Chinese characters, we express the patterns by the probabilities of the structural relationship.

2.0   Diagram of chinese character recognition approach

In this approach of   handwritten Chinese character recognition, after the pre-

132

processing of the primary image, at first we use the statistical features derived from the Rapid Transformation to realize the preliminary classfication and extract components by the sub-structure detectors. Then based on the result of the rough classfication, by matching the component structural dictionary, we accomplish the recognition of the whole character. The diagram is shown in Figure 1.

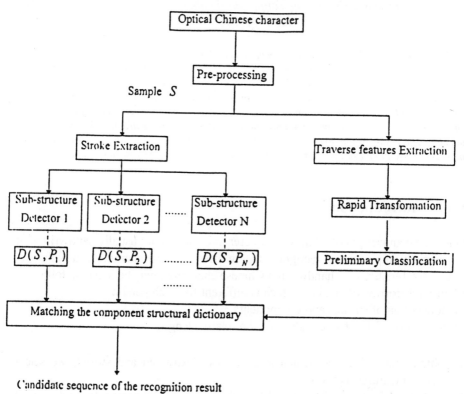

Figure 1: Diagram of this Chinese Character Recognition Approach

3.0   Rapid transformation of the traverse features

To extract stable traverse features, we should obtain the traverse numbers at suitable positions. The algorithm (Xia Ying,1991:p.235) below can extract the traverse features of Chinese characters precisely and rapidly. First, the primary image is normalized to a binary $N \times N$ character dot-matrix $F = \{f(i,j)|i = 1,\cdots,N, j = 1,\cdots,N\}$, $N = 2^l$, (here $l = 7, N = 128$). For black pixel (i,j), $f(i,j) = 1$, and for white pixel (i,j), $f(i,j) = 0$. From the $N \times N$ dot-matrix F, we can obtain the N-dimensional horizontal traverse feature vector

T_H and the N-dimensional vertical traverse feature vector T_V.

$$T_H = \left[t_H(0), t_H(1), \cdots, t_H(N-1) \right]^T \qquad \textbf{(Equation 3.1)}$$

$$T_V = \left[t_V(0), t_V(1), \cdots, t_V(N-1) \right]^T \qquad \textbf{(Equation 3.2)}$$

where $t_H(i)$ is the horizontal traverse number of the *ith* row, and $t_V(j)$ is the vertical traverse number of the *jth* column.

When the traverse flag changes from WHITE to BLACK, a traverse is supposed to happen. The algorithm of traverse feature extraction is as follows:

STEP 1. Set all horizontal traverse flags of N rows as WHITE, and all vertical traverse flags of N columns as WHITE. $t_H(0) = \cdots = t_H(N-1) = 0$,

$t_V(0) = \cdots = t_V(N-1) = 0$

STEP 2. Scan F. If all pixels of F have been scanned, then end.

STEP 3. Detect the 3×3 neighborhood of current pixel (i, j).

    3.1 If all pixels in the 3×3 neighborhood are white, then set the horizontal traverse flag of the *ith* row as WHITE and the vertical traverse flag of the *jth* column as WHITE.

    3.2 If all pixels in the 3×3 neighborhood are black:

        3.2.1 If the horizontal traverse flag of the *ith* row is WHITE, then the horizontal traverse number of this row $t_H(i)$ is added by 1, and the horizontal traverse flag of this row is set to BLACK.

        3.2.2 If the vertical traverse flag of the *jth* column is WHITE, then the vertical traverse number of this column $t_V(j)$ is added by 1,and the vertical traverse flag of this coloumn is set to BLACK.

STEP 4 Loop to **STEP 2**.

Because the dot-matrix is scanned only once, and the states of neighborhood are also concerned, this approach is rapid and tolerable to noise.

Considering the translation and revolution of handwritten Chinese characters, we conduct a Rapid transformation of the horizontal and vertical traverse features to extract stable recognition features. $T = \{ T_H', T_V' \}$, T_H' and T_V' are vectors while sampling T_H and T_V respectively at pitch 4. T_H and T_V are $N = 2^l$ dimensional vectors,thus T is a $M = 2^{l-1}$ dimensional vector.The Rapid transformation of T can be divided into l-1 steps, while the *Rth* and $(R-1)th$ steps meet the relationship below:

$$\begin{cases} T_{2i}^{(R)} = \left| T^{(R-1)}{}_i + T_{i+\frac{M}{2}}^{(R-1)} \right| \\[2em] T_{2i+1}^{(R)} = \left| T_i^{(R-1)} - T_{i+\frac{M}{2}}^{(R-1)} \right| \end{cases}$$

(**Equation 3.3**)

Where $i = 0,1,2,\cdots,(\dfrac{M}{2} - 1)$.

In Chinese character recognition, Rapid transformation is rapid and insensitive to translation and light revolution. For each $R(u)$ is the linear combination of original functions $T(i)$, it can comprehensively expressed the features of Chinese characters. For example, $R(0) = \dfrac{1}{M} \sum_{i=0}^{M-1} T(i)$ reflects the complexity of Chinese characters.

Through the Rapid transformation,the features are correlative,not all of them should be used to cluster.The features are selected as preliminary classification which take the smaller error probability in clustering.

In case of n classes,the error probability of Bayes classifier is as follows:

$$P(e) = \sum_{i=1}^{n} \int_{\bar{a_i}} p(x|\omega_i) P(\omega_i) dx$$

(**Equation 3.4**)

here, $\bar{a_i}$ is the areas other then ω_i.Then extend **Equation 3.4** to m-dimension:

$$P(e) = \sum_{i=1}^{n} \int_{\bar{a_i}} \int \cdots \int^{m} \bullet\bullet\bullet \int p(x|\omega_i) P(\omega_i) dx$$

(**Equation 3.5**)

Equation 3.5 is unfit for computing,for the limits of a_i of class ω_i is hard to be described.

Assume that there are N_i learning samples in the ith class of Chinese characters,when clustered by m features,the error numbers of samples is E_i,thus error probability may be estimated by:

$$P(e) = \sum_{i} \dfrac{E_i}{N_i} P(\omega_i)$$

(**Equation 3.6**)

While the learning samples are clustered with 1 to M features,the error probabilities are$\{ P^{(1)}(e), P^{(2)}(e),\cdots, P^{(M)}(e) \}$,the m features are selected to priliminary classification while $P^{(m)}(e)$ is the smallest of all.

In this paper, not all of $\{P^{(1)}(e), P^{(2)}(e), \cdots, P^{(M)}(e)\}$ are calculated. At first, the eigenvalues of global-divergence matrix $S_t = E\left[(T - M_0)(T - M_0)^T\right]$ are ranged from the biggest to the smallest, $\lambda_1 \geq \lambda_2 \geq \bullet\bullet\bullet \geq \lambda_M$, where T is the pattern feature vector of any learning sample of all Chinese characters, and M_0 is referred to the global average vector.

According to **Equation 3.6**, $P^{(m)}(e)$ is calculated while the m features taken to cluster which are correspondent to the biggest m eigenvalues.

4.0   Probability pattern and sub-structure detector

To imitate the process by which a person recognizies Chinese characters, we follow the way from strokes to components, and then from components to the whole character in this approach. Thus, we have a two-stage description of components and the whole character. In this approach, components are obtained from contours by the sub-structure detectors. For the sub-structure detector, we take the strokes as input, matching distance to its probability pattern as output, and through syntactic analyzing method realize the recognition from strokes to components. Each character is a high-dimension vector in the space of all components.

Because of the distortion of handwritten Chinese chracters, the stable structural relationship is valuable in recognition. So we define the mathing distance from a sample to its pattern based on the statistical probability, definition are presented as follows:

Definition 1. A structural compenent is described as $V = \left[v_1, v_2, \ldots v_{2k*(2k-1)}\right]^T$. Here v_i is refereed to the relationship between the terminal points of k strokes $\{(sx_1, sy_1, ex_1, ey_1)\ldots(sx_k, sy_k, ex_k, ey_k)\}$, and (sx_k, sy_k, ex_k, ey_k) is the coordinates of the starting point and the end point of the kth stroke. V is a vector of $2K*(2K-1)$ dimensions (Liu, Tang, Shu, 1994), where $v_1 = R(sx_1 - ex_1), v_2 = R(sx_1 - ex_2), \ldots v_{k*(2k-1)+1} = R(sy_1 - ey_1), \cdots$. Here $R(x) = 0$, while $x \leq 0$, and $R(x) = 1$, while $x > 0$.

Definition 2. Through the learning of M component samples $\{S_1, S_2, \ldots S_M\}$, we obtain a vector $T = \left[t_1, t_2, \ldots t_{2k*(2k-1)}\right]^T$ labeling the stable features of a structural

compnent and the happening probability pattern
$$P = \left[p(v_1 = 0), p(v_2 = 0)...p(v_{2k*(2k-1)} = 0) \right]^T.$$

Here Sj(j=1,...,M) is a vector as in definition 1, and $s_{j,i}$ is the *ith* element of S_j.

$$t_i = \begin{cases} 1, (\dfrac{1}{M}\sum_{j=1}^{M} s_{j,i} \le \alpha) OR (\dfrac{1}{M}\sum_{j=1}^{M} s_{j,i} \ge \beta) \\ -1, other \end{cases}$$

(here, $\alpha = 0.1, \beta = 0.9$)

t_i =-1 means the *ith* feature unstable.

Instead of the Euclidean-distance, we use the distance fuction based on probability as follows:

$$D(V,P) = \sum_{i=1}^{2k*2k-1} f(v_i, p_i) \qquad \text{(Equation 4.1)}$$

where function $f(v_i, p_i) = \begin{cases} 0, t_i = -1 \\ 1 - p_i, t_i = 1 \& v_i = 0 \\ p_i, t_i = 1 \& v_i = 1 \end{cases}$

In this approach, components are recognized by the relationship between strokes, and then the whole character is recognized by the combination of components. If we can't obtain the sequence of strokes and components, this approach won't be effective. For this point of view, we extract components from four sides and four corners. So while recognizing components, we have fixed the location of the components in a Chinese character. Also each sub-structure detector searches strokes according to its own stroke sequence to recognize components, which is from contours to center.

For a structural sample of Chinese characters, all sub-structure detectors will detect its stroke structure. The sub-structure detectors can be divided into nine classes based on the location of structure in a character: 1) Left radicals (such as 亻); 2) Right radicals (such as: 忄); 3) Top radicals (such as: 人); 4) Bottom radicals (such as: 灬); 5) Outside radicals (such as: 冂); 6) Top-left corners (such as: 厂); 7) Bottom-left corners (such as: 辶); 8) Top-right corners (such as: 乛); 9) Bottom-right corners (such as: 辶). The sub-structure detectors take the stable relationship between the terminal points of strokes as the main feature, and the connection of strokes as the supplementary feature.

5.0   Conclusion

A Chinese character recognition approach based on the statistical traverse feature and the contour structural features is proposed in this paper. It is highly parallel while extracting components and matching characters, and can tolerate the connection of strokes. In the test of 40,000 samples of Chinese characters written by different persons, the correct rate of component extraction is higher than 98%. If combined with a post-processing of contexts, this approach can be used to realize a practical recognition system.

References:

1. Xia Y., et al (1991), "A Suitable Approach for Chinese Character Recognition". *Proceedings of Pattern Recognition and Artificial Intelligence Conference 1991*, 235-238.
2. Zhang X.Z. (1992), Techniques of Chinese Character Recognition, Peking, *Tsinghua University Press.*
3. Liu J.F., Tang J.L., Shu W.H. (1994), "A Structure Similarity Analysis Method for On-line Recognition of Handwritten Chinese Characters". *Journal of Harbin Institute of Technology*, Vol. E-1, No.1,51-54.
4. Cao H.Y., Shu W.H. (1994), "Approach to Stroke Extraction of Handwritten Chinese Characters". *Proceedings of the Fifth National Conf. on Recognition of Chinese Characters and Speeches*, 1994.9,130-134.

PART 5

SYSTEMS DEVELOPMENT

5.1

MANAGING MULTIMEDIA PROJECT DEVELOPMENT: A SIMPLISTIC INSTRUCTIONAL DESIGN MODEL USING A PROBLEM-SOLVING APPROACH

Alfred Ko, & Lynne Chapman
University of New England, Australia

In developing educational multimedia, project management tends to be of most importance. We propose a simplistic four stage model for all team members in the development of educational multimedia packages. The model treats development as a problem-solving activity, identifies roles and reponsibilities and facilitates efficient team management.

1.0   Introduction

With the evolution and advancement of technology, the application of computer-based multimedia in education is growing rapidly. The skills and knowledge used for producing conventional materials in the past are no longer adequate to deal with the production of multimedia learning packages, knowledge and skills demanded are quite different. Moreover, multimedia projects are almost always developed by a team of experts, such as the subject expert, instructional designer, graphic artist/animator and programmer, who work together closely. An appropriate model which can guide the team in working efficiently from the beginning to the end of the project is essential.

Existing instructional design models have provided much help in developing various types of instructional media and in guiding academics in designing effective learning materials. However, there are few models specifically formulated for multimedia purposes. As multimedia development is closely related to software development, many colleagues have adopted software engineering models to develop their multimedia packages (Bergman & Moore, 1990; Howell, 1992; Yang, Moore & Burton, 1990). The former models stressing educational aspects and the latter, production aspects. It is useful, therefore, to formulate a model which can be used by different personnel in the multimedia team to enhance communication and aid effective work practices.

As a result of the problems we have encountered and the valuable experience we have gained from different projects, in this paper we propose a model which:
- provides a framework for the instructional designer (as a project manager) to manage all aspects of multimedia projects effectively and efficiently;

- provides guidelines for ALL members of the team to follow;
- clarifies roles and task responsibilities to improve communication;
- allows input from all team members but provides a structure to bring expertise together to achieve solutions along the way and for the final product;
- can be applied to future multimedia project development.

2.0 Inadequacy of models for developing multimedia projects

Looking at the development process of different multimedia projects, we discovered various problems that could not be resolved, in spite of using models as guidelines. These problems tended to be 'communication' problems or 'management' problems rather than technical problems. Problems can arise out of the expection of team members who have different expertise and usually have a different understanding of the project because of their background. Initial misunderstanding or misinterpretation of information can lead to greater problems in later stage. Unclear roles and responsibilites of each member can be created by the multidisciplinary nature of multimedia development. Unless precise roles and responibilites are defined, team members 'have to make assumptions, which lead to problems later' (Phillips, 1996: p.36). Of most importance is communication among team members. Team members may tend to work alone without sharing their ideas or problems with other team members. This is possibly because 'each member has a considerable creative investment in the work, and tends to claim intellectual ownship of the project' (Phillips, 1996: p.37), as a result, sharing experiences and ideas for improvement and enhancement can be minimised. Each problem mentioned above is related to the management of the project and people. Reviewing various models for developing instructional materials from a management perspective we have found existing models have not addressed this issue.

In developing instructional materials, the process is often guided by an Instructional Systems Development (ISD) model or an Instructional Design (ID) model. There are many instructional design models which help to achieve different instructional needs and contexts (Dick & Carey, 1996; Gagne & Briggs, 1979; Leshin, Pollock & Reigeluth, 1992; Maggs, McMillan, Moore, Mulligan & O'Brien, 1990; Romiszowski, 1981; Seels & Glasgow, 1990). These models, using a systematic approach, provide academics and instructional designers with guidelines for developing a learning package which is systematically designed, pedagogically sound and effectively delivered. However multimedia development is concerned, the contribution of other participants in the team.

Software engineering models when applied to multimedia development tend to focus on technical aspects only. The monitoring of the production process and the solution of the problems are always the goals of these models. Howell (1992) examined six models for developing multimedia projects. They provide software engineering personnel with guidelines as to what will 'work best' for ... [their] 'own particular situation and application' (Howell, 1992: p.29). The contribution to the development process of other team participants, was not considered.

In reality, developing a quality multimedia project requires a team effort from many different experts: academics to provide content; instructional designers to advise approaches; graphic artist/animators to suggest visuals and animation; production personnel to provide audio and video clips; and programmers to provide a user-friendly interface. The efforts of each of these experts needs to be coordinated into a cohesive final package completed within the budget and time line set. Hence management plays an important role and there is therefore a need to propose a model which not only looks at the instructional and technical aspects, but also at management issues seriously. More importantly the model should be compatible with existing instructional design and software engineering practice, and be simple enough for all team members to both understand the process and be comfortable working with it. The proposed model makes it crucial to investigate the nature of instructional design and the roles of instructional designers.

3.0 Instructional design: A process to solve problems

Rogoff (1987) describes the process of instructional design as: '... The systematic process of designing an instructional solution to an educational or training problem' (p.146). Instructional design as a discipline has developed through the contribution of many disciplines such as social science, information science and management science and it is 'both a body of knowledge about learning and learners, and a process for organising and managing the development of complex instructional programs' (Johnson, 1989: p.14). Numerous instructional systems have been proposed; for example Gagne and Briggs (1979) provide a comprehensive model consisting of fourteen stages; Romiszowski (1981) devised an instructional design model with five stages using Polya's problem-solving approach; and Heinich, Molenda and Russell's ASSURE model (1989) gives a six-step model to deal with different instructional system designs. Others (Seels & Glasgow, 1990; Maggs, 1990; Leshin, Pollock & Reigeluth, 1992; Dick and Carey, 1996) have also proposed models with various stages. All indicate that the instructional design process is a problem-solving activity which requires: identification of problem/situation; generation of possible solutions;

implementation of feasible solution; and evaluation of the outcome or the solution. Monitoring these problem-solving activities is part of the role of the instructional designer.

In the instructional design process, instructional designers work closely with academics subject to ensure that all content materials are effectively delivered and meet the goals of the subject expert. To achieve a quality product at the end of the process, instructional designers also need to manage the process so that each member involved is working effectively and harmoniously. This is particularly important when developing a multimedia project as the expertise and area of responsibility of other personnel involved in the process is clearly delineated, while the management task has increasingly fallen to the instructional designer to facilitate the interaction of content experts and production personnel. This dual-role assigned to instructional designers demands of them not only the monitoring of content and learning strategies, but also the coordination and management of people. Recent research shows that the managerial activities by instructional designers ranked as one of the five major activities among 29 other activities performed by instructional designers in Australia (Allen, 1996). Allen comments that 'instructional designers are not only concerned with designing the materials but also with ensuring that the development of materials is managed from start to finish' (1996: p. 24).

4.0 An instructional design model for managing multimedia project development

The growing importance of the managerial role of instructional designers combined with the inadequacy of existing models for developing multimedia projects has led to the model we propose, in order to address instructional, technical and management aspects. By management we mean all those activities which make the process more efficient and all those activities that contribute to individual motivation and harmonious working relations. Refined from Lawson's (1980) design model, our working model consists of four interconnected reversible phases: Identify problem/s; Develop Solution; Implement Solution; and Evaluate. A graphical representation of the model is shown in Figure One.

Note that the 'Evaluate' phase appears several times in the model as well as being the final phase of the development process. All activities are appraised following each phase. The result of each evaluation step either leads to a subsequent phase of development or back a step in the process. We see evaluation as an integral part of every phase and of such importance as to demand description first.

4.1   Evaluate

Throughout the whole developmental process, 'evaluate' is used as a mechanism to justify whether an activity should proceed. Evaluation provides information so that improvements can be made, and to justify whether a decision is made appropriately. All aspects and activities of the project should be appraised and revised until the project team is satisfied with their effectiveness. If this concept is applied to the whole project, the nature of 'evaluate' is then to appraise the quality of the product respect to the specifications defined as well as student learning outcomes as stated in the 'identify problem' phase. Tactful management of this aspect is vital to ensure everone's contributions are recognised and that creativity is not retarded for future stages in the process.

4.2   Identify problem

This phase of the development process involves activities such as: investigate the nature of an educational problem or a situation to be improved; identify the problem or situation; derive general and specific objectives for the project. General objectives are the ultimate goal of the project itself, i.e. to develop a multimedia project to solve an educational problem or to improve a situation for a particular target group of learners under a prescribed budget and an agreeable time frame. Specific objectives are the learning outcomes we expect from students.

Another issue associated with this phase is to decide who will be involved in the development process. In an educational setting, a multimedia team will be comprised of the Project Manager (the Instructional Designer (ID) in most cases), the Subject Expert (SE), usually an academic from faculty, the Graphic Artist/Animator (GA), the Authoring Expert (AE), usually, the programmer, and in some cases the Audio/Video Procuder (AVP).

At this initial phase, the managerial role of the instructional designer seems to be most important. His/her role as project manager is to ensure that the project is setting out in the right direction and will progress smoothly to the next stage. Some of the roles of a project manager at this stage are:

1.   to investigate/identify with the subject expert the problem to be solved;
2.   to confirm with the subject expert the use of multimedia to solve the problem;
3.   to identify the objectives of the project with respect to educational effectiveness; target learner; prescribed budget, and proposed time frame;
4.   to define with the subject expert the learning objectives of the project;

146

5.   to decide who will be involved in the process (except the subject expert); and

6.   to set team operational procedures and intitial schedules.

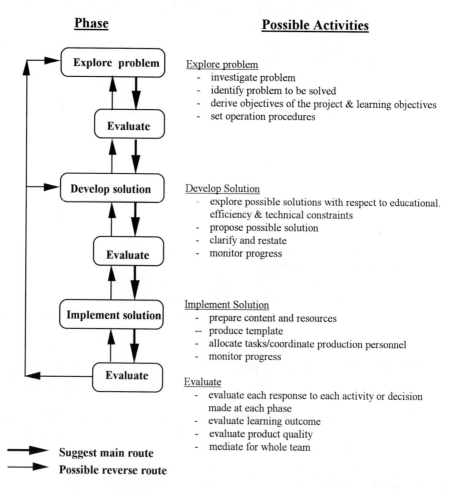

Phase   **Possible Activities**

Explore problem

Explore problem
- investigate problem
- identify problem to be solved
- derive objectives of the project & learning objectives
- set operation procedures

Evaluate

Develop solution

Develop Solution
- explore possible solutions with respect to educational. efficiency & technical constraints
- propose possible solution
- clarify and restate
- monitor progress

Evaluate

Implement solution

Implement Solution
- prepare content and resources
-- produce template
- allocate tasks/coordinate production personnel
- monitor progress

Evaluate

Evaluate
- evaluate each response to each activity or decision made at each phase
- evaluate learning outcome
- evaluate product quality
- mediate for whole team

Suggest main route
Possible reverse route

Figure 1: Illustration of the proposed model

4.3   Develop solutions

The major activities of this phase are to explore possible solutions and to choose one to implement. In exploring possible solutions, it is important to decide how to convert the 'content' of instruction into a multimedia environment. Conventional print-based instruction, with graphics as amplifiers and supplements, text, still images (diagrams and photographs) moving images as video or animation, and sound clips. How we apply multimedia to achieve our objectives is a key issue in this phase. Multimedia can be applied to different learning contexts such as tutorial, demonstration, simulation or games, etc. The decision to integrate different media and the preference of adopting a particular approach will depend on 'content', student learning style, availability of resources and preference of the subject expert.

In providing multimedia solutions to a problem, tools selected for development and delivery should be considered carefully. The choice of platforms, accessories for enhancing multimedia capability and productivity, compatibility between hardware and software, and compatibility between software are part of the solution. How and where the product is to be delivered should be taken into account in advance. In most educational settings, multimedia projects are run in computer laboratories so that students can work with the product at their own time and pace at no cost. However, if the product is going to be used outside a laboratory, the choice of delivery system should be examined more carefully, perhaps surveying the type of computers and peripherals students are using.

After exploring different solutions to the problem, the next step is to select the most feasible solution. In choosing a solution for implementation, evaluate whether the 'content' presentation will help achieve the learning objectives as stated in the 'identify problem' phase and whether technical constraints are minimised. The team will devise a set of specifications for the project. With mutual agreement among members, the specifications should provide solutions to the following questions: How is the package to be presented and deliverd? How is the package to be produce? Will the solution be accomplished within budget and time? What 'content' should be included and how will learning outcomes be assessed? What format (diskette, CD-ROM or other format), media (text, still images, videos, animation, audios etc) will be included? What user-friendly interface and navigation features will we use? What imaginative metaphor to arouse and maintain student interest can we create? The project manager's role in this phase includes:

1.　clarifying and restating solutions agreed to;
2.　determining learning strategies; and
3.　scheduling and maintaining progress of design phase.

4.4　Implement solution

Once specifications are defined precisely, the team can begin implementation. The subject expert works closely with the instructional designer to ensure that all the 'content' is correctly prepared and is ready to be converted into a multimedia format. Simultaneously other resources such as scripts, graphics,

148

animations, video and audio clips need to be prepared for implementation. It is also important at this phase for the instructional designer (project manager) to ensure both development and delivery systems are available and are functioning well and meet other programming time lines. Once the finalised 'content' and other resources are reviewed by the Instructional Designer, the authoring expert can begin the production of a template (or a prototype) which will form a trial version of the final product.

Once the template is tested with students, refinement or modification can be recommended. After refinement, the final product can be installed and used by students. For continuous improvement, we advise that on-going evaluation so that the educational effectiveness of a product can be further enhanced to cater for students' needs. The role of the project manager in this phase includes:

1.   allocating tasks;
2.   determining time lines;
3.   coordinating production personnel; and
4.   monitoring progress against the schedule.

As emphasised before we do not see the 'Evaluate' phase as the last phase of the model. Throughout the whole developmental process evaluation is used as a mechanism to justify whether a decision proceeds. Evaluation gives information for improvements and to judge if a decision has been made appropriately. The role of the project manager during evaluation includes:

1.   clarifying modifications;
2.   overseeing implementation of modifications; and
3.   maintaining continued commitment of team members.

5.0   How the model works

To demonstrate how this model works, we provide a matrix as Table 1which consists of suggested activities in the process and defines the primary role of each member. Suggested activities illustrates how the model works in a logical sequence. The explanation of the role of each member helps to clarify their responsibility in relation to each activity in the developmental process.

The responsibilities of each member in a multimedia team varies according to the nature of the project, the budget, time available, and the pratice and culture of the individual development unit. Different development teams assign different responsibilities to their members (Phillips, 1996; Bergman & Moore, 1990; Yang,

Moore & Burton, 1995). However, the responsibilities of some of the major members in the development generally are outlined.

5.1   Instructional designer

The instructional designer as project manager has the overall responsibility for the project—from start to finish. He/she has to oversee the design, development, implementation and evaluation of the project by constructing a feasible working schedule. Day-to-day operations such as controlling resources and progress, organising, leading and documenting meetings, coordinating different personnel in the team, resolving conflicts amongst team members and continually clarifying perceptions are typical examples. As project manager, it is the ID's task to outline the roles and responsibilies of each team member, facilitate input from all team members while remaining sensitive to the needs of all team members. The ID needs to ensure everyone holds the same view of the project before development begins. For harmonious and efficient development, it is essential that all decisions be the result of a 'team' decision giving all participants an equal sense of ownership. Evaluation of ideas and subsequent modifications of solutions have to be agreed to willingly for each person to be happy with the solution and to be motivated to continue working at the hectic pace necessitated by conflicting workloads and tight timelines. In the instructional design role, he/she is responsible for suggesting 'content' with the subject expert to meet the objectives; translating the content into the project; and advising of project structures based on the investigation conducted in the 'explore' phase. The instructional designer directs the effort to explore and design, and documents the most effective sequence, storylines, and strategies for the project. In some institutions, the instructional designer also shares the responsibilities of the managing producer, art director and video director in the production of visuals, audio and video portions of the product. In an academic setting the implementation phase is often a difficult time for the ID, as academics with heavy workloads require constant encouragement to provide all resources with agreed times. The ID needs to check all content and resources to ensure specifications are being met and that the resulting product remains educationally sound. A 'sign-off' system for each stage needs to be instituted to eliminate the possibility of a never-ending series of revisions. Clear guidelines must be set to indicate when changes are no longer negotiable.

5.2   Subject expert

The subject expert is content provider for the project who has in-depth knowledge in a particular subject domain. His/her prime role is to generate and provide precise and up-to-date content, and sometimes other resources, to the development team and to consult with the project manager/instructional designer and other experts on the appropriateness of the project's objectives and content. The subject expert also provides a continuing review of scripts, storyboards, and activities to ensure learning objectives are being achieved. The subject expert also plays an important role in evaluating prototypes.

5.3 Graphic artist/animator

The major role of the graphic artist/animator is to create screen graphics, either still or moving images, for the project so that the message conveyed by the content is effective (in a visual format). He/she has to work closely with the instructional designer and the programmer to ensure that all the graphics created are visually attractive and are suitable for integration into the interface. The overall 'appeal' of the final product for the student will depend on the graphic artist's expertise.

5.4 Authoring expert

The authoring personnel, or programmer, is responsible for translating the ideas and concepts of the development team into a working program using programming language or authoring tools to achieve the objectives of the project. His/her primary role is to: integrate the media prepared into the interface; code special routines; and create interactions in the interface to support the project. The authoring expert works closely with the instructional designer and subject expert in determining the approach and sequence of the project.

6.0 Conclusion

The tasks of the project manager are many and varied and are not always obvious to other team members. They are not of a nature easily listed in a description of team members areas of responsibilities—they are however essential to the successful completion of a project. The aim of our model is not to emphasise one set of tasks over another but rather to highlight tasks that have previously been glossed over or ignored. Multimedia development is very much a team event with every member's input essential. We believe however that every team requires a catalyst to motivate, encourage, maintain and monitor progress. Possibly one of the most important tasks is to ensure that all team members maintain a 'shared' vision of, and value for the final product throughout the development. This role in our experience usually falls to the project manager in the form of the Instructional Designer. It is our intention that our model for development be used in future multimedia projects and be presented to team members as a guide to follow from the start. Its advantage is in the area of role definition. With roles clearly defined the team should function efficiently and more harmoniously than it otherwise would.

Table 1: Activity matrix for team members

Activities/Team Member	ID	SE	GA	AE	AVP
Explore problem					
investigate/identify problem	s	P	s	s	
confirm the use of multimedia as a solution to problem	s	P	s	s	
prepare working procedures	P				
identify objectives of the project	P	s			
derive learning objectives	P	s			
decide other production personnel	P				
evaluate if objectives can help to solve problem	P	s			
evaluate appropriateness of personnel to be included	P				
Develop Solution					
explore & determine possible product format	s	P	s	s	s
explore & determine possible media to be included	P	s	s	s	s
explore & determine possible learning approaches/strategies	P	s			
explore & determine possible development & delivery tools	s	s		P	
analyse information explored & propose possible solution	P	s		P	
evaluate if solution is feasible	P	s	s	s	
Implement Solution					
prepare content/assessment	s	P			
determine time lines & monitor progress	P				
confirm availability of development & delivery tools & production personnel		P	s	s	
allocate tasks	P				
prepare resources/materials/ interface		s	P	P	P
produce template			s	P	
evaluate effectiveness of template in relation to objectives	P				
refine/modify template			s	P	
install & implement final product				P	
Evaluate					
clarify & oversee modifications	P				
evaluate learning outcome	s	P			
evaluate product quality	P	s	s	s	

Key: P = Primary responsibility
s = Secondary responsibility

References:

1. Allen, M. (1996), A Profile of Instructional Designers in Australia, *Distance Education*, 17(1).
2. Bergman, R., & Moore, T. (1990), Managing Interactive Video/Multimedia Projects, New Jersey, Englewood Cliffs.
3. Dick, W., & Carey, L. (1996), The Systematic Design of Instruction (4th ed.), New York, Harper Collins.

4. Gagne, R., & Briggs, L. (1979), Principles of Instructional Design (2nd ed.), New York, Holt, Rinehart & Winston.

5. Heinich, R., Molenda, M., & Russell, J. (1989), Instructional Media and The New Technologies of Instruction, 3rd edn, New York, John Wiley & Sons.

6. Howell, T. G. (1992), Building Hypermedia Applications, A Software Development Guide, McGraw-Hill, New York.

7. Johnson, K. A. (1989), "The Foundations of Instructional Design", In K. A. Johnson & L. J. Foa, Instructional Design: New Alternatives for Effective Education and Training, New York, Macmillan.

8. Lawson, B. (1980), How Designers Think, London, The Architectural Press Ltd.

9. Leshin, C., Pollock, J., & Reigeluth C. (1992), Instructional Design Strategies and Tactics, New Jersey, Englewood Cliffs.

10. Maggs, A., McMillan, K., Moore, J., Mulligan, I., & O'Brien, P. (1990), Instructional Design, A System Approach, Sydney, Science Research Associates Pty. Ltd.

11. Murphy, D. (1992), "Is Instructional Design Truly A Design Activity?" Education & Training Technology International, 29(4), pp.279-282.

12. Patten, J. V. (1989), "What Is Instructional Design?" In K. A. Johnson & L. J. Foa, Instructional Design: New Alternatives for Effective Education and Training, New York, Macmillan.

13. Phillips, R., (1996), Development Guide to Interactive Multimedia: A Methodology for Educational Applications, Australia, Curtin University of Technology.

14. Romiszowski, A. J. (1981), Designing Instructional Systems, London, Kogan Page.

15. Seels, B., & Glasgow, Z. (1990), Exercises In Instructional Design, Columbus, Merrill.

16. Yang, C., Moore, D., & Burton, J. (1995), "Managing Courseware Production: An Instructional Design Model with a Software Engineering Approach", Educational Technology Research and Development, 43(4), pp.(60-70).

5.2

AN IMPRECISE DCT COMPUTATION MODEL FOR REAL-TIME APPLICATIONS

*Kangbin Yim[1], Jaehong Shim[1], Hwaja Chung[2], Gihyun Jung[1],
Kyunghee Choi[1] & Dongyoon Kim[1]*
[1]Ajou University & [2]SNPU, Korea

We propose an imprecise computational model for the DCT (Discrete Cosine Transform). In this paper the DCT procedure is re-analyzed to fit to imprecise computation model. Since only several major DCT coefficients including a DC value influence the quality of the restored data significantly, the imprecise model may be very effective for the applications that hire the DCT coding algorithm and suffer from the resource limitation, such as the lack of computing power in real time operating system and the bandwidth limitation in the distributed multimedia application. The model is carefully tuned to get close to the ideal goal of imprecise computation. That is, the sum of the computation times taken for all imprecise computations is equal to that for the precise computation, and the quality of the imprecise computation is linearly improved with the increase in the imprecise computation steps. The proposed model is implemented on a real time micro kernel we have built. And the computation time and quality of the decoded data are empirically studied.

1.0   Introduction

The recent attempt to integrate various services into a system raises many problems that have never happened for the system with a single service. The lack of computing power or the bandwidth limitation in distributed real-time multimedia systems is included in the category.

In the case that many processes are competing the processing power, each process is scheduled based on the scheduling algorithm that the system hires, and the processing power is shared between them. The multimedia systems that provide continuous data such as video and audio information usually require real-time services between the information senders and the receivers. The characteristics of real time service impose some constraints on the service. It is possible that a specific real-time process has to wait for the completion of executing the predecessor process and misses its deadline. Even though many efficient scheduling algorithms (Andrews,1991;Tilborg,1991;Stenkovic,1993) have been reported to solve the problems related with deadline problem, there always exists the chance that they can not meet the real-time requirements for many concurrent services. The traditional deadline miss handling policies force the service whose deadline has been missed to be terminated. The timing guarantee is another requirement for real time service while a non real time system can fail only due to massive hardware and software failures.

If it is possible that a process with the hard deadline can be divided into several small processes and the results obtained by the sub processes are additive, the utilization of processing power can be increased dramatically. But we have to pay the significant cost to get the additive property. The cost includes the extra hardware and software capabilities. Another obstacle to make dividing the process hard is the fact that, generally, the sum of the processing times required for the small divided processes far exceeds the processing time required for the original undivided process. If the overhead and the processing time problem in real time services are resolved somehow, the utilization of processing power can be increased dramatically depending on the properties of applications. For example, many popular video processing techniques includes iterative computations. And in some techniques, the intermediate results of the iterative computations have an additive property. That is, the quality of video image is getting improved as the number of iterations increases.

The additive property allows real time service to relax its constraints. The intermediate result obtained from the incomplete processing that only certain amount of iterations have been completed due to the unexpected resource starvation can be utilized to meet the degraded QoS for the service. In addition, the processing time for the processes whose deadlines, otherwise, can not be met is saved, thus increasing the resource utilization. The above two advantages resulted from imprecise computation are very useful for many multimedia applications since fortunately, the QoS 's for multimedia applications are usually tolerable in a certain range and the resource starvation occurs frequently in the multimedia services (Steinmetz,1995).

The imprecise computation is also very useful to enhance the network utilization and to improve the computing power utilization for distributed systems. It is possible that the available network bandwidth is less than the capacity to service many incoming requests. In the case, the results of executing a few sub-divided processes are transmitted using the available network bandwidth (while the result of the whole process can not be accommodated) and the transmitted information produced by the imprecise computation restores a lower quality output which is still valuable in the receiver.

The DCT(Discrete Cosine Transform) is known as one of popular image data compression techniques and adopted in JPEG and MPEG algorithms since the DCT can remove the spatial redundancy of 2-D image data efficiently. Another reason behind its popularity is that it can be easily implemented in hardware since it has a very regular structure (Jung,1996). Even though many commercial data compression VLSI chips include the DCT hardware, the DCT computation is still very time consuming process and a lot of hardware resources are dedicated to the DCT implementation. When the amount of available resource changes dynamically, the DCT process included in a real-time service may not be completed in the given deadline. The result of uncompleted DCT process has no meaning and the processing time assigned to the process is wasted in the conventional DCT computation. This loss could critically degrades the performance of real-time service with the very limited resources.

We propose an imprecise DCT model to overcome the problems that prevent real time services from being partially serviced. The proposed model shows the advantages of imprecise computation mentioned previously. The characteristics of the proposed model are close to those of the ideal imprecise computation model (that is, the intermediate result is additive and the sum of processing times for the subdivided processes is equal to that of the original whole process). The DCT model has been implemented on the real time micro kernel we had built previously. The quality of imprecise computations is linearly improved and the total sum of imprecise computation times is very close to that of the original precise computation.

Section II describes the proposed DCT model. The empirical study is discussed in section III and section IV wraps up this paper.

2.0   Imprecise DCT computational model

For the DCT operations in JPEG or MPEG, an image frame is divided into multiple N×N blocks and the DCT operation is done with a single N×N block sequentially. The output of 2-D DCT is given as follows :

$$Y_{i,j} = \frac{4}{N^2} c_i c_j \sum_{m=0}^{N-1} \sum_{n=0}^{N-1} X_{m,n} \cos\left[\frac{\pi(2m+1)i}{2N}\right] \cos\left[\frac{\pi(2n+1)j}{2N}\right]$$

where X_{mn} is a pixel value located at [m,n] in a certain N×N block, $0 \leq i,j,m,n \leq N-1$ and $c_i, c_j = 1/\sqrt{2}$ for i, j=0, otherwise 1. The above equation can be re-written as matrix product form : $Y = C \times X \times C^T$ where Y is the output matrix, X input, and C cosine matrix. By applying the row column division algorithm Y is obtained in two steps : $G = X \times C^T$, then $Y = C \times G$, and the processing time is reduced by about 75%, compared with that for the direct implementation (Haque,1985).

For the DCT computation to be able to be applied to imprecise model, the following several points have to be cleared. The first point is that any one out of

156

NxN output values in a block has to be calculated independent of the rest (NxN−1) values. This independence requirement is quite obvious in imprecise model because the dependency between any two or more values implies that the granularity of output is degraded and the chance of imprecise computation is reduced. That is, a specific output value must contain the meaning, regardless of the completion of executing other (NxN−1) values. Without satisfying the independence requirement, imprecise computation is useless. Secondly, the output values have to be calculated in the order that we want, like the zigzag order recommended by JPEG. This point influences the effectiveness of imprecise model critically since the importance of the output values is increased as they are located in the top left side of the output Y in DCT. If it is not possible to complete the execution of all computation, it is natural to require more important output first. The third point is that the computation time for each output value is required to be equal or nearly equal. Without this requirement the operating system will have the trouble to schedule the processes. And the less important output may be calculated while the more important output can not be scheduled due to the lack of scheduling time. Finally the sum of computation times taken for each Y_{ij} has to be very close to (equal to or slightly larger than) that of one complete precise DCT computation. If the sum of all imprecise computation times is much larger than that of the complete precise model, the justification for the rationale of performing imprecise computation becomes weak.

To meet the above requirements the proposed DCT model is calculated as the following procedure. An image frame is divided into multiple of NxN blocks. For each block one coefficient value is calculated in the zigzag order for each scheduled computation time unit. After the completion of the first time unit for all blocks, all DC values for NxN blocks are obtained. In the next time unit, the first AC value right next to the DC value is obtained for each block, and so on. Figure 1 depicts the matrix operation to obtain one of the output values, Y_{ij}. As shown in the figure one column of G is needed to get Y_{ij}.

In the proposed model we modified the order of the DCT calculation to minimize the dependencies among computations , thus improving the steps of imprecise computations and maximize the regularity for hardware implementation (Jung,1996). The procedure for a block computation is summarized as follows :

$i=0 ; j=0 ;$
$While (sufficient resource available) \{$
$for (k=0; k<N; k++) \{$
$for (l=0; l<N; l++)$
$G_{kj} += X_{kl} * C^{T}_{lj} ;$

$$Y_{ij} \mathrel{+}= C_{ik} * G_{kj} ;$$

$\}$

$\{$ save Y_{ij} ; $\}$

$\{$ i, j, calculation for zigzag scanning ; $\}$

$\}$

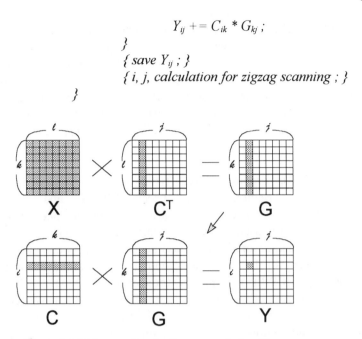

Figure 1: Matrix operation for the proposed algorithm

If it is found that no more available time is left for further computation at a certain instant, the output values obtained up to that instant are treated as the final output. The empirical study shows that the intermediate result is very valuable, and thus the proposed imprecise model is applicable to real-time services.

3.0   Empirical study

We have implemented the proposed imprecise model on our real-time micro kernel, Real-Time MIKE (MIcro KErnel). *Real Time Mike* is a microkernel-based real time operating system which has been developed at Ajou University (Shim,1996). Real-Time Mike implemented on T805 transputer board, consists mainly of three-layer structures : *microkernel layer, server task layer,* and *system call interface layer.* The microkernel layer, which is lowest layer, consists of three classes for communication processes: a task manager including a scheduler, the drivers for input/output devices and a timer handler. The memory manager, IPC facilities, and timer manager are not included in the microkernel layer. Instead, Mike provides only the infra structure for managing the server tasks that realize IPC facilities and resource management. The server tasks running on Mike that are scheduled as a Hoare's monitor (Hoare,1974) can be easily added, replaced and removed at run time when different IPC facilities or resource management policies are needed. This scheme maintains the benefits of the conventional microkernels without degrading the performance while it makes the kernel lighter and more flexible and increases configurability, extensibility, and portability. A server task is only a special application task that is executed in user mode. Application tasks do not call server tasks directly. Instead, they call the server tasks that correspond to the resource managers or the shared objects, indirectly by sending a message to microkernel layer via the system call interface layer.

Real-Time Mike provides three types of kernel services for imprecise computation : BeginIMPBlk(), ClearIMPBlk(), and AllocSieveTime(). BeginIMPBlk() and ClearIMPBlk() are used for the milestone method while AllocSieveTime() is used for the sieve method (Liu,1991). Application can use the milestone method or sieve method according to its computational algorithm and environment for the imprecise computation. The argument time of the service function BeginIMPBlk() means the total execution time which is required for complete execution of the optional part. The kernel that has received the time value computes the actual time to be preserved for the optional part of application and returns the preserved time. In this case, the kernel saves the context of application and sets the execution mode of application to the imprecise computation mode. And then the kernel sets the system timer to the preserved time. If the returned value from the kernel is larger than zero, the application processes the optional part iteratively. When the application completes the optional part, it should call the function ClearIMPBlk() to notify the completion of executing its optional part to the kernel. Then the kernel resets the system timer and sets the execution mode of application to the normal mode.

If the application is not completed within the preserved time, the kernel terminates executing the application and restores the application's context that has been saved when the kernel had called the service function, BeginIMPBlk(). And then the kernel returns zero to the application. AllocSieveTime() requests the admission for executing the sieve function to the kernel. The argument time of the function is the time to execute the sieve function. The kernel scheduler decides whether it has the additional time for the sieve function or not. If the returned value from the kernel is true, the kernel permits the execution of the sieve function and the application calls the sieve function. If not, the application skips the sieve function.

In the imprecise computation, every application is structured in such a way that it can be logically decomposed into two subparts: a mandatory part and an optional part. The mandatory part is the minimum portion of application that must be processed in order to produce a result with an acceptable quality. In the proposed model only all DC values in 8x8 image blocks are obtained in the mandatory part.

The optional part is performed only when the resource is available but the optional part is terminated if the resource becomes starved. The intermediate result of executing the optional part improves the quality of the result produced from the previous mandatory part.

The available processing times varied from nearly zero to sufficiently long time to see the performance of the proposed model. For a short processing time, only a few values (or a DC value) of the DCT outputs were produced and the restored image were obtained from those a few values. But for a long processing time, many DCT output values (a DC value and many AC values) could be calculated. For both cases, each output value was calculated independently with each other and all completed output values improved the quality of restored image.

We checked the processing time taken for each imprecise computation and the quality for each coefficient step. For the block size 8x8 was used, and thus maximum imprecise steps (the total number of DCT output coefficients) were 64. Akiko image was used for the test image. The accumulated processing times (x-axis) taken up to the specific steps are illustrated in figure 1. The i coefficients in the x-axis implies that the available processing time was just enough to complete the computation for i coefficients in each block. The elapsed time (y-axis) for each step is normalized by the time taken for the complete precise computation. That is, at the normalized elapsed time 1, the time taken for a complete precise calculation and the time for the imprecise computation are equal.

According to the figure, the imprecise model has an advantage in terms of the processing time up to around the 50th step. Above the 50th step, the accumulated processing time is greater than that for one complete precise computation. This is because for each Y_{ij}, all values of the n column in G matrix had to be calculated and the house keeping process such as buffer clearing operations between the consecutive blocks were included in the total accumulated processing times. The accumulated processing time of the proposed model is nearly increased proportional to the number of DCT coefficients and close to that of the ideal model. The total accumulated processing time (that is, the time taken for 64 steps) is also close to that of one complete precise DCT processing .

Figure 3 shows the restored images for the imprecise model with different coefficients (a DC value and i-1 AC values). When more than four coefficients for each block are obtained, the quality of restored image is comparable with the original image even though the sharpness of the image is slightly degraded. This result is very similar to that shown by Shenoy (Shenoy,1995).

160

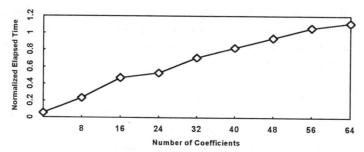

Figure 2: The normalized accumulated processing time

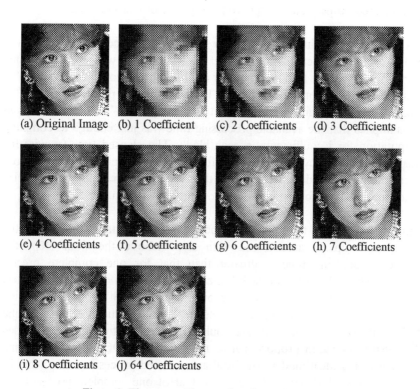

(a) Original Image (b) 1 Coefficient (c) 2 Coefficients (d) 3 Coefficients

(e) 4 Coefficients (f) 5 Coefficients (g) 6 Coefficients (h) 7 Coefficients

(i) 8 Coefficients (j) 64 Coefficients

Figure 3: The restored images from imprecise computations

Figure 2 and 3 show that the proposed imprecise DCT computation model shows the approximately ideal characteristics that a fine tuned imprecise model must have : accumulative property in terms of computation time and linearity property in terms of restored image quality.

4.0 Conclusion

We have proposed an imprecise model for the DCT and shown the feasibility of the proposed model through the simulation on a real time micro kernel. The proposed model behaves nearly same as the ideal model does. With the help of hardware, the proposed model may have a better chance to improve the linear property for calculation time and the linear property for restored image quality.

References:

1. Andrews, Gregory R. (1991), Concurrent Programming : Principles and Practice, Benjamin/Cummings.
2. Haque, M. A. (1985), "A Two-Dimensional Fast Cosine Transform", *IEEE Trans. on Acoustics, speech, and signal processing*, ASSP-33(6), pp1532-1539.
3. Hoare, C.A.R. (1974), "Monitors: An Operating System Structuring Concept", *Comm. ACM 17*.
4. Jung, J., Yim, K., Jung, G., Choi, K. et al (1996), "A 2-D DCT Architecture for Real-Time Resource Allocation", *Ajou University Technical Report*.
5. Liu, J.W.S., Lin, K.J., Shih, W.K., Chung, J.Y., Yu, A., Zhao, W. (1991), "Algorithms for Scheduling Imprecise Computations", *IEEE Computer*, pp58-68.
6. Shenoy, P. J. and Vin, H. K. (1995), "Efficient Support for Scan Operations in Video Servers", *Proc. Of the 3rd International multimedia conference and exhibition*, pp131-140.
7. Shim, J., Choi, K., Jung, G. et. al (1996), "A Real-Time Micro Kernel Implemented on Transputer", *Proc. Of PDPTA '96*.
8. Stankovic and Ramamritham (1993), Advances in Real-Time Systems, IEEE Computer Society Press.
9. Steinmetz, R. (1995), "Analyzing the Multimedia Operating System", *IEEE Multimedia*, 2(1), pp68-84.
10. Tilborg and Koob (1991), Foundations of Real-Time Computing : Scheduling and Resource Management, Kluwer Academic Publishers.

5.3

SUPPORTING REFERENTIAL INTEGRITY IN THE WORLD WIDE WEB

Eun-Sim Choi
Electronics and Telecommunications Research Institute, Korea

World Wide Web (WWW) is the universal network-accessible information based on TCP/IP. It is based on the client/server model in which the client application is connected to the proper server. The WWW client should identify the physical location of the server and document. In this paper, the extended model of WWW services to address the problem of referential integrity has been proposed. Providing a mechanism for managing resources by logical name, our WWW model addresses the referential integrity problem of current WWW system. Therefore, our model provides WWW service user with more reliable and seamless service to current WWW.

1. 0   Introduction

World Wide Web, which often called WWW, W3, or Web, is the universe of network-accessible information based on TCP/IP, which is the single interface that enables one to use and to access more easily and effectively the existing Internet protocols and services such as Hypertext Transfer Protocol (HTTP) (Berners-Lee, Fielding, Frystyk,1996), File Transfer Protocol (FTP) (Postel, Reynolds,1985), Telnet protocol (Postel, Reynolds,1983), Wide Area Information Servers (WAIS) (Fullton, Goldman, Kunze, Morris, Schiettecatte,1994), and Gopher protocol (Anklesaria, McCahill, Lindner, Johnson, John, Torrey, Alberti,1993). The WWW service system is based on the client/server model which is composed of protocols used for communications between server and client, browser running at client-site for displaying hypertext documents from local or remote servers, and hypermedia servers which browser can get documents from. From the viewpoint of protocols used in WWW service, the WWW services can be described as follows:

- Using HTTP, the client can get and browse some part of or full document (or file) from the server and also put document to the server by exchanging request/response messages between the client and server;
- Using FTP, the client can share files in server, including programs and data, that is, the client can get documents from the server and can delete and rename documents that located at the server, and also send documents to the server;
- Using Telnet, the client can establish a "Network Virtual Terminal" to the

server;

- Using WAIS, the client can access to bibliographic and non-bibliographic information including full-text and images by entering proper keywords;
- Using Gopher, the client can retrieve and search distributed documents spread over one or more hosts, that is, the client can get directory lists or documents of distributed documents with a file-system style hierarchy.

The majority of resources in WWW described above are documents, protocols, Internet addresses of server systems, and TCP port numbers assigned to servers, and each of resources has the following characteristics:

- Target documents on which clients operate: Documents of WWW is not only simple text documents, but also multimedia and hypermedia documents including audio and video information. Documents in current WWW are managed through their physical locations and names.

- Protocols used for communications between the client and server: WWW clients and servers can interact through standard protocol such as HTTP, FTP, Telnet, and Gopher, etc. Protocol is appropriately selected according to the requirements of user application.

- Internet protocol addresses of servers: To transfer data to target host, each host on network must be have a unique global network address (i.e., Internet address) and clients should know Internet addresses of hosts on which servers reside.

- TCP port numbers assigned to servers: Data is safely arrived at appropriate host on network by using Internet address, but it should be delivered to the proper server within the host. Each process within a host must have an address that is unique within the host, these addresses are known as TCP ports. So, clients should know TCP port number of server process within the host. Default TCP port numbers are assigned to processes of WWW servers: HTTP server is 80; FTP server is 21; Telnet server is 23; Gopher server is 70, and so on.

It can be considered that a system supports referential integrity only if it guarantees that resources will continue to exist as long as there are outstanding references to the resources. Within a complete request message, reference to resources such as name of documents, protocol to use, and server's location is represented as URL (Uniform Resource Locators) (Berners-Lee, Masinter, McCahill,1994; Berners-Lee,1994) that is formalized notation to identify resources. Resource is uniquely identified through URL in the WWW system. Concrete values that URL has such as physical locations lead to broken link after

164

the resource is moved or deleted, which is illustrated at Fig. 1. The current WWW system does not support referential integrity and cannot do so since the system is unaware of the number of references that exist to a particular resource.

In this paper, we define the extended model of WWW services to address problem of referential integrity. Instead of identifying resources through URL, our model chooses a mechanism for managing resources by logical name, which is meaningful even though the resource locations are changed. Section 2 of this paper presents the extended model of WWW services in which adding the component responsible for managing resources to the model of current WWW results, and defines each of components including the WWW client application, the Resource Administrator, The Resource Manager, and Application Specific Components, in our model. Section 3 describes naming schema, such as structure of logical name, the set of rules and constraints concerning its structure, for identifying resources in WWW, and section 4 describes service interfaces of the Resource Manager. Finally, some expected effects of our studies on definition of the model of enhanced WWW services to address problem of referential integrity and the further studies to be done in the future will be described.

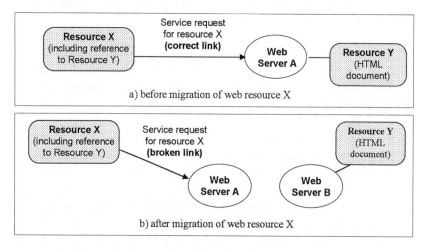

Figure 1: An example of the referential integrity problem

2.0   System model

To guarantee the referential integrity of WWW system, it should be provided a mechanism for maintaining correct reference to resources in the case of migration or deletion of resources. It is possible to support the referential integrity as references to the moved resources continue to be valid (Ingham, Little, Caughey, Shrivastava,1995), that is, whenever a resource is moved a stub representing the resource is left behind at the old. However, the referential integrity is also not guaranteed in case old server of the moved resource is not valid. Therefore, we define a component for managing resources in WWW, and add this component to the current WWW system.

Our system model for WWW services is presented in Fig. 2, for each of client-site and server-site. Our system model has several service components. At client-site, there must be a Web Client Application such as a browser, components processing application specific protocols, component for managing resources, and components for networking, and may be the resource administrator. At server-site, there must be components processing application specific protocols, and may be component for managing resources and the resource administrator.

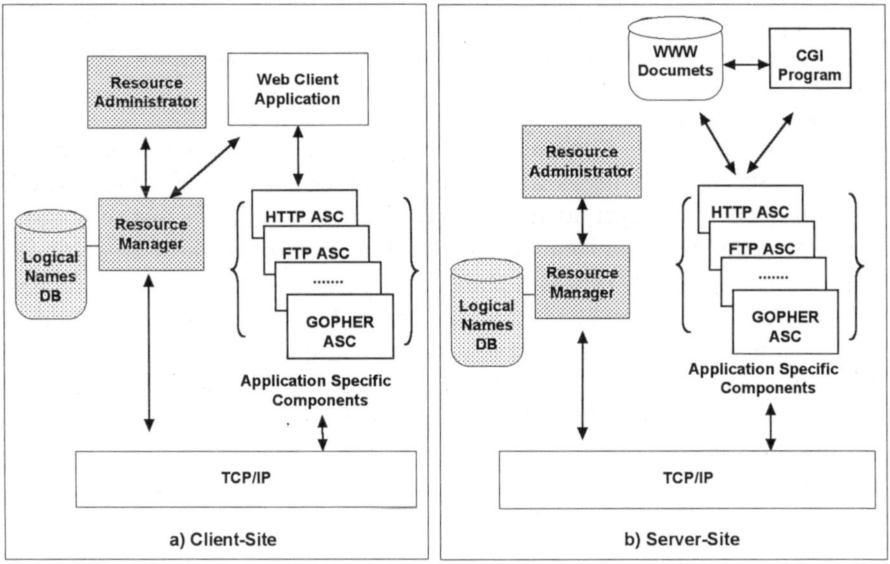

Figure 2: Extended web service model

3. 0 Schema for the logical name

In addition to functionality of the resource manager, it is necessary to define details of the logical name such as structure of logical name, the set of rules and constraints concerning its structure. All applications in our WWW system model identify their resources as logical names, and the Resource Manager manages all the logical names and their corresponding physical values.

The requirements on logical name of WWW resources are as follows:

- Global uniqueness: the same name never be assigned to two different resources, no matter how separated the objects are.
- Persistent naming: it is intended that the lifetime of a logical name is permanent. That is, the logical name will be globally unique forever, and may well be used as a reference to a resource well beyond the lifetime of the resource it identifies or of any naming authority involved in the assignment of its name.
- Sameness: there exists a mechanism for asking whether two resources are the same, based on their logical names without going to the naming authority.
- Scalability: the logical name can be assigned to any resource that might conceivably be available on the network, for hundreds of years.

In this section, structure and object classes of logical name to logically define WWW resources are described, satisfying requirements on logical name listed above.

When the Web Client Application makes a request message dependent on protocols used by it, it needs to identify resources such as the proper WWW server, protocol, and target document, if any. The WWW server that responds to the client's request can be identified by the IP address of the host at which that server is running and the TCP port number assigned to that server within its host. The WWW document can be identified by the globally unique name, the address of the host in which the document is residing, and the absolute path in the host file system. The protocol is identified by its name (Berners-Lee, Masinter, McCahill, 1994), i.e., http, ftp, telnet, gopher, and wais.

In this section, we define two types of objects to completely represent WWW resources. One is the host system that is composed of a number of servers, and another is the WWW document identified by the name, the address of the host in which the document is residing, and the absolute path of the documents in the host file system.

3.1   Structure of the logical name

Two types of objects that identify resources by logical name in WWW is constructed with the tree structure as in Fig. 3, this was derived from Directory Information Tree (DIT) structure of X.500 Directory (ITU-T,1992:Recommendation X.501; ITU-T,1992:Recommendation X.520; ITU-T,1992:Recommendation X.521).

The WWW document and host system are defined by "wwwDocument" and "hostSystem" object classes respectively. The logical name is composed of wwwDocument object class, hostSystem object class, and the number of object classes of X.500 Directory such as country, locality, residential person, organization, organizational unit, and organizational person.

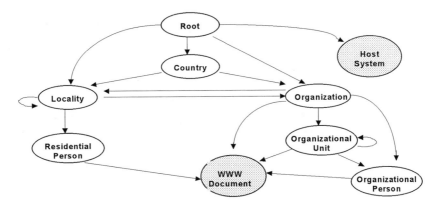

Figure 3: The logical name structure of resources in WWW

The wwwDocument object class represents documents used in WWW, while the hostSystem object class represents information concerning to various WWW servers. WWW documents are not only simple text documents, but also multimedia and hypermedia documents including audio and video information, and documents in the current WWW systems are managed through their physical locations and names. The object class wwwDocument may be the subclass of organization object class, organizational unit object class, organizational person object class, or residential person object class. The object class hostSystem is the subclass of top.

3.2   Definition of Object Classes for Logical Names

The object class for WWW document, wwwDocument, can be all kinds of documents such as simple text document, hypertext document, and document including audio, video data, etc. DN (Distinguished Name) (ITU-T,1992:Recommendation X.501) for the particular WWW document is defined according to the logical name structure of Fig. 3. Namely, an entry of the wwwDocument object class is subordinate for an entry of organization, organizational unit, organizational person, or residential person object class. The object class for host system, hostSystem, keeps the information about the WWW server running at particular host and its corresponding port numbers. Theses are defined as in Table 1, and its first attribute type is the RDN (Relative Distinguished Name) (ITU-T,1992:Recommendation X.501).

Table 1: Object classes and their attribute types

Object Class	Attribute Type
wwwDocument	• document name • host IP address • absolute path
hostSystem	• host IP address • the list of names and its port numbers of servers running at that host

The object class wwwDocument must have three mandatory attributes, document name, host IP address, and absolute path. The document name attribute type is the RDN of the wwwDocument object class, and has a printable string value constructing globally unique name dependent on its own hierarchy of logical structure. The host IP address attribute type represents the address of the host in which document resides. The absolute path attribute type is the absolute path in file system within its host. The object class hostSystem must have the host IP address attribute type and may have the list of names and its port numbers of servers running at that host as the optional attributes.

4. 0   Service interfaces of the resource manager

Service interfaces of the Resource Manager is described in this section. The Resource Manager interacts with its service users, the Web Client Application or the Resource Administrator, through its service interfaces in our WWW system model. The access permission to each resource item in LNDB is dependent on whether a service user requesting operation on the resource item is a creator of that resource or not. The creator of resource has the read/write permission to that, and anyone else has the read permission to that.

There are two types of service interfaces. One type is the administrative interface, which is for operations on resource items requiring a read/write permission, and another is the naming interface, which is for a operation on resource items requiring only read permission. The administrative interface is composed of LN_Register, LN_Delete, and LN_Modify operations for registration, deletion, and modification of the particular resource item, and the naming interface provides LN_Get operation for matching physical values to its logical name. Operations provided through service interfaces are described in Table 2.

Table2: Service interface operations of the resource manager

Service Interface Operation	Parameters In	Result Out	
LN _Register	• *logical name*: of newly created resource item, originally assigned by the resource creator. • *physical values*: of newly created resource item, originally assigned by the resource creator.	• *result*: indicates success or failure of the operation to register new resource item.	If the *result* is successful, new resource item which is uniquely identified by the *logical name* was added in LNDB. Otherwise, the operation is failed because of one or more reasons, and there is no change in LNDB.
LN_Delete	• *logical name*: of the resource item to be deleted.	• *result*: indicates success or failure of the operation to delete the resource item.	If the *result* is successful, the resource item by identified the *logical name* is deleted from LNDB. Otherwise, the operation is failed because of one or more reasons, and there is no change in LNDB.
LN_Modify	• *logical name*: of the resource item to be modified. • *physical values*: to be replaced by.	• *result*: indicates success or failure of the operation to modify the physical values of the resource item.	If the *result* is successful, old physical values of the resource item in LNDB which is identified by the *logical name* is replaced by new *physical values*. Otherwise, the operation is failed because of one or more reasons, and there is no change in LNDB.
LN_Get	• *logical name*: of the resource item of which service user attempts to get physical values.	• *physical values*: of the resource item in LNDB by identified by the *logical name*.	If the *physical values* are not null, those are matched physical values to the *logical name* that service user entered. Otherwise, there is no the resource item by identified the *logical name* in LNDB.

5. 0   Conclusion

In this paper, the extended model of WWW services to address problem of referential integrity has been presented for both client-site and server-site. Compared with the current WWW system, our model additionally has the component, the Resource Manager for taking the role of name server, which identify resource with its logical name, though its physical location changes. The Resource Manager at client-site is responsible for mapping logical names into physical values assigned to resources, and at both of client-site and server-site provides the component for administrating resources with services such as registration, modification, and deletion of resources. Service interfaces of the Resource Manager were described by their operations. We defined two types of objects to completely represent resources in WWW, such as WWW documents, protocols, Internet addresses of server systems, and TCP port numbers assigned to servers. One is the host system that is composed of a number of servers, and another is the WWW document identified by the name, the address of the host in which the documents are residing, and the absolute path in host file system. The structure and their attributes of these two object types that identify resources by logical name in WWW has been defined by Directory Information Tree structure of X.500 Directory Serivice.

Providing a mechanism for managing resources by logical name, our extended WWW model solves the referential integrity problem of current WWW system, that is, the broken link is not caused by migration or deletion of resources. Therefore, our model provides WWW service user with more reliable and seamless service to current WWW. Much more enhanced WWW services by adding more advanced services, including services such as real time service, collaboration service to the existing WWW system will be considered as the further studies in the future.

References:

1. Berners-Lee, T., Fielding, R., Frystyk, H. (1996), "Hypertext Transfer Protocol - HTTP/1.0", Internet Draft, URL: ftp://ds.internic.net/internet-drafts/draft-ietf-http-v10-spec-05.txt.
2. Postel, J., Reynolds, J. (1985), "File Transfer Protocol", Internet RFC0959.
3. Postel, J., Reynolds, J. (1983), "Telnet Protocol", Internet RFC0854.
4. Fullton, M.J., Goldman, K.J., Kunze, B.J., Morris, H., Schiettecatte, F. (1994), "WAIS over Z39.50-1988", Internet RFC1625.
5. Anklesaria, F., McCahill, M., Lindner, P., Johnson, D., John, D., Torrey, D., Alberti, B. (1993), "The Internet Gopher Protocol (a distributed document search and retrieval protocol)", Internet RFC1436.

6. Berners-Lee, T., Masinter, L., McCahill, M. (1994), "Uniform Resource Locators (URL)", Internet RFC1738.
7. Berners-Lee, T. (1994), "Universal Resource Identifiers in WWW", Internet RFC1630.
8. Ingham, D., Little, M., Caughey, S., Shrivastava, S. (1995), "W3Objects: Bringing Object-Oriented Technology to the Web", Proceedings of the 4th International World-Wide Web Conference,
URL:http://arjuna.ncl.ac.uk:80/w3objects/papers/www4/Overview.html.
9. ITU-T (1992), Recommendation X.501 - The Directory - Models.
10. ITU-T (1992), Recommendation X.520 - The Directory - Selected Attributes Types.
11. ITU-T (1992), Recommendation X.521 - The Directory - Selected Objects Classes.

5.4

ASPECTS OF VISUALIZING INFORMATION FOR A REAL-TIME HYPERMEDIA MUSICAL ENVIRONMENT

Kieslinger, M. & Ungvary, T.
Royal Institute of Technology, Sweden

Controlling complex musical tasks with real-time systems allow a more direct connection between the physical input and the musical result. The Cockpit, a hard- and software environment, has been introduced as a model for an optimized user interface supporting intuitive and rapid motion. One important aspect in designing such a cockpit is the implementation of visual feedback.As a result of our findings we present two aspects of visualizing information within a hypermedia musical environment: We describe visualization models supporting the change in the need of information, depending on the development stage of the user and the situation it is used in. Secondly, we discuss problems of interacting with complex data in real-time. Since a continous input is needed by the performer the interaction and information have to be quickly accessible to provide an intuitive use of such a system.

1.0   Introduction

The Hypermedia Musical Environment, further called Hypermedia-Instrument, is our concept of a real-time multimedia information system for music which adresses both the user, further called performer or composer, and its audience. On the one hand, it contains a computer musical system of integrated media which facilitates creative processes and expressive control of hyper-instruments through its intuitive link between the performers input and the music produced by the system. On the other hand it turns towards the audience conveying not only auditive but multimedial information about the ongoing process of the artistic activity. With the involvement of the audience we intend to introduce a large scale of social aspects in music, which represent an integrated part of the system design. We believe that this concept will highly influence our future work in various areas.

2.0 The computer music environment

2.1 Brief description

In order to discuss aspects and importance of visual feedback of a real-time computer music system, we have to describe its structure. The basic environment consists of four nodes, each of them customizable and modular. These are:
- a cockpit of input controllers
- high level music processing software with visual feedback
- software for combined pictorial and iconic input
- sound processing equipment

The nodes that may have various aims include different tasks which the system should be able to assist to. These include:
- composition in non-realtime with options for real-time actions and feedback
- improvisation with a hyper instrument
- interpretation with a hyper instrument
- the adaption of the system according to a later intended activity (learning, development, non-realtime composition with real-time action and feedback, improvisation on stage etc.) and intended musical and sonic structures development

These high level tasks do not represent separate entities in our design. They are integrated in a framework assisting musicians to bounce between improvisation, composition, and interpretation at any stage of an iterative creation process.

All of these activities must clearly be supported by a hyper instrument. For the instrument-design we use the Cockpit paradigm (Vertegaal et al. 1996) which is built around the Sentograph (Vertegaal & Ungvary 1995), a 3D pressure sensitive input device. The Cockpit, which entended to be an extension of the body, is a hard- and software environment, designed to control our interactive computer music system. It consists of a modular assembly of transducers, forming a variable number of sub-cockpits and monitoring devices. Depending on the type of transducer, it can be linked to a generator function (e.g., a 3D pressure transducer), a modifier function (e.g. a slider), or it may select, assign, or activate implemented functions.

The mapping of the control parameters onto the musical parameter space is provided by means of the IGMA software, which has moduls that support real-time high-level control. IGMA also provides fundamental compositional tools for recording, replacing, modifying, overdubbing, mixing and merging control signals.

174

Apart from haptic feedback, visual feedback is of key importance in the control of complex systems. The visual support is one of the common determinants of the problem-space variables defined by the objectives above.

2.2   The role of visual feedback

Traditionally, the performer interacts with the music directly through his hardware interface (instrument), where each psycho-acoustical property is represented by a well defined part, or a combination of parts, of a specific control-device. Hardware control-devices, i.e. instruments, take advantage of the kinetic memory of the performer and therefore increase the usability of the system. They also provide excellent compatibility between the input and the resulting output. The usage of the computer and its sound producing methods dramatically increased the number of possible controls, and, in the same time, lowered their representation from a psychoacoustical level to a parameter level. It is obvious that not every possible parameter can be connected to an individual controller. Even in the case of a fairly simple musical system the number of input devices would be to great to be controlled by a single person.

A possible solution to reduce the amount of external controllers is to use multiple software mapping. Multiple mapping dynamically links the controllers to the active parameters that are conditioned by the state of the system. The problem of this approach is that performers can easily get lost and their actions will have unexpected musical results. Visualization of the system's state can reduce the gap between the expected auditive result and the actual outcome of the system (Mont-Reynaud, 1993). The sound itself cannot give the performer all the required feedback (Preece, 1994) for a successful use. With the help of an appropriate visual information the user can more quickly learn and understand the underlying structure of the hypermedia-system. Additionally the incidence of errors can be reduced.

The design of our visual environment is based on the findings of Baecker & Small [1990] and Preece [1994], especially on the follwing four essential features of visual information:
- IDENTIFICATION - information about the actual state of the system
- TRANSITION - information about the movement between different settings
- CHOICE - information about the possibilities to interact
- FEEDBACK - show the input that has been received

2.3   IGMA

As mentioned above, IGMA (Interactive Gesture MApping) is a real-time interactive computermusic software package used for composition and improvisation. IGMA provides links between the refined physical controls and the sound the performer intends to produce. The graphical programming language MAX has been used for its development. IGMA has an underlying object oriented concept and is structured around four sections: Kernel, Moduls, Submoduls, and Editors.The Kernel forms a framework which manages the Moduls and offers fundamental services like global-recording, replacing, modifying, overdubbing, mixing, and merging of control signals. A Modul is defind by a certain characteristic of musically relevant behaviour. Technically, it contains Submodules and Objects which perform a certain task like sensing, processing, storing, displaying, or responding to data. Editors are used to initiate and modify data inside the Submodules and Objects.

The open concept of IGMA, defined by a set of programming constructs and conventions, provides a unified mechanism which allows the composer/performer to implement extensions or objects that enhance the capabilties of IGMA.

2.4 Aspects of visualization inside IGMA

Each parameter may be controlled either by a hyperinstrument or by means of direct manipulation on the screen. Both types of interaction require special appliances of the user interface design. Performers who interact with external hardware controllers like faders, buttons, or others need to have a visual feedback of their input-action and the system´s state. Direct manipulation requires a graphical interface which allows interaction by using either the mouse or the touchscreen.

2.5 Feedback of external controls

The visual feedback shows the perfromer his actions and allows him to see wether his input has been received and treated correctly or not. A good design is characterized by a high level of confidence that the user should have while running the system. Another important objective is to establish the coherence between the performers actions and the resulting alterations of visual elements on the screen. The spatial and conceptual outcome on the screen has to relate to the hardware controls in order to reduce the mental effort that is needed to transfer the visual information to the outside controllers and vice versa. The position of the visual objects on the screen should be analog to the arrangement of the physical transducers.

Figure 1 shows three different design strategies of visualizing data supplied by a 3D input device. The most appropriate feedback depends on several factors which may be clarified by asking the following questions: Does the user need exact information about the incoming data (number display)? In which situation

176

will it be used? Do input datastreams effect psycho-acoustically or musically closely related parameters? How often does the information need to be updated?

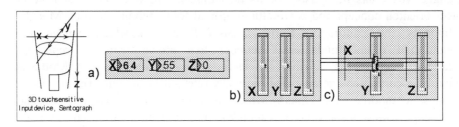

Figure 1

2.6 Adaptability of visualization

Inside IGMA the user can create and customize different display windows with the help of a visual object library which can be expanded by the user. The user can take objects from this library, place them in one of the display-windows of a IGMA Modul and connect them to the parameters he wants to represent visually. In combination with the Kernels mangament capability this facility allows not only the alteration of the design of the visual feedback, but also the creation of appropriate display sets. This allows the user to bounce between them according to his needs inside the multilevel taskspace described earlier. Furthermore, this concept facilitates the filtering of information in different displays at different stages of a learning process.

The multiple display-windows, that can form nodes which are connected via links, can be activated either manually or automatically by an internal timing schedule. This feature allows the design of an Interactive Score. The composer can use any graphical program to create his score and integrate it into this hypermedia environment.

2.7 Low structure, quick access

A flat hierarchical structure of information on the screen is another important factor. During a live-performance the user has no time to select from several menues or to scroll through windows. The amount of steps that are needed to send a command defines the speed in which the system can be used. The steps will increase along with the complexity of the system. Empirical laws that estimate the performers interaction help to design a efficient user interface.

Figure 2 shows three different ways how to select a scale for a musical algorithm. a) menu-selection with continuous faders:

It helps the user to find a particular item of data. Menu-based navigation is not a particulary rapid way of accessing information when its location is already known to the user (Newman & Lamming 1995). More experienced users switch from selecting by verbal clues to selection based on spatial locations of the items (Kaptelinin 1996). Therefore, the next two interaction styles will be faster.
b) selection with external buttons:
Interaction with external buttons is fast and relyable and the user has tactile feedback of his action. It takes a long time to learn the underlying functions of the buttons, especially when buttons have multiple functions.
c) selection by means of graphical direct-manipulation interfaces:
Newmann & Lamming (1995) state that graphical manipulation has high usability but is sometimes slower than performing tasks by pressing one or more keys.

2.8   Support of Cognitive Ergonomy

The use of graphical based selection techniques, supported by pointing devices or touchscreens, allow a more open approach to the design of menus. The user may define background images as well as the appearance of buttons which can include:

- filenames
- thumbnail-pictures of the linked window (in case of an existing link)
- thumbnail pictures of the sound-information (e.g. sonogramm, envelops),
- notes showing a sequence in the score

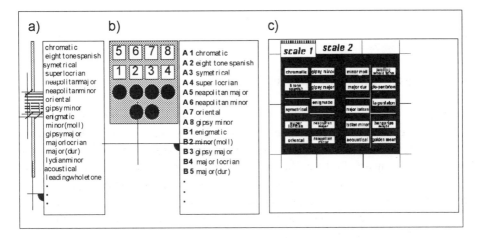

Figure 2

Preece(Preece 1994) states that a combination of pictorial images, names, and icons for interactive elements reduces the ambiguaty of interactive elements The implementation of the hypertext-concept to structure the visual information

178

supports a intuitive access to the underlying data and enhances the usability of the system This is especially important for novices .

Figure 3 shows a screenshot of a prototype. It was developed with authoring tool Macromind-Director which communicates with IGMA via MIDI. The screen has two main parts: the frame, which includes links and navigational commands, and the "action" field, which changes according to the state of the hypermedia-system. The action field shows the area where the user can store and recall system snapshots.

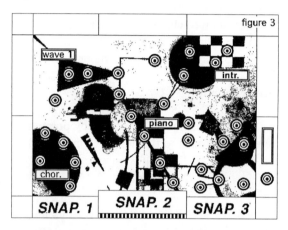

Figure 3

3.0   Presentation for the audience

Usually, the design of a computer music system does not take into consideration a socially determined performance situation. The visual presence and personal charisma together with the gestics are an integrated part of a traditional instrumental concert. Perhaps the two most important visual factors concerning the performer and the perception of the audience are: the preparatory phase of an instrumental gesture and the physical effort by playing the instrument which is obviously perceivable. While the preparatory gesture generates expectation the gesture itself, by playing, rewards the expectation since the instrument usually sounds according to the applied force of the gesture.

As soon as the computer substitutes a traditional instrument, or a part of it, the impact of the above mentioned objectives are dissapearing. With our concept of a

Hypermedia-Instrument we try to take into account these facts by means of multimedia technology.

3.1   The First Attempt

Our first undertaking is to connect the Interactive Score, described earlier, to a set of modular and interlinked applications. The actions of the performer with the Interactiv Score will trigger commands which control both the content and the appearance of the generated projection. The application uses visual elements from the Interactive Score, from a user created database, and from life video input. They are processed by various means and the visual outcome is projected onto a screen.

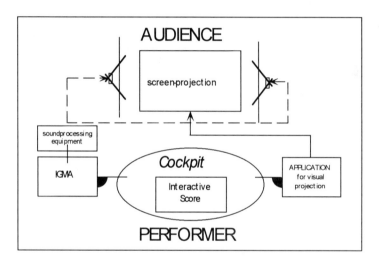

Figure 4

References:

1. Backer, R., and I. Small (1990), "Animation at the interface", *The Art of Human Computer Interface Design*, Brenda Laurel ed., Reading, MA: Addison-Wesley Publishing Company
2. Kaptelinin, V. (1996), "Computer-Mediated Activity: Functional Organs in Social and Developmental Contexts", *Context and Consciousness. Activity Theory and Human-Computer Interaction*, Bonnie A. Nardi ed.,Cambridge, MA: The MIT Press.
3. Mont-Reynaud, B. (1993), "SeeMusic: A Tool for Music Visualization", *Proceedings of the ICMC 1993, 457-460.*
4. Newman, W.M., and M.G. Lamming (1995), Interactive System Design, Wokingham, England: Addison-Wesley Publishing Company.

5. Polfreman, R. and J. Sapsford-Francis (1995), "A Human Factors Approach to Computer Music Systems User-Interface Design", *Proceedings of the ICMC 1995, Banff, Canada,* 381-384.

6. Preece, J. (1994), Human-Computer Interaction, Wokingham, England: Addison-Wesley Publishing Company.

7. Vertegaal, R., and T. Ungvary (1995), "The Sentograph: Input Devices and the Communication of Bodily Expression", *Proceedings of the ICMC 1995, Banff, Canada.*

8. Vertegaal, R., T. Ungvary and M. Kieslinger (1996), The Musician's Cockpit: Transducers, Feedback and Musical Function", *Proceedings of the ICMC 1996, Hong Kong.*

5.5

APPLYING SOFT SYSTEMS METHODOLOGY TO MULTIMEDIA SYSTEMS REQUIREMENTS ANALYSIS

D. Z. Butt, T. Fletcher, S. MacDonell, B. E. Norris & W. Wong
University of Otago, New Zealand

The Soft Systems Methodology (SSM) was used to identify requirements for the development of one or more information systems for a local company. The outcome of using this methodology was the development of three multimedia information systems. This paper discusses the use of the SSM when developing for multimedia environments. Namely, this paper covers the problems with traditional methods of requirements analysis (which the SSM addresses), how the SSM can be used to elicit multimedia information system requirements, and our personal experience of the method. Our personal experience is discussed in terms of the systems we developed using the SSM.

1.0   Introduction

Towards the end of 1995, the Multimedia Systems Research Laboratory (MSRL) at the University of Otago was approached by a local manufacturing firm to address the problem of disseminating technical and product information throughout the organisation. In addition to textual data, technical and product information often include engineering drawings, assembly and repair illustrations. Due to the large size of the organisation and the complexity of the environment in which it operated, the MSRL adopted the Soft Systems Methodology, or SSM (Checkland and Scholes 1990), to requirements analysis. Furthermore, we were also interested in determining whether it could be used to identify a need for multimedia.

With traditional methods, the system's developer tends to push a certain type of solution which is usually within the bounds of the developer's expertise. The outputs of requirements analysis "..too often contain elements that are designs rather than essential requirements" (Booch 1994), p. 5). While focus has shifted to getting the requirements right in the early stages of systems definition and new methods for requirements gathering have been created, there are still some fundamental problems inherent in both the new and traditional approaches. The focus is on modelling the system to be developed rather than trying to understand the problem and its relationship within the organisational environment. Without this understanding, solutions are only partially defined and in some cases may confound the problem. According to (Avison 1985, p9) inadequate systems:

- do not account for a natural change in user requirements over time, and incur heavy maintenance costs,
- require the user to change their behaviour to accommodate the system, rather than the reverse, and
- reflect the data captured by the organisation instead of the information people need.

The traditional system development life cycle, and the new methods for requirements analysis which are based on it, explicitly refer to only one system (Winter, Brown et al. 1995) p. 140). In real world situations, more than one system is usually required to meet user needs. It is for this reason that we attempted to see if the SSM approach might be beneficial in addressing these shortcomings.

Furthermore when using new technologies like multimedia there is always the tendency to incorporate more features than is necessary. For example:

- users may be inadvertently lured into using unnecessary 'bells and whistles' which complicate communication between the system and users, rather than enhance it,
- conventional approaches to requirements gathering (i.e. the data base approach) may lack the robustness to include new forms of information (such as video) and in effect be tied to 'captured' data (which in turn relies on prior technology), and
- there may not necessarily be a need for a 'high-tech' or computer based solution at all.

It was envisaged that through the use of SSM, we would be able to identify the needs in context and hence the features of the system that will enhance the delivery of information. Therefore in order to achieve more complete solutions we need to address the "problem of how to expand our understanding...of the environments and activities of system use" (Suchman 1995) p. 33). The Soft Systems Methodology (SSM) is a set of "principles of method" (Winter, Brown et al. 1995) which facilitates understanding of the problem and its domain.

2.0   Using the SSM in a multimedia development environment

At the start of this project, a meeting was arranged with a manager and a systems engineer of a local whiteware manufacturing firm. The firm designs, produces, and distributes the products it manufactures. The meeting took place in a room which had a large whiteboard which was used to draw rich pictures as part of the analysis. The atmosphere was uninhibited and all members participated freely in the analysis. One member of the MSRL, with experience using the SSM, guided the meeting and ensured that the steps described in the last section were followed. To complete the SSM process and evaluate the model, subsequent meetings were held with individual actors identified during the CATWOE analysis.

2.1   The relevant systems

The identification of relevant systems begun by discussing the primary tasks. A division of the organisation was broken up into subdivisions which interacted with one another. The primary tasks that identified the relevant systems are collection, preparation, and the delivery of technical and product information between the organisational subdivisions. Through this analysis, our understanding of the issues influenced our view of how the relevant systems were defined. The following two characteristics were included in our definition of relevant systems: 'a system to produce technical information easily and unobtrusively' and 'a system to communicate directly to a subdivision about a problem or change'.

2.2   The root definition

The next step was to define a root definition. This was done by naming the activities conducted by, and understanding the relationships between, the relevant systems. CATWOE was used. Again, the iterative nature of SSM became apparent, entities within CATWOE were added as our understanding of the current situation increased. The analysis identified the following Customers, Actors, Transformations, Weltanschauung, Owners and Environmental Constraints. Each entity was tagged with additional information, giving us a quick reference to the reasons they were there.

The *Customers* of the system were identified as:
_   Service Centre. They benefited through cost savings by reducing inefficiencies in the system.
_   Consumer. The consumer needs a problem resolved.
_   The Organisation, consisting of the Engineering Design, Plant and Tooling, Product Servicing, and Product Improvement Departments. They benefitted by reducing the cost of disseminating information, get product to market more quickly, and reduced warranty servicing costs.

The *Actors* were:
•   Service Centre. The service centres co-ordinate repair jobs and pass on warranty information Service Technicians to the Quality Department.

- Service Technician. They service one or many products and provide warranty information to the Service Centres from .
- Technical Representatives. They train and update Service Technicians with hints and service procedure.
- Engineering Designers. Engineering designers enter initial Computer Aided Design (CAD) models and other relevant design information.
- Plant and Tooling Designers. They enter CAD models for the design of plants and tool equipment.
- Assembly Line Management. They receive training information and plant and tools specification. They also train workers. Assembly line management are part of the Plant and Tooling department.
- Product Improvement Designers. They enter changes to CAD designs and other relevant design information.
- Store Technician. Store Technicians provide spare parts and pass warranty information to the Service Centre.
- Telephone Staff at place of purchase. They handle initial customer queries and complaints.
- Customer Care Centre. A centralised telephone service staffed by trained technicians with good interpersonal skills to answer customer queries.
- Printery. The Printery prints and distributes information such as training manuals and publicity material.

Two *Transformations* were identified. The first transformed product technical information into technical manuals, technical bulletins, magazines, marketing information, tool list, and training information for assembly and maintenance of the various products. The transformation extracted structured knowledge by the specific sub-divisions of the organisation. In the second transformation, marketing and industrial design recommendations, product costing information, warrantee information , and component information were transformed into new or modified product specification information.

The *Weltanschauung* or world view, was stated as 'better collection, preparation, and dissemination of technical information will result in better product design, assembly, and maintenance'.
The *Owners* of the system were identified as:
- Top Management
- The Technical Information Group
- The Project Champion

A number of *Environmental* constraints were also identified. They were:

Time. Technical information must be released before actual product releases, revised information must be released before changes take effect.

185

Resources. Limited resources are available for the documentation of technical information.

Quality control. Industry standards for quality control need to be adhered to.

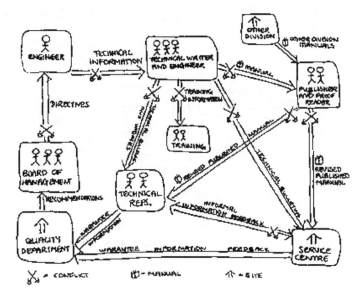

Figure 1: The current system

A rich picture was drawn and modified to clarify our understanding of CATWOE and the current system. What evolved is shown in Figure 1.

As our understanding of the system became clearer through the CATWOE analysis, the root definition of the system crystallised and is summarised below:

"A system to improve the existing process of collection, preparation, and delivery of accurate technical information in an efficient, timely, and effective manner by, and for the use of, Product Design, Plant and Tooling Design, Product Servicing, and Product Improvement."

2.3   The relevant system

The final model of the relevant system was created iteratively by performing steps three and four of the SSM. The final model of the system is represented in figure 2.

186

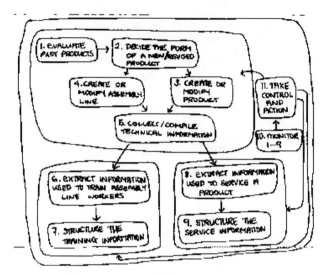

Figure 2: A model of the relevant system

The model was compared with 'perceived reality' by conducting twenty informal interviews with a cross section of the individuals or groups identified in CATWOE. Over time, the model was revised to include the interests of all parties; namely, Engineers from Plant and Tooling, Product Design, Product Servicing and Product Improvement.

There was a marked difference between the model of the present situation (Figure 1) and the model of the relevant system (Figure 2). As the relevant system emerged, it became clear that the focus of this system needed to focus more on the initial collection, capture and structuring of information, rather than on transforming the source data as is the case with the current system. In the current system, technical information had to undergo two separate transformations before it was distributed to service personnel. This was in addition to the initial preparation of the information by the engineers. Line workers were less fortunate. The information with which they learned to assemble products was reviewed and corrected only once. Hence there were often errors in their manuals. On the other hand, the model of the relevant system indicates that the collection and compilation of technical data should be encapsulated as one system. Rather than being transformed and heavily revised, information relevant to product assembly and servicing should be extracted from the core system into peripheral training and mobile service support systems. Once the information is extracted, it is then presented to those who need it, e.g. training and service personnel, in a structure that is useful to them. Further analysis of our relevant system suggests that the information could only be multimedia in nature.

2.4   The identification of multimedia systems through the SSM

After constructing a model of the relevant systems, the model was then subject to further evaluation based on the 3Es, Efficacy, Efficiency, and Effectiveness. It was during this stage that identified the need for multimedia systems. Based on the relevant system (Figure 2) three information systems were identified. They were 1) a system for the collection, initial preparation, and storage and retrieval of technical information, 2) a mobile service support system, and 3) an assembly line training system. The three systems are currently in their prototype phases.

2.5   The collection system

The Collection System will use intranet technology to tie the other systems together. Its aim is to facilitate the capture and storage of relevant technical information created by product design engineers, product improvement engineers, plant and tooling engineers, and service personnel. This information system will also reflect the natural workflow of each party. It will automatically place shared technical information in context for users, e.g when a plant and tooling person needs to re-design a tool, his starting point will be CAD models of the product. The system will also extract relevant technical information for training and service 'on the fly'. It will rapidly disseminate notification of product changes via the equivalent of technical bulletins to the other information systems and users.

This system will meet the long-term efficacy goal of an improved process of collection, preparation, and dissemination of accurate technical information in several ways. First, the system provides a unified and structured approach to entering technical information into a corporate 'database'. At present, no such unified system exists. Secondly, the system will collect all relevant technical information relating to a product. At present, information is stored in filing cabinets, on disk, and in several stand-alone databases. Third, the system provides a consistent entry point and method (a web browser) for the storage and modification of information across the board. Fourth, the system will allow ease of sharing technical information to those who need it. Finally, the system administers greater centralised control over the quality and structure of information to be stored.

Compared to the current system, there are less steps needed to collect, prepare, and disseminate technical information. An example of this is the process of collecting CAD drawings, a form of technical information, from the product designers, and its subsequent transformation into a manual for service personnel. In the current situation, this process passed through many steps and many hands, from engineer to technical writer, to publisher and proof readers elsewhere in the country, before finally reaching service personnel. The information system identified by SSM does away with the 'middlemen'. As stated above, the emphasis was on extraction rather than transformation. In this way, the new relevant system would be more efficient than the current system.

As the required techical information would be extracted rather than transformed, there would be benefits if the information remained as close as possible to its original form, e.g. CAD models and designs, mock-ups of products and components. Thus the most expedient way to capture and transmit this sort of information would be via multimedia technology which would increase the bandwidth of communication, rather than lose valuable information by transforming the original work into written documents.

2.6   The mobile service support system

The second information system provides service information and procedures to service personnel in the field. It is envisaged to utilise web technology, and is expected to provide a means of communicating feedback directly between service personnel and design engineers, product improvement engineers and plant and tooling engineers.

In order to remain efficient and effective, the information system would use the same multimedia information captured by the Collection System. The information would only be restructured to suit service personnel. Additionally, as the repair of products is mostly done at the customers residence, and the service person works in 'eyes busy, hands busy' situations, written manuals are not effective. Manuals are difficult to manage. It is difficult to search quickly for specific information, the service person doesn't have a free hand to keep his place, and frequent visual movement between the document and the product wastes valuable time. A solution to this is the use of non-textual multimedia methods of communication, i.e. video, animation and sound. The service personnel think in terms of the physical object they see before them. By using video, for example, they are *shown* rather than *told* how a product is repaired. Additionally, it is envisaged that service personnel would be able to communicate problems directly to engineers through the use of video conferencing, voice mail, or electronic mail to which original product information relating to a specific problem can be readily tagged. These changes alone would meet the long term goal to improve the collection, presentation, and dissemination of technical information to service personnel.

2.7 The assembly line training system

The third system deals with communicating manufacturing and training procedures from product designers to line workers. The system will show them how to piece together a product as they work on the assembly line or during training. This system would be more efficient than the current method of training. At present, assembly line workers use a physical mock up of the product and technical specifications and diagrams to learn to assemble the product. There are several problems with this approach. More often than not the physical mock up is not available, or it takes too long to modify, or is being used elsewhere. As such many line workers end up learning the assembly on the factory floor instead. A high number of errors result, causing frequent delays in the assembly line and high warranty costs.

As with the service personnel, the most appropriate way to present information on how to assemble the products, which is procedural knowledge, is to show rather than tell. This can be done through the use of voice and video, voice and graphics, or video alone. As a training system there was a need to incorporate practice as well. The prototype that was built incorporated a module which allowed the user to graphically and interactively assemble a product on screen. The module provides auditory feedback such as a fan starting up, and graphical feedback e.g. number of errors vs. number correct, and the cooking elements 'lighting' up. The use of this feedback gives deeper meaning to the assembly of the product. It is no longer a matter of connecting Wire A to Slot B. It becomes 'attaching the power source so the element will work'. It was the line workers which identified the need for and asked for this deeper meaning.

The system would also keep track of general scores (not individual's scores) which would identify problem areas within the individual assembly of products. This would open a statistically backed dialogue between line workers and engineers. We recognise that line workers are not entirely at fault for poor assembly. In this manner, and by being more efficient and effective, the training system would help meet the long term goals of improving the capture, preparation and dissemination of information for training.

3.0 Conclusion

The reported work indicates that the Soft Systems Methodology was useful in identifying multimedia requirements for information systems as demonstrated by the development of the three prototype multimedia information systems. More research is underway to evaluate the suitability of this approach in developing other systems.

190

References:

1. Avison, D. E. (1985). <u>Information Systems Development: A Database Approach.</u> Oxford, Blackwell Scientific Publications.
2. Avison, D. E. a. F., G. (1988). <u>Information Systems Development: Methodologies, Techniques and Tools.</u> London, Blackwell Scientific Publications.
3. Booch, G. (1994). <u>Object-oriented analysis and design with applications.</u> Rerdwood City, CA., Benjamin / Cummings Publishing Co., Inc.
4. Checkland, P. and J. Scholes (1990). <u>Soft Systems Methodology in Action,</u> John Wiley & Sons.
5. Suchman, L. (1995). "Representations of Work." <u>Communications Of The ACM</u> **38**(9).
6. Winter, M. C., D. H. Brown, et al. (1995). "A Role For Soft Systems Methodology In Information Systems Development." <u>European Journal of Information Systems.</u> **4**: 130 - 142.

5.6

IMPRESS : INTERACTIVE MULTIMEDIA SERVICE PLATFORM

Young-Duk Park
ETRI, Korea

IMPRESS (Interactive Multimedia exPRESS) is a service platform that supports various interactive multimedia services. The main objectives of developing IMPRESS are to implement DAVIC compliant service platform to verify DAVIC specification and to support new service developing and testing environment. IMPRESS includes video server, set-top box, delivery system and SRM (Session Resource Manager). Interactive multimedia services such as movies on demand and home-shopping were developed via the IMPRESS. In this paper, we describe the overall architecture of our approach to the IMPRESS and the system implementation on the video server, set-top box, and service protocol based on the DAVIC specification.

1.0   Introduction

There are three key technologies which influence interactive multimedia service environment: high speed networking based on the ATM (Asynchronous Transfer Mode) technology, digital multimedia compression and presentation technology, and worldwide standardization activities for the end to end multimedia services[1]-[3]. The ATM technology provides high speed data transfer between user and service provider system, and allows a single network for all traffic types of media. Because of the integration of various traffic types and its high speed, the ATM technology makes it possible to create and expand new application services. The second key technology, multimedia technology is used on many computers and telecommunication systems for data storage and information presentation. The MPEG and the MHEG standard defines a compression and interchange format for motion pictures and interrelationship between the multimedia presentation. The contents of multimedia interactive services will follow these multimedia standards[4]. DAVIC leads the worldwide standardization for the end to end multimedia services. The purpose of DAVIC is to advance the success of emerging digital audio-visual applications and services by the internationally agreed specifications of open interfaces and protocols [5]. DAVIC specification 1.0 covers typical interactive multimedia services of nowadays such as movies on demand, news on demand, home-shopping and home-banking. DAVIC specification solves the problems in proprietary standard based digital audio-visual services that are incompatible with service systems.

Information superhighway is being constructed step by step in Korea, and optical fiber is supposed to be supplied to every house until 2015. Since the final infrastructure of information superhighway will be a B-ISDN, the research on the B-ISDN has been carried out since last five years. ATM core switch, an ATM access network equipment, a transmission equipment and B-ISDN terminals have been developed as the results of the research. Therefore, we set a new plan to integrate network equipment developed and interactive multimedia services. We have implemented a service platform called IMPRESS (Interactive Multimedia exPRESS) to support developing environment for the interactive multimedia services. Research on the interactive multimedia systems, the creation of new services, and the verification of service specification will be performed based on the IMPRESS.

In this paper, described are the overall architecture of IMPRESS and the current activities on the server, set-top box, and service protocol based on the DAVIC specification. The conclusion and our future directions are mentioned at the end of this paper.

2.0   System architecture of IMPRESS

The main objectives of developing IMPRESS are to implement DAVIC compliant service platform to verify DAVIC specification and to support an environment for new service developing and testing.

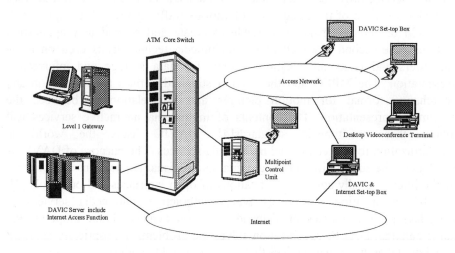

Figure 1. Overall architecture of IMPRESS

Fig. 1 shows an overall architecture of the IMPRESS. As the services implemented in IMPRESS environment, selected are movies on demand, multipoint videoconference service, and Internet service. These services are supposed to be built in next two years. After that, applications such as tele-education, home-shopping will be developed continuously based on the built system. Table 1 is a list of service equipment that will be used for IMPRESS Among these services, we have implemented MPEG-2 quality movies on demand service based on the DAVIC specification. For the delivery system, ATM switch is used as a core network and CANS (Central Access Node System) and DANS (Distributed Access Node System) are used as access networks. All the service equipment are connected with 155Mbps STM-1 interface.

Table 1. List of equipment in IMPRESS service platform

Core network	ATM switch
Access network	CANS (Central Access Node System)
	DANS (Distributed Access Node System)
Server	SUN sparc 20 with DAVIC S2,S3 protocol
Pump	SUN Ultra sparc with DAVIC S1 protocol
L1 GW	Pentium PC with DAVIC S3 protocol
MCU	MCU(Multipoint Control Unit) with MCS protocol
Terminal	MPEG-2 Set-top box
	PC based MPEG-2 set-top box
	PC based DVT (Desktop Videoconference Terminal)

Protocol stack of IMPRESS is compliant to DAVIC 1.0 specification. Table 2 shows an implemented protocol stack for the IMPRESS. S1 information flow for a content-information flow use MPEG-2 systems, video, and audio[6]. For the S2 information flow that is a control-information flow from an application service layer source object to a peer destination object, MPEG-2 DSM-CC (Digital Storage Media Command & Control), User-to-User Interface is used[8]. S3 is control-information flow from a session and transport service layer source object to a peer destination object. The DSM-CC User-Network signalling is used for the session control protocol. S4 is control-information flow from a network service layer source object to a peer destination object. The standard B-ISDN call/connection control protocols (ITU-T Q.2931, Q.2130, and Q.2110) are used for S4 flow.

Table 2. Protocol Stack for the IMPRESS

S1 Flow	S2 Flow	S3 Flow	S4 Flow
	DSM-CC U/U		
MPEG-2 A/V ES	OMG CDR/UNO	DSM-CC U/N	Q.2931
MPEG-2 PES	TCP	TCP/UDP	Q.2130
MPEG-2 TS	IP	IP	Q.2110
AAL Type 5			
ATM Layer			
Physical Layer			

A/V : Audio/Video, DSM-CC U/U: DSM-CC User to User, DSM-CC U/N: DSM-CC User to Network,
MPEG-2 A/V ES : Audio/Video Elementary Stream, PES : Packetized Elementary Stream, TS : Transport Stream
OMG CDR/UNO : Object Management Group Common Data Representation/Universal Networked Object

3. 0   Implementation of IMPRESS terminal

3.1   Hardware architecture

IMPRESS terminal is developed in the form of two add-on boards in PC system hardware: MIBA (Media Interface Board Assembly), NIBA (Network Interface Board Assembly). Fig. 2 shows the hardware architecture of the IMPRESS terminal [9].

MIBA is the main unit for the correct demultiplexing and decoding of the multimedia information that is to be displayed on the TV or computer screen. MIBA consists of three modules: Media Processing Module for the decoding of MPEG-2 video and audio, Mux/Demux Module for the demultiplexing of MPEG-2 transport stream, and Media Input Output Module for the media input and output function.

NIBA is the network interface between an ATM access network and an IMPRESS terminal. NIBA consists of three modules: Physical Processing Module for termination of optical signal, ATM Processing Module for ATM processing function, and AAL Processing Module for the AAL type 5 and SAAL processing function. NIBA provides 155Mbps STM-1 interface.

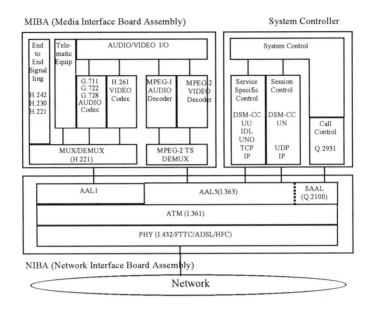

Figure 2. Hardware architecture of the IMPRESS terminal

3.2 Software Architecture

Software functions of IMPRESS terminal operate in the Windows NT environment. They can be classified as the CB (Connection Block) that control the low layer connection between IMPRESS terminal and server, SM (Session Manager) for session management, and AB (Application Block). Fig. 3 shows the software functional blocks of the IMPRESS terminal.

Connection Block consists of ATM Control Module for B-ISDN call connection protocol and User-to-Network Communication Module defined in DSM-CC. Being installed on a PC, ATM Control Module is connected to the network-connecting hardware and API (Application Program Interface) that follows the native ATM service recommended by ATM Forum. ATM Control Module provides the functions of data transmission, establishment/release of SVC (Switched Virtual Channel) and PVC (Permanent Virtual Channel), traffic management, OAM protocol, and etc. DSM-CC U-N module performs the functions of user-network configuration, session control for session establishment/release, resource allocation/deallocation for the session, and status management. Session Manager establishes and manages sessions for service. It receives the request of session establishment/release from Application Block, and asks Connection Block to serve the request. Application Block consists of four

196

modules: 1) DSM-CC U-U, 2) Media Decoding, 3) MHEG-5 RTE (Runtime Engine), and 4) Digital A/V Application module. DSM-CC U-U changes the request from MHEG-5 RTE into the DSM-CC U-U messages in order to get the running result from the server. Media Decoding Module decodes and processes all media received from the server such as MPEG, Bitmap, Text, and Audio. MHEG-5 RTE decodes MHEG-5 object files transmitted from the server in the form of coding stream for describing MHEG-5 information, then analyzes them according to the object [7]. As an upper layer of above modules, Digital A/V Application supports the interaction between system and users. MHEG-5 RTE analyzes the MHEG-5 data to run application.

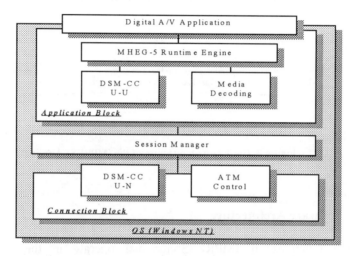

Figure 3. Software functional blocks of IMPRESS terminal

4.0 Implemenation of IMPRESS video server

4.1 Hardware Architecture

IMPRESS video server consists of application server and video pump as shown in Fig. 4. Because our main goal of video server part is to implement DAVIC compliant protocol, we use the general purpose workstation for the hardware platform. The application server is based on the commercial SUN sparc 20 workstation and Fore ATM board is added to provide ATM interface function. To process DAVIC service protocol in the application server, we implemented DAVIC's S2, S3, S4 information flows in SUN workstation, and connected video pump for DAVIC's S1 information flow via internal API. To provide real-time stream pumping function, we used high speed SUN Ultra workstation for the video pump hardware platform. For video stream storage, we added

20Gbytes hard disk to the video pump via fast wide SCSI interface. Fig. 4 shows the basic system architecture of the application server and video pump.

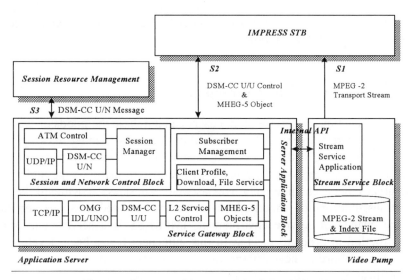

Figure 4. System Architecture of the IMPRESS Video Server

4.2   Software Architecture

Protocol software of IMPRESS application server operates in the SUN UNIX environment. Application server's protocol software consists of four blocks: Session and Network Control Block, Server Application Block, Subscriber Management and Supplementary Service Block, and Service Gateway Block. Session and Network Control Block performs the network connection control, user-network   configuration,   session   establishment/release,   resource allocation/deallocation for the session, and status management for session and network connection. Server Application Block controls the other block in application server and video pump via internal API. Subscriber Management and Supplementary Service Block manages subscriber information and provides supplementary services such as client profile, download, and file service. Service Gateway Block is the core function block in application server. It has the responsibility to provide user's navigation and application selection function. The work flows between the STB and Service Gateway Block is as follows. First, STB connects to a Service Gateway Block and gets an application list. A MHEG-5 RTE on the STB displays the list on the user's screen and the user chooses an application from the list. DSM-CC UU sends the user's request to the Service Gateway Block. The Service Gateway Block possesses DSM-CC objects that are encoded by MHEG-5 and other DSM-CC objects together. Both of them are sent to the STB through DSM-CC UU and MHEG-5 objects are displayed by the MHEG-5 RTE. The application server controls one or more video pumps, which store MPEG-2 stream. The user's request about MPEG-2 streams is sent to the video pump via internal API (Play, Stop, FF, REW), and the MPEG-2 stream is delivered to the STB.

5.0   Conclusion and future directions

With interactive multimedia service, home users can purchase the goods or watch the latest movies interactively. Office applications such as training, messaging, and cooperated working will be provided as new interactive multimedia ones. Interactive multimedia service is the main service in information superhighway and it has great influences upon daily lives as well as business activities. Like in other countries, information superhighway being implemented in Korea should consider the change of service environment. IMPRESS is a service platform under construction in order to meet with this influence. It has been developed specifically for supporting new service developing environment, and verifying service specifications and its validity. Using ATM-based B-ISDN as a basic infrastructure, IMPRESS includes various service components such as server, set-top box, videoconference terminal, and level 1 gateway. Interactive multimedia services such as movies on demand and home-shopping those are based on the DAVIC specification 1.0 have been implemented via the developed service system. Research on the DAVIC Internet access and other interactive multimedia application service will be kept going continuously.

References:

1. Bohdan O. Szuprowicz, (1994) ``Multimedia Networking and Communications'', Computer Technology Research Corp.
2. IGI Consulting Inc. (1994), ``Video Dialtone and Video on Demand''.
3. Tim Kwok, (1995)``A Vision for Residential Broadband Services: ATM to the Home'', IEEE Network, pp. 14 ~ 28, September.
4. T. Meyer-Boudnik, W. Effelsberg, (1995) ``MHEG Explained,'' IEEE Multimedia, Vol.2, No.1, pp.26~38.
5. Digital Audiovisual Council, (1995) ``DAVIC 1.0 Specifications'', Berlin 11th Meeting, December.
6. ISO/IEC JTC1/SC29/WG11, (1996) ``Information Technology: Generic Coding of Moving Pictures and Associated Audio Information IS 13818-1,2,3''.

7. ISO/IEC JTC1/SC29/WG12, (1995) ``Multimedia and Hypermedia information coding Export Group DIS 13522-5''

8. ISO/IEC JTC1/SC29/WG11, (1995) ``Digital Storage Media Command & Control DIS 13818-6''.

9. J.H.Park, J.S.Choi, S.J.Kim, Y.D.Park, (1995) ``Multimedia Terminal in ATM Network'', KICS Proceeding Vol.14, No.2, pp. 1014 ~ 1018.

5.7

"BRINGING IT ALL TOGETHER": THE DEVELOPMENT OF AN INTEGRATED COMPUTER LANGUAGE LEARNING NETWORK

Bruce Morrison
Hong Kong Polytechnic University, Hong Kong

This paper examines the development of a networked computer system within a self-access language-learning centre. The system incorporates five key elements: access to the Internet, Computer Assisted Language Learning (CALL) programs, multimedia CD-ROM programs, E-mail and word processing. The system has been set up to provide an integrated language-learning resource which is designed to encourage learners to be more independent in, and responsible for, their own learning. The paper describes some of the main stages in the system's development including the design of the computer/user interface and questions of learner access to the various elements that comprise the system.

1.0   Introduction

Warschauer identifies that, increasingly, in foreign language learning, the focus is on learner-centred methodologies where the individual learner is expected to take more responsibility for their own learning, and a central goal of modern language teaching is to "enhance student autonomy and control over the language learning process" (Warschauer 1994: p.1). Reflecting this, there has been a growing awareness of the potential value of self-access language-learning centres in providing language-learning opportunities supplementary to classroom teaching provision. The role of the computer in self-access language learning, both in terms of the potential pedagogical benefits of the technology in general, and particular applications in specific, has been discussed (eg. Ehrmann, 1996; Sheerin, 1989; Sorge, 1994). There has been less focus, however, on pedagogical questions concerning the integration of individual computer-based learning tools into a self-access language-learning centre's infrastructure and language-learning approach.

This paper will describe the development of a networked system that has been designed to draw together some of the main computer-based learning tools and to integrate these into the infrastructure of a self-access language learning centre. It will examine the stages of the system's development in terms of some of the questions that have had to be addressed and subsequent decisions that were made, and highlight some of the issues concerning such integration that have been raised.

2.0 Background

The Centre for Independent Language Learning (CILL) is a self-access centre where learners are encouraged to develop their independent language-learning skills to enable them to continue their learning outside a formal educational context. They are expected to decide for themselves when to study, their pace of study, the level and type of materials that they use, and the type of learning tasks that they undertake - with little explicit guidance from a language tutor.

3.0 The stages of development

While a number of planning decisions were made prior to the physical setting-up of the CILL, much of the computer system's development has been "organic" and part of a learning process both technically and administratively. Thus, the system is still seen as very much as part of an ongoing "process" rather than constituting a finished "product".

Stage 1: Identifying the role of the computer

There were five main reasons why it was decided that computers should be a major pedagogical focus in the CILL.

Firstly, a number of studies have indicated that computer-mediated instruction is generally an effective learning tool in a wide variety of instructional settings (e.g., Doughty, 1995; Dalton, 1986) and perceived as such by learners (e.g., Skinner, 1988; Stevens, 1991). Specifically, support for the adoption of interactive multimedia computer materials is provided by Fletcher (1990) who reports that "researchers have found that people retain only 20% of what they hear, 40% of what they see and hear, and 75% of what they see, hear and do" - quoted in Athappilly (1994: p.108). Secondly, the computer can be an empowering tool that helps in the development of learner autonomy (e.g., Doughty, 1995). It does this in two main ways: by providing the learner with a degree of choice of learning style (in terms of the huge variety of material-types available through multimedia CD-ROMs, the Internet and CALL materials); and by enabling them to "...choose their own learning path through the material, making sense of surrogate experience according to their preferred learning styles and strategies and prior knowledge" (Yildiz & Atkins, 1993: p.136). This is an element of control that is not usually associated with linear, textual, audio or video based materials. Thirdly, computer-mediated materials can be a motivating factor for learners who are working without the presence of a teacher (Stevens, 1991). Fourthly, the computer can provide instant, personalised feedback to a learner for whom the only other source is the answer key of a book. Fifthly, it can provide a virtually limitless source for communicative language practice through the use of E-mail and the Internet.

Stage 2: Initial planning

In the initial planning stage, a number of decisions had to be made and these included the hardware, network software and (initial) program software to be purchased, and the facilities that we wanted to be available to learners.

It was decided that the Centre's initial network should comprise the following. For the twenty workstations, Pentium computers with CD-ROM drives and 16MB RAM (to ensure full audio, video and multimedia capabilities) were purchased and networked with Novell Netware 3.1 run on a Pentium 100 server with a 2GB hard disk.

In terms of software provision, six program types were identified to meet initial learner needs. A word processor (MS Word) provides learners with a tool to practise various academic writing skills such as report writing and referencing. A range of CALL programs (such as "Story Board" and "Tense Buster") help meet the needs of those learners who want to focus on linguistic accuracy. Multimedia CD-ROMs provide the main focus with a range of program types which can provide both linguistic input and tutoring, as well as content-based opportunities for language practice. E-mail provides learners with an opportunity for "real" communication with other learners as well as a way of contacting the tutors working in the Centre for help with language problems. A World Wide Web navigator (Netscape) provides access to the CILL homepage on the Internet from where learners can access both language-learning sites and other language-rich resources. Finally, a database (Paradox format) provides learners with on-line access to the Centre's materials catalogue to locate the materials that match their learning criteria.

Stage 3: User access and interface development

From the outset, a primary concern was to make the system as user-friendly and easy to access as possible while, at the same time, ensuring systems security through a system of Learner IDs and two levels of virus protection. It was decided that, since we would be running both DOS and Windows based programs, a Windows environment was necessary to avoid learners having to launch Windows each time a Windows application was required. However, while it was decided that Windows should be launched on power-up, we felt that the standard Windows interface was not the most suitable for our purposes - particularly in the light of the wide variety of different program-types and facilities we wanted to be able to offer to learners. Therefore, Windows is used only as the platform to launch a custom-designed menu program written in DELPHI.

A major question was how learners were to launch the various language-learning floppy disk-based CALL programs and multimedia CD-ROMs - we were keen to avoid the cumbersome necessity of learners having to write commands to execute the program files. For the CALL programs, we were able to negotiate site licences that allow the Centre to have the program residing on the server for multiple-user access. For the CD-ROMs, a series of EXE files to reside on the server which are executed from the menu after the learner has placed the appropriate CD-ROM into the drive.

For access to E-mail, two options were made available: international key-pals to enable learners to get more practice using English for "real" communication not necessarily related to language learning (accessed through the Internet); and communication with the CILL tutors for language learning advice and correction. The Internet was initially accessed through the departmental homepage but is now accessed through the CILL homepage (see below).

During the development of the computer-learner interface, we followed five guiding principles (derived from both our own experience and factors noted in the literature - eg. Sutcliffe, 1988; Duchastel, 1993). These reflected Duchastel's view that "the key to a good learning environment lies in the notion of access" (Duchastel, 1993: p.229) and that structured guidance should be provided that ensures the language environment is such that it meets, as fully as possible, the needs of the learners. Among the factors we took into consideration were:
- the type of learner (in terms of computer literacy, linguistic capabilities, predicted frequency and patterns of usage);
- the physical design and layout of the computer work-islands;
- the different modes of use (eg. CD-ROMs, E-mail, word processing, Internet);
- the amount and type of learner-support available and the need to be able to provide a clear representation of the Centre's systemic structure.

The first principle was that the interface should be clear and simple; the second was that it should offer the learner a choice of clearly defined learning options grouped according to criteria that are easily identifiable by the target learners; thirdly, that all programs and features are accessed through the menu system; fourthly, that the interface can be easily adapted and further developed; finally, it is important that the interface reflects, in style and presentation, the philosophy and image of the Centre.

In the light of initial informal feedback, the menu was designed to represent a series of twelve file dividers with the organising criteria at the top. The criteria (modified in the light of learner feedback) now represent four categories: Language (Speaking & Listening, Reading & Writing, Grammar and Vocabulary), computer mode (Internet, Utilities, and E-mail), learning materials (Multimedia materials, Course-specific materials and access to the Materials Index) and a multimedia introduction to the Centre.

Stage 4: Pedagogical dvelopment of individual applications

While there are a large number of excellent EFL-specific and general-interest programs available, for use in a self-access environment the guidance and instructions provided are often insufficient to enable individual learners to use the programs effectively. This is particularly true in the case of multi-media packages as highlighted by Sorge (1994: p. 510): "Multimedia-based learning does not work just by having the hardware and software available for the learner....one needs to provide on-going support". We have identified four major, learner-related problems in the use of the system in general, and multimedia programs in particular:
- a technical one - the problem of program access;
- a conceptual one - how the learner selects a program-type and, specifically a particular program, to meet their individual learning needs;
- a cognitive one - exactly how a learner interacts with a program;
- how the various system components can be integrated into a pedagogical framework.

The technical issue we have addressed, as discussed above, through the use of a menu system.

The conceptual issue is how one can enable learners to make an appropriate choice of program. For this, the pedagogical value and purpose, and a description of activities in the program, should be clear before the learner loads the software.

We have addressed this issue in four main ways:
- each CD-ROM box/case is labelled indicating a suggested language level and broad program-type (eg. "Business English");
- the menu screen will include a brief overview of the program features;

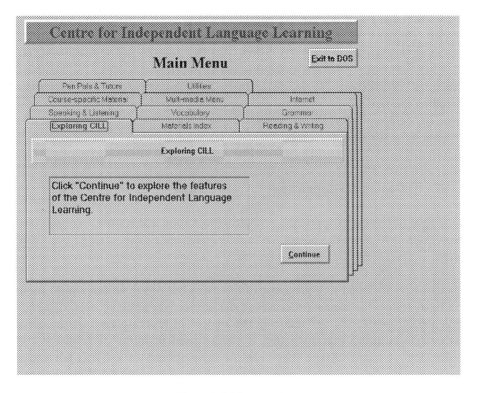

Figure 1: Main menu screen

- thirdly, on the shelf, next to each CD-ROM, there is a very brief description of
  the program and the language level it would be most appropriate for;
- a system of data-based indexes help learners identify materials that are
  potentially relevant to their needs.

The cognitive issue is how to facilitate learner-program interaction. For this,
learners in the Centre are provided with a hard-copy menu overview with a brief
description of each menu selection while each program has (or will have) a "User
Guide" which is designed to act as a simple, jargon-free computer-learner
interface to help learners focus their attention on the language-learning task
rather than working out how to navigate the program. This reflects Conklin's
(1987) view that the price to be paid for giving the learner complete freedom to
browse a program without support can be disorientation. This view, in turn, is
supported by comments in Learner Diaries such as: "I'm not familiar with
controlling the computer. It wasted me a lot of time to learn to control it. If there
is a simple manuale, it will help me to concentrate on learning English" (from an
intermediate learner's diary) .

Lastly, three means of integrating multimedia have been initiated in the Centre: relevant elements of the program features (topics, grammatical structures, vocabulary areas etc.) have been included in the indexes and a "Multi-media" index has been added; we are in the process of developing a series of "Learning Directions" Worksheets to guide learners to non-computer based materials related to the unit of the program they are using; thirdly, we are developing a series of "Strategy Worksheets" which suggest ways that learners can use the program as a stimulus for other language learning activities. (See also page 8 below.)

Stage 5: On-going development

In the light of our own experience, technical innovation and learner feedback (see below), we have, from the outset, constantly re-evaluated and adapted our initial system.

Changes have included a re-grouping of the menu options in an attempt to more accurately reflect the mental processes of the learner when attempting to access a particular program-type, and reducing the amount of text displayed on the menu cards while ensuring that such text is standardised in terms of language and appearance. A major change, has been the development of a CILL homepage which may later be used as the menu to not only access the World Wide Web but also to launch our Centre-based applications.

The past year has seen the introduction, and wide acceptance, of Windows '95 as the successor to Windows 3.1 as an operating system. After trialling, we are now in the process of upgrading our machines and expect the change to impact in two main ways. Firstly, as a real multi-tasking environment, we are hoping it will increase the reliability of the system; and secondly, future 32 bit applications - and in particular the 32 bit companions to World Wide Web (WWW) applications (for sound or video for example) - should run faster and be more reliable.

4.0   Learner feedback

While the Centre has not conducted large-scale formal analysis of learners' reactions to the system, learner feedback so far, comments in Learner Diaries and on-going monitoring by tutors produced a number of observations and, in response to these, we have made corresponding changes to the Centre's infrastructure. These observations and changes are summarised overleaf.

5.0   Issues of integration

Through the menu system, it has been possible for us to bring together for our learners a set of learning modes and activity options which encompass a wide range of language-learning opportunities from controlled CALL "drill-and-kill" exercises to unmonitored communicative practice through E-mail or on the Internet. This presentational integration is not, however, sufficient on its own to ensure effective use of the various resources. There is a need for the various components to be integrated into the language-learning objectives of the individual learners, the Centre's other learning materials and the pedagogical infrastructure of the Centre - to help avoid learners perceiving the computer options as "game-like" activities unrelated to their learning goals.

5.1   Integration into the learner's language-learning objectives

At the level of the individual learner, integration is encouraged in four main ways. Firstly, the orientation session, that every new learner attends and part of which consists of an in-house produced, interactive program, introduces the computer network as central to the working of the Centre. Secondly, each learner keeps a "Learner Diary" in which their learning aims and the materials used are recorded together with comments on each learning session. Thus, the computer-based learning tool is identified as the learning material which was instrumental in the achievement of the learner's objective. Thirdly, the "User Guides" (discussed on page four) are designed to increase learners' awareness of the pedagogical value of individual programs and thus encourage learners to include them in their learning programme. Lastly, the tutors in the Centre provide the learners with an opportunity - through face-to-face interaction or through learner and tutor comments in the Learner Diaries - to ask about the programs and for the tutors to situate them in the learning scheme of the Centre.

5.2   Integration with the centre's other learning materials

Integration with the other learning materials in the Centre is primarily acheived through the use of the "Materials indexes" which list materials of all types by topics, language function, grammatical structure, vocabulary area as well as by media type. Additionally, a number of multimedia programs have accompanying "Learner Directions" worksheets which suggest other learning materials (mainly text or video based) which learners can use to further practise the language items encountered in the computer program.

Table 1: Learner feedback and action taken

Feedback	Action
Learners were not easily able to identify the menu categories to which their target program/activity belonged	The categories were re-assigned to more closely correspond to existing infrastructure classification
Learners reported that the menu background colours were too bright and distracting	The backgrounds were changed to display "softer", pastel colours
The menu background colours were found to be inconsistent	The backgrounds are being changed to correspond to the label colours used by all materials (eg. vocabulary - brown)
Learners had problems understanding how to access some of the multimedia programs from their introductory screens	Additional, help options have been added to some of the menu screens
Many learners had problems getting into the E-mail	A window now appears prompting the learner to enter their e-mail ID whenever they try to access e-mail

5.3   Integration into the pedagogical infrastructure of the centre

Duchastel, writing about the principles of Learning Environment Design, talks about the need for "the learning support structure that is placed over the information in the learning environment" to be the "orientation and guidance structure that particularly tunes the learning environment to the requirements of learning" (Duchastel 1993: p.230). In the Centre, we have tried to integrate the various learning tools, human resources and materials to provide such a structure. The elements we have utilised in attempting to provide such an integration are: the menu system, materials indexes, the CILL WWW homepages, learning strategy worksheets, the tutors, and the orientation session.

Some writers (eg. Barnett, 1993) have expressed reservations about the value of menus in a self-access environment. However, the menu system in CILL is the primary tool for integrating the various computer programs into a language-learning environment which depends on its infrastructure for much of the support usually provided by the teacher in a classroom situation. The integration is primarily achieved by the grouping of programs, and/or elements of programs (eg. particular exercises) into readily-recognised language-learning categories: for example, the "Vocabulary" entry leads learners to various CD-ROM multimedia dictionaries, an in-house produced multimedia program, two vocabulary-based CALL programs and an on-line dictionary. These categories are also those that are used in the materials indexes and then reflected in the colour-coded, text-based materials shelving system.

Further integration is provided by the WWW homepages which provide an overview of the Centre in terms of its structure and the facilities and materials available, and the new learners' orientation sessions. Pedagogically, further integration is provided by the "Strategy" worksheets. These unlike the "Learning Directions" worksheets and User Guides" which provide guidance on how to use a program, suggest ways that learners can more fully exploit the computer programs as effective language-learning tools. Finally, the tutors encourage learners to view the computer as one part of an integrated learning environment.

6.0   Conclusion

The on-going development of the Centre's system has reflected, and brought into focus, a number of pedagogical and administrative issues central to the question of the type and extent of learning autonomy that we encourage our learners to develop. In particular, the fine line to be drawn between "help" and "control" has been highlighted with our initial conclusions tending towards Garrison and Baynton's view that learner-control "can be achieved only by striking a balance between independence and ...power and support" (Garrison & Baynton, 1987: p. 5).

References:

1. Athappily, K.K., Durben, C. & Woods, S. (1994), "Multimedia Computing: An Overview", in Reisman, S. (ed.).
2. Barnett, L. (1993), "Teacher Off: Computer Technology, Guidance and Self-Access", System, 21(3), 295-304.
3. Conklin, J. (1987), "Hypertext: An Introduction And Survey", IEEE Computer, 20(9), 17-41.
4. Dalton, D.W. (1986), "How Effective is Interactive Video in Improving Performance and Attitude?", Educational Technology, 31(2), 27-29.

5. Doughty, G. (et al) (1995), Using Learning Technologies: Interim Conclusions from the TILT Project, Glasgow, University of Glasgow Press.
6. Duchastel, P. (1993), "Learning Environment Design", Journal of Educational Technology Systems, 22(3), 225-233.
7. Ehrmann, S.C. (1996), "Asking the Right Question: What does Research Tell Us about Higher Learning?", World Wide Web paper, [http://www2.ido.gmu.edu/AAHE/Change/March/Erhmann.html].
8. Fletcher J.D. (1990), "Effectiveness and Cost of Interactive Video-disk Instruction in Defense Training and Education", Institute for Defense Analysis, 1990/July, 2372.
9. Garrison, D.R. & Baynton, M. (1987), "Beyond Independence IN Distance Education: The Concept Of Control", The American Journal of Distance Education, 1(3), 3-14.
10. Goforth, D. (1994), "Learner Control = Decision Making + Information: a Model and Meta-Analysis", Journal of Educational Computing Research, 11(1), 1-26.
11. Reisman, S. (ed.) (1994), Multimedia Computing, London, Idea Group Publishing.
12. Sheerin, S. (1989), Self-Access, Oxford, Oxford University Press.
13. Skinner, M.E. (1988), "Attitudes Of College Students Towards Computer-Assisted Instruction: An Essential Variable For Successful Implementation", Educational Technology, 1988, 7-15.
14. Sorge, D.H., Russell, J.D. & Weilbaker, G.L. (1994), "Implementing Multimedia-Based Learning", in Reisman, S. (ed.).
15. Stevens, V. (1991), "A Study Of Student Attitudes Toward CALL In A Self-access Student Resource Centre", System, 19(3), 289-299.
16. Sutcliffe, A. (1988), Human-Computer Interface Design, London, Macmillan.
17. Warschauer, M., Turbee, L. & Roberts, B. (1994), "Computer Learning Networks & Student Empowerment", National Foreign Language Resource Centre at University of Hawaii Research Notes, 10.
18. Yildiz, R. & Atkins, M. (1993), "Evaluating Multimedia Applications", Computers and Education, 21/1, 133-139.

5.8

EARLY EXPERIENCES IN MEASURING MULTIMEDIA SYSTEMS DEVELOPMENT EFFORT

Tim Fletcher, Stephen G. MacDonell & William B.L. Wong
University of Otago, New Zealand

The development of multimedia information systems must be managed and controlled just as it is for other generic system types. This paper proposes an approach for assessing multimedia component and system characteristics with a view to ultimately using these features to estimate the associated development effort. Given the different nature of multimedia systems, existing metrics do not appear to be entirely useful in this domain; however, some general principles can still be applied in analysis. Some basic assertions concerning the influential characteristics of multimedia systems are made and a small preliminary set of data is evaluated.

1.0   Introduction

With its inherent use of original and pre-sourced media components as fundamental building blocks and a focus on screen-oriented authoring, multimedia systems development does not lend itself easily to the 'traditional' software processes commonly used in other domains. Multimedia information systems (MMIS) development has therefore evolved as its own sub-discipline over the last ten years to a point where a range of high productivity specialist tools and more appropriate development methodologies have been formulated. This is a reflection of an increasing maturity in MMIS development. Another outcome of this greater maturity is a realisation that the development process must be managed effectively, so that it can be measured, controlled and improved (Gao and Lo, 1996) - for *all* systems, we are concerned with increasing quality and productivity whilst minimising cost.

Despite tool and methodology advances, MMIS development continues to demand significant effort. England and Finney (1996) believe this is because multimedia development projects have so many influencing variables (more than for other system types) that must be considered, while Marshall et al. (1994) suggest that the development of system content is the major constraint to the widespread use of commercial multimedia, despite faster cheaper hardware and more powerful authoring environments. In terms of the current project, we are concerned with the implications of the 'non-standard' MMIS development methodologies and the particular characteristics of MMIS in terms of software development effort measurement.

The next two sections of the paper consider the specific characteristics of MMIS that mean that commonly used measurement methods in the business software domain are less applicable. This is followed by a discussion of the current empirical study. Preliminary data analysis is then presented and the implications of the findings are discussed. The limitations of the study are described and the paper is concluded with a short summary of ongoing work.

2.0   Special characteristics of multimedia systems

Multimedia information systems development is sufficiently different from that of other development paradigms to mean that models, tools and methodologies from these domains are not entirely suitable (Marshall et al., 1994; Gao and Lo, 1996). Four important differences have particular impact: the use of specialised high productivity authoring tools, the preparation of the media content, the cross-functional composition of many development teams, and the methodology phases applicable to MMIS development.

Authoring tools are used in a similar manner to the way in which fourth generation languages (4GLs) are used in business-oriented systems development. In general, authoring tools are utilised to integrate and build the *system* (rather than the content) at a very high level of abstraction. Of concern is what the system should do, rather than how it should do it (hence the analogy with 4GLs). These environments offer very high productivity, and some even allow systems to be built without coding or scripting. Research into development effort associated with the use of authoring tools is not widespread, however. Moreover, this mirrors a similar dearth of knowledge in regard to 4GL-based development in the business domain. Thus the degree of impact of the use of such tools on development effort is unclear.

The authoring process generally occurs after the development of the specific media components. Construction of the media is arguably the most difficult task in the overall MMIS development process - it certainly appears to be the most time consuming. Marshall et al. (1994) and others (Merrill et al., 1991) indicate that elementary computer-based training (CBT) software requires 100 hours of effort per delivery hour, a figure that can rise to 800 hours or more per delivery hour if multimedia elements are added (Beautement, 1991). Unfortunately, these figures are generally anecdotal - it is to be hoped that continued empirical work may provide more objectively derived indications of effort required.

The media preparation component has further implications for effort from a personnel perspective. Whereas 'traditional' development of information systems is generally dependent on a team of software specialists (albeit with particular strengths), the development of MMIS is often undertaken by cross-functional development teams, with one group responsible for the software and the other responsible for the content and design. This can bring added complications to the development process, given that communication even among software specialists is notoriously poor, particularly as the size of the team increases. The impact of a 'non-software' design team on development effort may be significant.

Finally, the overall development methodologies and the activities that occur within them are by necessity quite unique to the development of multimedia systems. As a consequence, many of the components or models on which measurement has been based in the past are simply not available in the multimedia domain. For example, data-oriented specification methods and models used in commercial transaction-based systems development are not easily mapped to multimedia projects. Similarly, the algorithm-centred models used in scientific systems development are also inappropriate for multimedia systems. Multimedia information systems development processes are probably most similar to prototyping methodologies in that significant emphasis (and hence effort) is required in the iterative development of a suitable and appropriate interface with adequate system functionality, although Marshall et al. (1994) have used an adapted waterfall model to represent multimedia courseware development (Figure 1). It should again be acknowledged, however, that the inherently necessary media preparation stage is a key distinguishing factor. The IBM Multimedia Consulting Methodology (Gruskin, 1994) shown in Figure 2 provides a useful illustration of this consideration, with media preparation depicted as a separate and important activity that is carried out concurrently with authoring and integration.

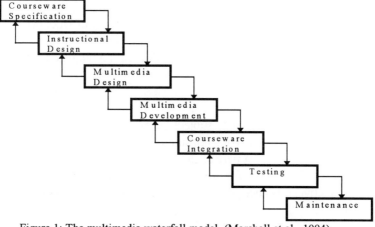

Figure 1: The multimedia waterfall model (Marshall et al., 1994)

214

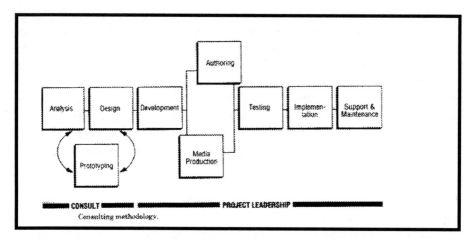

Figure 2: The IBM multimedia consulting methodology (Gruskin, 1994)

3.0   Mesuring development effort

Almost all current effort assessment and early prediction methods assume the existence of data-centred products (e.g. data flow diagrams, data models, screen and report layouts) and/or a 'traditional' development process (incorporating analysis, design, coding and so on). As previously discussed, multimedia systems development incorporates little of these aspects. A more appropriate assessment and estimation method is therefore suggested here.

3.1   Existing measurement methods

Development effort estimation is primarily undertaken using either a size-based measure or a function-based measure. The most popular size-based methods use estimated product lines of code as input to a derivative of Boehm's Constructive Cost Model (COCOMO) (Boehm, 1981) with adjustments for various 'cost drivers'. Marshall et al. (1994) have adopted an adjusted version of this approach in their analysis and prediction of multimedia courseware development effort, incorporating consideration of course delivery time and a large number of drivers (influential factors) under four classes of course difficulty, interactivity, development environment and subject expertise. Although their general approach seems sound, the work considered here has no courseware emphasis, so the use of this factor as a part of the model is inappropriate for our purposes. Furthermore, the inclusion of more than twenty drivers, some of which must be assessed subjectively, is an aspect that should be avoided if possible.

Determining effort using function-based measures may be useful for multimedia systems. Albrecht's function point analysis (FPA) method (Albrecht, 1979) considers the contribution of system inputs, outputs, enquiries and files to system scope and complexity, with final adjustment based on the characteristics of the development and operating environments. As defined, however, the approach is not entirely appropriate for MMIS development, for several reasons (Gao and Lo, 1996): MMIS make use of large databases but these are not actually maintained by the system; MMIS development tends to adopt extensive component reuse; and the output forms for MMIS are far more complex than for standard business systems. Gao and Lo (1996) have therefore produced an adjusted FPA assessment method that has attempted to take account of these differences, with some success. In their model, however, output forms (text, sound, animation) are weighted equally whereas it may be that some forms of output are significantly more influential than others in regard to their contribution to effort. Moreover, the subjectivity of FPA in general has been widely questioned (Jeffery and Low, 1990), so an alternative approach may be desirable.

3.2   The proposed measurement approach

When compared to existing assessment/estimation methods, the proposed method considers software products more relevant to multimedia systems (e.g. animation sequences as opposed to data entities) and examines their contribution to systems development effort. Measurement of development effort is itself made more relevant to multimedia systems, in that it is suggested that effort data be recorded alongside tasks such as audio/visual editing, digitising, video recording and sound capture. (It should be noted that the empirical analysis described below does not fully evaluate the proposed method, for reasons discussed in the Lessons Learned subsection. In the interests of research, however, the approach is more fully described here.) The proposed approach is based on the assertion that MMIS development effort is a function of (i) building the system content and (ii) authoring the system. Each of these tasks is evaluated in terms of the components manipulated and the activities carried out:

(i) building the system content - for each media component created, the following data items were to be recorded: filename, media type (graphic, audio, video, animation, photograph, scan), original or pre-existing, creation effort (for original media), digitising effort (for scans, video and audio), editing effort, and component duration (for temporal media i.e. animation, sound and video). The assumption underlying this collection is that each media form may have a different impact on development effort.

(ii) authoring the system - for screen authoring the screen name and authoring effort were to be collected for each screen. An inspection of each project was also to be conducted to ascertain the 'complexity' of each piece of media and each screen. The data to be collected for each screen were: the number of objects on the screen (including sounds), the number of links between that screen and other screens, the number of events on a screen and the average number of actions per event. Procedures that respond to a mouse being clicked, or any other scripted actions, are considered as events. The associated task is normally a generic activity to be performed; typically most link buttons contain only two actions for the click event: play 'click' sound and go to another screen. The media complexity was to be based around graphics data: the number of objects on the component, whether it had been reused elsewhere in the project, and the form it took (button, toolbar, screen, background, component i.e. part of the foreground or a source in an animation sequence). This approach is based on the assumption that a screen that incorporates a greater number of objects and events will take proportionally greater effort to develop.

4.0   Small-scale empirical investigation

In order to test the validity of the approach and to determine which factors were the main contributors to development effort, data were collected from several senior student projects.

4.1   Data collection

Preliminary data was gathered from five 4th-year group projects in multimedia information systems from a joint course taught by the Information Science and Design Studies departments at the University of Otago. The group sizes were four (three groups) or five (two groups) and the ratio of Information Science to Design Studies students were 3:1 (two groups), 2:2 (one group) and 3:2 (two groups). As described previously, this mixture of personnel is common in commercial projects where groups are frequently made up of people from very different backgrounds, such as graphic design, programming, video/audio production, project management and interface design (England and Finney, 1996). This situation should therefore be considered as reflective of the commercial environment.

For most of the class this was their first exposure to MMIS development. Projects were to be delivered in two phases: the prototype then the final system. During the prototype stage students were 'learning by doing', gaining experience with the various tools and technologies. While most students had little experience of multimedia *per se* when entering the course, they did have sufficient training is the various areas of multimedia listed above. Typically the Information Science students were skilled in the areas of programming, requirements gathering and systems management while the Design students had skills in the areas of graphic design, interface design and the preparation of audio-visual material.

The projects were undertaken with the goal of producing a cross-platform system. Applications included an interactive shopping mall, a guide to mountain bike tracks and a music catalogue. Media components were built with commercial development packages and two authoring environments were used. The choice of environment was important since it affected authoring time and the manner in which the media components were prepared. The two environments were Macromedia Director and Apple Media Tool (AMT). These tools employ quite different metaphors. Director uses a time line with media included on different channels, while AMT uses an iconic metaphor with individual screens (see Figures 3 and 4). The time line approach is more ponderous for interactivity since each screen is simply a point in time. This means that an interactive session will consist of 'jumping' around a timeline; this is not as straightforward as using links between screens. However, Director uses Lingo, a powerful scripting language, whereas AMT has no scripting language as such. This means that although AMT is easy to use for simple systems, for more complicated projects Director's scripting capability may prove to be more useful. It would be interesting to have some appreciation of the impact of each environment on development effort.

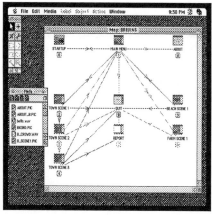

Figure3: AMT screen map

Figure 4: A director 'score'

4.2 Analysis

Two sets of data were available for analysis, the first being the data related to the creation of media components. This data set included 45 observations all associated with graphic media components (thus no comparison of the influence of different media types on effort was possible, for reasons discussed below). For each component, the creation effort, development (authoring) environment, number of objects and component form were recorded. Correlation analysis was performed across the data set to check whether any of the characteristic variables were related to development effort. Although no significantly useful relationships were identified, some observations were made. It was evident that the development environment had some impact on effort (so analysis was performed on two data subsets but with no further success), as did the component form, in that the few screens took significantly greater effort to develop than buttons and animation sequence components.

The screen authoring data set comprised eighteen observations, for which authoring effort, authoring environment, number of links, number of objects and number of events were recorded. It was evident from examining the data that again the two environments showed differing characteristics - the set was therefore split into one of eleven observations and one of seven. Relationship analysis using scatter plots and correlation assessment for the eleven observation data set showed that none of the screen characteristic measures were related to the associated development effort. Analysis of the smaller data set, however, revealed a very strong and significant linear relationship between both the number of objects and the number of events and development effort (the correlation coefficients are shown in Table 1).

Table 1: Effort-screen characteristic correlations

	Effort and No. objects	Effort and No. events
Pearson's correlation	0.98	0.98
Spearman's correlation	0.88	0.94

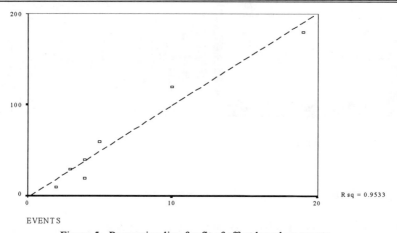

Figure 5: Regression line for fit of effort based on events

Figure 5 illustrates the goodness of fit for the regression of screen authoring effort based on the number of screen events for one of the authoring environments. Although the data set is very small, the strength of the relationship gives us encouragement for further investigation.

4.3   Lessons learned - observations, limitations and difficulties

Clearly much of what we set out to achieve in this study remains unresolved at this stage. The most significant problem was data capture - the students were simply most reluctant to complete the data collection sheets, directly contributing to (i) the very small data sets and (ii) the infeasibility of undertaking much of the planned analysis. For example, all temporal media (video, audio and animation) should have had an associated duration entered on the datasheet. However this was rarely provided. In all cases video and audio pre-existed and only needed to be digitised and edited - however, no records of even these tasks were taken. Similarly, digitising and editing small pieces of audio were seen as 'unimportant' and therefore the times were not recorded. In the final analysis, only three video-associated records were received, too few to be of any use, and no sound or animation data was received. Our objective of assessing the effort needed in the development of various media types was therefore not possible.

A computer-based collection system could solve many of these problems. For example, valid fields only would be highlighted for a particular media type and integrity rules could be enforced at data entry to ensure that all required fields had been completed with valid values. This would also have the effect of streamlining what is at present a tedious, time consuming two stage process (collecting the datasheets and entering the data). Moreover, developers should where possible be given some form of incentive for participation - in a class situation marks may be a possible reward. If developers are educated concerning the benefits of and rationale for a metrics program they feel part of the process and are more likely to cooperate. Another limitation should also be acknowledged at this point. Student data is often criticised as being unrealistic in terms of 'real' development. Admittedly, the effort required may not be comparable to that needed by commercial developers, particularly as the learning curve formed part of the effort. On the other hand, all of the students began the projects with the same level of experience, so the figures should be appropriate in relative terms for the sample.

5.0   Conclusion and ongoing work

It remains our belief that media type, development environment and media component characteristics all have an impact on associated development effort.

Although this preliminary study has been unable to empirically illustrate some of these assertions, there is adequate justification to continue with the work. At present, further data collection is being performed under more controlled supervision (something that was lacking in the original exercise) in the hope that larger data sets will enable us to more effectively determine whether useful relationships exist among the data items of interest.

References:

1. Albrecht, A.J. (1979), "Measuring application development productivity", in *Proceedings IBM Application Development Symposium*, Monterey CA, 83-92.
2. Beautement, P. (1991), "Review of interactive video systems and their possible application to training in the 90's", *Interactive Learning International*, 7, 45-54.
3. Boehm, B. (1981), Software Engineering Economics, Englewood Cliffs NJ, Prentice Hall.
4. England, E. and Finney, A. (1996), Managing Multimedia, Harlow, Addison-Wesley.
5. Gao, X. and Lo, B. (1996), "A modified function point method for CAL systems with respect to software cost estimation", in *Proceedings of the Software Engineering Conference SE:E&P '96*, Dunedin, New Zealand, 125-132.
6. Jeffery, D.R. and Low, G. (1990), "Calibrating estimation tools for software development", *Software Engineering Journal*, 5(4), 215-221.
7. Gruskin, L. (1994), "Multimedia consulting", in Keyes, J. (ed), The McGraw-Hill Multimedia Handbook, New York, McGraw-Hill, 24.1-24.11.
8. Marshall, I.M., Samson, W.B. and Dugard, P.I. (1994), "A proposed framework for predicting the development effort of multimedia courseware", in Kappe, F. and Herzner, W. (eds) Multimedia/Hypermedia in Open Distributed Environments, Springer-Verlag, 161-180.
9. Merrill, M.D., Li, Z. and Jones, M.K. (1991), "Limitations of first generation instructional design", *Educational Technology*, 30(1), 7-11.

5.9

THE IMPACTS OF ALTERNATE INFORMATION PRESENTATION APPROACHES UPON TASK PERFORMANCE IN A TASK SUPPORT SYSTEM: EXPERIMENTS AND ANALYSES IN A TEAM DECISION MAKING SETTING

James R. Marsden[1], Ram Pakath[2] & Kustim Wibowo[2]
[1]University of Connecticut & [2]University of Kentucky, USA

We describe an experimental platform for assessing user preference for, and performance under, different information presentation approaches in a computerized task support system. The tasks involve repeatedly classifying computer-generated objects of varying complexity levels. Rules for classification and "snapshots" of each object are provided using information sources that involve textual displays, image displays, and voice, each at various possible speeds. We use this platform to assess subject performance, in terms of decision-making rate and decision correctness, under specific "task complexity--information mode--presentation speed" combinations and to contrast pre-experimental attitudes towards information sources and task complexities with experimental findings.

1.0   Introduction & literature overview

In this research, we seek to study the impacts of alternate computerized information presentation sources upon the efficiency and effectiveness of repetitive, computerized-task performance by human subjects in a tightly-controlled laboratory setting. During an experiment, the "work" done by a subject involves interacting with an IBM PC-compatible using a mouse and his/her powers of sight, hearing, memory, and intellect. Each subject is one entity (i.e., the human entity) in a joint human-computer decision-making team. The other entity is a computerized task support system (TSS).

TSS is a broad label that encompasses the gamut of personal and business systems in an organization such as Management Support Systems (i.e., EDPSs, MISs, OASs, EISs, DSSs (and variants), and CSSs), Operational Support Systems (i.e., EDPSs, DSSs (and variants), ..), Personal Support Systems, Research Support Systems, and so on (Holsapple and Whinston, 1996). Here, we use the term TSS to denote a specific Research Support System. Our research is an extension of prior work in the fields of IS evaluation and UI design and assessment.

The business computing literature documents abundant work (e.g., Mahmood and Medewitz, 1985; Sanders and Courtney, 1985; Snitkin and King, 1986; Sharda et. al. 1987; Money, Tromp, and Wegner, 1988)on the ex-post evaluation of DSSs (i.e., evaluating operational systems in actual and/or hypothetical task settings). More recent studies stress the benefits of ex-ante (i.e., evaluating hypothetical systems in similar settings) and combined ex-post – ex-ante evaluations of DSSs (Gardner, Marsden, and Pingry, 1993a). A relative assessment of the two approaches may be found in (Gardner, Marsden, and Pingry, 1993b). In virtually all such work, the system-user interface (UI) is held invariant as the predominant focus is not on the evaluation of alternative interface designs.

Studies on UI design and assessment have appeared in forums representing the education (e.g., Mcfarland, 1995; Park and Hannifin 1993), computer science/engineering (e.g., Bieber and Isokowitz, 1995; Garzotto and Mainetti, 1995; Kimura et al., 1995), behavioral science (e.g., Chen and Tsoi, 1988; Ware, 1988; Fisher et al., 1989; Fisher and Tan, 1989; Travis et. al., 1990; Kirschenbaum, 1994), and business computing (e.g., Sleeth, Wynne, and Saunders, 1988; Carr, 1992; Zeffane and Cheek, 1995) fields. Our work differs from such prior work in the following important respects: (a) we take the ex-ante approach to system evaluation where the hypothetical task (which has several real-world parallels) must be performed a time-constrained environment, and (b) we offer performance-based monetary rewards to the subjects where performance is measured in terms of speed, accuracy, and the extent of system help facility-independent action by the user.

Decision-making under externally-imposed time pressure has been studied both theoretically (e.g., Hwang, 1994) and empirically (e.g., Chen and Tsoi, 1988) before. Similarly, our reward mechanism draws on the pioneering work by Vernon Smith (Smith, 1976, 1982, 1985) in experimental economics and induced value theory. In the business computing arena, it has been used before (Gardner, Marsden, Pingry, 1993a) for ex-ante system evaluation. Both time pressures and performance-based rewards are factors that system users must contend with in the real-world. We explore some of the impacts of such factors (and others such as varying task complexity and information flow rates) upon human subjects given three different means of machine-to-human communication in a repetitive, hypothetical task environment.

2.0   The experimental platform

2.1   Platform and experimental highlights

Each laboratory session (in which a subject participates) is made up of 54 experiments and was designed to last no more than about 2 hours in duration (different subjects could take different times to complete a session). Each experiment involves a subject first learning a set of computer-presented classification rules. He/she then applies these rules to help classify each object, in a series of computer-generated objects (or samples), as belonging to a certain class or bin.

The classification rules describe how a computer-generated object with specific characteristics ought to be classified. These rules are presented to a subject using one of three information presentation modes called *text*, *image*, and *audio*. As the names imply, a rule set may be displayed in text form (on the computer screen), displayed in image form (on the computer screen), or in computer-replayed recorded human voice form (through computer-attached headphones).

Apart from the fact that a source presents information in a certain mode, the source supplies this information at a predetermined rate (i.e., speed) of information flow. There are three speeds: *slow*, *normal*, and *fast*. A subject is allowed to repeatedly invoke and study the rule set, as often as he/she desires, for a predetermined amount of time (called the Standard Rule Learning Time). Once this time has elapsed, or once the subject indicates that he/she is ready to start, the subject is presented with sample object information, one after the other, and is asked to apply the learned rules to classify each object, in turn, as belonging to one of several bins, based on its characteristics.

An object is characterized by a certain number of *views* (maximum of 6) and the number of *pins* in each view (maximum of 4). A specific experiment displays an object of a specific *complexity*. The greater the number of views displayed and the greater the possible number of pins per view, the more complex the object is regarded as being.

The information about a sample is provided using the same mode and flow rate as those used for the associated decision-rule set presentation. Once the information has been presented, a subject is given a predetermined amount of time (called the Standard Decision-making Time) within which he/she could: (i) seek re-presentation of sample information, (ii) seek information on which specific classification rule is applicable based on his/her recollection of sample characteristics (i.e., use the system's help facility), and (iii) make a classification decision. Whereas the original presentation of object information is for free,

224

seeking re-enforcement of object information through re-presentation requests incurs imputed costs in terms of delayed decision making: the longer a subject takes to make a correct final decision, the lesser the gross reward for that decision. Finally, an incorrect final decision, or not making a decision within the available time, results in a penalty (i.e., a negative reward). Depending on factors like the extent of information re-presentation demanded and the time in which a final decision is made (or no decision is made), a subject earns a net reward (or penalty).

The subject is then presented either with information on the next object in the series or the next rule set, if any. At any point during the session, a subject may look up his performance history to see statistics related to past samples and the total reward/penalty accumulated thus far. A session ends with each subject being paid a total amount which is the sum of a show-up fee (US$5/-) and any (positive) rewards earned. (In the case of a net penalty, a subject will only be paid the show-up fee.) The reward/penalty structure is set up such that the maximum payment a subject can earn in one session (including the show-up fee) is US$25/-

The platform, as it now stands, does not use color (the display uses various shades of gray). This was a deliberate choice made for the first set of experiments wherein we did not wish to have color as one of the variables.

2.2   Prototyping and refinement

The platform is implemented on a set of Gateway 2000 P5-120 machines using the Multimedia Toolbook 3.0 software. Prototype assessment and refinement was done over a period of several months with the assistance of 31 individuals (9 Ph.D. students (6 information systems majors, 1 decision science, 1 economics and 1 agricultural economics) 6 Masters students (3 information systems majors, 1 mechanical engineering, 1 electrical engineering, 1 computer science), 10 undergraduate students (6 information systems majors, 1 marketing, 1 accounting and economics, 1 mathematics, 1 electrical engineering), and 6 university employees (1 MIS manager, 1 MBA coordinator, 4 staff assistants).

These individuals also gave us their feedback on a Computerized Training Tool Set for use with actual subjects. We use the TSS itself as an instructional facility to help subjects learn how to use it proficiently and to become familiar with the experiment, its goals, and such. The resultant tool set contains 3 modules – an Experimental Overview, a Guided Platform Tour, and a Hands-on Session Provider. Their criticisms have enabled us to significantly refine the training capabilities of this tool set.

Finally, these individuals also provided us with feedback on the experimental environment – i.e., the temperature, lighting, and noise conditions in the laboratory, the seating arrangements for the subjects, and such. This feedback has enabled us to focus on a number of environmental issues to help subjects be as comfortable as possible when performing the experiments.

2.3   Real-world parallels

The hypothetical decision-making scenario described above encompasses characteristics similar to those of several realistic special cases. Examples include decision-making by crisis managers (such as the 911 system operators, the police department, the fire department, oil spill cleanup crews), stock market investors/brokers, and medical personnel such as doctors and nurses.

Situations handled by such individuals often have the following characteristics: the decision maker must operate under (sometimes severe) time constraints; the payoff (monetary or otherwise) is performance-based; the complexity of the situation could differ from instance to instance; the complexity of the situation could vary during the same instance. All of these decision-making settings involve (or could involve) the use of a computerized TSS. TSSs could assist by providing the decision maker with signals describing a situation, permit the review of those situational signals, store prescriptive rules for action, and assist with the recall and application of these rules.

2.4   Platform capabilities and possible extensions

The platform and approach described above may regarded as a "base scenario" for our experiments. This scenario may be customized and extended in a number of ways, depending on specific experimental goals, to create a number of special variants. Notably, one may:

(a) choose to hold constant or suitably vary the presentation mode, the flow rate, and/or the task complexity within a session, depending on experimental goals. Varying the mode and/or flow rate is tantamount to creating different information sources.

(b) create "composite" sources that can mix various modes and/or flow rates within an experiment (e.g., part of the information is presented in "audio" mode at the "normal" flow rate whereas the rest is presented in "image" mode at a "faster than normal" rate).

(c) allow a subject to pick an information source of his/her choice that is used with *all* experiments in that session or allow a subject to pick a mode of his/her choice for *each* experiment within the session,

(d) add color as yet another variable.

(e) extend the team decision-making scenario/platform to the more general case where one human deciding participant and one or more human supporting participants are involved. Each participant, in turn, forms a decision-making team with a computerized support system assisting him/her. Essentially, we have a team of teams.

(f) extend the scenario/platform to accommodate competitive decision-making situations where group members compete with one another for performance-based rewards. Each member may be a human-computer decision-making team or a team of teams as in (e).

(g) extend the scenario/platform to handle decision making with possibly less than complete information in the simple team, team of teams, and competitive group scenarios.

We hope to examine several such variants and extensions in the future.

3.0   Our experiments

We have been using the basic platform to examine one set of experiments from the many possible using 27 paid subjects. Each subject participates in three sessions spread across three consecutive days. In each session, we hold the mode constant. Thus, a subject may operate with text mode on day one, audio on day two, and image on day three. We picked the following three ways of sequencing the sessions: (a) <Text, Image, Audio>, (b) <Audio, Image, Text>, and (c) <Image, Text, Audio>. Nine subjects are assigned to each of these session orderings. Within a session, tasks are arranged in increasing order of task complexity. We consider three complexity levels, C1 (i.e., 1 view with a maximum of 4 pins), C2 (i.e., 2 views with a maximum of 4 pins/view), and C3 (i.e., 3 views with a maximum of 4 pins/view). Within each complexity level, subjects participate in experiments involving the three information flow rates Normal, Slow, and Fast. At each rate, the subject is offered a total of six experiments. A rule set precedes every two experiments in this subset of six experiments.

Before the subjects participate in the sessions, they go through the computerized tutorial session (made up of an introduction, an animated platform tour, and a hands-on practice session). Subjects are allowed to ask clarifications at any stage of this process and prior to beginning actual experiments. Before they begin the first session, the subjects also sign an agreement that explains the rules for participating in the study and payment terms. They then answer a short questionnaire that seeks to capture their pre-experimental attitudes toward information mode, flow rate, and task complexity. The subjects are offered the choice of accepting payment after each session or following all three sessions.

To help us determine values for the Standard Rule Learning and Standard Decision-making times for use in the actual experiments, we conducted a pre-study using 27 volunteer subjects (from a variety of backgrounds such as finance (7), education (5), information systems (3), english (2), and others (10)). All of these were undergraduates as we wished to limit the actual experiments to undergraduate subjects. Only one of the pre-study subjects had also participated in the prototyping process.

This is how the pre-study was conducted: We have 3 modes*3 flow rates*3 complexity levels = 27 possible experiments that a subject may be exposed to. We randomly picked 6 experiments for the first subject, two from each of the three possible modes but of different complexity levels. We repeated this process for each of the remaining subjects such that each of the 27 possible experiments had exactly 6 subjects participating in it. We allowed each subject to take as much time as he/she wanted for the rule learning and decision making activities for each experiment. We used the data gathered from the pre-study to establish the Standard Rule Learning Time as 180 seconds and the Standard Decision-making Time as 42 seconds. Of the 27 subjects in the real study, 9 had participated in the pre-study.

We are using the data gathered from our experiments to examine subject performance in terms of decision making effectiveness and speed under the different conditions mentioned. Also of interest to us are questions related to learning both within a session and across sessions and the impacts that such learning has on performance. Lastly, the actual data is being contrasted with pre-experimental data (gathered through the questionnaires) to help contrast perception with reality. The presentation will encompass the key issues discussed in this paper as well as the results of our data analysis.

228

References:

1. Bieber, M. and Isokowitz, T. (1995), "Designing Hypermedia Applications," *Communications of the ACM*, 38(8), 26-29.
2. Carr, H. H. (1992), "Factors that Affect User-friendliness in Interactive Computer programs," *Information and Management*, 22, 137-149.
3. Chen, H. And Tsoi, K. (1988), "Factors Affecting the Readability of Moving Text on Computer Display," *Human Factors*, 30(1), 25-33.
4. Fisher, D.L., Coury, B. G., Tengs, T. O., and Duffy, S. A. (1989), "Minimizing the Time to Search Visual Displays: The Role of Highlighting," *Human Factors*, 31(2), 167-182.
5. Fisher, D. L. And Tan, K. C. (1989), "Visual Displays: The Highlighting Paradox," *Human Factors*, 30(1), 25-33.
6. Gardner, C., Marsden, J. R., Pingry, D. E. (1993a), "The Design and Use of laboratory Experiments for DSS Evaluation," *Decision Support Systems*, 9, 369-379.
7. Gardner, C. Marsden, J. R., Pingry, D. E. (1993b), "DSS Evaluation: A Comparison of Ex-ante and Ex-post Evaluation Methods," in *Recent Developments in Decision Support Systems*, (Holsapple, C. W. and Whinston A. B., eds.), Berlin, Springer-Verlag, 439-455.
8. Garzotto, F. And Mainetti, L. (August 1995), "Hypermedia Design, Analysis, and Evaluation Issues," *Communications of the ACM*, 38(8), 74-86.
9. Holsapple, C. W. and Whinston, A. B. (1996), Decision Support Systems: A Knowledge-based Approach, Minneapolis/St. Paul, West.
10. Hwang, M. I. (1994), "Decision Making Under Time Pressure: A Model for Information System Research," *Information and Management*, 27, 197-203.
11. Kimura, T. D., Apte, A., Sengupta, S., Chan, J. W. (March 1995), "Form/Formula, A Visual Programming paradigm for User-definable Interfaces," *IEEE Multimedia*, 27-35.
12. Kirschenbaum, S.S. (1994), "Effects of Graphics and verbal Probability on Command Decision Making," *Human Factors*, 36(3), 406-418.
13. Mahmood, M. A., and Medewitz, J. N. (1985), "Impact of Design Methods on Decision Support System Success: An Empirical Assessment," *Information and Management*, 9.
14. McFarland, R.D. (Feb. 1995), "Ten Design Points for the Human Interface to Instructional Multimedia," T.H.E. Journal, 67-69.
15. Money, A., Tromp, D., Wegner, T. (June 1988), "The Quantification of Decision Support benefits Within the Context of Value Analysis," *MIS Quarterly*, 223-236.
16. Park, I. And Hannifin, M. J. (1993), "Empirically-based guidelines for the Design of Interactive Multimedia," *Educational Research and Technology Development*, 41(3), 63-85.

17. Sanders, G. L., and Courtney, J. F. (1985), "A Field Study of Organizational factors Influencing DSS Success, *MIS Quarterly*, 7.
18. Sharda, R.., Barr, S. H., McDonnell, J. C. (1988), "Decision Support System Effectiveness: A Review and an Empirical Test," *Management Science*, 34(2), 139-159.
19. Sleeth, R.G., Whynne, J., and Saunders, G. S. (1988), "The Case for Speech Synthesis: An Experiment in Human Engineering," *Information and Management*, 14, 225-233.
20. Smith, V. L. (1976), "Experimental Economics: Induced value Theory," *American Economic Review*, 66 (2), 274-279.
21. Smith, V. L. (1982), "Microeconomic Systems in Experimental Science," *American Economic Review*, 72(5), 923-955.
22. Smith, V. L. (1985), "Experimental Methods in Economics," in *The New Palgrave: A dictionary of Economic Theory and Doctrine*, (Eatwell, J., Milgate, M., and Newman, P., eds.), New York, Macmillan.
23. Snitkin, S. R. And King, W. R. (1986), "Determinants of the Effectiveness of Personal Decision Support Systems," *Information and Management*, 10, 83-89.
24. Travis, D. S., Bowles, S., Selton, J., and Peppe, R. (11990), "Reading from Color Display: A Psychophysical Model," *Human Factors*, 32(2), 147-156.
25. Ware, C. (1988), "Using Color Dimensions to Display Data Dimensions," *Human Factors*, 30(2), 127-142.
26. Zeffane, R. And Cheek, B. (1995), "The Differential Use of Written, Computer-based, and verbal information in an Organizational Context: An Empirical Exploration," *Information and Management*, 28, 107-121

PART 6

MULTIMEDIA EDUCATION

6.1

APPLICATION OF WORLD WIDE WEB ON CIVIC EDUCATION: A PROPOSED MODEL

Alfred Loo, Raymond Fu & Alan Lam
Lingnan College, Hong Kong

The Internet currently reaches over 30 millions of people in over 61 countries and there are around 300,000 internet users in Hong Kong. The number of Internet Services Providers (ISP) increases rapidly to over 40 in a years' period. The Internet is revolutionizing the way we work, learn and play. Although there are many different services on Internet, World Wide Web (WWW) is the most interesting browsing method. WWW is a distributed hypermedia system embedded in the Internet and it is a powerful education tool due to its multimedia capabilities. People can access the information stored in remote computer sites in any place, any time as long as they have a computer with suitable communication facilities. This is a paper to evaluate on the performance of the application. The paper allows not only the public access but also a promotion channel for Civic Education to exchange information with all participants.

1.0   Introduction

The Internet currently reaches over 30 millions of people [GVU's WWW User Surveys 1995] in over 61 countries [Comer 1995]. In a recent survey [Foley 1996], there are over 300,000 internet users in Hong Kong. The number of Internet Service Provider [Loo & Lo, 1995] increases rapidly to over 40 in a years period. The Internet is revolutionizing the way we work, learn and play [Boutel, et al, 1994; Crispen 1994; Foley 1996; Hoffman & Krol, 1993].

Although there are many different services on Internet [Loo & Chan 1995], WWW (World Wide Web) is the most interesting browsing method. WWW is a distributed hypermedia system embedded in the Internet, initiated by the European Laboratory for Particle Physics (CERN). In WWW, information, files, messages, images, sound clips, animation, etc. are displayed in hypertext (or hypermedia in the cases of sound & images) format. The specialty of hypertext is the ability to link to other sources. By clicking words or images, the users can be linked to other Web pages, this is idea of hypertext. The user could "jump" around in the Web from documents to documents without knowing where exactly the next stop will be, this is called "Web/Net Surfing". This is a very efficient way to access information in terms of time and manpower. These information may or may not be formally published paper, journals, or technical

Appendix 1

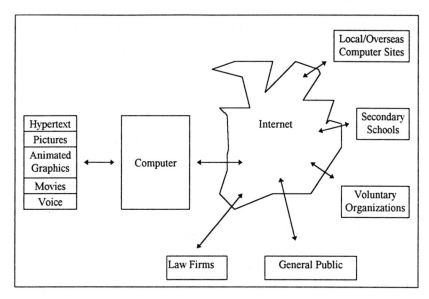

Figure 1: Proposed computer system

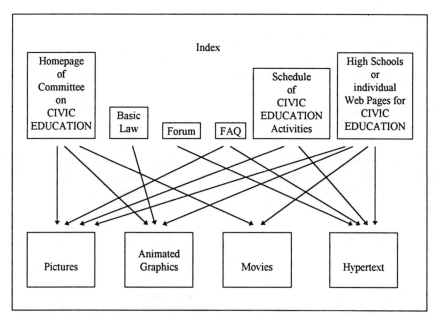

Figure 2: Hierarchy of design

menu, but this is a quick way to bypass the librarian, administration, snail-mail and to pick up the required information in this centralized but vast network.

The WWW is a powerful education tool due to its multimedia capabilities. The learning process can be more interesting than a regular classroom teaching. People can access the information stored in remote computer sites in any place, any time as long as they have a computer with proper communication facilities. We proposed to install a computer site (for civic education to promote Basic Law) which allows public access using the Internet technologies, particularly the WWW.

2.0   Aims and objectives

Aims :
- promote the concept of using Information Technology for the civic education
- provide an information center for Civic Education
- to evaluate the impact of using Information Technology on civic education

Objectives :
- set up a computer site (Fig. 1, 2 in Appendix 1) in Lingnan College which allows public access using the Internet technology:
    - to store the Basic Law (both Chinese and English version) with hypertext, pictures, animated graphics, movies and voice
    - to store the "promotion of civic education activities" by other organizations
    - to maintain a FAQ (Frequently Asked Questions with answer) for the civic education
    - to provide a forum on the Internet for the public to express their view or discuss issues about the civic education
- to produce CDs which contains the Basic Laws and related materials
- to set up a homepage for "Committee on Promotion of Civic Education"
- to provide computer aided education facilities for secondary schools for Civic Education
- to measure the efficiency of using Information Technology for civic education
- to provide seminars to secondary school or general public
    - to teach individual/organization to use Internet software such as Netscape, Java, etc.
    - to teach individual/organization to create Web pages for civic education
- to organize competition for Web pages design (about civic education)

- to provide facilities for secondary schools of HK & Overseas to exchange information of civic education
- to provide an archive site and to store historical civic education information for future research and planning related to civic education

3.0 Systems development

The proposed project requires the testing of the internet service using modems and telephones, and the technical set-up . In addition, how to generate computer art works for the internet sites, thus the project demands a large amount of memory and to create CDs for distribution in order to promote the site.

In bandwidth, the public will access our internet site through the high speed T1 telephone line. The telephone line is sponsored by JUCC and 7 higher education institutions in Hong Kong. The cost is roughly 6 millions per year. As traffic will increase due to public access to our internet site, $10000 will be allocated to computer service centre of Lingnan College as an additional cost.

estimated charges :

3000 M bytes x $1.75 (prime hours rate) + 4000 M bytes x $1,25 (non-prime rate)
= $10,250

Human Resources, the development and maintenance of the computer system will be a time consuming job,   thus a part-time experienced programmer is required for the job.

4.0 Pomontion and evaluation

There are several ways to promote this Web Site:

- advertise the web site through the homepage of the Government, Tertiary Institutes, Internet Service Providers
- distribution of CDs to secondary schools and companies
- use of conventional methods such as posters, mass mailing, competitions etc.

In addition, the project could be evaluated by monitoring the login rate of the users.   A survey will be carried out in the Web page, via email or by questionnaires and also aim at various levels of the general public.

5.0   Activities and schedules

Major activities of this project include:
- Installation of an Internet Web site
- Production of CDs with civic education material
- Competition for Web pages design
- Presentation of Seminars for Internet related technologies
- Evaluation of the efficiencies in using Internet technologies for civic education (The results will also be compared with traditional method)

Expected Outcome of this project
- Better educated people
- CDs
- a Web site
- Research papers
- Seminars
- Competition

(Tentative schedule is described in Figure 1.)

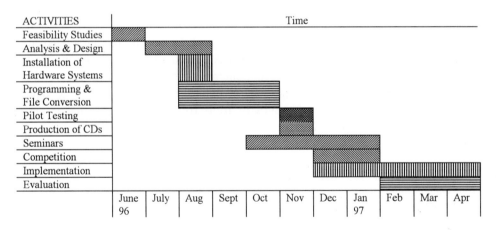

Figure 1: Schedule of the project

6.0   Limitations and constraints

Although the project is still under construction (by referring to fig.1), we encountered the following problems during application.

The cost of keeping a web site. It is necessary to forecast the volume of traffic on information transfer and the frequency for the information updating on the

238

site. If the frequency of updating is huge ,the speed on data transmission will be lowered and so as the transmission cost will be higher in maintaining the web site. **Systems maintenance.** To have a good quality web site, a steady and an experienced computer personnel (e.g. a programmer) is needed to modify the homepage or responsible for the normal routine maintenance process on the site. **Administrative work load.** Since the web site allows the public access, a lot of feedback will require further elaboration , analysis and even answer back. Hence, some expertise (e.g. the executive officers of the Civic Education Committee) have to work closely with the people working on the web site.

7.0   Conclusion and recommendations

The project certainly achieve objectives as listed in the above. In addition , we may consider that such homepage would certainly act as a rapid and cost-effective communications, in terms of worldwide information dissemination. Others, like marketing research, seeking for expert advice, peer communications and even advertise for recruitment. However, It is important to notice that since there is no central control of the information dissemination in internet services. Some information may be false and in some case, to create different problems about computer security.

To improve the situation, an experienced programmer is recommended to monitor the operation of such internet services, secondly, careful "filtering" of the information by some authorised administrative personnel to secure the proper handling for FAQ from the general public. Finally, it is better to have some more user-friendliness languages or tools (other JAVA) so that it may beneficial to more computer layman to write or to modify their own homepage.

Acknowledgment: I would like to acknowledge the following persons for their valuable contributions to this study, the executive officers of the Civic Education Committee and thanks are particularly made to the technical advice from Able Computer Consultants Co. Ltd. Lastly but not the least, I would like to thank for the cooperation and hard work from all the authors towards this project.

References:

1. Boutel, T, Torkington, N, Andreessen, M, Johnson, T (1994), *World Wide Web frequently Asked Questions,*
   http://sunsite.unsite.unc.edu/boutell/faq/www_faq.html

2. Crispen, P.C. <pcrispel@ua1vm.ua.edu> (1994), *Roadmap Workshop*, <listserv@ua1vm.ua.edu>,
3. Comer, Douglas E. (1995), *The Internet Book - Everything you need to know about computer networking and how the Internet works*, Prentice Hall International
4. Electronic Frontier Foundation (1994), *EFF's Guide to the Internet, v.2.21.*
5. Foley, Anna (1996), *Hong Kong Net account holders top 100,000 mark*, ComputerWorld Hong Kong, Vol XII No 18, March 14, 1996
6. GVU's WWW User Surveys (1995), http://www.cc.gatech.edu/gvu/user_surveys/survey-10-1995/, 15th May, 1996
7. Hoffman, E and Krol, Ed (1993), *What is Internet?*, University of Illinois
8. Krol, Ed (1992), *The Internet User's Guide and Catalog*, O'Reilly & Associates, Inc.
9. Liu, C, Peek, J, Jones, R, Buus, B, Nye, A (1994), *Managing Internet Information Services*, O'Reilly & Associates, Inc.
10. Loo, Alfred & Chan, Max (1995), *A Survey of On-line Services and their Applications*, The conference guide of the 3rd conference of HK Association for Education Communication and Technology, 1995
11. Loo, Alfred & Lo, David (1995), *Internet*, Able Computer Consultants Co. Ltd.

240

6.2

INTEGRATING THE WORLD WIDE WEB INTO MULTIMEDIA COURSES

David Inman
South Bank University, UK

The advantages of publishing on the World Wide Web have been reported on extensively. We encourage our students to publish on the Web, here at South Bank, but this would require students to learn to author material for publication on the Web. We have developed software at South Bank that allows automatic Web page generation from a Hypercard database of student content. This content is a set of reference reviews that encourage active reading. The practical details of how this is done are reported in this paper, and results and implications are presented.

1.0   Active reading

Like many University courses, particularly at post graduate level, we want our students to read around their subject as much as possible. Just giving out lists of material to read is rarely effective, however. Most students put reading from such lists as a low priority task, especially with the trend towards heavily assessed units.

We have developed an active reading approach based on the PQ4R technique of Anderson [1995], Gibson [1975], & others. This requires active reading, by focussing on questions, rather than passive attempts at absorbing the material. Advantages of active learning have been described in Bloom [1976].

The basic approach we adopt, is a modified version of the above, and works as follows:
1. Students choose their reading material (with tutor's guidance)
2. Students produce a structured review of the reference, which is input to a Hypercard database.
3. The structured review requires them to read actively, by producing several levels of abstraction. For example, this requires them to set a series of questions addressed by the reference, and then to answer these questions.
4. Students spend typically 10 - 20 hours on a 20 page reference. This encourages an in depth understanding of the original reference.

The end result of this is that each student has an excellent grasp of one reference in a subject area. However we want that understanding to be shared with their class mates, and future cohorts. As each review is input to a database, we can export all the reviews to Web pages, to achieve this aim.

2.0 Database structure

In order to encourage active reading, along the Anderson PQ4R model, each student must produce a reconstruction of the original reference in 4 layers. These give increasing detail:
1. The top layer gives the title, author, source and the student adds a set of key words.
2. The next layer is a brief abstract, which must be in the student's own words even if the original reference has an abstract.
3. Next are 10-15 questions which are addressed by the original reference. These act as a summary layer, and is often the most effective way to see if the reference is of interest. The questions are set and then answered. Student find this particularly difficult.
4. Finally there is an overview, or rational reconstruction of the original reference, in about 2000 words.

These layers are input to a Hypercard database, which performs some routine input checks, and gives feedback on word counts. This shows the top layer of one reference review:

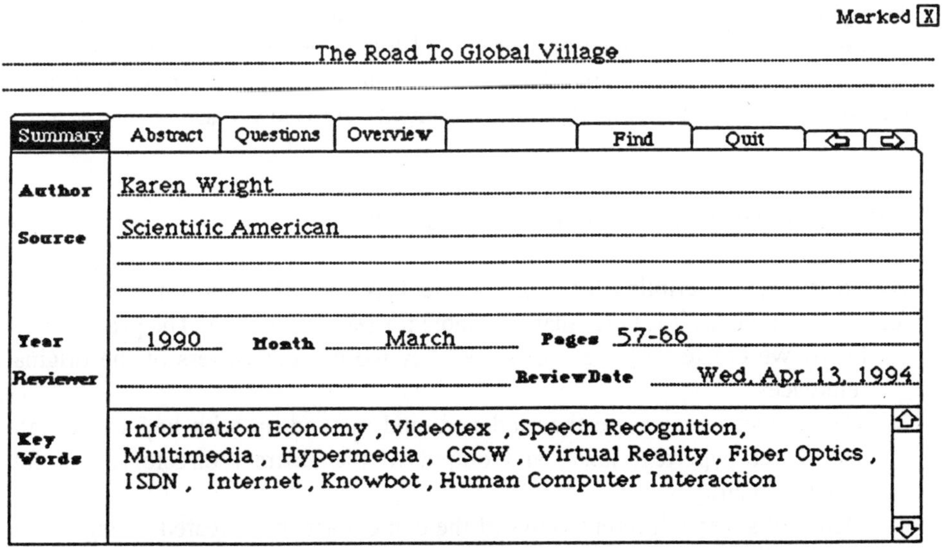

Marked ☒

The Road To Global Village

| Summary | Abstract | Questions | Overview | | Find | Quit | ⟲ | ⟱ |

Author Karen Wright

Source Scientific American

Year 1990 **Month** March **Pages** 57-66

Reviewer **ReviewDate** Wed. Apr. 13. 1994

Key Words Information Economy , Videotex , Speech Recognition, Multimedia , Hypermedia , CSCW , Virtual Reality , Fiber Optics , ISDN , Internet , Knowbot , Human Computer Interaction

Figure 1

3.0   Exporting from the database to the web

Any database has structure, and we can use this to produce several views of the content. These views can then be exported to Web pages, with suitable menu and overview pages giving access to the different views as well as the content itself.

The database has HyperTalk scripting additions that allows the database to be marked up into linked Web pages. We hope this makes the students' work widely available for future cohorts, gives them pride in creating and viewing their work and further encourages active reading.

These pages represent all the reviews created by all students. For example it is easy to see all the reviews which share a common key word.

There are many such views. You can view all the reviews in the subject area by:
*   title
*   abstract
*   key word
*   questions posed by reference
*   writer
*   date
*   reviewer

and there are extensive hypertext links between these views, and the main review itself.

This shows the directory structure of the Web pages created. This structure allows the content to be well organised, and for the Web pages to be re-used as much as possible. For example there are many links to the full reference reviews directory from the key word view of the content, and vice versa.

4.0   Scripting to generate the web pages

Hypercard uses a scripting language "HyperTalk" and this has some advantages for the task here, as it is particularly suitable for text processing. The process is:

1. Firstly we create a glossary of sorted key words, and writers of the original references.
2. The student reviews are then indexed, and marked up with key word, date and writer hypertext links, and output to the abstract directory, and full review directory.
3. Menus of several different views of the content are then created, along with a top level overview. For example, this allows key words to be viewed

alphabetically and by frequency, with links to all the references which contain the given key word, and further links to the actual occurrence of the key word in the full review.

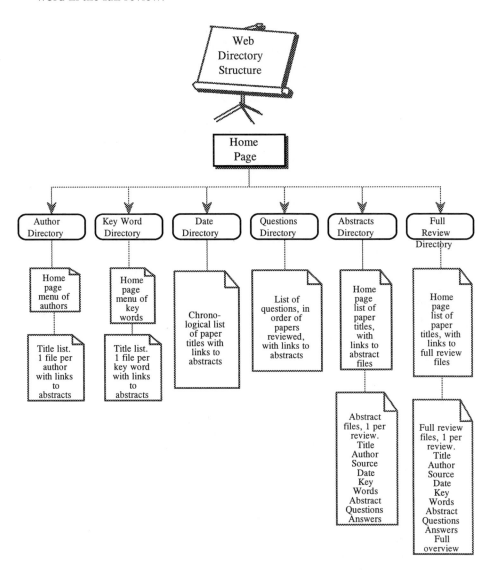

This shows a sample of HyperTalk script that takes a set of key words "kws" and marks up a piece of text "text" with links from each key word to the main key word page. The main loop is on each key word "kw". If the key word is found in the text (offset returns the start character if found, 0 otherwise) a link is made to the main key word page. There is the option of tagging the key word in the text as well, to allow a jump directly to the key word in the text later.

```
    repeat with i = 1 to the number of lines in kws
        put line i of kws into kw
        put the number of chars in kw - 1 into NC
        put offset(kw,text) into sc
        if sc is not 0 then
          put "</A>" after char sc + NC of text
          put "kw"&i into kwd
          if noTag is "" then
            put "<A NAME="&kwd&"></A>" into t
          else
            put "" into t
          end if
          put "<A HREF="&quote&
            "../keywords/"&kwd&quote&">" after t
          put t before char sc of text
          exit repeat
        end if
    end repeat
end repeat
```

This shows some of the HTML generated from the HyperTalk script. As you can see no attempt has been made to make is particularly easy to read. Instead comments in the HyperTalk explain functionality.

```
<HTML>
<HEAD>
<TITLE>Key words Index : Hypermedia</TITLE>
</HEAD>
<BODY>
<h1> Key words Index : Hypermedia </h1>
<HR>
<h5>
<A HREF ="../index.html">Menu</a> |
<A HREF ="../review/index.html">Titles</a> |
<A HREF ="../abstract/index.html">Abstracts</a> |
<A HREF ="../keywords/index.html">Keywords</a> |
<A HREF ="../author/index.html">Writers</a> |
<A HREF ="../date/index.html">Dates</a> |
<A HREF ="../question/index.html">Questions</a> |
<A HREF="./reviewer/index.html">Reviewers</A> |
<hr> </h5>
```

Welcome to the key word index for Hypermedia <P>

Click here to view key words by
<A HREF="#freq"><B>frequency</B></A> </UL>
<HR><H3>Alphabetic keywords </H3>
<UL>
<A HREF="kw1">Activation</A>

This piece of HTML is to create a menu bar at the top of an introductory page, for a set of reviews on Hypermedia.

A small set of reference reviews on Hypermedia can be viewed at:

http://www.scism.sbu.ac.uk/~inmandw/review/hypermedia/index.html

5.0   Alternative views of the content

There are several ways that the content of each reviewer is combined into a whole. Hypertext links provide the connections between different reviews, and different views of the reviews, and separate overview pages allow this structure to be navigated.

If the browser clicks on a key word, perhaps from the frequency sorted list of key words, they will be taken to the titles of the references that contain that key word. Clicking on a title takes the browser to the first occurrence of that key word in the full reference review. Clicking on a key word in a review, on the other hand, links to the key word view, and shows all titles that contain that key word.

One problem with hypertext links, is that it can be easy to be disorientated. To help with this each Web page has a menu of navigation buttons at the top to allow easy re-entry. The menu is consistent across all Web views, and the linear sequence corresponds to the depth. This helps to orientate the user.

6.0   Evaluation

We will evaluate the system from a systems point of view and also from the users perspective.

6.1   System

The HyperTalk code is about 32K in total, and being semi-compiled (ie compiled on first interpretation) is not especially fast. We found that it takes about 30 minutes to create a set of Web pages from about 1Meg of content.

For about 1 megabyte of review content produced by students:
- 2 megabytes of linked, marked up and indexed web pages are produced
- The process is completely automatic. The user needs only specify the name of the top level directory, and all sub-directories, marked up reviews, menus and links are created automatically.
- Large databases can thus be processed overnight

Processing is carried out on the client machine, not the server. The Web directory structure produced is then ftp'd to the server. All file names are created by the HyperTalk, and are unique within the top level directory. All links are relative links, so the top level directory is completely portable.

Our experience of using Hypercard is that it has good text processing functionality, and so makes creation of HTML quite easy. It was easily extended (via XFCNs written in C) for file/directory management. The scripting language is easy to learn, but has limited array handling. It is semi-compiled , and so it is rather slow, but this is no real problem for Web page generation with an update cycle of perhaps twice a year.

It has also been used for some Web directory management, such as updating links throughout a directory of Web files. Several hundred files can be examined and have their links updated in less than 15 minutes.

6.2   User

Students seem pleased to find that they can publish their reviews at a push of a button, and can easily browse other student's work. Because their review appears as part of a much larger linked set of pages, it seems to add more value to their work. They seem to take more care when producing their review if they know it will appear on the Web!

7.0   Alternative systems

We already had the database of reviews in HyperCard format, so we scripted that to export the Web pages. However if you started without a database, and wanted a well supported product, it might be worth evaluating "Internotes". Lotus Corp. released in April 1996 "Internotes" which extends Lotus Notes. It lists the database views as hypertext links on the home page, and converts each Notes document into an HTML file. It converts Notes doclinks into hypertext links and Notes tables into HTML tables. It also converts bitmaps in Note documents into inline .GIF files. For more info on Internotes see: http://www.internotes.lotus.com/

8.0   Future enhancements

At present, the students input their reviews to a HyperCard database. This is inconvenient for students who like to work on PCs at home, so using Web forms to capture reviews would be sensible.

The key words used at present are those from an edited list of the students' key words (excluding some). It would be better, perhaps, to obtain a list of standard glossary items for the domain, and use these instead. Minority key words would thus be excluded, and important key words would definitely appear.
It would be useful also to allow links to key word roots, or to similar entries, perhaps by using some thesaurus. In addition, links to key words should perhaps show the most important key word entry first, rather than jump to any occurrence of a key word.

Finally, and definitely for the future, it would be good to apply natural language processing techniques, to obtain a summary of review by content as well as key word. Similar content could then be shown by similarity maps for example.

9.0   Conclusion

We have found benefit in converting a database in one format (HyperCard), into another (linked Web pages). The process is automatic, requires no HTML coding, and is tolerably fast. We found the HyperTalk scripting language suitable for the task.

Student seem to enjoy seeing their original content published widely, which allows wider distribution of each student's work both within their cohort and between cohorts. This seems to encourage better quality work on production of the content, and a more valuable resource is created from this work.

We plan in the future to use NLP techniques to make this conversion process more valuable.

248

References:

Web URLs
1. Example reviews on the Web
2. http://www.scism.sbu.ac.uk/~inmandw/review/hypermedia/
3. Lotus Internotes info at http://www.internotes.lotus.com/

Books:
1. Anderson, J.R. "Cognitive Psychology and its Implications" Freeman, 1995
2. Bloom, B. S. , "Human characteristics and school learning", McGraw Hill, 1976
3. Gibson, E.J., Levin, H. "The psychology of reading" MIT Press , 1975

Periodicals:
1. Inman, D. and Davies, G., "Computer Assisted Student Centred Assessment ", Proc. 3rd Annual Conference of the Teaching of Computing ", Dublin, Sept. 1995

6.3

UNIVERSITY OF LA VERNE AND GTE: A PARTNERSHIP IN DELIVERING GRADUATE BUSINESS PROGRAMS THROUGH INFORMATION TECHNOLOGY

A. Ispahani, D.S. Kung and E.J. Pilafidis
University of La Verne, USA

This case study describes a pilot program between the University of La Verne and GTE Corporation to provide business programs to GTE employees, who are dispersed in many locations throughout the western U.S. The paper explores the challenges facing the University (curriculum, faculty-student interaction, program effectiveness), and GTE's concerns (technology selection, remote sites, personnel training and related costs). It is concluded that such new delivery systems in business education open opportunities to serve students' needs. Yet, they also represent significant departures from traditional instructional methods, and require careful discussion among faculty, and with potential Corporate sponsors to insure program quality.

1.0 Introduction

The use of information and multimedia technology in universities in the United States is rapidly expanding, with more schools providing information and multimedia equipped computer labs and classrooms. Another trend is the establishment of on line institutions, "virtual universities," to serve students in new and innovative ways. Furthermore, according to the Chronicle of Higher Education, 64% of business studies courses require students to purchase their own personal computers (Wilson, 1993).

This explosion in the use of information technologies in universities is supported by extensive research on how such technology should support the knowledge-based organization, and how partnerships between information systems and business management should be formed and operated (CIO, 1994). In Business Schools another application of information technology is gaining favor, namely group support systems for teaching case-based classes ((Lewis, 1996). Research on how multimedia technology can be used to bring new depth and dimension to classrooms and laboratories extends beyond business programs, and includes sciences and engineering as well (Illman, 1994).

In this dynamic environment it is useful to study the issues that universities and corporations are facing as they implement and use such powerful new tools and processes.   In this regard, this paper describes a pilot program under development between the University of La Verne in California and GTE Corporation's Western Regional organization, headquartered in Dallas, Texas.

The program involves the delivery of business education programs and courses by the University to remote GTE sites (such as small offices, stations, and service centers), through the use of information and multimedia technology.   Even though this potential partnership is in the early stages of definition and negotiations between the university and GTE, it nevertheless represents a useful case study of the rationale of using such technologies in the higher education arena, particularly for programs involving working professionals in multiple sites.

The paper will outline the relevant background information on both organization, the University and GTE, will review the motivations and potential benefits for establishing such programs and delivery methods, and finally the managerial challenges facing both ULV and GTE in the design and implementation phases of this potential cooperative arrangement will be examined.

2.0   Organizational background

In order to develop an understanding of the considerations in both   organization of how to best design and deliver ULV business courses to remote GTE locations throughout the western United States, the following background information is offered:

2.1   GTE corporation

With revenues of $20 billion in 1995, GTE is one of the largest publicly held telecommunications companies in the world.   GTE is also the largest U.S.- based local telephone company and a leading cellular-service provider -- with wireline and wireless operations that form a market area covering more than one third of the country's population.   GTE also is a leader in government and defense communications systems and equipment, aircraft-passenger telecommunications, directories and telecommunications-based information services and systems.

Internally, GTE comprises many divisions located throughout the United States, with operations that extend throughout the world.   GTE World Headquarters, located in Stamford, Connecticut is home of GTE International, GTE Foundation and major staff functions for the corporation.   In addition to traditional and cellular telecommunications products, GTE is active in offering products and services in video games, CD-ROM computer games, video-based communications solutions for businesses, Internet and intelligent network services, and advanced software services for the wireless industry, among others.

In the United States, GTE is organized regionally, and by product division. Its telephone operations based in Dallas, Texas, provide voice, video, and data products and services through more than 23 million access lines in the western U.S. and some international locations. These telephone operations have linked eight technology solutions centers around the country with real-world multimedia applications (Pappalardo, 1995).

These Operations employ thousands of technical, marketing, sales, and administrative personnel. Such a large organization has diverse training and educational needs. The regional GTE human resources department in Dallas, and particularly the Training Section, is responsible with developing a variety of training programs, as well as working educational institutions to support the needs of their employees. For example, using CD-ROM products, GTE's training archives include sales training with audio, video and high motion sequence for installation/repair training materials (Trowbridge, 1994).

2.2   University of La Verne

The University was founded in Southern California in 1891. It is a comprehensive Institution offering bachelor's, master's, and doctoral degrees to over 6,000 students. Major units of the University are located throughout California, Alaska, and Europe; Central America, Asia and Africa are to have satellite operations in the near future. La Verne is a private university, accredited by the Western Association of Schools and Colleges, offering a student/faculty ratio of 19:1, and professors give the student one-on-one academic and advising support.

The School of Business and Economics, with a student body of 2,500, offers undergraduate and graduate programs in Management, Marketing, International Business, Accounting, Finance, Economics, Human Resources, and joint programs in Health Care Administration and a joint MBA - J.D degree. In 1968 the University began an innovative outreach initiative by establishing the School of Continuing Education and offering the opportunity to earn degrees at over 150 locations in California, Alaska, and overseas. This outreach provides an opportunity for people to take ULV programs at geographic locations convenient to their homes or work places.

This core competence that ULV has developed over the last thirty years has been of benefit to numerous employers who have supported the education of thousands of their employees through tuition refund programs at many such ULV locations and centers. The reputation that these programs have enjoyed, resulted in GTE approaching ULV with the idea of a pilot program for employees in remote locations, utilizing information and multimedia technology.

3.0   GTE'S needs and motivations

Even though GTE's training organization in Texas develops and delivers many programs to groups of employees, there is still an important need to be resolved, namely to deliver educational programs to remote employee populations. Throughout the Western U.S. GE has numerous small offices in remote sites, which todate have not been reached by traditional Schools. Since GTE is very decentralized, the needs of such employees in those locations are the responsibility of the Dallas, Texas training department.

As a result, GTE contacted the University of La Verne's School of Continuing Education to explore the joint development and implementation of such a delivery system, specifically for business courses. The vision for such a delivery system included information and multimedia technology and courseware, and excluded any on site instruction. GTE's interest in ULV's programs is   based on ULV's long history of off site adult education, and contacts in California between both organizations.

4.0   Benefits of a potential partnership

Both GTE and ULV would benefit from such a partnership. For GTE, the potential of customizing business education programs and courses for clusters of their employees, in remote sites, is an important benefit. Also, since GTE's network and expertise could be part of   the eventual delivery system, no new training would be needed on how to use such an information system, and related costs would be reduced.

For ULV, this approach to education represents an opportunity to increases competencies in multimedia technologies, and to learn from this pilot program how to deliver courses to individual students, or small clusters of students, in remote sites. Additionally, this expertise in information technology based delivery systems of graduate and undergraduate academic programs, fits with the University's vision of addressing and meeting the emerging life-long needs of a diverse student body.

5.0   Academic considerations

For the pilot program the potential partners have selected ULV's graduate business program for experienced professionals (MBA), since this best suits GTE's population in the   various remote Western locations.   At ULV, the program calls for quantitative and qualitative content, and requires up to fourteen courses, most of which involve heavy interaction between   professors and students.

Methods of instruction include, lectures, student presentations, student team projects, in-class discussions, guest speakers, and others.   Technology in the classroom includes the traditional audio/visual equipment, as well as lab top computers and CD-ROM multimedia, for simulations, presentations, Internet access and research, library access, etc.

For student assessment purposes, each of these courses involve exams, term papers, and individual and team student presentations.   Course and instructor assessment is based on student feedback and collegial reviews.

1. Even though the delivery of such courses over the GTE Network is technically feasible, there are a number of questions to be resolved in order to design an academically acceptable system of on- line instruction:
2. How to achieve a significant level of interaction between instructors and students, and among students themselves?
3. How to best utilize Internet technology with a student body in different time zones and locations, and with students that travel frequently, and who potentially may be relocating during the degree program?
4. How should the curriculum and/or course content be changed to fit the needs of this student population (and others like it)?

From the perspective of ULV's faculty, these are important issues, representing drastic departures from more traditional instructional methods, and requiring careful consideration.

6.0   Technical considerations

From a system design stand point, this pilot program requires delivery of lecture and other instructional material to multiple locations, each representing one or more students. Delivery system cost considerations are also a significant factor. For example, video teleconferencing, in its present form, appears to be uneconomical when the multiple locations of the students are considered.

Internet and multimedia technologies therefore represent the more viable approaches. Interactive technologies, including e-mail, electronic bulletin boards, multimedia/CD-ROM, in some combination and depending on the particular course, would be essential for such a program. Yet, it is also important to consider the complexity of multimedia technology from a user standpoint, since often users need to be both creative artists and integrators if all-in-one, almost plug-and-play capabilities are not available in the system (Trowbridge, 1994). In this regard GTE has already built-in multimedia capability between most of their sites and will utilize it in this partnership.

Yet, some amount of "hard copy" and in person communications will remain essential. According to Cabbell Smith, assistant director of communications at The Fuqua School of Business at Duke University "there likely always will be many contexts where written pieces and other forms of communication are more appropriate and effective in communicating with targeted audiences, such as at school forums." (Smith, 1995).

7.0   Conclusion

A pilot program between GTE and ULV to deliver business programs, through information technology, to GTE employees in remote locations in the western United States, has many significant benefits. Namely, students who would otherwise have very limited access to academic programs, other than through correspondence, would greatly benefit from on-line and multi-media technology.

Faculty would also be able to benefit from this delivery approach in many ways. For example, the access of up-to-date information and the opportunity to interact with experts in various disciplines, are important advantages. As a sign of such interest, the Governor of California and higher education leaders are planning the launch of a collaborative on line college, a "virtual university" that could deliver instruction to students from Fresno to Tokyo.

Yet, if the program is designed to be delivered largely on line, many traditional academic approaches would not be possible. Clearly the most fundamental change involves the loss of direct human contact between professors and students. It is therefore important that before a collaborative effort between a University and a corporate sponsor is established for delivery of academic programs in the on line environment, the following considerations must be addressed:

1. How will the academic integrity of the programs be safeguarded? Is there potential for on site instruction to supplement on line programs?

2. What resources and expertise will each organization commit to the program?
3. What structural and operating mechanisms need to be set up for the effective design and implementation of the program?

It is therefore recommended, largely based on the literature of strategic alliance management, that potential partners consider the following (Pilafidis, 1995):

1. A joint steering committee should be established by both organizations, at the earliest stages of negotiations.
2. Program and delivery system decisions should be made jointly by the partners.
3. Conflicts should be addressed directly and early-on.
4. The motivations, interests, and expectations of both organizations need to be discussed openly, and in the early stages of partner selection and subsequent negotiations.

If such an approach can be agreed on, both organizations can look forward to a potentially rewarding experience as they further develop this collaborative effort.

References:

1. Anonymous (1994), "A Valuable Return Engagement," CIO, 7(14), 1-4.
2. Illman, D.L. (1994), "Multimedia Tools Gain Favor for Chemistry Presentations," Chemical & Engineering News, 72(19), 34-40.
3. Lewis, L.F. (1996), "Using Group Support Systems in the Teaching of International Business," Journal of Teaching in International Business, 7(4), 31-47.
4. Papparaldo, D. (1995), "GTE Connects Centers," Communications Week, (562), 28.
5. Pilafidis, E.J. (1995), "Managerial Operating Mechanisms in Non-Equity Strategic Alliances," Academy of International Business, Annual Conference Proceedings.
6. Smith, C. (1995), "Business Schools Stake Their Claim In Cyberspace: Harnessing The World Wide Web," Newsline AACSB, 25(4), 2.
7. Trowbridge, D. (1994), "Doceo Dumps Multimedia Guesswork," Computer Technology Review, 14(7),19.
8. Trowbridge, D. (1994), "Multimedia Ready for Plug 'n Play?," Computer Technology Review, 14(7), 1-8.
9. Wilson, D.L. (1993), "Computer Revolution Changing the Way Business Schools Teach Their Courses," The Chronicle of Higher Education, 40(8), 31-32.

6.4

ARCHITECTURE ELEMENTS FOR HIGHLY-INTERACTIVE EDUCATION-ORIENTED APPLICATIONS

C.K. Leung
Lingnan College, Hong Kong

Traditional teaching is carried out through lectures and tutorial lessons, which heavily relies on individual teachers and textbooks. Such method has shortcomings. For example, it is difficult to grip everyone's attention within a class, and it lacks mutual communications especially when introducing those difficult and "boring" subjects, or in big classes. Thus, students are usually unable to achieve the best result of learning. To counter these problems, in this paper, a detailed review of the requirements of education-oriented applications and current research issues is presented, and thereafter, a project of multimedia application in education is introduced aiming to build a common framework of design principles of good educational software.

1.0   Introduction

Today, traditional teaching through lectures alone is not sufficient for good student learning. Teaching students especially in big class is not an easy task due to their different levels of learning abilities, and it lacks communications. In addition, certain aspects of subjects may be difficult for students to learn merely with lectures and textbooks. Therefore, lots of effort is usually required to smooth the knowledge building after lecture, such as tutorial lessons.

To improve the quality of teaching and learning, many innovative measures have been introduced into traditional teaching method, such as radio, TV, audio and video tapes, and computer-assisted instructions. However, many of these measures have failed to improve or have little impact on the quality of learning. A phenomena as described by (Adam, 1993), "The history of educational reform has shown that 'innovative' technologies that use a different medium from paper have done little to benefit learning." Adam (Adam, 1993) further stresses that "The content of instruction, not the means of its conveyance is what influences performance results." So far, there is still no generic principles about the design of educational systems.

With the technology advances, in particular, multimedia technologies which are able to combine audio data, video, text, graphics, and animation into an unified application, it appears that the real opportunity has come for computer assisted teaching and learning applications. From the research point of view, further work is required on the design principles of educational software in terms of Human-Computer Interactions (HCI) and Graphical User Interface (GUI) design.

2.0 Characteristics of using educational software

Using educational software has many advantages over the traditional teaching method. Generally, by contrast, a educational software can make learning on an one-to-one or as-needed basis, which have individualized attention, immediate interaction, and feedback, present users with tasks that interest them, and the audio-visual presentation readily absorbed, allow users to be inquisitive and explore, offer users the possibility of recovery from failure by asking persistent questions and mastering the material before moving on without embarrassment, put learners in control of a task, and encourage students to take most efficient path to mastery, and be consistent in instruction.

Because of these claimed advantages, it has become possible that using educational software can overcome the conceived shortcomings of traditional teaching. Therefore, significant research has been carried out in this area to pursue such goals (Dewey, 1916) (Schank, 1993,1994).

3.0 Problems with current educational software

Computer-assisted instruction has been playing a major role in educational reform. When multimedia technology emerged and proliferated, the belief of using of computer system in education is getting even stronger. Consequently, many educational software were developed. However, not many of them were applied successfully. The reason, as Schank (Schank, 1993) explained, is that the dominant educational paradigm in computer based instruction has been what can best be described as "page-turning architecture," and therefore, they asked students to do little more than "press button for next page" for video or graphics. Such software shows no creativity in terms of innovative educational method, and exposes lack of understanding of the problems with current education system among those developers.

Most designers of educational software lacked computer science expertise, and they tried to implement outdated theories of learning. Even when designers did have computer science expertise, their lack of knowledge about learning and teaching forced them to copy existing programs. Today, though there are multimedia computers with exciting new capabilities, the content of instruction, not the means of its conveyance is what influence performance results (Adam, 1993). This is in line with Scardamalia's comments (Scardamalia, 1993), who says "Traditional knowledge reproduction strategies limited potential for advancing knowledge, and often are not even very effective for purposes of memorization and organization of knowledge." He regards that the most conspicuous failure is of those educational software is in the development of understanding.

Creating educationally effective multimedia software means taking seriously the idea of learning by doing, which was first introduced by (Dewey, 1916), and focusing on understanding and supported learning in entirely new ways, with vital attention to the skills of social interaction and participation. Pea (Pea, 1993) points out, "In contrast to learning-before-doing, which is the model of most educational settings, learning-by-doing is a model in which learners are increasingly involved in the authentic practices of communities through learning conversations and activities involving expert practitioners, educators, and peers." Thus, good educational software is active, not passive, and ensures that users are doing, not simply watching.

4.0   Development requirements

The overall architecture of the multimedia educational system is summarized by (Schank, 1994) as follows:
1. A simulation of the task to be learned is needed.
2. An on-demand video database that can supply relevant video as needed is necessary.
3. Controls must be given to the student that allow user control of the process.

Like any educational environment, multimedia systems should be designed for compatibility with people's powerful natural learning mechanism. A simulation-based learning environment implies that students have access to video clips of teachers commenting on what they had just done and answering questions that arose. Therefore, in a multimedia environment, it is necessary to have anticipated where questions might arise and to have previously videotaped and catalogued the answers to these questions. Such measures are also applicable for social simulations (Blevis, 1991)(Kass, 1994).

One method to shift control from a programme itself to the user, as suggested in (Schank, 1993), is to use a set of buttons, such as Why, How, What, Too Hard, No Way, and Boring, thus allow a student to stop anything that is going on and find out what he/she needs to know.

For those topics which are difficult or boring to learn, the incidental learning architecture was introduced (Schank, 1993). It creates tasks whose end results are inherently interesting and can be used to impart dull information, such as Geography (Kass, 1994) and Biology (Edelson, 1993).

5.0   Research issues

For a successful educational software, research on the framework of an all encompassing task that both motivates the students and guides the teaching is crucial, which becomes a hot research topic today. Also, the applications of educational software in different aspects of learning, such as teaching, tutoring, and doing exercises, and in different fields of education, such as Business and Engineering, are very challenging. Distributed multimedia learning environments which extend teaching, learning, and material resources beyond the limits of individual classrooms is a more advanced issue (Hewitt, 1992). Then, established collaborative technology learning environments enables project-enhanced science learning among remote project partners using telecommunication networks (Pea, 1993).

Apart from these issues, there is also urgent need for powerful software development tools or toolkits, which will make the development easier and quicker. To develop a good multimedia educational software, using a multimedia-support tool or toolkit is crucial for the successful implementation of the framework built. An ideal software tool will allow teachers and other experts without programming experience to construct educational software. Thus, in the near future, it is expected to see more software tools being developed, and to provide the right environment for fundamental reforms in education.

6.0   Project initiation

Through the above review, it has shown that multimedia computing has real potential in education. An intelligently designed computer program can make a significant and positive difference in the way that people learn. Such technology will engage users by drawing upon and cultivating people's natural inclination to learn. As concluded in (Scardamalia, 1993), a real educational software will alter educational discourse so that knowledge reproduction processes give way to knowledge-building processes.

At Lingnan College, there are enormous opportunities for the research and development of multimedia educational systems. For instance, some introductory courses at the College about computer systems could be partially or fully taken by using multimedia programs. Also, many tutorial lessons which usually require repetitive efforts of the tutors can be carried out in a similar way. By doing so, many man hours can be saved to be spent on research, and more importantly, the quality of learning can be increased through the use of well designed and highly interactive multimedia packages.

A research project is then proposed to explore the viability of using multimedia programs in education, and to build a common framework of design principles of good educational software. Then, the framework could be used to develop more profound applications in other aspects of teaching, such as tutorial and exercise, and in other areas, e.g. Business and Engineering.

To achieve these objectives, there were several major tasks laying ahead: firstly, identifying suitable areas for the development, secondly, exploring and specifying the requirements of educational software for achieving the best learning result through user and computer interactions, thirdly, developing and evaluating the multimedia software for the areas identified, and finally, expanding the framework to other fields.

6.1   Requirement analysis

One of the objectives of this project is to construct a general framework of educational software for development. In this respect, some starting work has already been done. In particular, the work by (Schank,1993) was very significant. He summarizes some general requirements of educational software:

1. Software should encourage learning by doing by providing no-easily accomplishable tasks that motivate students.
2. Recognizing what to do is much easier than recalling what to do. Multiple choice must be eliminated.
3. Most interesting questions have no agree-on answers. Software should encourage students to explore a variety of possible answers.
4. Students respond to well-told stories. Software must have good stories to tell.
5. No computer should be allowed to be in control of the educational process. Students should have the power to determine what is coming next.

Though some of these points may not be relevant or sufficient for this research, they provide a good starting point, rather than starting from scratch. Through the development of this project, it is expected that these requirements are verified and enhanced, and more comprehensive framework is developed for multimedia educational software development.

6.2 Current Development

Currently at the College, the demand for educational software is strong. Along with this project, there is another teaching development project, also led by the Writer, aiming to improve the quality of teaching on a College-wide basis. It is encouraging to see that the potential of computer-assisted learning has now been widely recognized by the public. Their acceptance has proved crucial for the success of this research and development.

1. Student controls with buttons, such as Why, How, What, Too Hard, Boring, Back, Forward, and Stop on the screen.
2. Providing no-easy questions (no multiple choices) after each session, and only satisfactory answers will lead to the next session.
3. Hints and suggestions for additional preparation to the students who have performed poorly in answering the questions.
4. Different methods of presentation of same materials for different levels of students, i.e. Hard, Medium and Easy.
5. System logs to monitor the progress of students, in particular regarding poor performance records.

Initial development was concentrating on the subject of Marketing Management within the Department of Marketing and International Business. The main features of these software could be summarized as follows:
Multimedia based with sound, picture and video clips.

6.3 Future Work

Current development is limited within the tutorial lessons, and it is expected to introduce such applications to the classroom as well as doing exercises or assignments. They do have different requirements in terms of interactions. Also, more topics and subjects need to be covered, such as Information Systems Management and Computer Networks. Moreover distributed educational system is the likely direction to go for in the near future, and new technology, such as Teleconferencing, will be helpful if it is introduced into the system. Thereafter, the framework built could be used as reference for more profound applications in other areas, such as Business and Manufacturing. The ultimate objective of this research would be to create a common conceptual framework which is necessary for IS in general to be productive.

262

7.0   Conclusion

Through this research, it was intended to clarify several issues concerning education-oriented applications, such as system framework and application domains. The objective has been to apply multimedia technology to various domains, such as teaching, tutoring, and exercise, then, to build a common framework of an all encompassing task that achieve the optimum result of understanding. In this paper, much effort was devoted to the analysis of human factors within teaching and other related aspects regarding computer assisted learning, i.e. the architecture elements that should be considered in building an education system. It also explained the environment chosen for the development, and the features of the developed system, and results of using such a system.

References:

1. Adam, J A (1993), "Applications, Implications," IEEE Spectrum, Vol. 30, No. 3, pp. 24-31.
2. Blevis, E B et al. (1991), "Teaching by Means of Social Simulation," Int'l Conf. on the Learning Science, Birnbaum, L. (Ed.), Assoc. for Advancement of Computing in Education, Evanston, pp. 45-51.
3. Dewey, J (1916), Democracy and Education: An Introduction to the Philosophy of Education, Macmillan, New York.
4. Edelson, D E (1993), "Learning from Stories: Indexing and Reminding in a Socratic Case-Based Teaching System for Elementary School Biology," Tech. Report No. 43, Inst. for the Learning Sciences, Northwestern Univ., Evanston, Ill.
5. Hewitt, J et al. (1992), "Designs to Encourage Discourse in the OISE CSILE System," Poster Presentation at the Computer Human Interaction Conference, Calif.
6. Kass, A et al. (1991), "Environments for Incidental Learning: Taking Road Trips Instead of Memorizing State Capitals," Proc. Int'l Conf. on the Learning Sciences, Assoc. for the Advancement of Computing in Education, Charlottesville, Va., pp. 258-264.
7. Kass, A et al. (1994), "Constructing Learning Environments for Complex Social Skills," Journal of Learning Sciences, Vol. 3, No. 4, Lawrence Erlbaum Assoc.
8. Pea, R D (1993), "The Collaborative Visualization Project," Communications of the ACM, Vol. 36, No. 5, pp. 60-63.
9. Scardamalia, M et al. (1993), "Technologies for Knowledge-Building Discourse," Communications of the ACM, Vol. 36, No. 5, pp. 37-41.

10. Schank, R C (1993), "Learning via Multimedia Computers," Communications of the ACM, Vol. 36, No. 5, pp. 54-56.
11. Schank, R C (1994, Spring), "Active Learning through Multimedia," IEEE Multimedia, Vol. 1, No.1, pp. 69-78.
12. Silicon Graphics Inc. (1995), Company Product Brochure.

6.5

PHOENIX QUEST: LESSONS IN DEVELOPING AN EDUCATIONAL COMPUTER GAME FOR GIRLS ... AND BOYS

Maria Klawe, Marv Westrom, Kelly Davidson & Doug Super
University of B.C., Canada

This paper describes our experience in developing and evaluating Phoenix Quest, a computer game designed to encourage children of ages 10 - 14, especially girls, to explore concepts in mathematics and language arts. We include preliminary results from a recent study of approximately 200 school children's playing Phoenix Quest over a period of several weeks. The data reveals interesting gender differences in both attitude towards, and actual playing of, the elements of the game. Girls chose significantly more of the game elements as fun, important and challenging than the boys did, while the boys made more progress in completing the game.

1.0   Introduction

Phoenix Quest is one of the prototype games being developed by the E-GEMS project. E-GEMS is a large-scale collaborative effort by university researchers in computer science and education, teachers, children, and commercial electronic game developers, to develop and do research on electronic games that increase children's interest and achievement in math and science. The E-GEMS participants include the University of British Columbia, Queen's University, Electronic Arts, Creative Wonders, and elementary schools in Vancouver, BC and Kingston, Ontario.

2.0   The development experience

In October 95, we started testing version 2 of Phoenix Quest in two grade 4 and one grade 7 classrooms. The game contained a 65 chapter story, over 100 story illustrations, correspondence with the four main characters of the story, and 12 interactive mathematical puzzles, many of which had several levels of difficulty. We observed many problems in terms of its educational effectiveness. For example, students seemed to be ignoring the mathematical concepts in several of the puzzles, succeeding only through trial and error. Students seldom replayed the more difficult puzzles. During our observations few of the students seemed to be actually reading the story chapters, though in discussions with the students we found that most of the students had absorbed a great deal of knowledge about the story. Usage of the postcard correspondence feature of PQ varied greatly among students.

In January 96 we began developing the next phase prototype (PQ v.3), making a variety of changes to address these issues. The four major areas of focus during this phase of development were as follows:

a) We made improvements to mathematical puzzles to increase their educational effectiveness.

b) We added a card game, Keeper's Strife, as the game's final challenge, and added Strife cards as rewards for replaying puzzles and completing other educational activities to increase the motivation for doing these tasks. Keeper's Strife was designed to include a number of mathematical elements, and to be gender inclusive.

c) We added cloze passages (text passages in which the player must fill in many of the characters) as summaries of story chapters to raise the incentive for reading the story. Cloze passages are a familiar language arts activity for many teachers, and are the basis of a number of successful educational games. Strife cards are provided as rewards for completing each cloze passage.

d) We improved the conversation nets to reduce the number of off-topic responses.

This version (PQ v.3) was essentially completed by the end of April, and we entered another round of evaluation.

2.1   Phoenix quest, the game

Julie, a young girl, is trapped in the Phoenix Archipelago, a mythical set of islands off the coast of Hong Kong. By magical means, she is able to send and receive postcards to and from your computer. A desperate message asking for help is waiting for a response. Will you help Julie? If you agree, you will learn about Julie's fall into the Archipelago, how the world is turning dark, and how the stolen Phoenix feather must be found to stop this diabolical progression. You will meet a trapped boy, Darien, and you will help Julie and Darien pass tests of math and logic to unlock secrets, reveal chapters of the whole story as told in Saffron's magic journal, and acquire valuable Strife cards for the final confrontation with the mastermind, the mysterious Keeper.

Phoenix Quest is based upon a story written by the award-winning Canadian childrens' author Julie Lawson in collaboration with members of the E-GEMS research project. You interact with the other characters and participate in this adventure in a number of ways. The initial contact is a postcard from Julie; you start the game by replying to this with a postcard of your own. As the game proceeds, you can send postcards to Julie at any time. And as you learn about the other characters, you can send postcards to them too. One of the characters, Saffron, has a journal telling the events happening in the Archipelago, i.e. the Phoenix Quest story. At various times, in response to your actions and achievements, you receive chapters of Saffron's journal. Unfortunately you do not normally discover them in sequential order, but you can still use the information to piece together an understanding of what is going on this world.

The chapters contain power words that are the answers to clues and riddles sent in postcards from Saffron. Finding the power words reveals illustrations, adds chapters and provides access to new islands in the Archipelago as well as to the mathematical puzzles. Strife cards are given as rewards for completing cloze passages and solving the puzzles. The Strife cards are kept in a special album where they can be examined and reorganized at any time. Most of the puzzles have several levels of difficulty, and more valuable Strife cards are given as rewards for completing more difficult levels.

Table 1 outlines the twelve types of mathematical puzzles in Phoenix Quest. There are two distinct puzzles for three of the types (maze, robot and logic) and one for each of the others.

Table 1: Mathematical puzzles

Puzzle	Math Concepts, Skills, and Strategies	Brief Description
Mazes Cave / Spider	- 90° rotations - working backwards	The player rotates from 1 to 3 path tiles to complete a connecting path through the labyrinth for Julie.
Bees	- degrees 0° to 360°	The player chooses the angle and timing for Darien to lob honey at bees attacking him.
Fishing	- degrees 0° to 360° - relative distance - polar coordinates	The player chooses the angle, distance and timing for Julie to cast a fishing line.
Stepping Stone	- translations - rectangular coordinates	The player chooses coordinates specifying vectors for Julie to cross a river by stepping stones.

Table 1: Mathematical puzzles (Con't)

Shrine	- addition - closed path - travelling salesman	The player chooses a path for Julie to visit each shrine and return to the first. The length of her path must be less than a given number.
Paddy	- addition - tree diagram - minimum spannng tree	The player selects trenches for Julie to dig tó connect all the paddies to a water source. The total length dug must be less than a given number.
Robot Mask / Key	- simple programming - translations - planning	The player programs two robots to push pieces together to form a key or a mask. The directions are represented by beads strung on a string.
Logic - 2 door - 3 door	- rubic cube-like puzzle - sliding fifteen puzzle - logical reasoning	The player must unscramble two sentences and then solve a Lady and the Tiger logic puzzle.
Gears	- geometric patterns - equivalent ratios - factors and products	The player chooses an inner and outer gear to draw a specified spirographic pattern.
Coins	- deduction - logical progression - tabular representations	The player determines the false coin by weighing groups of coins against each other. A table helps the player analyse the result of each weighing.
Hexagons	- number sequences - factors, progressions - primes, squares	The player chooses Julie's path across hexagonal tiles. Numbers on the correct path follow a pattern which the player must discover.
Poison	- adding fractions - equivalent fractions	The player must build a target fraction from other fractional components that are found.

3.0 The research setting

A six-week study designed to evaluate children's response to Phoenix Quest when played without mediation was conducted at Clinton Elementary School in Burnaby, Canada. Eight classes volunteered to participate by devoting pre-scheduled computer lab time to playing the game. Several grades were represented: 3/4, 4, 4/5, 5, 5/6, 6 and two grade 7 classes. The amount of time spent in the lab varied across classes; with two classes beginning one and two weeks, respectively, after the study began. Students were instructed to work in self-selected, same-gender pairs. As the weeks progressed, there was some breakdown of this structure with a few students choosing to work on other software, leaving others to work alone or form groups of three.

There were 62 male groups and 58 female groups in the study. Students played the Phoenix Quest game during regular class periods of about 40 minutes. Each time a same-sex group played was recorded as a session, and the students cumulatively generated over 1800 playing sessions. Each session terminated with the students responding to a three-page on-line session-exit questionnaire. On each page the group was asked to 'vote' for the activities that they considered to be fun, important, and challenging, respectively; the list of activities on the pages were identical. One of the pages is shown in Figure 1. Data was also collected in log files that recorded all of the postcard correspondence and game events (loading of puzzles, completion of puzzles, time spent on various tasks). Players were asked to rate the appropriateness of each postcard reply they received on a scale from 0 to 4. In addition, researchers informally observed behaviour in the computer lab and conducted interviews with six teachers and 15 pairs of students during the final week of the study.

The first few weeks of the study were hampered by recurrent system crashes due to a combination of bugs in Phoenix Quest and incompatibilities with the system configurations in the computer lab. Thus the researchers spent much of their time resetting the students' machines. By the fourth week most of the problems had been resolved and both students and researchers were able to focus on playing the game.

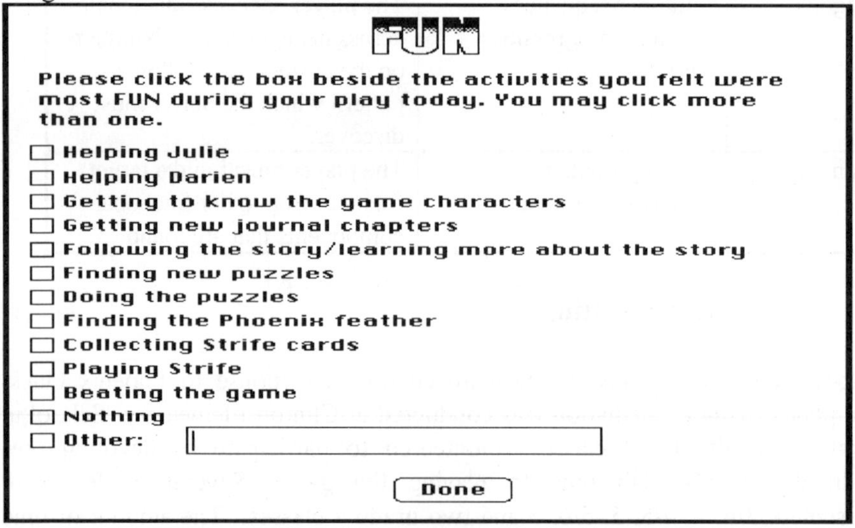

Figure 1: The "FUN" page of the session-exit questionnaire

4.0   Preliminary results from the Clinton study

As shown in Table 2, the log files indicate that 618 of the 1806 sessions (34%) ended prematurely, which we attribute to the many system difficulties encountered during the first half of the study. To exit from most of these aborted sessions, students still had to complete the session-exit questionnaire (SEQ) and they were instructed by session supervisors to reply "Nothing" to speed the exit process. Although students could choose "Nothing" for a normal session-exit, it is clear this was not a common choice since the "Nothing" choice was only selected in 37% of the Fun, 35% of the Important, and 37% of the Challenging SEQs. In the analysis that follows the "Nothing" responses have been deleted to facilitate comparision of the other responses.

On average, females selected more items as fun, challenging and important than males on the SEQ (see Table 3). One also notes from Table 3 that the number of votes tended to drop off from the first SEQ page (Fun) to the last (Challenging).

Table 2: Sessions terminated with system problems

	Males	Females	Total
Sessions terminated with a problem	376	242	618
Sessions completed normally	654	534	1188
Total	1030	776	1806

Table 3: Average number of votes on the SEQ by gender

	Fun	Important	Challenging	Average
Males	3.8	3.2	2.9	3.3
Females	4.3	4.0	3.5	3.9
Average	4.0	3.6	3.2	3.6

The choices selected by males and females is shown in Table 4. For example, on the Fun pages completed by boys, on average 0.4208 of them contained a vote for "Helping Julie". The girls' average for this item was 0.5969. The boys' and girls' averages are significantly different ($p<0.001$).

The girls cast significantly more votes for the first five items than did the boys. The girls' average response to any particular item is higher in all of the significantly different means, and higher in almost every case.   Following are three charts showing the responses to the three pages (fun, important, challenging) of the session-exit questionnaire arranged to compare responses by gender. On the FUN page, Figure 2, players felt that "Doing the puzzles" and "Helping Julie" were the most motivating aspects of Phoenix Quest. In both cases males and females differ significantly with the females casting more votes for the activity ($p<0.001$).

The second graph shows ratings by males and females of the IMPORTANCE of different aspects of the game. These measures matched rather closely the results for FUN for most aspects except in several intriguing areas. The girls rating for "Doing the puzzles" fell by 15% and the boys rating for Helping Julie rose by 5%.

The third graph shows rating of CHALLENGE for differenct aspects of the game. There were fewer votes overall for this page.

From the action log files we extracted data on student playing of the games. Table 5 shows the number of male and female groups who reached each of the puzzles and the two locations in which the Strife card game can be played. There are many different possible paths through Phoenix Quest resulting in many possible orders in which the puzzles can be encountered; however, the order shown in Table 5 is the most common one. Table 5 shows that on average the male groups made significantly faster progress through the game than the female groups.

5.0   Conclusion

There are differences between the way males and females reported their opinions on the session-exit questionnaire (SEQ). On each of the three pages of the SEQ, students could cast up to 12 votes for activities they found fun, important, or challenging. Females cast almost 20% more votes, and their pattern of votes was different from the males. In particular, they voted significantly ($p<0.05$) more often for "Human" aspects of Phoenix Quest: Helping Julie, Helping Darien, Getting to know the characters, Finding new chapters, and Following the story. They voted more often, but not significantly more often for the "Game" aspects: Finding new puzzles, Doing the puzzles, Finding the Phoenix feather, Collecting Strife cards, Playing Strife, and Beating the game.

Table 4: Mean gender differences on session-exit questionnaire

Activity		Fun	Important	Challenging
Helping Julie	boys	0.4208	0.4685	0.3083
	girls	0.5969***	0.5935***	0.4271***
Helping Darien	boys	0.3441	0.3288	0.2641
	girls	0.4134*	0.4014**	0.3122

Table 4: Mean gender differences on session-exit questionnaire (Con't)

Getting to know chars	boys	0.2828	0.2181	0.1516
	girls	0.3671**	0.3310***	0.2058*
Finding new chapters	boys	0.3543	0.3356	0.2419
	girls	0.4717***	0.4271**	0.3448***
Following the story	boys	0.2896	0.2726	0.1840
	girls	0.3551*	0.3808***	0.2864***
Finding new puzzles	boys	0.4327	0.3714	0.2964
	girls	0.4614	0.4031	0.3379
Doing the puzzles	boys	0.5026	0.3935	0.3867
	girls	0.5952**	0.4408	0.4305
Finding Phoenix feather	boys	0.2692	0.2709	0.2555
	girls	0.2504	0.2539	0.2762
Collecting Strife cards	boys	0.4106	0.3765	0.3049
	girls	0.4545	0.4168	0.3568
Playing Strife	boys	0.2129	0.1925	0.2232
	girls	0.1901	0.2007	0.2213
Beating the game	boys	0.1618	0.1908	0.2606
	girls	0.2007	0.2384*	0.3002

* $p<0.05$, **$p<0.01$, ***$p<0.001$

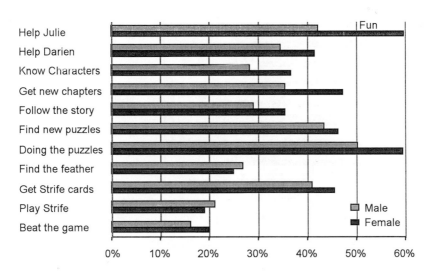

Figure 2: Percent of choices on FUN page by gender

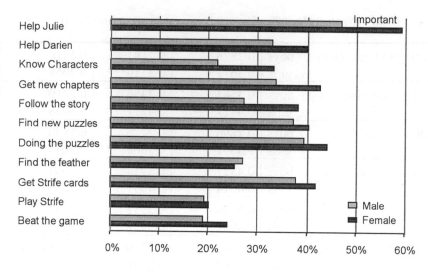

Figure 3. Percent of choices on IMPORTANT page by gender

There were three choices that girls voted for almost 60% of the time: they said it was fun to help Julie, fun doing the puzzles, and important to help Julie. Since the primary purpose of PQ is to interest girls in mathematics, the female FUN result for "Doing the puzzles" is encouraging. The males had only one choice selected more than 50% of the time: they voted for "Doing the puzzles" as FUN. Thus it would seem that doing the puzzles was fun for both genders.

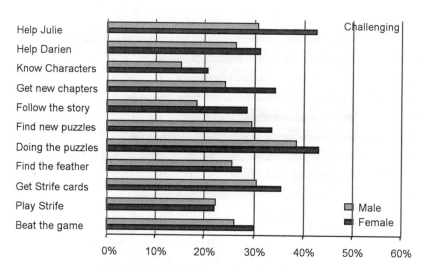

Figure 4: Percent of choices on CHALLENGING page by gender

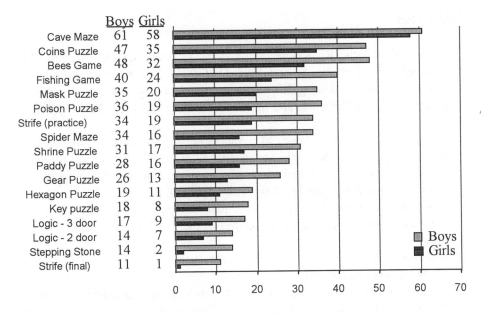

	Boys	Girls
Cave Maze	61	58
Coins Puzzle	47	35
Bees Game	48	32
Fishing Game	40	24
Mask Puzzle	35	20
Poison Puzzle	36	19
Strife (practice)	34	19
Spider Maze	34	16
Shrine Puzzle	31	17
Paddy Puzzle	28	16
Gear Puzzle	26	13
Hexagon Puzzle	19	11
Key puzzle	18	8
Logic - 3 door	17	9
Logic - 2 door	14	7
Stepping Stone	14	2
Strife (final)	11	1

Figure 5: Number of players reaching each mathematical puzzle

From Figure 5 it is clear that the boys played many more of the games than the girls. For the students who played most of the games, the number of times they played them and the amount of time they spent was relatively uniform, but because the girls did not play as many of the games, they are under-represented in the game achievement data. We plan to study this issue further to determine what factors contribute to the rate of progress made by boys and girls.

The Children understood that one of the main underlying goals of Phoenix Quest was to help the lead character Julie with her predicament, and that students could differentiate between the motivating experiential aspects of the game and the socially important objective. In other words, they saw playing puzzles as merely a means to the end of helping.

In future research on Phoenix Quest over the next few months we will be using revised versions of SEQs and action-log file collection to study gender, grade level and time-profile differences. With more stable software and a research design that follows each student team from the first login with Phoenix Quest until the final conclusion of the game, we expect to increase our understanding of how students interact with this type of educational software, what maintains their motivation, and how their experience with multi-media software relates to their learning.

References:

1. Inkpen, K., Upitis, R., Klawe, M., Lawry, J., Anderson, A., Ndunda, M., Sedighian, K., Leroux, S. and Hsu, D. (1994) "We have never-forgetful flowers in our garden: girls' responses to electronic games". Journal of Computing in Mathematics and Science Education , Vol. 13, No. 4, pp. 383-403.
2. Lawry, J., Upitis, R., Klawe, M., Anderson, A., Inkpen, K., Ndunda, M., Hsu, D., Leroux, S. and Sedighian, K. (1995) "Exploring common conceptions about boys and electronic games". Journal of Computers in Mathematics and Science Teaching Vol. 14, No. 4, pp. 439-459.
3. Upitis R. and Koch C. (1996). Is Equal Computer Time Fair for Girls? Potential Internet Inequities. Proceedings of the INET Conference, Montreal, June 1996.
4. Upitis R. (1996). Profiles of Adolescents using Information Technology. MSTE Newspostcard, No. 2, pp. 3-5.
5. Westrom M. and Super D. (1996). Click Smart: Some Considerations for the Design of Click-ons in Educational Games. Conference Proceedings, Computer Game Developers' Conference, Santa Clara, March 1996.
6. Westrom M. Super D. and Klawe M. (1996)., Design Issues involving entertainment click-ons. Computer-Human Interaction '96 Conference Companion, Vancouver, April 1996.

6.6

A RECENT DEVELOPMENT IN EDUCATIONAL SOFTWARE IN ECONOMICS: THE MICRO GRAPHICS TUTOR (MGT)

Michael Swann
Charles Sturt University, Australia

With its source code written in Borland C^{++} the Micro Graphics Tutor (MGT) is the first of a new generation of generic educational software which provides the student with an electronic textbook in the principles of microeconomics. Consisting of seven modules covering all the major areas of microeconomics, each module comprises a group of options on specific microeconomic topics. Mouse driven and operated with a user-friendly toolbar, MGT allows the undergraduate student to experience a new degree of computer interface. Complete with wide ranging parameters, formulae files which complement the diagrams and the ability to print diagrams and text files. MGT brings microeconomics alive for the information technology conscious student today. Moreover, MGT can be used in a Windows environment in association with other Windows applications and tools such as Paint Brush, Word or Works to give the assignment writing student an enhanced sense of MGT's uses in a business communications context. The pedagogical implications of the use of educational software in economics in terms of its measurable benefits, is still in its early days. Initial results at CSU in first year microeconomics offered by both internal and external modes suggest grounds for cautious optimism.

1.0   Introduction

The Micro Graphics Tutor (MGT) is not simply another piece of educational software attached to a particular undergraduate textbook. MGT is the first of a new generation of *independent generic software* which represents an initial attempt at producing an authentically student inter-active *electronic textbook*.

With its source code written by a programmer and consultant in the state of the art language, Borland C^{++} MGT is an inter-disciplinary effort aimed at using information technology to efficiently and effectively facilitate the student learning process in economics.

As explained below in this paper,MGT generates potential benefits in modifying and facilitating both the internal and external (distance education) learning modes. Indeed the importance of relating social science disciplines such as economics to information technology not simply as an academic innovation, but

276

more importantly, as a career skills learning/training process cannot be over-estimated.

For students in the 1990s seeking professional careers in an age of increasing technological awareness and rapid technological change in the modes of business and professional communication, the measured use of appropriate software is becoming an essential part of their curriculum work.

2.0   Brief description of MGT

While MGT reflected an inter-disciplinary team effort involving Borland C^{++} programming and micro economics, the format and structure of MGT is *economics driven* in that the program responds to the needs of the undergraduates in microeconomics and does not assume per se any previous knowledge of information technology. MGT is essentially user friendly.

Figure 1 below shows the on-screen title page of MGT with the seven modules (with mini-diagram icons) which represent seven major chapter headings typically covered in any microeconomics principles course which first year students are likely to encounter at Australian universities. Within each module a selection of options is available to the student corresponding to the range of the specific sections available within each chapter in any of the standard undergraduate textbooks.

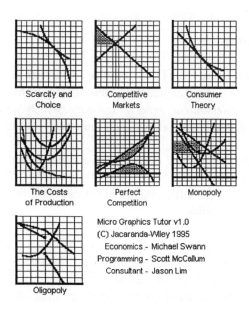

Figure 1: MGT module icons

The generic flexibility of MGT as essentially a 'smorgasbord' of standard topics arranged in modules and options simulating the chapters and sections of any standard text book is reflected in its current use in both semesters at CSU in 1996 for both the large group introductory principles course in first year economics (ECO110 Microeconomics) and also the small group, intermediate level, second year economics course (ECO200 Microeconomic Analysis).

In 1996 MGT at CSU is proving to be an exciting and genuinely innovative approach to the teaching of undergraduate economics. So much of the currently available educational software in economics uses information technology simply as a cosmetic afterthought to the text book, an optional addition to the printed text which is either quickly relegated to the "too hard" basket or marginalised as a largely irrelevant electronic toy with little pedagogical substance for the adopting lecturer and his/her course.

In marked contrast, MGT is a genuine innovation-a working tool, seeking to bring the full value of the printed textbook to the PC screen with the measurable benefits of computer inter-action and of CAL - computer assisted learning - for both on campus and distance education modes as briefly outlined below.

3.0   Guided tour of the MGT format

MGT is essentially mouse-driven through the use of a Windows compatible *toolbar* which focuses on user friendly direct inter-face between the student and the PC screen. It is important that the first year student is not burdened unnecessarily by an excessive reliance on keyboard skills or any requirement for a high level of familiarity with Windows software.

MGT is designed to be a self-contained Windows application which once loaded to the hard drive can be used continuously in isolation or alternatively, by the student more familiar with a PC, in conjunction with a suite of other Windows applications such as *Paint Brush* and *Word or Works* etc., as explained below.

Figure 2: Toolbar buttons for MGT

The toolbar shown in Figure 2 above provides the mouse-driven basis for student and computer interface in a manner familiar to Windows users and consistently friendly for first time computer users from purely social science backgrounds.

MGT seeks to give the student as much inter-active control of diagrams/text/formulae as is consistent with the constraints of the program language.

Some of the features of the MGT toolbar are briefly outlined below.

⊒ = ?
parameters This toolbar button allows the student to access key economic **parameters** behind the particular curves so that eg, a change in disposable income shifts the demand curve or a change in technology shifts the supply curve in option 1 of Module II on the topic of supply and demand.

𝜋𝑓 𝒞𝑓
formulae Selection of **formulae** allows the student to access a new set of files associated with selected pages within options where tables and formulae are used and changed with changing parameter selection. For example, the firm's revenue table (total, marginal and average) in option 3 (the marginal approach) of Module V on perfect competition responds to changes in the market price above or below its initial equilibrium (default setting).

𝒞
resize A unique feature of the MGT format is that it allows the student to vary i.e. resize the default screen settings of a 50:50 split between diagram (left hand side) and accompanying economics text file (right hand side). Frequently the student wished concentrate on the diagram, exploring the visual effects of parameter changes etc.. By simply mouse selecting the resize button in the toolbar either full screen diagram or full screen text file may be selected as well as the 50:50 screen split.

∿ print
graph One of the most important features of MGT is that students are able to not only work with and modify diagrams on screen but also **print graphs** through standard Windows mode or post the diagram to anther Windows tool or application such as *Paint Brush* (for additional and powerful editing) or directly to a word processor such as Word.6 or Work.3. This provides the student with states of the art diagrams in his/her assignment or essay work consistent with desk top publishing quality. (Note: if the student has access to a colour laser or dot matrix printer, then all MGT diagrams can be printed in the same colours as they appear on screen.)

⊒ print
text This feature allows the student to inter-act with any part of the current text file in any option by use of the **print text** button. This student may choose to directly print a part of a file or a selects built in microeconomics *glossary* definition and use it in an assignment or essay context. Moreover, the word-processor *Notepad* is built into the text file mode, so that students may choose to type in their won text combined with selected *glossary* definitions or default text. Print text also allows students to print any of the formulae files so that the tables

or selected formulae can be incorporated in class assignment work. Moreover, the student can also print-out any of the myriad mouse selected *hypertext* files behind key intersections, points, lines and areas on the graphics by use of the print text button.

The **exit** button is particularly user-friendly as it allows the student new to both economics and computers to not only switch between options and modules easily but also returns the student to any option in its default mode so that work can resume on any particular diagram(s) with "a clean board" approach. This facilitates the student's inter-active and progressive learning which is a feature of computer aided learning (CAL).

4.0   MGT-modules

In working with MGT the student is made aware of the module approach to the teaching/learning process in economics. With its essentially generic and *smorgasbord* approach to topic development, MGT groups a selected number of core economic topics as options under a particular module. Thus the student selecting Module II *Competitive Markets* finds the following *four options* under this module icon dealing with several core aspects of basic market analysis as illustrated in Figure 3 below.

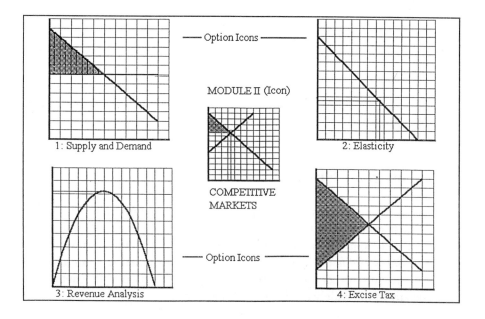

Figure 3: The icons of the four options of Module II and its module access icon

Once the student selects a particular option within a Module, eg, option 1: *supply and demand* or option 4: *excise tax*, the page 1 default mode graphics and text appear and the student is in a position to commence work on the microeconomic topic under consideration in wither the on-campus class or off-campus distance education home environment.

MGT has proved particularly useful with distance mode students. Office consultation time be converted into a *virtual classroom* with the lecturer and student both access the same graphics within a particular option. The student can be directed to eg, mouse select and discuss the economic meaning and interpretation of the graphical and/or tabular results in *real time* - although the lecturer is in NSW while the student is in eg, WA or Victoria or Queensland.

The full benefits of this mode of delivery are yet to be explored. But the anecdotal student feedback is encouraging suggesting that this approach has potential for motivating and focusing students in their study of economics.

5.0   MGT options

Consider for instance option 1 of Module II which introduces the student to the elements of competitive market analysis over four on-screen pages 1 and 2 deal with defining, explaining and using demand and supply curves respectively while page 3 brings the two sides of the market together in a standard market equilibrium - Marshallian scissors - microeconomic diagram.

However, page 4 of the option introduces the student to the methodology of *comparative statics* by inviting him/her to change any one of a set of purely *quantitative* parameters behind either the supply curve or the demand curve and observe, on the computer screen the *direction of change* in the market equilibrium price/quantity configuration.

6.0   Study guide format

The MGT software is accompanied by its own generic *Study Guide* which works through each option within each module systematically providing the student with a detailed explanation and illustration of the content and purpose of each topic. The *Study Guide* is viewed as 'generic' in the sense that it is not associated with any one current economics textbook but may be used with equal facility alongside any of the widely used undergraduate texts.

For example, at CSU in 1996 internal students used the MGT *Study Guide* with the Nelson text, Quale and Robinson, while the external students used the *Study Guide* with the McGraw-Hill Text, Samuelson *et al.* The chapters of the *Study Guide* have the following standard format learning objectives, option outline, default graphics, student participation, multiple choice questions, review questions/problems.

7.0   Windows 3.1 environment for MGT

Once loaded onto the computer, students, are encouraged to use MGT in a Windows 3.1 environment - viewing MGT as educational software which accommodates a wide range of other Windows applications and tools. For example, via *Paintbrush* under *Program Manager* it is possible to copy and paste any form of customized editing of diagrams, tables, economic formulae, glossary definitions or pieces of standard texts. This provides a virtually open ended basis producing state of the art professional quality work in semester assignments, essays or tutorial exercises.

Thus MGT not only provides a powerful and inter-active computerized learning tool for the student but also helps motivate the student to produce the type and range of quality work output which bears favorable comparison to the professional standards expected by the employers of graduates in both the public and private sectors in the communications driven work places of the highly competitive labor markets of Australia in the 1990s.
For instance, in writing a term paper on aspects of perfect competition, the student would access any of the six options under Module V. Perfect Competition, selecting the relevant diagrams with appropriate parameter changes and associated tables and text files as required. Assuming that a sequence of graphics editing was required before pasting the MGT diagrams to say a *Word. 2* file, the student would typically employ the following Windows sequence.

Task List MGT (eg. Module V: Option1, Page2) => *Paint Brush* => *Word.2*(File)

8.0   Pedagogical features

Arguably, one of the most important and challenging aspects of CAL - Computer assisted learning - is the task of determining the optimal way in which it can be appropriately and effectively integrated into conventional teaching methodologies at Australian universities. As we move from the comfortable and familiar

282

conventional teaching modes of "chalk and talk" to across the threshold into the computerized age of electronic blackboards and electronic texts like MGT, the watchword should be *festina lente* - make haste slowly.

The use of information technology in the social sciences is not simply a matter of quantitative difference: replacing books, note paper and pens with PC terminals and mouse-driven inter-active software. The methodologies of effective communications are quantitatively different in that type of cognitive response(s) generated by economics undergraduates in the 1990s reflects their continuing exposure to and increasing facility in coping with multimedia technologies.

Hence pedagogically, lecturers in economics will be required to not only develop their personal skills in the use of information technology but will need to trial different modes of teaching and assessing student performance to accommodate the new technologies. For example assignment and essay writer will be able to access discipline based software libraries via networking, modifying significantly the conventional concept of student bibliography.

Some of the initial impacts which MGT has facilitated at CSU are outlined below in terms of its use with wither on-campus internal students or its off-campus distance education students. In passing, it is observed that in 1995, external mode students in first year economics (ECO 110) represented more than two-thirds of total student enrollment in the subject.

8.1   Internal students

Large Lectures. For lecturers taking the large first year group (200 to 300 students) in a computerized theater MGT used in conjunction with any of the standard laptops provides a basis for generating state of the art diagrams with the mouse used as a very effective screen pointer. From personal experience, I have found that this frees me up to concentrate on my overheads and the intellectual content of the lecture topic and its delivery rather than having to concentrate on the geometry of tangency with free hand construction of the more involved diagrams.

Lab Sessions: (Campus Computer Centre) for small group tutorial mode interaction lab sessions allow for monitored classes by the lecturer with students working individually with their PC on a particular MGT option as directed by the session tutor. Although still in an early phase, lab sessions have the potential to replace the traditional tutorial format - subject to the constraints of university costs and the politics of on-campus room allocation administration.

8.2   External student

The introduction of GMT at CSU has represented a major advance in providing teaching support for the very large numbers distance education students enrolled in first year economics. In its initial phase through 1995-96 external students are being offered a binary mode of assessment; computerized assignments (using MGT) or noncomputerised (i.e. printed material only) assignments.

Preliminary inferential statistics analysis of the results between the two large sample groups in the first semester of 1995 indicated that average scores by the computerized students were significantly higher (at the 95% confidence level) than those obtained by the noncomputerised students. Statistically consistent results were obtained in 1996.

While this is potentially encouraging, it is still early days and much more student data and statistical analysis will be required before and firm conclusions can be drawn.

The effective use of educational software in disciplines such as microeconomics with its strong bias towards technical analysis and use of diagrams for topic exposition has greatly improved student involvement and interaction in the subject. Lecturer office consultation time is now no longer a frustrating talk at cross purposes with external students who are experiencing difficulty with particular microeconomic diagrams. With MGT both the lecturer and the student can have the same diagram on-screen in eg, Wagga and Sydney, and use the mouse to work together to make the necessary explanatory diagrammatic changes.

Thus for distance education students working at their own pace and at irregular intervals, subject to job and domestic commitments, MGT provides a 'private on-screen tutor facility' which increases their work flexibility and gives them an enhanced sense of participation in the learning process. The generic nature of the MGT *Study Guide* allows the student to use it effectively alongside any prescribed text in microeconomic principles and to observe how the diagrams and tables of their course text 'come alive' on the screen.
For distance education students this adds a new dimension to their sense of participation in a lining discipline rather than merely rote learning . Distance mode students are gaining a sense of active involvement in the learning process and establishing a new base for more effective electronic communication with their course lecturer.

9.0 Measurable outcomes

From the pedagogical perspective, it is essential that the use of educational software be related to measurable outcomes in terms of the benefits to students and to university staff involved in teaching these courses. For instance, the MGT *Study Guide* provides a set of multiple choice questions for each option within each module - with the correct answers given at the back of the book. This provides a potential basis for *diagnostic testing* of student performance as the choice of an incorrect answer can be self-corrected by the student leading to the student producing a new on screen correct diagram which the student can then proceed to print and file away as a right answer.

In the 1997 academic year it is planned to establish a data base derived from student surveys and spreadsheet data of semester results. The large numbers of both internal and external students combined with the different sources of data access should provide a meaningful basis for drawing relevant conclusions about *inter alia* the teaching effectiveness, degree of student acceptance, pedagogical advantages and academic performance changes for both internal and external students, as well as assessments of its impact on teaching modes and the general effectiveness of the delivery of educational services - especially through distance mode.

10.0 Conclusion

While it is still very early days for the introduction of effective - and mot purely ancillary or cosmetic - educational software in the social sciences such as economics in Australian universities, initial response would appear to be favorable but with reservations. Microeconomic software such as MGT is not and never can be a substitute for the hard grind of individual study, requiring self discipline and regular commitment by all students - irrespective of their study mode.

However, in an age of rapid technological change and innovation, educational software has an increasing role to play both in terms of its pedagogical benefits in the learning environment - on or off campus - and because it reflects, and participates in, the contemporary communications revolution which is increasingly the basis of the professional work environment of the modern graduate.

References:

1. Swann M. McCallum. Lim J. (1995) *Micro Graphics Tutor* (MGT), Brisbane Jacaranda-Wiley.
2. Walbert, M.S., *Writing Better Software for Economics Principles Texts*, Journal of Economic Education, (Summer 1989)

6.7

INTERACTIVE MULTIMEDIA COMPUTER-ASSISTED INSTRUCTION SYSTEM — FOR INFORMATION MANAGEMENT SYSTEM

Jui-Che Tu and Wen-Yi Pai
Da-Yeh Institute of Technology and Industrial Technology
Research Institute, Taiwan

Modern education is a kind of learner-based education. How to provide a effective teaching methodology and a good learning environment to keep learners realizing the content of courses well is the goal of all people that are concerned with education. Utilizing the computer-assisted instruction (CAI) can keep learners realizing the content of courses well and keep more interested in study. Comparing with the traditional CAI tools, the most difference of the Interactive Multimedia Computer-Assisted Instruction (IMMCAI) is the capability of offering different kinds of media such as animation, text, sound, and video to state the content of courses and demonstrate the examples or instances and the interaction between systems and learners. This study emphasizes that it needs considering the interaction that a Interactive Multimedia Computer-Assisted Instruction system is to be developed and evaluated. The IMMCAI system should support a good communication with the learners so as to be a better learning environment to promote the interest of the learners. As the results, the study has concluded the evaluation of effectiveness from system and given some recommendation for developing a better IMMCAI system in teaching and learning.

1.0   Introduction

Researches on the area of CAI are receiving more and more emphasis. Utilizing the computer-assisted instruction (CAI) can match the requirements of distinct learners and adapt the difference among learners to accomplish the best learning effect. Since the computer technology developing widely and rapidly, CAI has evolved from the traditional teaching tools into a new multimedia learning environment, called Multimedia Computer-Assisted Instruction (MMCAI). Beside the medium change, the interaction is too important to ignore.

The research compared with the traditional CAI tools, the most difference of the Interactive Multimedia Computer-Assisted Instruction (IMMCAI) is the capability of offering different kinds of media such as animation, sound, text, and video to state the content of courses and demonstrate the examples or instances and the explanation make the learners to keep more interested in courses and enhance the realization and reaching motive for the teaching topics.

Therefore, the purpose of the study is to discuss the teaching and learning theory of Interactive Multimedia Computer-Assisted Instruction (IMMCAI), and the application of Interactive idea of Interactive Multimedia Computer-Assisted Instruction (IMMCAI) design process. The IMMCAI prototype of the Information Management system is also developed to match the develop process and IMMCAI theory, at last, the study has concluded the evaluation of effectiveness from system and given some recommendation for developing a better IMMCAI system in teaching and learning. Since the traditional CAI can not satisfy requirements of learners, an Interactive Multimedia Computer-Assisted Instruction (IMMCAI) system is developed to accomplish the purpose of the study.

2.0   Procedure

This study emphasizes that it needs considering the interaction while the interactive multimedia CAI systems is developed. The system should support a good communication with the learners so as to be a better learning environment to promote the interest of the learners. In the research section, it states a research structure (see Figure 1). At first the structure includes the research background, research object, data collection and researches the IMMCAI teaching theory, development process, and system construction. Next, it decides system development process, system construction, and then selects a proper system platform and design language. In the meantime, it makes a script of IMMCAI for the management information system course. Then, the study implements the prototype of IMMCAI system using the selected design language on the specific system platform according to the definite script. After the IMMCAI system is completed, the study also evaluates its effectiveness and adaptiveness through the formal statistic method. In the end, it concludes the evaluation result and give some recommendation.

Beside the research of the application of the ineractive teaching idea and the development of the construction of IMMCAI teaching course, the study also states a sytem development process (see Figure 2). The IMMCAI prototype of the Information Management system was developed according to the concept of interaction and learner-dependent adaptation. The whole system is separateed as two subsystem: the teaching subsystem and the learning subsystem (see Figure 3).

288

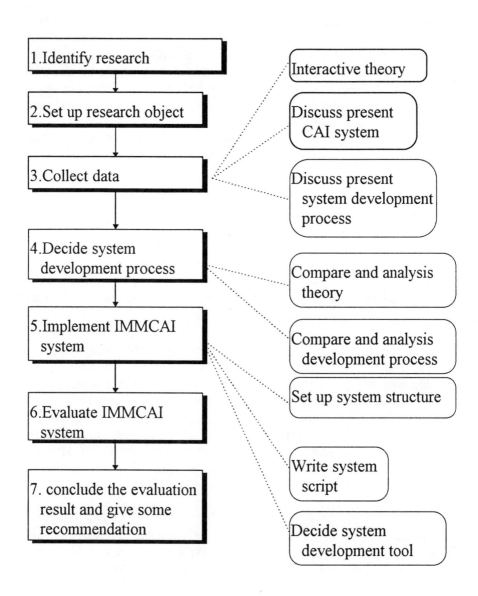

Figure 1. Research structure

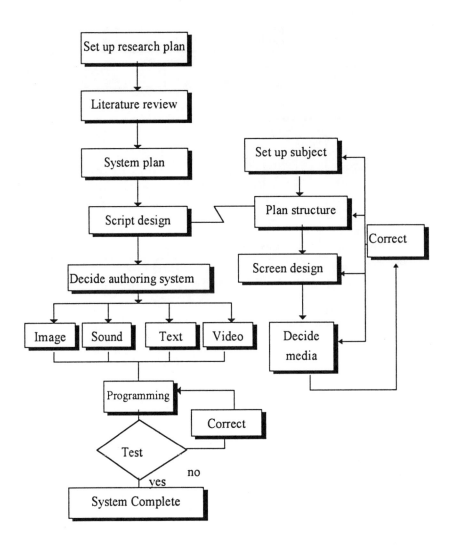

Figure 2: System development process

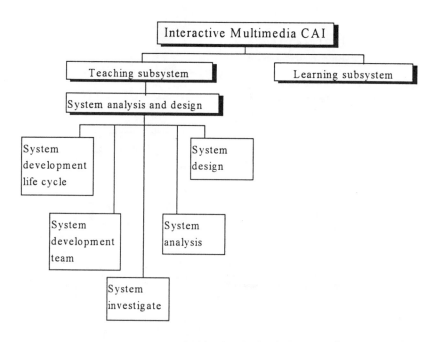

Figure 3: Interactive multimedia CAI

The study used the advanced multimedia environment to construct an effective learning course in the teaching subsystem. The system development process is partitioned into three phases: 1) Script design, 2) Media construction, and 3) Programming. The detailed steps are discussed as following:

1) Script design

Since the context of the teaching course must be complete and comprehensive in the meanwhile the messages provided by the system should be also simple and clear, the script design (see figure 4) is the most time-consuming but key part of the whole IMMCAI system development process. In this phase, the study researches the related topics associated with the course in order to get the main idea and setup the subjects. Furthermore, it plans structure and designs screen. The study selects the demonstration media so as to offer the great impression of the screen. After all, it repeats the above steps until finalize the context of the script.

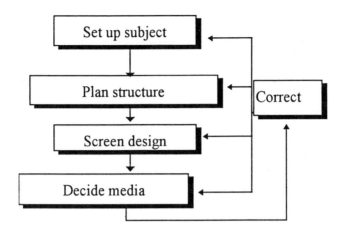

Figure 4: Script design process

The construction of a IMMCAI system is a team-work, and it is important to make the colleague to realize the content of script to be a seamless communication. Therefore, the study states an IMMCAI system script format in order to communicate between the team workers (see figure 5).

2) Media construction

The media of IMMCAI prototype of the Information Management System include text, graph, image, video and sound. And the integration of all media is the authoring tool discussed below (see Table 1):

Table 1: Apparatus of the IMMCAI prototype

Authoring Tool	Delphi 1.0
Graph/Image	MediaStudio/Photoshop 3.0
Video	Premiere 4.0
Audio	Digital Domain/ Noise Master 2.01
Text	Delphi 1.0

Project :_____

Unit:	Unit No:	Screen No:

Screen

Control:	OS:
	1.content:

Image:	Music:
1.*Image No:_____	1.in:
*File name:_____	*Sound No:_____
*File Format:_____	*File name:_____
2. *Image No:_____	*File Format:_____
*File name:_____	*Time:_____ sec

Video:	2.out:
*Video No:_____	*Sound No:_____
*File name:_____	*File name:_____
*File Format:_____	*File Format:_____

Figure 5: IMMCAI script format

- Text: Create the special text effect in the IMMCAI prototype by VCL (Visual Component Library) of Delphi 1.0.
- Graph and Image: Produce the graph and image using two software, one is MediaStudio of U-lead, scanning the graph and image on the scanner; another is Photoshop 3.0 of Adobe, making the special effect on graph and image.
- Video: Proceed the video frame using two software, one is UPMOST MTV of UPMOST that catches the video frame from Hi-8 to personal computer; another is Premiere 4.0 of Adobe that makes the effect of video.
- Audio: Edit the audio wave using two software, one is Digital Domain, which records the music from CD and turns into WAV format; another is Noise Master 2.01, which makes the effect of audio.
- Authoring tool: Use Delphi 1.0 of Borland International, Inc. to integrate the IMMCAI prototype system. Basically, Delphi is an integrated environment which suits to develop IMMCAI system. It is a component-based application development environment supporting rapid development of highly efficient Microsoft Windows-based applications with a minimum of coding. Delphi also provides design tools such as form templates and class library, so programmer can quickly create and test the IMMCAI prototype system. The components of Delphi do not only integrate text, graph, image, video and audio but also develop powerful desktop database.

The Interactive function of the learning subsystem is developed by components of Delphi in the IMMCAI prototype system. Because Delphi is a visual and object-oriented development environment, programmers can easily produce the IMMCAI prototype system. Therefore, the CAI system is not an invariable teller, but it can promote the learners' intention to use the interesting CAI system which give the interaction with them.

3) Programming

The authoring tool of the IMMCAI prototype system is Delphi 1.0, programmers write the programs and integrate the media according to the written script. The programming principle is to design separate modules based on the one-page-one-module rule. The screen swapping is done by the background operating unit. Therefore, the system is highly adaptive. The designer may change the displaying order or modify the context of each page without intercepting other modules. Furthermore, recording learning history and implementing hyper-linking become uniform and easily accomplished, too.

The IMMCAI prototype of the Information Management System is separated into the teaching subsystem and the learning subsystem. The study used the advanced multimedia environment to construct an effective learning course in the teaching subsystem. The learners may travel in the different topics freely and find the most important knowledge they need. The most distinction between the IMMCAI prototype and other CAIs is the construction of the learning subsystem. In the IMMCAI prototype learning subsystem, the learners face a smart interactive virtual-teacher. They answer the questions provided by the virtual-teacher and get feedback associated with the answer they give. The learning subsystem examines the answer and offer the proper hint to the learners so as to they can realize the question and the right answer deeply. In addition to the proper hint, the virtual-teacher records the results of the interaction of learning and gives some recommendation to the learners to improve the learning. As the result, the class teacher may also analyze the recording data with statistics to enhance the content of the IMMCAI to get a better teaching process.

3.0   Apparatus

The IMMCAI prototype of the Information Management system is developed using Delphi 1.0, the product of Borland International, Inc. The media of IMMCAI prototype are processed using Premiere 4.0, Photoshop 3.0, Mediastudio, Digital Domain and Noise Master 2.01. These software operate on IBM PC and compatible machines (see Table 1).

4.0   System

The IMMCAI prototype of the Information Management system is implemented according to the system development process. It begins from a welcome screen (see Figure 6) and jump into the introduction page (see Figure 7). In the welcome screen, the title characters rotate continuously. From the introduction page, the learner will know the author and the source of the content of the whole system.

After the system introduction page, the system moves into the main screen (see Figure 8), which displays the entries of distinct modules. The learner may freely select any module which interests him by the mouse. The system includes several subsystems: system development life cycle, system development participants, system investigation, system analysis, system design and the learning result evaluation. The entries of the above modules are shown on the left side of the main screen, which compose the teaching subsystem, and the learning subsystem is located on the right side of the main screen.

Figure 6: Welcome screen

Figure 7: Instruction page

296

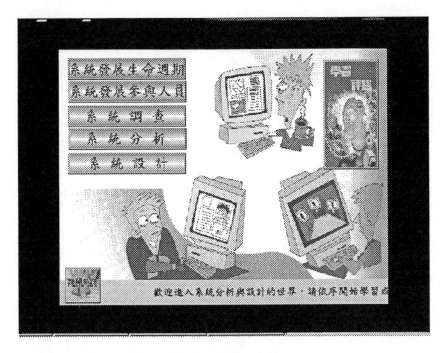

Figure 8: Main screen

5.0 Evaluation

To evaluate the effectiveness, the IMMCAI system is open to the sophomores in the department of the management information system of the Da-Yeh Institute of Technology.
This research collects the evaluation feedbacks of learners. The feedbacks include questionnaire, learning result evaluation scores of the learners who take the test in IMMCAI prototype system and learning result evaluation scores of the learners who answer the evaluation form. Through the statistic analysis, the result correspond to the feasibility and the effectiveness. The evaluation steps (see Figure 9) and result are stated in detail as following:

1) Research evaluation steps:

Step 1. Assure the research object.
The purpose of the research is to discuss the teaching and learning theory of IMMCAI, the design process of the Interactive idea of IMMCAI application, and implement the IMMCAI prototype of the Information Management system to match the develop process and IMMCAI theory. The researcher makes evaluation to correspond to the learner-central rule which the main goal of the system.

Step 2. Set up the population of the samples of the research.
The sophomores in the department of the management information system of the Da-Yeh Institute of Technology are the population. The evaluation data are collected by the questionnaires.
The sampling method is randomly to select about 30 people from the population and let them use the IMMCAI system, take the experiment and fill the questionnaires.

Step 3. Design research tools.
Research tools are composed of the IMMCAI prototype system, the questionnaires and the evaluation form. The content of the questionnaires includes acceptance, system contents, and global evaluation.

Step 4. System evaluation.
The IMMCAI system is open to the samples. They take the experiment and fill the questionnaires.

Step 5. Data collection and analysis.
The sources of the data comprise the questionnaires, the scores of the on-line evaluation in the system, and the scores of the evaluation form. Completing the data collection, the researcher adopts the frequency distribution as the statistic method.

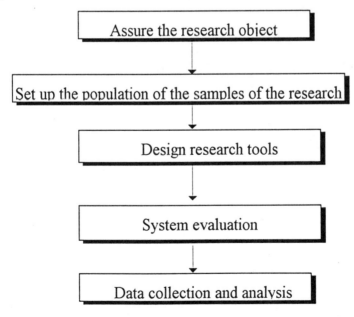

Figure 9: Research evaluation steps

298

2) System evaluation result:

The phenomenon of the promotion about the score of the on-line evaluation and the score of the evaluation form indicate that the IMMCAI system corresponds the capability of the IMMCAI system to enhance learning effect of the learners. Beside that, the comments filled on the questionnaires by the users to the system provide many references to refine the behavior of the IMMCAI system.

There are thirty questions in the on-line evaluation of the learning subsystem of the IMMCAI system. Whenever the learner selects the learning evaluation module, he need complete ten questions extracted randomly from the questions pool in the learning subsystem and the system will record the score of the evaluation. To verify whether the learner makes progress or not, the system requires every learner completing the on-line evaluation three times. After finishing the on-line evaluation, the learner accept a paper-form evaluation. Finally the research makes the comparison between the total average of the on-line evaluation and that of the evaluation form so as to realize the progress of the learners.   Table 2 shows that the learning result of the learners through the IMMCAI system. Analyzing the result, it is clear that almost learners make great progress by repeating using the system. Among them, only three members obtain about seventy and the others get more than eighty. The total average is even over ninety (see Figure 10).

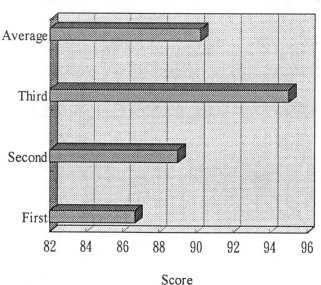

Figure 10: Learning result evaluation scores (in IMMCAI prototype system)

Table 2: Learning result evaluation scores (in IMMCAI prototype system)

Number	First Score	Second Score	Third Score	Average
1	100	80	100	93.33
2	100	90	100	96.66
3	70	90	100	86.66
4	100	100	100	100
5	100	100	90	96.66
6	100	100	100	100
7	90	100	100	96.66
8	80	90	100	90
9	70	70	90	76.66
10	80	90	100	90
11	100	90	100	96.66
12	90	60	100	83.33
13	90	90	80	86.66
14	80	100	100	93.33
15	60	80	90	76.66
16	80	100	100	93.33
17	90	100	100	96.66
18	100	100	100	100
19	80	70	90	80
20	100	80	80	86.66
21	70	80	80	76.66
22	90	100	100	96.66
23	70	90	100	86.66
24	90	90	80	86.66
25	80	70	100	83.33
26	100	100	100	100
27	90	90	90	90
28	90	90	90	90
29	80	100	100	93.33
30	80	80	90	83.33
Average	86.66	89	95	90.22

- The scores of the evaluation form filled by the learners are shown in Table 3. The questions on the evaluation form are partially extracted from the same question pool as the on-line evaluation module use. In addition to those, there are three questions directly extracted from the text book. They are not available to the learners before they take the evaluation form. When the learners take the evaluation form, there are no feedback to them, just as the normal testing happens. Even in such environment, the average score of the learners is over eighty five, which demonstrate the same phenomena of the result of the learning effect of the learners learn by the IMMCAI system. This confirms the great effectiveness for the assistance of the IMMCAI system to the learners.

Table 3 Learning result evaluation scores (in evaluation form)

number	Score
1	90
2	90
3	70
4	100
5	90
6	90
7	90
8	80
9	100
10	90
11	90
12	90
13	90
14	80
15	90
16	80
17	70
18	90
19	70
20	80
21	100
22	70
23	90
24	90
25	70
26	60
27	100
28	90
29	90
30	90
Average	85.67

● The result of the questionnaires provides the opinions about the IMMCAI system and as the fundamentals to refine the behavior of the system in order to accomplish the goal to make the practical system match the interactivity theory. The questionnaire form is designed by referring the form of paper used in the National Science Council project Dr. Chou is responsible to. There are five grades to evaluate different aspects of the system as best, good, no comment, bad, and worst. (see table 4).

In the item of system acceptance, almost all samples select good or best. In the item of system content, sixteen members select good and ten members choose best, that they occupy ninety percent of the population. In the item of general evaluation, twenty eight members express good or best. In the item of interactivity, which is the key topic of the research, there are twenty eight members from thirty populations thinking that the system possesses high interactivity. As a matter of fact, the results demonstrate the high acceptance from the learners the IMMCAI system developed in the research (See Figure 11).

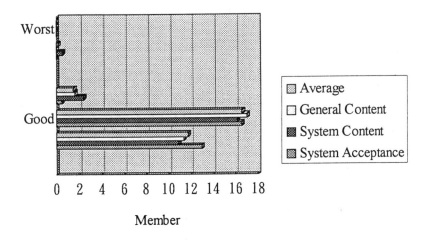

Figure 11: Questionnaire evaluation results

6.0   Conclusion

The purpose of the study is to discuss the teaching and learning theory of Interactive Multimedia Computer-Assisted Instruction (IMMCAI), and the application of Interactive idea of Interactive Multimedia Computer-Assisted Instruction (IMMCAI) design process. In the process of the developing the practical system, the researcher adopts the spiral life cycle model. A initial prototype is developed rapidly and is the center of the model. And then it is modified repeatedly according to the feedback of the learners, which is just like the spiral proceeds. Finally the general-acceptable version of the system emerges. Since the development of the IMMCAI needs the team-work, the spiral life cycle model is suitable to be applied into this process. In the developing process of the IMMCAI system, the researcher repeats refining the system four times according to the opinions of the experts.

There are four common multimedia constructions: hierarchy, linear, multitrack, and interactive stories. The study mixes the hierarchy and multitrack structure to form a hybrid multimedia style which has the constructions of easy implementation and high adaptiveness. The learner may get more information by traveling on self-defined route.

At last, the promotion about the score of the on-line evaluation and the score of the evaluation form approves the capability of the IMMCAI system to enhance learning effect of the learners. Beside that, the comments filled on the questionnaires by the learners correspond to the interactivity between the system and the learners. The multimedia used in the IMMCAI system give a great incentive to utilize the system to accumulate knowledge.

Table 4: Questionnaire result

Evaluation Content	Best	good	No Comment	Bad	Worst
1.icon use easily	16	14	0	0	0
2. System use easily	10	19	1	0	0
System Acceptance	13	16.5	0.5	0	0
3. System Content is clear	11	13	4	2	0
4. Screen is active and harmony	13	14	2	1	0
5. System is interactive	7	21	2	0	0
6. Comparing the traditional learning, I like learning style	16	14	0	0	0
7.The effect of the learning style is better than traditional learning	10	15	5	0	0
8. Learning subsystem has suitable feedback	10	19	1	0	0
9. Learning subsystem provides suitable test	9	17	3	1	0
System Content	10.86	16.14	2.43	0.57	0
10. The system deserves high degree	8	21	1	0	0
11. Would you like to introduce the IMMCAI system to others	13	14	3	0	0
12. Would you use other CAI system having this experience	13	16	1	0	0
General Evaluation	11.33	17	1.67	0	0
Average	11.73	16.55	1.53	0.19	0

References:

1. 周惠文（民82）。多媒體電腦輔助學習系統，行政院國家科學委員會專題研究計劃。計劃編號：NSC82-0111-S008-005。20-35頁。
2. 教學科技與媒體，"正視互動式科技時代的來臨"，教學科技與媒體，第12期。2頁。
3. 黃清雲（民83）。"互動式多媒體的功能及其應用—以體育教學為例"，教學科技與媒體。第16期，21-26頁。
4. 詹國群（民81）。"影像、動畫、CD、MIDI多媒體"，PC Magazine中文版，第11卷，第6期，91-100頁。
5. 羅綸新（民82）。"以互動模式設計互動式多媒體教學軟體"，教學科技與媒體，第12期，21-27頁。
6. 羅綸新（民83）。多媒體設計。松崗電腦圖書資料股份有限公司。1-17頁。
7. 鐘樹橡（民82）。互動式在電腦輔助教學設計上之必要性，教學科技與媒體，第12期，15-20頁。

8. Cotton, B., and Oliver, R. (1993). Understanding Hypermedia. Phaidon Press Ltd., 12-19.
9. Gregory, W. J. (1990). Software Engineering. John Wiley & Sons, 72-75.
10. Guan, S. U., Su, W. J., and Huang, Y. Y. (1994). "The Design of a Multimedia Hyperbook—紅樓夢". 94' Pacific Workshop on Distributed Multimedia System, Feb, 43-50.
11. Lopuck, L. (1996). Designing multimedia. Peachpit Press, 21-29.
12. Martin, J. and Odell, J. J. (1992). Object-Oriented Analysis and Design. Prentice Hall, Inc., 441-448.
13. Ralph, M. S. (1996). Principles of Information System. (2nd ed.). Boyd & Fraser Publishing Company, 408-481.
14. Roth, C. H. (1993). "Computer Aids for Teaching Logic Design". Frontiers In Education Conference, 188-191.
15. Yourdon, E. (1989). Modern Structured Analysis. Prentice-Hall, Inc., 77-83.

6.8

AN EXPERIMENTAL SURVEY ON MULTIMEDIA EDUCATION

W. Gowri Shankar and S. Raman
Indian Institute of Technology, India

This paper focuses on the various issues in the development of Multimedia Education from the perspectives of product research, design, implementation, financial and marketing techniques. We have created a set of modules targeting students from high school to junior college levels which highlights the salient features and advantages of multimedia education. These modules were demonstrated to the students and teachers from schools belonging to different parts of the city of Madras, and a feedback was obtained from them about the demo, existing facilities, and future plans on Multimedia Education. A report of the analysis made on the feedback is presented, which estimates the popularity, feasibility, and the existing scenario of multimedia education in this city.

1.0   Introduction

The main aim of Multimedia Education is to make the teaching and learning process an active one, thus improving the people's inclination to learn. These modules should help the learner to probe, discover and understand the concepts, and provide an effective replacement to certain dull and passive aspects of the process of learning with text books. To achieve this, these modules should not have a mere page turning mechanism, i.e., the learner should not be provided just with the control to cover the contents page by page. Instead, the modules should be highly interactive and involve the user in every stage of the learning process. This interactive capability of the multimedia systems has generated many interesting applications in the areas of education, entertainment, and training. The rapid advancements in the hardware technology have led to the evolution of more complex applications such as video on demand, teleconferencing, and computer supported cooperative work.

We have chosen multimedia education as our application domain due to its vast target audience. The population explosion and the associated increase in thirst for knowledge require new institutions, distance learning programmes, and self-study opportunities to satisfy their learning needs. The advances in networking technology and the advent of Internet make Multimedia Education a key factor in mass education.

These modules prepared introduce the capabilities of multimedia education rather than provide a complete coverage of the subject. We have chosen the subject of Physics for our initial phase of development. The live experiments and the associated graphical descriptions have been brought to the students through movie clips and animations, which help them to comprehend many abstract concepts very clearly. The modules provide an elaborate coverage on a few topics in Physics such as mechanics, atomic physics, hydrostatics, and measurement using vernier calliper along with a few short presentations on Tamil alphabet, setting up of distillation apparatus, periodic table, photography, etc. Each topic consists of a tutorial and a question and answer session. A few interactive experiments, wherein the student can interact with the system to setup and observe the progress of the experiment have been created. Finally, the students can also take a quiz, consisting of objective type questions, which is evaluated automatically.

We have created the modules using Authorware, which runs under the MS-Windows environment. The modules can be packaged as executable files and can be ported to any other system in a dedicated or a networked environment. The modules were tested on systems with different hardware configurations in order to arrive at an optimum design of the module. The processor power, memory size, and display types of the system form the key factor in the performance of these modules. Currently, there are problems in displaying the true colors, animations with the required speed, synchronized playback of video and audio data in the 80386-based systems with 8 or 16MB of main memory and a VGA display. However, the performance is very good on 80486 and Pentium based systems with 32MB main memory and dedicated display boards which reduce the overheads of the CPU for displaying the animations and movie clips. We loaded the modules on a Pentium based Multimedia System, carried it to different schools in and around the city, and demonstrated them to the students and staff of these schools. After the demonstration, the students and staff were requested to answer a questionnaire. These questions aim at providing us the feedback about the quality of the demo, existing popularity of multimedia education, the available infrastructure, and the financial capabilities of these schools.

2.0 Module creation

The selection of topics for the multimedia title creation depends on the target audience, their pre-requisites, and the depth of information to be conveyed through the titles. In our case, since we have decided to target the school students upto a junior college level, the contents of these modules follow the academic curriculum of the schools and thus serve as an aid to the class room teaching. The popularity of any multimedia title lies in the degree of interactivity provided to the users, and the navigational facilities which allow one to browse the entire contents, choose any topic of their interest and jump to a different topic with ease. This can be implemented by making use of hypertext and hypermedia features, which make multimedia education stand apart from its counterparts. These features allow the provision of several levels of description for the same topic, each one being more fundamental in nature, catering to the users who cannot comprehend the description currently provided. These layers of information are linked to each other in a particular order, and information about this linkage is indicated to the users in some form. For example, in between the text descriptions, a few key words can be displayed in a different color, style or font. This serves as an indication to the user that some more information on this keyword is available. The user may click on this word to display the associated information.

The key to the success of teaching is to attract and hold the attention of the learner. This is possible in multimedia education through exciting audio-visuals, and effective user interface designs. The different user interface types such as text response, pushbuttons, hot spots, clickable objects, drag and drop, etc., which can be implemented using simple devices such as keyboard and mouse can be used to design any kind of user interaction required for such applications. Elegant mechanisms for displaying the data using attractive wipe and dissolve patterns is very helpful to arrest the attention of the users. In addition to these, there is an urgent need for novel teaching mechanisms which make extensive use of the interactive features provided by this technology. Roger Shank (1995) has described several new models of teaching suitable for multimedia education. We have designed a few sessions based on these models, and have found it to be effective for teaching the students. We present a brief discussion on these models in the following paragraphs.

2.1   Learning by practice

We all learn better while doing or attempting to do something. The interactive features can be used to provide this kind of a learning environment, wherein the students can be instructed to perform a task step by step, correcting them when they do a mistake, and guiding them properly to accomplish the task. For example, in the interactive session of assembling a distillation apparatus, the parts of the apparatus are shown separately, and the students are required to assemble them by dragging the individual parts with the mouse and dropping them at appropriate positions. Proper feedback is provided after every interaction, which ensures that the students commit no mistakes while assembling. Figure 1 shows an interactive experiment of measuring the length of objects using vernier calliper. The students can measure the length of various objects using this module which is a simulation of the laboratory exercises. The student can move the arm, insert the object for measurement, readout the scales from the display, and type-in the readings after hearing suitable audio prompts from the system. A hint button helps the student to arrive at the correct reading, and several hypertext links are available on the different parts of the calliper containing appropriate message which can be activated by the student by clicking on those hot spots. This approach not only teaches the concept behind these experiments, but also makes them confident while actually performing them in the labs. Moreover, experiments which are costly, hazardous, and time consuming can be made available to the students through these modules.

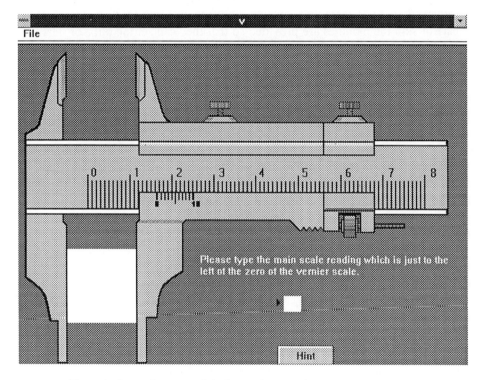

Figure 1: A sample screen of the interactive experiment on vernier calliper

2.2   Learning to discover, probe and question

The tutorial sessions describe the abstract concepts in these topics through well designed audio-visuals. For example, the description and comparison of atomic models proposed by various scientists, experiments to determine the mass of atoms, calculation of resultant of forces, definitions like torque, moment of inertia, formulae of motion, etc., explain the fundamental ideas very clearly in unambiguous way through carefully prepared animations. These animations stimulate the students to visualise the concepts, apply them to other similar phenomenon and comeup with several interesting questions and new ideas. After the tutorials, the students can take an objective type question and answer session which test the level of understanding of the students rather than repeating the materials taught. The main aim of these modules is to encourage the students to learn by understanding and not through rote memorization.

2.3 Learning in a convenient way

The learning process should be simple, convenient and be under the control of students who can develop their knowledge on the subjects gradually. User Interfaces like VCR metaphors which allow the students to start, stop, pause, replay or skip the modules are provided so that they can set the pace of learning according to their levels of comprehension. A brief description of the navigational buttons and pull-down menus is flashed on the screen once the cursor enters these hot spot areas which is helpful for the students to know about functions of these metaphors. Even though the systems cannot provide the empathy which the human beings are capable of, they are more suitable for such repetitive tasks which may cause many humans to become impatient.

It is found that the students who are used to group studies find this method of study more convenient than those students who indulge in self-study. This may be due to the reason that students who do self-study have less opportunity to gather different ideas, and this leads to the memorisation of the text book materials. Moreover, such students are found to be closed, in the sense that they do not raise their voice for clarifying their doubts or come forward and part with their knowledge. Multimedia education can play a vital role to benefit these students in several ways. It is possible to provide individual attention to every student, which, by itself, can help the students grasp the subject better. Moreover, students who feel shy to express their inability to comprehend will feel comfortable with these modules, since they could repeat the lesson any number of times till they become thorough with it. Also, the modules provide a safe place for failures for students who do not perform well in quizzes. The students should neither be discouraged nor belittled for their failures, but should be encouraged to correct their mistakes. This is done through these modules by way of encouraging remarks and providing the solutions to those questions for which the students answer incorrectly.

2.4 Learning is fun

It is very important to be relaxed while learning as this makes the students pay more attention and also enjoy the learning process. We have provided soft background music throughout the modules in order to enable the students to concentrate better on the material taught, which has found to be very effective for the students. The modules have been designed with attractive audio-visuals, which make extensive use of cartoon figures, special effects, and interesting feedback for the user interaction. At the end of the quiz session, an animation with encouraging audio will be flashed on the screen depending on the students' performance, with the most attractive animation played for the highest scorers. This motivates the students to try harder in the forthcoming quiz sessions.

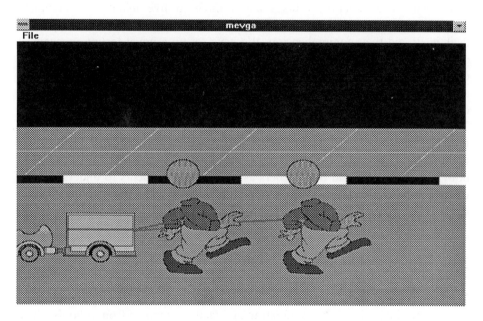

Figure 2: A sample screen illustrating the idea that learning is fun

Moreover, if a student does not respond for a long duration, simple animations are played on the screen which remind the students about their response. Figure 2, a sample screen of one of the modules, defines the resultant of forces using cartoon-like characters. These techniques make the learning process an effective one for the students.

2.5   Learning by understanding

It is found that many of the students use the rote memorizing technique for learning instead of trying to comprehend the contents. The main aim of multimedia education is to make the students understand the concepts through well-designed audio-visuals. In our modules, we have implemented this by allowing the students to answer several objective type questions after each tutorial session. If the student answers incorrectly to any question, the solution is provided immediately, which enables a spontaneous correction of their mistakes. These questions test the understanding of the students and encourage them to learn by recalling in small steps, instead of following the brute force method of memorization.

To emphasise this concept, we have created a tutorial session on Rutherford's gold foil experiment, which illustrates the entire experiment through carefully prepared animations and approriate narration describing every step in the experiment. The experiment takes about three to five minutes to complete depending on the students' interaction, as we have provided several hypertext facilities to aid their comprehension. We have set up a novel testing mechanism of this experiment in the quiz session. Several short sentences which describe the experiment is arranged in an improper order and the students are prompted to arrange the sentences in the proper order which describes the experiment correctly by dragging and dropping a graphical object attached to each sentence. The idea is to allow the students to form the description of the experiment which they had learnt earlier. This interactive session corrects the students and guides them to form the experiment correctly. This kind of an approach is appreciated both by the students and the teachers as it allows the students to understand the complex experiments in simple steps, and also tests their understanding effectively.

3.0   A report on the feedback

We have covered about twenty five different schools belonging to different parts of the city which have diverse infrastructural facilities ranging from schools which have no computers to the schools which already have started implementing multimedia education for a few classes of students. We have obtained feedback from about one hundred and fifty students and one hundred teachers through separate questionnaires. The questions aimed at the students mostly concentrated in finding out their response on the various technical aspects of the demo such as user friendliness, coverage of the subjects, ratings of this demo, their usage of computers, etc. The questions to the teachers and the administrative staff aimed at gathering information on the existing infrastructure, future plans of their schools, their interest to implement multimedia education, and so on. The students ranged from highly intelligent to the below-average categories and we found that every one equally enjoyed going through the demo sessions.

The demo has evoked a terrific response from the students and the teachers who welcomed this kind of education to be introduced in their schools. A qualitative analysis of the feedback given by the students and the teachers has raised several points worthy of consideration from technical, marketing, financial, and psychological aspects. It is found that almost all the schools have computers, and the students are being exposed to them at various levels. However, not many schools have the necessary infrastructure for multimedia education. The computers have been mainly used for developing programming skills among the students. However, multimedia systems are slowly making their entry into the schools. Most of the students were curious and excited about a demo of this kind, as their knowledge on computer applications was limited to programming, word processing, office automation and accounting. Eventhough multimedia titles like encyclopedias are available, modules on subject-specific coverage like these which cater to their academic curriculum, evoked a widespread interest among students and teachers. The students were comfortable with this kind of learning mechanism and felt confident to face an examination, with this kind of preparation. This kind of learning method has helped the students to pay more attention to learning, which became evident in the quiz sessions, in which the students answered many questions properly. The students wanted more descriptive type questions and numerical problems, which showed their enthusiasm towards these modules.

We have learnt from the students' feedback several requirements in navigational mechanisms of these modules. The students felt comfortable with the browsing mechanisms provided like content buttons, history, forward, backward and search commands, etc. However, every student wanted to browse in a style comfortable to them, and hence a successful multimedia title should contain all the browsing mechanisms mentioned above, in addition to special ones which may be specific to a particular title. For example, in geographical descriptions, a map of the area under discussion will be a better browsing mechanism than the traditional tools. The response to the interactive experiments and quiz was overwhelming. Though some of the students found it difficult to interact with the mouse at the beginning, they felt comfortable after a few sessions. The students showed maximum interest wherever interactive features are more, and the contents have plenty of graphics. We found that the different scoring methods in the quiz, the timing parameters for the question and answer sessions, questions of varying levels of complexity, providing answers to the questions, feedback comments for incorrect answers which add fun and encouragement to the students are some of the important areas to be concentrated in such multimedia titles.

The teachers found this very interesting, and many were even willing to learn authoring so that they can use their teaching experience and create such modules. The authoring tools, such as Authorware, do not demand any programming skills on the part of the authors to create multimedia presentations. This is ideal for teachers, as they can concentrate on the contents of the modules rather than their implementation. They suggested the provision of two modes of control of navigation of the contents - the supervisory and the user mode, in these modules. The supervisory mode allows the teachers to decide on the contents the students can see at any time, and thus control and plan the course according to their curriculum. It also prevents the students from wandering into areas which have not been covered in the classroom. The user mode is for the students, who can be allowed to view the modules according to the teachers plan.

3.1   Marketing and financial scenario

The educational multimedia titles can be produced and marketed in a large scale throughout the nation. However, the language medium of education and the syllabus vary in different parts of the country. This calls for special preparation of multimedia titles which should be able to switch audio and text in the presentation according to the required medium of education. It is very cumbersome to create such titles as it becomes difficult to meet the required timing constraints in playing the audio files belonging to different languages along with the same animation and video sequences. This necessitates the use of sophisticated authoring tools and demands some programming expertise from the authors. Hence, niche marketing is likely to be more popular where the multimedia titles target a limited audience belonging to a particular region or language. In fact, there are many small entrepreneurs who prepare such modules according to the specific requirements of some schools, colleges and institutions. The charges for developing such modules vary from a few hundreds to several thousands of rupees depending on the complexity of the contents, time for development, and volume of the title.

Another important area which needs to be given due consideration is the copyrights and intellectual rights issues. It is important to note that these modules have to be prepared according to the needs of the individual schools, and hence, we found that several constraints arise on marketing similar products to different schools. Many teachers have posed several questions on proprietary issues which call for greater insight, uniform rules and regulations, and general consensus which are outside the scope of this paper.

4.0   Conclusion

The exercise reported in this paper shows that multimedia education is entering the schools in a big way, and there is a huge market for such modules not only in our country but throughout the world. The schools welcome this approach, and many have already started implementing in a phased manner. While this survey was being carried on, we found that several schools have entered into contracts with big software houses to develop multimedia modules for them. Several schools have acquired Multimedia computers, Internet connection and are implementing this method of education. There is an increased demand for authors who create such modules, and training centers have come up which specialise on multimedia authoring packages. The integration of TV with multimedia computers will bring down the price of such systems, which will expand the market for this product. Though it is not affordable for many at present, we hope that multimedia systems will become household items in the future, due to its application in the fields of education and entertainment.

References:

1. Bajaj, N.K. (1993), Physics for Class XII, New Delhi, Tata McGraw-Hill.
2. Macromedia Inc. (1993), Authorware: Users Guide and Reference Manual.
3. Robert, R. and David, H. (1960), Physics for students of Science and Engineering.
4. Roger, C.S. (1995), "Active Learning through Multimedia", IEEE Multimedia, Vol. 1, No. 1, pp.69-78.

PART 7

MULTIMEDIA TRAINING

7.1

THE FUNCTION EXTENSION OF AUTHORWARE AND ITS APPLICATION IN POWER INDUSTRY TRAINING

Yingli Luo, Jianhua Zhang, Lianguang Liu, Xiaofang Liu, Ying Pu, Xiqiang Chen, Henan Qu, Yongshu Gao[1], & Feng Liang[2]
North China University of Electric Power (Beijing), [1]Panjiankou Pumped Storage Power Plant, [2]Peking University, PRC

The functions of Authorware Professional have been extended using C++ programming according to the special requirements of the power engineering training. The dynamic data exchanging between the main Authorware program and power system analysis procedures. This technique lays a foundation for the study of multimedia development platform specially needed in power engineering training.

1.0   Introduction

In order to ensure the security, reliability and economics of power system operation, the operation staff should be regularly trained. Taking into consideration of the complexity of the modern power equipment with the physical procedure varied instantly, the training system is required to possess the following functions.

1. With friendly multimedia interface, making use of the synthetic effects of text, graphics, sound, video and animation for the training.

2. Man-machine interactive functions, the real operation circumstance can be simulated during the training.

3. The coordinating operation between multimedia display in the front platform and the analysis and calculation program running in the back platform, the related physical parameters should be calculated and the operating results performed by the trainee should be judged and corrected in time. According to the specified requirements, it is usually needed to solve linear or nonlinear equation sets with a lot of unknown variables. When dynamic procedure is involved, it is also required to solve more complicated partial differential equation sets.

Taking the multimedia simulating experiment of reactive power control in power systems as an example, this paper suggests that Authorware Professional, the powerful multimedia authoring tool, can meet the needs of power industry training in developing multimedia interface and man-machine interaction, and has shown its prospective application in power industry training. Meanwhile, it is also proposed in this paper that the concurrent functions provided by Authorware should be extended when it is necessary for the trainee to draw color graphics himself during the training, especially when the coordinating operation is required between the multimedia interface in the front platform and the simulation program in the back.

Authorware functions of graphics, dynamic data exchanging and control for the simulation program in the back platform are extended and performed using Borland C++ programming to form several useful dynamic linking library. Perfect effects have been achieved applying the extended functions to the training.

The extended functions of Authorware can be found a larger scale application and provide a new technical means for the developers.

2.0   The necessity of function extension for authorware

Authorware is considered to be one of the most powerful multimedia tools in the world, but when used in power system in the following areas, it still needs to be further exploited.

1. Authorware supplies a convenient drawing tool box during development, but when a platform is developed and packaged to form an executable file, the user have no means to access the drawing tool box.

2. Authorware supplies many functions and variables, but most of them are aimed to generate flexible interface and animation. For power system training, simulated operation, control adjustment and complex calculation should be integrated forming a powerful system. For example, in a simple power network as shown in Fig. 1, when calculate the power flow, a nonlinear deferential equation group including 18 variables should be solved. So the calculation function in Authorware needs to be further developed.

3. A lot of real time data should be exchanged between the front interface and the calculation programs in power system training. Although Authorware provides necessary functions to exchange data with the outside program, it is satisfactory to process small amount and static data exchanging. When running power system analysis program, large amount of data have to be real time exchanged dynamically. Dynamic data exchanging technology (DDE) is used to do so instead of making use of the existing Authorware functions.

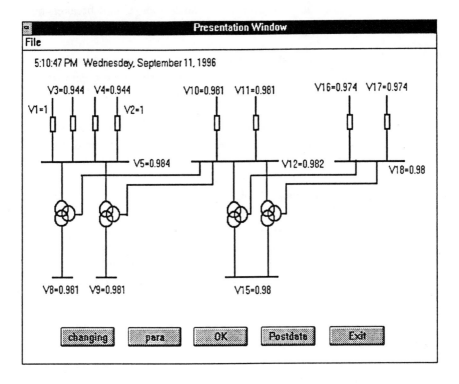

Figure 1: Topology graphics of a sample power network

3.0   Extension contents for authorware functions

3.1   The developing environment before and after extension

Before extension, Authorware provides two ways for programming, one is using Authorware icon program, another is applying the system functions and variables supplied by Authorware. After extension, the developing environment becomes a more powerful tool for the special application in power industry training. Apart from the existing functions, the extended contents includes the following activities.

1. Custom DLL function library which adds many custom functions such as colored graphing when packaged for delivering to end users, function for retract color palette, etc.

2. Power system component library which includes the typical graphics of power system components, such as turbogenerator, transformer, circuit breaker, busbar, switches.

3. Program library for power system analysis and calculation which is compiled to .exe Windows file and can be separately run by Authorware application using DDE technology.

4. Dynamic Data Exchanging model which can exchange data between Authorware display and analysis and calculation programs operated in the back platform.

3.2   Function extension using DLL

Authorware enables the user to develop new dynamic link library using C++ programming. For example, in power system training, it is necessary for the trainee to draw a power network. A powerful graphical library has been specially designed to draw various power system elements, including colored busbar and feeders, circuit breakers, isolators, transformers and generators.

3.3   Function extension using DDE

Authorware has also provided an interface to run the outside program. The system function "JumpOutReturn" enables users to run outside programs from Authorware application. The power system analysis program is compiled to form an independent Windows's .exe file using C++. The multimedia training program is developed by Authorware.

In fact in power system training, it is necessary to calculate the power flow along various feeders by real time solving nonlinear equation group with hundreds of variables. For the training of transient procedures, it is also necessary to solve nonlinear differential equations. The input data for the calculation should be send to the back platform program, and the calculated results are to be transferred to the front plat for display. The data exchange is carried out dynamically with real time operation. Dynamic Data Exchanging (DDE) is introduced to extend Authorware functions so as to ensure the coordinating operation between the multimedia interface in the front platform and the calculation program in the back. Under the management of Windows, the processing step of DDE is as follows.

1. Design and compile C++ functions to initialize, terminate and control data exchange to form corresponding DLLs. The training program will call for these functions and supervise the whole procedure of the data exchanging.

2. According to the requirement of the training, several statements are added to both Authorware training program and the back platform calculating procedure. Hot link is used in data exchanging for power industry training. After setting up the hot link, DDE is proceeded automatically whenever new results are solved out.

3. After receiving the new data, Authorware training program will call for the corresponding DLLs to display the results on the screen. From the trainees point of view, the display they can see on the screen are updated according to what they have just adjusted by mouse or keyboard through man-machine interface.

4.0 Authorware application in power industry training

4.1 Power system analysis and calculation program

In order to realize the coordinate operation with the training program developed by Authorware, the back platform operated power system analysis and calculation program is designed with the structure as shown in Fig. 2.

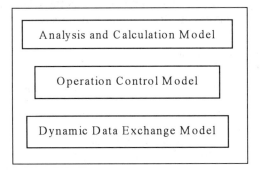

Figure 1: The structure of analysis & calculation

It can be seen that there are three models in the program.

The analysis and calculation model is usually transferred from the ordinary application, in this case, it is translated from a Fortran language to C++ Windows program.

The operation control model is used to set up the operation conditions. That is to specify under which condition and how long of the interval the program runs. In

322

general in the training procedure, the analysis program will run as long as the trainee modifies parameters or make an operation in the front platform.

The DDE model for analysis program servers two functions. One is to receive initial data from the training application, for example, the juncture number, branch number and impedance's of an electric topologic network. Another function is to send the calculated data to the front platform for display.

4.2   The DDE between training application and analysis program

1. Conditions for DDE between Two Programs

The two Windows applications must possess the properties of calling Windows system functions and transferring Windows message between each other. After translated to C++ program, the back platform analysis program has already had the ability. But the training application developed by Authorware is not able to call Windows system functions directly. A special DLL function is developed to equip Authorware application with DDE ability. This DLL is called by Authorware application and promote dynamic data exchange with the back platform analysis program. In this paper, the analysis program is used as the Server of DDE, and the Authorware application as the Client. For simplification, they are called DDE Server and DDE Client respectively.

2. The Structure of DDE Client

Fig. 3 shows the structure of the DDE Client, which includes 4 models.

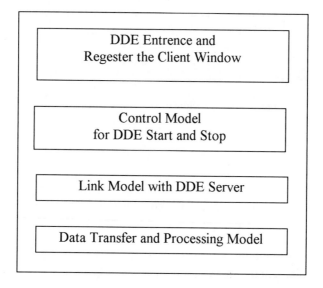

Figure 3: Structure of DDE client

3. Mutual Linking between Authorware Application and Analysis Program

The analysis program running in the back platform will send the analysis results to the multimedia interface continuously for display. The hot linking is adopted to link the two programs. Under hot link, the procedure of Windows message transfer to each other is shown in Fig. 4.

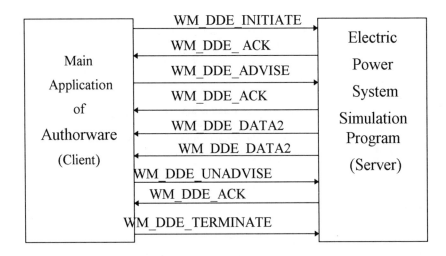

Figure 4: The hot link between Authorware application and the simulation program

5.0   Conclusion

Authorware is a convenient, powerful multimedia development tool for interactive training programs. DLL and DDE technology are introduced to extend Authorware functions so that Authorware can be extensively used to develop more complicated training program. Using the extended functions Authorware has been successfully used to develop a simulation training program for operators in pumped storage power plant, which is illustrated in another paper in this conference.

References

1. He Liqi, Borland (1994). C++ Windows Programming. The People's Posts and Telecommuni-cations Publishing House.
2. Zhang Jianhua, Luo Yingli (1996). Graphical Modeling in Multimedia Development for Power Systems,   Modern Electric Power

APPLICATION OF MULTIMEDIA TECHNOLOGY FOR TRAINING OF OPERATORS IN PUMPED STORAGE POWER PLANT

Jianhua Zhang, Yingli Luo, Lianguang Lui, Xiaofang Liu, Xiqiang Chen, Henan Qu & Yongshu Gao[1]
North China University of Electric Power (Beijing), [1]Panjiakou Pumped Storage Power Plant, PRC

The general scheme of the multimedia training system for operators in pumped storage power plant is illustrated in this paper. It is demonstrated that it is more effective using multimedia technology than the traditional methods for training. The training logic can also be applied in other fields of the energy engineering.

1.0   Introduction

The development of pumped storage power plant in China is now just in its primary stage. The training for the operators in pumped storage power plants is of urgent necessity because of the following three reasons.

a. The operators lack of experience in both operation and management,

b. There are more operating states in pumped storage power plants than in ordinary ones, and the control for transferring from one operating state to another is much more complicated as it is quite different between the control and adjustment of the ordinary water turbine-generators and the reversible pump-turbine and generator-motor machines,

c. The main equipment in the limited pumped storage power plants in China are all imported from abroad, and it is urgently needed to absorb and digest the imported advanced technology.

Taking the above into consideration, in order to enhance the operation and management level so as to ensure the secure, stable and economic operation in pumped storage power plant, the training of operators must be achieved as soon as possible. The most suitable solution to meet such requirement is the application of multimedia technology.

This paper proposes the general structure, functions and method of realization of the multimedia training system for the pumped storage power plant.

2.0 Suitability and specialty of multimedia training system for pumped storage power plant

2.1 Suitability

The system is suitable for operators, and also takes into account of the technical training for managers working in pumped storage power plant. For the operator training, the system is aimed to enhance the capability of experienced operators who graduated from specialty institutions, or provides systematic training for those who graduate from general high school and lack of special knowledge and experience.

2.2 Specialty of the training system

Multimedia technology can synthetically process graphics, text, sound, video and animation using computers. In the man-machine interface of the front platform, the training system provides strong interactivities. The trainees can be involved in the training procedure at any time, such as adjusting the operation parameters, operating with a circuit breaker, reference an operating regulation, entering an exercise or transfer to another procedure. And in the back platform, it possesses remarkable functions for calculation, analysis and logic reasoning so that performs a training simulation for pumped storage power plants. Several types of information effect on the human senses so that the trainees can actively study under the circumstance of excited man-machine dialogue environment. Such a training scheme can greatly increase the learning interest and the amount of information accepted by the trainees, which achieves a much more perfect training effect than the conventional training methods.

In China the operators are quite different in their education background. The fact that the trainees stay in a different knowledge level before training and are required to reach to a unified criterion after training makes the training system developed to possess the following features.

a. The knowledge training and operation training have a close relationship. The knowledge training supplies the necessary preparation for the operation training, which makes the trainee know not only how to operate, but also why to do so.

b. Both parts of knowledge and operation training include different level of contents. So the trainees with different background can conveniently access their corresponding entrance in the system.

2.3 The main functions of the training system

Fig. 1 illustrates the functions of the system. They are summarized as follows.

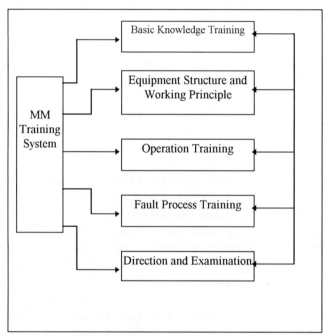

Figure 1: General structure of the training system

a. Basic Knowledge Training

Including the basic knowledge involved in the areas of electrical engineering, hydraulics, machinery, electronics, computer application, etc.

b. Training for Equipment Structure and Working Principles

Including the training of the main primary and secondary equipment in pumped storage power plant with their structure, principle and the associated key advanced technology. The training materials are carefully selected in accordance with the needs of operation training and fault processing training.

c. Operation Training

This part is focused on the training of operation and control for generator-rotor and pump-turbine equipment. It also provides training for operating regulations and the usage of ordinary instruments.

d. Fault Processing Training

According to the varies types of faults listed in the operating regulations, the system supplies a training program for the operators to enhance their capability to deal with the faults which may occur very occasionally in their operation career but may cause serious results.

e. Intelligent Direction and Examination for the Trainees

The training system is capable to analyze and determine which level the trainee stands and intelligently introduces the trainee to enter his corresponding entrance, so as to realize the so called teaching in accordance with capability. It also possesses functions of systematic appreciation and examination for the trainees, and establishes the training documents which make record of the all trainees.

The whole system is open to the developer. According to the requirements from the power plant, some special training contents as well as more management functions can be added.

3.0   Training methods

Different training methods are adopted for the two kinds of training, that is, knowledge training and operation training.

3.1   Method for knowledge training

In order to suit for deferent levels of trainees, the training contents are so arranged that they can be either gradually introduced from easy to difficult, or entered directly to the interested topics. As far as the specified principle is concerned, it can be mastered by the trainee through three key procedures, that is, learning, exercise and examination.

a. Learning

"Learning" procedure is performed by demonstration, lecture and man-machine interaction. According to the features of the electrical equipment, special

328

attention is paid to make the full use of the powerful graphical presentation in multimedia courseware during demonstration and lecture. At the same time, the timing logic of the procedure is also taken into consideration. The coordination between time and space should be presented as far as possible. For example, when introducing the principle of voltage wave of a generator and that of harmonics which the generator produces, the contents shown in Fig. 2 are presented to the trainees on the screen.

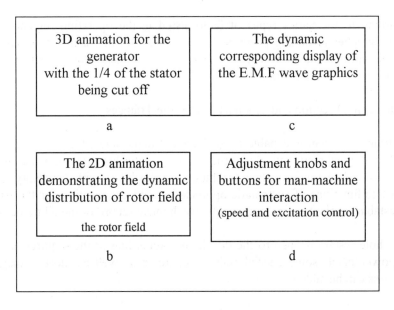

Figure 2: A demonstration interface for knowledge training

When the trainee adjusts the speed knob in Fig. 2d, the rotor speed displayed with 2D and 3D animation in Fig. 2a and 2b will be changed in accordance, and the period and frequency of E.M.F in Fig. 2c will also be altered coordinately.

b. Exercises

"Exercises" can be performed by means of various types of multi-choice fillings. When the trainee has selected a correct choice, he will be informed with the correct answer by text and sound. If the trainee could not understand the correct solution and needs to proceed further learning, the program will introduce him to enter the corresponding contents.

c. Examination

The difference between "examination" and "exercise" is that the former does not show the correct answers and adds several functions such as time limit and examining results statistics. The whole training procedure for the knowledge training is shown Fig. 3.

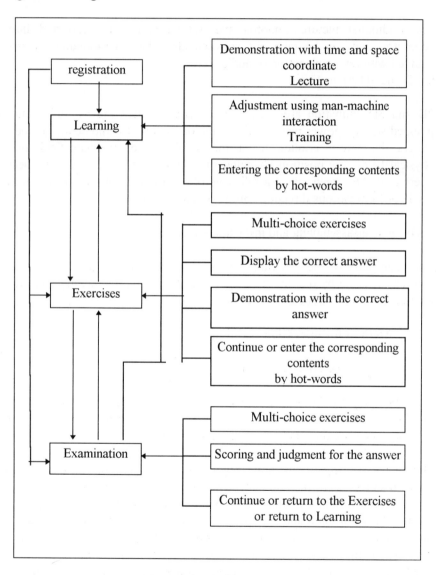

Figure 3: The typical procedure for knowledge training

3.2   The graphical function in knowledge training

In order to illustrate the structure and principle of the power plant equipment, the following graphical functions are adopted in the knowledge training.

a. The 2D and 3D static graphics

The traditional pictures, photos and 3D structures are imported into the computer, and can be take out conveniently. The corresponding images are coupled with text explanation or audio lecture.
b. 2D and 3D Animation

2D and 3D animation are used to imaginary simulate the dynamic actions in pumped storage power plants, such as the operation of equipment, the update of meters, the flow of cooling media, the distribution of magnetic fields or other physical fields, the position changing of circuit breakers, etc. The trainees can operate on the screen, make a full scale observation, from the outside, from the inside or from various directions of the objects.

c. Dynamic disassembling and installation graphics

The main parts of the generator-motor and pump-turbine can be disassembled and installed one by one by the trainees on the screen by clicking and dragging the mouse. Some parts can be cut out to see their inner structure.

3.3   Method for operation training

a. Training for Operating Regulation

The operating regulations can be referenced on the screen by means of text, graphics, sound or video pictures so as to make the trainees familiar with the regulations before they enter the operation training.

During the training of operating regulations, the operation among the control panel, the main network and the generator set is directly displayed simultaneously on the screen with multi-windows setting. For the mutual coordinate operation of the three parts in time and action order, a combination method is adopted, with multimedia display in the front plate associated with the simulation program running in the back plate. The information exchange between the main multimedia program and the simulation procedure is made by means of the dynamic linking library (DLL) which establishes the dynamic data exchange between the two programs (Fig. 4).

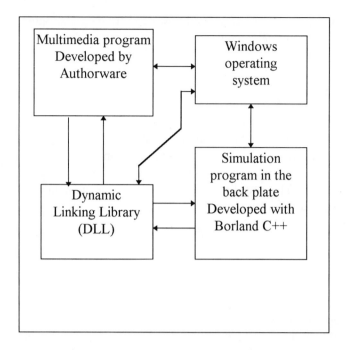

Figure 4: DDE between MM main program and simulation in the back plate

b. Training for the Ordinary Operation and Fault Processing Operation

In operation training, the operation states may be proposed by the computer, or setup by the trainer. The trainee has to determine how to make a correct operation in a limited time. This part of training has fully absorbed the experience from the sophisticated operators, and especially presents such operation modes which may cause serious accidents if incorrectly operated.

The control panel displayed by the computer is similar to the real one. Limited by the screen resolution, if the whole console is displayed, the buttons and knobs are too small to be operated. When operate with some parts or read from a special meters, the interested objects are enlarged to give a clear display.

3.4 The coordination between knowledge training and operation training

In the exercise part of operation training, the trainee can either reference the operating regulations at any time, or conveniently enter the corresponding knowledge training contents. When an error operation takes place, the training system can automatically introduce the trainee to learn the related regulations or knowledge, and then return. Thus the knowledge training and operation training form an entity with mutual interaction.

4.0   Conclusion

The multimedia training system for operators in pumped storage power plants is developed and presented in this paper which makes a combination of knowledge training and operation training to form an entity of an interactive system. Such a training scheme can greatly enhance the training effects and is suitable for various levels of operators. The coordinate operation between the multimedia display in the front plate and the simulation program in the back reflects the advancement of the system.

References

1. Zhong Yuzhuo (1995). "The Industrialization of Multimedia Technology" Computer World, 1995 (1) (In Chinese)
2. Farr MaShell J and Psotka Joseph (1992). "Intelligent Instruction by Computer -- Theory and Practice" Taylor & Francis, Washington
3. Duchastel Philippe C (1992). "Integrating HyperMedia into Intelligent Tutoring" Interactive Multimedia Learning Environments Edited by Max Giardina Springer-Verlag Berlin Heidelberg

7.3

DESIGNING MOTIVATING INTERACTIVE MULTIMEDIA LEARNING ENVIRONMENTS

S.B. Wynn, and R. Oliver
Edith Cowan University, Australia

This paper describes how to design a multimedia program to meet both emotional and cognitive needs. Much of the educational multimedia being produced is dry and unengaging and does not motivate the learner, nor does it promote a desire to continue learning about the subject once the class has finished. This paper identifies eight critical features which can be taken into account when developing engaging and motivating IMM. It briefly describes a program which has been written encompassing these critical features in order to attend to the affective needs of the learner as well as cognitive needs.

1.0   Introduction

Interactive multimedia (IMM) is gaining widespread use as an instructional medium for the flexible delivery of education and training in universities and higher education. Its increase in popularity is due in part to an effort by universities to cut costs, and partly by a need to deliver education to remote locations and to a wide variety of students.

The ability of IMM to improve performance whilst teaching content and in significantly less time, makes it extremely attractive to universities and training institutions (eg. Dalton, Hannafin, & Hooper, 1989; Kulik & Kulik, 1986). In the current frenzy of IMM production, it is predicted that by the Year 2000 more than half of education and training will involve computers in some form (Harrington, McElroy, & Morrow, 1990). To bring about this prediction, educators have to adapt and modify their teaching strategies to accommodate the technology and its impact on the learners. In particular, when designing IMM, recognition must given to not only cognitive outcomes of the programs, but also to the affective requirements of learners.

The affective domain is often overlooked despite evidence that affect and cognition exist in a dynamic spiral and that one cannot exist without the other (Csikszentmihalyi, 1990). There appear to be a number of reasons for this. In the first instance, the affective domain is often not considered part of "serious" scholarship. It is difficult to quantify in educational evaluative terms and research in this area is less common (Goldfayl, 1995). With IMM, the affective domain is associated with the entertainment end of an entertainment-education continuum, comprised of appealing graphics, sounds and low level educational content. On the other hand, the education end of the continuum tends to be occupied by dry and unengaging content (Goldfayl, 1995).

In order to build affect into the design of IMM, it is necessary to have an understanding of the way learners interact with the material. IMM has the capacity to frequently affect changes as learners progress through a program moving from low level understanding to a degree of expertise. Our investigations of the literature and previous research have identified a number of effects which when induced in the learner lead to motivation and engagement. We contend that consideration of these effects in the design process for IMM will lead to more effective learning materials.

2.0   Motivation and interactive multimedia

Many writers provide suggestions for developing IMM which can motivate the learner. For example Gould (1995) states that a motivating multimedia program tends to include fewer productivity features and more experiential and exploratory features. Elements borrowed from gaming multimedia can be substituted for elements borrowed from productivity software and fashioned into an instructional landscape which includes authentic and anchored instruction (Laurel, 1991). The program should be interactive, challenging, include guided discovery and expert performance (Hedberg & Harper, 1996). Norman (1994) suggests the use of a microworld as being able to provide these ideals as well as providing relevant and meaningful material. Motivation also stems from giving the learner an element of control with appropriate feedback on actions taken (Csikszentmihalyi, 1990). When the literature describing motivation in learning environments is taken as a whole, it is possible to distill clear patterns describing learner behaviour and motivation. The following learner effects appear clearly associated with motivation and learner achievement.

2.1   Immersion

Motivation and engagement, whilst having cognitive components, is primarily an emotional response to activities (Laurel, 1991). Learners need to be engaged at a visceral level so that they can temporarily suspend disbelief and feel as though they are part of the program both physically and psychologically (Low, 1994; Laurel, 1991). For engagement, a program must incorporate both experiential and productive activities. Most effective in this regard are programs which are relevant, free of gender bias, provide authentic contexts for learning and which are anchored in everyday, realistic activities. When learners find themselves in situations which make them uncomfortable (e.g. non-realistic situations, or incorrect gender biases), they often cease to be immersed and capable of operating the program using surface thinking only (e.g. Lave, 1988; CTGV, 1993; Brown et al 1989 and Norman, 1994).

Although the gender specific differences found by various studies may simply be a reflection of the ways males and females are socialised, a study by Huff & Cooper (1987) revealed that educational software designers tended to design games for males and learning tools for females. Designing games or microworlds specifically for females can reinforce societal sex stereotypes and raises the ethical issue of the need to produce educational and recreational software which appeals to both sexes (Chaika, 1995).

An effective strategy for incorporating motivating dimensions into IMM programs is to design theme based activities in the form of simulations or microworlds. Microworlds situate learners in an environment that is both meaningful and relevant and allow them to experience a situation which would not normally be available to them.

Situated cognition gives learning a context similar to that of the real world and therefore provides an authenticity to learning. This is tied closely to the theories of adult learning. Knowles (1980), for example, claims that adults learn in the most meaningful way when the learning is anchored to their everyday lives. Jarvis (1987) argues that learning is intimately related to the world and is affected by it. Wilson (1993) extends this argument with the assertion that for any educational process to be truly motivational, it must be located in an authentic activity where it can be based on cognitive practices rather than decontextualised processes and principles. There are a number of ways to create a sense of immersion in a program. Microworlds are gaining in popularity because they can accommodate so many of the above effects.

2.2 Reflection

Immersion in a multimedia program can lead the learner to reflection, a process which is too often neglected in student-centred learning environments (Laurillard, 1995). Reflection can be stimulated in many ways. For example, when buttons and menus are eliminated or substantially removed from a multimedia program, the user must make decisions as to where to move next and how to explore the environment. This act of decision-making involves time (and therefore engagement) and a degree of reflection which cannot be emulated with software with a productivity-based click and read type of interface (Gould, 1995). If this experiential technique is to be successful however, the interface should be intuitive and simple and students may have to be taught to explore if they have never used this type of program before. The program should be truly interactive with a variety of choices and paths so that students may construct their own learning.

Reflection and decision making can lead to higher order thinking and problem solving, but the program must encourage the learners to remain on each task long enough to absorb the information or become expert (Resnick, 1987).

2.3   Transfer

One of the main aims of adult education is to facilitate transfer of learning. Transfer is believed to increase as the similarity between the learning and the real situation increases (Fleming & Levie, 1978). Again, theme based, real-world activities presented in a variety of scenarios and incorporating relevant problem solving activities can accomplish this objective. Situated learning has been attributed with improving transfer of learning to new situations, although some of the literature is divided on this view (eg Park & Hannafin, 1993; Young, 1993, CTGV, 1993).

2.4   Collaboration

Although computers are often viewed as being a tool which students use in isolation from each other, they are readily used by students in small collaborative groups. There is substantial support in the literature of developmental psychology and social cognitive theory that justifies the use of groups as an instructional strategy (eg. Wild, 1996; Vygotsky, 1978). The value of student-student collaboration, however has been called into question by a number of authors (e.g. Laurillard, 1993) who believe that students can "wallow around in mutual ignorance" and may only identify what it is that they don't know, rather than provide mutually beneficial support and instruction.

Specially designed computer-based learning environments can provide for forms of collaboration that can overcome this problem. Such environments support collaboration between the learner and the computer, and it is from this that IMM shows considerable promise in promoting motivation. An IMM program with expert performance built in, can provide opportunities for students to model processes and observe expert performance prior to attempting similar tasks (Herrington & Oliver, 1995). The use of collaborative activities in the design and implementation of IMM provides learning settings that are motivating and engaging for learners of all ages.

2.5 Control

Learner control has been one of the most researched areas of computer based instruction. It is that aspect of design which allows the learners to choose the paths, content, pace and nature of the feedback they receive (Reeves, 1993). A crucial aspect of interactive learning is the way in which control is handled (Kinzie, 1990; La Follette, 1993). There are three basic issues for interactive learning: learner control, self-regulation of learning and ongoing motivation to learn (Kinzie, 1990). When control is given to the learner, adaptive instructional decisions can be made, whereas with system control, instructional decisions are made for the student. This association between the learner and the environment is important in determining the degree of interactivity of the program. Learner control together with coaching is more effective than total learner control or browsing, as the learner is not always capable of maximising use of the control capabilities even when the technology provides unlimited learner control; therefore guided discovery is superior (Hannafin, 1992).

Proponents of learner control believe that it facilitates greater achievement, but Steinberg (1989) found that learner control could create better engagement and attitudes, but not necessarily greater achievement, and that not all students were motivated by being able to control their learning (Reeves, 1993). This finding has been replicated by Murphy & Davidson (1991) who found that learners completed the tasks faster but did not have superior recall or retention of concepts. These findings would suggest that a balance between learner and system control may enhance learning whilst retaining the motivational effects of control; a microworld is capable of being programmed to accommodate different levels of learner control on a continuum from linear or system control, through guided discovery to a browsing mode. One such compromise is known as an *advisement* orientation, where the system makes suggestions to the learner which they can follow or ignore (Ross & Morrison, 1988).

In a business education environment, the microworld can present a view of the business world not previously observed by the students such as ethical standards and behaviours. This builds on the principles of higher order learning where students can be guided into heuristic problem solving and logical thinking.

2.6 Curiosity

Curiosity is an important element in attaining and keeping the learner's attention. The learning environment should be neither too simple, nor too complex, but should be novel and surprising (Malone, 1980). In order to achieve this, the IMM program needs to have elements of exploration, with changing facets to maintain

338

interest and ensure that the learner continues to explore. A program which has only the elements of productivity software, for example, task-oriented procedures and content-free activities, will not stimulate curiosity to the same degree as another with elements that cause curiosity in the learner (Gould, 1995). A microworld is one of the more common learning environments with this capacity.

2.7   Fantasy

Malone (1980) defines a fantasy inducing environment as one that evokes "mental images of things not present to the senses or within the actual experience of the person involved". Fantasy has long been recognised as a key factor in motivating learner activity. To incorporate elements of fantasy, an IMM program needs to build in enough sensory experiences that the learner can actually believe or fantasise that they are in the situation. A distinction can be made between an extrinsic fantasy, where the fantasy depends on the use of skill, but not vice versa, and intrinsic fantasy, where the fantasy depends on the skill, and the skill depends on the fantasy. Intrinsic fantasies are usually better than extrinsic fantasies because not only does the fantasy depend on the skill being used correctly, it also incorporates corrective feedback (Malone, 1980).

2.8   Challenge

Challenge describes the capacity of an IMM program to confront the learner in a manner that evokes some form of competitive activity in the learner. To be effective in motivating and engaging learners, the program should have goals which are challenging without being impossible; they should be more than just read and absorb, or even read and answer questions. More motivating IMM settings have goals with several levels, variable levels of difficulty, hidden information, an element of randomness and contain both relevant and irrelevant material so that the learner has to make decisions about what to accept and reject (Malone, 1980; Brown, Collins & Duguid, 1989; Herrington & Oliver, 1995).

3.0   Developing IMM incorporating these learner effects

When these factors are taken together, they present a strong framework for the development of motivating and engaging IMM programs. The table below provides a summary of the learner effects that are characteristic of motivated learners and describes the educational attributes of IMM learning environments able to create the stated effects.

4.0   Summary of features of a motivating multimedia program

Desired Learner Effects	Educational Attributes
Immersion	Situated cognition, authentic and anchored activities, experiential and productive, relevant. Free of gender bias, theme based activities, microworld, simulation (eg Lave 1988; Brown et al, 1989; CTGV, 1993; Norman, 1994)
Reflection	Higher order thinking, problem solving, exploratory, experiential, time on task (eg Laurillard, 1993; Resnick, 1987b)
Transfer	Situated cognition, authentic and anchored activities, relevant, productive, appropriate feedback (eg Bransford et al, 1993)
Collaboration	Interaction, feedback, learner control (eg Laurillard, 1995; Kinzie, 1990)
Control	Guided discovery, scaffolding, modelling (eg Ross & Morrison, 1988)
Curiosity	Experiential, exploratory, optimally complex, sensory, completeness, consistency, parsimony (Malone, 1980)
Fantasy	Sensory stimulation, engaging, intrinsic and extrinsic, transfer, (eg Low et al 1994; Malone & Lepper, 1987)
Challenge	Problem solving/higher order thinking, appropriate level of difficulty reflective review of strategies (eg Grundy, 1991)

We are currently in the process of developing an interactive multimedia program for use in a local course that incorporates features to induce each of the learner effects shown in Table 1. The program, Principles of Investment, is being designed for adult learners enrolled in a tertiary course of study. The attempt to include a high degree of motivation for the learners is based on our previous observations of adult learners in this setting, many of whom showed disinterest and ambivalence to computer-based training materials.

The design of Principles of Investment has attempted to include elements able to produce each of the eight learner effects. The table below shows the program characteristics that have been employed to achieve this.

5.0   Program attributes in principles of investment

Desired Learner Effects	Program Attributes in Principles of Investment
Immersion	A microworld of a relevant and realistic setting which is easy and intuitive to navigate round.
Reflection	The learner has to decide where to go next, making investment decisions based on the information given to date. The contemplation on the next move creates reflection. Learners can also decide whether to repeat sections based on their understanding.
Transfer	The program aims to instil an understanding of market forces on investment. These are comparable to real-world events
Collaboration	Students are encouraged to collaborate with each other to provide coaching. The system also collaborates with the learner providing coaching and scaffolding. Expert performances are also integrated into the program so that learners can compare their decisions with those of an expert.
Control	Students can explore or get help and hints. They can also choose their own path through the program, revisiting sites where necessary.
Curiosity	Learners' curiosity is constantly stimulated with changing elements, extra features, such as ethical questions posed, and random events.
Fantasy	This program capitalises on the desire to invest in stocks and shares and perhaps to make an investment profit. During the process of investing and making investment decisions, students are taught important financial principles.
Challenge	Surprise elements are included which constantly challenge decision-making principles. Students compete against themselves and also the resident "expert".

The development of Principles of Investment is proceeding and our progress to date suggests that the quest to incorporate each of the eight elements will be successful. Use of a microworld has provided a landscape capable of supporting many of the attributes while discrete aspects within the program design have enabled us to include the remaining elements. On completion of the project, we intend to conduct a thorough investigation of the capacity of the program to motivate and engage learners and will be reporting this research in due course.

6.0 Summary and conclusion

This paper has described a number of attributes of IMM programs which can assist in helping instructional designers to create learning environments that not only attract the attention of users but which are able to hold that attention to assist in the attainment of the desired learning outcomes. Motivation has always been seen as a key element of conventional classroom teaching but tends to be neglected in the design of computer-based products where it is often assumed that the novelty of the technology will provide this component of the learning environment. Our review of the literature has revealed a number of learner effects which have been found to lead to increased motivation. We contend, and are supported by the literature in our contention, that if designers of IMM are able to create learning environments that induce these effects in learners, then such programs will likely lead to higher levels of motivation and engagement with the subsequent prospect of enhanced learning outcomes.

Our review of the literature has shown what it takes to produce a motivating and engaging piece of multimedia. There are, however, very few programs being produced for the education market that contain these features. There are many instructional designers and producers who are creating linear programs with relatively low levels of interactivity but which are easy and cheap to produce. Such materials are limited in their application and can be limited in their effectiveness because of their lack of affective appeal and subsequent lack of utilisation. It does take more time, effort and money to generate motivating learning environments within multimedia programs. To develop IMM programs with some or all of the eight criteria described above, requires careful and deliberate planning and often clever and innovative instructional design. In the long run, the heightened planning and effort can provide significant returns in terms of the scope and extent of the learning outcomes that can be achieved. We believe that this effort is desirable in any form of instructional materials development but particularly in the case of IMM which is developing as a very common form of instructional delivery medium.

References:

1. Brown, J. S., Collins, A., & Duguid, P. (1989). Situated Cognition and the Culture of Learning. *Educational Researcher*, 18(1), 32-42.
2. Chaika, M. (1995). Ethical considerations in gender-oriented entertainment technology. In http://info.acm.org/crossroads/xrds2-2/gender.html
3. Cognition & Technology Group at Vanderbilt (1993). Toward integrated curricula: Possibilities from anchored instruction. In M. Rabinowitz (Ed.),

Cognitive Science Foundations of Instruction Hillsdale, NJ: Lawrence Erlbaum Associates.

4. Csikszentmihalyi, M. (1990). Flow: The psychology of optimal experience. New York: Harper & Row.

5. Dalton, D. W., Hannafin, M. J., & Hooper, S. (1989). Effects of individual and cooperative computer-assisted instruction on student performance and attitudes. *Educational Technology Research & Development*, 37(2), 15-24.

6. Fleming, M., & Levie, W. H. (1978). Instructional message design: Principles from the behavioural sciences. Englewood Cliffs, NJ: Educational Technology Publications.

7. Gardiol-Gutierrez, C., & Boder, A. (1992). Multimedia and Training: Practice and Skills of European Producers, Results of the European Project "START-UP" (Part 2). Educational Media International, 29(3), 120-128.

8. Goldfayl, D. (1995). Affective and Cognitive Domain Learning with Multimedia: Two Sides of the Same Coin. In ASCILITE '95, . Melbourne:

9. Gould, E. J. (1995). Empowering the audience: the interface as a communications medium. *Interactivity*, 1(4), 86-88.

10. Hannafin, M. J. (1992). Emerging technologies, ISD, and learning environments: critical perspectives. *Educational Technology Research and Development*, 40(1), 49-63.

11. Harrington, K. V., McElroy, J. C., & Morrow, P. C. (1990). Computer anxiety and computer-based training: a laboratory experiment. *Journal of Educational Computing Research*, 6, 343-358.

12. Hedberg, J., & Harper, B. (1996). Interactive educational technologies: Effective design and application in the classroom. In C. McBeath & Atkinson, R. (Ed.), 3rd International Interactive Multimedia Symposium, (pp. 160-168). Perth, Western Australia: Promoco Conventions Pty Ltd.

13. Herrington, J., & Oliver, R. (1995). Critical characteristics of situated learning: Implications for the instructional design of multimedia. In J. M. &. E. Pearce A (Ed.), ASCILITE'95 - The 12th Annual Conference of the Australian Society for Computers in Learning in Tertiary Education, Melbourne: University of Melbourne.

14. Huff, C., & Cooper, J. (1987). Sex Bias in Educational Software: The effect of designers' stereotypes on the software they design. *Journal of Applied Psychology*, 17(6).

15. Jarvis, P. (1987). Adult Learning in the Social Context. London: Croom-Helm.

16. Kinzie, M. B. (1990). Requirements and benefits of effective interactive instruction: learner control, self-regulation, and continuing motivation. *Educational Technology, Research & Development*, 38(1), 5-21.

17. Knowles, M. S. (1978). The Adult learner: a neglected species (2nd ed.). Houston, Texas: Gulf Publishing Co.

18. Knowles, M. S. (1980). The Modern Practice of Adult Education: From Pedagogy to Adragogy. Chicago: Follett Publishing Company.

19. Kulik, C. L., & Kulik, J. A. (1986). Effectiveness of computer-based education in colleges. *AEDS Journal*, 19, 81-108.

20. La Follette, J. J. (1993). Interactivity and Multimedia Instruction: Crucial attributes for design and instruction. In Selected Research and Development Presentations at the Convention of the Association for Educational Communications and Technology Sponsored by the Research and Theory Division, . New Orleans, Louisiana:

21. Laurel, B. (1991). Computers as Theatre. Reading, Mas: Addison-Wesley Publishing Company.

22. Laurillard, D. (1993). Rethinking University Teaching. London: Routledge.

23. Laurillard, D. (1995). Multimedia and the changing experience of the learner. *British Journal of Educational Technology*, 26(3), 179-189.

24. Lave, J. (1988). Cognition in practice: Mind, mathematics and culture in everyday life. Cambridge, UK: Cambridge University Press.

25. Low, M., Venkataraman, S., & Srivatsan, V. (1994). Developing an entrepreneurship game for teaching and research. *Simulation & Gaming*, 25(3), 383-401.

26. Malone, T. W. (1980). What makes things fun to learn? A study of intrinsically motivating computer games. Technical Report CIS-7, Xerox Parc.

27. Murphy, M. A., & Davidson, G. V. (1991). Computer-based adaptive instruction: Effects of learner control on concept learning. *Journal of Computer-Based Instruction*, 18(2), 51-56.

28. Norman, D. (1994). First Person: Defending human attributes in the age of the machine. InNew York: Voyager.

29. Park, I., & Hannafin, M. J. (1993). Empirically-based guidelines for the design of interactive multimedia. *Educational Technology Research and Development*, 41(3), 63-85.

30. Reeves, T. C. (1993). Interactive Learning Systems as mind tools. *Viewpoints, 2*

31. Resnick, L. B. (1987). Education and Learning to Think. Washington, DC: National Academy Press.

32. Ross, S. M., & Morrison, G. R. (1988). Adapting Instruction to learner performance and background variables. In D. H. Jonassen (Ed.), Instructional Designs for Microcomputer Courseware (pp. 227-245). Hillsdale, NJ: Lawrence Erlbaum Associates.

33. Steinberg, E. R. (1989). Cognition and learner control: a literature review 1977-88. *Journal of Computer based instruction*, 16(4), 117-121.

34. Vanderbilt, C. a. T. G. a. (1993). Toward integrated curricula: Possibilities from anchored instruction. In M. Rabinowitz (Ed.), Cognitive Science Foundations of Instruction Hillsdale, NJ: Lawrence Erlbaum Associates.

344

35. Vygotsky, L. (1978). Mind in Society. Harvard University Press: Cambridge, MA.
36. Wild, M. (1996). Investigating verbal interactions when primary children use computers. *Journal of Computer Assisted Learning, 12*(2), 66-77.
37. Wilson, A. L. (1993). The promise of situated cognition. In S. Merriam (Ed.), An Update on Adult Learning Theory San Francisco: Jossey-Bass Publishers. Young, M. F. (1993). Instructional design for situated learning. *Educational Technology Research and Development*, 41(1),

7.4

MULTIMEDIA AND NEW MODELS OF LEARNING IN THE INTERNET

Jyrki Pulkkinen and Esa Niemi
University of Oulu,Finland

An important challenge facing the development of educational programs has been to find the relation between the contents and the method of study. The problem in Web based courses has been the lack of functional, practical models and tools. The guiding principle of our Web based open learning environment is that the studies proceed as a project from the student's point of view. The backbone for the OLE and it's learning tools is provided by a study server on which information systems have been constructed to support the studies, especially project study. Multimedia is an essential part of the learning environment. These models and tools are suitable for in-service training of schools and enterprises.

1.0   Introduction

An important challenge facing the development of educational programs has been to find the relation between the contents and the method of study. This model of thinking has traditions which date back to the remote past. John Dewey, the American philosopher and researcher, crystallized the principle of his "problem method" in the early 20th century in the concept of "Learning by Doing". Dewey thus thought that study meant problem-solving that would be most successful through practical research activities. The same model of action is also present in the "project method" introduced by Kilpatrick. Today these principles have re-emerged as educational challenges thanks to the so-called constructive psychology, in which the basic idea is that the student must construct his knowledge and skills through his own experiences. Systemic psychology has also placed emphasis on independent research as the cornerstone of all study, but it has emphasized the social nature of learning to a larger extent than constructive psychology.

The problem in Web based courses has been the lack of functional, practical models and tools for the construction of the students' own knowledge. Mere reading does not open the contents of courses, as the participants need to be allowed to do things and produce knowledge themselves. The student who is struggling alone with a bunch of WWW learning materials may well be longing for the strained atmosphere in the classrooms of his childhood. In our developmental work, an effort has been made to construct a new kind of open learning environment on Web which enables distance learning from work or home, adds the social dimension to study and helps the student to develop his thinking further.

2.0   Pedagogical principles of open learning environment (OLE)

In learning theoretical or practical skills mere experience adds to the student's knowledge level but is not sufficient, however, in order to reach for higher learning processes. This would presuppose so called reflection, which can be described as a general term for those intellectual and affective actions with which an individual handles his experiences in search of a new kind of understanding and evaluation. As far as reflection is concerned, it should be remembered that although an individual controls the reflection process himself, he needs also social interaction for reflecting and comparing his own ideas with those of others. Individual learner can process his own experiences and link new ideas and insights into the cognitive schemes of other people. Teacher's role is to assist and support this process.

A reflective process cannot develop in a void. We stop to reflect because some things require reflection before action or a particular situation we are in calls for a need to reflect. Situations like this can occur in everyday life, but they can also be situations which have been created on purpose, like in our Open Learning Environment (OLE). Project learning situations arise from practical or theoretical problems related to student's own learning goals, earlier experiences or related learning materials. For reflecting these problems, students can use the questions presented in the learning materials or "bookmarks" as a starting-point. Special tools for reflection and discussions are created on this purpose in our OLE. Reflective discussions are very important in order to make the students feel that they belong to the group which has come together to try and learn, to find a deeper understanding to the matter they are learning about.

Learning through own experience and reflection emphasizes the student's own activity to a great extent. The guiding principle of our OLE is that the studies proceed as a project from the student's point of view. This means that the student's first task is to get oriented towards the field of topics to be learned, and to *determine a goal* for his studies which is sensible and challenging from his own viewpoint. The goal is reached gradually through *project work* supported by different *learning materials* and joint discussions. In this practico-theoretical project work, students can put together all the knowledge which they have experienced meaningful in the learning materials and discussions.

Because the project work will be finished slowly as students proceed in their studies, it has been useful to develop so-called "portfolio study" for organization and joint evaluation of knowledge. Students have to gather any thoughts directly provoked by each section of learning materials to the relevant portfolios. On this basis it is possible to enter into a discussion with the other students and with the tutor. Through this reflective and social activity on the web, the students are able to finish their project papers trying to improve their design and expertise.

3.0   Project tools for learning (Proto)

The backbone for the OLE and it's tools is provided by a study server (http://edtech.oulu.fi) on which information systems have been constructed to support these studies, especially project study. This information server is based on World Wide Web technology and also provides E-mail and capabilities. The learning materials and learning tools are implemented in HTML format and Allaire's Cold Fusion. This will offer quite a robust system, because all database interactions are encapsulated in a single database processing engine.

One tool for project learning consists of a remote editor for portfolios and project pages and special discussion areas for reflective discussions. The remote editor system enables the students to produce their project pages easily on the web, even without knowledge on how to use the HTML language. At the moment it will be sufficient to mark only links and images with HTML tags. In addition, students can send HTML page scripts made by another editor to our server. On the Proto pages there is also a possibility to add links to multimedia applications created by using Toolbook. To achieve system security, students have access to edit only their own pages, but they can read all the pages of other students. The tutors and administrators have access to edit all the pages. That way they can assist the students in their work, for example.

In addition to traditional information presentation, it is possible for the students to take part in discussions based on their project papers and other learning experiences. The discussion tools have been developed to support argumentation and reflective discussion. The progress of discussion is shown as a thread and students can use filters while browsing the messages. Discussion tools are also a field where the students will get assistance from the tutor, both in technical as well as in content problems.

4.0   Multimedia as a part of OLE

Generally, multimedia as a tool in learning process is more interesting than multimedia as a source of information. Of course, in instruction, the properly structured multimedia presentation can help student to form an image about the subject, but reaching deeper understanding, producing the multimedia (hypermedia) presentation seems to be the only way. You can compare these processes to reading and examining. In multimedia authoring process the learner have to make the structure of the subject very clear, before he can construct the presentation. This process can be based to the literature and own experiences. Relevance of the knowledge should be judged in social context by the teacher and the peer group of the student. Therefore, if there is need for socially relevant learning, as the cases in our own experiences,   there should be a human interaction in the multimedia authoring process, too. (e.g. tutoring, guidance and assessment at the distance).

Understanding multimedia and hypermedia more as tools than as an information source, makes it difficult to help and support student's multimedia projects at a distance. Reflective discussions are not very effective, if there are no productions to show.   In our learning model and PROTO environment, it is essential that students can present their project works irrespective of the multimedia authoring tool. Currently it is easy for students to select different backgrounds on PROTO pages and link other multimedia components (i.e. sound, pictures, animated images) only by selecting and pasting the required links on their pages from distance.

To helping students we have already made it possible for students to convert, link and show PowerPoint, Microsoft Word documents and present Asymetrix ToolBook applications on their Proto pages. Students are also encouraged to examine live video clips and real time video conference via tcp/ip when it gives added value for their projects.

In near future it will also be possible for students to transfer images and binary programs via PROTO pages to the database. This way students can have own image library related in their work. In some cases there might be a need for transfer programs. From student's point of view, one user interface in all distance study activities is the major advantage. It saves time and money and can make learning meaningful and effective.

5.0   OLE in in-service training of schools and enterprises

A traditional way to implement training in organisations is to teach the individual members. As the activities and tasks become more and more complicated, co-operation is required in order to handle various entities, individual-centered way to develop things is no longer sufficient by itself. Often the aim is to reach deeper levels of learning and such tools and environments are needed, which enable a group to make use of both common and individual experiences while in pursuit of these deeper levels.

The meaning of a group in an experimental or reflective learning is important. On one hand a group brings in new ideas and comprehension, it works as a kind of mirror, where an individual can reflect his own experiences and ideas and receive feedback from. The feedback in turn initiates and supports the reflection process. On the other hand, the group functions as a kind of shelter for the individual against difficult and threatening things, which become inevitable once deeper levels of learning are sought and familiar ways of thinking and functioning have to be given up.

It is necessary for an individual and groups to learn, but from the point of view of an organisation functioning in a complex environment this is not enough. The work of separate people and groups have to be linked together and the whole of organisational functioning will have to be developed as a result of a group work. When this occurs, we can speak about a learning organisation. This can be portrayed as a cycle where individual cognitions work their way via group work into organisational functions and thereafter via surrounding functions and reactions back to individual cognitions. This kind of cycle and its various phases can be practised also in a simulated environment.

As the OLE has been developed, the principles of the previously mentioned functioning models of a learning organisation have been considered. A simulated situation where a group processes together the task at hand can be built in the environment. Group work becomes possible with easy dissemination and processing of the output in PROTO environment. The group can either produce one output as a solution to a problem, or each of the group members produces their own solution, after which the results are discussed together and they are further developed in a PROTO environment. The process leader may simulate an organisation or its functions by using various tools and thus guide the process to take the desired direction. The discussion topics are in a tree-format and this makes it easy to follow the course of discussion. The process controller may observe how active each member in the group is to participate. The system can be protected in such a way that the group enters the system either with a common pass word, in which case they all share the same resources and are able

350

to produce documents together, or, they each have a pass word of their own. In this case, a member can follow the output of all the other members of the group, but produce and edit only his own document. When the system is in www-environment the group does not have to be physically in the same place, it will be sufficient that they all have access to www-pages. The system can be protected with pass words so that outsiders cannot access the area and the simulated situations can therefore rise directly out of the everyday work of the organisation.

References:

1. Boud, D, Keogh, R and Walker, D. (ed).(1987). Reflection: turning experience into learning. London: Kogan Page.
2. Jonassen, D.H. (1994). Thinking Technology. Toward a Constructivist Design Model. Educational Technology April/1994, 34-37.
3. Järvilehto, T. (1994). Learning and the new educational technology. In Proc. Int. Workshop on CLCE, ed. by Levonen, J.J. and Tukiainen, M.T., 58-60.
4. Järvelä, S. (1996). Cognitive apprenticeship model in a complex technology-based learning environment. Universitas Ostiensis, University of Joensuu. Publications in Education. N:o 30.
5. Pulkkinen, J. (1996). Technology Changing the Pedagogical Culture. The Thirteenth International Conference on Technology and Education, ICTE, March, 17-20, 1996. New Orleans, USA
6. Pulkkinen, J. & Niemi, E. (1996). Kohti sisällön ja muodon integraatiota - koulutusteknologia 15 ov. Koulutusteknologia-lehti 1/96, 14-15.
7. Pulkkinen, J. (ed.). (1996). Introduction to Telematics in Teacher Training: First flexible learning material package of T3.
8. Sweefers, W. (1994). Multimedia Electronic Tools for Learning. Educational Technology May-June/-94, 47-52

7.5

THE INTERACTION OF COGNITIVE STYLES WITH VARYING LEVELS OF FEEDBACK IN MULTIMEDIA PRESENTATION

Swe Khine Myint
University of Brunei Darussalam, Brunei

The concept of feedback and its role in instruction has historically received a great attention in the instructional design literature. While feedback seems to be crucial to effective instruction, research indicated that this is true only under certain conditions. Some of the findings suggested that elaboration of feedback did not necessarily increase in test performance. In an attempt to improve learning efficiency and address to individual differences, research frequently focused on the relationship between different learner aptitudes and different instructional methods, particularly on the concepts of cognitive styles such as field-dependent-independent (FDI). Recent development in multimedia presents opportunities and challenges for educators who want to develop effective instructional programs. A study was carried out to investigate the interactive effects between varying levels of feedback among students who were field-dependent-independent in a multimedia presentation. This paper describes the findings from the investigation and discusses some of the implications to the design of multimedia instruction.

1.0   Introduction

One challenging task of instructional designer-developer in the field of media and communications technology is to improve the design of instructional systems and materials in achieving better learning outcomes. The technology of instructional design looks for a prescription specifying which instructional strategy or combination of strategies most effectively enhance the human learning. The concept of feedback and its role in instruction has historically received a great deal of attention among instructional designers. While feedback would seems to be crucial for learning enhancement, it was found that it is only true under certain situations and conditions.

Clarina, Ross and Morrision (1991) noted that while the benefits of feedback in general is taken for granted, uncertainty still exist as to how to select and optimize the uses of different forms of feedback depending on characteristics of students and learning situation. The effectiveness of feedback is a basic component of instructional theory that has been demonstrated by many researchers. Frequent and consistent use of feedback is also recommended in variety of teaching situations.

In a learning situation, feedback may be broadly defined as information obtained by students regarding the correctness of their performance in a learning task. Different types of feedback can be categorized according to their functions and characteristics (Dempsey and Sales, 1993). Knowledge of results (KOR) is the simplest level of feedback which provides responses such as "right" or "wrong", "true" or "false and "correct" and "incorrect" without giving the correct answer.

Elaborative feedback (EF) is a higher order post-response information which not only contains result on the appropriateness of a learner's response, but also provides reasons for why it was wrong and gives the correct answer. No feedback (NF) allows the learners to proceed the instructional sequence without receiving any post-response on what they have tried.

The research literature so far has focused on numerous aspects of information feedback. Studies have examined immediacy of feedback, amount of information in feedback, the type of task involved, the importance of error analysis, and response certitude. Researchers agree that informative feedback does benefit learning under certain conditions, but whether it enhance performance for all types of learning tasks and all types of learners is still not clear.

Hedberg and McNamara (1985) examined the effects of type of feedback (knowledge of results and informative feedback) and cognitive styles (field-dependence-independence and reflectivity-impassivity) on response time, error rate, number of attempts, and correct score. Their results indicated that field-dependent students had higher response rates and fewer errors when knowledge of results was given. Based on the results reported in the literature, it is evident that there is a possibility that different forms of feedback might have differential effects on different types of learners.

Almost all of the existing literature suggested that manipulation of levels of feedback research used printed materials or computer assisted instruction. The development of technology assisted learning is rapidly moving from the simple use of computer as a text and graphic generating device to more integrated multimedia.

The purpose of the study was to investigate the possible interaction effects between three levels of feedback and level of field-dependency in multimedia presentation. The achievement of posttest scores of field-dependent and field-independent students was compared among different levels of feedback treatments.

2.0   Method

2.1   Subjects

The subjects for thus study were 105 upper secondary school students with the age ranged from fifteen to twenty. Eighty three percent of the group were between the ages of sixteen and seventeen. Of these students, 52 percent are male (N=55) and 48 percent are female (N=50). From the questionnaire from the pilot study, it was found that the experimental students have not been exposed to the content of the multimedia instruction used for the study. The student's cognitive style of field dependence-independence was assessed by means of Group Embedded Figure Test (GEFT)(Witkin, Oltman, Raskin & Karp, 1971).

The overall mean GEFT score of the 55 males was 12.45 with a standard deviation of 4.74 while the overall mean GEFT score of the 50 females was 10.86 with a standard deviation of 4.45. For the purpose of the study, the 105 students were divided in thirds based on their scores. Those with mean score higher than half of the standard deviation were placed at the upper third level and labeled field independent. Those with the mean scores lower than half of the standard deviation were labeled field dependent. This strategy allows for the comparison of definite cognitive style tendencies by extreme groups for comparison without losing valuable data.

2.2   Material

Multimedia Presentation. A commercially produced multimedia presentation on Dinosaurs was used as stimulus material. The multimedia program consisted of verbal information and presented in text, graphic and sound. The content presented in the program consisted of six major sections.

Practice Test. A practice test with different levels of feedback was developed by the investigator. The practice tests were designed to include three different levels of feedback namely No feedback (NF), Knowledge of results (KOR) and Elaborative feedback (EF). Each subjects answered ten practice questions and observed the corresponding feedback.

Posttest. The on line posttest was administered after the practice session. Each posttest included 20 multiple choice questions on the stimulus material. The score on each test were used as the dependent variable in this study. The KR-20 reliability coefficient was found to be 0.668.

Procedure. Subjects were assigned in random to one of the three treatment. Each student spent about an hour on the stimulus material presented in multimedia mode. Upon completion of the presentation, each subject individually completed the on line posttest.

Design and Data Analysis. The study employed 2 x 3 factorial design. The two independent variables were the different levels of feedback (No feedback-NF, Knowledge of results -KOR) and Elaborative feedback -EF), and the students' level of field orientation (field-dependent-independent). The learning outcomes as measured by the posttest were the dependent variable. In order to determine the effects of feedback and level of field dependency, one-way ANOVA was used. To measure the Post Hoc Multiple Comparisons, Scheffe' Multiple Range Test with a significance level of .05 level was used. Two-way ANOVA was performed to test the interactive effects between the level of feedback and the level of field-dependency.

3.0   Results

3.1   Achievement

The first research question in this experiment addressed whether or not provision of different levels of feedback has any effect in terms of test performance. The second research question explores whether the students' level of field-dependency would have any effect on their test performance. Table 1 shows the breakdown of treatment groups by level of field-dependency of these 105 experimental subjects.

Table 1: Summary of means and standard deviations of treatment groups by field-dependency

	NF		KOR		EF	
	Mean	S.D	Mean	S.D	Mean	S.D
Field Dependent	8.27	3.19	13. 50	1.17	11.89	2.57
N=	11		10		9	
Field Independent	10.72	2.39	14.75	2.37	14.88	1.96
N=	18		12		16	

The preliminary data showed that subjects in the field-dependent group score higher in knowledge of results (KOR) treatment (Mean=13.50, S.D=1.17) than those with the same level of field-dependency in elaborative feedback (EF) treatment (Mean=11.89, S.D = 2.57). Similarly those in the knowledge of results group (KOR) scored higher than those with the same level of field-dependency in the no feedback group (NF) (Mean=8.27, S.D=3.19).

For field-independent subjects those who were in the elaborative feedback (EF) group (Mean=14.88, S.D=1.96) scored higher than those who were in the knowledge of results (KOR) group (Mean=14.75, S.D=2.37). While at the same time subjects in the knowledge of results (KOR) group scored higher than those in the elaborative feedback (EF) group (Mean=10.72, S.D=2.39).

In order to test the hypothesis on whether or not provision of vaying levels of feedback has significant effect on the posttest, group means were computed. Table 2 indicates the means and standard deviations of posttest scores by each treatment group. As a whole group, subjects in the elaborative feedback (EF) group scored highest (Mean=14.22, S.D=2.37) as compared to those in the knowledge of results group (Mean=13.50, S.D=2.85). Subsequently subjects in the knowledge of results (KOR) group scored higher than those in the no feedback (NF) group (Mean=9.85, S.D=3.1).

The one-way analysis of variance of the treatment groups was performed in order to find out the efficiency of different level of feedback. The results showed that the value of $F = 24.7059$ is significant at p =.0000. However, it was not possible to conclude whether the significant difference among the group means reflects exclusively the positive effect of level of feedback, or if this significant difference also indicated superiority of other experimental conditions.

Table 2: Means and standard deviations of treatment groups

Treatment Group	Mean	S.D.	Cases
No Feedback	9.85	3.1	35
Knowledge of Results	13.50	2.85	34
Elaborative Feedback	14.22	2.37	36

In order to clarify the true significant mean difference, a Scheffe's Multiple Range Test was used for the *a postteriori* multiple comparisons, with an Alpha set at the .05 level. The results showed that there is a significant difference in posttest

356

scores between the NF group and KOR, NF and EF groups. However, a significant difference was not detected between the KOR and EF groups.

Table 3: Analysis of variance of feedback efficiency for three treatment groups

Source of variation	DF	SS	MS	F	Sig. of F
Between Groups	2	385.1254	192.5627	24.7059*	.0000
Within Groups	102	795.0078	7.7942		
Total	104	1180.1333			

* Significant at the .05 level

3.2 Effects of field-dependency

The second reserach question is to find out whether or not the students' level of field-dependcy have any effects on posttest performance. As shown in Table 4 the group mean score for field independent subjects was Mean=13.21, S.D=2.98 is higher than the field dependent subjects Mean=11.1, S.D=3.31. The mean score of the field independent subjects in Program 2, Mean=14.10, S.D=3.62 is again higher than that of the field dependent subjects, Mean=11.66, S.D=4.61.

Table 4: Means and standard deviations of field-dependency groups

Treatment Group	Mean	S.D.	Cases
Field Dependent	11.1	3.31	30
Field Independent	13.21	2.98	46

One-way analysis of variance as shown in Table 5 indicated that there was a significant difference between different groups of field-dependency. Significant difference between three groups of field-dependency was detected at $F = 4.0965$, p = .0194.

Table 5: Analysis of variance of field-dependency

Source of variation	DF	SS	MS	F	Sig of F
Between Groups	2	87.7452	43.8726	4.0965*	.0194
Within Groups	102	1092.3882	10.7097		
Total	104	1180.1333			

* Significant at the .05 level.

3.3 Interactive effects

The analysis of variance was conducted for the purpose of establishing the homogeneity of the three groups (NF, KOR and EF) and field dependency. The results are presented in Tables 6.

It indicated that there were significant main effects on the field dependency and type of treatment. For the main effects of field dependency, significance difference, $F=16.136$, $p=.000$ was detected. The results also show that there was a significant difference in feedback level, $F=28.369$, $p=.000$. However no interactive effects were detected at .05 level of significance.

4.0 Discussion

This study was to ivestigate the effects of vaying level of feedback and cognitive styles of students (field-dependent-independent) in a multimedia presenatation.

The results of the study yielded a significance difference between No feedback (NF) and Knowledge of results (KOR) and No feedback (NF) and Elaborative feedback (EF). However a significant difference between KOR and EF was not detected. The results also confirmed that field independent students performed significantly better than field dependenet students in all treatments.

The results of this study are supportive of the positive value of higher level feedback to enhance the performance of the student on verbal information. These results are consistent with the findings from previous investigations on the provision of varying levels of feedback when compared to a no feedback situation. Several studies can be cited, whose conclusion on the value of feedback for enhancing the performance are similar to the results of this study (e.g. Kulhavy and Wager, 1993, Dempsey, Driscoll and Swindell, 1993 and Ross and Morrison, 1993).

Table 6: Analysis of variance on Posttest with treatments and field-dependency as main effects

Source of variation	SS	DF	MS	F	Sig of F
Main Effects	395.857	3	131.952	23.980	.000
FIDN	88.789	1	88.789	16.136	.000
Treatment	312.212	2	156.106	28.369	.000
Two-way Interactions	8.846	2	4.423	.804	.452
FIDN X Treatment	8.846	2	4.423	.804	.452
Explained	416.752	5	83.350	15.147	.000
Residual	385.182	70	5.503		
Total	801.934	75	10.692		

It is important to note that most of the studies cited before used mainly text-based or computer assisted instruction modes. The subjects engaged in those studies used no more than two sensory channels. This study extended to multimedia instruction which incorporated sound, animation and video clips in the presentation.

It would be possible to include other dimensions in feedback apart from audio and visual responses. Visual dimensions include those that can be observed by the learner such as written text, pictures and icons as visual stimuli. Using slightly more sophisticated technology, a recorded or synthesized human voice might be used in the feedback. In fact, the range of emerging technology feedback applications that can be supported is potentially overwhelming. Designers must consider how, when, and why such technologies can be used to promote meaningful learning in a given task.

Hannafin (1992) noted that the overall framework of effective feedback centers on three lesson design foundations: psychological, technological and pedagogical. Psychological foundations are based in learning theory and research, and emphasize the role of the individual in organizing and restructuring knowledge and generating response. Technological foundations focus on the capabilities of the hardware itself, the various devices available for providing output, receiving input, and processing appropriately the myriad of program code, data, and so forth. Pedagogical foundations are rooted in beliefs about how to organize lesson knowledge, sequence lesson activities and to support the learner in acquiring knowledge (Hannafin, Hannafin and Dalton, 1993).

The literature suggests that feedback is more effective when it relates to the correct answer (right or wrong), but adding further information to the feedback message has no consistent effect on instructional performance (Kulhavy and Wager, 1993).

Much research has demonstrated how field dependence-independence can affect performance on a variety of psychological and academic tasks. Several recent investigations have suggested a consistent relation of field dependence-independence to tasks involving memory efficiency (Davey, 1990). In most research studies, relatively field dependent individuals tend to perform differently and generally less successfully than their more field independent persons due to the tasks of varying degree of memory load (Descy, 1990 and Davidson and Smith, 1990).

Wager and Mory (1993) pointed out that feedback served different purposes at different stages in learning. It was also concluded that it is unlikely to find any universal agreement on the "best" type of feedback. It will depend upon the type of question, the stage of information processing, and conditions within the learner to arrive at an answer.

Hoska (1993) also argued that there are no easy answers or guaranteed techniques to providing feedback that will influence all learners to invest effort in a learning task. This is based on the fact that individuals differs. No two learners are alike, and the process by which each individual decides in their effort to learn is a complex matter.

The analysis of the data indicated that the raw scores of field dependent students in the knowledge of results group were higher than those in the elaborative feedback group, but raw scores of field independent students in the knowledge of results groups were lower than those in the elaborative feedback group. In other words, field independent students benefited as the level of feedback increased and, for field dependent students, simple correct or incorrect messages seemed to work better.

It would be interesting to see if the same trends take place if the number of students assigned to each group is increased. The present study was limited to 105 subjects and each cell consisted of 9 to 18 students.

Little research on feedback has been done on how the level of difficulty influences the effectiveness of varying level of feedback. Some researchers felt that too much feedback might distract learners (Phye, 1979). According to

Kulhavy (1979) when learners fail to understand the content, the feedback will make little sense to them.

Furthermore, extra time should be allocated to each program. In the present study, time was limited to an hour for each program. Participants had to rush to get through the program, possibly penalizing participants who were slow learners.

It would also be useful if some qualitative data could be obtained during the experiment. Some information such as how students approach the learning task, whether they prefer to view the program in a group or individually, why and how they choose particular answers to the questions and whether they think the feedback in practice tests helps them to learn more about the content.

Other information which could be obtained by structured interviews might concern which particular aspect of the program content was difficult to understand. This would also provide some detail information into the process of student learning using a multimedia lesson.

Some tentative recommendations for instructional designers and classroom teachers concerning the use of varying levels of feedback to enhance retention of verbal information can be derived from the results of this study. It is recommended that in multimedia instruction, knowledge of results and elaborative feedback be provided to students after every testing situation. The students should not only be informed of the correct or incorrect answers to each item, but also to elaborate on the those answers.

This study confirmed some of the hypotheses by using a multimedia program. In general the study confirmed that varying levels of feedback had some effect on the student performance. Since multimedia is an emerging educational technology, teachers should explore the use of such innovations in an effective manner. One of the possible ways is to add on a teacher-made feedback practice program based on the original information, as was done in this study.

Multimedia technologies have advanced a great deal in the past few years, and impressive multimedia programs are now within the reach of every educator. Multimedia involves students in active learning through physical interaction. Such active learning can serve to maintain attention, create new knowledge, and improve achievement. Research in learning styles indicated that some students learn better through specific modalities. Multimedia provides instruction through multiple sensory channels, allowing students to use the sensory modes that they prefer.

From an educational technology perspective, there are many possibilities for conducting research into feedback when using multimedia instruction. There is a range of presentation dimensions available for feedback. Feedback can be provided through visual, verbal, sensory, or multiple modalities. The motivational impact of feedback should not be underestimated. Affective feedback engages learners primarily through eliciting, then sustaining interest and engagement (Hannifin, Hannifin and Dalton, 1993).

The efficiency of different feedback, timing, complexity and certitude will be most useful in improving the instructional design of multimedia presentations. By using authoring systems, a classroom teacher can construct practice tests and questions in multimedia to supplement and complement the commercially available multimedia lessons to suit the particular needs of the students.

References:

1. Clariana, R.B., Ross, S.M. and Morrison, G.R. (1991). The effects of different feedback strategies using computer-administered multiple-choice questions as instruction. *Educational Technology Research and Development.* **39**(2), 5-17.
2. Davey, B. (1990). Field dependence-independence and reading comprehension questions: Tasks and reader interactions. *Contemporary Educational Psychology*, **15**, 241-250.
3. Davidson, G.V. and Smith, P.L. (1990). Instructional design considerations for learning strategies instruction. *International Journal of Instructional Media*, **17** (3), 227-243.
4. Decsy, D.E. (1990). Effect of colour change of the ground of a visual on picture recognition of field dependent/field independent individuals. *International Journal of Instructional Media*, **17** (4), 283-291.
5. Dempsey, J., Driscoll, M. and Swindell, L. (1993). Text-base feedback. In Dempsey, J. and Sales, G. (Edited). *Interactive instruction and feedback*. Englewood Cliffs: Educational Technology Publications.
6. Dempsey, J. and Sales, G. (1993) (Edited). *Interactive instruction and feedback*. Englewood Cliffs: Educational Technology Publications.
7. Hannafin, M.J. (1992). Emerging technologies, ISD, and learning environments: Critical perspectives. *Educational Technology Research and Development*, **40** (1), 49-64.
8. Hannafin, M., Hannafin, K. and Dalton, D. (1993). Feedback and emerging instructional technologies. In Dempsey, J. and Sales, G. (Edited). *Interactive*

9.   *instruction and feedback.* Englewood Cliffs: Educational Technology Publications.
10. Hedberg, J.G. and McNamara, S.E. (1985). *Matching feedback and cognitive styles in visual CAI tasks.* Paper presented at the meeting of the American Educational Research Association, Chicago, IL. (ERIC Document Reproduction Service No. ED 260 105)
11. Hoska, D. (1993). Motivating learners through CBI feedback: Developing a positive learner perspective. In Dempsey, J. and Sales, G. (Edited). *Interactive instruction and feedback.* Englewood Cliffs: Educational Technology Publications.
12. Kulhavy, R.W. (1977). Feedback in written instruction. *Review of Educational Research.* **47** (1), 211-232.
13. Kulhavy, R.W. and Wager, W. (1993). Feedback in programmed instruction: Historical context and implications for practice. In Dempsey, J. and Sales, G. (Edited). *Interactive instruction and feedback.* Englewood Cliffs: Educational Technology Publications.
14. Phye, G. and Andre, T. (1986). *Cognitive classroom learning.* Orlando, Florida: Academic Press.
15. Ross, S. and Morrision, G. (1993). Using feedback to adapt instruction for individuals. In Dempsey, J. and Sales, G. (Edited). *Interactive nstruction and feedback.* Englewood Cliffs: Educational Technology Publications.
16. Wager, W. and Mory, E. (1993). The role of questions in learning. In Dempsey, J. and Sales, G. (Edited). *Interactive instruction and feedback.* Englewood Cliffs: Educational Technology Publications.
17. Witkin, H.A., Oltman, P.K., Raskin, E and Karp, S.A (1971). *A manual for the embedded figures test.* Palo Alto: Consulting Psychologists Press.

7.6

LANGUAGE NEEDS ANALYSIS SUPPORTED BY PROTOTYPE EASY-ACCESS AUTHORING KEYS LANA SPEAKS

Nigel Reeves[1] & Joe Farrell [2]
[1] Aston University & [2] Crystal Presentations Ltd, UK

*Traditional language learning methods have undergone a number of major changes. Grammar and translation methods have given way to the communicative method - a method which has fulfilled the needs of large numbers of adults who wish to communicate in a foreign language. The communicative method, however, falls short of natural language acquisition in several respects and the SPEAK (**S**upported **P**rototyped **E**asy-access **A**uthoring **K**eys) multimedia & on-line authoring, tutoring and learning system aims to compensate for many of the drawbacks of communicative language acquisition (shortage of time, lack of exposure to authentic learning experiences and low learner motivation) by providing not only improved learning routines, but also ensuring that the contents meet precisely the user's language learning requirements. The use of LANA software (**LA**nguage **N**eeds **A**nalysis) ensures that the selection of content and usage is functional and relevant.*

For some twenty five years both the theory and the practice of language teaching have been dominated by the doctrine of the communicative method. The apparent failure of the grammar and translation approach (translation, that is, into the target language as a way of instilling and testing grammatical knowledge) which had been derived from the traditional methodology of teaching Classical Languages, coincided with an urgent need for large numbers of adults to communicate in a foreign language. This was the consequence of the vast increase in world trade in the 1960s as post World War II recovery came into full swing and in Europe, for example, the creation of the European Economic Community and European Free Trade Area.

Children appeared to have no difficulty in acquiring not only their mother tongue but in tri- or bilingual family or social circumstances, a second or even third language. The view that language learning for children in non-bilingual circumstances and for adolescents and adults should seek to copy the natural acquisition process was promoted by theoreticians, by national policy proposals and in new approaches to language analysis such as the functional/national schema published by the Council of Europe. The Council of Europe papers were driven by the idea that growing numbers of European citizens, young and old, were travelling in Europe and therefore had easily identifiable needs associated with travel, tourism, and, it was hoped, the exchange of experience and opinions, as would befit an educated citizenry in a continent seeking ever closer political ties.

The two principal strands of the new teaching and learning philosophy were, thus, the attempt to replicate as far as possible the learning, or rather acquisition, circumstances that surround a child when acquiring a language naturally and, secondly, the identification of the communicative needs encountered by travellers and tourists. The two approaches were fused in teaching that exposed the learner to authentic and quasi-authentic materials, encouraged communication in the classroom through the recreation of everyday situations and sought to make the learning environment more real and vivid by the use of the new audio and especially video and later satellite television technology. (It should be added that behaviourist audio drills favoured by the Skinner School, which led to the popular use of the so-called language laboratory rapidly fell out of favour again because of the sheer tedium and decontextualized learning they involved.)

Unfortunately there are four central characteristics of child language acquisition which are difficult, if not practically impossible to reproduce in the normal language learning environment. These can be particularly problematic for adult learners, the learners with whom we are primarily concerned in this paper. They are:

1. Exposure to the target language on a massive scale (and related to that:)
2. Time. (A five-year old child has had some 17000 hours of potential exposure to its mother tongue. Arguably an educated first language user needs twenty to twenty-five years or more to become an articulate speaker and writer of that language).
3. Motivation (and related to that:)
4. Relevance of language input. (For the child acquiring language it is a matter of survival. She is embedded in situations where understanding, and, soon linguistic response become vital, where the relevance is obvious and communication is with trusted, sympathetic co-communicators).

Added to this is the usual question whether the acquisition should be accompanied by reflective, systematic based knowledge of the language. In the heyday of the communicative method a grammatical underpinning was frequently eschewed to maintain the alleged spontaneity of the acquisition process, a practice contrary to the approach in any of the other subjects learned by children, particularly in secondary schooling and adulthood when the cognitive process is different and the use of reason, encouragement of reflection and analytical skills and the search for principles become central. This is true both for the study of science and the arts (if only, in the latter case, to test the validity of ideas or hypotheses and use them until falsified by experience, experiment or argument).

The SPEAK approach does not claim to have found a single answer to these issues. But it tries to tackle, modestly at least, the four obstacles to the adult language learner sharing some of the benefits enjoyed by the younger person acquiring a language naturally. And through the use of on-line multimedia technology it retains, in far more flexible form than conventional audio and video language learning, the advantages of offering authentic materials that can be seen and heard but also controlled in output to suit the learner, i.e. used at his/her pace, repeated as required, and moreover with the option of both formal explanation and exposure to a large number of further examples presented as patterns.

The flexibility of on-line learning cannot substitute for the sheer time available to the natural learner but it can *maximise* the time available to busy adults.

But this anticipates the second half of our presentation. Let me take up the remaining two factors, motivation and relevance. Adult learners relate no less than children to communicative situations that they face in their professional life. The adult professional learner possesses a substantial conceptual knowledge or 'knowledge frames' through the practice of his or her profession. Indeed in many cases it is precisely this conceptual field within which the adult learner for professional purposes wishes to operate in the target foreign language. In much language teaching, especially that based primarily on a cultural content, the learner is faced with three unknowns or semi-unknowns - concepts, vocabulary (terminology) and forms. If the material through which the learning occurs is familiar conceptually - that is the knowledge frames are familiar, neither the vocabulary nor the semantic relationships (that is the meaning) presents the same level of difficulty in comprehension as decontextualised and conceptually unfamiliar language materials. Vocabulary of a general nature can be learnt on the foundation of the specialist vocabulary that itself is learnt through subject familiarity. Mastering of forms can be assisted through practice that centres on messages of familiar meaning. The motivational thrust that comes from this appeal to the learners' own knowledge and the relevance of the material for their needs parallels the circumstances of natural language acquisition.

A key to the SPEAK approach is thus the LAnguage Needs Analysis which precedes the selection of learning materials. This front end, which we have called LANA, will also be available in free standing software form is based on the language auditing methods developed and explained in the recent book by Reeves and Wright, *Linguistic Auditing, A Guide to identifying Foreign Language Communication Needs in Corporations.* (published by Multilingual Matters,

Avon, UK). This auditing system offers a range of techniques for identifying those needs not only at an individual and departmental (or operational) level but at the strategic level as part of the strategic planning process. SPEAK can potentially be deployed as a follow up to the strategic analysis of needs occurring primarily through qualitative analysis by an auditor, consultant or trainer.

LANA takes up analysis at the operational and individual levels.

It identifies the need for foreign language competence by organisational function, thus establishing a process-based map of the organisation's complete foreign language needs in the context of its whole operation. At the same time the program helps to identify the foreign language communicative tasks that individual postholders and their departments have to - or should in the name of efficiency and effectiveness - carry out in the foreign language.

The program further establishes which general professional/business vocabulary the postholder requires (that is at a generic level such as quantities and times) and which specific specialist terminology is required - and for which communicative tasks. These tasks may involve any one or all of the four language skills, listening, speaking, reading and writing.

The program also identifies the types (or genres) of written material with which the learner is confronted and may need to produce, varying from e-mail and fax to technical reports, categorised in the analytical procedure by likelihood of occurrence in the postholder's function.

The results of this on-screen analysis can be presented both as a profile for the individual and as a profile for the postholders' department. The profiles form the basis for a needs-driven curriculum, related to the learners' professional requirements and building on their professional, specialist knowledge and communicative circumstances.

The SPEAK system, which can be used for distance learning with a tutor or without a tutor, can be customised for its learning materials either through the establishment of a specialist language database created in cooperation with an organisation, professional or trade association or by calling on its own database.

Alternatively LANA can be used as a stand-alone by auditors, trainers or training managers to develop a needs-specific curriculum for face-to-face tuition, or at the level of the organisation, to provide a basis for a training tender or for checking and monitoring the appropriateness of proposed or on going language training.

But identification of language learning needs of a company is of limited benefit unless positive action can be taken to overcome the language deficits that such an analysis identifies. In the context of, for example, international business negotiations or multinational joint research and development clarity and speed of communication is vital.

Acquiring the fluency for effective foreign language communication is therefore becoming a necessity rather than a desirable option. The time and training for such a task is constrained by the economic and practical pressures of any professional job. However, just as technology has made possible the concept of **just-in-time stock control** and **just-in-time manufacturing** this principle can now be applied to language learning skills (**just-in-time language learning**).

To communicate effectively at a rudimentary proficiency level in any foreign language, as has already been described, a minimum foundation course is essential. There is no satisfactory instant easy formula that can short circuit the lengthy natural acquisition process. However, with the advancing uses of audiovisual resources accelerated learning systems provide excellent innovative "say and do" techniques, frequently within a range of cognitive, affective and psychomotor mechanisms, to maximise the pace and quality of initial language learning. Most systems emphasise one or two features and neglect or down grade others. But the addition of multimedia drill and practice routines, on-line tutoring dialogue and help facilities can enhance further the learners ability to experience 'total immersion' foreign language learning without leaving the home or the workplace.

This introductory process can take the foreign language learner to a level of competence beyond which it is then necessary to move from 'simulated total immersion' to real life communicative interaction. It is at this point, however, that the future trends in language learning could be sharply differentiated from traditional methods and practices. Much less priority and, therefore, less time and resources will be given to acculturation skills and know-how and more will be devoted to specialist and sharply focused business related content and processes. If allowed to proceed unchecked there are considerable dangers inherent in this approach - the objectives and content of communication can be obscured or lost in the failure to take proper account of the cultural context within which it is delivered.

We can accept that the world would be a much more manageable place if we all spoke the same language, but a much poorer place if we were deprived of the richness and range of conceptual and cultural richness embedded in the global language spectrum. But are these considerations an obstacle to effective foreign language acquisition? Can the objectives of delivering acculturation and content be combined in bespoke language learning packages without hindering the relentless push towards speed and efficiency in business related language acquisition and communication? SPEAK, in concept and design, aims to address these issues in a comprehensive flexible system.

So what does SPEAK consist of ? SPEAK is an innovative language learning software delivery system consisting of a comprehensive range of language learning facilities. It is designed to be Supported by standard commercial resources such as electronic dictionaries, grammars and text analysis in delivering essential aspects of language acquisition. It provides Prototypes of its applications and offers Easy-access Authoring and tutoring Keys to its commercial as well as personal end users. SPEAK aims to break the mould of prepackaged, inflexible, all embracing commercial language learning packages. It aims to be compatible with the immediate language learning needs of industry and consistent with their evolving use of multimedia. Its objectives are to develop and bring together the key components in an integrated language learning development and delivery system that encompass authoring, tutoring and learning.

SPEAK's target market is not the individual user. It is the mediating user - the teacher, the tutor, the language school or the commercial training department. Essentially it incorporates the elements of best practice and teaching techniques developed to date and makes them accessible within a single framework. It will aim to provide the means and the incentive to mediating users to upgrade and reposition their range of language learning services by providing customised multimedia products for their customers. Customised in this context refers to the empowerment of language tutors through the use of multimedia and on-line systems to deliver the precise content, format and exercises needed by their customers. Thus, using SPEAK, language schools and training departments will be able to incorporate their own contents for their own clients stated language learning needs.

The SPEAK project will pilot and test the system with the active commitment and involvement of these users. A network of language learning trainers and their customers is in place. This will enable the piloting of realistic and relevant contents to be used to test SPEAK's features and its effectiveness in real life applications. These customers will be taken from key automotive industries, initially in France, Italy and the UK. In addition, as sponsoring partners, two major publishing companies will provide business training contents for more general applications of the system.

SPEAK, by demonstrating its potential and relevance, will aim to stimulate the market for extending the use of multimedia in work-related language learning. It will provide added value training and cost effectiveness and a reduction of learning lead times. For the language learner, SPEAK offers the means for increased speed of acquisition of language learning skills in a user friendly framework. In addition it frees the user from the constraints of time and place for language learning and the contents can be selected to be directly relevant to their learning needs. An on-line version of SPEAK is being prepared which will be piloted in the context of home and distance on-line learning projects. SPEAK will contribute to industrial communication, training and the principle of life-long learning.

The SPEAK language learning development and delivery system is designed to work on four levels as illustrated in Figure 1.

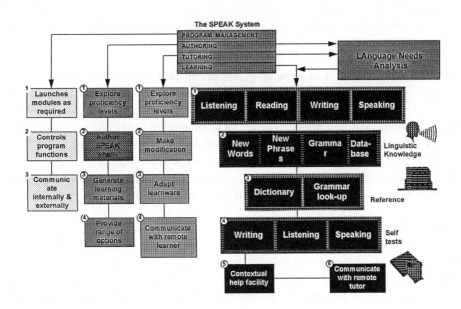

Figure 1

Based on language needs analysis the author will either call up existing SPEAK packages and modify them accordingly or create his/her own customised packages built up from various exercise templates available from the SPEAK template library. At the same time an author can choose which reference materials he wishes to associate with each specific package in accordance with the learners' needs. A tutor would then be able to call up any of the previously authored SPEAK packages and modify them according to their learners' profiles and their own preferred teaching style thereby providing the learner with customised learnware packages designed to support their specific needs.

In the near future, the traditional broad based, generalist language production and literacy skills are increasingly likely to be replaced by more sharply focused work-related content and activities. These will be selected by criteria determined by the extent to which these are consistent with and relate directly to the subject matter and range of communication skills required by the commercial, industrial and scientific foreign language users. Such a change of emphasis implies, of course, the possession of a basic grounding in the target foreign language on the part of the user. This basic level is already widely available in high quality multimedia and tutoring formats for most languages. Here with the growth of ever more powerful multimedia delivery systems and the reduction in costs for the preparation and presentation of multimedia language learning packages, the basic building blocks of foreign language learning will become ever more accessible for personalised self paced learning. The logical sequence to this will be a demand for customised material for specific second language communication tasks in a work related environment.

The development of **just-in-time** language acquisition will tend to focus on the professional, commercial and practical needs of industry and commerce. Such a system implies that the language learner is in a position to specify precisely his/her language learning needs. These can be quantified in specific terms as seen in the LANA audit. Examples such as *"I need to negotiate by telephone on the purchase and resale of oil cargoes still on the high seas."* or *"I have a weekly requirement to update my overseas colleagues in their own language on progress in the genetic engineering trials underway in our laboratory."*

Both of these instances provide a starting point from which the learner can request assistance in vocabulary, idiom and syntax related precisely to his or her language for special purpose requirements. This can now be achieved in a way in which traditional language learning providers are not as yet equipped either in expertise or technology. These requirements call for specialist tutoring resources and teaching strategies as well as easy access to specific subject matter. The solution to the learners needs is an obvious one - custom build the users learning experiences and empower the language learning providers to deliver, mediate and manage this learning. This is the planned function of the SPEAK utilities and learning environment.

PART 8

TELECOMMUNICATIONS & TECHNOLOGY

8.1

AUGMENTING VIDEO INFORMATION: CONTENT BASED HYPERLINKING

Nuno Correia, João Martins, and Nuno Guimarães
INESC/IST, Portugal

This paper presents tools and applications for augmenting video information using content based processing and hypermedia techniques. Video processing is used to find the indexes in the video stream corresponding to events where hypermedia links will be established. These anchors give access to other information, either video or other materials, available on the local machine or over the Internet. This task is carried out using two applications: the Annotator applies video processing algorithms to the video stream and is used to establish the links; the Player is used to play the hypermedia network that was set up using the Annotator.

1.0   Introduction

Video information is progressively being used in computer systems and applications. Despite its enormous advantages and "life like" characteristics, a lot remains to be done regarding the integration of video with other media. This is partially caused by the intrinsic difficulties posed by video information, such as the amount of data to represent it and the acquisition process, usually requiring special hardware. Partially because of these reasons until recently video content was not considered. Video was seen as an opaque data type and research was mainly oriented towards compression and coding mechanisms.

The consideration of content and of the diversity of video information sources, suggests the usage of hypermedia mechanisms to complement it or provide additional insight. These video hypermedia mechanisms should be integrated in application construction frameworks according to some design principles: (1) they should, as much as possible, reuse other mechanisms for establishing relations between media objects, i.e., synchronization mechanisms; (2) they should take in consideration the specific properties of video information, such as its dynamic nature and the narrative process that is usually employed.

In this paper we propose a model and tools for dynamic information hyperlinking. The model is based on previous work on synchronization mechanisms given the similarity of purposes in both models: to establish temporal relations between media objects. The model is described in section 4 along with the extensions required for hypermedia. The remainder of the paper is organized as follows: the next section presents some related approaches to content analysis and video hyperlinking. Section 3 describes previous work on video processing applications. Section 5 describes the tools for establishing the hyperlinks and finally, section 6, includes the conclusions obtained so far and directions for futures work.

2.0   Related work

Much of the work on content based video processing attempts to identify the structural units in a video stream by detecting the boundaries of these units (Otsuji,1993;Dailianas,1995;Deardoff,1994).These algorithms employ techniques that use the differences of content between images as the main criteria for separation. Some of the systems use models to help the parsing and segmentation process (Zhang,1995;Correia,1995). Our work on video modeling reported below is an attempt to generalize this concept. Additional attributes such as camera movements, dominant color detection (Tonomura,1993) are also used to characterize video streams.

After identifying the relevant events in the video stream, hyperlinks can be established at the points where those events occur. Although some systems consider the possibility of establishing the links semi-automatically using content processing techniques the integration of these techniques is still under development.

The work reported in (Hardman,1994), provides mechanisms for hyperlinking dynamic media as an extension to the Dexter model (Halasz,1990). Important concepts are the structuring mechanisms and the notion of link context. The system uses the notion of composite as a collection of media nodes with temporal dependencies. Composite are useful to hide the complexity of managing a large set of media nodes. Link contexts provide information about the state of source and target nodes when the link is traversed. A more specific hypermovies model is described in (Gessler,1996). This work uses a track model for each component of the movie. Links are temporal relation between tracks and they can be content dependent (although the processing techniques were not integrated yet). It's a simple and interesting model, but given its track based approach it lacks some of the flexibility needed for integrating heterogeneous information sources.

Both (Liestol,1994) and (Sawnhey,1996) are primarily concerned with aesthetical and rhetorical aspects of hyperlinking in video. The former is a hypermedia environment for public access in a museum. It discusses the integration and linking of video and text in hypermedia documents. The problems of continuity when changing the presentation medium are also discussed. It suggests that the continuity may be stressed by given temporal properties to static media. This concept suggested some of the work in the object model reported in section 4. The later system, HyperCafe, is an interesting experimental hypermedia prototype, developed to illustrate hypervideo concepts. The system allows the user to follow different conversations by offering opportunities to follow links. As an aesthetic design option the film sequences play continuously, to simulate the visit to a real cafe. The video scenes are logically organized in a hierarchy creating linked narrative references. Link opportunities are presented temporally in the form of one or more previews of related video scenes that fade in, determined by the progression in the current video scene. Some video scenes have spatial opportunities, that can trigger other video sequences. Both these systems use only materials that were specifically designed for a given hypervideo. They provide valuable suggestions regarding the narrative structure of hypervideos, but they are limited as a platform for constructing and integrating existing heterogeneous materials.

3.0   Video processing framework and environment

This section describes previous work leading to a framework for video processing. Currently it comprises a toolkit for application construction, a video model definition environment and several applications, built with preliminary versions of the toolkit.

3.1   Object model

The object model for video processing has its roots in early work in the MADE (Multimedia Application Development Environment) EEC funded Esprit project (MADE,1992). This project had the goal of defining an object oriented framework for construction of multimedia applications. Time based media classes, such as audio and video derive from a superclass where all temporal management and synchronization mechanisms were introduced. Similar mechanisms exist in our video processing toolkit.

The Media class inherits temporal attributes from the TimeSync class and includes generic application independent media manipulation through the encapsulation of a time ordered set of frames or samples. A derived class, CompositeMedia supports hierarchical composition of media objects. Media objects include a set of methods for activity control (play, pause, suspend, resume) and manipulation of temporal properties such as the duration and frame rate control. Media objects rely in a set of Stream handler objects for low level cache management and input/output. Image processing tools, such as cut detection, can be applied to the video segments resulting in labeled media objects. These tools are also modeled as classes in the toolkit.

The mechanisms for hyperlinking are introduced at the level of the class representing a media object and are also based in the synchronization mechanisms introduced in the MADE project. Section 4 describes this synchronization model and the necessary changes for hyperlink support.

3.2   Video information model

In previous work we have defined a language and an editor for video information modeling. This environment allows for the definition of models based on samples of the original content. Models represent video streams in terms of basic blocks with start and stop conditions and are useful for repetitive processing of video information of a given type.

The block start and stop conditions are defined in terms of signal processing functions such as histogram differences exceeding a pre-defined threshold. Conditions represent, in general, semantic events such as the start of a block of commercials in a TV program or the appearance of a given character in a movie.

The result of applying the model is a set of media objects describing the video stream. These objects can be used for interactive browsing and manipulation of the video stream or they can be transmitted or stored in multimedia databases. The objects may include annotations at certain points in time that will be used to establish hyperlinks as described in section 4.

3.3   Applications

The above components were used to build several video processing applications. Some of these applications are:

Video browser: The video browser is used to visualize video streams. The browser can load a stream and split it in its shot components using cut detection algorithms. Each shot is represented in the browser main window by an icon (the first frame in the shot). The shots can be played using several view objects.

WeatherDigest: This application generates HTML documents from TV weather forecasts. The temporal sequence of maps presented in the forecast is mapped to a sequence of images in the HTML page. The application illustrates the importance of information models.

News Analysis: We developed a set of application to be used by social scientists in content analysis of TV news. The analysis was centered in filling forms including news items duration, subjects, etc.. Our system attempts to automate the process so that all repetitive tasks are carried out automatically. The system generates HTML pages with the images and CSV (Comma Separated Values) tables suitably for use in spreadsheets such as Excel. Additionally, the generated HTML pages can be used for news browsing. We are also developing Java based tools for accessing this information. Preliminary results (depicted in fig. 1) can be accessed at `http://amadeus.inesc.pt`.

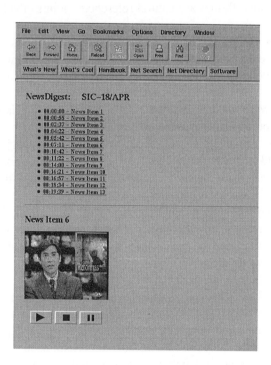

Figure 1: Java applet for news browsing

4.0 Hyperlinking in dynamic media

This section describes the model for video hyperlinking and the requirements for a toolkit supporting hyperlinking. The model is an extension of a previous synchronization model developed in the scope of the MADE project and partially adopted in the PREMO ISO standard (ISO/IEC 14478, see http://www.cwi.nl/Premo). The description of the model, presented next, highlights the necessary elements to support hyperlinks and is followed by the description of the path mechanism for video augmentation. The section concludes with some issues related with the presentation and generation of link representations and the integration of static/dynamic media types. In the MADE synchronization model (Correia,1994), relations between objects are based on reference points and synchronization elements. These concepts can be summarized as follows:

Reference points: are points in the internal scale of the object and are media dependent (e.g., video frames are natural reference points in video objects).

Synchronization elements: are attached to reference points and define what happens when a reference point is reached. This information includes the objects and method to invoke when the reference point is reached.

These concepts were used to express relations between media objects, defined for presentation purposes, that were not, in general, content based. An example of these relations can be: play audio obj2 when video obj1 reaches frame 1000. This would correspond to the creation of a synchronization element in obj1 at frame 1000, with the specification of an action (play) in obj2.

In the current hyperlinking model relations will, in general, be derived from information content, e.g., display other images related with the current news story. These relations can be established by hand or preferably using content analysis of video information.

In static media, link traversal is usually triggered by user actions on link representations (anchors). Anchors are always visible as long as the document is visible. On the other hand links in dynamic media are time dependent and their representations should only be visible for a certain span where the link is meaningful. Hyperlinking and link traversal in dynamic media are modeled as triggering of actions at certain points in time. The actions can be the display of other document as in traditional hyperlinks or other complex action. This suggests the usage of the above synchronization model for establishing the temporal relations between media objects.

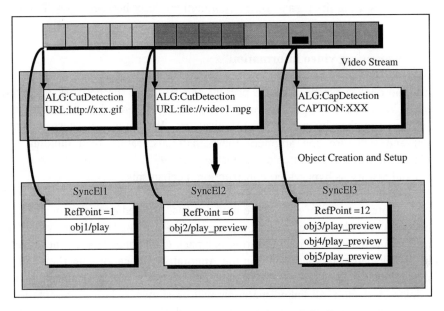

Figure 2: Annotations and hyperlinking mechanisms

4.1   Establishing the hyperlinks

Hyperlinks are established in two steps: (1) in the first step the video streams are annotated, in general with text tags; (2) in the second step, the objects representing the synchronization elements and the link targets are created.

The annotations are, usually, text or bitmaps that have a specific position in the objects timeline. Possible annotations include the algorithm that was used to find the time index (such as cut detection), the captured caption in the case where such an algorithm is used (Lienhart,1996), a keyword for use in later queries, and references to other media materials. References are URLs (Uniform Resource Locators) given its ability to represent local or remote media segments and its wide usage. This information will then be used to create the appropriate synchronization elements defining the actions as depicted in fig. 2. In the figure, three annotations were made to the video stream. The first is a reference to a static remote image. The second is a reference to a local video file and the third one, resulted from a caption detection algorithm and is the captured string. These annotations are then used to create the appropriate media objects. The first one, obj1, is able to display images, the second one is a movie player and in the third situation the captured string is used to perform a query that returns several references (used to create several media objects). The actions specified in the synchronization elements will act upon these objects so that they (or their link representations using the play_preview method described below) will play at appropriate times.

4.2   Augmenting video information

Several approaches can be taken to present and structure the network of linked materials. We choose an approach where structuring is derived from the original content put together by movie or TV directors. We intend to reuse existing content and structure and augment these materials, rather than building the complete structure from scratch as in (Davenport,1995). This suggests the usage of path and history as hypervideo construction mechanisms.

A path is a presentation of successive media items, ordered such that most or all of the decisions about the order of presentation are made by the author in advance rather than by the reader during playback (Zellweger,1989). These paths can be established at the beginning, in the Annotator application, but they will be mainly defined and used in the Player application: when establishing the hyperlinks, by default, all linked materials will be shown as link representations. Depending on users actions, if the links are selected they are kept in a path mechanism and next time the stream will be played the linked materials will also be fully played. This behavior could be changed at any time. A path is implemented as a group of synchronization elements defining the appropriate actions.

4.3   Converting between static and dynamic media

Transformations in dimensions are a very important aspect when considering hyperlinking in video. These transformation are useful when:

Converting from static media to dynamic media. When presenting a video linked with other materials, it is not convenient (Liestol,1994) to switch the browsing mode from watching the video to link following in static documents. This suggests that static   documents should be presented in a dynamic way. Examples of this conversion can be automatic scroll of a text or speech synthesis for text presentation.

Changing the dimensions of dynamic media. The anchors indicating   links to other video or audio sources can be moving icons   (introduced at the   MIT Media Lab), representing the content. These link indicators can be generated by the Media objects (upon request)   in a way that they are sensible to the content. This requires   support for generation of content based anchors in the objects integrating the hypervideo.

It is also possible to consider transformations of dynamic media to static media, as our previous experience of HTML generation from TV programs. This is however a particular situation of the above transformation (with target duration 0).

These transformations have corresponding methods in the Media class. The `resize` method accepts as parameter a duration and tries to accommodate the object to this duration. The `create_preview` method also accepts a duration but it does not change the original object, creating instead another object with the appropriate duration. The newly created object, can be controlled with a set of methods similar to the ones used to control the main media object.

5.0   Video annotation/Visualization tools

This section describes the two basic tools for video annotation and visualization. The first one, the Annotator, is used mainly to establish the points in the stream where external actions are needed. The Player enables visualization of the resulting annotated hypervideos.

5.1   Annotator

The Annotator application (fig. 3) is used to establish links between the video source and external information in different formats. The process can be entirely manual or can be optimized using video analysis tools.

The developed application is a video (object) player with additional facilities for annotation of the objects. Several algorithms can be applied to the video stream described by the current objects. The results of applying the algorithms is a set of annotations indexed to video frames.

The VCR like buttons can be applied to move forward and backward between these annotations, allowing to associate actions with each of the annotations. The tool has the notion of current algorithm and movements triggered by control buttons will consider only annotations made by the current algorithm or technique. The Annotator can also use the models described above for video segmentation and annotation. The result of a model driven processing is a set of annotated media objects, to which synchronization elements can be attached.

382

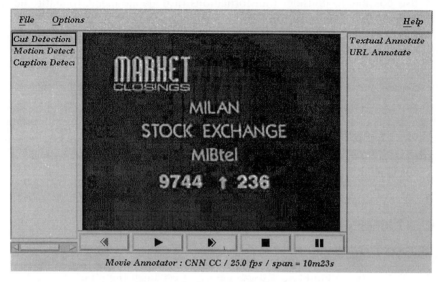

Figure 3: The annotator application

5.2 Player

The Player application has a main window displaying the master stream and several additional windows where link representations will be displayed. These representations will appear according to the temporal progression of the media object displayed in the main window. The representations give access to the linked materials. This access is made through selection of the appropriate link representation causing the node to be displayed in the main presentation window.

5.3 Using the System

Our first experiments with the system used business news video information. The annotations were established with the Annotator and the video program was mainly linked with HTML pages resulting from queries related with the topic of each news item. Other possible use is to provide context when the viewer is not familiar with the video subject. This happens in foreign news or documentaries.

5.4 Implementation Issues

The current implementation includes the object model, and preliminary versions of the Annotator and the Player. These were developed in C++, using M-JPEG (Moving JPEG) video decompressed in software. Some of the concepts above, mainly in maintaining video properties while linking to static materials available in the Internet, are still under testing. Implementation of the Annotator and the Player in Java is under way, so that hyperlinks between video information and other information available in the Internet could be easily established.

Given current limitations of networks main video segments are local to the system, linked to remote materials, essentially text and pictures but also some video and audio clips. The Player loads the necessary materials for the presentations, considering the timing constraints in the hyperlinks and it will use native methods for accessing software/hardware video decompression.

6.0   Conclusion and future work

In this paper a model and tools for content based hyperlinking were presented. Main characteristics of the model are reuse of previously defined components for multimedia synchronization and the support for specific narrative properties of video information. An important issue that influenced the design is the fact that materials from different sources, not originally designed for a specific hypervideo, should be integrated.

Besides some implementation issues mentioned earlier, future work on this area, will be centered on improving the Annotator application by adding other means for detecting content based indexes in the stream. We will also consider means for automatic linking, using pre-defined information models or algorithms such as caption detection.

An important area of application, to explore as future work, is to provide contextual information when the viewer is not familiar with the topic of the video. The video augmented with the hyperlinks can be used to provide the network of references that is needed as background in order to understand a given topic. We intend to study the way the mental process of gathering contextual information work and try to partially reproduce these processes in the video hyperlinking system.

Acknowledgments This work was partially financed by JNICT (National Board for Scientific and Technological Research). We would like to thank Inês Oliveira, António Grilo and Artur Caetano for their contributions and also Teresa Chambel for reviewing early versions of the paper.

References:

1.   Correia,N. and Guimaraes,N.(1994), "Time and Synchronization Objects for Multimedia Application Construction", *Proceedings of the Fourth Eurographics Workshop on Object Oriented Graphics,* Sintra, Portugal.

2. Correia,N.,Oliveira,I,Martins,J, and Guimaraes,N.(1995), "WeatherDigest:An Experiment on Media Conversion", *Integration Issues in Large Commercial Media Delivery Systems*, vol. SPIE 2615, 50-61.

3. Dailianas,A.,Allen,R.,England,P.(1995), "Comparison of Automatic Video Segmentation Algorithms", *Integration Issues in Large Commercial Media Delivery Systems*, vol. SPIE 2615, 2-16.

4. Davenport,G.,Murtaugh,M.(1995), "ConText: An Associative Media Browser", *Proceedings of the ACM Multimedia Conference*, San Francisco, CA, USA.

5. Deardoff,E.,Little,T.,Marshall,J.,Venkatesh,D.(1994), "Video Scene Decomposition with the Motion Picture Parser", *Proceedings of the IS&T/SPIE Symposium on Electronic Imaging Science and Technology*, vol. SPIE 2187, 44-55.

6. Gessler,J.(1996), "Surfing the Movie Space: Advanced Navigation in Movie Only Hypermedia", *Proceedings of the ACM Multimedia Conference*, San Francisco, CA, USA.

7. Halasz,F.,Schwartz,M.(1990), "The Dexter Hypertext Reference Model", *Proceedings of the Hypertext Standardization Workshop*, NIST, USA.

8. Hardman,L.,Bulterman,D.,van Rossum,G.(1994), "The Amsterdam Hypermedia Model; Adding Time and Context to the Dexter Model", *Communications of the ACM*, 37(2), 50-62.

9. Lienhart,R.,Stuber,F.(1996), "Automatic Text Recognition in Digital Videos", *Image and Video Processing IV*, vol. SPIE 2666-20.

10. Liestol,G.(1994), "Aesthetic and Rhetoric Aspects of Linking Video in Hypermedia", *Proceedings of ECHT (European Conference on Hypermedia Technology)*, Edimburgh, Scotland.

11. MADE(1992), "MADE 1 (EP 6307): Technical Annex".

12. Otsuji,K.,Tonomura,Y.(1993), "Projection Detection Filter for Cut Detection", *Proceedings of the ACM Multimedia Conference*, Anaheim, CA,USA.

13. Sawhney,N.,Balcom,D.,Smith,I.(1996), "HyperCafe: Narrative and Aesthetic Properties of Hypervideo", *Proceedings of the ACM Hypermedia Conference*, Washington, USA.

14. Tonomura,Y.,Akutsu,A.,Otsuji,K.,Sadakata,T.(1993), "VideoMAP and VideoSpace Icon: Tools for Anatomizing Video Content", *Proceedings of INTERCHI*, Amsterdam, The Nederlands.

15. Zellweger,P.(1989), "Scripted Documents: An Hypermedia Path Mechanism", *Proceedings of the ACM Hypertext Conference*, Seattle, USA.

16. Zhang,H.,Yihong,S.,Smoliar,S.,Yong,T.(1995), "Automatic Parsing of News Video", *Proceedings of the IEEE ICMCS Conference*, Boston, MA, USA.

8.2

DUAL-VIDEO-SCHEME VIDEOCONFERENCING

Junhui Zhou[1], B. Cousin[2] & Hong Wang[1]

[1]Northwest Institute of Nuclear Technology, P.R.C & [2]IRISA, France

The videoconferencing system delivers video and other real time multimedia data in multicast mode through a data network. A source in videoconferencing usually generates a single video stream. Multicasting such a single video stream in a heterogeneous network such as the Internet may cause some network links to be overloaded and some other network links to be under-loaded. In this paper, we propose to deliver two type video streams in two different schemes which have different bandwidth requirements to adapt to the heterogeneous network environments. The two sub-trees over which the two type streams are sent and two approaches for video translation between two video schemes are first described. Then the architecture for dual video scheme videoconferencing is discussed. This paper finally presents a videoconferencing system operating in dual video schemes and its typical application.

1.0   Introduction

The past years have been seeing rapid development of videoconferencing technology. The videoconferencing system delivers real time multimedia data such as video and audio data through a data network. It allows people at different locations to attend a videoconference. This will bring great facility to us in modern society.

Among traffic flows of videoconferencing, the video stream has comparatively high data rate, sometimes much higher than all other traffic flows, so in videoconferencing, the issue of video transport is peculiarly important. The video streams generated by participants of the videoconference will be sent in multicast mode (Baker,1994) to a multicast tree where all the participants spread. A source usually generates a single video stream. Sending such a single data stream in multicast is suitable for the homogeneous network where the bandwidth is identical everywhere. However for heterogeneous networks such as the Internet where the links may possess different bandwidths, multicasting a single data stream to a multicast tree may cause some links to be overloaded and some other links to be under-loaded. A solution to this problem is limiting the data rate of the stream to the minimum bandwidth of the network. But this solution is not fair because those who are not at the narrow-band links are forced to lose some video quality that they are able to obtain. An alternative solution is delivering multiple data streams which have different bandwidth requirements to adapt to different network bandwidths.

386

Two layered coding (Hoffman,1993) is such an idea. The sender encodes video data in two layers: the basic layer and the enhanced layer. The basic layer ensures basic video quality, while the basic layer + the enhanced layer gives a better quality. The data stream of the basic layer is delivered over all the multicast tree, and that of the enhanced layered is only delivered over a sub-tree of the multicast tree. This sub-tree has enough bandwidth to accommodate those two streams. Clearly layered coding streams can achieve better utilization of the bandwidth resources of the heterogeneous network than a single data stream.

In this paper, we will propose another approach to generate and deliver multiple video streams in videoconferencing.

Because of the diversity of video coding techniques, we can find a lot of video coding schemes, and some of them have become international standards such as JPEG, MPEG, and H261 (Aravind,1993). A video source, using different coding schemes, may generate video streams of different data rates and have different bandwidth requirements. For example, intraframe coding scheme generally produces video streams of high data rate, and in contrast, interframe coding scheme produces video streams of low data rate because it takes advantage of correlation of consecutive frames. Data streams in intraframe coding need much greater bandwidth than those in interframe coding. But intraframe coding is superior to interframe coding in capacity of tolerating data loss. Data loss may occur in the network at any time for various reasons. That will impose serious influence upon interframe coding, but don't impose much influence upon intraframe coding (Aravind,1993). Hence intraframe coding can ensure better video quality in the presence of data loss. When a source sends video data to a multicast tree in a heterogeneous network, we construct two sub-trees: one consists of broadband links and the other is the rest of the multicast tree, and install a video gateway at the common node of the two sub-tree. Then the source sends a data stream in intraframe coding to the former, and send another data stream in interframe coding to the latter. (In fact, one of the video streams is generated and sent by the gateway.)

In this way, we can also achieve better utilization of the bandwidth resource as layered coding. We refer to two different video coding schemes as dual-video-scheme. Further analysis and comparison of dual-video-scheme among the video coding schemes is interesting, but this is beyond the scope of this paper. Our focus will concentrate on transport of dual-video-scheme data streams.

Videoconferencing falls into two categories: interactive videoconferencing and non-interactive videoconferencing. Interactive videoconferencing allows every participant to send video data (and audio data), while non-interactive videoconferencing only allows one participant to do so. That is, in the interactive case, there are multiple video sources, while in the non-interactive case, there is only one single. If we use dual-video-scheme in interactive videoconferencing, the overhead of sub-tree construction and video gateways may be too large to be accepted, so dual-video-scheme is only suited for non-interactive videoconferencing. Hence in the following, we will only investigate the case of non-interactive videoconferencing.

In the following section, we will address the issues related to the video gateway. Section 3 will discuss architectural considerations for dual-video-scheme videoconferencing. In Section 4, we present a dual-video-scheme videoconferencing system IVS-H261/JPEG. Section 5 concludes the paper.

2.0   Video gateway

In dual-video-scheme videoconferencing, two video data streams which carry the same video information are multicasted on two sub-trees of the multicast tree, separately. In order to save bandwidth resources, the two sub-trees of the multicast tree are supposed to have no common link (but they have a common node). This differs from layered coding. In the case of layered coding, data streams are multicasted to overlapped sub-trees (the data stream of the enhanced layer is sent to a sub-tree of the tree where the data stream of the basic layer is sent).

The construction of the two sub-trees depends on bandwidth characteristics of network links. Suppose in a multicast tree T illustrated in Fig.1, the bandwidth of each link directly attached to the source is 10Mbps, and the others links have bandwidths of 64Kbps, 1.5Mbps or 10Mbps. The links directly attached to the source can form a broadband sub-tree T_1, and the others form another sub-tree T_2. T_1 has enough bandwidth to accommodate a video stream in some intraframe coding scheme, while T_2 can only accommodate a video stream in an interframe coding scheme such as H261. Therefore we can multicast a video stream in intraframe coding on T_1 and another video stream in interframe coding on T_2.

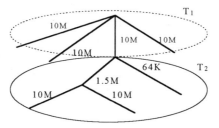

Figure 1:   Multicast tree T for a videoconference

In fact, the multicast tree T has been divided into two multicast trees T_1 and T_2. We need to give each of T_1 and T_2 a host group address that will be different from the group address of T. Logically, T, T_1 and T_2 can be considered to be three parallel multicast trees. As we see later, according to the architecture proposed in this paper, a dual-video-scheme videoconferencing system will no longer multicast data on T.

Clearly, at the common node of T_1 and T_2, a video gateway is required to receive data from T_1, and translate to another data stream then multicast to T_2.

Translation from a video scheme S_1 to another one S_2 can be achieved through direct conversion. Direct conversion is an effective approach to translate video data. However in practice, conversion methods are very difficult to find for some schemes (or don't exist at all).

Another approach to translate video data is first decoding then encoding, that is, first decoding video data in S_1 to get original data, then encoding in S_2. Conversion may not be realized for some schemes. But this method can always be realized. Such translating processes can be described as a directional pair:
$P(S_1->S_2)$: $<S_1$ decoding, S_2 encoding>.

Of course $P(S_1->S_2)$ could also be regarded as a type of special conversion. $P(S_1->S_2)$ may need certain time overhead, but its influence on non-interactive videoconference can be ignored. In our implementation of dual-video-scheme videoconferencing prototype IVS-H261/JPEG, we adopted the approach first decoding then encoding.

3.0   Architectural considerations

A dual-video-scheme videoconferencing system will operate in two different video schemes. It can be implemented as one single system with two video codecs, or two sub-systems, each of which contains one video codec. We can find that the latter gives an open system structure for dual-video-scheme videoconferencing. It allows us to adopt some existing systems to implement a dual-video-scheme videoconferencing system. This is just the approach to implement our dual-video-scheme videoconferencing system IVS-H261/JPEG. Therefore in the following, we will consider that the dual-video-scheme videoconferencing system consists of two   mono-video-scheme videoconferencing systems operating in different video schemes with a gateway.

The two sub-systems in a dual-video-scheme system are expected to have the same architecture. Otherwise the system complexity increases unnecessarily, and it may be difficult for the sub-systems to implement communications. The gateway should also have the same architecture as the sub-systems. Thus both the sub-systems are similar except for their different video codecs. This implies the optimized way to implement the two sub-systems is first developing an one-video-scheme videoconferencing system or selecting an existing videoconferencing system then substituting   the video codec in it by another one to obtain the other system. We will discuss further the architecture for dual-video-scheme videoconferencing systems in a particular example in the following section.

4.0   Dual-video-scheme system IVS-H261/jpeg

IVS-H261/JPEG is a dual-video-scheme videoconferencing system on the Internet. It consists of two   videoconferencing systems IVS-H261 (Turletti,1993) and IVS-JPEG (Patrice,1994) with a gateway IVS-SERV (Cousin, 1996). IVS-H261 and IVS-JPEG had been developed successively, then we have developed IVS-SERV which allows them to become a dual-video-scheme videoconferencing system.

IVS-H261 and IVS-JPEG adopt the video scheme H261 and JPEG, respectively. IVS-261 is also known as IVS on the Internet. We refer to it as IVS-H261 in this paper to explicitly point out the video scheme used. The data rate of video codec in IVS-JPEG can reach about 1.5Mbps, while that in IVS-H261 is relatively low, about 30Kbps. The difference is great. This is because, first, H261 is an interframe coding scheme, and JPEG is an intraframe coding scheme; second, the video codec in IVS-H261 is implemented in software while that in IVS-JPEG is hardware codec in XVideo Parallax card, and the speed difference of hardware codec and software codec makes the difference of those two data rates even greater. Clearly, IVS-H261 is suitable to narrow-band links of   the Internet. And IVS-JPEG is suitable to broadband links of the Internet (We assume the hosts involved are equipped with Parallex card). Although IVS-JPEG requires a comparatively high bandwidth, it can tolerate data loss occurring in the network. Both IVS-H261 and IVS-JPEG have the same architecture, illustrated in Fig.2. They are based on the User Datagram Protocol (UDP). Compared with another protocol TCP on top of IP, although UDP doesn't ensure reliable data transport, it generates small transport delay that is essential for real time network applications such as videoconferencing.

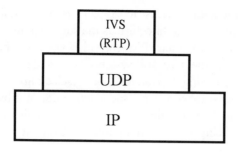

Figure 2: Architecture of IVS-H261 and IVS-JPEG

IVS-H261 and IVS-JPEG use the Real-Time Transport Protocol (RTP) (Schulzrinne,1995) to deliver video and audio data. RTP is proposed by the Internet Audio-Video Transport Working Group to implement real time video and audio data transport in packet-switched networks such as the Internet. RTP is comprised of two sub-protocols: RTP Data Transfer Protocol and RTP Control Protocol. The former provides data delivery service including data type identification, data packets sequence numbering, and data samples timestamping. The latter monitors the quality of service (QoS). In either IVS-H261 or IVS-JPEG, RTP doesn't emerge as a separate layer. It is integrated into the two systems, as illustrated in Fig.2.

Video transport and audio transport multiplex the same multicast tree. That is, they multiplex the same IP host group address. The two types of data streams are demultiplexed through different UDP ports.

IVS-H261 and IVS-JPEG are incorporated into the dual-video-scheme videoconferencing system IVS-H261/JPEG. The typical application case of IVS-H261/JPEG is where some participants are in the same local area network (LAN) as the conference speaker, and the others are in other LANs connected with that LAN through backbone links. The first set of participants can take advantage of the broadband links of the LAN. They use IVS-JPEG. The bandwidths of backbone links on the Internet are not too great (1.5Mbps, 384Kbps, or even 64Kbps). In addition, there are various traffic flows on backbone links. The bandwidth available will only accommodate IVS-H261 traffic. The two sets of participants form two host groups, and each group is given a unique IP group address. The two multicast trees corresponding to the two host groups are, in turn, created. In fact, these two trees are two sub-trees of the original multicast tree which contains all participants. At the common node of the two tree, the video gateway IVS-SERV will translate video data from JPEG to H261.

The gateway IVS-SERV is supposed to have the same architecture as IVS-H261 and IVS-JPEG. It is based on UDP and uses RTP to implement real time transport. Since the gateway is the common node of the two sub-trees, it needs to join the two host groups corresponding to the two sub-trees. The gateway receives video data in the host group which the speaker is in, translates and sends to the other host group. The method of video translation is first decoding then encoding, that is, through the directional pair
<JPEG decoding, H261 encoding>.
The JPEG codec and H261 codec in IVS-SERV are hardware codec and software codec, respectively, as in IVS-JPEG and IVS-H261.

The speaker also sends audio data. Since audio transport multiplexes the same multicast tree with video transport in IVS-JPEG, those who are in the host group using IVS-H261 are not able to receive audio data sent by the speaker. In order to enable all participants to hear the speaker, the gateway needs to forward the audio data, from the host group using IVS-JPEG to the other. IVS-JPEG and IVS-H261 can operate in the same audio scheme, say PCM or ADPCM, to have audio interoperability. Therefore audio translation is not required.

A videoconferencing system should perform QoS control. The gateway IVS-SERV can be regarded as a destination in one host group and the source in the other, so we can consider that dual-video-scheme videoconferencing creates two separate videoconferencing sessions, and QoS control will be performed within each session separately. In the IVS-JPEG session, as a destination, the gateway sends QoS monitoring data to the source, while as the source in the IVS-H261 session, the gateway receives QoS data from the participants and control its data rate through the same QoS control mechanism as in both IVS-H261 and IVS-JPEG (Bolot,1994).

5.0   Conclusion

We have investigated the use of dual video schemes in videoconferencing. Dual-video-scheme videoconferencing can generate two type video streams to adapt to heterogeneous network environments. The architecture for dual-video-scheme videoconferencing is proposed. A dual-video-scheme   videoconferencing system consists of mono-video-scheme sub-systems with a gateway. The gateway translates video data between the two sub-systems. Translation for different video schemes can be achieved in two ways. One is direct conversion; the other is first decoding then encoding. Direct conversion is more effective but cannot always be achieved. The translation in the way   first   decoding then encoding is implemented in IVS-SERV, the gateway for IVS-H261 and IVS-JPEG. IVS-SERV allows two existing videoconferencing systems to become a dual-video-scheme videoconferencing system IVS-H261/JPEG. IVS-H261/JPEG can well adapt to heterogeneous network environments of the Internet.

References:

1. Aras, M. et al. (1994), "Real-Time Communication in Packet-Switched Networks", *Proceedings of the IEEE*, 82(1), 122-139.
2. Aravind, R. et al. (1993), "Image and Video Coding Standards", *AT\&T Technical Journal*, January-February 1993, 66-89.
3. Baker, S. (1994), "Multicasting for sound and video", *Unix Review*, Feb. 1994, 23-29.
4. Bolot, J-C. et al. (1994), "A rate control mechanism for packet video in the Internet", *Proc. IEEE INFOCOM'94*, June 1994, Toronto, 1216-1223.
5. Cousin, B. et al. (1996), "Translation gateway for videoconferencing systems", *Proc. IMAGE'COM 96*, May 1996, Bordeaux, France, 133-138
6. Hoffman, D. et al. (1993), "Network support for dynamically scaled multimedia data streams", *Proc. NOSSDAV'93*, Lancaster, UK, Oct. 1993, 240-251.
7. LeGall, D.J. (1991), "MPEG: A video compression standard for multimedia applications", *Communications of the ACM*, 34(4), 47-58.
8. Liou, M. (1991), "Overview of the p times 64kbps video coding standard", *Communications of the ACM*, 34(4), 59-63.
9. Macedonia, M.R. et al. (1994), "Mbone provides audio and video across the Internet", *IEEE COMPUTER magazine*, April 1994, 30-36.
10. Patrice, L. Q. et al. (1994), "Analyse et modification d'un systeme multimedia", *Rapport de projet* DIIC 3 LSI, IFSIC, France.
11. Schulzrinne, H., S. et al. (1995), "RTP: A Transport Protocol for Real-Time Applications", *Internet-Draft*, March 21, 1995.
12. Turletti, T. et al. (1994), "Issues with multicast video distribution in heterogeneous packet networks", *Proc. 6th. International Workshop on Packet Video*, Porland, Oregon, Sept. 1994, F3.1-3.4.
13. Turletti, T. (1993), "H.261 software codec for videoconferencing over the Internet", *Research Report* 1834, INRIA Sophia Antipolis France.
14. Wallace, G.K. (1991), "The JPEG still picture compression standard", *Communications of the ACM*, 34(4), 31-44.

8.3

IMPLEMENTATION OF MANAGEMENT BUS FOR A HETEROGENEOUS NETWORK INTERWORKING SUBSYSTEM IN ADVANCED COMMUNICATION PROCESSING SYSTEM

Hyeon-sik Shin , Won Ryu, and Dong-Won Kim
Electronics and Telecommunications Research Institute, Korea

Advanced Communication Processing System(ACPS) is a gateway system among various access networks under developing in Korea. It is aimed to support a flexible and efficient provision of value-added services. A high-speed interconnection subsystem, named HSSF(High-Speed Switching Fabric), carries out interconnecting and switching among various network access subsystems in ACPS. For diagnosis and management of HSSF, we have adopted a Management Bus(M-Bus), which is separated from packet data path so as not to interfere service traffic transportation. In this paper, we propose management methods including fault, configuration and duplication control with M-bus to accomplish the rapid, flexible, and reliable operation of HSSF.

1.0   Introduction

Communication Processing System (CPS) has been developed to support the HiTEL service, which is a nation-wide information retrieval system for PC communication. Currently, Korea Telecom has been serving the subscribers of HiTEL with CPS since 1994. The object of CPS is to support an efficient interconnection between PSTN(Public Switched Telephone Network) and PSDN(Public Switched Packet Network), called HiNET-P in Korea. But, we have several problems in provisioning global and flexible value-added services using CPS because it had been designed to operate only in a single service provider environment, to accommodate limited subscriber and service links and to support only PSTN and PSDN. To overcome these problems, we introduce ACPS(Advanced Communication Processing System), which is able to accommodate multiple service providers and to interface among the various heterogeneous networks, such as Frame Relay, ISDN, B-ISDN, etc. ACPS consists of a high speed interconnection subsystem called HSSF, various services or Network Access Subsystem(NAS)s and OAM(Operation, Administration and Maintenance) Subsystem. OAM Subsystem provides overall ACPS system management functions, such as configuration, fault and performance management(Kim et al., 1995; Jang et al., 1992).

HSSF is very important subsystem to regard the function that is interworking among various network access subsystems and service modules in ACPS. To allow the indications of abnormal status and to report its status to the OAM Service Subsystem as soon as possible in the HSSF, we have designed and implemented the management functions using special M-Bus. In this paper, we overview the architecture of HSSF, present the configurations of M-Bus for HSSF and propose an method of resource and fault management using M-Bus.

2.0   ACPS configuration and HSSF architecture

To get over the limitations of CPS mentioned above chapter, the gateway system, which is called ACPS, must have simultaneously a flexible and open architecture to accommodate the existing various networks, sufficient processing power to handle the service control, and support functions for a number of users. The system must have switching capability to interwork among the various heterogeneous access networks and service modules.

As a consequence, the general reference architecture for an ACPS as shown in Figure 1 is proposed to exploit the emerging communication technologies, such as ISDN, ATM and Internet. The NAS(Network Access Subsystem) has module-based architecture, which is composed of specific network interface units, a network service processor unit(SPA, Service Processor board Assembly) and a HSSF interface unit named HSNA(High-Speed Network Adapter). The adoption of modular architecture makes it possible to accommodate easily the various type of networks and service functions. As a result, already developed modules of CPS can be used in ACPS without any modification of them. In current situation, the major considerable networks are PSTN, ISDN, PSDN, Frame Relay, ATM and Internet. Frame Relay, ATM and Internet access subsystems are under development for incorporating the future multimedia service and VOD(Video On Demand) in the platform service domain.

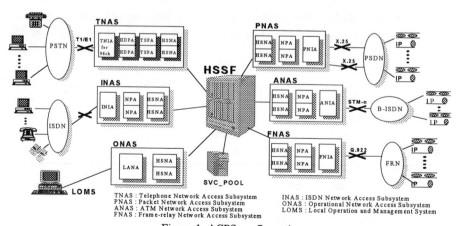

Figure 1. ACPS configuration

2.1 HSSF architecture

HSSF subsystem is capable of interconnecting among various NASs and service interface modules. HSSF is designed for applications in high-speed and highly reliable distributed computing systems for data communication services. HSSF consists of HSSU(High-Speed Switching Unit), HSCU(High-Speed Channel Unit)s and HSBB(High-Speed Back Board) as shown in Figure 2. The architecture of HSSF is based on the High-speed common Bus(H-Bus) technology that is easy to implement and cost effectively. HSSF can accommodate up to 32 channel nodes, that is 16 HSCUs, in a single unit configuration, which can be configurable for expanding up to 128 channels by cascading with multiple units. The switching capability of HSSF is about 640 Mbps(Kim et al., 1995). Table 1 shows the specifications and functions of each unit for HSSF.

HSSU has a MC68030 microprocessor and its peripheral devices like MFP(Multi Function Peripheral), LANCE(Local Area Network Controller for Ethernet), H-Bus controller, and HSCU emulation block. The host microprocessor is used for general management of the unit and M-Bus control with operating in the VRTX real-time operating system. H-Bus controller polls the buffer status of each HSCU channel and moving a packet frame from source channel to destination via H-Bus. The HSCU emulation function that enables host processor to transfer a packet frame related on OAM functions to all of NASs or OAM service subsystems. HSCU has frame buffers as FIFO and serial TAXI (Transparent Asynchronous Xmiter - receiver Interface) devices to interface with HSNA of each NAS by a coaxial cable(AMD,1992). HSNA can communicate with SPA via VMEbus in NAS.

Taking into account the role of HSSF in ACPS, it is important to manage HSSF efficiently for configuration, fault and performance management. Therefore, we have designed the M-Bus for the purpose of only management functions without using packet frame path. ACPS system is configured with duplication of each subsystem for reliability. Also HSSF is duplicated with Load-sharing method as shown in Figure 3. At the initial state HSSF(A) and HSSF(B) nodes share the service traffic equally. If HSSU(A) detects a fault state from the node (A), it is notified to HSSU(B) via DCC. Then HSSU(B) broadcasts a fault management packet to all of HSCUs when receiving this indication. SPA linked with the fault node would transfers all the traffic to node HSSF(B).

Table 1. Specifications and functions of HSSF

Unit	Functionality	Capability
HSSU	Packet switching control using H-Bus	32x32 ch., 640Mbps transfer rate, self-routing architecture
	System management using M-Bus	Configuration, fault and performance monitoring
HSCU	Packet frame buffering	TX : 8Kbyte, RX: 16Kbyte
	Serial Communication with NAS	TAXI with coaxial up to 100Mbps
HSBB	H-Bus	Packet frame transfer path
	M-Bus	Management control path

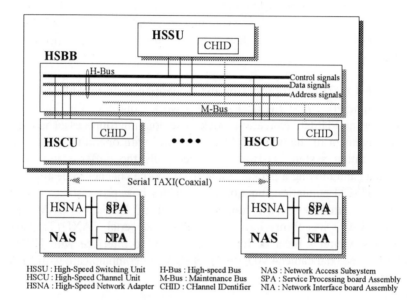

HSSU : High-Speed Switching Unit   H-Bus : High-speed Bus   NAS : Network Access Subsystem
HSCU : High-Speed Channel Unit   M-Bus : Maintenance Bus   SPA : Service Processing board Assembly
HSNA : High-Speed Network Adapter   CHID : CHannel IDentifier   NIA : Network Interface board Assembly

Figure 2: HSSF configuration

3.0 M-bus configuration

Figure 4 depicts the configuration of M-Bus in HSSF. M-Bus is made up of address(HMA:HSSF Management Address), data(HMD:HSSF Management Data) and control(HMC:HSSF Management Control) signals. With this bus, the host processor in HSSU can write and read registers of HSSU and HSCUs. Registers in HSSU and HSCUs consist of status, command and multicasting group identifier register. The status registers contain the abnormal state such as fault of the serial link between HSCU and HSNA or H-Bus control, the state of frame buffer, the state of which unit is inserted in the shelf, etc. The command register can use to reset for the self-recovery from the abnormal condition. The host processor also can configure the MGID(Multicasting Group IDentifier) to designate the destination channel in case of frame multicasting function.

HMA allows M-Bus controller to select the channel number of HSCUs and to discriminate registers between MGID and command/status. HMA[6:1] is used selecting the HSCU channels. With these bits, the host can select up to 64 channels. On the other hand, HSSF accommodates only 33 channels in a shelf including HSCU emulation port of HSSU. HMA[0] bit is used to discriminating access of MGID or command/status register. The data is transferred through the HMD in writing or reading. Control signals(HMC) are used to select the directions of data, to validate address bus and to acknowledge data transferring.

3.1   Registers in HSSU

The command register in HSSU can order to initialize the H-Bus controller and all the functions of HSCU emulation at the same time. This causes itself to recover from switching control failure and to initiate all of HSCUs.

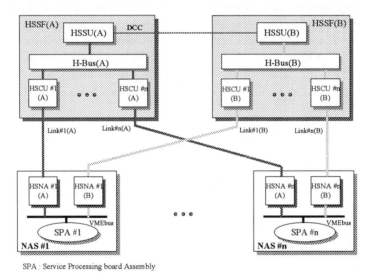

SPA : Service Processing board Assembly

Figure 3: Duplication configuration of HSSF

The status registers in the HSSU denote the abnormal behavior of H-Bus controller and the status of HSCU emulation buffers like half full and frame empty. These states can be used in fault management and performance measurement of HSSF system. The detailed bit format of the status registers is as follows :

- b0 : status of polling for bus arbitration in H-Bus controller

- b1 : status of data empty of receive buffer
- b2 : status of data half full of transmit buffer
- b3 : status of frame empty of receive buffer

3.2   Registers in HSCU

In HSCU, the command registers also are able to initialize the TAXI control part and frame buffers and to start checking of the TAXI link availability between HSCU and HSNA. The format of the command registers in HSCU is as follows :

- b0 : channel soft reset(CH_RESET)
- b1 : loopback link between HSCU and HSNA
- b2-7 : reserved

For the purpose of TAXI link verifying, first of all, the host has to set b1 of the command registers to send a loopback code of TAXI device which is decoded at TAXI control part of corresponding HSNA and returned into HSCU immediately. If the host checks serial TAXI link failure, it can order to initialize that channel TAXI control part using bit 0 (CH_RESET) of the command registers. Also, the host can try to recovering from local channel fault, for example a specific link failure between HSCU and HSNA, using the CH_RESET command register.

HSSF can accommodate up to 16 HSCUs, that means HSSF can control switching among 32-channel in/out ports. Each channel of HSCU can report internal device states for management of the system through the status registers. The status registers in HSCU indicate conditions of each channel as follows :

- b0 : status of link between HSCU and HSNA
- b1 : status of data empty of receive buffer
- b2 : status of data half full of transmit buffer
- b3 : status of frame empty of receive buffer
- b4 : status of power provisioning

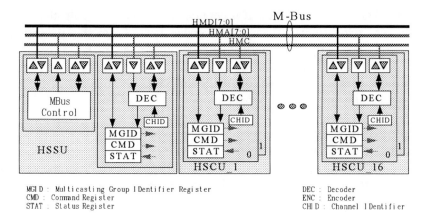

MGID : Multicasting Group Identifier Register
CMD : Command Register
STAT : Status Register

DEC : Decoder
ENC : Encoder
CHID : Channel Identifier

Figure 4. M-bus configuration

4.0   Management procedures in HSSF

The MC68030 micro-processor in HSSU is the host of the M-Bus and can manage the configuration, fault and performance of the HSSF. The host collects information on the system management by accessing the status registers of the each unit through M-Bus.

4.1   Configuration Management

As a configuration management, Figure 5(a) shows that the host will get the knowledge of the system configuration, such as which HSCU is inserted in the shelf and which is linked with HSNA. At first, the host collects information about which HSCU is inserted into the HSSF shelf after powered. Next, it checks inserted HSCU is linked with corresponding HSNA. This results in making initial configuration table. The table can be used to monitoring a valid HSCU, which is in fault or not.

Another function of configuration management is setting up a MGID, which is used to delivering the packet frames to the specific destination group during switching control. The MGID register is written or read also by the host through M-Bus.

4.2   Fault Management

For fault management as shown in Figure 5(b), if the host detects a fault status, at first, it will be trying to recover itself from abnormal condition using the command register. Nevertheless, if it continues to detect the fault, the host will indicate that self-system has an unrecoverable fault. From this indication via DCC, HSSU that is operated normally at the other node, makes a management packet frame and broadcasts to all the HSCUs. This result in requesting of maintenance to OAM subsystem of ACPS and SPAs will transfer all the packet frame through the other node operated properly.

The host monitors states of the switching controller and HSCU channels that is inserted into the shelf and linked with HSNA. If it detects the switching controller being suspended abnormally, first of all, it will try to recover from the abnormal condition by the initialization command of system level. As a result of this, if the abnormal condition continues, the host asserts failure of H-Bus operation and reports to the normal HSSU in duplication configuration.

5.0   Conclusion

We have presented M-Bus architecture and management methods using it in HSSF system. A flexible and rapid configuration and fault management can be performed by means of extra M-Bus, which is separated from packet frame switching path, named H-Bus. We have implemented configuration and fault management of HSSF system and are implementing performance measurement for traffic management and connection admission control.

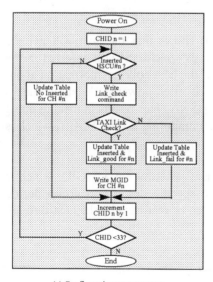

(a) Configuration management

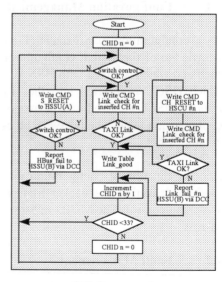

(b) Fault management

Figure 5. Management flow

Acknolwledgment: The authors wish to thank all the colleagues in our development department. This work was sponsored by Korea Telecom.

References:

1. Kim, D.W., Ryu, W., Kim, D.U., and Bae, H.D. (1995), "A Large-scaled Advanced Communication Processing System for an Open Vlaue Added Network," *Proceedings of MICC '95.*, Vol.2, 9.4.1~9.4.4.
2. Jang, J.W., Kim, D.W., Kim, T.J., and Lee, J.T. (1992), "A Configuration Management System in HiTEL Platform - Call admission control and continuous service," *proc. ICCS/ISITA '92*, 989~993.
3. AMD (1992), Am7968/Am7969 TAXIchips Handbook, , Sunnyvale, Advanced Micro Devices.

8.4

DESIGN OF THE REAL-TIME MULTIMEDIA SERVER WITH FINITE BANDWIDTH

Quanwen Mai, Guangzhao Zhang
ZhongShan University, PRC

The network bandwidth and storage I/O bandwidth are bottleneck parameters in real-time multimedia servicing, and they are interrelated. They must be considered simultaneously when designing real-time server. In this paper ,we analyse real-time servicing process, estimate the maximum simultaneous subscribers and buffer size based on $M^k / M / 1$ queuing system. In order to improve its property, we propose "Time Inverse Proportion Multisubscriber Servicing"(TIPMS) algorithm, which is more effective than QPMS. At last, we evaluate the performance of the TIPMS.

1.0   Introduction

Video On Demand is one of important applications in interactive multimedia communication. It is possible to be achieved in the area of metropolitan with the development of wideband network and Redundant Arrays of Inexpensive Disk(RAID). Multimedia server is one of the important parts in the system.While how to design Real-time multimedia server is one of the most important and diffcult problem.Because it not only decides whether the real-time media is continously played but also affects the cost of the system and subscriber. By far, it still suffur from two bottleneck parameters, one is network bandwidth, the other is storage I/O bandwidth, and the two factor are interrelated. Harrick et al. (1993) deveoped a algorithm to estimate the Maximum Simultaneous Subscribers(MSS), but they neglected the affect of network bandwidth Harrick et al. (1993) , they presented the QPMS alogrithm to improve it. Buddhikot et al. put forward a kind of massively-paralled and real-time storage hardware system structure based on ATM Port Interconnect Controller(APIC) (Millind et al. 1994) . It is a good way to improve the server property in the lerver of hardware. But even in this condition, the network bandwidth and storage I/O bandwidth must be finite, and should be considered in order to guarantee the real-time servicing. In this paper, we present a way to calculate the MSS and buffer size based on $M^K/M/1$ queue model under finite network bandwidth and storage I/O bandwidth. According to the estimated result, we develop Time Inverse Proportion Multisubscriber Servicing(TIPMS) algorithm. At last, we evaluate the performance of the TIPMS.

The rest of this paper is organized as following: In section II, we present real-time multimedia system. In section III, we develop a algorithm to estimate the MSS and buffer size under the condition of finite bandwidth. In section IV, we give the TIPMS alogrithm to imporve the MSS and evaluate the performance of the TIPMS. Section V concludes the paper.

2.0   Real-time multimedia service system

Considering the real-time VOD system given in Figure 1. Requests coming from subscribers are transferred to the Access Unit (AU) in server, AU dispatches the program message to the Storage Interface Unit (SIU) under the control of the Center Manager Unit(CMU). This is upstream, which constituts of program items and control messages. SIU reads data from RAID to Sending Unit (SU) parallelly, and the SU sends program stream to subscribers . SU services one subscriber each time, and then switch to the next subscriber. All the sequence of services constitute a service round. So, the down subsystem is the system bottleneck, its parameters are given as following.

Program stored in the RAID is divided into several blocks. Blocks which could be read simultaneously constitute a strand. We define storage pattern of the program i with pair $S_i = (M_i, G_i)$, where M_i is the mean size of each strand, G_i is the mean size between successive strand .The scatter parameter of programme is Δt_s^i . The SIU read data from RAID to Sending Unit(SU) for N requests. There are N buffers in SU, each size is L_i , $L_i = k_i M_i$, while k_i is a constant which is decided by the type of programe and its quality. The SU tranfers all the blocks in buffer i before switch to the next request. All sequence of tranfer $k_1, k_2,...k_N$ constitute a service round (Anderson et al. 1992).

If all the N requests are real-time data stream, Equation (1) must be satisfied in order to guarantee the programme being played continously.

$$\sum_{i=1}^{N}\left(k_i \Delta t_s^i + \max_{j\in(1,kiMi)}(\Delta t_s^{ij}) + \frac{k_i M_i}{R_d} \right) \le \min_{i\in(1,N)}\left(\frac{L_i}{R_p^i} \right) \qquad (1)$$

Where R_d is RAID I/O bandwidth, R_p^i is the playback rate of programme i, Δt_s^{ij} is the delay of bit j in buffer i, B_d is the bandwidth of downstream.Equation (2) must be satisfied also in order to guarantee the data having been read to buffer I completely in a round servicing.

$$\frac{\sum_{\substack{j=1 \\ j\neq i}}^{N} L_j}{B_d} \geq k_i\left(\Delta t_s^i + \frac{M_i}{R_d}\right) \tag{2}$$

It is clear that the sending system is the bottleneckof the server. So, in the next section, we analyse the sending system., and give the way to estimate the maximum simultaneous subscribers and buffer size, which are refrred to as the real-time property parameters when designing server.

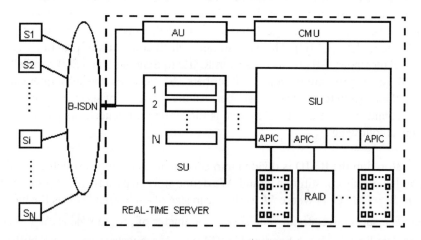

AU: AECESS UNIT ;   CMU: CENTER MANGER UNIT ;   SU: SENDING UNIT ;   Si : SUBSCRIBER i;
RAID: REDUNDANT ARRAYS OF INEXPENSIVE DISK ; APIC : ATM PORT INTERCONNECT CONTROLLER ;

Figure 1 : Real-time servicing system

3.0   Estimate real-time property parameters

To simplify the analysis, frist we assume all the the N programmes are stored in the same pattern, and played in the same playback rate. Then, we get
$$\forall i, j \in [1, N]$$
$$M_i = M_j = M; G_i = G_j = G; k_i = k_j = k; R_p^i = R_p^j = R_p; \Delta t_s^i = \Delta t_s^j = \Delta t_s;$$
Because the maximum value of Δt_s is G/R_d , Substitute these equation in (2), we get

$$R_d \geq \frac{B_d}{N-1} \cdot \frac{M+G}{M} \tag{3}$$

Equation (3) must be satisfied when we choose RAID, Suppose the process that blocks reach sending unit is a batch poisson process, and the batch size is kM , Fig2 can be referred as $M^k / M / 1$ queuing system, which service rate $\mu = B_d$, arrival rate $\lambda = \dfrac{1}{kM} R_d^{avg}$, where R_d^{avg} is the mean bandwidth of the RAID, its maximum value is $\dfrac{M}{M+G} \cdot R_d$.

For each buffer , the mean delay Δt_d^{avg} is given by (Robertazzi 1990)

$$\Delta t_d^{avg} = \frac{kM+1}{2\left(B_d - R_d^{avg}\right)}$$

and the maximum delay is given by

$$\Delta t_d^{\max} = 2\Delta t_d^{avg} = \frac{kM+1}{B_d - R_d^{avg}} \tag{4}$$

Substitute equation(4) in (1), we get

$$N \cdot \frac{kM}{R_d} + N \cdot \frac{kM+1}{B_d - R_d^{avg}} + N \cdot k \cdot \Delta t_s \leq \frac{kM}{R_p}$$

Considering $kM \gg 1$, rearranging above equation, yield

$$N \leq \frac{\dfrac{1}{R_p}}{\dfrac{\Delta t_s}{M} + \dfrac{1}{B_d - R_d^{avg}} + \dfrac{1}{R_d}}$$

So, the MSS is given by integerring right side of above equation

$$N_{\max} = \left\lfloor \frac{\dfrac{1}{R_p}}{\dfrac{\Delta t_s}{M} + \dfrac{1}{B_d - R_d^{avg}} + \dfrac{1}{R_d}} \right\rfloor \tag{5}$$

If the value of bandwidth is infinite, and rearrange equation(5), it can be found that the equation is the same as what given by the reference Harrick et al (1993), but as B_d and R_d^{avg} are considered, the MSS estimated by equation(5) is less than that estimated by the reference Harrick et al (1993), If B_d is big enough, substitute $B_d - R_d^{avg}$ with B_d and let $\Delta t_s = 0$, it can be found that the $N_{\max}$ is equal to $\dfrac{B_d}{R_p}$, It is an ideal condintion without considering the RAID I/O bandwidth.

Some examples are given in Figure 2, one of the example is that when B_d is equal to 2.5Gps, the storage pattern $S = (0.5Mb, 16.66Mb)$, 195 subscribers can be suppoeted, while it is 222 subscriber without considering B_d.

According to Little Law, the mean queue length ΔL is given by

$$\Delta L = \frac{R_d^{avg} \cdot (kM + 1)}{2(B_d - R_d^{avg})}$$

The size of each buffur is

$$L \approx kM \left[1 + \frac{R_d^{avg}}{2N \cdot (B_d - R_d^{avg})} \right] \tag{6}$$

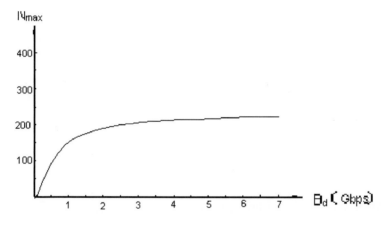

$S = (0.5Mb, 16.66Mb); \quad R_d = 1Gbps; \quad \Delta t_s = 1ms; \quad R_p = 1.5Mbps$

Figure 2: The MSS value changed with bandwidth

When the programme are different , It can also be referred as $M^k / M / 1$ queue system , but the batch size , $\{k_i M_i, i \in [1, N]\}$, is random variable. The mean delay for each buffur is given by

$$\Delta t_d^i = \frac{E\left[(k_i M_i)^2\right] + E(k_i M_i)}{2(B_d - \frac{R_d^{avg}}{k_i M_i} E(k_i M_i)) E(k_i M_i)} \tag{7}$$

Where $E()$ is expectation, and the maximum delay in buffur i is given by

$$\max_{\substack{i\in[1,N]\\ j\in[1,k_iM_i]}} \left(\Delta t_d^{ij}\right) = 2\Delta t_d^i = \frac{E\left[(k_iM_i)^2\right] + E(k_iM_i)}{\left(B_d - \dfrac{R_d^{avg}}{k_iM_i}E(k_iM_i)\right)E(k_iM_i)} \tag{8}$$

Because

$$E\left[(k_iM_i)^2\right] = Var(k_iM_i) + \left(E(k_iM_i)\right)^2 \tag{9}$$

$$E(k_iM_i) = Cor(k_i,M_i) + E(k_i)\cdot E(M_i) \tag{10}$$

Where $Var()$ and $Cor()$ indicate variance and covariance. So

$$E\left[(k_iM_i)^2\right] \ge (E(k_iM_i))^2$$

$$E(k_iM_i) \ge E(k_i)\cdot E(M_i)$$

Define $E(k_i)=k^{avg}$; $E(M_i)=M^{avg}$ and Δt_s^{avg} to indicate mean value of $\{k_i, i\in[1,N]\}$; $\{M_i, i\in[1,N]\}$ and $\{\Delta t_s^i, i\in[1,N]\}$. Substituing (9) and (10) in (8), we get

$$\max_{\substack{i\in[1,N]\\ j\in[1,k_iM_i]}} \left(\Delta t_d^{ij}\right) \le \frac{k^{avg}M^{avg}}{B_d - \dfrac{R_d^{avg}}{k_iM_i}E(k_iM_i)} \tag{11}$$

Continue to substitute (11) in (1), yield

$$N\cdot\left(k^{avg}\Delta t_s^{avg} + \frac{k^{avg}M^{avg}}{B_d - R_d^{avg}} + \frac{k^{avg}M^{avg}}{R_d}\right) \le \min_{i\in[1,N]}\left(\frac{k_iM_i}{R_p^i}\right)$$

we get

$$N \le \frac{\min\limits_{i\in[1,N]}\left(\dfrac{k_iM_i}{R_p^i}\right)}{k^{avg}\left(\Delta t_s^{avg} + \dfrac{M^{avg}}{B_d - R_d^{avg}} + \dfrac{M^{avg}}{R_d}\right)}$$

The MSS is given by

$$N_{max} = \left\lfloor \frac{\min\limits_{i\in[1,N]}\left(\dfrac{k_iM_i}{R_p^i}\right)}{k^{avg}\left(\Delta t_s^{avg} + \dfrac{M^{avg}}{B_d - R_d^{avg}} + \dfrac{M^{avg}}{R_d}\right)} \right\rfloor \tag{12}$$

The way to estimate the buffur size is given as

1. Calculate $E(k_i M_i)$
2. Calculate Δt_d^i according to equation (7)
3. Calculate the mean queue length $\Delta L = E(k_i M_i) \cdot \Delta t_d^i$
4. The buffur size is given by $L_i = k_i M_i + \dfrac{k_i M_i}{\displaystyle\sum_{i \in [1,N]} k_i M_i} \cdot \Delta L$

4.0   Time inverse proportion multisubscriber servicing

The MSS is the key parameter in designing real-time multimedia server. Equation(12) shows it relates not only to playback rate, but also to its storage pattern. Vin et. developed QPMS algorithm, which is that the number of blocks accessed during each round for each subscriber request is proportional to its playback rate. Based on this idea, $k_i \propto R_p^i$, substitute it in equation(12), induce to

$$N_{max}^{(1)} = \left| \frac{\min\limits_{i \in [1,N]} (M_i)}{R_p^{avg} \left(\Delta t_s^{avg} + \dfrac{M^{avg}}{B_d - R_d^{avg}} + \dfrac{M^{avg}}{R_d} \right)} \right| \tag{13}$$

If we allocate values k$_i$ inverse proportional to the time which a block would play in, it should be $k_i \propto \dfrac{R_p^i}{M_i}$ and equation (12) will became

$$N_{max}^{(2)} = \left| \frac{M^{avg}}{R_p^{avg} \left(\Delta t_s^{avg} + \dfrac{M^{avg}}{B_d - R_d^{avg}} + \dfrac{M^{avg}}{R_d} \right)} \right| \tag{14}$$

We call this way Time Inverse Proportion Multisubscriber Servicing (TIPMS), let we compare the QPMS and TIPMS as following

It is certainly that $\qquad\qquad M^{avg} \geq \min\limits_{i \in [1,N]} \left(M_i \right)$

So , it must exit that $\qquad\qquad N_{max}^{(2)} \geq N_{max}^{(1)}$ $\qquad\qquad$ (15)

It shows that TIPMS can improve real-time property more effectively than QPMS.

Table 1 Storage patterns and system parameters

programmes parameters		MPEG I	MPEG II	SDTV	HDTV
prog -ramme para -meters	playback rate (Mbps)	1.5	5	9	18.8
	storage pattern(Mb)	(0.1,35)	(0.33,58)	(0.3,18)	(0.63,26)
	programme number	35	35	15	15
RAID para -meter	bandwidth	1Gbps			
	scattering parameter	1ms	1.5ms	0.6ms	0.8ms

In order to evaluate the performance of TIPMS algorithm, we calculate the MSS under the same programme storage pattern and system parameters with TIPMS and QPMS ways. The system parameters are given in table 1 and the results are given in Figure 3.

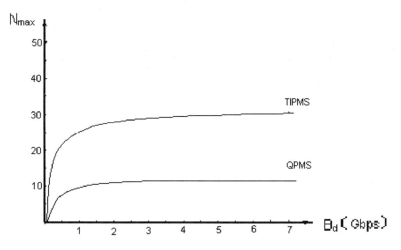

Figure 3: The calculation results of qpms and tipms

From the results, conclusions are gotten as follow:

1. Compared to QPMS, the TIPMS increases the MSS effectively. For example, when B_d is equal to2.5Gbps, The MSS of QPMS is 10, while it is 30 with TIPMS. So, the cost of subscribers would decrease by the way of TIPMS.

410

2. At the beginning of bandwidth increasing(Such as 100Mbps-2Gbps), The MSS increases swiftly, but if the bandwidth increases continously, it doesn't show distinct improvement, it indicates that to improve the MSS though increasing bandwidth won't work.

5.0   Conclusion

The network bandwidth and storage I/O bandwidth are interrelated in real-time multimedia server ,and must be considered simultaneously. After analysing real-time servicing process, we give the way to estimate the maximum simultaneous subscribers and buffer size based on $M^k / M / 1$ queuing system. According to the estimated result, we develop the Time Inverse Proportion Multisubscriber Servicin(TIPMS) algorithm, compared to QPMS, it is more effective to increase simultaneous subscribers. At last, we evaluate the performance of the TIPMS.

References

1. Harrick et al.(1993). "Designing a Multiuser HDTV Storage Server", IEEE Journal On Selected Areas in Communications, 11(1), 153-164.
2. Millind et al.(1994). "Design of a large scale multimedia storage server",Computer Network and ISDN Systems, 27,503-517.
3. Anderson et al.(1992). "Real-time disk storage and retrieval of digital audio and video", ACM Trans. Comput. System.
4. Robertazzi, Thomas G. (1990). Computer Network and Systems:Queueing Theory and Performance Evalution, Springer-Verlag.

8.5

A DIRECT TRANSMISSION METHOD OF MULTIMEDIA DATA

Ha-Jae Chung, Dong-Won Han & Bae-Wook Park
Electronics and Telecommunications Research Institute, Korea

This paper describes a direct transmission method of mutimedia data streams between a multimedia processor and a network interface without using system memory. We propose the direct transmission method of multimedia data through a single data path, without additional data path between the multimedia processor and the network interface card in a multimedia platform. The hardware architecture and functions for direct transmission is defined. Procedure to transmit multimedia data to and from the multimedia processor is described from the viewpoint of control flow. Comparing the proposed method with general methods, we show that the direct transmission method can decrease the number of bus accesses and bus cycles.

1.0   Introduction

Recently, many efforts have been made in both software and hardware to make various multimedia applications possible. This paper is on a direct transmission method of multimedia data streams between a multimedia processor and a network interface card without using system memory. We propose the direct transmission method of multimedia data through only a single data path, without using additional data path between the multimedia processor and the network interface card in a multimedia platform.

2.0   Multimedia H/W platform

From a hardware point of view, a multimedia platform generally has to support the functions shown in Figure 1. The video Codec and the audio Codec are designed to capture audio-visual data from input devices and compress these data. Data are compressed in each Codec and passed to the multimedia processing block for synchronization and mixing. And the multimedia data stream is transmitted to a display monitor and a speaker, otherwise is saved in a hard disk.

In many cases, multimedia functions are implemented and integrated in various forms of hardware boards which connect with the system bus of the multimedia hardware platform. For example, mutimedia hardwares such as video Codec, audio Codec, video overlay and network interface transmit and receive multimedia data using the system bus.

In the computer systems which transmit or receive multimedia data stream through networks, the sequence of the internal data flow in multimedia systems is as follows.

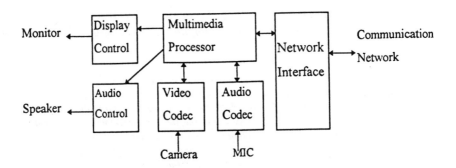

Figure 1 : Functional structure of multimedia platform

3.0   General method for multimedia data transceiver

In the case of transmission, data streams generally flow from the multimedia processor to the network interface card by way of a system bus, a main memory and the system bus in turn. In the case of receiving, data streams proceed from the multimedia processor to the network interface card, in the reverse order of the transmission sequence. Of the system resources in this sequence, the main memory is not necessary for transceiving multimedia data in the computer system the multimedia processor board of which is connected to the network interface board through the system bus.

Though the source and destination of multimedia data streams, in both receiving and transmission, is the network interface card and the multimedia processor, data streams are sent from source to destination by way of the main memory. The access to this main memory makes the load of the main processor and system bus increased. As the result of the frequent use of the system bus, the processing speed of the main instruction processor and the multimedia processor becomes slow. Eventually the system performance is more decreased.

4.0   Direct transmission method

To minimize data traffic on the system bus in a multimedia hardware platform, we propose a method to directly transmit multimedia data between the multimedia processor and the network interface card. This method is called Pre-Tx/Post-Decision & Control method. (Figure 2)

Adding a hardware module for direct transmission functions to the multimedia processors and the network interface card, the Pre-Tx/Post-Decision & Control method can be implemented. To support the direct transmission function, the direct transmission controller shown in Figure 2 must include various functional blocks such as bus snoop controller, media analyzer, hold status register and sequence controller.

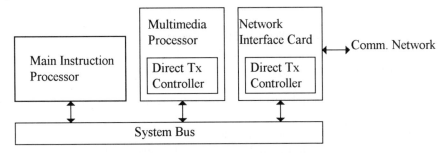

Figure 2: Direct transmission method

On input operation, the multimedia processor concurrently receives data moving from the network interface card to the main memory in the same cycle. And if some data are available for the multimedia processor, these data are saved in the multimedia processor, otherwise these data are not used. On the other hand, the multimedia processor sends data to the system bus on output operation. Subsequently the network interface card also takes these data and processes them in the same manner as the main instruction processor.

5.0   Architecture for direct transmisson

This paper is about the method which analyze and adjust its related status after receiving a multimedia data stream from a multimedia processor or network interface board.

This direct transmission method for multimedia data by means of analysis and adjustment enables a transmission method to bring about the same result as direct data transmission between the multimedia processor and the network interface performed.   The direct transmission method we proposed is summarized as follows.

414

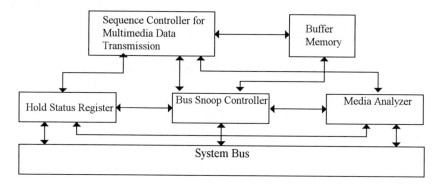

Figure 3: Functional block of direct transmission

5.1   Feature

o Direct transmission between the multimedia processor and the network interface
o Direct transmission without using the system memory
o Direct transmission through only the system bus without additional data path
o Bus based architecture system that the multimedia processor connected to the network interface through the system bus

5.2   Architecture

The direct transmission controller is composed basically of the following entities :
o Sequence Controller for Multimedia Data Transmission
o Media Analyzer
o Hold Status Register
o Bus Snoop Controller
o Buffer Memory

5.3   Operation

o Sequence Controller for Multimedia Data Transmission :
This controller controls the status transition and the operation of the bus snoop controller, the media analyzer, the hold status register and the buffer memory, according to the system bus and functional modules related.
o Media Analyzer :
This module analyzes the multimedia data stream just latched by the bus snoop controller for the next operation, and decides to use or discard it.
o Hold Status Register :
This register holds the status to decide that the multimedia data stream buffered is effective data or not.

o Bus Snoop Controller :

This controller snoops and indicates to receive the multimedia data on the bus. And also this snoops and indicates to drive out the multimedia data on the bus.

o Buffer Memory :

This is the temporary storage for buffering the multimedia data stream which is scheduled to transceive to/from the multimedia processor or the network interface.

5.4 Functional Block Diagram

Figure 4 shows the relations between the direct transmission controller and other functional modules in a multimedia hardware platform. The block diagram can be classified into two parts. The upper side of the system bus is the main instruction processor that performs functions like a mother board in the conventional PC. The other side is a multimedia processor or a network interface controller which includes the data transmission controller supporting the direct transmission method.

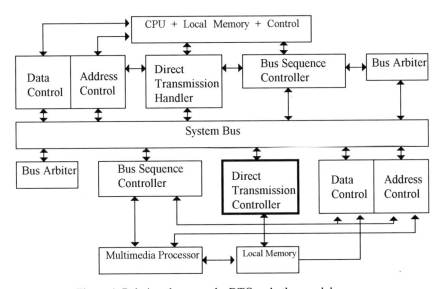

Figure 4: Relations between the DTC and other modules

6.0 Example and processing rate

In this chapter, we intend to compare the general transmission method with the direct transmission method from the viewpoint of processing rate. Figure 5 is a system block diagram which is consisted of the number of n multimedia processors, two network interface controllers, a main instruction processor, a main memory and a system bus.

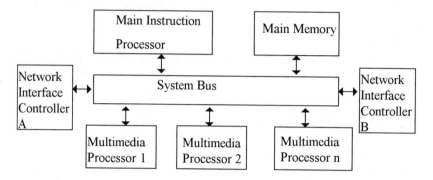

Figure 5: System block including multiple components for direct transmission

In this kind of systems, we define a comparing model as following;
The same size of the multimedia data as system bus width is transfered from the network interface controller A to the multimedia processor 1, from the network interface controller B to the multimedia processor 2, from the main memory to multimedia processor n.

In the general transmission method, the network interface controller A and B access the main memory by means of using the system bus only once, and the main memory uses the system bus 3 times. In case of the former, the internal operation for storing data into the main memory takes about 2 system bus cycles time. Therefore total time for all operation on the comparing model defined will be taken about 9 system bus cycles time.

$$\text{NIC A} \xrightarrow{\text{1 BC}} \text{Bus} \xrightarrow{\text{2 BC}} \text{Main Memory} \xrightarrow{\text{1 BC}} \text{MM Processor 1 (2 BU)}$$

$$\text{NIC B} \xrightarrow{\text{1 BC}} \text{Bus} \xrightarrow{\text{2 BC}} \text{Main Memory} \xrightarrow{\text{1 BC}} \text{MM Processor 2 (2 BU)}$$

$$\text{Main Memory} \xrightarrow{\text{1 BC}} \text{MM Processor n (1 BU)}$$

In the direct transmission method, the network interface controller A and B use system bus only once, and also the main memory uses the system bus once. Therefore total time for all operation needs just 3 system bus cycles time. We are able to know that the rate of the number of the system bus for the general method to the direct transmission method is 5 to 3, and the rate of total time for completion of operation is 9 to 3.

$$\text{NIC A} \xrightarrow{\text{1 BC}} \text{MM Processor 1 (1 BU)}$$

$$\text{NIC B} \xrightarrow{\text{1 BC}} \text{MM Processor 2 (1 BU)}$$

$$\text{Main Memory} \xrightarrow{\text{1 BC}} \text{MM Processor n (1 BU)}$$

The following table is results from making a comparative study. Comparing the proposed method with general methods, we show that the direct transmission method can decrease the number of bus use and bus cycles.

Table 1 : Comarision of processing rate

	# of Bus Use	# of Bus Cycles
General Method	5 BU	9 BC
Direct Tx Method	3 BU	3 BC

7.0   Transmission control flow

In this chapter we describe the internal operation and state of the direct transmission mechanism. In the initial status, the Direct Transmission Controller (DTC) checks the bus state every bus cycle. If it is a receiving state, the receiving state machine of the DTC starts. If it is a transmission state, the transmission state machine of the DTC starts. And if neither receiving nor transmission it is, then the DTC checks the bus state repeatedly.

In the previous stage, if the bus state is a data receiving state, the bus snoop controller is checked. If it is an enable state for data copy, the DCT reads data into the buffer memory and if it is not, the DTC checks the bus state continuously.

After the above step, if the bus state is valid, the DTC read data. Otherwise, the state machine returns to the Tx/Rx check state.

And then the bus snoop controller checks the acknowledgement state for the address just received. If the acknowledgement state is normal, the internal buffering condition is checked. If abnormal, the DTC returns to the beginning state.

The DTC decides whether the internal status of the multimedia data processor board including the DTC is valid for buffering data on the basis of the state known by investigating the previous bus operation. If invalid, the DTC makes the possession status flag non-possessive, then it returns to the beginning. If valid, it checks the media analyzer and decides the media data is same kind or not.

In the previous stage, if the DTC decides the media is not the same kind as the DTC expected, then the media analyzer is initialized and the DTC state machine returns to the beginning state. If the DTC decides the media is the same kind of one, the DTC stores the data received from the system bus into the buffer

418

memory, and makes the hold status register possessive, and then returns to the Tx/Rx check state.

After the above step, if the multimedia processor receives the information that the data stored in the local memory is valid, from Direct Transmission Handler in the main instruction processor, then it progresses the next stage operation such as data compression.

In the bus state check stage, if the bus state is a data transmitting state, firstly the DTC prepares the data to be transfered in the reverse order of the operation for receiving data, and it generates an address for transmission, and then requests the bus use through the bus arbiter, and lastly enters into the bus competition state.

If the DTC loses, it enters into the bus competition state again. If the DTC wins, the DTC drives data on the system bus. And if the result of transmission check is normal, the DTC initializes the hold status register and the media analyzer, and then it returns to the initial status. If abnormal, the DTC returns to a bus requesting state again

8.0   Conclusion and future work

In this paper, we proposed a method to minimize data traffic on the system bus in a multimedia hardware platform. We show that multimedia data streams such as audio and video data can be directly moved through a single data path between a multimedia processor and a network interface card without using main memory. We defined a hardware architecture and functions for this direct transmission function.

We described the procedure for data transmission from a control point of view and compared the general transmission method with the direct transmission method from the viewpoint of processing rate. Our aim is to build a multimedia processor and a network interface which are able to provide high-end multimedia services. To test the Pre-Tx/Post-decision & Control method, hardware implementation is essential to us. Therefore we are designing a silicon that supports the direct transmission method. To verify the suitability of our proposed mechanism we are currently working on simulations and analysis of various different strategies.

References:

1. Chung, H.J., Han, D.W., Lee J.W. (1996), ``On the Design and Analysis of Multimedia I/O for Video Conference'', *The Transactions of The korea*

Information Processing Society, 3(3), 608- 616.

2. Khayat, S.H., Bovopoulos,A.D.,(1994), "A proposed bus arbitration scheme for multimedia workstations", *Multimedia*, IEEE

3. Rothlisberger U. (1992) " A multimedia Network interface", *Multimedia'92 4th IEEE ComSoc International Workshop on Multimedia Communications*, 80-88

4. Shin, O.K., Kim, H.K., Chae, Y.D. (1995), " An Architecture of Multimedia Platform for Integrated Audio-Visual Data Processing", *WSCG 95*, Conference Proceedings volume 1, 273-282

5. Song. D.H., Shin, O.K., Min, B.E., Lim, Y.H. (1994), "CombiStation: A Platform and Frameworks for Multimedia CSCW", *First Joint Workshop on Multimedia Communications 94*, 54-64

6. Borko Furht (1994) "Multimedia systems:An overview", *Multimedia*, IEEE

7. PCI Local Bus specification Revision 2.1, PCISIG, 1995

8.6

REAL-TIME COMMUNICATION IN A SIMPLIFIED TIMED TOKEN PROTOCOL

Ming Li & Koppenhoefer Shawn
Swiss Federal Institute of Technology, Switzerland

Our problem consists in determining if the bounds on deadlines for time-critical traffic in PROFIBUS, can be respected, given that the worst-case is known. We perform an analysis of the real-time characteristics using a formal model, Stochastic Timed Petri Nets. To our knowledge, there exists no other published material on Profibus that uses this particular formalism. The main results of this paper are two-fold: a formal description (an STPN model of Profibus) with analysis, verfication, and validation; the schedulability condition for time-critical traffic on Profibus.

1.0 Introduction

Profibus is a German standard for fieldbus [1] [2], and is now widely used in industrial applications. Profibus is a three-layer communication architecture, composed of a Physical layer, a Fieldbus Data Link (FDL) layer and an Application layer. The Physical layer uses the standard RS-485 for transmission and reception. The main function of FDL layer is to perform the medium access control (MAC). MAC protocol used in Profibus is a simplified timed token protocol. The application layer contains two sublayers — FMS (Fieldbus Message Specification) and LLI (Lower Layer Interface). The former supports the 39 FMS services which are used for remote control of manufacturing devices and data sampling; the latter performs the connection management and maps the FMS services to the FDL services or vice-versa.

In Profibus, there are two types of stations — masters and slaves. A master is able to control the bus. In contrast a slave is only able to acknowledge a received frame or transmit a frame in response to a remote request.

Profibus is designed for the industrial applications where real-time communication is often required. In such an environment the problem is to determine whether the scheduling of the time-critical traffic is feasible at all. An alternative formulation of the real-time communication problem consists in determining the bounds on deadlines for the time-critical traffic, given the maximum offered time-critical traffic. In order to solve the above problems, real-time performance analysis for Profibus MAC protocol, which is subject of this paper, must be performed. In this paper, we also present a formal model of Profibus MAC protocol using Stochastic Timed Petri Nets (STPN). Our model totally conforms with the Profibus standard and corrects the Profibus model presented in [3]. We will show that our model is well suited for analyzing the real-time performance of Profibus.

2.0   Traffic model and notations

2.1   Traffic model

The Profibus standard defines three classes of traffic: the high-priority traffic, the cyclic traffic and the low-priority traffic.

(1) the high-priority traffic must be guaranteed to meet the deadlines. The deadline guaranty implies that some restrictions are imposed on the arrival rate of the high-priority traffic. This is usually done by assuming that the high-priority traffic is sporadic, which means that there is a minimum delay between two successive message arrivals within a given stream. Since the high-priority data streams are not synchronized, all their samples may be offered simultaneously for service by the stations.

(2) the cyclic traffic corresponds usually to the reading and writing of sensor and actuator values that is performed at regular intervals. This is done through the polling tables in stations that are set and updated by network management. Here the traffic is obviously bounded and can be considered as predictable and known beforehand. The time constraints on this traffic depend on the application, and the traffic may be considered as non time-critical traffic if it is acceptable to use occasionally an old sample value in the image memory when the refreshing service has missed its deadline. If this is not acceptable, the cyclic traffic must be considered as time-critical traffic. In this paper we consider the cyclic traffic as non time-critical traffic.

(3) the low priority traffic is not periodic and there is no minimum interarrival time between successive bursts of data. However we arbitrarily model this traffic and the constraints we impose upon it

by considering that there is at most one data stream of low-priority traffic in a station.

2.2   Notations

In this paper, the following notations are used:

N_s: Number of master stations
T_t: Duration of a token transmission in seconds/token transmission

T_h: Largest service time of all high-priority service times
TS_h: Service time for all high-priority traffic data streams
P_h: Minimum interarrival time among all data streams of high-priority traffic
TTRT: Target Token Rotation Timer

3.0   Medium Access Protocol

The MAC protocol in Profibus belongs to the class of token-passing protocols. To transmit, a station must hold a token that circulates around a logical ring. To become a member of this ring, a station must wait for an invitation from an in-ring station. Once in the ring, a station is guaranteed to receive cyclically the token and to be allowed to transmit. The rule that a station cannot transmit unless it holds the token is not always valid: in the immediate response mode, a station can send a response frame although it does not hold the token. A master with the immediate response looks like a slave (recall that slaves are not involved in the ring) when this slave transmits a frame to a master.

In Profibus, the service time for frame transmission depend on the last token rotation time. When a station receives the token, it calculates the difference between the Target Token Rotation Time (TTRT) and the actual rotation time of the last round, which defines the Token Holding Time (THT). The THT is then decremented by a timer and as long as the residual THT is positive, the station is allowed to transmit frames, i.e., only if the token arrived earlier than expected.

In order to guarantee the transmission of urgent frames the station is allowed to transmit at the beginning one high-priority frame upon receipt of the token, even if the THT is negative. After this frame, if any, the rest of the frame transmission by the station is controlled by the residual value of the THT, with the sending of high-priority frames which continues until either the THT is negative or the supply of high-priority frames is exhausted. In the last case, the station enters the polling cycle mode and sends the frames that pertain to this second highest priority class. The frames pertaining to this class are referenced in a polling table that keeps track of the frames that pertain to a given polling cycle. Should the polling table step-through need be interrupted because the THT has expired, its execution will resume at that place in the table in the next round after handling any subsequent high-priority frames.

After the polling table has been scanned and if the THT has not expired, lower priority frames are sent until the timer expires. If no low priority frames are present, the token is passed without delay.

An exception to these events occurs when no time remains to send low priority frames after the polling has been completed. In that case, the low priority packets are sent immediately after the high-priority at the next token round. The medium access method is summrized in Fig. 1.

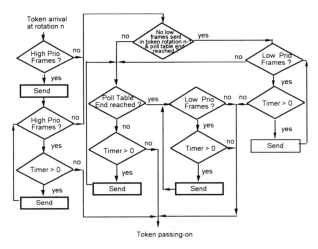

Figure 1: medium access flow chart of the profibus

4.0   Real-time performance analysis of profibus MAC protocol

In this section we analyze the case where only the high-priority traffic is time-critical. This is equivalent to lumping together the cyclic and the low priority traffic into non time-critical traffic. We make no assumptions about the traffic distribution over the stations and we seek to determine the bounds on the deadlines of the high-priority traffic. The worst case allowable interarrival time between successive samples occurs when the network is constrained to serve as little high-priority traffic as possible. Since each station is allowed one extra high-priority service even if the residual value of its TRT is negative, the worst case condition requires that all the high-priority traffic be concentrated on a single station. Moreover, in order to achieve a worst case condition for the high-priority traffic, we must assume a situation where all the stations attempt to serve as much lower-priority traffic as allowed by the residual value of their TRT. This leads to a situation such as shown in Fig. 2.

In the example of Fig.2, we assume that all the high-priority traffic is concentrated in station 1. Then, after an empty token rotation, station 1 services cyclic or low-priority traffic during TTRT - N_sT_t time units if no high-priority traffic is pending at the token arrival in this station. Assume now that a burst of high-priority traffic arrives at station 1 just after this station has started servicing the lower priority traffic. Then obviously station 1 cannot serve the high-priority traffic at this token visit.

Since TRT = TTRT, the succeeding stations cannot serve any lower priority traffic and since all the high-priority traffic is concentrated in station 1, stations 2 and 3 do not serve either any high-priority traffic. The process continues until the next token visit to station 1, at which time we still have TRT = TTRT. However station 1 is allowed to provide one service of duration Th on high-priority traffic that is pending. Then station 2 can serve lower priority traffic for TTRT - $N_s T_t$ - T_h time units.

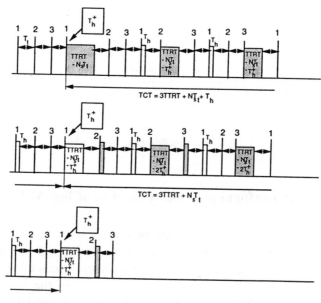

Figure 2: worst-case cycle time for high-priority traffic in profibus

It can be seen on the example that station 1 provides only one service of duration T_h at each token visit until the fourth token visit where it can serve the residual high-priority traffic for TTRT - $N_s T_t$ - T_h time units.

Thus in the general case of a N_s master station network, the period of the high-priority traffic cannot be less than N_s*TTRT + $N_s T_t$ + T_h. During this time, the network can be accessed for high-priority in station 1 during $N_s T_h$ time units for a single service and during TTRT - $N_s T_t$ - T_h for the residual service. Hence we must have (1)

$$TS_h = TTRT - N_s T_t + (N_s - 1)T_h \qquad (1)$$

Thus,

If $N_sT_h < TS_h \leq TTRT - N_sT_t + (N_s - 1)T_h$

$$P_h \leq N_s*TTRT + N_sT_t + T_h \qquad (2)$$

If $TS_h \leq N_sT_h$

$$P_h \leq \lceil TS_h/T_h \rceil TTRT \qquad (3)$$

In the rest of this chapter, we always assume $N_sT_h < TS_h$. The setting of the TTRT can be expressed from Eq. 1 and Eq. 2 as

$$TS_h + N_sT_t - (N_s - 1) T_h \leq TTRT \leq (P_h - N_sT_t - T_h)/ N_s \qquad (4)$$

Where the first inequality expresses the constraint on the service time of the high-priority traffic and the second inequality represents the constraint on the interarrival time.

Eq. 4 implies the feasibility condition

$$TS_h + N_sT_t - (N_s - 1) T_h \leq (P_h - N_sT_t - T_h)/ N_s \qquad (5)$$

5.0 Formal model of profibus using STPN

The objective of this section is to present a formal model of the data link layer of Profibus using Stochastic Timed Petri Nets (STPN). With the STPN model, we can unambiguously analyze the behavior of the data link layer, and evaluate its performance using an approach presented in [4].

To our knowledge [3] is the only paper that evaluates the performance of Profibus based on an extended stochastic Petri net model. However, this paper gives only a simplified representation of the protocol where the low priority frames are never transmitted before cyclic data. This work reports results on the mean node service time but does not consider hard real-time environments. Moreover this evaluation is based on the following assumptions:

The token holding time THT_j at each station j is predetermined and fixed to the estimated mean traffic transmission at this station. In effect, this reduces the Profibus network to a simple fixed TDMA system, which is a gross simplification.

In this section we present a Profibus STPN model that corrects the errors and the deficiencies in [3]. Our model is totally conformant with the Profibus standard and can be used for analyzing the hard real-time performance of Profibus.

5.1   STPN model for profibus

The complete Petri net, as we will soon see, is relatively complex so that its description is more easily understood by presenting separately its different parts. Therefore, we will organize the presentation in several pieces: (1) Timer mechanism (2) High-priority services (3) Cyclic services (4) Low-priority services. In the following we have a potential conflict in the use of the word "token", since the network operation is based on the circulation of a token while the Petri net operation is usually described by the evolution of tokens in the graph. In order to avoid any confusion we will reserve the word "token" for the token that is used in Profibus and we will refer the tokens in a Petri net place as "markings". In our representations of STPN nets, the coloring of transitions in the graphs will indicate the class of the transition from the standpoint of its firing time characteristic; white transitions are assumed to fire immediately, while gray transitions are time-delayed transitions.

5.2   Timer mechanism

The data link layer of Profibus uses two timers, the THT and the TRT. Timer THT counts down and timer TRT counts up. Upon the token arrival, the THT and the TRT are reset as follows: THT := TTRT - TRT; TRT := 0. The Petri net model for the TRT and THT timers is shown in Fig. 3.

The sequence P3, t4, P4 models the TRT timer. The number of markings in place P3 represents the time interval TTRT - TRT; here each marking represents an elementary time unit1, denoted as τ. Obviously, TTRT - TRT = $M3*\tau$ where M3 is the number of the markings in P3. M3 is equal to zero if the TTRT value is less than or equal to the TRT. The timed transition t4 and place P4 are used to perform the time counting. At each time unit t, the timed transition t4 fires and a marking in place P3 is consumed. So, if N_T = TTRT/τ markings are placed into P3 upon the token arrival, then the number of markings in P3 corresponds to TTRT - TRT time units upon the next token arrival.

The sequence P5, t6, P6 models the THT timer. The number of markings in P5 represents the value of the THT timer. Obviously, THT = $M3*\tau$ where M5 is the number of the markings in place P5. The timed transition t6 and place P6 are used for the THT time counting. In each time unit τ, the timed transition t6 fires and a marking in place P5 is consumed.

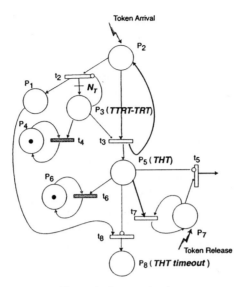

Figure 3: time mechanism

5.3   High-priority service

We model the high-priority traffic at a station as a set of k high-priority streams which are periodic. In practice the high-priority traffic corresponds primarily to the service of alarms which is best described as a sporadic traffic that is characterized by the minimum interarrival delay between two successive services in a given stream. However, we are mainly interested in evaluating the real-time performances of Profibus, which obviously correspond to the worst case traffic configuration. For a sporadic traffic, the worst case situation occurs when the a service is requested at the end of each inter-arrival time, that is when the stream is periodic. Each high-priority stream is characterized by its period2 and its service time. The Petri net for the high-priority service is shown in Fig. 4.

The places and transitions $P9_{h(1)}$, $t9_{h(1)}$, $P10_{h(1)}$, $t10_{h(1)}$, P12, P11, $t11_{h(1)}$ model the production and servicing of the high-priority stream h(1). The markings in $P10_{h(1)}$ indicate the number of pending high-priority messages in stream h(1). In each period, the timed transition $t9h(1)$ fires once and a marking is placed into $P10_{h(1)}$. The timed transition $t10_{h(1)}$ (or $t11_{h(1)}$) defines the service time for a high-priority message in the h(1) stream by delaying its firing by the service time of the message.   Each high-priority stream is modeled similarly, with a set of places and transitions $P9_{h(k)}$, $t9_{h(k)}$, $P10_{h(k)}$, $t10_{h(k)}$, P12, P11, t11 $_{h(k)}$ that models the production and servicing of this stream h(k). Now let us explain how high-priority traffic is serviced.   The services time for

428

high priority traffic is controlled by the THT timer. However, the service for one high-priority message is guaranteed upon receipt of the token, even if the THT is negative. Place P12 is designed for this function. Upon the token arrival, one marking is deposited in place P12 and this allows one high-priority message to be serviced through the transitions $t10_{h(1)}$ to $t10_{h(k)}$ if there is at least one marking in places $P10_{h(1)}$ to $P10_{h(k)}$, that is if there is at least one pending high-priority message. After one high priority message is serviced, the marking in place P12 is consumed and one marking is added into place P11. Then, the high-priority messages are serviced through the transitions $t11_{h(1)}$ to $t11_{h(k)}$ until either the THT is negative (place P8 is marked) or the supply of high-priority messages is exhausted. For the former case, t14 fires and the token is released. For the later case, t13 fires and the station begins to service the cyclic traffic. If there is no high-priority traffic upon the token arrival, then the cyclic traffic should be serviced immediately. From the figure we see that t12 fires immediately if there is no marking in the places $P10_{h(1)}$ to $P10_{h(k)}$.

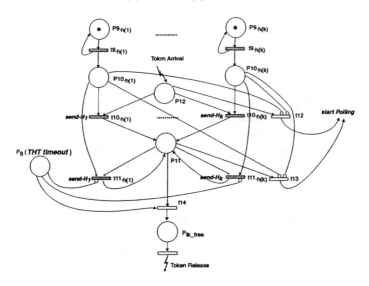

Figure 4: high-priority service

5.4   Cyclic service

The Petri net for cyclic services is shown in Fig. 5. The places and transitions t16, p17 model the production of cyclic traffic. The markings in P17 represent the pending cyclic services. After all pending cyclic services are serviced, T16 fires and L (recall that L is the number of cyclic services in the poll list) markings are added into P17.

Place P19 is designed to take into account the priority inversion in Profibus. If a marking exists in this place, it means that low-priority frames are transmitted ahead of cyclic frames at the next token visit.

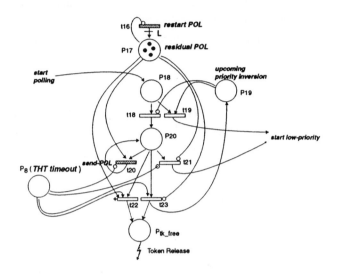

Figure 5: cyclic service

The operation of the Petri net for cyclic services can be described as follows. When P18 is marked (i.e. when cyclic services begin to be serviced) and there is a marking in P19, then t19 fires and the access control is passed to the sub-network that serves the low-priority traffic. If there is no marking in P19, then t18 fires and the cyclic services are serviced. This is done with the place P20 and the timed transition t20 model the service for cyclic services. In our model, we assume that the service time for each cyclic service is the same and is determined by the delay that is associated with this transition. Each time a cyclic service is serviced though the firing of the timed transition t20, a marking in P17 is consumed. Note that transition t20 is conditioned upon P8 being empty, which ensures that the cyclic service do not exceed the service quota specified by the THT.

5.5   Low priority service

The Petri net for low-priority service is shown in Fig. 6. The low priority traffic is normally not periodic and there is no minimum interarrival time between successive burst of data. However, the low-priority traffic must be limited if strict deadlines are to be guaranteed for high-priority traffic and cyclic traffic. One way of doing this is to assume that there is a single stream for low-priority

430

traffic at each station and to assume a distribution for the low-priority services. In our model we choose to model the limitation on the intensity of the low-priority traffic by imposing a minimum inter-arrival time in the low-priority stream. The Petri net for low-priority service is very similar to that for high-priority service except for the following differences:

(1) Upon the token arrival, the service for one high-priority message is guaranteed, even if the THT is negative.

(2) After all pending low-priority traffic is serviced, the token is passed to the next station.

For Fig. 6, we see that if the THT is zero or negative, then no low-priority traffic can be serviced, since t26 cannot be fired.

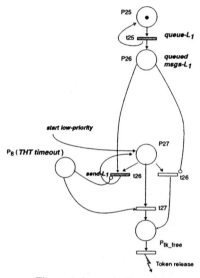

Figure 6: low-priority service

5.6   Complete profibus STPN model

Now we assemble separate parts into a complete Profibus Petri net (Fig. 7). For this STPN model, the following assumptions are made:

(1) only one high priority stream is considered

(2) the service time in each traffic class is constant and the same for each for each service invocation in that class. From the figure we see immediately that the Profibus SPTN model is a deterministic one. Our discussion in the preceding sections has also shown that this model faithfully accounts for the operation of the Profibus access control mechanism.

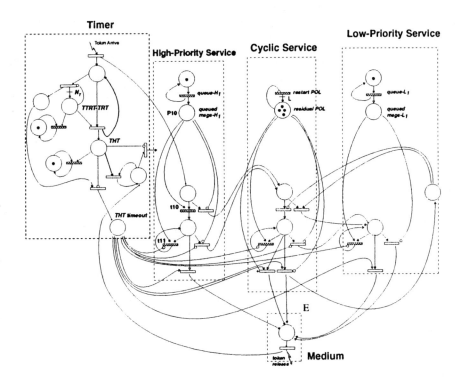

Figure 7: profibus sptn model

6.0 STPN real-time analysis

The real-time analysis for a standard Profibus aims primarily at determining the medium access delay for high-priority traffic. With the medium access delay, we can easily establish the schedulability condition for high-priority traffic (i.e, the minimum interarrival interval for high-priority traffic must be greater than or equal to the medium access delay). In Section 4, we have present an analytic approach to perform the real-time analysis for a standard Profibus. In this section we perform the real-time analysis using STPN approach. We will compare the results obtained from these two approaches.

6.1 Configuration

For our experiment, we assume that Profibus is configured as follows:

(1) The network contains two masters. When STPN approach is used for the performance analysis for Profibus, we must strictly limit the number of masters in order to reduce complexity of SPTN model.

(2) Service time for each high-priority frame, cyclic frame and low-priority frame is the same and is equal to 0.4 ms. In fact, service time for cyclic frame and low-priority frame is not important because we assume that each stations attempt to serve as much lower-priority traffic as allowed by the residual value of their TRT.

(3) The token passing time is 0.16 ms.

6.2   Results

Given the different value of N_T in Fig. 8, we can get the medium access delay as a function of the TTRT. The results obtained by SPTN approach and the analytic approach given in Section 4 are listed in Table 1.

From Table.1, we see that the results obtained from SPTN approach is very close to that obtained from the analytic approach. The error caused by SPTN approach is 0.04 ms. This error depends on the elementary time unit used by TRT timer in the Profibus SPTN model. Because each station has a TRT timer, the error generated by it is less than $\tau*N_S$. In order to reduce the error, we must choose a small τ. However a small τ means that a large number of marks in places P3 and P5 (see Fig. 8) is needed in order to represent the TTRT (recall $N_T = TTRT/\tau$). Thus, the complexity of SPTN model will increase. For our experiment, we choose τ to be 0.1 ms. The error caused by SPTN approach is 0.04 ms (2τ). With $\tau = 0.1$ ms, $N_T = 20$ for TTRT = 2 ms, $N_T = 80$ for TTRT = 8 ms.

Table 1: latency value for the various implementations

TTRT (ms)	Access delay in analytic approach (ms)	Access delay in SPTN approach (ms)
2	4.72	4.76
2.8	6.32	6.36
3.6	7.92	7.96
4	8.72	8.76

7.0   Conclusion

In this paper we have studied the capabilitiesreal-time performance of the standard Profibus. We have presented the schedulability condition for the time-critical traffic. To our knowledge, this topic has not yet been addressed in the literature with this formulation.

In this paper, we have also presented a formal model of the Profibus protocol using Stochastic Timed Petri Nets (STPN). This STPN model totally conforms with the Profibus standard and improves upon the Profibus model presented in [3]. We have shown that our STPN model is well suited for analyzing the real-time performance of Profibus.

The analysis presented in this paper shows that the real-time performance of the standard Profibus network is poor. In [7], we present a way of improving the real-time performance of Profibus.

References:

1. Deutsche Industrie Norm, (1989) "Profibus Standard", DIN 19245 Part 1, Beuth-Verlag, Berlin.
2. Deutsche Industrie Norm, (1989) "Profibus Standard", DIN 19245 Part 2, Beuth-Verlag, Berlin.
3. J. W. Park, S. Moon, W. H. Kwon, (1996) "Analytical Evaluation of the Token Rotation Time of PROFIBUS Networks" Technical Report, Dept. of Computer Science, Seoul of University.
4. G. Juanole and L. Gallon, (1995) "Formal modelling and analysis of a critical time communication protocol", WFCS'95, p.107-115 Lysin, Switzerland, October 4-6.
5. Li Ming, (1996) "Real-time communication in an industrial network --- Profibus", Thesis, Dept. of Computer Science, Swiss Federal Institute of Technology.

8.7

UNITED INTEGRATED SERVICE NETWORK OF WHOLE PROVINCE

Xianming Zhao, Dingjie Xu, and Xiuming Huang
Harbin Institute of Technology, PRC

This paper concisely describes a united integrated service network which is being prepared to set up in two or three years in our province of Heilongjiang. The LANs of every city are all based on CATV network. Its construction model and operation are illustrated, and an experimental scheme of TV/Tel/Data integrated service network is proposed.

1.0   Introduction

In 1990's, with the development of social economy, the need for Broad-band telecommunication service has greatly increased. Communication services are developing towards digital, intellectual, personal, broad-band, and integrated direction.

The construction of Information Super-high-way and Broad-band ISDN have been becoming focus of all kinds of trades in our country. Now the domestic departments concerned have been known the latent large market of Broad-Band communication service. They have been preparing and trying to do this work actively. Look from all development situation, it will start soon. Against this background, exploiting superiority of oneself and trait and considering practical local situation to build High-speed information network of independence, and being in advantageous status in the future market competition for the integrated service, is of momentous current significance and future significance.

In our province of Heilongjiang, an integrated service network is being prepared to set up, which will interlink LANs of several major cities. The LANs are all built by changing the existing CATV networks in every city.

At present, the services of an experimental integrated service network should include TV , telephone, data services, etc. These are briefly introduced in the following.

435

2.0   Topology structure of the network

The united integrated service network is set up by interlinking   the integrated service LAN of every city(at fist step, several major cities are considered, next, other cities will be included) through transmission truck,   which is broad-band, high speed, integrated, intelligent communication network, offering video, data, voice, and the other integrated services by telephone, broad-casting, computer, fax and TV . See Figure 1.

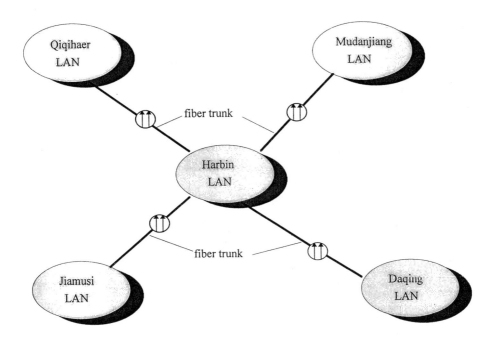

Figure 1: Topology of Uniter Integrated Service network of whole province

2.1   Transmission trunk

Fiber-optic communication, satellite communication, and radio communication are three major technologies using in modern communication network. Band-width of fiber-optic communication is very enormous (about 5 Ghz)and the cost of it is little. So it has become principal in communication network, all of transmission trunks (the trunk of Laval network) use fiber cable.

436

network, as shown in Figure 2.

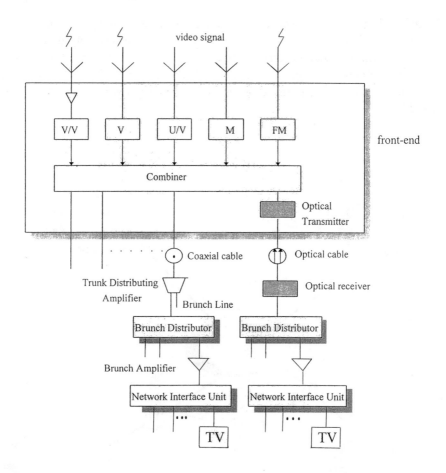

Figure 2 CATV System

Front-end is a core-part of network. It's main functions are signal-receiving, processing and mixing before transmitting. To the signals of wireless-receiving, some of them will be V/V channel transferred, another need to be enlarged in antenna amplifier (weak-signal) and the rest need to be UHF/VHF channel transferred and necessarily enlarged, these signals will be mixed in mixing unit.

Video program of autoplaying (for example recorder program, signal of camera, video signal of satellite receiver) need to be modulated to be sent to mixer. Mixer realizes sending multiple channel signals by neighboring channel. The frequency resource used has changed from radio to cable, the utility rate has improved, the number of channel also has increased from dozens to hundreds.

2.2 Exchange mode

ATM exchange is implemented ,which is a core of every LAN network, and carry out exchange of broad-band signal of the network. The signal is distributed dynamically to every subscriber's receiver module on command. It is high speed and is flexible to the multimedia services.

2.3 Subscriber access network

It is a end part of the whole network, which sends information to user at last and is the foundation of the whole communication network. Because it interlinks directly to every user and users have all kinds of types, too dispersedly, too hybrid, and it is concerned with all network terminals, and investment is so big that it will be kept for some time after its setup, the construction scheme of user's access network ,whether it is good or bad , is most important to the whole network.

These years, CATV business in our country has developed so fast, almost every metropolis and city has its own CATV network with high generalization percent. And its user's access mode is usually fiber coax distribution combined way, it can reach users by broad-band, therefor, changing the available CATV network to offer integrated business services such as voice, data, TV services, is a shortcut to set up effective user's access network.

3.0 Construction and characteristics of CATV network

The traditional broadcast, one-way, single TV video transmission system will be made two-way, interactive, video, digital, audio, Integrated Business Local Network by analyzing, studying, and reforming the existing CATV networks of every city, and then these LANs are interlinked to the united high-speed information network of while province with fiber trunk.

CATV is a kind of TV broadcast mode called cable TV, comparing to radio TV. Its signal transmission mode, program service mode and business running mode are all different to radio TV. But it reserves radio broadcast system and it does not change fundamental function of TV receiver.

With rapid development of modern science and technology, transmission technology and network structure of CATV have become consummate. CATV network provides services from one-way broadcast to interactive receive-on-command, telephone, and data communication services.

CATV is composed of the front-end and transmission system and user distribution

The transition system exploits fiber-optic cable or coaxial cable. The trunk transmission system send the multiple channels programs from front-end to each subscriber administration area, the trunk usually use fiber-optic cable or wide-band coaxial cable. The fiber-optic cable can increase the transmission distance to 25km or more without the trunk amplifier. It not only improve the transmission reliability and the quality of image transmission but also can achieve more transmission capability than coaxial cable. When the trunk link length is beyond 3km, the cost of fiber-optic cable trunk is apparently lower than coaxial cable trunk. When there is need for the trunk line to distribute one signal system to the brunch line, it can be done by connecting distributor or amplifier. The brunch line usually use the coaxial cable, but sometimes can use fiber-optic cable.

Subscriber assignment network is connected with the brunch line or subscriber line, and assign the signal from the transmission trunk to subscriber. It usually use short-diameter coaxial or source delay amplifier.

The system of which topology is that trunk line use fiber-optic cable and subscriber line use coaxial cable, is called Hybrid Fiber/Coax (HFC)system . Subscriber line can also use fiber-optic cable, that is to say, the whole signal transmission line is fiber-optic cable. This is called Fiber to The Home. Such a system has a wide transmission band. It is adapted to development of B-ISDN and it will be the end result of development of CATV network .But the experimental result shows that the cost of   FTTH is high, so it is impossible for FTTH to be applied on large scale in this century. Some experts consider that HFC is now the best wideband transmission architecture and becomes the principle aspect in the CATV network.

The CATV system has the following features:

1. Wide frequency band, a great number of channels. During the beginning of CATV ,it has 77 channels at most .With 8MHz per channel, the 300Mhz system can achieve 12 channels, 450MHz system can achieve 28 channels (subscriber-end need the subscriber transfer unit).
2. It can offers TV ,telephone, and data integrated service.
   Because the CATV system can support more channels, the channels beyond the TV channels can be used to transmit the voice and data.
3. The CATV system is common, and is implemented into home, enterprise, hotel, and etc. It is an economical choice to use CATV system to transmit voice and data.

The application potentiality of CATV system is so large that besides providing various TV programs(TV broadcast , TV services on command in the future), it can also provide telephone , fax, and various data network connecting services to families and offices. In future information super-high-way, CATV system may play a very important vole.

4.0   Experimental scheme of TV/telephone/data integrated service network

To develop CATV integrated services, first may be specified as implement of TV, Telephone and Data hybrid system at present, and so be the base to develop farther higher-level, more advanced function, more all around integrate services.

CATV network can implement connection with other all kinds of network. Such as PSTN Gold-Bridge information network of our country. Ethernet and X.25 protocol telecommunication network etc., so that making user of various terminal devices to communication with other users of other network, as shown in Figure 3. This system should employs hybrid structure of optical fibers and coaxial cables, it may provide users TV video, telephone, data communication services. During data communication, users-end needs MODEMs yet.

There are two fundamental schemes.

1.Implementing TV/Tel hybrid system, voice/data communication through telephone transmitting lines.
2.Implementing TV/Tel/Data hybrid system.

4.1   TV/telephone hybrid system

In this kind of system, there are front-end, optical node(ON) devices and network interface unit(NIU) in common.

Front-end consists of host digital terminal(HDT), video optical transmitter and telephone optical R/T instrument. The HDT may be connected to PSTN and other network switch, it sends telephone multi-routing signals to analog optical transmission devices to implement optical/electronic transforming, then transmits the optical signal to optical node devices.

Optical node is equal to distributor, and classified video optical receiver, telephone optical receiver and telephone optical transmitter three parts. It mixes downward telephone optical signal with CATV downward video optical signals, and at the same time, optical node implements O/E transforming of these two down-ward signals.

440

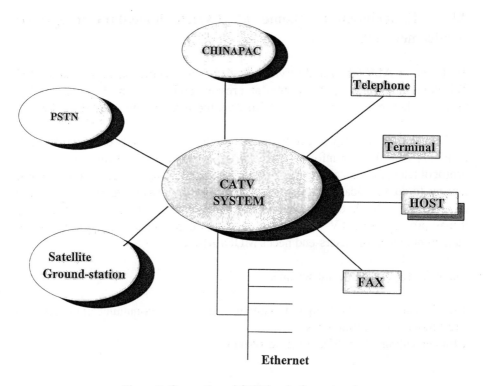

Figure 3: Connection of CATV and other networks

Connecting to optical-knot afterward, it is a traditional coaxial cable distribution network, which extends to user (some users' house) by coaxial cable. The network interface unit is equal to distributor and used to connect branch line to user's line. Data communication passes through MODEM connecting with network interface unit. With the network intelligence interfacing unit, data interface needed by users will be offered. Figure 4 shows how to use network intelligence interfacing unit, and network intelligence interfacing unit's structure is showed in Figure 5. Network interfacing unit has several uses, such as TV service on command in broadcast mode, telephone service (be used by family and miniature business)and data service (LAN/WAN connection and multi-medium),etc.

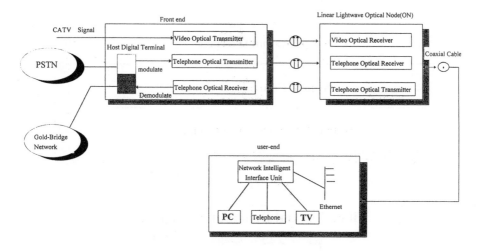

Figure 4: TV/Telephone Hybrid System

4.2   TV/telephone/data hybrid system

In such system, a single independent frequency-band is selected to support data communication. Its structure is showed is Figure 6. The difference from the TV/Tel system is that data optical receiver/transmitter is added between HDT and ON equipments to transfer data.

4.3   TV/telephone/data integrated local network frequency partition

In integrated service CATV system, frequency 5MHz-1GHz are used commonly in different countries and manufacturers concerned have different ways of signal band-width and frequency partition. In our country, bandwidth of TV image and accompanying sound is 8MHz.

In TV/Telephone/Data integrated local network, Frequency partition will accord to relevant national regulations and refer to international conventions. In TV/Telephone hybrid system, frequency partition is showed in Figure 7.
and frequency-band of 750MHz-1GHz is used for data communication.

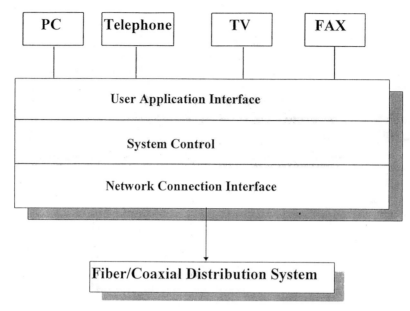

Figure 5: Network intelligent interface unit structure

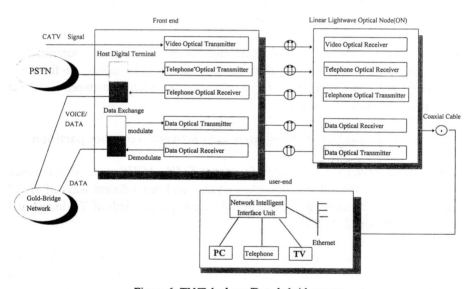

Figure 6: TV/Telephone/Data hybrid system

4.4 TV/telephone/data integrated local network interface stipulation

1. Host Digital Terminal and PSTN interface
   According to standard E1 interface, it connects to PSTN in E1 or NXE1.
2. Network intelligence interface unit and user interface

Network intelligence interface offers not only TV interface but also telephone and data communication interface, telephone is connected by -standard telephone interface (two lines or four lines) and offers interface of V.35, V.24, X.21, RS232 and ETHERNET network and other standard data interfaces to users.

3. MODEM interface

MODEM will be used in data communication through telephone line. MODEM interface standard of integrated service network is identical with that of common PSTN. It's speed usually achieves to 9.6KBPS or 19.2 KBPS.

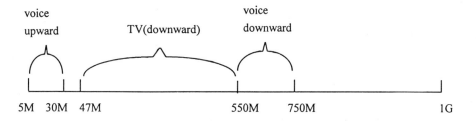

Figure 7: Frequency partition of TV/Telephone hybrid system

8.8

MAGNET: MALAYSIAN GIGABIT NETWORKING TESTBED

Kamaruzzaman Seman, Norsheila Fisal, Jaafar HM Abu Bakar,
Alias Mohd and Fatimah Mohamad
Universiti Teknologi Malaysia, Malaysia

Future network should be able to support a very high speed, unlimited bandwidth and an acceptable quality of service (QOS). It should also be able to cater for heterogeneous traffic such as voice, video, data, and a mixture of any of them for multimedia application. ATM has emerged as the most promising transfer protocol to support future broadband multimedia communication services. MAGNET (Malaysian gigabit network) is an ATM test-bed implemented in UTM (University Technology of Malaysia) in collaboration with TMB (Telekom Malaysia Berhad), the main carrier operator in Malaysia.. The test-bed will be expanded nation-wide in phases. The interconnectivity to the campus local area network and to wide area network will provide excellent platform for research in the area of high-speed networking and multimedia communication development. MAGNET is also envisioned as the country's future network infrastructure that will serve the government, industry and individual user requirements.

1.0   Introduction

The so-called information highway has attracted a great deal of attention. However, a precise definition is still eluding. It seems to be the results of definition of convenience and overuse of the road system analogy. There are two trends towards the information highway. The first trend is the expansion of the Internet. The impact on the Internet stems directly from the scale of the networks involved, the services that the Internet provides and the fraction of the population which can access them. The other trend is the technological changes in the high performance networking elements which can accommodate high bandwidth services. This trend line allows backbone technology to extend their reach to the offices and homes. In Malaysia the first trend is initiated by an Internet service provider and the later trend is promoted by the network provider. These two trends are happening in Malaysia and will enhance the process towards the development of the national information.

An important feature of the future national information infrastructure is that it will be heterogeneous in its physical network connections, in the end-user terminals attached through these connections, and in the applications that runs on those end terminals. It is expected that ATM will provide the region wide transport for a variety of useful information right to the desktop service for high bandwidth users. However, a mixed combinations of connectivity options to the end users may be exploited. For example, the end user terminal may include ISDN, Ethernet and wireless networks. At the same time, the end user terminals might be as simple as a telephone and as complex as a high performance multimedia personal computer. A main feature of the future network is that the user interface must maintain consistency although the architecture of the terminal on which it runs and the characteristics of the network to which it is attached can vary.

Realising on the potential future that ATM can provide, network providers and operators has embarked on the future ATM based technology. Today, in Malaysia many higher learning institutions and private organisations has begun upgrading their local network infrastructure to take advantage of the future services that can be applied on ATM network. Meanwhile the public carrier operators have been upgrading their backbone capability to serve the growing demand from the users.

2.0 Malaysian national information infrastructure

Malaysian national information infrastructure is governed by the Department Of Telecommunication Malaysia (JTM), a government body under the jurisdiction of the Ministry of Post and Telecommunication. Malaysian National Information Infrastructure Forum (MNI2F) is an ad-hoc committee setup to look into the various issues pertaining to the formation of a national information infrastructure. One of the issues being setup by the committee is the formation of the national ATM test-bed. The formation of the test-bed is the initiative of the government and will be funded jointly by the government and the telecommunication service and network providers.

The concern and commitment towards the formation of advanced information infrastructure to support the growth industries and the country's economy is initiated by the Prime Minister. The effort has resulted in the formation of the Multimedia Super Corridor (MSC). The MSC will cover Klang Valley area, the heart of Malaysia's economic activities. The location covers the Kuala Lumpur International Airport (KLIA) which is to be the biggest airport in South East Asia, Kuala Lumpur City Center (KLCC) which houses Petronas Twin Tower, the tallest building in the world and Putra Jaya which will be the new government complex.

University Teknologi Malaysia as a member of MNI2F and is actively involved in research implementing its own local ATM test-beds. The test-bed will be part of the national ATM test-bed and the work is carried out in collaboration with Telekom Malaysia Berhad. The following sections will describe in detail the

MAGNET network infrastructure and the phases of the project being implemented. This will be followed by descriptions of the research and the trial work involved.

3.0   MAGNET configuration

The tested (MAGNET) is located at the Broadband ISDN/ATM laboratory, Faculty of Electrical Engineering, Universiti Teknologi Malaysia (UTM), Skudai, Johor Bharu, Malaysia. The network configuration is shown in Figure 1.

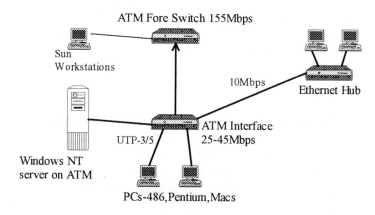

Figure 1: MAGNET configuration

MAGNET will be initially developed as a local area network (LAN). It comprises of five major components: ATM FORE switch (ASX-200), 25 Mbps switch, SUN workstations, Ethernet hub and a cluster of PCs and MACs. The FORE switch has been equipped with two type of network interfaces: 155 Mbps (OC-3) and 100 Mbps (TAXI). The former can support up to four ports per interface card, whereas, the latter provides six ports of 100 Mbps each. Each SUN workstation uses either 155 Mbps or 100 Mbps, depending on the network interface card being used. Communication between these two elements are achieved through the use of optical cables.

The FORE switch is also connected to the low speed ATM switch of 25 Mbps to enable us to use the widely available PCs and MACs. Transfer of information between PCs or MACs to the 25 Mbps switch is done using the 25 Mbps interface cards housed in both ends. Such connection not only open opportunities for developing applications using the ubiquitous PCs and MACs, but also enables us to experiment on the internetworking with UNIX based SUN workstations through the FORE switch.

4.0 Applications

As mentioned earlier, one of the main objectives of setting up MAGNET is to develop application related softwares by utilising the hardware infrastructure. The development of such application software has been identified necessary in order to determine the viability of the ATM based systems. In addition, it can be used to measure or study the flexibility of the API (Application Programming Interface) routines provided by the equipment vendors. Prime applications developed for MAGNET are multimedia communications. These include transport of real time video, parallel computation on ATM connected workstations on clusters, development of new transport protocol for distributed multimedia applications. The API in the FORE system can be linked to the device drivers through software programming to allow any real time traffic to be sent directly over an ATM connection with or without AAL processing. At present research works are being undertaken by staff of Switching Network Research Group assisted by undergraduates as well as postgraduates. Some of the research works are in collaboration with TELEKOM MALAYSIA.

5.0 Future Development

Future development of MAGNET has been grouped into two parts: infrastructures and applications. The latter is concerned on the expansion of MAGNET beyond the LAN environment. This expansion is necessary so that we can experiment on many issues regarding the connectivity and the operability of various networks. The network expansion activities will be done in several phases, as follows:

o   phase I - connection to TELEKOM MALAYSIA ATM testbed
o   phase II- connection to Faculty's ATM backbone
o   phase III- connection to APII Technology Center, Japan
o   phase IV -connection to narrow band ISDN (N-ISDN) testbed

The proposed expansion works can be illustrated in Figure 2.

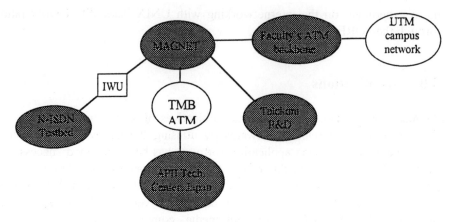

Figure 2: Future development of MAGNET

In phase I, MAGNET will be interconnected to the TELEKOM MALAYSIA's ATM testbed located at the broadband laboratory in the R&D division in Kuala Lumpur. TELEKOM MALAYSIA is our research partner in this project. A point to point communication link will be established between UTM and TELEKOM using an OC-3 fiber cable provided by TELOKOM MALAYSIA. The main issue that will be investigated is on the testing and the development of new multimedia protocols to be used across the ATM based wide area networks (WAN).

The second phase would be the connection of MAGNET to the proposed faculty's ATM backbone. The ATM networking at the Faculty of Electrical Engineering is expected to be ready by the end of 1996. Initial proposal for the network configuration will have three ATM switches which make the backbone of the network. The switch will be linked to each other using 155 Mbps (OC-3) fiber cables.

The next phase of the development will be to interconnect MAGNET via Telekom Malaysia's ATM backbone network to the newly proposed Asian Pacific Information Infrastructure (APII) Technology Center which will be situated at Kansai City, Japan. The Technology Center was proposed by the Ministry of Posts and Telecommunications Japan during the 15th AIC Meeting Tokyo 1995. The detail concepts and the framework of the APII Technology Center was further elaborated during the 16th Meeting held in Surabaya, Indonesia in December 1995. The main objective of setting up the APII Technology Center was to establish a new technology cooperation for the growing information infrastructure activities in the Asia-Pacific region.

The APII will be used as a means of providing the connection for various testbeds and pilot networks of countries in Asia-Pacific region. This can provide a great opportunity of having joint research activities among the participating countries in which the Technology Center will become the main center. The technology center is expected to be used by other testbeds to test on the issues of interconnectivity and interoperability among various testbeds and pilot networks. Besides that, the Technology Center will also be the center for training in all aspects of information infrastructure, application experiments facilities, and joint support facility. It is expected that future development of applications will include video on demand (VOD), news on demand (NOD), electronic library, and remote education. It can be seen that a lot of benefits can be harvested through the participation of MAGNET in the APII.

Experimenting on various issues pertaining to narrowband ISDN (N-ISDN)/ATM connectivity will be done in the next phase when MAGNET is connected to the N-ISDN testbed in the same research laboratory through an internetworking unit (IWU). The IWU will perform necessary protocol adaptation between these two different worlds. The connection enables researchers to study the transmission of constant bit rate services (CBR) such as voice and video, that can be transmitted to the ATM networks and vice versa. Potential contributions would be on the standardization of the AAL-1 protocol. Another interested issue is on the impact of cell delay variation (CDV) introduced by the networks to the quality of CBR services.

The final phase of the MAGNET's infrastructure development would be on the connection to the UTM campus networking. At present, campus networks is still based on Ethernets and FDDI. Introduction of ATM will not be expected in a short time period due to the presence of the existing LAN equipments.

6.0   Conclusion

This article has described the implementation of MAGNET for ATM related research activities at the Universiti Teknologi Malaysia. The benefits that can be obtained from having such project can be classified into direct and indirect beneficiaries. Direct beneficiaries of research agenda will support and enhance the product-oriented developments. In addition, such project would also benefit a particular telecommunication provider which is in this case TELEKOM MALAYSIA. Above all, MAGNET enables the university to become the training center in all aspects of ATM technology which would help the nation progress. Indirect beneficiaries will include private and government organizations which could directly access to information superhighway for increasing their level of competitiveness.

References:

1. Decina, M., Mossoto, C. and Roveri, A. (1994 Oct). "The ATM Testbed: An Experiment Platform for Broadband Communication, IEEE Communication Magazine.
2. Choi, Y. (1992). "Research Network Testbed: SMART (Seoul Multimedia Advanced Research Testbed," Proc. of Singapore ICCS/SITA.
3. Lewis. D. and Kirtein, P. (1994 June). " A Broadband Testbed for the investigation of multimedia services and teleservices management", Proc. of 3rd International Conference on Broadband Island, Hamburg, Germany.
4. Black, C. (1995). "Foundation for the Broadband Networks", Prentice Hall.

8.9

PERSONALIZED TRAILER MAKING OF MPEG SEQUENCES

Anand Rangarajan and S. Srinivasan
Indian Institute of Technology, India

With Video-On-Demand revolutionizing the multimedia entertainment industry, video distributors are switching over to digitizing movies and rendering them to houses by computer networks. The need for a trailer in such a context can hardly be overemphasized. The opportunity for exploiting the random access feature of MPEG sequences and the widespread usage of MPEG in video transmission have been the prime motivation for this venture. The issues considered here are segmentation of MPEG sequences based on some fundamental characteristics, their subsequent playback and the alteration of the user profile using relevance feedback. The quality of the fringe frames of trailer shots is also analyzed.

1.0   Introduction

As on-demand multimedia services keep increasing by the day, it is becoming increasingly necessary to develop effective tools (Zhang and Smoliar, 1994) for efficient access mechanisms and manipulation of MPEG (Gall, 1991) sequences. In Video-On-Demand, it has often been found that trailers for MPEG movies (Smith and Pincever, 1991) need to be stored and retrieved. Since on-demand services are highly user interactive and user sensitive, it is important for them to employ personalized expert systems. A software has been developed to provide support for tagging/annotation of MPEG movies to facilitate personalized playback. For personalization, every user is identified with a profile that captures the user's interests. In the case of movies (Arman et al, 1993), some basic components of the movie have been identified based on which the user interests are quantified. These fundamental features, that have been used to broadly characterize the contents of movies are "Adventure/Action"(a), "Romance"(r), "Comedy"(c), "Musical"(m), "Violence"(v) and "Emotional"(e). To provide flexibility and scope for expansion, another feature "Others"(o) has also been included. After personalized playback of the trailer, the user gives a feedback based on the contents of the movie, and this helps in modifying the user profile using widely used linear relevance feedback principles.

2.0   Annotation

Since content based retrieval of information from frames is extremely difficult (if not impossible), manual annotation of MPEG movies is essential to decide the parts of the sequence that are fit for trailer making. The seven features (as mentioned earlier) that are assumed to specify the contents of a movie, are the tools for annotation. An expert trailer maker or any other film expert would first watch the entire movie, and tag specific parts of the sequence with relevant features. Let us show the process with an example. He would stop at some frame, and indicate that a feature (say) "Comedy" begins at that frame. He would then stop at some subsequent frame, and indicate that the context "Comedy" has ended. Such a tagging would be done for the whole sequence. This information about the parts suitable for trailer making is stored in a form as shown in Fig. 1

a 20 46 c 79 145 r 189 225 c 256 289 a 299 327 m 357 398 v 420 456

Figure 1: Parts identified as "suitable for trailer making"

We will call the parts 20 - 46, 256 - 289, etc., as trailer shots, and a collection of trailer shots as shown in Fig. 1 as trailer sequence.

3.0   Profiling

The user interests are captured with a profile similar to the one shown in Fig. 2. The profile indicates that if the user watches 100 movies, he would watch 15 pure adventure movies, 7 pure romance movies, and so on.

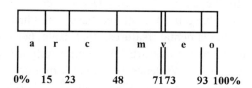

Figure 2: a typical user profile and a movie profile

When a user registers with an on-demand service, he will have to give his profile, after which the system would try to understand his changing interests using his feedbacks. A typical movie profile is also similar to the one shown in Fig. 2 but its interpretation is that the percentages shown in the profile are representative of the relative proportion of the features of the movie. The movie, as represented by the profile, contains 15% of adventure, 25% of comedy, and so on. These percentages are called feature percentages (fp).

4.0 Personalized playback

After the annotation of a sequence has been completed, the necessary sections from the trailer sequence need to be played depending on the user profile. If the trailer is for 'm' minutes, the number of frames that would fit in that time frame (N_f) can be calculated by knowing the picture frame rate. The picture frame rate depends on the size of each frame, and also the kind of the frame. A nominal frame rate is calculated initially, or the value given in the MPEG stream is used. In this way, we can get N_f. Using the user profile as shown in Fig. 2., we know that we have to play only $0.15N_f$ number of "Adventure" frames. From Fig. 1., it can be seen that there are only 54 Adventure frames in the trailer sequence that we can choose from. If N_f is 100, we have to cut 15 frames from the sequence. Now, how these 15 frames are chosen from the 54 available frames is another bone of contention. We have, on a test basis, cut frames from different trailer shots in proportion to the length of the trailer shots. For example, in the case of Fig. 1., for adventure, there are 26 frames in the first trailer shot and 28 in the second. So, seven frames from the beginning of the first trailer shot and eight frames from the beginning of the second trailer shot were cut. Such an exercise would be carried out for all other features. If a feature is not present in the trailer sequence, we would not be able to give the user that particular aspect. If the available number of frames is lesser than that the number of frames to be displayed to the user (calculated from his profile), all the frames would be displayed. Two people with very great interest in "Adventure", would get to see all "Adventure" shots in a trailer of a predominantly comic movie, and their relative difference of interest in "Adventure" would be obscured. This means that tagging should be as elaborate as possible, lest the full effect of personalized playback be lost.

5.0 Alteration of the user profile

After a trailer or a movie is played, the user would be asked for a feedback on a scale of 1 to 9. Depending on the user's feedback, the change in user interests is detected and his profile would change. The formulae for changing the user profile based on feedback 'f' are shown in Fig. 3. In a movie, some features are called predominant features if their feature percentages are greater than or equal to a threshold 'T'. Since this threshold is critical to decide which features are going to be predominant and the way in which they are going to be altered, it is important for them to be carefully chosen. It may even be apt to choose a T for every movie. We have used a T of 20% for all the 20 MPEG sequences we tested. The more the T, the slower is the rate of change of the user profile.

Predominant features change to
$$fp = fp + (f - 5) / weightage$$
where *weightage* is a parameter which decides the amount of sensitivity in the system, and
non-predominant features (other than "Others") change to
$$fp = fp + np * (f - 5) / (weightage * (7 - np))$$
where *np* is the number of predominant features.

Figure 3: Formulae for alteration of profile

The underlying assumption is that the movie profile is perfect and if the user is not fully satisfied, or if he considers the trailer or the movie extremely good, his interests have changed. If the user gives a feedback of 5, then the user indicates that he would prefer to get movies and trailers with the content profile similar to what was rendered this time. If the user gives a feedback other than 5, the user profile linearly approaches the movie profile. It is very important that the user give his feedback based on only the content of the movie and not on how much he likes the way the contents were presented. It is very difficult to quantify the quality of the movie. So, we will stop with quantifying only the content. Another point to be noted is that the movie profile is never changed.

6.0   Methods of trailer making

Three ways of trailer making have been employed here : 1) by playing only specific GOPs, 2) by playing only frames from one number to another and 3) by playing only trailer shots beginning from the point of I frame. The first method is an implied suggestion of the MPEG draft, where a GOP was introduced for the sole purpose of random access. But the biggest problem with this method is the unreliability of the size of GOPs, a factor decided by the encoding process. Since sometimes, GOPs can be very long, the number of tag points in the sequence will become too small to have many trailer shots, and hence this method is very inflexible. In the second method, the trailer shots are played as decided during tagging. If a trailer shot begins in a P or a B frame, the motion vectors used for predicting the first frame of the trailer shot will be the ones obtained from an I or a P frame that occurs much before in the sequence and hence will be flawed. This error will propagate until an I frame is reached. In the third method, since any trailer shot is played only from an I frame, the blurring during trailer shot boundaries will be absent. If there is no I frame in a trailer shot, the whole trailer shot will be skipped. This method also suffers from the same inflexibility of the first method due to scarcity of I frames in sequences.

7.0   Results

All the three methods of trailer making were tested on a DEC 100MHz machine with about 20 MPEG sequences. It was found that the second method was the best among the three, but it suffered from partial haziness during trailer shot boundaries. The GOP-wise method was the least effective. It was also found that each trailer shot should have more than 5 frames for it to be conspicuous in a trailer. The amount of blurring depends on the frame rate. It was found that the same tests on a DEC 150MHz machine gave significantly less amount of blurring. With the third method, no blurring could be detected even in a 100MHz machine. As processor speeds are increasing nowadays, the blurring effect between trailer shots may become insignificant in the future. It is hence likely that the number of available tag points would be the most important yardstick for choosing from, amongst the methods of trailer making, hence making the second method the best choice.

References:

1. Le Gall, D. (1991), "MPEG : A video compression standard for multimedia applications", Communications of the ACM, 34, 47-58.
2. Aguierre Smith, T.G. and Pincever, N.C. (1991), Interactive Cinema Group, The Media Lab, MIT, "Parsing of Movies in Context", Usenix, Summer.
3. Zhang, H.J. and Smoliar, S.W. (1994), "Developing Power Tools for Video Indexing and Retrieval", Proceedings of IS&T/SPIE Conference on Storage and Retrieval of Image and Video Databases II, San Jose, CA, 140-149.
4. Arman, F.,Hsu, A. and Chiu, M.-Yi, (1993), "Feature management for large video databases", Proceedings IS&T/SPIE Conference on Storage and Retrieval of Image and Video Databases, San Jose, CA, 2-12.

8.10

DESIGN AND IMPLEMENTATION OF A HIGH SPEED SWITCHING FABRIC FOR MULTIMEDIA TRAFFIC SERVICES IN AN ADVANCED COMMUNICATION PROCESSING SYSTEM

Won Ryu[1], Hyeon-Sik Shin[1], Dong-Won Kim[1] & Jin-Wook Chung[2]
[1]Electronics and Telecommunications Research Institute &
[2]Sungkyunkwan University, Korea

Nationwide advanced communication processing system(ACPS), as a network node, links various user terminals over ordinary public switched telephone network(PSTN) with information providers(IPs) connected to the public switched data network(PSDN) to provide subscribers with the value added network(VAN) services. Through the ACPS systems, subscribers can easily get information services using only modems without any extra devices. The ACPS system has been promoting a more information-oriented society in Korea. It is needed to develop more powerful advanced functions for ACPS systems in order to provide more convenient methods both for service subscribers and IPs. This paper focuses the design and implementation of a high speed switching fabric(HSSF) system with a switching function needed to interconnect various access networks in an ACPS system.

1.0   Introduction

With existing information communication processing systems (ICPSs), small-scale IPs almost always have a lot of difficulties in account management and prepare the great amount of initial investment[4][5]. The automatic account management function may solve one of the problems and accelerate the growth of IPs. Thesedays, the change from the registration system to the admission one is one of the major factors for booming and maturing VAN businesses in Korea[6]. However, many different networks cannot afford the interworking capabilities with each other and there are lots of problems such as utilization of facilities, system and network management, etc. So, it is inevitable to integrate these VANs with the ACPS system and to provide the interworking capability with one another effectively. Multi-VAN processing function will vitalize information services in such an environment[1][2]. In addition, one of our research objectives is to promote high performance information services like multimedia communications. It is also that national competition power in communication area will be increased by constructing a nationwide ACPS system network through the Korean Information Infrastructure, so called KII. The ACPS system can have a capacity of 960 channels and 256 ports (56 kbps) for the subscriber and the IP sides, respectively. It also can transfer data at high speed, i.e., 28.8Kbps. In addition, it has the dial-out service function which calls the subscriber side from the network side, the audiotex service function that converts text into voice, and finally the interworking function with the Internet[2][4].

Development of the ACPS system is scheduled to be completed by 1996 and the field test for commercialization will be enforced in 1997. Interworking the ACPS system with PSTN and PSDN is supposed to be performed by the middle of this year. On the other hand, the Large-scale capacity and multi-VAN processing function is also considered to be developed. At the present time, researches are being carried out for the realization of the interworking between to the ACPS system with ISDN, frame-relay, and ATM networks.

The ACPS system in Fig. 1 should accommodate various public networks such as PSTN, PSDN, frame-relay network, integrated digital network(ISDN), and ATM network, so its structure has to be significantly different from the existing ICPS and needs more general interworking methods with these networks[1].

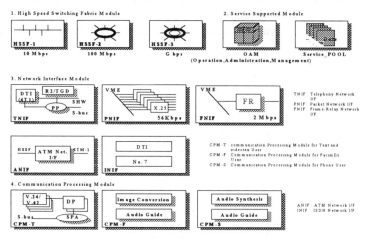

Figure 1: Composition family of the ACPS

2.0   An advanced communication processing system platform

An ACPS system is composed of network access subsystems(NASs), and a HSSF subsystem. And also NAS subsystems are made up of telephone network access subsystem(TNAS), packet network access subsystem(PNAS), ATM network   access   subsystem(ANAS),frame   relay   network   access subsystem(FNAS). We design the structure of an ACPS system supporting various access network interfaces and standard protocols. The Platform of the

458

ACPS system is shown in Fig. 2.

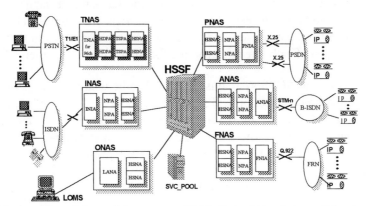

TNAS : Telephone Network Access Subsystem   PNAS : Packet Network Access Subsystem
INAS : ISDN Network Access Subs   HSSF : High Speed Switching Fabric
ANAS : ATM Network Access Subsystem   ONAS : OAM Network Access Subsystem
SVC_POOL : Service_POOL   FNAS : Frame Relay Network Access subsystem
LOMS : Local Operation and Maintenance Subsystem

Figure 2: The platform of an advanced communication processing system(ACPS)

The physical structure and protocol stack for HSNA(High Speed Network
Assembly) is shown in Fig. 3.

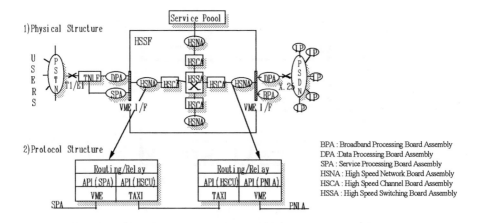

BPA : Broadband Processing Board Assembly
DPA :Data Processing Board Assembly
SPA : Service Processing Board Assembly
HSNA : High Speed Network Board Assembly
HSCA : High Speed Channel Board Assembly
HSSA : High Speed Switching Board Assembly

Figure 3: Physical structure and protocol stack for HSNA

3.0   HSSF subsystem H/W configuration

3.1   A H/W architecture for a HSSF subsystem

We designed and implemented the HSSF subsystem as the core function of the

ACPS system. And the HSSF subsystem has the capacity of 32 X 32 switching function. The H/W structure for HSSF in our ACPS system is depicted in Fig. 4. A HSSF subsystem is capable of interconnecting among various NASs and service interface modules. A HSSF subsystem is designed for applications in high-speed and highly reliable distributed computing systems for data communication services. A HSSF subsystem consists of HSSA(High-Speed Switching Assembly), HSCA(High-Speed Channel Assembly)s and HSBB(High-Speed Back Board) as depicted in Fig. 4. The architecture of HSSF subsystem is based on the High-speed common Bus(H-Bus) technology that is easy to implement and cost effectively. A HSSF subsystem can accommodate up to 32 channel nodes, that is 16 HSCAs, in a single unit configuration, which can be configurable for expanding up to 128 channels by cascading with multiple units. The switching capability of HSSF is about 640 Mbps.

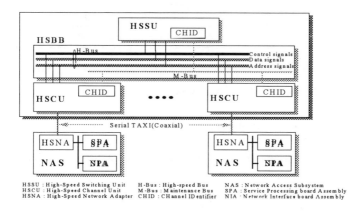

Figure 4: A H/W structure for High Speed Switching Fabric(HSSF)

3.2   A H/W configuration for a HSSF subsystem

An HSSA has a MC68030 microprocessor and uses its peripheral devices like multi-function peripheral (MFP) and local area network controller for ethernet(LANCE), H-Bus controller, and HSCA emulation block. The host microprocessor is used for general management of the unit and monitoring_bus(M_Bus) control with operating in the VRTX real-time operating system. H-Bus controller polls the buffer status of each HSCU channel and moving a packet frame from source channel to destination via H-Bus. The HSCU emulation function that enables host processor to transfer a packet frame related on OAM functions to all of NASs or operation, administration, and maintenance(OAM) service subsystems. HSCA has frame buffers as FIFO and serial transparent asynchronous xmiter - receiver interface(TAXI) devices to interface with HSNA of each NAS by a coaxial cable.[3] HSNA can communicate with SPA via VMEbus in NAS. Taking into account the role of HSSF in ACPS, it is important to manage HSSF efficiently for configuration, fault and performance management. And specifications and functions of a HSSF subsystem is depicted in table 1.

Table 1: Specifications and functions for HSSF

Unit	Functionality	Capability
HSSU	Packet switching control using H-Bus	32x32 ch., 640Mbps transfer rate, self-routing architecture
	System management using M-Bus	Configuration, fault and performance monitoring
HSCU	Packet frame buffering	TX : 8Kbyte, RX: 16Kbyte
	Serial Communication with NAS	TAXI with coaxial up to 100Mbps
HSBB	H-Bus	Packet frame transfer path
	M-Bus	Management control path

4.0   Communication primitives

4.1   Configuration S/W description

Communication primitives between HSNA in the HSSF subsystem and the processor board in the NAS subsystem and their packet format are as follows(depicted in Fig. 6);

a) Communication Primitives

hsna_send(packet)   **hsna_recv(packet)**
struct   hsna_packet *packet;   **struct   hsna_packet *packet;**

Return codes   0x0000   *RET_OK   successful return*
*   0x000f*   *ERR   failure return*

dma_send(bid)
int   bid;

b) Packet Format

8 7 6 5 4 3 2 1	8 7 6 5 4 3 2 1	8 7 6 5 4 3 2 1	8 7 6 5 4 3 2 1	
flag	primitive	length		DPRAM
mode	mcga	sid	iid	TAXI
pad		len		Header
packet_type				HSNA
dest_addr	dest_bid	dest_chid		Packet
src_addr	src_bid	src_chid		Header
packet_len				
data[0]				
				HSNA
				DATA
			data[1023]	

Figure 6: Communication primitives and packet formats for HSNA

And hsna_send( ) and hsna_recv( ) primitives are used for sending and receiving control data and user data between processor board(e.g. SPA/NPA) and HSNA board. The packet types can be described as depicted in Table 2.

Table 2: Packet types for HSSF

Packet Type	Value	Description
Call_Request	0x00	Call Request
Incomming_Call	0x01	Operation about Call Request
Call_Accepted	0x02	Acknowledgment of Call Request
Call_Connected	0x03	Call Connect
Data	0x10	User Data
Clear_Request	0x20	Request for Call Clear
Clear_Indication	0x21	Indication for Call Clear

4.2   Communication method between HSSF abd NAS subsystems

A communication method between HSNA in the HSSF subsystem and processor board for NAS subsystem is communicated via an interrupting scheme. A communication flow from Processor Board Assembly to HSNA is described as depicted in Fig. 7-a. The reverse flow is shown in Fig. 7-b. The structure of dual port random access memory(DPRAM) is shown in Fig. 7-c.

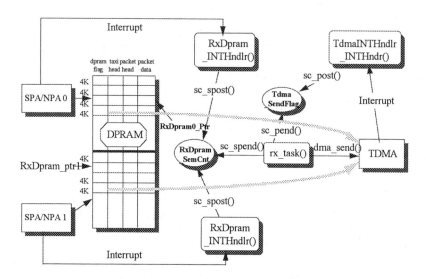

Figure 7a: Communication flow from processor board assembly to HSNA

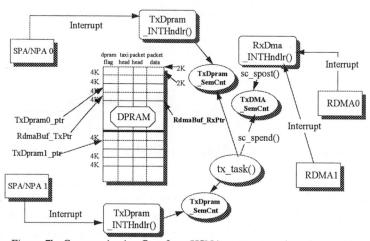

Figure 7b: Communication flow from HSNA to processor board assembly

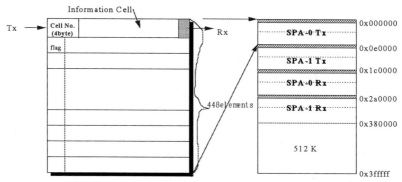

Figure 7c: Communication flow and structure of DPRAM, structure of DPRAM

4.3   Internal procedure in HSNA

The transmission of direct memory access(DMA) interrupt handler routine in the HSNA is described as shown in Fig 8-a. And the receiving side is described as shown in Fig 8-b. The dataflow of dma_send( ) routine is in Fig. 8-c.

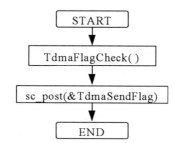

Figure 8a: Flowchart of sending DMA interrupt handler routine

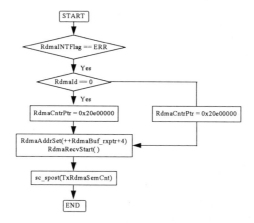

Figure 8b: Flowchart of receiving DMA handler routine

464

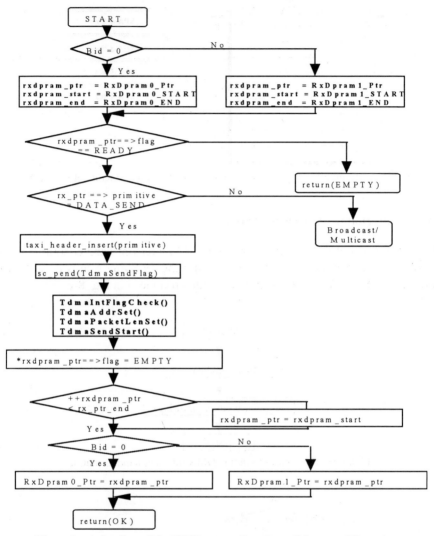

Figure 8c: A dataflow of the HSSF system, flowchart of dma_send( ) routine

5.0   Conclusion

In this paper, we mentioned the ICPS and the ACPS system to strongly support the efficient VAN services. The ICPS was already developed and in commercial service. We propose a new information retrieval method for various user terminals over PSTN, PSDN,ISDN, ATM, Frame Relay to various databases over PSDN, ISDN, ATM, etc.. We realize a prototype of the data communication processing system, and are in the field test for the verification of the HSSF subsystem, the network access subsystem, and local operation and management subsystem(LOMS).

Acknowledgment: The ICPS and ACPS system is the result of the project 'Development of the Service system for PC Communication Network' sponsored by Korea Telecom.

References:

1. Smith, C., Milham, D.J and Mulcahy, C.(1990) "OSI Systems Management Networks," British Telecom T.J. Vol.8, No.2,pp.78~127, Apr.
2. Embry, J., Manson, P. and Milham, D.(1990) "An Open Network Management Architecture : OSI / NM Forum Architecture and Concepts," IEEE Network Magazine, Vol. 4, pp.45~52, July.
3. Am7968/Am7969 TAXIchips Handbook, AMD, Sunnyvale, 1992
4. Jang, J.W., Kim, D.W., Kim, T.J .and Lee, J.T. (1992) " A Configuration Management System in HiTEL Platform," ICCS/ISITA `92, Nov.
5. Hong, H.S. (1992) "The Communication Processing System," The Proceeding of the Korean Institute of Communication Science, Vol.9, No.5, pp.11~22, May.
6. Kim, D.U. (1992) "A View of the Communication Processing Service," The Proceeding of the Korean Institute of Communication Science, Vol.11, No.3, pp.10~20, Mar.
7. Yoon, B.N.(1993) "Application of the Communication Processing System to an Open Value Added Network," Proceeding of the 6th JC-CNSS, pp.34~38, Jun.
8. Kim, D.Y.(1993) "Flexible Architecture for Communication Processing Service between PSTN and PSDN," JWCC-8, Taipei, B2.2.1~B2.2.6, Dec., 1993.

8.11

THE DESIGN OF INFORMATION PROCESSOR BASED ON THE MHEG FOR THE ON-DEMAND SERVICES

Mi-Young Huh & Gwang-Su Kim
Electronics and Telecommunications Research Institute, Korea

This paper presents the MOBIL and MORE within on-demand service system. The MOBIL is a core component of service consumer system within on-demand service system and it's a multimedia information browser which it presents the multimedia application service to user and processes the user interaction. We describe the architecture and function of the MOBIL and presents the MORE, a MHEG-5 object processor, a core component of the MOBIL. Because this system supports the on-demand service based on interactive TV using remote control, the MORE processes the related MHEG-5 objects. We also describe the architecture and function of the MORE.

1.0   Introduction

As increase the interests of multimedia application services the DAVIC (Digital Audio VIsual Council) was made by various companies and institute to promote upcoming digital audio-video applications and services. DAVIC specification 1.0 was developed for the on-demand services such as movie on demand, teleshopping, karaoke on demand in December 1995 (DAVIC, 1995). Therefore, we developed the on-demand service system based on DAVIC Specification 1.0 (Park, 1996). In this paper, we describe the MOBIL (Multimedia Object Browser for Interactive Looking-in) and MORE (Multimedia Object Representation Engine). The MOBIL is a multimedia information browser and the component module of IMPREES (Interactive Multimedia exPRESS) system, the service consumer system of on-demand service system. The MORE is a core module of the MOBIL and it processes the MHEG-5 (Multimedia and Hypermedia information coding Expert Group - part 5) objects (ISO 13522-5, 1996). The MHEG-5 is selected as a representation and encoding method of multimedia and hypermedia information in the DAVIC Specification 1.0.

The on-demand service system and the IMPRESS system are introduced in chapter 2. In chapter 3, we present the MOBIL system which is capable of presenting the multimedia application services to the user and processing of user interaction. The architecture and component module of the MORE are described in chapter 4. In chapter 5, the available on-demand services in this system are presented. They were based on interactive TV using remote control. Also we introduce the creation method of MHEG-5 objects and implementation environment. We'll make an end with the conclusion and further studies.

2.0   On-demand service system

The major difference between on-demand services and existing services is whether the interaction function is provided or not. In other words, service provider supports the appropriate information responding client's request and service consumer acquires the necessary information. Our on-demand service system is based on DAVIC Specification 1.0 and its configuration is shown in figure 2-1. Our on-demand service system consists of a Service Provider System, a Session Resource Manager, a Delivery Network, and a Service Consumer System. Service Provider System consists of a content server which distributes MPEG-2 transport stream and an application server which provides service menu navigation and stream control. Session Resource Manager manages sessions and resources between Service Provider System and Service Consumer System. Delivery Network is an ATM network. Service Consumer System is called the IMPRESS and is built in a PC equipped with ATM and MPEG-2 decoding capable hardware board.

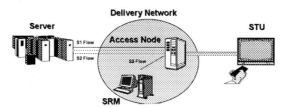

Figure 2-1: Configuration of on-demand system

3.0   Multimedia information browser (MOBIL) system

The MOBIL is in the IMPRESS system. As shown in figure 3-1, the MOBIL system is composed of Communication Manager, the MORE, and Presentation Manager. Communication Manager has the function to transfer MHEG-5 objects, the MORE has the function to handle MHEG-5 objects and Presentation Manager has the function to present the MHEG-5 objects to user and processing the user interaction. Communication Manager consists of DSM-CC and Local File Manager. Local File Manager has a role to retrieve the MHEG-5 objects stored in this system and DSM-CC has a role to retrieve the MHEG-5 objects transferred from the server (Kim, 1996).

468

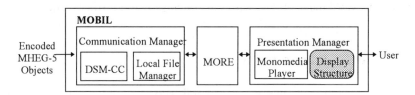

Figure 3-1: System architecture of the MOBIL

3.1   Communication manager

Communication Manager transfers the encoded MHEG-5 objects according to the request of Internal Behaviour Processor within the MORE. Encoded MHEG-5 object is stored in this system or transferred from server system. Any communication method does not be described in the MHEG-5 standard. So, some methods such as tape, diskette, compact disk, communication network is possible. In this paper, we utilize the DSM-CC defined in DAVIC Specification 1.0 (ISO 13818-6, 1995). The DSM-CC is charged with transferring the MHEG-5 objects and controlling the MPEG-2 stream.

3.2   MORE (multimedia object representation engine)

The MORE is a core component of the MOBIL. It consists of a Decoder, an Object Manager, an Internal Behaviour Processor, a Link Manager, and an Action Manager. Information representation method and the function of each component module in the MORE system are described in chapter 4.

3.3   Presentation manager

Presentation Manager initializes the screen of the MOBIL and initiates the MORE. But, Its main role is presenting the MHEG-5 objects and transferring the user input to the MORE. Presentation of MHEG-5 objects is occurred by the request of Activation module within Internal Behaviour Processor. The inherent information in MHEG-5 object and additional information necessary to present the MHEG-5 object is stored in Display Structure by Presentation Manager and then the MHEG-5 object is displayed in the monitor. In this case, Presentation Manager keeps the sequence of the presentation in Display Structure, because the requests of the MORE such as SetSize, SetPosition happen to redraw the shaded object by overlapping. Meanwhile, user interaction is treated as an event, it is transferred to the Link Manager.

4.0   Mheg-5 objects processor (MORE) system

4.1   Information representation method in the MORE

The MORE processes the created objects based on MHEG-5 which is selected as a multimedia information representation method in DAVIC Specification 1.0. MHEG is started with necessity to standardize information representation independent of application and platform to enable various applications easily share high-priced multimedia and hypermedia information. Because our section has an interest in this area, we have studied about MHEG since 1993 (Sung, 1994:p.67; Huh, 1995:p.6-2-1)

ISO/IEC JTC1/SC29/WG12 MHEG group developed the MHEG-1 standard as a first part of MHEG standards (ISO 13522-1, 1995). Because MHEG-1 standard is too generic and complex to adapt simple multimedia and hypermedia application, MHEG group developed the MHEG-5 standard to support the base-level of interactive application services defined in DAVIC specification 1.0. MHEG-5 guarantees the portability of multimedia application services and also defines the synchronization, link, and composition relationship among monomedia data. In addition, it is possible to reuse the existing multimedia information and supports the user interaction. Figure 4-1 shows the inheritance tree of MHEG-5 classes. Object oriented approach is used to express the inheritance relationship of attribute among classes.

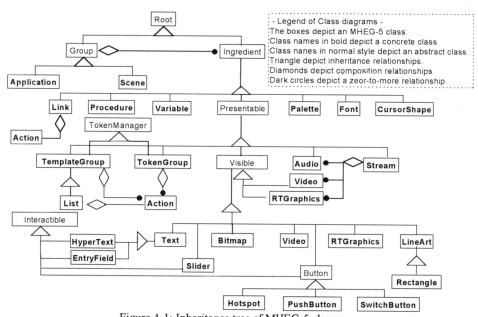

Figure 4-1: Inheritance tree of MHEG-5 classes

4.2 Architecture of the MORE

The MORE is a core element in the MOBIL. Its architecture is shown in figure 4-2. In this paper, MHEG-5 object has the following two types. First one is the encoded type by BER (Basic Encoding Rule) for ASN.1 (Abstract Syntax Notation One) which guarantees the portability of multimedia application services (ISO 8824-1, 1994; ISO 8825-1, 1994). This information is transferred from Communication Manager to the MORE system. Second one is the stored internal class structure type for handling within the MORE system. This information is converted by Decoder within the MORE system.

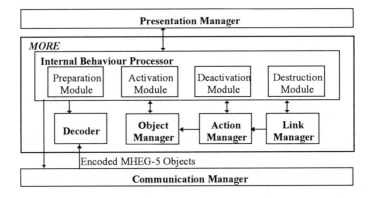

Figure 4-2: Architecture of the MORE

● Decoder

Decoder decodes the encoded MHEG-5 object and then stores it to the Internal Class Structure within the MORE system. Encoded MHEG-5 object is transferred from Communication Manager. In this system, Decoder is created using ASN.1 compiler of Open System Solution corporation (OSS, 1995). Internal Class Structure consists of different format according to each class. It includes both the fields for class inherent information defined MHEG-5 standard and the fields for additional information to use in the MORE.

● Object Manager

Object Manager manages the available or activated MHEG-5 objects within the MORE. It performs the InitObject, InsertObject, FindObject, and DeleteObject function according to the request of Internal Behaviour Processor or Action Manager. The processing block diagram of Object Manager is shown in figure 4-3.

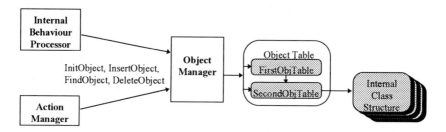

Figure 4-3: Processing block diagram of object manager

MHEG-5 class is classified into Group class and Ingredient class. Application or Scene object is an instance of Group class and includes the Ingredient objects as a component item. Internal behaviour for Group class inherits its property to the included Ingredient classes. In other words, if Scene object is activated, included Ingredient objects are activated and if Scene object is deactivated, included Ingredient objects are deactivated. Therefore, Object Table consists of FirstObjTable and SecondObjTable. FirstObjTable has a pointer to the SecondObjTable, and SecondObjTable has a pointer to the Internal Class Structures of Group object itself and included Ingredient objects.

● Internal Behaviour Processor

The life cycle of MHEG-5 object is shown in figure 4-4. First one is an available status in the MORE. It is occurred by Preparation of internal behaviour and it is possible to reuse of MHEG-5 object in this status. That MHEG-5 object is managed by Object Table and its available_status has an 'available' value. Second one is an activated status in the MORE and it is occurred by Activation of internal behaviour. If that MHEG-5 object is a Presentable object, it is presented to user and then it is possible to interact with user. That MHEG-5 object is managed by Object Table and its running_status has a 'running' value. Third one is not an activated status in the MORE and it is occurred by Deactivation of internal behaviour. If that MHEG-5 object is a Presentable object, it is disappeared from user. That MHEG-5 object is managed by Object Table and its running_status has a 'not_running' value. Fourth one is not an available status in the MORE and it is occurred by Destruction of internal behaviour. That MHEG-5 object in this status is not found in Object Table.

Internal Behaviour Processor consists of Preparation, Activation, Deactivation and Destruction module and the role of each module is as follows;
  ◇ Preparation module
    – Request the FindObject() to Object Manager in order to find the MHEG-5 object in Object Table. If that MHEG-5 object is not found in Object Table, request GetObject() to Communication Manager in order

to receive that MHEG-5 object and then request InsertObject() to Object Manager in order to register that MHEG-5 object in Object Table.
- In case of Group object, propagate the Preparation internal behaviour to included Ingredient objects.
- Set 'available' value to its available_status.

✧ Activation module
- In case of Presentable and Scene object, request the PresentObject() to Presentation Manager in order to present the MHEG-5 object to user. In this case, real content data can be included or referenced in MHEG-5 object. Bitmap data was included and video data was referenced in our system. In case of referenced data, request the GetData() to Presentation Manager.
- In case of Link object, request the AppendLink() to Link Manager in order to register that Link object in Link Table.
- In case of Group object, transfer the Action object defined in its on_start_up to Action Manager and propagate the Activation internal behaviour to included Ingredient objects.
- Set 'running' value to its running_status.

✧ Deactivation module
- In case of Presentable and Scene object, request the DisappearObject() to Presentation Manager in order to disappear the MHEG-5 object from user.
- In case of Link object, request the DeleteLink() to Link Manager in order to delete that Link object in Link Table.
- In case of Group object, transfer the Action object defined in its on_close_down to Action Manager and propagate the Deactivation internal behaviour to included Ingredient objects.
- Request the FindObject() to Object Manager and then initialize the additional field of that MHEG-5 object.
- Set 'not_running' value to its running_status.

✧ Destruction module
- In case of Group object, propagate the Destruction internal behaviour to included Ingredient objects.
- Request the DeleteObject() to Object Manager in order to delete the MHEG-5 object in Object Table.

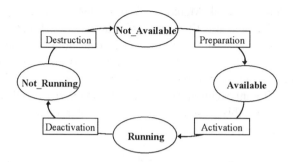

Figure 4-4: The state transition diagram of MHEG-5 object

● Link Manager

Link Manager is started by event. Event is occurred by user interaction or the change of status in object. If event is occurred, Link Manager finds the mapped Link object according to the event and then it transfers the Action object defined in link_effect of Link object to Action Manager. The processing block diagram of Link Manager is shown in figure 4-5.
In general, they say that application service consists of a sequence of "if xx_condition is satisfied, perform the yy_action". In this case, 'xx_condition' and 'yy_action' is variable and frequent. "if xx_condition is satisfied, perform the yy_action" can be expressed as a Link object. Because the processing request of Link object is frequently occurred, it is important to decrease processing time of Link object. Therefore, Link Manager manages the Link Table for Link object. Link Table is a linked list and it has a pointer to Link class structure. Link Manager performs the AppendLink, DeleteLink function according to the request of Activation and Deactivation.

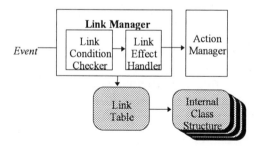

Figure 4-5: Processing block diagram of link manager

● Action Manager

When the link_condition defined in Link object is satisfied, Action Manager is started by the request of Link Manager. Action Manager requests the MHEG-5 object to Object Manager and then performs the inherent function to it. Action object has the functionality of executing, in synchronous sequence, a series of elementary actions. Targeting an elementary action to an object corresponds to calling a method of an object in any ordinary object oriented programming language. Many different elementary actions are adapted to each class. Because on-demand service in this system is based on interactive TV using remote control, we implemented the elementary actions of Table 4-1.

Table 4-1: Implemented elementary actions

class name	implemented elementary actions
Application	Launch, Spawn, Quit
Scene	TransitionTo, SetTimer, KillTimer, RunTimer, StopTimer
Link	Activate, Deactivate
TokenGroup	CallActionSlot, Move, MoveTo, TransferToken, Run, Stop
Stream	SetData, Run, Stop
Audio	SetData, Run, Stop, SetVolume
Video	SetBoxSize, SetData, SetPosition, Run, Stop, SetSpeed, ScaleVideo, BringToFront, SendToBack, PutBefore, PutBehind, SetTransparency
RTGraphics	SetBoxSize, SetData, SetPosition, Run, Stop, BringToFront, SendToBack, PutBefore, PutBehind, SetTransparency
Bitmap	SetBoxSize, SetData, SetPosition, Run, Stop, ScaleBitmap, BringToFront, SendToBack, PutBefore, PutBehind, SetTransparency
LineArt	SetBoxSize, SetLineColor, SetLineWidth, SetPosition, Run, Stop, BringToFront, SendToBack, PutBefore, PutBehind, SetTransparency
Rectangle	SetBoxSize, SetFillColor, SetLineColor, SetLineWidth, SetPosition, Run, Stop, BringToFront, SendToBack, PutBefore, PutBehind, SetTransparency
Text	SetBoxSize, SetData, SetPosition, Run, Stop, BringToFront, SendToBack, PutBefore, PutBehind, SetTransparency
PushButton	Select, Deselect, SetBoxSize, SetLabel, SetPosition, Run, Stop, BringToFront, SendToBack, PutBefore, PutBehind, SetTransparency
SwitchButton	Select, Deselect, SetBoxSize, SetPosition, Run, Stop, Toggle, BringToFront, SendToBack, PutBefore, PutBehind, SetTransparency
Hotspot	Select, Deselect, BringToFront, SendToBack, PutBefore, PutBehind, SetTransparency

5.0   Supported services and implementation environment

Movie on Demand service, Home Shopping service and Presentation service of Test object are available in this MOBIL system. In case of Movie on Demand service, user can select the necessary movie from the list of movies in service provider system and then user can control the selected movie like VCR (Video Casette Recorder) function such as Stop, Rewind, Play, Forward, and Pause. Meanwhile, we expanded the function of PushButton object to have bitmap data as a label. Figure 5-1 shows the snapshot of Movie on Demand service.

a) Initial scene

b) List of movie

c) Selection of movie

Figure 5-1: Snapshot of movie on demand service

a) Home shopping service

b) Presentation service of test objects

Figure 5-2: Snapshot of home shopping service and presentation service of test objects

In case of Home Shopping service, user can select the necessary goods from the list of goods in service provider system and then user can look up the information about selected goods with text, bitmap, audio and video type. Meanwhile, in Presentation service of Test object, the Test object was created by MHEG group. If the Test object can be presented in MHEG-5 engine, that engine conforms to MHEG-5 standard. Therefore, we presented the Test objects in the MORE. Also, we created our test objects for classes described in table 4-1. Figure 5-2 shows the snapshot of Home Shopping service and Presentation service of Test object.

Because this MOBIL system is a browser, it did not support the authoring function. So, to create the MHEG-5 objects in service, we used the value notation method of ASN.1 compiler by OSS corporation. The procedure of creation is following; First, append the value notation to ASN.1 of MHEG-5 class. Second, using ASN.1 compiler and ASN.1 of MHEG-5 class, create the encoder and related C structure. Third, if the size of real content data included in MHEG-5 object is large, write the content data to the correct position of C structure directly. Fourth, store the value of C structure in file by calling the encoder.

This MOBIL system implemented on Microsoft Windows NT 3.5 using Microsoft Visual C/C++ 2.0 language and we used the Microsoft Win32 library to process the graphic data. Also, we used the ASN.1 compiler by Open System Solution corporation to encode and decode the MHEG-5 objects and used the CORBA 1.2 by Digital Equipment Corporation for implementation of DSM-CC.

6.0   Conclusion

In this paper, we present the MOBIL, interactive multimedia application service browser, and the MORE, MHEG-5 object handler. Both the MOBIL and MORE system were based on DAVIC Specification 1.0 and can process and present the available on-demand services on interactive TV. Especially, in this MORE, the extension of MHEG-5 standard to support user friendly interface and composition of internal tables to fast access MHEG-5 objects were considered.

Because this MOBIL system is a browser for services based on interactive TV, it did not support the service using keyboard and mouse device and it did not support the authoring function to create the MHEG-5 objects. But, to widely prevail the multimedia application service based on MHEG-5 standard, it is necessary to develop the authoring system which supports the easy and friendly user interface to service provider. Therefore, in a future, we'll extend the MOBIL and the MORE to support mouse and keyboard device and then we'll develop the authoring system. Meanwhile, the MHEG group is developing the MHEG-6 standard to support the script and is studying the interface between MHEG-5 standard and Java language. Therefore, we'll extend the MORE for MHEG-6 standard.

References:

1.   DAVIC (1996), "DAVIC 1.0 Specifications". Digital Audio Visual Consortium
2.   Park Y.D., Kim S.J. (1996), "Interactive Multimedia Service System in

Information Superhigh way", Seventh Hungarian-Korean Seminar, 5-14.

3. ISO 13522-5 (1996) , "Information Technology - Coding of Multimedia and Hypermedia Information, Part 5: MHEG subset for base level implementation", ISO/IEC SC29/WG12 DIS 13522-5.

4. Kim S.J, Park Y.D (1996) "Design and Implementation of the Interface between MHEG-5 and DSM-CC in a Service Consumer System", HNTTI'96(High-New Technology and Traditional Industry)

5. ISO 13818-6 (1995), "Information Technology - Coding of Moving Pictures and Associated Audio, Part 6: Digital Storage Media Command & Control", ISO/IEC SC29/WG11 DIS 13818-6.

6. Sung J.J, Huh M.Y., Kim H.J. (1994), "Hypermedia Information Retrieval System Using MHEG Coded Representation in a Networked Environment", Proc. 2nd Int'l Workshop on Multimedia Advanced Teleservices and High-Speed Comm. Architectures, 868, 67-77.

7. Huh M.Y., Kim G.S., Hahm J.H (1995), "Design of Multimedia/Hypermedia Information Processor for VoD Services", Proc. 2nd Joint Workshop on Multimedia Communications, 6-2-1~6-2-8.

8. ISO 13522-1 (1995), "Information Technology - Coding of Multimedia and Hypermedia Information, Part 1: MHEG Object Representation, Base Notation : ASN.1", ISO/IEC SC29/WG12 IS 13522-1.

9. ISO 8824-1 | ITU-T Recommendation X.680 (1994), "Information technology - Abstract Notation One (ASN.1): Specification of basic notation"

10. ISO 8825-1 | ITU-T Recommendation X.690 (1994), "Information technology - ASN.1 encoding rules: Specification of Basic Encoding Rules (BER), Canonical Encoding Rules (CER) and Distinguished Encoding Rules (DER)"

11. OSS (1995), "OSS ASN.1 Tools Version 4.0 : User's Manual", Open System Solutions.

8.12

IMPLEMENTATION OF MULTISTAGE CONTROLLED PSTN-PSDN COMMUNICATION PROCESSING SYSTEM

Jae Doo Huh[1], Kyung Pyo Jun[1] & Eon Kyeong Joo[2]
[1]Electronics and Telecommunications Research Institute &
[2]Kyungpook National Univ., Korea

Recently considerable research has been done on interconnection networks for multiprocessor systems. In this paper, we present the implementation of multistage controlled PSTN-PSDN communication processing system(CPS) that provides automatic fee collection, billing data management of special subscriber and new information provider(IP) registration functions. By using the developed CPS, many IPs can manage the business without worrying about manual fee collection and easily participate in value added network(VAN) business. And a PC communication user can connect any IP without service identification on the network.

1.0   Introduction

Until recently, information retrieval services are actively increased the use of telephone network for everyday living information and acoustic response such a 700-service and the Internet service especially. Nowadays most IPs adopt closed access type for the special interest group in which all information users must register service account and pay entrance fee in advance to utilize the database system except the Internet service. The closed access methods may have problems that an information user has service account for each IP and registers service account for new IPs. These kinds of closed services are not suitable for information communication society in that many users demand various types of services. Therefore, there is a great need of open access information service without a user account. Everyone who wants to use on-line service can access all database systems.

Communication service consists of users, databases supplying information, and communication networks. Since the users are usually attached to the public telephone network, if the information centers are operated as a type of local telephone subscriber, then all communication traffics are concentrated on a constructed databases for a specific telephone exchange. Finally the load for a switching system designed to process only telephone calls becomes large and in the worst case there is the possibility for the system to go down.

To solve this problem, all of the supplied databases should be connected to the packet switched data network and the generated traffic by each local switch should be bypassed through a network facility. PC communication users can access to a specific IP at any time. A nationwide CPS is expected to be an important infrastructure for VAN services(H.S. Hong et al., 1992; D.U. Kim et al., 1992; B.N. Yoon et al., 1993)

2.0   System configuration

The implemented multistage controlled PSTN-PSDN CPS is a gateway system that supports user services by connecting the public switched telephone network(PSTN) and public switched data network(PSDN), executing media conversion and implementing protocol conversion functions with a 96 channel unit. The CPS has several multiple access points which consist of telephony network interface part, user data multiplexing part, main service control part, and packet network interface part. Each part is managed by a Mediation-Operation, Administration and Maintenance(M-OAM) system. Figure 1 shows the internal system structure and general service configuration.

The CPS is categorized into PSTN and PSDN block for the heterogeneous inter-networking, the multiplexing and service control block for the user data processing, and the OAM block for the service management and guidance. The data multiplexing block performs multiple user data handling, physical layer adaptation, media and protocol conversion, etc. The service control block provides attribute information that a user is to desire, which has independent function to the characteristics of network interface and user terminal. The overall description of system architecture can be shown as in Figure 1(D.Y. Kim et al., 1993). In Figure 1, integrated services digital network (ISDN) and the Internet services are still in field test. And highly telecommunication (HiTEL) and Magic call are the sampled PC communication services in Korea.

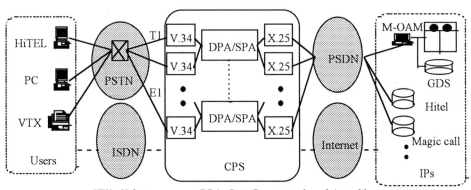

VTX : Videotex,   DPA : Data Processing board Assembly
SPA : Service Processing board Assembly,   GDS : Guidance Subsystem
Figure 1: System configuration

480

2.1 Network interface part

There are two network interface blocks for data communications in CPS, PSTN and PSDN. The PSTN interface block consists of digital pulse coded modulation(PCM) trunk interface module, clock generation and switching module, modem pool with V.34/V.42bis function for the local service, PSTN control processor module, and fault management module. The block diagram of Figure 2 shows the hardware structure of PSTN interface. The digital trunk interface block provides digital T1 or E1 link matching. Its block performs T1/E1 frame information handling of the trunk signal, status monitoring and carrier recovery function. The clock generation and switching block receives a network synchronization reference clock and provides a 8KHz phase locked loop(PLL) reference clock by detecting of phase difference between the internal reference clock and the received synchronization clock. The local service part controls R2MFC(Multi-Frequency Code) signals and busy tone. The fault management part detects PSTN-related to hardware fail and reports it to PSTN control processor. Finally the PSTN control processor manages telephone network call processing and transfers inter-processor communication(IPC) message to service control module. And its processor extracts the originating call number after a completed call for the billing. The PSDN interface block provides X.25 networking for the data delivery service. It performs standard X.25 protocol function including the physical line supervision, free-running timer and data stream control. The architecture of PSTN interface is proposed to deal with flexible changes on demand for a user terminal, that is, modem.

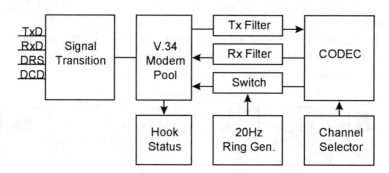

DRS : Data Rate Select   DCD : Data Carrier Detect

Figure 2: Structure of PSTN interface

2.2 Data Processing/Control Part

The data processing block takes care of the user terminal characteristics and subscriber modem negotiation. The flexible architecture for various types of user modem or terminal is prepared to cope with changes of new media or modem protocol by simply upgrading the function separately. It is the first level flexible capacity by distributing input/output data. The number of data processing blocks can be extended or reduced according to the service rate.

2.3   Subsystem Management Part

The OAM subsystem can check the overall system management locally. Its system is connected to PSDN via X.25 and run remotely. Management application has five functional block of configuration management(CM), fault management(FM), security management(SM), performance management(PM) and account management(AM). CM of OAM performs system startup, application program loading, status control of remote site. PM does overload estimation, traffic limitation to prevent system down. FM reports online supervision by automatic and manual test for the peripheral fault. SM controls access privilege, user password by data encryption. AM executes billing data management, recording and backup. The management software is implemented with the user interface based on menu driven, graphic user interface, and mnemonic code as operators are requested.

3.0   Implementation of multi-stage controlled system

3.1   Architecture of hetrogeneous inter-networking

The main framework of gateway system is interconnection between heterogeneous networks. The major part of CPS is SPA. The service processing block consists of multiple function modules related to attributes on CPS which are independent on the characteristics of user terminal. All service functions are performed independently based on real time multitasking operating system(OS) and IPC among tasks by the control of service controller. In Figure 3, we present the block diagram of main service control in CPS. The PSTN interface block is mapped to PCM signal of T1 or E1 trunk link. The PSTN control processor provides telephone call procedure by means of IPC with a network interface.

The major role of the PSTN-PSDN interface part is call connection and its maintenance, call termination and idle channel management. The service program is loaded from OAM server at the initial stage and updated the running program if it is necessary. It is called as a loader manager in CPS. Also there is PAD controller function because of heterogeneous network connection. For example, when Q-bit in the packet is set to `1`, it means a packet which is not use the data but control information. For the control of X.3 PAD parameters according to X.29 would be data echo on/off a host IP respectively. The PSDN interface part uses the standard X.25 protocol for the connection of packet data network.

482

All of the application software run on real time multitasking based environment.

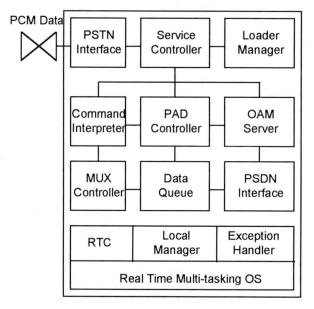

PCM Data

PSTN Interface	Service Controller	Loader Manager
Command Interpreter	PAD Controller	OAM Server
MUX Controller	Data Queue	PSDN Interface
RTC	Local Manager	Exception Handler
Real Time Multi-tasking OS		

PCM : Pulse Code Modulation, RTC : Real Time Clock
PAD : Packet Assembly and Disassembly

Figure 3: Implementation architecture of PSTN-PSDN CPS

3.2   Experiment proof

A CPS provides a transmission channel that can be prepared by various types of modem since most of users can access IPs through a telephone network, and the resource of the database can be shared through a packet network and can be protected by the overload of telephone exchange equipment due to the excessive traffic. A CPS has the identification function of the various types of user terminals such as accessing a HiTEL service retrieval terminal, PC and videotex terminal to provide specific services. And it also supports communication protocol function for media conversion, protocol conversion, and service provision function for user management, fair retrieval function of IP, and information guidance service. Therefore, this system can provide convenient and diverse information circulation service to users and IPs (see Fig. 1 : System Configuration). The user can access nationwide databases with a local call by establishing a telephone network facility. The service providers lighten the burden on a matter of user management and information record. The network vendors have an effect upon increasing the circuit utilization due to the separation of communication traffic and service expansion. A CPS consists of line interface part that PSTN users can access to multiplexing module for several user's data, dual linked main service control parts, and packet data network interface part that IPs are connected to(see Fig. 4 : Test Model)(Leonard, 1975; C.D. Shin et al., 1996).

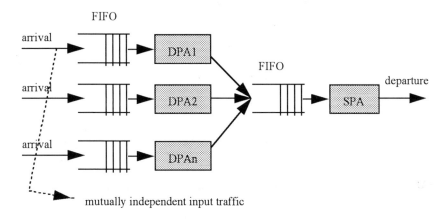

Figure 4: Test model

The major role of CPS is interconnection between the PSTN users and the PSDN IPs. The message that is generated by telephone users is transferred to the main service processing part, and the packet network interface part with other user's data respectively. And its data is multiplexed in the data processing module(DPA). The IP's data coming from the packet network are transmitted to a user through a packet module, a service control module, and an input/output processing module sequentially. At this time, the messages that are made by a IP may have a delay in service processing applications. This processing delay can be considered as a low element of quality of service. Therefore, this drawback is analyzed by the data delay time in service control part by the analytical method.

When a user sends a call-connection-request protocol, call indication data is sequentially transmitted through a routing path from terminal to PSTN, CPS, PSDN, and IP. And the service indication is returned reversely. At this time, the data probably has no effect on the CPS since it possesses much smaller quantitative receiving message than that of the incoming call. Consequently, this paper considers only data flow from a IP side to a terminal side. It assumes that an information from a user terminal has one-to-one correspondence to a IP data, and the IP data are arrived to user screen as soon as requested. It can not measure the system performance of the CPS for the mixture of delay value in network. This paper excludes their effect of the above external element for evaluating the system itself. Besides the system processing elements, it is assumed that they have a infinite capacity. It can be modeled as a memoryless

484

system that user data are already arrived at CPS on requesting a call connection(J.D. Huh et al., 1994; C.G. Park et al., 1993). Figure 5 shows the input/output relation between inter-processor module of the data processing and service control. The data in the packet assembly part is transmitted to the data processing part by the application program if the service processing application is in an available state. Otherwise, it becomes in a wait state. For an analysis, the following assumptions are made;

(1) Information arrival pattern of the connecting users is mutually independent, and arrival rate follows a
     Poisson process.
(2) The batch data size has a uniform binary distribution since IP data is provided with the byte format.
(3) The data processing time of the service application follows an exponential distribution with a finite service
     rate.
(4) The behavior of SPA can be modeled using queuing network technique.

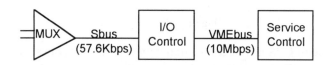

Figure 5: I/O relation between inter-processor module

Figure 6 shows the load of SPA for incoming user data manipulation as time changes. By the simulation result, in case that processing rate of service control part is below 120kbps, main service control processor becomes the bottleneck of the system due to the delayed processing rate which is compared to the multiple input data, and eventually the system goes to the unstable state. When a user connects a call with 28.8kbps modem, the multiplexing part, which is processed 96 channel unit, has 57.6kbps rate at least. And SPA rate of processing capacity has to get the range of 904.190k ~ 1707kbps for the bi-directional communications. In Figure 6, the average processing rate of the accumulated data of service control part is $1.125 * 10^{+6}$/sec when the input traffic is occurred every 5 seconds. The maximum processing capability of SPA is $1.625 * 10^{+6}$/sec. This means that the system has the initial load of data processing because of the simultaneous input traffic. With the lapse of time, the queued data is fairly distributed and gets the sequential number. For reference, the minimum processing load of SPA is $1.0525 * 10^{+6}$. In Figure 6, the variable of top.m1.queue[0].mean_bitsize represents the average length of processing data in SPA at a time.

This paper focuses on the experimental results in the main service control that processes incoming data that can estimate the system performance based on service delay time and waiting queue length. These items depend on the quality of service in case of multiple I/O processing. Most of the previous work on the multiprocessor interconnection networks has assumed that fixed small-sized packets are transmitted. In this paper the inter-connection strategies and their performance for switching variable length and relatively long message need further study.

4.0   Conclusion

Some of the earliest work on multistage interconnection networks has been done in the context of telephone switching networks. The emphasis here was on designing non-blocking networks which use fewer cross-points than a full mesh switch. These networks had a centralized controller for setting the subsystems respectively. This was adequate since the networks were circuit switched and connections were held for a relatively long period of time. Subsequently, many multiple interconnection networks have been studied for connecting multiple processors and memories in computer systems.

In this paper the change of input traffic was measured by processing queue length and delay time for the effect of service provision. It is assumed that input traffic satisfies the Poisson distribution, - average occurrence event is 0.04 per second - that is, when the packet data is come in 25 frames/second, service processing module becomes load unbalance state as the processing queue length abruptly. The increased processing queue in the system is the primary factor of the QoS degradation and also adds the processing load. This paper will be further studied for more accurate analysis.

A developed CPS is being serviced for the PC communication users. This system provides not only useful information but basic communication tools for the distributed database. The multistage/multiprocessor controlled architecture suggests several data communication areas for further research.

486

top.m1.queue[0].mean_bitsize (x1e÷06)

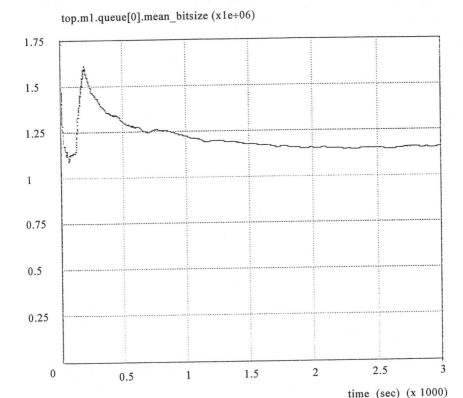

Figure 6: SPA capacity as function of input traffic

Acknowledgment: The authors would like to thank all the members of Intelligent Network Department of ETRI for their valuable advice and collaboration. Especially thanks for the members of LGIC Co. and SEC Co. This work is a part of the project, 'Development of Advanced Functions for Communication Processing System', sponsored by Korea Telecom.

References:

1. Hong, H.S. (1992), "The Communication Processing System," The Proceeding of the Korean Institute of Communication Science, Vol.9, no.5, pp.11~22
2. Kim, D.U. (1992), "A View of the Communication Processing Service," The Proceeding of the Korean Institute of Communication Science, Vol.11, no.3, pp.10~20
3. Yoon, B.N. (1993), "Application of the Communication Processing System to an Open Value Added Network," Proceeding of the 6th JC-CNSS, pp.34~38

4. Kim, D.Y. (1993), 'Flexible Architecture for Communication Processing Service between PSTN and PSDN," JWCC-8, Taipei, B2.2.1~B2.2.6
5. Leonard Kleinrock, (1975), "QUEUEING SYSTEMS VOLUME I," A Wiley-Interscience Publication
6. Shin, C.D., Huh, J.D., Yun, S.J., Cho, P.D. and Jun, K.P. (1996), "The Implementation of a Billing Data Processing Mechanism for Open Access to Information Services," Proceeding of the ICCT '96, China, pp.1067 ~ 1070
7. Huh, J.D. (1994), "Performance Analysis of a Communication Processing System using a Queueing Model," Proceeding of the ICOIN-9, Japan, pp.357~361
8. Park, C.G. (1993), "Analysis of Statistical multiplexing of Multimedia traffic in Packet network," Proceeding of the 6th JC-CNSS, pp.76~81

PART 9

BUSINESS APPLICATIONS

9.1

MULTIMEDIA TECHNOLOGY AND COST SAVINGS IN HOTEL APPLICATIONS

Tat Y. Choi & Robert Law
The Hong Kong Polytechnic University, Hong Kong

The recent development in multimedia technology has produced tremendous impact on hospitality industry. Multimedia, an interactive information technology, provides an effective means for the hospitality industry in such areas as training, marketing, hotel reservations, guest room entertainment and network delivery services. The interactive way of presentation and communication has immense flexibility in configuring business transactions to meet the customers' and users' requirements in hotel and tourism related industry.The explicit effectiveness of adopting interactive computer-based multimedia technology can be measured in accounting terms by cost reduction and processing time. Yet, there are various implicit savings from the employment of multimedia technology. This research explores the applications of multimedia to Hong Kong hotel industry. The present travellers demand more sophisticated information about facilities and services that are available to them. Multimedia is an apparent tool providing the customers with valuable intrinsic needs in hotel and tourism industry. Being a renowned city with many first class hotels, Hong Kong inevitably needs to adopt the latest information technology to achieve its competitive edge in the global information environment. Also, this research attempts to investigate the implicit cost savings arising from the applications of multimedia technology in Hong Kong hotels. This research will offer insights into the features of successful development of a computer-based interactive multimedia system, and the perceived significance of using multimedia technology in local hotels to retain Hong Kong's relative competitiveness.

1.0   Introduction

The recent development in multimedia technology has produced tremendous impact on hospitality industry. Multimedia, an interactive information technology, has no unique definition. Broadly classified as an application of computer technique in information technology, multimedia involves two or more of the following interactive forms: plain text, graphics, images, audio and video. Mainly used for communication and information processing, multimedia is now a technology with wide applications in most environments. Some typical examples of multimedia applications, among others, are Internet information processing, Video conferencing, CD-ROM diskettes, Electronic mail, and Virtual reality.

While multimedia technology has been adopted at full speed in most industrial sectors, it has not been widely accepted as a common base for information distribution in the hospitality industry in Hong Kong. At present, most multimedia applications to the local hotel industry are on teleconferencing in the hotel's business centre, if there is one. However, the application of multimedia, as far as hotel application is concerned, is more than just teleconferencing. On the other hand, multimedia provides an effective means for the industry in areas such as: training, marketing, hotel reservation, guest room entertainment and network delivery services. For example, a user in a multimedia environment can directly control the operations of a mixture of computer-based text, audio, visual, graphics and animation relevant to his needs. The interactive way of presentation and communication has immense flexibility in configuring business transactions to meet the customers' and users' requirements in the hotel and tourism related industry.

The explicit effectiveness of adopting interactive computer-based multimedia technology can be measured in accounting terms by cost reduction and processing time. Yet, there are various implicit savings from the employment of multimedia technology. This research explores the applications of multimedia to the Hong Kong hotel industry. Furthermore, this research attempts to investigate the implicit cost savings arising from the applications of multimedia technology in Hong Kong hotels. This research will offer insights into the features of successful development of a computer-based interactive multimedia system, and the perceived significance of using technology in local hotels to retain Hong Kong's relative competitiveness.

2.0 Multimedia applications in the hotel industry and cost savings

Hong Kong hotels are still not adopting multimedia at a scale that can match their western counterparts. The nature of service industry in hotels always makes customer services and their satisfaction the highest priority, leading to the incorporation of multimedia primarily installed in hotel business centres but not in other departments. The growing popularity of Internet furnishes an endless frontier that allows users to communicate worldwide.

Multimedia applications to a hotel environment can be summarized in the following categories:

> -Internal Management,
> -Training,
> -Marketing,
> -Central Reservation System and,
> -Entertainment

Figure 1 shows how a hotel's multimedia environment can be connected by its internal and external (internet)environments.

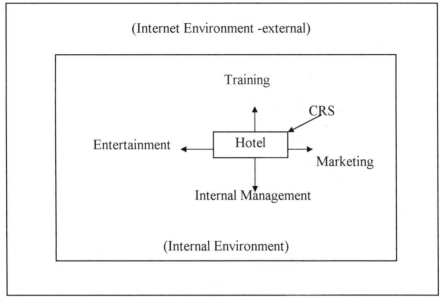

Figure 1: A multimedia in a hotel environment

A multimedia in a hotel environment includes an internal network, which links to the hotel's overall operation. The Internet provides an external network that can link to the internal environment of the hotel.

2.1 Internal management

While a hotel in a city/region can have its own operation autonomy, most hotels are owned by hotel chains or hotel management firms. For example, Four Seasons Hotel is a chain operation having its hotel operations all over the world with its management team operating in Toronto, Canada. To maintain its blend name and unique quality hotel services, the management in Canada must provide concerted information to its hotel operators in various regions. Multimedia plays an essential role in hotel management in that it not only provides information to its members all over the world but with much faster and lower cost of operation. Multimedia in this category can be applied in teleconferencing but with much more direct and explicit communicating point. To fully exploit the potential usefulness of the multimedia system, one can use, during the process of information transmission, plain texts, graphics, images, audio and video. Since a hotel with an information technology multimedia provides a focal point to its delivery partners, a hotel partnership can effectively obtain convenient information from the hotel chain's headquarter where individual hotels are thousand miles away. The transmission of communication among members of the hotel group can be improved through the internet with virtually no additional marginal cost involved.

494

2.2   Training

Multimedia can be applied in hotel staff training in almost all hotel departments. A contemporary hotel basically has the following departments to take care of, as far as training is concerned:

-Front office operations, central reservation system
-Room services, guestroom entertainment/services
-Back office operations, revenue and sales management
-Staff benefit management
-Property management, energy management and safety and security
-Sales and catering
-Training and implementation

While multimedia presentations are combinations of instructional resources controlled by a single operating system, the operating system itself enables the presenter to design a lesson or demonstration using a mix of such resources as text, audio, still and motion video, graphics and animation controlled and manipulated through a computer program. The presenter has great flexibility in formulating a program that will best meet the needs and learning levels of the audience (Harris and West, 1993).

With the proper administration, training for hotel staff can be more efficient and effective with the help of multimedia technology. For example, a new staff can acquire a front office training with a multimedia visual and audio facilities before actually being put into the front office's working environment. This, in turn, will assist the provision of better quality services.

The hospitality industry has many successful stories in multimedia applications in staff training. For example, Marriott has been using multimedia for employment marketing since the early 1990s (Jonker, 1993). Other successful stories using multimedia facilities include Holiday Inn's training system. Since a hotel such as Holiday Inn, needs "an awful lot of people, an awful lot of time, and an awful lot of money to make sure that everybody is trained all the time," said Mr. Leven, CEO of Holiday Inn. Front desk personnel have to master the hotel's property management system, which handles registration and accounting for each guest from arrival to departure. The system is essential to keeping each hotel functioning smoothly and paying customers satisfied. The challenge is complicated by constant addition of new workers - many of whom have not been adequately trained (Wallace, 1993). Multimedia comes to the help.

Replacing traditional classroom instruction with multimedia will cut training time tremendously. For example, a one-hour tour through a multimedia simulated hotel that exposes a general manager to many business problems, such as hotel property management, would probably take a week to do all in a traditional classroom environment. Also, a multimedia environment actually gets the trainee into the training environment where the hotel employer wants to teach. This training environment is different from the 'plain' vedios which does not allow the trainee to interact. Multimedia, however, allows the trainee to interact with the system as they would in their actual job. Moreover, the workstation in multimedia can stay behind after training and the learning can be sustained in the future. As Wallace (1993) puts it: multimedia training resolves many logistic and resource issues of training and enables the hotel to spend training dollars more effectively.

2.3   Marketing

Multimedia applications in hotel marketing can be divided into two main categories: sales at point and sales promotion. The former is a direct sale at which the front desk or a travel agent may involve while the later involves hotel advertising or promotional campaign. In direct sales, customers normally demand full information about the services and the facilities the hotel provides. Through multimedia interaction, services can be explained more thoroughly and more effectively thus improving the competitive edge of the hotel. Direct sales now have a broader definition with the advance of the internet (World-wide-web). Through the world-wide-web, point of sales can be carried out via the internet system.

The multimedia plays an important role by providing instant interaction between the hotel provider and the client. For example, if a client in the US wants to know a hotel's exact location in Hong Kong, the multimedia program can be constructed in such a way that the client can be brought to the computer monitor (via internet) so that he can be led through the exact routes leading the the hotel after he lands in Hong Kong. A travel agent can apply the same technology in explaining, through visual, audio and interactive techniques, in exactly the same way as that described above to its clients of how and in what ways a packaged-tour is going to be arranged. By the same token, the world-wide-web can provides the same facilities for multimedia for hotel sales promotions.

2.4   Central reservation system (CRS)

Theoretically, the CRS should be considered part of the marketing system. However, CRS represents a more complex information system, which provides the hotel's partners with a complete delivery system in the travel market. For example, CRS in a hotel may link its system to resort centres, airlines CRS, conference facilities, travel agents, cruise, theatres, other hotels and other transportation modes (Choi, Law and Au, 1996). And simply because of its complex system, multimedia technology can provide a simpler yet comprehensive interaction to both the users and providers. Savings can be quite substantial if one adds up all the details for providing such services.

2.5   Entertainment

The last multimedia application is on hotel entertainment. Virtual reality and guest room amusements are two major functions that are applicable to the hotel industry. The availability of the latest technology enables a hotel to remain competitive by providing more sophisticated entertainment services. As hotel users' expectations of quality services and products become more demanding, managers of the hospitality firms are discovering that they must provide quality services preferred by hotel clients. The development of multimedia programs has helped managers perform those tasks. For example, some hotel rooms are installed entertainment programs with interactive video compact disc either alone or in network applications. Furthermore, a hotel client can, via the hotel's interconnected system, access to various service information. For example, the client can get into his updated account, screen through the hotel's entertainment facilities and food and beverage services.

Holiday Inn was probably the first, in 1993, to introduce its multimedia automated Holiday-Inn-Worldwid hotel reservation system. With 1,700 hotels worldwide, Holiday Inn was probably the largest single corporate user of multimedia technology and save million of dollars (Fitzgerald, 1993). Besides training, Holiday Inn also uses multimedia capabilities to handle hotel selection and property management.

With a multimedia environment, a front desk employee uses a mouse to click on various features on a screen, such as a computer or customer, and the selected items interact to the users. On the other hand, a manager can screen through the employee's concern about the hotel's problems that must be addressed.

3.0   Final Remarks

Computerized multimedia environment offers interactive and tracking capabilities that can reduce a hotel's overall operating costs and improve its efficiency and effectiveness of its management. Because of the different style of individual hotel management in the industry, managers must choose desirable systems and programs designed for its own needs. One advantage of the computer-based multimedia is that the message can be delivered instantly and consistently. The forms of multimedia, however, continue to evolve with the development of new capabilities and formats. For example, the sophisticated window version and touch-screen version allow users to interact virtually without any difficulties. Besides, many new systems in multimedia and peripherals are both affordable and common to most hotel organizations. As Harris and West (1993) mention: PC-TV (Personal computer television) and PIP (Picture in a picture) are two systems that couple a regular television with a personal computer, giving the user the option to toggle between videotapes and the working being done on the computer. Those systems are useful for hotel organizations that are prepared to invest in state-of-the-art multimedia systems.

Interactive multimedia environment allows the world to communicate much faster. The development of multimedia of the 1980s and early 1990s has helped organizations to save time and energy and improve communication. A hotel chain without a computerized multimedia system would probably require more time to make reservation, to train its new staff, to produce more paper work to update information about its clients and services. In a time when saving costs, providing quality services, and reducing staff turnover are the bottomlines, the hotel industry needs to invest in a technology system that allows the hotels to adopt the many forms of multimedia that are easy to operate and can be upgraded in the future with multimedia enhancement (Harris and West, 1993). The obvious benefit with the multimedia system is that it gives managers what they need when they need it (Wallace, 1993).

References:

1. Choi, T. Y., R. Law and N. Au (1996). "Techno Bytes--Hotels slow to adopt IT", *Asian Hotel and Catering Times*, August, pp10-12.

2. Fitzgerald, M. (1993). "Multimedia to Save Hotel Time, Money", *Computerworld*, Vol. 27, Issue 18, May, pp.94.

3. Harris K. J. and J. West (1993). "Using Multimedia in Hospitality Training", *The Cornell HRA Quarterly*, pp. 75-82.

4. Jonker, P. and P. Rowson (1993). "How Marriott Uses Multimedia for Employment Marketing", *The Cornell HRA Quarterly*, pp. 78-79.

5. Wallace, P (1993). "Multimedia Boots Holiday Inn's Training System - Case Study", *Info World*, June 14, V15, 24, p. 62.

A STUDY OF APPLYING INTERACTIVE MULTIMEDIA FOR TOURISM IN HONG KONG

Frankie Chi-bun Lo, John Kin-man Ng, and Albert Cheong-kei Leung Lingnan College, Hong Kong

This paper presents a study of interactive multimedia applications for tourism in Hong Kong. The main objectives of the study are to survey the market potential of using multimedia kiosks for tourism, and to investigate the expectations of the tourists in terms of using the kiosks. During the study, several tasks were accomplished. First of all, the market of interactive multimedia, in particular, the needs of in-bound and out-bound tourists, was investigated. Secondly, the features and functions that multimedia kiosks should provide for tourists were reviewed. Then according to the findings of the survey, a prototype was developed to show the new features generated in this study. In this paper, thorough analysis is described, and detailed results and discussions on the applications of multimedia kiosks for tourism in Hong Kong are presented. Finally, limitations and recommendations of this research are given in the paper.

1.0   Introduction

In Hong Kong, Tourism industry brings the second largest income to the territory. As reported by the Hong Kong Tourist Association, over 9.3 millions overseas tourists including those from Mainland China and Taiwan visited Hong Kong in 1994, which represented a 4.4 percent growth over 1993 [1]. On the other hand, with the rise of disposable income of Hong Kong households, more and more Hongkong residents travel overseas, e.g. around 2.7 million people in 1994 alone [1].

With this large amount of both in-bound and out-bound tourists in Hong Kong, there is a huge demand of travel information. Thus merely providing travel information for them through brochures and verbal description is not sufficient, because very often, tourists want to see the actual scene of the destination. Therefore, use of multimedia presentations may satisfy their requirements or expectations, as they can get information through video, sound, text, animation provided by the multimedia kiosks.

Many evidences have shown that using interactive multimedia presentation that combines photo, sound, animation and video to provide information has high potential in tourism [2-5]. For example, at airports, customers can look for hotels or restaurants, make reservations, and print out a map for direction. In travel companies, customers can use multimedia kiosk to get impressive travel information [6]. As discussed in [7], a computer-based system can save money and help visitors to gather the information needed. An interactive kiosk can also provide better information and services, and can even act as a point of sales, promotion channel and the place to get the data from the targeted customers.

Nowadays, interactive multimedia applications are widely used in many service industries in Hong Kong, such as banking industry [8]. However it is still not common to use such applications in tourism. Most of the travel companies in Hong Kong use only text, photo and direct dialogue to provide limited information to their customers. Though tourist guides using multimedia presentations have been developed for a few years in the U.S. and some European countries, there are still few multimedia applications in the tourism industry in Hong Kong and few researches in this field.

2.0   Problems and opportunities

To ensure the satisfaction of tourists, good images and better services are important for tourism industry. The functions of allowing tourists to acquire and transmit unbiased information through interactive kiosks in a courteous, efficient and timely manner will be their competitive advantages. Although there are many problems when implementing a multimedia travel system, it is beneficial for a company to have such a system in the long run.

Owing to the increasing popularity of multimedia kiosks, many companies are undertaking different research and plans to gain the competitive advantages over their competitors. For example, many hotels introduce new multimedia kiosks with self-check-in check-out system to ease the manual process [9]. With the use of ATM machines, customers can reserve rooms or check-in/check-out by themselves with credit cards.

However, simply implementing a multimedia kiosk does not mean a guaranteed success. It may fail. Those who tried and failed to develop multimedia system did so for three main reasons [10]: 1) People regard multimedia as an information provider and not as a sales channel. 2) Systems were designed by technologists who were familiar with multimedia technology rather than with commercial environment. 3) Customers found these systems difficult to use or not user friendly. Overall, profitability is the key to the future of travel kiosks [10].

As concluded in [11], there are two factors which will affect the chance of success of a kiosk. The first determinant of success is the amount of time the people need to look at the kiosk, which is affected by many factors, such as the scale of the information coverage, options offered, number of choices and time responding to a search. The second success factor is novelty: the more frequently the information is updated or new information added, the more likely people will continue to use the kiosk.

Therefore, the objectives of this study are to locate the market of interactive multimedia in Tourism in Hong Kong, to survey the expectations of multimedia kiosks from in-bound and out-bound tourists, and to generate a framework for such development.

3.0 Market for multimedia kiosks

3.1 In-Bound Tourist Market

We chose the arrival area of Hong Kong Kai Tak International Airport to collect our data. A total of 336 in-bound tourists responded to our survey, while a prototype system was used to demonstrate our ideas during the survey. All the attributes in the questionnaire were rated on a five-point scale from "very desired" to "very undesired".

The survey results of service requirements indicate that most of the in-bound tourists perceived "Providing travel information" as the most desirable attribute in multimedia kiosks, while "Reservation service" is regarded as very desirable. Details of the results are shown in Table 1.

Table 1: Ranking of perceived desirable of service providing in the system

Attribute	Mean	S.D	Ranking
Providing travel information	4.23	0.95	1
Reservation service	4.12	1.01	2
Providing other local information	3.12	1.16	3
Inquiry Hotline	3.01	1.13	4
Self Check-in/Check-out services	2.69	1.26	5

Table 2 shows the results of some specific functions which the respondents rated during the survey. Overall, the respondents regarded "Resort places" as the most desirable information in a multimedia kiosk, followed by "Shopping places", "Restaurant/bar", "Transportation" etc. Among the respondents, those from Europe and North America perceived information about transportation as more desirable than other information, whereas tourists from Taiwan and Mainland China required more information of shopping places.

Table 2: Ranking of perceived desirable of information providing in the system

Attribute	Mean	S.D	Ranking
Resort place	4.72	0.58	1
Shopping place	4.38	0.82	2
Restaurant / Bar	4.12	1.01	3
Transportation	4.06	1.00	4
Hotel service	3.65	1.19	5
Exchange shop /Bank	3.58	1.21	6
Tour Guide service	3.21	1.18	7
Entertainment place	3.10	1.18	8
Cinema	2.11	0.97	9

We also carried out a survey on other issues, such as extra features desired and kiosk locations etc., and the results are shown in Table 3 and Table 4 respectively.

Table 3: Ranking of perceived desirable of extra functions/features attached in kiosk

Attribute	Mean	S.D	Ranking
Multi-language	4.69	0.60	1
Laser printer attached	3.12	1.20	2
More video	3.05	1.26	3
In-room services	2.65	1.21	4

Table 4: Ranking of perceived desirable of location that kiosk should be installed

Attribute	Mean	S.D	Ranking
Tourist center	4.12	1.01	1
Hotel mall	4.06	0.99	2
Airport	3.75	1.09	3
Shopping plaza	3.51	1.23	4
Restaurant	2.62	1.15	5

3.2 Out-Bound Tourists Market

We chose the departure area of Hong Kong Kai Tak International Airport to collect our data. A total of 383 Hong Kong residents responded to the questionnaire. Again, all the attributes are rated on a 5-point scale varying from "very undesired" to "very desired."

The survey results, shown in Table 6, indicate that the out-bound tourists perceived "Specific destination in regions or state" as the most desirable travel information in a kiosk, followed by "Specific plan of journey", "The beauty of place before visit" etc.

Table 6: Ranking of the perceived desirable of travel information attribute to be got in kiosks

Attribute	Mean	S.D	Ranking
Specific destinations in region or state	4.22	0.71	1
Specific plan of journey	4.17	0.71	2
The beauty of a place before visit	3.91	0.86	3
Prices of hotel and attraction	3.72	0.99	4
The guide to use vacation time	3.51	1.11	5
Recognition of landmark	3.41	1.03	6
Aspects to be prepared for the journey	3.03	1.16	7
Bargains or coupons	2.74	1.28	8

Regarding the regions of travel attractions, "Southeast Asian countries" was the most desirable region that the out-bound tourists wanted to know more. Detailed results are listed in Table 7.

Table 7: Ranking of perceived desirable of region's travel attractions providing in the kiosk

Attribute	Mean	S.D	Ranking
Southeast Asian countries	4.04	1.13	1
Africa	3.93	1.08	2
Europe	3.70	1.22	3
North America	3.43	1.22	4
Japan	3.39	1.38	5
Taiwan	3.32	1.26	6
Mainland China	3.30	1.36	7
South America	3.11	1.25	8

Other issues, such as kiosk locations and extra features desired, were also surveyed, and detailed results are shown in Table 8 and Table 9 respectively.

Table 8: Ranking of perceived desirable of location that kiosk should be installed

Attribute	Mean	S.D	Ranking
Shopping plaza	4.10	0.77	1
Travel Agent	4.09	0.77	2
Airport	3.82	0.89	3
Restaurant	3.01	0.99	4
Cinema	2.56	1.14	5

Table 9: Ranking of perceived desirable of services providing in the kiosk

Attribute	mean	S.D	Ranking
Providing travel information	4.43	0.48	1
Provide a hard-copy of the information	4.08	0.76	2
Inquiry Hot line	3.55	1.04	3
Reservation services	3.29	1.02	4

3.3 Findings

The response of the tourists to our survey was overwhelming and encouraging. Most of them showed enthusiasm to the idea of multimedia kiosk. This reinforced our assumption that using multimedia in tourism has high potential in Hong Kong. Another important implications of our survey is about the language. As the majority of the tourists in Hong Kong are Chinese [1], and most of our respondents indicated that a Chinese version kiosk would be more helpful, thus the language factor is worth considering in actual development.

Through our survey, the views of both in-bound and out-bound tourists on the essential attributes of multimedia kiosk, such as functions, extra features, locations were investigated. These data are very useful for the later development.

4.0   Prototype development

The kiosk was initially developed as a prototype for demonstration during our survey. Due to the time constraint, it did not provide much information for tourists and simply equipped with some basic features which could explain our idea to the respondents. Obviously the prototype cannot fulfill the requirement of a real tourism kiosk.

After our survey, we re-designed the kiosk for both in-bound and out-bound tourists on the basis of original one to reflect exactly what the tourists want. According to the analysis of the survey, most of the services and features which were rated over 3.0 by the respondents are included in the new tourism kiosk. The layout of the kiosk is shown in Figure 1.

504

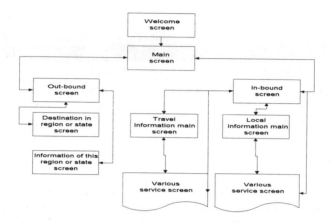

Figure 1: Layout of the multimedia kiosk

The re-designed kiosk can basically reflect the requirement of a travel kiosk. Though it is still preliminary, it provides some fundamental services for tourists. Figures 2-3 show a few clips extracted from the program.

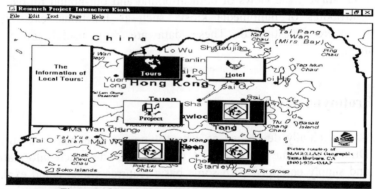

Figure 3: One of screen showing the services required

Figure 4: Transport information

5.0 Conclusion

Through our survey, we reached the following conclusions: 1) Multimedia kiosk has high potential in the tourism industry. 2) Developing Chinese version kiosk should be a major consideration to accommodate the majority of Chinese tourists. 3) Multimedia kiosks should include the travel information for both in-bound and out-bound tourists. Other services such as reservation, resort place and shopping place should also be included. A prototype was then developed during the study, which demonstrates the fundamental functions to meet the tourists requirements.

The results generated in this study basically satisfy our objectives. Overall, they could be regarded as an integrate framework, and therefore, can be used by both travel companies and developers as reference who intend to commit into such development.

6.0 Recommendations

Several restrictions must be acknowledged which limited the depth of this study. Firstly, tourists in different seasons may have different requirements, and this study only surveyed the tourists in the Spring season. Secondly, the cost implications of developing such multimedia kiosks was not discussed in the study. Thirdly, a successful kiosk must help a company to boost sale. In this study, the role that the kiosk should play in a company was not clarified.

References:

1. Hong Kong Tourist Association, Annual Report, 1994.
2. Goodpasture, V.A., Mountain Travel*Sobek And The Adventure Disc:, CD-ROM Professional (July / August 1994), 7683.
3. Bredin, A., Hotels checks out lobby kiosks, Advertising Age (August, 1994), p16.
4. Poon, A., Tourism Technology and Competitive Strategies (1994).
5. Fisher, C., Hotel check hits lobby Kiosks, Advertising Age(August8, 1994), p16.
6. IW, Presentation authoring packages offer balance of power, INFOWORLD (March 27, 1995), p106.
7. Schneider, B., Using interactive Kiosks for retail research, Marketing News (August 8, 1994), p13.
8. HKEJ, Multimedia, Hong Kong Economic Journal (July 2, 1995), p7.

506

9. CRN, Improving the Inns & Outs; Hyatt Hotel is using ATM-like kiosks to speed up customer reservations, Computer Reseller News (July 31,1995), p11.
10. TIGUKI, Profitabiliy is the key to the future of travel kiosks, Travel Trade Gazette UK & Ireland (June 1, 1994), p66.
11. CPW, The Write Stuff, Personal Computer World (Aug 1995), p518-539.

9.3

A CASE STUDY ON THE USE AND SUITABILITY OF THE WORLD-WIDE WEB FOR A TOURIST INFORMATION SYSTEM

R.J. Millar and J.R.P. Hanna
University of Ulster, N. Ireland

This paper reports on the experiences in designing, constructing and operating an Internet-based world-wide web server for tourist information. The Tourist Board's marketing approach before the development of the Web system is described together with their aims and objectives in pursuing this marketing medium. The type of information included in the system is justified and results are included to indicate the most popular information, the origin of users and the hourly load on the server. An analysis of visitors' book comments is given and the paper concludes that the Internet is a viable technology through which to promote tourism as long as it is properly resourced by the information provider.

1.0   Introduction

Many national tourist boards currently market their countries as a tourist destination using magazine and television advertising, literature distribution through airlines and travel agents, as well as responding to postal and telephone enquiries. They will often establish a local office in those countries which they perceive as their main markets. The growth of the Internet and, in particular, the growth of one of its services, the world-wide web (WWW Consortium, 1996), has introduced a new marketing medium. With some consultants predicting that as much as 20% of shopping will be carried out electronically by the year 2000 (Glyn-Jones, 1996), it is a medium which deserves serious attention.

This paper reports on the construction and operation of a prototype world-wide web tourist information system. The system was introduced, in conjunction with a local tourist board, to supplement their existing marketing media. The main aim in producing the prototype was to study the benefits and implications of using the Internet to promote tourism. The Tourist Board wanted to investigate the popularity of their web pages and the information they contained. This would determine whether or not they would go ahead with a full web system in the future and the content which it should have. In addition to this, the geographical location of many inquiries could be determined.

The results and conclusions presented in this paper will inform management decisions on the implementation of a world-wide web server in terms of its growth, the type of material to include and the overhead required to maintain the information.

2.0   Why use the internet?

As an advertising medium, the Internet is a relatively cheap means of distributing information on a global scale. With the improvements in hypertext mark-up language (HTML) (Erwin, 1995) tools (Elliot, 1995; Frentzen, 1994), it is possible to produce web pages in-house in much the same manner as many design departments produce desktop published documents destined for printing. However, the HTML documents are immediately ready for publication on the web without the higher costs of paper and printing. Additionally, the documents can also be used within the organisation on its intranet by (say) counter staff in remote offices, whereby ensuring that they are referring to the latest edition.

The HTML documents can be continually updated and immediately republished - although this has resource implications. This makes the medium particularly suited to rapidly changing information sources such as Event Programmes and Accommodation Availability in the context of tourist information. Also, the full multimedia capabilities of the HTML document allows the publisher to incorporate video and sound - something which would be prohibitively expensive in conventional document distribution.

The disadvantages in using the Internet and HTML pages are:

- although the advances in the language and protocols have been upwards compatible, it is an evolving technology and therefore pages can quickly look dated if they do not incorporate the latest trends;
- the marketing only reaches a specific breed of client, for example those with a credit card or bank account - but this scenario is changing also with the rapid growth of the Internet to the home and the inevitable increase of the average age of Internet user;
- the need to create new promotional material.

However, given that many other organisations (including tourist boards) have now at least a presence on the Internet, there is a sense that 'everyone else is using the Internet and so must we'!

3.0 The prototype structure and page content

The content and design of the pages was decided by the design and marketing department of the Tourist Board. The 'welcome page', usually the first page to be accessed by a caller, was constructed around the Tourist Board logo and was intended to be visually attractive. This page provided the links to pages with more detailed information. In addition, the welcome page had links to other relevant sites, for example, to airlines serving the region, as well as a Visitors' Book to record comments as a means of feedback on the prototype.

A brief description of each page category follows, to indicate the content initially thought important by the Tourist Board and, more importantly, the rationale behind its inclusion. On each main page, links were provided to the other page categories and to the welcome page.

3.1 Travel and geography

These pages had a simple map of the region as their main feature, identifying the major towns and cities as well as the airports. Distances between these locations were provided by means of an HTML table. For backwards compatibility, a non-tabular form of these distances was also provided for those using a browser which did not support tables. Details of transport and its approximate cost to and from the airports to connecting cities was also provided. Finally, contact details for the airports were provided.

The feedback from users confirmed this information to be invaluable in trip planning-especially the inclusion of air routes to the region. An added bonus was the availability of the arrivals and departure screens for the international airport on the Internet. Lessons to be learnt from the page design were: to be careful on the use of too many different colours in the map (other users might only have 16 colour screens), to keep the resolution of the map low (reducing the download time and hence communications costs for dial-up Internet users) and to quote telephone numbers in the contact details in international format.

3.2 Information services

This page listed local tourist information centres throughout the region, grouped by county. Against each centre an indication was given of the services on offer. Many tourists to the region would plan a touring holiday and this information allowed them to incorporate stops at local offices on their route. Once again, contact details for each office were provided.

3.3 Reservation services

The accommodation services provided by the local tourist offices were described on this page. Obviously this page was important for tourists planning an independent trip to the region. Although the Tourist Board operate a computerised reservation system for accommodation at their offices, it was not linked to the prototype web system to reduce the development costs for the prototype. Much of the accommodation on offer in the region is based on small independent hotels and guest houses. Properties of this size rarely appear on the airline central reservation systems and thus it was considered important that visitors have some means of access, albeit by telephone and fax, to the Tourist Board reservation system.

3.4 Board details

This page was rather formal in nature. It presented the background to the Tourist Board, quoted the Board's mission statement, objectives and funding sources and give a list of Board members. Some statistics on the number of visitors to the region were included. Initially, the inclusion of this material was not intended by the marketing department but it was forced upon them by more senior management levels within the Board.

3.5 Events calendar

These pages presented lists of past and forthcoming events, organised chronologically by month. Brief details were given for each event together with contact details for the event organiser. This information was also of value to non-tourists living in the region. These pages made the biggest demands on resources for keeping them up to date.

3.6 Conference bureau

This was a new service being offered by the Tourist Board and they were keen to publicise it. The Bureau were offering their services in organising conferences in the region. The page was simply a means of publicising the service with a name and address for further details.

4.0 Development costs

The development of the web pages, in terms of creating their content and programming their layout, cost approximately £1,000 Stg. The recurring costs were approximately £150 Stg. to cover Internet access, serving the pages and the provision of statistical monthly usage reports. These costs do not include the 'hidden' costs for the Tourist Board in attending meetings with the developers, in collating the material for inclusion in the pages and in responding to the user feedback. However, given a commitment from the organisation, they do illustrate that establishing a useful presence on the world-wide web does not have to be costly.

5.0 Publicising the site

When the web site went 'live', an entry was added to each of the major (and minor) search sites, for example Lycos (Lycos, 1996) and Yahoo! (Yahoo, 1996). The site was advertised on several 'What's New' lists and free advertising of the site was also obtained from traditional, paper-based Internet magazines. The statistics which are presented below demonstrate that there is a 'lead-in' period as awareness of the site grows.

A further method of publicity is to approach the operators of other relevant sites to request links from their site to yours. Often this needs to be a reciprocal agreement. It was the authors' experience that all sites which were approached were very happy to provide links. For the Tourist Board, the relevant sites were: airlines which served the region, companies which operated in the region and government departments.

6.0 Usage statistics

The statistics presented below represent an analysis of the first five months of operation of the web server. Figure 1 illustrates the number of 'hits' (i.e. page accesses) per month on the server. It illustrates the progressive growth of interest in the server and the fact that it took roughly one month for knowledge about the server's existence to spread. The use of the server seemed to level out at approximately 10,000 hits per month after this period. This could be due to server and/or network limitations.

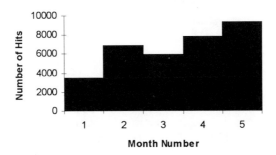

Figure 1: Number of server hits per month

512

Figure 2 presents an analysis of server usage by time of day. It is interesting to note the usage peak around the end of the UK working day (17 hours GMT), which is also the start of the US lunch break (GMT - 5 to 8 hours), when users are obviously surfing the net! Usage is otherwise fairly constant throughout the day except from 6am to 12noon. The most likely reason for this, given the origin analysis (see below), is that the US has largely gone off-line.

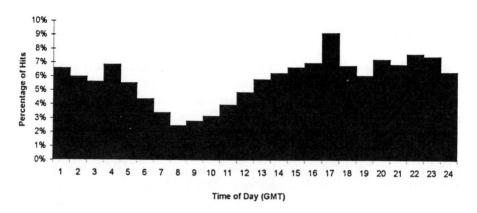

Figure 2: Percentage of hits by hour

The Tourist Board were particularly interested in knowing the origin of their callers. Figure 3 shows the percentage hits by country or world area. It should be realised, however, that these figures can only be an approximate guide; for example, a caller using CompuServe would appear as US in origin even though they could be using the CompuServe network from almost anywhere in the world. However, these percentage figures tied in closely with the Tourist Board's previous experience in servicing conventional inquiries.

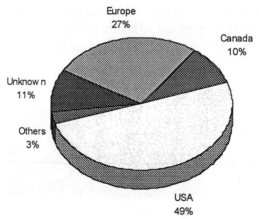

Figure 3: Percentage hits by country / area

Finally, an analysis of hits per page was carried out to determine the most popular type of information on the server. Figure 4 illustrates the percentage of hits per server page category. Not surprisingly, the Welcome page is the most accessed page. The popularity of the photographs confirms the importance of visual material on a web server. It was surprising that the Reservation Services page was so unpopular - feedback would indicate that most tourists leave this up to their travel agent. On average, each caller read 3 pages of information - which is most likely to be the welcome page plus two further pages. This is a good indicator of how effective the pages are at holding the reader's attention.

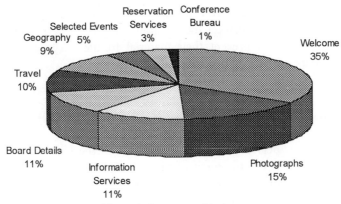

Figure 4: Percentage hits by page

6.1 The Visitors' book

This feature recorded over 1000 comments in the first four months. Most comments fell into the following categories:

- comments encouraging more of this type of information;
- requests for specific information;
- comments on recent visits to the region; and
- comments from home sick emigrants!

Only three of the comments were negative and in fact made very valid points that the information could be more extensive (the server did not advertise the fact that it was a scaled-down prototype). Three particular comments are quoted below to illustrate specific points:

"A well organised, easy to move around in source. Look here before paying US$15 for a travel guide."

This would confirm that the information provided is useful to potential tourists and that the page structure and inter-linking is effective.

"British Embassy, Press and Public Affairs Dept, Washington DC - very interesting."

This illustrates that you never know who is reading your pages - or where!

"As a travel agent I found very valuable info for my clients - thanks."

Increasingly the travel industry are using the Internet as an information source. Tourist boards who do not market their region using the Internet are going to miss the opportunity to present their material to the very people who are advising the tourists - the travel professionals.

7.0 Lessons learned

In the initial meetings between the Tourist Board and the University, it became clear that page design is not the remit of IT specialists. The initiative to launch the prototype server came from the IT Department of the Tourist Board and, at first, it was thought that they and the Computing Department at the University could handle the whole project. Inevitably, the first page drafts looked 'flat' and contained too much textual information. The lesson learned from this was that the IT specialists should restrict themselves to technical server issues and engage designers for page layout.

A further lesson learned in the page design process was that web pages are not merely an electronic version of existing paper-based catalogues. Apart from the fact that a direct transfer would not make use of the multimedia facilities provided by HTML and the Internet, it tends to generate pages which contain too much text, too little graphics and not enough 'punch' in their appearance.

In the technical authoring of pages, care must be taken in making the pages portable between different web browsers and indeed different platforms. It has been our experience that developers tend to use high-end machines with high resolution monitors and full-colour graphics. Thought must be given to the user with a VGA, 16 colour system using a different browser which is probably not even the latest release. Lesson: check out the created pages on a basic system, preferably on a different platform and using an alternative browser.

The main lesson to be learned from the prototype trial is the management implications. These fall into two categories: keeping the system up to date and responding to users. Updating the system is not simply a process of keeping (say) an events calendar current, although this is part of it, but it is also keeping abreast of the technical developments in HTML and web browsing. For example, many sites are now offering 'shocked' versions of their pages, others are making use of Java (Flanagan, 1996) applets and others are linking into on-line databases to provide live information. Failure to maintain a site in this way will make it less attractive to users and this ultimately means a drop in the number of hits. Certainly a site which offers the latest in web page appearance will attract surfers purely for the effect. However, while they are accessing the pages they might read them as well!

The second implication for management is from a site which allows users to place on-line orders, brochure requests or even just to sign a visitors' book. The Tourist Board did not anticipate the number of comments which would be made in their visitors' book and initially did not have the facilities to answer them by email (they were using a bureau service to serve the web pages). The Board had taken a deliberate decision not to offer brochures in the trial but they got requests for them via the visitors' book anyhow - the intention in providing the latter being for feedback. For an organisation which must maintain an excellent public image it would not suffice to ignore any form of request. Ultimately, the Board plans to integrate a brochure request mechanism into their computer system to eliminate this problem. However, there will still be questions for information asked in the visitors' book and human systems for processing them need to be established.

8.0   Conclusion and suggestions for further work

This limited trial of using the Internet to promote tourism has demonstrated that there is a demand for this service. This demand comes from tourists wanting to plan a trip, seeking information on air routes, distances between cities and towns and accommodation booking. The demand also comes from travel professionals who want information in advising their clients. Finally, those who have emigrated from the region use the information to stay in touch and as a promotional 'brochure' for their friends. With the rapid growth of the Internet, this demand is likely to increase.

The trial has shown that users want mainly travel-related information together with pictures of tourist attractions. Lists of events seemed to serve mainly those who live in the region. The server could usefully be extended to handle requests for brochures (perhaps with the provision of a credit card number to cover a small postage charge and/or to establish the legitimacy of the request) and maybe

516

automated accommodation booking - although the trial would indicate that this has a lower priority than one might initially have expected.

Finally, the trial has brought to light the resources which must be provided to adequately support such a system. Dynamic information, such as event calendars, require an automated tool to convert them from a desktop published form into HTML pages. Such tools are beginning to appear on the software market. Management systems are also required to handle electronic requests from users in the same way that telephone and postal enquiries might be processed - with the additional requirement that email users expect a fast response to their enquiry.

References:

1. Elliot, J. (1995)., "Write your own pages the easy way", *Internet*, 11, 47-50.
2. Erwin, M. (1995)., "Publishing on the Web", *Boardwatch*, 9(2), 45-49 and 9(3), 44-47.
3. Flanagan, D. (1996)., "Java In A Nutshell", USA, O'Reilly.
4. Frentzen, J. (1994)., "HTML Editors for Creating Web Documents", *PC Week*, 11(43), 21.
5. Glyn-Jones, F. (1996)., "Electronic Trading - The World is About to Change", *Cambridge*, 38, 115-118.
6. Lycos (1996)., http://www.lycos.com/
7. WWW Consortium (1996)., http://www.w3.org/pub/WWW/
8. Yahoo (1996)., http://www.yahoo.com/

9.4

BANKING INFORMATION SYSTEM MIGRATION TO MULTIMEDIA

V. Pantovic
Energoprojekt Holding, Yugoslavia

In this paper implementation of banking information system based on multimedia technology is presented. We analyzed if conventional methodology was acceptable for development planning and modeling of multimedia information system and submitted conclusions and proposals for modification. The pilot applications using signature database in existing IBM mainframe environment are evaluated. The implementation of an information system for banking cheques handling using Unix and Windows client/server environment is presented, too. Bar code on cheque is proposed, as an enhancement for document processing.

1.0   Introduction

Multimedia processing will develop from an esoteric, expensive technology to an indispensable tool used by modern business. The need to manage the flow of information has become more and more apparent to corporations everywhere. As people became more able to append text files with video, sound, and images, the need to figure out how to store this stuff and find it again has exploded (Appleton, 1995). Modern banks have already used multimedia points of information, videoconferencing, smart cards, cash dispensers, automatic teller machines, telephone banking, but the most important multimedia application is document processing (Pantovic, 1994).

Current banking information systems are specific systems that have many characteristics of a business information system as well as some characteristics of a public information system (Starcevic, 1995). In fact, due to the wide application of information technologies we now have companies whose primary activity is not banking which are in competition with banks. In order to protect their interests, banks have to appear more aggressively on the market and "go" not only to the companies, but to the homes of their clients. New services are offered and current services considerably improved on the basis of new technological solutions.

The text is further organized in such a way that the next Section presents a brief overview of the use of conventional methodology for development planning and modeling of multimedia information systems and some conclusions and proposals for modification. The third section presents the use of multimedia technology in banking. The processing of the most important document in banking, cheque, is presented in the fourth Section through its life cycle and several pilot applications. The conclusions are outlined in the final Section.

2.0   Modeling a multimedia information system

Time-based media, including digital audio and digital video, music and animation, involve notions of data flow, timing, temporal composition and synchronization. These notions are foreign to conventional data models and, as a result, conventional database system in general (Gibbs, 1994).

We applied conventional methodology (BSP - Business System Planning, SSA - Structured System Analyze, EER - Extended Entity Relation model) for development planning and modeling of information system. Conventional methodology is an acceptable approach for multimedia information system in general. Conclusions and proposals for modifications are:

• Planning for specific multimedia equipment appears in BSP.

• SSA for modeling processes is acceptable in general. In specification for multimedia processes appears some new functions (image compressing, sampling, producing sound, voice recognition,...). There exists a need for new domain in data dictionary for sound, image, video,...

• We propose modification of graphic concepts in EER image and sound attributes. In that way the semantic of model will be improved.

• It is necessary for CASE tools to include new domains for multimedia data and concepts.

3.0   Multimedia in banking

The most frequent and the most attractive application of multimedia computer systems is for marketing purposes (Pantovic, 1995). A successful performance or presentation is often of multimedia nature. With that we have stressed the strong information flow between the performer and the participant of the event. The information flow is multiple and simultaneous by occurrence and transmission paths. When graphics, animation, immovable and movable colour images are added to classical alpha-numeric data, the material which is presented becomes much more interesting, attention and understanding are improved, information is better memorized. All those who will try in the future to convey information only through the means of letters and numbers, are bound to lose the race with multimedia. Multimedia presentations will also be attractive for training and disseminating information to bank's employees and users of banking services. Multimedia equipment plays an ever growing role in the realization of bank security.

Implementation of multimedia systems in video-conferencing is very attractive for large banking systems, covering enormous geographical expanses. Their implementation provides savings in time, and the savings in travel costs very quickly pay off the initial investments.

Modern banking activities make use of specialized devices - automated teller machines, which are having increasing multifunctional purposes and multimedia characteristics. Automated teller machines most often include devices for self-service cash withdrawal (cash dispensers), supplied in models for external and internal use. These devices also provide some other banking services such as statement of account query and electronic funds transfer.

Mass usage of plastic cards has contributed to ever wider implementation of non-cash payment. Most of these cards have a magnetic stripe storing data which can be used for on-line transactions. Cards are enhanced by implementation of memory or processor chips allowing execution of transactions in off-line mode. This manner of payment reduces the time needed for transaction execution and telephone expenses. There are special devices in the market for reading these smart cards, thus expanding the use of electronic funds transfer.

In addition to implementation of these services for non-cash payment at points of sales, banks have an essential need for fast and multimedia provision of information (point of information). Communication with these devices is very simple, because it uses, beside classical textual information, images, animation, video records and voice, and commands are most often entered by touching the monitor.

Modern banks provide to their customers certain banking services without their having to come to the bank (home banking, telephone banking). The expansion in the use of voice technologies allows various general pieces of information to be supplied by unilateral implementation of voice devices. Interactive communications are an advanced aspect of implementation of voice-response automated devices allowing the user to get his account balance statements and to request cheque books. A simpler level of communication is achieved by pulse or tone dialing, while the more complex by computer's direct voice analysis.

Image processing has in recent years evolved from an inarticulate, expensive technology into a indispensable tool used by modern companies for managing overwhelming paper flood. Regardless of the type of the organization, the prevailing communication medium is paper, so that information, being a critical resource, is mainly stored on paper. Delays in collection and processing, document misplacement, wrong document distribution, the problems of storage, are formidable obstacles in operation of many companies. Modern transaction-oriented companies require very fast action in the reception and processing of information, which necessitates image processing on the computer. Many companies are potential users of such systems, but traditionally banks are most interested, primarily because of enormous amounts of transaction documents, where speed and quality of processing are essential, as well as the fact that large financial means are concentrated there.

4.0 Processing of banking cheques

The automatic teller machines, plastic cards and electronic money transmission in the business world have had continuously a growing share in all banking transactions. However, it is a fact that in the developed countries cheques are still the most popular payment method. For example (Austin, 1995), in Great Britain about 42% of all payments are done by cheques and about 28% by cards. In the business world about 80% of all payments are done by cheques. In order to retain the cheque as a popular payment method the banks are forced to raise the quality of transactions, to reduce considerably the cheque realization time and to reduce the cost of cheque processing.

The Postal Savings Bank, where we made some practical investigations, maintains one million accounts. Cheques remain the most popular method for personal sector non-cash payments. Cheque is an instrument that gives close control over cash flow and has the physical safeguard of signing cheque. The daily number of cheques is very large. The Postal Savings Bank processed up to 800,000 cheques per day at the period of hyperinflation. According to legal regulations, the realized cheque must be saved for some time. As the microfilm record is an authentic document by law, it is usual to use it in the archiving information system. All cheques are microfilmed at the end of document processing, but images can't be delivered electronically when needed.

On account of its great influence to bank's business activities and potential benefits, one of the top priority subsystems to be implemented is the document processing subsystem which should provide information support for everyday processing and archiving, primarily of all transaction documents. Speed and accuracy in financial transactions processing is the key for each financial institution in delivering quality services. The essential characteristic of this subsystem is that it runs the functions of keeping master data, i.e. the functions generating a class of data without using other data classes. These functions are the points of departure for information system implementation.

4.1 Life Cycle of Cheque

Due to enormous space and costs involved in cheque keeping, usage of microfilm copies is legally prescribed. Lack of legal regulations concerning the use of digital images and prices, as well as the need for the concept of memory hierarchies to be implemented, necessitate implementation both of the digital and analog images. That is why in process and data modeling both archiving methods are concurrently modeled. That such modeling approach is justified, is best shown by the chart in Figure 1, which is presented in logarithmic scale for easier reference.

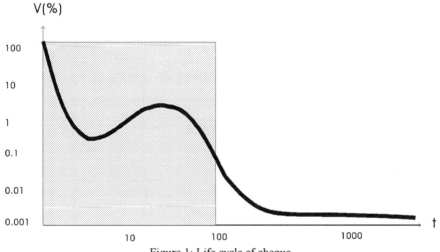

Figure.1: Life cycle of cheque

For analysis, explanations of extreme points are important. The first day, when a cheque enters the bank, is characterized by a hundred percent activity, because it requires the coding of the information from each cheque (data entry), that is microfilming and scanning. During the next few days it is necessary to take a look at the appearance of the cheque, on account of possible controls and corrections of errors made in data entry. Requirements for cheque visualization reach their maximum after thirty days when there are customer complaints. In practice, after three months requests for cheque visualization are very rare, and after three years the legal obligation for storage of microfilm copies expires.

4.2   Signature database in mainframe environment

We made pilot application using signature database in order to test the possibility of image implementation under the existing conditions. Signature database is also very important for identification of cheque holders. Existing hardware environment was mainframe computer IBM 9000/330 with MVS operating system networked with three smaller systems, 500 personal computers, 2000 terminals, microfilm center with 6 KODAK cameras. The open systems and the client/server approach allow new applications to access data held in older systems. 3270 emulation lets PC users connect to an MVS mainframe, to take advantage of host capabilities. Client/server will be sufficient to retain existing systems on existing hardware platforms, and simply add graphical user interface on PC. We have used the High-Level Language Application Program Interface. EHLLAPI by using a Language Interface Module (LIM) as a bridge, interprets the information from the application program on PC and passes the request on to the IBM Personal Communications/3270 Emulation Program which performs the task. (Fig. 2). After the task is completed on the host computer, EHLLAPI returns control to the application program. With the applied imaging technology, all the processes related to the management of signatures (customer images or account documents) can be delivered from mainframe to the point of service, either by fax or the branch PC.

4.3   Information system for cheques handling

The second pilot application has been developed in a different   environment (Starcevic, 1995). We have started from the already widely applied practice in the world that the cheque is considered a multimedia entity and that the cheque characteristics described by standard data types in a data model are supplemented by a front and a back side of the cheque image. Client photographs and client signature images are saved in the banking cheque card database, also. Such reasoning brings us to a changed concept of the realized cheque processing. Now, the computer readable cheque form as a multimedia entity is enough for all standard cheque operations. It means that the electronic cheque image is created in the bank immediately and after that it circulates inside the information system in place of the cheque. For example, the data entry from a cheque that cannot be done automatically, is performed by an operator which looks into the cheque image on the screen (videocoding). In this way, organization is simplified, the security is considerably increased and the total cheque processing time is reduced. This approach provides a remarkable improvement in bank office operations. Assuming that between the computer equipment in the bank office and the central bank there exists a communication link, a bank clerk can check the client identity on the basis of his signature or photograph at any moment.

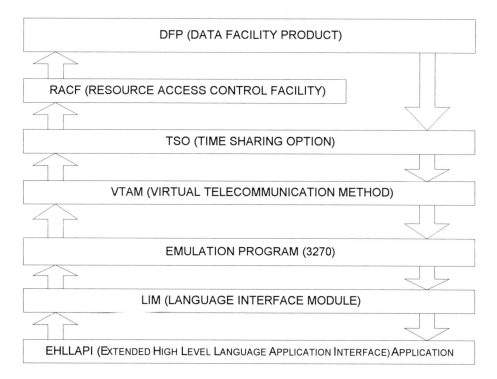

Figure.2: Ehllapi application

Also, now a client's complaint in relation to the banking report about realized cheques can be instantly resolved without waiting for many days or going round other organizational bank units. In fact, the client can see the image of a suspicious cheque on the screen and he/she can visually check all relevant elements of the cheque. Just to say that the mentioned checking can be made even the bank office has only a fax device.

Having in mind that a bank is as a rule a geographically distributed organizational system, which consists of the center, branches and subbranches, the information system for banking cheques handling is not only multimedia, but distributed. The database of the distributed multimedia bank office information system is logically and physically divided into two parts: an alphanumeric database and a multimedia database (Grosky, 1994). Our demo banking MMIS as well as most of the new distributed information systems has been implemented according to the popular client-server paradigm (Bucci, 1994).

In order to minimize development and maintenance expenses of our information system, to ensure adaptability, portability and interoperability, along with maximum reliability of the whole system, the basic idea is to realize the system as an open system. The system should consist of the dominant world standard modules, using elements available, off-the-shelf and checked in practice.

Having in mind the processing nature on the server side we selected UNIX operating system as the standard for an open multi-user multitasking system. On the other side, the client side, respecting the importance of the Windows, as the dominant graphical user interface on personal computers, operating systems can be DOS/Windows, Windows NT or Windows '95. Also, the client should communicate with the server by SQL, whenever possible. Application elements are defined by the system functions required. For example, in our case for electronic images of cheques, clients and their signatures only, it is necessary to provide the electronic images archiving and searching. In these circumstances the system should dispose of an image digitalization function, an image compression, indexing, storing, searching, protecting and reproducing.

4.4   Bar code on cheque

In the third pilot application we have investigated the usage of bar code on cheque as a enhancement for document processing. Bar codes are proving indispensable as a compact, efficient way to convey information. The number of uses for bar codes is growing. We applied a "picket fence" bar code to each cheque. Cheques contain OCR (Optical Character Recognition) human readable text and bar code printed on IBM 3835 laser printer (5 cheques/sec). Automatic bar code identifications provides data entry with cost savings and improved efficiency. Bar code reading can be used to provide automatic image indexing. Image address can be generated automatically from bar code during scanning/filming cheque and transferred to the image application as part of an image header file. The advantage of bar code usage on cheques would be especially emphasized at point of sale (cash registers equipped with bar code reader).

5.0   Conclusion

Multimedia information technologies give an answer to certain problems, but there arises the problem of integration into the existing data processing environment and therefore it is very important to analyze such systems in good time and develop technology and standards of banking activities to allow efficient application of multimedia technologies.

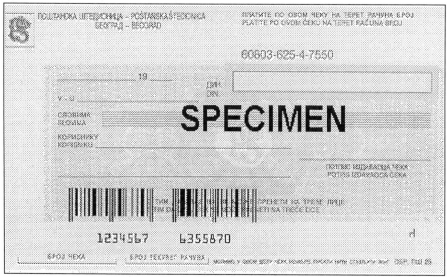

Fig. 3: Bar code on cheque

The paper points out that multimedia computer systems are a natural technical and technological environment for implementation of banking information systems and that implementation of archiving functions is of top priority in possible multimedia applications. We analyzed migration from conventional system to multimedia information system in which cheques would be simultaneously scanned and microfilmed at the entrance of system. Through the practical realization of signature database it has been shown that the existing resources can be used for implementation of multimedia processing. It has been confirmed that the client/server architecture is extremely favourable, because maximal use is made of the advantages of mainframes and personal computers. Document processing as images has become one of basic strategic requirements in information systems. It is essential that the documents in their appearance, colour and data arrangement are adapted to digital processing, and therefore it is necessary to adjust them in good time, standardize and obligate all participants creating and using documents to comply with the agreed-upon standards. The suggested modification of the banking cheque through inscription of the bar code would enhance security and speed up automated data coding.

The advance in telecommunications and the ability to use voice as well as data will bring a new simplicity to doing banking through electronic networks. Moving away from face-to-face banking implies significant cost savings for banks, and a more convenient service for customers. We believe that the majority of all system spending in the banking sector will be on client/server computing.

The existing mainframe systems would continue to play an important role and would act as an application server within the client/server strategy.

References:

1. Austin, D. (1995), "Cheque Out Time", Banking Technology, London (UK), March 1995, 42-44.
2. Appleton, E.L. (1995),"The Document Explosion:Take Control", Datamation, November 1, 64-68.
3. Bucci G., Detti, R., Pasqui, V. "Sharing multimedia data over a client-server network", IEEE Multimedia, 1(3), 44-55.
4. Gibbs, S. (1994), "Data Modeling of Time-Based Media", SIGMOD 94-5/94, Minneapolis, Minnesota, USA, 91-102.
5. Grosky, W.I. (1994), "Multimedia Information Systems", IEEE Multimedia, 1(1), 12-24.
6. Pantovic, V. (1994), "An Approach in the Use of Multimedia Computer Systems in Implementation of Archiving Information Systems", Faculty of Electrical Engineering, Master thesis, (in Serbian).
7. Pantovic, V., Starcevic D. (1995) "Multimedia in Banking", Proc. YU-INFO '95, Brezovica, Vol. 2, 455-459.
8. Starcevic D., Simic D., Radetic A., Pantovic V. (1995), "Information System for Banking Cheques Handling", Conference on Operational Research, Thessaloniki, Greece.

9.5

A DISTRIBUTED MULTIMEDIA BANK OFFICE INFORMATION SYSTEM

B. Simic[1] and Dusan Starcevic[2]
[1]Institute Mihajlo Pupin and [2]University of Belgrade, Yugoslavia

For a bank's success in the world it is critical to provide all services efficiently, accurately, timely and appropriately. The best way to do that is improving the traditional way of work by using a new technology or technologies. Today, an emerging technology with exponential growth is the multimedia technology. Having this in mind, in this paper a framework for a distributed multimedia bank office information system is presented. Special attention is dedicated to a multimedia management subsystem.

1.0 Introduction

It is well known that information technology continually changes. Information technology is revolutionizing our lives. Nearly every aspect of our society is involved: how we communicate, how we learn, how we do business. Digital computer systems - "computers" celebrate their fiftieth anniversary. In this period of time the use of computers has caused great changes in the world. Namely, a powerful positive feedback effect is characteristic of computer usage in the development cycle: science - technology - production. The use of computers in various scientific research areas has allowed discovering and mastering complex technological processes and, consequently, the appearance of new or improved products. This effect is specially evident on the example of the computer product itself, because hardware possibilities of computer systems have multiplied in no more than a few years. The described process has repeated itself on new computers and the cycle duration has decreased. Simply stated, an explosion of knowledge and of the way of production and application, with a frightening exponential growth speed, is in progress. As far as software support is concerned, issues have developed at a different pace. The available software has increased with the increasing number of computers. But, until recently, the annual productivity growth in software "production" has been of the order of several percents. Hence the well known term "software crisis" that expresses the impossibility to utilize the new hardware potentials. Starting from the attitude that the features of program support determine the system architecture, we conclude that only several dominant paradigms of computer application have determined the direction of architecture evolution during the past fifty years. The appearance of new paradigms has caused jumps not only in the quality of information systems, but also in performance improvement, both in the development and exploitation phases. The importance of understanding the information systems architecture evolution in the past half-century period is in that it may help us to better solve the problem of adequate computer usage in business automation and specially in the distributed multimedia bank office information systems.

At the beginning of the past decade, according to data given in (Cox, 1987: p.4), only 2% of delivered information systems was successful immediately, that is, real user needs were satisfied! According to research by Butler - Fox foundation "at the end of the past decade one installation was a complete success, one a complete failure and eight were nothing special from a total of 10 installations". Nevertheless, it should be mentioned that in comparison with corporate management information systems, which were evaluated almost catastrophically, office automation results are described as "often disappointing", because they did not utilize the offered potentials (Noble, 1991). American company Business Research Group (BRG) states that there is no general advice for computer usage, because "solutions are by definition exceptionally individual and idiosyncratic, so cultural habits, the structure and way of work in the respective organisations must be taken into consideration".

This paper is organized as follows. Section 2 describes the evolution of information systems. Section 3 introduces the proposed architecture of a distributed multimedia bank office information system. Section 4 describes the basic components of the system. We present a framework for a distributed multimedia bank office information system that works with both text and image documents. Section 5 focuses on multimedia management subsystem. Conclusions are given in Section 6.

2.0   The evolution of information systems

In the first phase of the architecture evolution, that is from 1948 to 1965, the dominant characteristics of the information system based on the use of electronic computers were determined by the computer hardware of that time. The hardware was extremely expensive. The cost of computer user personnel per unit time was nearly negligible in comparison with the equivalent cost of hardware. So, software support, as the interface between a user and machine, was in the first place adapted to the hardware requirements. The user had to "think like the machine". This was the phase of monolithic program support. The runtime code that results from the algorithm of problem solution "coalesces" with the routines of input-output devices and monitoring program (See Figure 1 a) (Morland, 1985), level I). Solving some problem was treated as a highly creative programmer's work.

The phenomenon of positive feedback, described in the introduction, led to the appearance of computer systems with better characteristics than their predecessors in the world market. This, in turn, resulted in an increased number of computer systems and in a wider application domain. The concept of monolithic program support was no longer the best solution. First of all, lower computer cost does not justify neglecting the personnel expenses, even in the first approximation. The hardware vendors started to offer to the potential users not only the hardware, but also a part of program support that was required for computer systems exploitation. This part of program support is known as the system software and it is located between the computing hardware and the application (See Figure 1 a), level II). The system software consists of the operating system and the auxiliary programs. The most important characteristic of this phase is the portability and the portable application gained the attributes of finished goods. Roughly, this phase lasted from 1965 to 1985.

A big jump in the information systems development was recorded in the 1980s by the appearance of a cheap personal computer, PC. The appearance of personal computers led to a new paradigm in computer systems usage, that is, to a new architecture of the program support. A typical user of a personal computer has very little knowledge about the technical characteristics and potentials of the computer. It is important to note the user interface system (See Figure 1 a), level III). In fact, it is a graphical user interface, such as for example MS Windows, or Motif Windows. In the last half of the 1980s, the development of non-standard database management systems, including image and document databases, started to become interesting for investigation (Milenkovi}, Star~evi}, Mu~ibabi}, 1987).

The appearance of personal computers emphasized not only the graphical user interface, but also introduction of the local area networks. In Figure 1 b) is shown one more software layer - the distributed operating system shell. Just this architecture, shown in Figure 1 b), is used as a framework for implementation of a distributed multimedia bank office information system and it is outlined in the next Section.

530

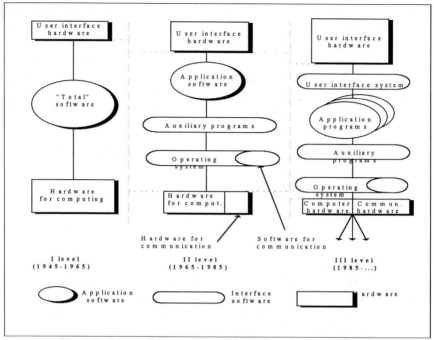

Figure 1a: The evolution of information systems from 1945 to 1990

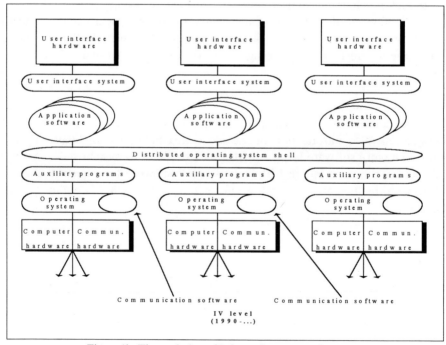

Figure 1b: The evolution of information systems from 1990

3.0   An architecture of a distributed multimedia bank office information system

Figure 2 shows the architecture of the distributed multimedia bank office information system that we propose. The system is based on the standard client/server architecture. The client/server architecture assumes that the processes which make an application can be divided into the client processes that need services and the server processes that give services. We suppose that the bank has a hierarchical organization and consists of a centre, branches and subbranches. The central host should be some mainframe or some RISC machine, because on the centre side, usually, such systems already exist. On the branch and subbranch levels, the servers should be UNIX - based systems. We have selected the UNIX operating system, because it is the standard for an open multi-user multitasking operating system. Today in the world, the personal computer usage predominates in the implementation of open information systems. So, on the client side we have selected Windows 95 operating environment. The clients take advantages of Windows graphical user interface and utilize the highly distributed environment of the bank. The distribution relates to geographically distributed bank offices.

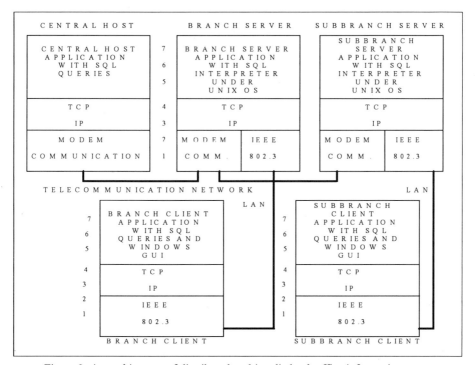

Figure 2: An architecture of distributed multimedia bank office information system

532

The database of the distributed multimedia bank office information system is logically and physically divided into two parts: an alphanumeric database and a multimedia database. It is a variant of Grosky's generic architecture for a multimedia information system (Grosky, 1994). The alphanumeric database should be implemented in some commercial relational database management system. The multimedia database may also be implemented in the same chosen relational database management system, but better performance results will be attained using ordered files and modified B^+ algorithm (Star~evi}, Jovanov, 1993).

Figure 3 shows the main parts of the network system. The network is necessary to provide high bandwidth and low latency, specially for the large number of clients and extensive use of the multimedia. Better integration of diverse media, such as text and images, is enabled by high-speed fiber-optic networks. The architecture of the clients themselves must provide high bus bandwidth and efficient I/O.

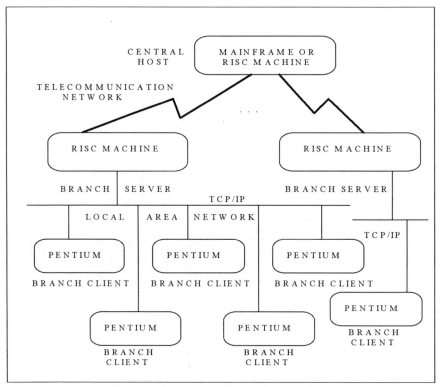

Figure 3: The centre and branch levels of the bank

4.0   The system description

It is a fact that in the developed countries bank cheques are still the most popular payment method. In the business world about 80% of all payments are done by cheques. In our implementation the cheque is considered as a multimedia entity. In the system the cheque characteristics are supplemented by a front and a back side of the cheque image.

The multimedia information system provides all necessary information about customers including their images, the images of their cheque cards and the images of their realised cheques. The images are stored in the multimedia database, while the alphanumeric data are stored in the alphanumeric database. For example, the basic alphanumeric data about a customer are customer identification number, name, address, phone number, account number, etc. On the client side, bank personnel using the multimedia and the alphanumeric database, get a complete financial picture of the customer, instantly. At the same time, high security is guaranteed.

The described solution can be realized completely in Internet environment. Having in mind Internet weaknesses in data security and knowing that the proposed architecture of the distributed system must provide high network bandwidth and efficient I/O, today it is better to implement such a system as a private computer network where only the predetermined points are available to Internet.

The development of complex distributed multimedia information systems requires a systematic approach. There are many open problems in system design and development resulting from the introduction of multimedia entities into the information system. According to our opinion the following problems are the most important: current versions of SQL do not support an image as an abstract category, commercial relational database management systems in the first place have primitives that are not adequate for modelling of multimedia entities, for very large databases the system should possess better indexing, storing and searching algorithms. Some possible solutions to the mentioned problems are given in (Star~evi}, Simi}, 1995).

Our framework for implementation of a distributed multimedia bank office information system is reactive in nature. This means that it efficiently and successively reacts to input stimuli issued by its environment.

5.0   Multimedia management subsystem

The multimedia management subsystem is located on the branch and subbranch server sides (See Figure 4). Clients communicate with the server by messages. On the server side a special process - a demon process keeps communication with the clients. The demon sends input messages into the server input queue and it sends answers from the output queue back to the clients. The server process is a process that reads messages from the input queue, analyses them, calls the corresponding procedure, makes the answer and puts it in the output queue. The server process uses an existing file system on UNIX.

Data processing in the multimedia management subsystem is very intensive. On the other hand, it is well known that the execution time of memory operations compared to disk access time could be neglected. In order to increase the number of transactions per second and to satisfy the requirements of interactive multimedia applications, we need to minimize the number of disk accesses. This can be achieved by optimization of the number of disk accesses. The new algorithm, which is based on synergism of B^{+} tree and hashing mechanism, provides increasing of the server throughput (Star~evi}, Jovanov, 1993). A possible way to solve the same problem is based on a database hardware accelerator. This is outlined in (Jovanov, Star~evi}, 1992).

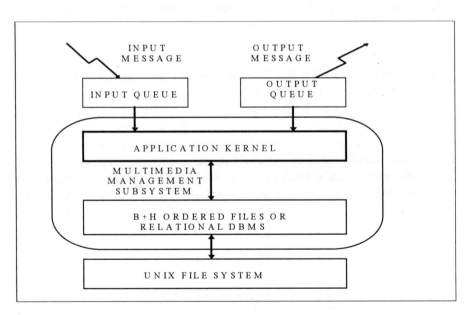

Figure 4: The branch and subbranch server architecture

6.0 Conclusion

The paper has described the basic characteristics of a distributed multimedia bank office information system. The distribution relates to geographically distributed bank offices. We have supposed a hierarchical organization of the bank, such that the bank consists of a centre, branches and subbranches. The demo system is implemented using the standard client/server architecture. Multimedia computer systems proved to be convenient technical-technological environment for improvement and expansion of bank office services.

The system is distributed by local and telecommunication networks and the application is based on the client/server architecture. On the client side we have chosen Windows and on the server side a UNIX environment. The transport and the network levels use the standard TCP/IP protocols. The described solution can be realized completely in Internet environment. Having in mind Internet weaknesses in data security, today it is better to implement such a system as a private computer network where only the predetermined points are available to Internet.

The implementation of a distributed multimedia bank office information system is relatively simple and it does not take very much effort and time. It is important to note that the system can be realized not only from scratch, but by additional development of an already existing system.

References:

1. Cox, J. B. (1987), Object Oriented Programming - An Evolutionary Approach, Addison-Wesley.
2. Grosky, I. W. (1994), "Multimedia Information Systems", *IEEE Multimedia*, 1(1), Spring, pp. 12-24.
3. Jovanov, E., Star~evi}, D., Aleksi}, T., and Stojkov, Z. (1992), "Hardware Implementation of Some DBMS functions Using SPR", in *Twenty-fifth Hawaii International Conference on System Sciences*, Kauai, Hawaii, Vol. 1, January, pp. 328-337.
4. Milenkovi}, ^., Star~evi}, D., Mu~ibabi}, B. (1987), "PC-based Multimedia Messaging Systems", in *Proc. of the Thirteenth Symposium on Microprocessing and Microprogramming Euromicro 87*, Portsmouth, Great Britain, September 14-17.
5. Morland, D. V. (1985), "The Evolution of Software Architecture", *Datamation*, February 1., pp. 123-132.

6. Noble, F. (1991), "Seven Ways to Develop Office System: A Managerial Comparison of Office System Development Methodologies", *The Computer Journal*, 34(2).

7. Star~evi}, D., Jovanov, E. (1993), "Large file operations support using order preserving perfect hashing functions", *Yugoslav Journal of Operations Research*, 3(2), pp. 171-188.

8. Star~evi}, D., Simi}, D., Radeti}, A., Pantovi}, V. (1995), "Information system for banking cheques handling", *3rd Balkan Conference on Operational Research*, Thessaloniki, Greece, 16-19 October.

9.6

MULTIMEDIA INFORMATION SYSTEM FOR COMMODITY EXCHANGE OPERATIONS UNDER THE CONDITIONS OF TRANSITION

Vinka Filipovic, Nevenka Zarkic-Joksimovic, Vesna Milicevic,
Bojan Ilic & Petar Jovanovic
University of Belgrade, Yugoslavia

The paper deals with the introducing multimedia information system for commodity exchange operations under the specific conditions of the transition to a market economy. The focus is on the application of the concept of automated commodity exchange and on its main characteristics.

1.0   Conditions of transition to a market economy

Under the conditions of transition toward a market-oriented economy managers need to be fast in bringing their business decisions with acceptable risks. To meet such requirements managers can make use of Multimedia Information Systems that ensure support to decision making and to a multiple flow of information between the performers and participants. In user communication multimedia information systems thus simultaneously use different practical forms of information such as text, graphs, pictures, pieces of music, speech, all this aiming at improving the quality of the manager -system communication. This is also achieved through connection of new input/output units (camcorders, microphones, scanners, and the like).

Integral market creation under the conditions of transition also understands introduction and functional operations of commodity exchanges. Exchange operations are characterized by utilization of modern information technologies; thus commodity exchange-intended modern information systems mean rather specific systems featuring characteristics of a business information system. Indeed, the broad information technology implementation makes it possible to reach relevant information in a fast and effective manner and complete all the business transactions successfully.

2.0 The concept of multimedia information system for commodity exchange

The abovesaid is what induced the authors to conceive and engage in development of a multimedia information system for commodity exchange operations under the conditions of transition. The system bases on its client/server structure amidst local and telecommunications computer networks. On the server-offering side there is the base of commodities as multimedia entities, comprising conventional bases of data on types of goods, commodity prices, financial standing of potential business partners participating in exchange transactions, as well as the base of images of individual items, and photos of vendors and purchasers active in exchange operations. The system thus offers information to all participants on relevant features necessary for decision making, ensuring communication of all the commodity exchange participants for the purpose of trade exchange. Participants connected technically in this manner are able to much more effectively mitigate the problems inevitably faced under the present conditions of their performance and business operations.

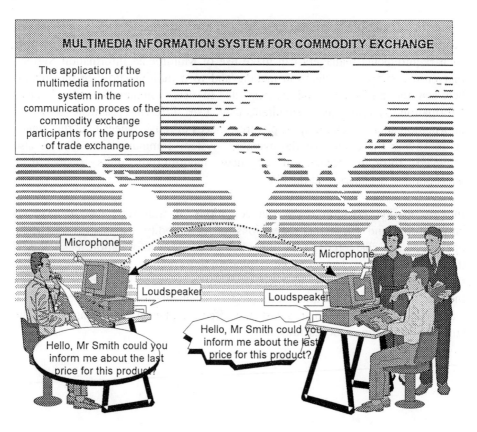

3.0   Main characteristics of the automated commodity exchange

The automated commodity exchange system operations assure:
- Direct entry of Supply/Demand conditions
- Insight of other participants' Supply/Demand conditions
- Prompt access to all relevant information in contacts with potential partners
- Possibility of automated telephone dialing via utilization of special-purpose programme packages
- Printing of currently relative documents and reports following arrangement conclusion immediately
- Mailing of circuit messages via electronic media
- Utilization of computer conference links (up to four participants at a time).

Individual computer unit operations are organized in an ON-LINE regime; the ask "system enables updating and entry of data on supply and demand, as well as answers to requests in form of information, data visible on monitor screens or printed.

The paper describes characteristics of a multimedia information system for commodity exchange operations, demonstrating the same as a technological milieu suitable for introduction and improvement of exchange operations.

References:

1. Bucci, G., Detti, G., Pasqui, V. (FALL 1994), Sharing multimedia data over a client-server network, IEEE Multimedia, vol. 1, p.p. 44-55.
2. Star~evi}, D. (1995), Multimedia (Multimedij), Info, no.1, p.p. 14-18.
3. Star~evi}, D., Radeti}, A., Simi}, D., Pantovi}, V. (1995), Multimedia banking information system, SYM-OP-IS `95, Belgrade.
4. Group of authors (1995), Yugoslav Financial Markets (Finansijsko tr`i{te Jugoslavije), Savez ekonomista Srbije, Belgrade.

9.7

PROSPECTIVE OF MULTIMEDIA MARKET IN CHINA

Xiao Wang & Hongsheng Xia
Jinan University, PRC

This study intends to show the prospective of the multimedia market in china. Here are three stages to do that : First of all, the study provides the general situation of the multimedia market in china through several dimensions including speed of development, volume and structure of the market etc.; Secondly, by means of factors analysis , some important factors are drawn out to illustrate the environment of the multimedia market in China such as technology factors, economical factors and legal and management factors; At last, a case --Multimedia CAI application in Guang Dong province, is presented in detail in order to give a living example to show the properties and opportunities of multimedia market in China.

1.0   Introduction

Multimedia technology is derived from computer interface graphics. At the very beginning, multimedia technology and product were incorporated in computer hardware, software and service. From the beginning of 1990s multimedia section had been separated from it Gradually. Today, the scope of the market run so fast that most of electronic companies envelop multimedia into their development strategy because of the gigantic market volume: 9000 US dollar in 2000 as estimate approximately now.

Beginning with the Audio-Video entertainment through CD-ROM and sound card, multimedia technology extended very fast to management, Computer Aided Instruction(CAI), presentation etc. Multimedia market has become one of the most important part of computer market in china. For the sake of grasping market opportunity and making profits, it is necessary for any traders and analysts to follow the situation and features of multimedia market. The following study will give the information of general situations(volume, structure, speed) and features of multimedia market in china in form of statistical data. Most of data came from three main periodicals: China Infoworld, China Computer World and Electronic Today from 1994 to 1996.

2.0   Survey of multimedia market in China

2.1   Variable system and data preparation

No one takes multimedia as a separated market until the beginning of 1990s. According to a sample investigation [1], we can determine a rough proportion which multimedia took up in domestic computer market . so that the volume and structure of multimedia market can be estimated . First of all, from the purpose of my study, a data model(variable system) must be defined to embody the situation of different phase of multimedia market. The Predefined model is listed below:

● general situation (total sale of whole computer market, PC sale, software sale) ;
● multimedia market sale (MPC sale, board & card sale, CD-ROM, software sale) ;
● number of people engaged in computer market (software, manufacture, marketing, R&D) ;
● number of company in computer market (software, manufacture, marketing, R&D) ;

The general situation will offer the macro environment for multimedia market study. The number of engaged company and people give us a signal to identify the scope and trend of the market. Data (in table 1) came from several related studies including market study by means of sample investigation. Volume, structure and development speed of multimedia market will be found in it.

Table 1: General situation of computer market in China

(a)   Unit: billion yuan

	computer sale			multimedia	sale		
	total	PC	software	MPC	board & card	software	CD-ROM
1995	55	16	14	1.9	0.0375	2	0.06
1996	67	24	25	507	0.08	4	0.12

(b)

	number of company				number of people		
	software	manufacture	marketing & service	R&D	software	manufacture	marketing & service
1995	1000	1000	13000	50	80,000	100,000	120,000
total	15,050				300,000		

Datasources: / The Overlook of Computer Market, China Infoworld, 1995, 1, p35;
/ Market Analysis, Electronic Today, 1996, march, 25, p141;
/ The Development of Computer Industry during 1996--2000, China Infoworld, 95, 41, p99

2.2   General situation

Table 1 listed the quantitative of market in four dimensions. And now, let's pay

542

attention to the proportion which multimedia take up in the whole market. Another table that is calculated according to the upper table will tell us the scope of multimedia market in more detail (Table 2.).

Table 2: Proportion of multimedia in domestic and world market

		MPC	board & card	CD-ROM	software	total sale
In domestic	1995	3.45	0.07	0.11	3.636	7.29
market(%)	1996	8.51	0.12	0.18	5.97	14.93
in world	1995	0.1	0.002	0.003	0.1	0.2
market(%)	1996	0.19	0.003	0.004	0.133	0.333

From table 1, we can see great change in Chinese computer market, the total volume of Chinese computer market is 55 billion yuan (about 6.63 US$) and 67 billion yuan (8.07 US$) in 1996 as estimate [2]. The proportion of multimedia market is 7.29% of whole volume and will probably rise to 14.93% in 1996. Comparing with the worldwide multimedia market(24 billions US$ volume), Chinese proportion is 0.2% in 1995 and 0.333% in 1996, which is forcasted by a study [2].

2.3 Market structure

We can describe market structure from different angle of view. In this study, three kind of structure would be taken into account: (1) product structure; (2) application structure; (3) company and personnel structure. Product will emphasis on the multimedia hardware sale structure. Application structure will provide the a rough rank list of multimedia application in domestic multimedia market and the situation of company and personnel distributions will be displayed in the third part.

Product structure. From views of product sales, the market structure changes hardly in 1995 and 1996(see chart 1). Sales of Multimedia Personal Computer(MPC) have been promoted so fast that it will become the main part of the market and software and service take the second rank in the meantime.

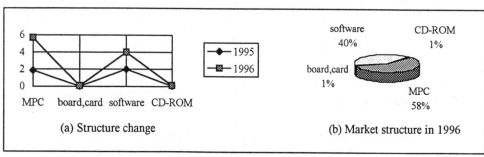

(a) Structure change   (b) Market structure in 1996

Chart 1: Product structure of multimedia market

Application Structure. Anyway, the motivation of the market growth is public AV entertainment. And entertainment multimedia will be the leading section in the long run from views of application structure analysis. Following chart (Chart 2) illustrates us the marketing rank of multimedia application. Data came from a sample test in November, 1995 which is taken by China Infoworld press[3]. The rank data marks the percentage of cases which are interested in certain application.

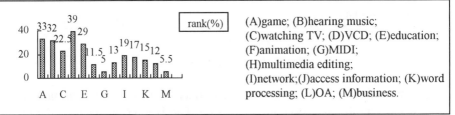

Chart 2: The application rank in multimedia market

Company and Personnel Structure. As a sample investigation [1] indicate, about 95% PC vendors were engaged in multimedia market. it divided vendors into 3 groups: (1)lower 20 employees, (2)20 to 50 employees and (3)over 50 employees. Half vendors belong to the first group. The second group has 12.5% of all. The rest belong to the third group--about 37.5%. Small vendor is still the main bone of present multimedia market.

2.4 Speed and Stage

We have referred to the high speed of market changing during 1990-1995. Depending on historic marketing data [2][3], we can evaluate the speed of whole market as well as multimedia section and mark their developing stage.

Table 3: The historic data of China computer market

	90	91	92	93	94	95	96
total sale	33.5	70.4	198.9	284	407.4	550	670
PC sale	10	18	37.5	63.4	110.8	160	220
multimedia	N/A	N/A	N/A	10	40	100	N/A
software	10	25	40.6	89.87	107	140	250

using the upper table, we calculate the respective average increase rate (in term of %, see chart 3):

544

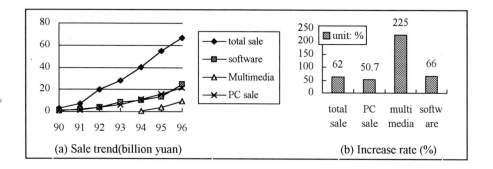

Chart 3: The market increase rate

Comparing with the other market, we can conclude that multimedia market in china have enter into high speed growth period. The average annual growth rate is 225% now. And the rate will be maintained at 100% in the future 3 years. The mature period will appear in the next century.

3.0   Factors of multimedia market environment

3.1   Market environment

The development of market will be decided by its environment. So it is important for trader to comprehend the market envionment. Some studies such as Business Environment Risk Index(Haner,1960), integrated analysis(Rummel;Hlluan)[4] give us different variable system to evaluate the market environment. From the views of integration, I want to simplize these model to 3 factors which are market demand factor, technical factor and legal factor: **Market demand factor** comprises two aspects: Macro economy which is explained by total quantitative of economy, financial state and taxation etc. and Micro economy which indicates supply and demand of market. **Technical factor** should be consider as infrastructure of market . Quantitative of hardware keeping, technician and R&D institute situation and technical standard will be discussed in it. **The policy and legal factor** will concentrates on laws of intellectual property protection and national industry policy concerning with multimedia market. Further study is listed in the following.

3.2   Market demand

From 1990 to 1995, the high speed of economy development is impressive(rate over 10%). Consistent with macro environment, many opportunities are created for participants. Two things-- Purchasing power and potential client will be discussed to show the demand of flourishing market:

Purchasing Power. From views of micro economics, we can estimate the quantitative of purchasing power by means of bank deposit of resident and enterprise. Considering Chinese resident's bank deposit takes up the 90% of total bank deposit[5], we have the quantitative of market purchasing power approximately: that is about 3 trillion yuan(about 1/3 trillion US$) in the end of 1995. If a considerable part of the great purchasing power is led to multimedia market, large marketing will be surely engendered. By the end of august, 1996, the Central Bank has pulled down interest rate to the lowest of historic record, which means a great stimulation to realizing of the purchasing power.

Potential Client. It is up to the quantitative of multimedia consumer that How much power will be led into. Visible and invisible consumers is often called as "author" of market. Let's see who has the honor to be the author. (1)College student is the largest user group. Sample test[2] show over 95.8% of students would like to use computer and 94% of this group know multimedia and need it in Beijing, Shanghai and Guang Zhou. (2)Family consumers, which is related to student group very closely. China has 7300 city family and only 0.25% of them have computer. According to the "Family Computer Impelling Plan", the rate of family computer popularization will be 1% in 2000. About 20-30% of family computer will be MPCs as estimate. On the other hand, the popularization of family electrical equipment (such as TV, refrigerator)has come to a stable stage. Purchasing of House and mobile still need long term fund. In favor of integration of entertainment and education,
the family will be happy to invest in the new hot spot. (3)Schools and institutes. There are about 800,000 primary to high schools and 2,000 post high schools in china, and only 300,000 PC is kept by them. Education committee of china plans to equip 1% of primary to high school by computer every year. that will about 20 - 30 thousands PCs. For the sake of CAI, many of them will be MPCs. In addition, china has 500,000 R&D institutes which are also big consumer groups. Companies. Advertising and marketing company in Guang Zhou city developed very fast: 2000 in the end of 1995 and only 700 in 1994. they need lots of professional multimedia equipment for producing advertisement, training clerk, guest and so on. These companies are also important for traders to notice.

3.3   Technical status

Technical Status will effect the market directly. Let's see the following 3 aspects:
Quantitative of technical institute and person. There are 500,000 R&D institutes by the end of 1995, and only 800,000 software workers are working now. the average annual developing speed is only 25%-- much lower than the

546

increasing rate of computer marketing which is 62%. **Hardware and Software Keeping**. There are about 1 billion software, 80 thousands on-line database and 1,299 million computers(80.83% are PCs) in 1995 market and about 22.3% of them connected to network Now. 25% users are thinking of local Network(Ethernet:85%, FDDI: 15%, other: 5%)[6]. But the poor datacommunication status limited the application of multimedia very much. PDN(x.25) only built in main cities. ISDN is still the plan of next century[7]. It is the reason why 12.5% users don't want to purchase networking-based multimedia application[1]. **Standardization** is another problem. MPC level I-III had been very popular. But to the network's multimedia, there are still not anything to do with the multimedia data interchange protocol. This situation prevent large data network from multimedia application. From the aspect of Application., the most important standard is of the video decoding. MPEG I has been accepted by many consumers and vendors. But to MPEG II, many consumers are waiting for the price lowering of DVD.

3.4   Policy and legal status

Industry Policy brought good news to multimedia market. According to the computer industry developing plan [3], computer industry will become the pillar industry in next century. Many related policies are issued to support it, which include policies of finance, taxation, labor, anti invalid competition and Intellectual Property Protection(IPP) etc. Because IPP problem is too much serious in china, the following will be concentrated on the legal status in IPP. Based on content, we can divided IPP into 4 types: trade secret, copyright, trademark and patent. From another dimension, Irah think that objects of multimedia IPP may include hardware, software, audio and visual entertainment and interactive interface mechanism [8]. That is the very structure used in the following, and the critical information is filled in table 4.

Table 4: IIP status in China

properties	objects / regulations and laws	hardware	software	AV record	interface mechanism
trade secret	Anti Invalid Competition Law	V	V		
copyright	Copyright Law and Formalities		V	V	
	Software Registration Regulation and Formalities		V		
	Software Protection Regulation		V		
	International Copyright Regulation		V	V	
trademark	Trademark Law	V	V		
patent	Patent Law	V	V		V

Trade Secret is formula, equipment or method of operations used in business and have commercial value. This type of IPP is pretty dangerous because it doesn't prevent competitors from getting the secret through valid path. Its owner must be sure of that. But accessing trade secret from invalid way such as stealing and cheating will infringe the Anti Invalid Competition Law. **Copyright** gives owners the exclusive right to copy their work, such as literary work, pictures, sculptures, sound recording, motion picture and computer software in any medium of expression. Five laws and regulations concerned with copyright. The main arbitrator is National Copyright Bureau. **Trademark** is a symbol to distinguish your product in the market. "Trademark Law" protect it from infringing. If you meet any troubles concerned with trade marks, Industry and Commercial Bureau will arbitrate it. **Patent** prevent all others from making selling and using the invention, even though they developed new version independently. So it is a ultimate protection to a invention. National Patent Bureau will manage the affairs of patent depending on the Patent Law.

4.0   Case study: multimedia CAI in Guang Dong

Guang Dong province is one of most developed zones in china. City family computer popularization   lies in the first rank among big cities in china: rate is 8.3% in Guang Zhou and 17% in Shenzhen, much higher than Beijing(7.2%) and Shanghai(4.7%). But multimedia is not familiar in Guang Dong until schools and families found its magic power in CAI recently. The following two parts will show the CAI situation in Guang Dong, which will reflect the market present situation and future partially.

4.1   Present Situation of Computer Aided Instruction(CAI)

It's in 991 that CAI was led into universities and colleges in Guang Dong. Limited by computer's performance and price, the developing is not used practically and broadly. Since the entering of   practical Multimedia technology, CAI has been applauded by both teachers and students. Any way, the multimedia CAI has not been spread in all level of schools. Things will be better in posthigh school than in primary to high school according to investigation. The following table(Table 5) shows the situation of education and CAI in Guang Dong province.

Table 5: Situation of CAI and education in 1995

school level	students	schools	computers	CAI rooms	CAI softwares	CAI investment(yuan)
post high	215,000	43	8000	10	78	2,150,000
under high	6,880,000	17,200	15,000	N/A	N/A	N/A

datasources: / Guang Dong Statistic Yearbook, 1995;
/ "Electronic Education evaluation n posthigh school", Posthigh Education
Bureau 1995;
/ Zhang Tailing(1995), "Electronic Education in Guang Dong's higher schools"

4.2   Market Opportunity in Multimedia CAI

In 1994 and 1995, multimedia had been the most splendid word in education field. Many schools began to make their own plans for it. "Handreds" plan which means to build 100 CAI rooms,100 multimedia CAI softwares began to be impelled by the Posthigh Education Bureau. PC's increasing rate will be higher than 1%. That means 50,000 PCs will go into these schools. Internet became a hot spot in the end of 1995. The market is not so clear . But many big companies (such as Guang Dong telecommunication company, Guang Zhou information service international)began to invest on on-line family education and entertainment services, which proved internet application a new large market. Another hot topic in family is MPC. Sample test [9] show 52% PC consumer would like to buy MPC, only 23% persons want to purchase multimedia card. That means MPC's popularization rate will be climbing up continually, which will bring demand of software and service to the market.

In present. 4 multimedia application are being proved to be prospective: Education presentation; Audio and vedio entertainment; Graphics and animation; Game. To the extent of whole country, the total volume of these four fields may be 6.9 billion yuan (see table 6; chart 4 show the proportion of different applications might take up in market) which will take up 56.3% of ultimate multimedia market -- that is about 12 billion US$[10].

Table 6: Proportion of multimedia application

number	1	2	3	4	5	6	7	8	9
application	edu.	AV	graphics	game	communication	database	mgnt.	word proc.	developing tool
proportion	19.1	16.2	10.8	10.2	8.9	7.9	6.9	6.8	5.7

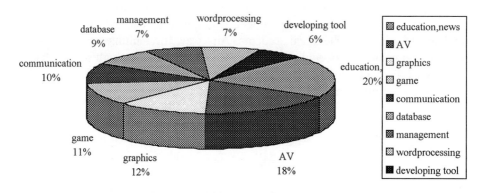

Chart 4: Multimedia application structure

References:

1. Investigation Report(1995), "Multimedia Market Investigation", *China Computer World*, Nove. 20;
2. Investigation Report(1996), "China Computer Market Analysis", *Electronic Today*, March, No.25;
3. Yang Tianxing(1995), "Computer Industry Status and Development", *China Computer World*, no.41, p63;
4. Irah H, Danner(1995), "Intellectual Property Protection for Multimedia Application", *Computer*, June, p99.
5. Xie Qinan; Han Zhaozhou(1995), Commercial Statistics, Guang Zhou, Jinan University Press;
6. Investigation Report, "China Computer Network Investigation", *China Computer World*, No.22, p40;
7. News Report, "10 Billion Yuan invested in Telecommunication", *China Computer World*, No.16 1996, p85;
8. Irah H, Danner(1995), "Intellectual Property Protection for Multimedia Applications", *Computer*, Aug., p92;
9. Investigation Report(1995), "Multimedia Computer Consuming Demand Investigation", *China Infoworld*, No.41 p37;
10. Investigation Report(1995), "Multimedia Software Market investigation", *China Infoworld*, No.44, p37.

9.8

PROS AND CONS OF SETTING-UP A "VIRTUAL" LABORATORY ON THE INTERNET USING THE DSMAC PROCESS-TRACING INTERFACE

Gad Saad
Concordia University, Canada

In a sequential-sampling task, an individual must decide after each piece of acquired information whether to make a choice or collect additional information. The SMAC and DSMAC interfaces (Saad, 1996a; Saad, 1996b) were developed to investigate the cognitive processes leading up to a final multiattribute choice in such a task environment. Currently, I am investigating the feasibility of downloading DSMAC onto a web page, resulting in the creation of a self-contained "virtual" laboratory on the Internet. Following a brief review of DSMAC, the pros and cons of setting-up such a laboratory on the Internet are discussed.

1.0   Introduction

It has been estimated that close to 80 million people use the Internet everyday. This figure is estimated to grow to 180 million over the next 3 years (Wilde, 1996: p.1). Originally, the Internet was predominantly used by academics in university settings as a means of communicating with one another. Looking back at the early interactive platforms, one realizes that the Internet was too difficult to use by the typical layperson. However, the advent of the World Wide Web and user-friendly interfaces such as Netscape has permitted for the Internet's rapid diffusion in both industry and private homes. The adoption of the Internet as a viable mode of communication has not only spurted the growth of new services and industries (e.g., Internet provider companies, electronic cafés, web-site developers) but also created new ways of doing old things (e.g., advertising, home shopping, information gathering). The purpose of the current paper is to discuss the viability of using the Internet as a vehicle for collecting psychological data. In other words, is it feasible to construct a "virtual" laboratory on the Internet and if so what are the associated pros and cons of such an endeavor?

As a behavioral decision theorist, I am particularly interested in understanding the cognitive processes leading up to a final multiattribute choice (e.g., choice between cars to purchase, apartments to rent or jobs to take). For example, how does an individual decide when he/she has acquired sufficient information to make a final choice? In what order will the decision maker acquire the information in? How does his/her mood affect the amount of information that will be acquired prior to choosing an alternative? In a recent paper, I described the SMAC interface (Saad, 1996a), a computerized data collection tool for investigating Sequential Multiattribute Choices. In such an environment, it is assumed that an individual acquires one piece of attribute information at a time, across pairs of competing alternatives, until sufficient discrimination is achieved to permit a final choice. Within SMAC, three distinct stages of the sequential-sampling process can be addressed: (a) attribute selection, i.e., if additional information is desired, deciding which attribute information to acquire next; (b) information integration, namely the processing of newly-acquired information; and (c) backtracking, i.e., the review of previously-acquired information. The SMAC interface has been used to investigate a myriad of behaviors in each of the latter three stages (see Saad, 1994; Saad, 1996c; Saad and Russo, 1996). Recently, the DSMAC interface (Saad, 1996b) was completed. It is a more dynamic and elaborate version of SMAC. It too is a process-tracing methodology that allows a researcher to investigate individuals' behaviors in a sequential-sampling task. Unlike SMAC which consists solely of a subject interface, DSMAC is bi-modular, consisting of both an experimenter and a subject interface. In the former, a researcher interactively specifies all of the relevant experimental parameters (i.e., stimuli and task) for a given study. Subsequently, the subject interface uses the latter specifications as input and accordingly "adjusts" itself. Both SMAC and DSMAC were written in ThinkPascal 4.0.1 and can be run on any Macintosh machine which uses a system 7.0 (or higher) operating system. An equivalent IBM version of DSMAC will soon be developed, using in all likelihood a more powerful (as compared to ThinkPascal) fourth-generation, object-oriented language such as Delphi.

When conducting studies using the latter methodologies, the interface is downloaded onto diskettes, and these are subsequently run on several stand-alone Macintoshes in a laboratory. Thus, if a laboratory is equipped with 10 machines, one can simultaneously have 10 subjects participating in the study. Over the next few months, I am hoping to develop a "virtual" psychology laboratory on a web page. In other words, the interface would be downloaded to a website and accordingly net surfers interested in participating in the particular study would transfer the interface onto their machine via a program such as FTP and subsequently would run the interface from their machine. Having completed the task, they would send back via FTP the output files that were generated. These files would automatically be stored in a predetermined memory block in my e-mail account. In the ensuing section, I shall briefly discuss some of the relevant literature followed by a detailed account of the advantages and disadvantages of setting up such a system.

2.0   Literature review

Early work in decision making research stemmed from economics where the focus was and continues to be on developing normative theories of how individuals ought to behave given a set of axioms of rational choice. On the other hand, prescriptive theories attempt to identify an optimal course of action for an individual facing a choice. A decision tree analysis, whereby it is prescribed that, the set of actions along the path leading to the highest expected value should be followed, is one such example. In contrast to the above two schools of thought, descriptive theories of decision making attempt to understand the exact cognitive processes taking place when individuals are actually making choices (process-tracing research). The reader is referred to Bell, Raiffa and Tversky (1988) for a good synopsis of the three schools of thought.

Within the descriptive tradition, the informational display board (IDM) methodology has been the dominant approach in investigating the cognitive processes leading up to a final choice. An IDM is an m x n matrix whereby the m rows correspond to the m competing alternatives and the n columns represent the n attributes defining the alternatives (see Ford et al., 1989 for a review of process-tracing work that has utilized IDBs). Hence, cell (i,j) corresponds to the value of alternative i on attribute j. Studies that have employed the IDB approach have typically investigated the decision rules (an example would be the Lexicographic rule, i.e., choosing the alternative that is superior on the most important attribute) that individuals apply in reaching a decision via an analysis of various measures of search such as the depth, sequence, content and latency of search (see Ford et al., for an explanation of these characteristics). Early studies that utilized this methodology used physical representations of an IDB (e.g., Jacoby, Chestnut and Fisher, 1978) through the use of cardboard (to construct the m x n matrix) and envelopes (to represent the attribute values in each cell). Hence, if a subject wished to acquire the attribute information corresponding to cell (i,j), he/she would physically have to look inside the envelope corresponding to that cell. An obvious improvement to the latter methodology occurred when computerized versions of IDBs and other related process-tracing software packages were developed (cf. the Mouselab interface as described in Payne, Bettman and Johnson, 1993 or Search Monitor by Brucks, 1988). Thus, one of the methodological trends in process-tracing research has been a gradual shift away from the traditional paper-and-pencil tasks and other "physical" representations to more elaborate computerized tasks. For the interested reader, Brucks (1988) provides an excellent discussion of the pros and cons of using computer interfaces in process-tracing research.

In the same vein that there has been an increase in computerized tasks in process-tracing research, I foresee a similar trend occurring for research conducted via the Internet. Currently, most of the relevant experiments and studies available on the Internet consist of surveys and questionnaires (i.e., paper-and-pencil tasks). The difficulty in setting-up a computerized interface on a website is due to technological limitations. Existing Web browsers can solely support very basic commands (e.g., point and click and dialogue boxes). As such, more intricate interfaces cannot be developed using the browser's hypertext markup language (HTML). ["The current technology is very powerful, but it is also very limiting in terms of interactivity," says Adams of Poppe Tyson. "For the most part, the presentation of information on the Web is done through static pages. But that is changing as we speak. We will quickly be moving away from viewing Web pages and moving toward dynamic Web systems."] (Koprowski, 1996: p.52). That being said, several companies have recently developed more powerful languages permitting for improved interfaces on the Internet (e.g., Java or Shockwave). One of the key benefits of this new technology is its cross-platform nature. In other words, an interface that is developed using such a programming language can be run, irrespective of the type of machine a net surfer is using to access the particular website.

While the latter technology is a considerable improvement over the traditional capabilities of an HTML, it requires substantial and extensive programming expertise. In light of the latter impending limitations, the "FTP solution" is probably the most viable current option for researchers wishing to conduct computerized experiments on the Internet. As previously mentioned, DSMAC will hopefully be available in both an IBM and a Mac version. As such, depending on whether potential participants are using an IBM or Mac machine, the appropriate version of the interface will be sent to them via FTP. There are two obvious disadvantages to such a solution: (a) potential participants must have access to the FTP program (or some other file transfer program); (b) given that the interface is not cross-platform, only those subjects accessing my website via a Mac or IBM machine will be able to participate in the experiment.

3.0   Setting up a virtual laboratory on the internet

(i) Advantages

The most obvious benefit in setting-up a "virtual" laboratory is that it alleviates many of the logistical problems inherent in conducting experiments in a "physical" laboratory (e.g., lab availability). Second, while in a "physical" lab, a researcher is bound in the number of subjects that can be run simultaneously, clearly this is not a concern in a "virtual" laboratory. As such, the total amount of time needed to collect data on the required number of subjects will be shortened. Parenthetically, it is worth mentioning here that in constructing the website, one should set-up a counter which would ensure that the desired number of subjects for a given study is not exceeded (e.g., if the counter is greater than 100, disactivate the website). Such a precaution need only be taken if subjects are being financially remunerated, in which case one would want to place an upper limit on the number of participants. Third, given that it is less effortful for subjects to participate in a "virtual" study (e.g., not having to brave a snow storm and drive to the laboratory on a Saturday morning) , the response rate to a call for participation is likely to be higher. On a related note, Dickson and MacLachlan (1996) found that faxed surveys yielded higher response rates than their mailed counterparts. Fourth, studies conducted in a "virtual" laboratory would not be prone to any experimenter bias (Hewson, Laurent & Vogel, 1996). Fifth, collecting cross-cultural data via the Internet becomes a much simpler and less expensive endeavor, given that users from over 100 countries are now connected. Case in point, one of our doctoral students has been collecting cross-cultural data on the differences in reaction to one-sided versus two-sided advertisements of English and Chinese Canadians. The process has been a difficult and arduous task, one which would have undoubtedly been facilitated through the use of the Internet.

(ii) Disadvantages

In the long-standing epistemological debate between laboratory and naturalistic modes of inquiry, the most cited advantage of the former is the tremendous control that can be imposed on potentially confounding variables. The predominant drawback to conducting experiments in a "virtual" laboratory is precisely the loss of such a tightly-controlled environment as found in the "physical" laboratory. For example, two subjects participating in a "virtual" study might be doing so in drastically contrasting environments. One subject might be listening to loud music while completing the task while the second one does not have any music in the background. On a related note, subjects will oftentimes require assistance as they complete an experimental task. Clearly, in a "virtual" setting, access to an experimenter would be limited if at all available, a further source of loss of control. A more sinister disadvantage, also related to loss of experimental control, is the potential for malfeasance by dishonest subjects. For example, the same subject might try to participate in the experiment on several occasions as a means of obtaining multiple financial remuneration. One possible method to combat such behavior would be to include a security algorithm that would check for duplicate e-mail addresses (assuming that the participant is logging in from the same account). Another potential source for dishonest behavior would be if subjects tried to alter the contents of the generated output files, via the use of a text editor. Clearly, the output files can be designed as to solely permit the interface to write into them in an on-line manner. All subsequent attempts to reopen the generated output files would be blocked off.

One of the dependent measures that is collected in DSMAC is reaction times. For example, the interface keeps track of the number of seconds that an individual took to decide which piece of attribute information to acquire next. Clearly, in a "virtual" laboratory, reaction time studies can potentially yield erroneous data. For example, a subject might decide to take a coffee break during the experimental task, yet another manifestation of loss of experimental control. The interface would nonetheless wrongly keep track of the total time that the subject spent at that particular stage. One possible solution would be to program the interface to recognize unduly long delays, i.e., wherein the subject does not produce a single concrete action. Subsequently, the interface could flag the subject for a response (e.g., "are you deliberating or are you busy doing something else?"). Failure to reply within a certain time limit would lead to the disabling of the interface. The difficulty in setting up such a safeguard is in determining the appropriate length of the inactive period, an issue that can be solved empirically with the use of pilot studies.

A third disadvantage might be the non-random and unrepresentative nature of subjects willing to participate in a "virtual" experiment, i.e., a form of a self-selection bias. For example, potential "virtual" subjects are likely to be younger, more computer-literate and more educated than the general population. Having said that, a similar issue has been raised in the context of standard experiments in psychology, whereby the overwhelming trend has been to use undergraduate students as the main source for subjects (see Gordon, Slade and Schmitt, 1986 for a more thorough discussion). The archetypal reply to the latter concern is that as long as the "unrepresentative" dimensions (e.g., age, income or education) are not expected to moderate the issue(s) under investigation, one need not worry about this point.

4.0   Recruiting "virtual" subjects

There has been a tremendous proliferation of websites on the Internet and this trend will continue to grow over the next few years. As such, if a researcher's goal is to randomly sample from the general "surfer" population, one of the likely problems that he/she might face is the small likelihood that a user would stumble upon the particular web page. Thus, while the Internet would theoretically increase the representative nature of a sample in comparison to that which would be obtained in standard experiments, accessing the general "surfer" population might prove difficult. Those researchers willing to restrict the sample of "virtual" subjects to undergraduates will nonetheless have a much larger population to choose from in comparison to those that can be sampled in standard experiments. Typically, in the latter studies, most if not all of the recruited students attend the same university. However, calls for participation placed on Internet academic discussion lists (e.g., the elmar list for marketing academics) or the set-up of Internet subject cooperatives/pools (e.g., that which was set-up by the Society for Judgment and Decision Making) would both increase the population size and ameliorate its representative nature.

5.0   Conclusion

Burke et al. (1992) compared search behavior as obtained from both naturalistic and computer-simulated environments. Overall, the two sets of behavior displayed substantial convergent validity. A similar approach can be taken to gauge the methodological validity of behavior collected in a "virtual" laboratory. The same experiment could be conducted in both a physical and "virtual" laboratory with a subsequent comparison of the two sets of data. Should the two data sets accord with one another, this would satisfactorily address most of the cited disadvantages associated with setting-up a "virtual" laboratory on the Internet, especially those relating to the potential loss of experimental control. On the other hand, if the two data sets yield disparate behavior, one could hopefully identify those conditions under which a "virtual" laboratory would or would not be an appropriate data collection medium (see Hewson, Laurent & Vogel, 1996 for a discussion of the type of experiments that are more amenable with cyberspace). All pros and cons considered, it is my opinion that in most instances, setting-up a "virtual" laboratory for the implementation of process-tracing research in decision making would prove to be a fruitful exercise.

References:

1. Bell, D. E., Raiffa, H. & Tversky. A. (1988), "Descriptive, Normative, and Prescriptive Interactions in Decision Making", *In Decision Making: Descriptive, Normative, and Prescriptive Interactions.* Bell, D.E., Raiffa, H. & Tversky, A. (Eds.), New York: Cambridge University Press, 9-30.
2. Brucks, M. (1988), "Search Monitor: An Approach for Computer-Controlled Experiments Involving Consumer Information Search", *Journal of Consumer Research*, 15, 117-121.
3. Burke, R. R., Harlam, B. A., Kahn, B E. & Lodish, L. M. (1992), "Comparing Dynamic Consumer Choice in Real and Computer-simulated Environments", *Journal of   Consumer Research*, 19, 71-82.

4. Dickson, J. P. & MacLachlan, D. L. (1996), "Fax Surveys: Return Patterns and Comparison with Mail Surveys", *Journal of Marketing Research*, 33 (February), 108-113.
5. Hewson, C. M., Laurent, D. & Vogel, C. M. (1996), "Proper Methodologies for Psychological and Sociological Studies Conducted Via the Internet", *Behavior Research Methods, Instruments, & Computers*, Vol. 28 (2), 186-191.
6. Ford, J. K., Schmitt, N., Schechtman, S. L., Hults, B. M. & Doherty, M. L. (1989), "Process Tracing Methods: Contributions, Problems, and Neglected Research Questions", *Organizational Behavior and Human Decision Processes*, 43, 75-117.
7. Gordon, M. E., Slade, L.A. & Schmitt, N. (1986), "Science of the Sophomore" Revisited: from "Conjecture to Empiricism", *Academy of Management Review*, 11, 191-207.
8. Jacoby, J., Chestnut, R. W. & Fisher, W. A. (1978), "A Behavioral Process Approach to Information Acquisition in Nondurable Purchasing", *Journal of Marketing Research*, 15, 532-544.
9. Koprowski, G. (1996), "Marketing on the Information Superhighway: The Next Big Wave", *American Demographics*, Marketing Tools Supplement, Jan/Feb, 51-52.
10. Payne, J. W., Bettman, J. R. & Johnson, E. J. (1993), The Adaptive Decision Maker, Cambridge: Cambridge University Press.
11. Saad, G. (1994), "The Adaptive Use of Stopping Policies in Sequential Consumer Choice", *Unpublished doctoral dissertation*, Johnson Graduate School of Management, Cornell University.
12. Saad, G. (1996a), "SMAC: An Interface for Investigating Sequential Multiattribute Choices", *Behavior Research Methods, Instruments, & Computers*, Vol. 28 (2), 259-264.
13. Saad, G. (1996b), "DSMAC: A Dynamic Interface for Investigating Sequential Multiattribute Choices", Submitted for publication.
14. Saad, G. (1996c), "Attribute Acquisition and Backtracking Behavior in Sequential Choice", Submitted for publication.
15. Saad, G. and J. E. Russo (1996), "Stopping Criteria in Sequential Choice", *Organizational Behavior and Human Decision Processes*, (forthcoming).
16. Wilde, C. (1996), "Internet Growth Through 2000", *Internet and Electronic Commerce Conference Special Supplement*, Sept. 4-6, 1.

9.9

THE ROLE OF MULTIMEDIA TECHNOLOGY IN THE DELIVERY OF ACADEMIC PROGRAMS IN SATELLITE FACILITIES

Ahmed Ispahani[1], David S. Kung[1], Emile Pilafidis[1], and Mabel T. Kung[2]
[1] University of La Verne and [2] California State University, USA

The Education Industry is one of the more traditional industry that is currently facing fundamental shift of the operating environment. It has created the need of development of alternative delivery system. This research discuss the role Multimedia Technology plays in such transformation.

1.0   Introduction

In the past fifteen years, it is well documented that Information Systems/Information Technology(IS/IT) had made significant positive, but yet sometimes negative, impact in most industries around the world. For example, the use of state-of-the-art Information Technology had allowed the banking industry to streamline and automate most of their operations including the check processing operations and on-line banking. In some of the major banking operations, most of the check-clearing operations do not require human handling anymore and billions of dollars are changing hand electronically each day. Even in these IT driven industries, the road to today's highly automated environment has been difficult and at times confusing. There are no industry that has not been affected by IS/IT. It is usually just a matter of the level of impact, both positive and negative. The intent of this research paper is to analyze the role of IS/IT, in particular Multimedia Technology, in the Higher Education Industry during its current re-engineering of itself, driven by market-related changes for the Twenty First Century. The market forces driving Higher Education will first be discussed. A theoretical model for the future will then be presented. The role of IS/IT and Multimedia Technology in accomplishing the theoretical model and the corresponding implementation issues will be studied thoroughly. It will be followed by an analysis of the current and near future situation in the United States of America(USA). The purpose of utilizing the USA as a base line for discussion is the recognition of the trend that in the economic environment, USA has been a leading country with other nations typically will follow the footsteps both in positive and negative ways. In the conclusion, some of the more long term issues will be raised so as to begin the thought process of tackling this tradition-rich industry. In order to keep the discussion manageable, this research will involve professional education only, such as business programs. Obviously, similar concepts and issues can be applied to other disciplines.

2.0   The changing environment in higher education

Through out the 1980s, certain factors had changed the critical factors of the academic industry drastically. First of all, minimum academic requirements in significant amount of the jobs in organizations had been elevated from high school diploma to university level degrees. This is especially true in professional disciplines. With the change in requirements, a large volume of professionals and staff employees had decided to be re-trained academically in order to maintain their current situations or to be in a position to advance themselves in organizations. This had led to a dramatic increase of adult professionals to find ways of attending academic institutions while maintaining their current jobs. As a matter of fact, in 1994, for the first time in the USA, there were more adult entering colleges than traditional age students. Coupled with the demographic shift(decreased college-going age people), academic institutions had to commit to major changes in order to maintain enrollment level.

Adult professional students had created different types of problems for traditional academic institutions. The two most significant factors that mandate adjustment are as followed:

2.1   Logistics

Students have to work in the day time and can only attend classes at night and on a part time basis. Also, it is not possible for students to go to the campus. A student that is more than 30 miles from a university has no chance of taking courses from that university.

2.2   Curriculum

The educational needs of the students are different when they are with working experience as compared to traditional twenty year-old students without experience. For example, adults prefer and excel in participating in class discussion based on their experience and thus forth can learn well among students instead of just with the instructor.

Regarding the curriculum, the challenge is then to adjust the academic curriculum to include the needs and experience of adult professionals. Normally, academic institutions can handle this issue by creating two separate paths after some common core requirements. The logistics issue is rather difficult for most academic institutions due to the traditional setup of having a physical campus where all the services, faculty, and administration are resided. Students will then come to the campus and normally will attend school full time. Due to the demographic shift and the remedial needs of adult, the academic institutions of the future have to be very different then today's'. The following section is a description of the academic environment of the future. It will then follow by the discussion of the role of Information and Multimedia Technology in that future environment.

3.0 Model of the future environment (delivery alternatives)

It is inevitable that academic institutions of the future have to be able to accommodate the non-homogeneous student body in terms of logistical issues. A very hard-to-deal-with factor is the inability of students to congregate in a central campus to take classes. From the students point of view, both traditional and adult, the delivery system of academic programs has to be flexible. It needs to have various alternatives. Flexibility in the area of physical location and contact time/duration are particularly important.

Delivering academic programs at multiple sites outside the traditional central campus is a proven concept that have been practiced by numerous academic institutions with a wide range of success. In particular, facilities can be contracted practically everywhere, such as conference room in business premises, community properties, and hotel proprietors. Clearly there are certain type of academic courses where it is difficult to conduct outside a central campus. For example, courses requiring a laboratory or computer equipment. This will limit the delivery of certain programs outside the central campus. But experience have shown that, at times, regional satellite facilities can be useful in overcoming this shortfall. For example, in some highly populated area, multiple sites within a certain geographical area can all be linked to a satellite facilities where more elaborate equipment such as computer laboratory can be made available. Within a specific academic program, a student may attend most of the course work at the nearest site with the understanding that a very few number of courses will require the student to travel to the satellite facilities to complete.

Ideally, in the future, the concept of a virtual university is the most appropriate. The idea is such that a university will not necessary be tied to any physical locations. It is the authors' opinion that the concept of a central campus that serve some common, general functions should prevail. There really is no economic and practical purpose/benefit of not having a central campus. But from the students' point of view, where does one go to attend classes should be full of convenient alternatives and transparent to the academic program. A major problem still exist is the situation whereby the students may be isolated geographically and do not have satellite facilities close by. In other words, it is not economically feasible to service certain students due to not enough quantity. That is a case where Information and Multimedia Technology can help. The role of such technology in these situation will be discussed in the next section.

4.0   IS/IT (Multimedia) support

In order to arrive at the future environment of academic institution, universities have to transition first to operate with multiple sites with satellite facilities. If successful, later on the concept of a virtual university can then be implemented. A critical resource in such implementation is the availability of faculty for teaching in all these sites and in particular, the idea of educating students where quantity is a issue. Obviously physical limitation in terms of numbers and faculty cannot be in two places at the same time can be resolved by the use of Information and Multimedia Technology. In the case of satellite facility serving multiple sites, through Multimedia Technology, a professor can be located at the satellite facility and conduct class sessions with students that are coming in from their office or home via some form of regional networks. The bandwidth required for on-line video is definitely an issue. Teleconferencing cost over long distance is still prohibitive. But since the students are typically either work or live within very short distance, high capacity connections should not present a problem. The type of video-conferencing software necessary is becoming readily available and stabilized Of course, it is not necessary that the student will never come into the satellite facility through out the course. Multimedia Technology will reduce the necessary physical meeting but not illuminate all contacts.

The concept can be established between the central campus and numerous satellite facilities also. But then since this is normally over a much longer distance, cost can become a determining factor. In the long run, with the establishment of ATM as the back bone network, cost will not be an issue In order to avoid failure, it is important to keep in mind that the intent of the use of Multimedia Technology should be to enhance and increase the flexibility of the delivery of academic programs, but not to completely replace the existing delivery system. Group dynamics of human beings and needs of adult students will not allow the complete replacement to happen without failure. The issue is usually to what extend it should replace. It will not be a technical issue but more

562

of a human issue. In the next section, the current situation in the USA will be presented for reference.

5.0　Logistics issues for USA academic institutions

In the USA, unlike majority of the world, the reality of educating non-homogeneous students has been well accepted. Significant number of universities had invested in the satellite facilities concept with mixed results. In terms of Multimedia Technology to support the new delivery alternative, often times, universities will use technology for all or nothing. In other words, either a whole course will be electronically driven with insignificant physical contact or follow the traditional approach. The ultimate purpose of Information Technology as a supportive tool and not a replacement is many times misunderstood. It had led to unsatisfactory results from the students' point of view. Obviously, like any new ideas, most universities are going through a learning process with hits and misses. Another misunderstood factor is that it is mostly a technical issue but in reality the most difficult part is in gaining the acceptance and co-operation of faculty, which a tremendous change in approach/preparation is required.

6.0　Conclusion

It is estimated that the learning curve will be about ten years in terms of stabilizing the concept of appropriate and effective use of Information and Multimedia Technology in the delivery system of academic programs. Obviously, from a technology point of view, whatever capacity and technical issues will not exist any more as academic institutions move on down the path. From a global perspective, there is no doubt that academic institutions in the USA will most likely be pioneers in this effort and will have to suffer the consequences of no bench marking. But this will afford the same institutions the opportunity of being one step ahead in this increasing competitive world of education.

References:

1.　Chang, Chia-Hao & Chen, Yubao (1995), "A Study of Multimedia Applications in Education and Training", Computers & Industrial Engineering, Vol 29, Issue 1-4.
2.　Fox, Edward & Kieffer, Linda (1995), "Multimedia Curricula, Courses, and Knowledge Modules", ACM Computing Surveys, Vol 27, Issue 4.

3. Halal, William & Liebowitz (1995), "Telelearning: The Multimedia Revolution In Education", Futurist, Vol 28, Issue 6.

4. Ingram, Albert (1996), "Teaching With Technology", Association Management, Vol 48, Issue 6.

5. Jordahl, Gregory (1995), "Global Multimedia Moves to The Head of The Class", Inform, Vol 9, Issue 4.

6. Matson, Elaine (1996), "Multimedia in Higher Education: A Practical Guide to New Tools for Interactive Teaching and Learning", CD-ROM Professional, Vol 9, Issue 5.

7. Rappoport, Jon (1996), "Cyber-grads: Savvy Students Hit the Net", Advertising Age, Vol 67, Issue 20.

8. Schank, Roger & Korcuska, Michael & Jona, Menachem (1995), "Multimedia Applications for Education and Training: Revolution or Red Herring?", ACM Computing Surveys, Vol 27, Issue 4

9. Shimizu, Yasutaka (1996), "Tokyo Institute of Technology's Application & Evaluation of Long-distance Education", Japan 21st, Vol 41, Issue 3.

10. Wong, Henry (1995), "ATM: Tomorrow's Technology is Here", Computer Technology Review, Vol 15, Issue 11.

11. Wulf, Katie (1996), "Training via the Internet: Where Are We?", Training & Development, Vol 50, Issue 5.

9.10

Automatic Video Editing by Filmic Decomposition of Non-Filmic Queries

Butler, S. and Parkes, A. P.
Lancaster University, UK.

In this paper we describe an approach to generic automatic intelligent video editing, which has been implemented in the LIVE system. We discuss Cinema Theory, and earlier systems which recombine film fragments into sequences. We introduce our system, describing the implementation and the main components of the system architecture. We then examine the generic film fragment generation rules implemented within the system, with examples. Finally, we discuss the future direction of our research.

1.0   Introduction

Reduction in storage costs and increases in computing power, combined with the success of video compression techniques, is rapidly leading to a situation where computer video retrieval and presentation is becoming an unwieldy process. One approach to reducing the size of video databases is to facilitate re-use of individual video clips. That shots of film can take on differing meanings according to context has been established since the early days of the cinema, when experiments showed that even neutral material, when juxtaposed with other material, could result in different meanings being attributed to the material.

We focus on assembling meaningful sequences of film from fragments stored in an annotated video database. The sequences satisfy an externally generated query. The query is essentially a conceptual specification of a very simple story (i.e. event of sequence of events). From this specification, which contains no filmic directions, our system creates one or more alternative queries, each representing the realisation of the simple story as a sequence of film fragments. Thus, our system could be regarded as a (simplified) representation of a film editor who is given a collection of film fragments and told to produce a given story.

2.0   Cinema theory - context, order and meaning

Like most "languages", film does not have a definitive specification of its syntax and semantics, but a loose collection of descriptive and prescriptive statements of particular effects from a wide variety of sources. (Andrew, 1976; Arnheim, 1958; Balasz, 1972; Branigan, 1984; Carroll, 1980; Eisenstein, 1949; Eisenstein, 1948; Metz, 1974; Parkes, 1989a; Pudovkin, 1968; Spottiswode, 1955; Tudor, 1974). However, some results of cinema theory are of particular relevance, and will be discussed here.

Pudovkin (1968) identifies an effect he calls "creative geography". This is occurs when successive shots are assumed to depict events in the same location, even though the shots were actually filmed in different locations. Similar effects to creative geography can be found in terms of film portrayal of events. In other words, we can create fictional *space* with editing, but we can also create fictional *narratives*. Obviously, the juxtaposition of several shots of disjointed locations will not in itself create a coherent filmic space in the spectators mind. Further constraints must be placed on the content of the shots for a filmic space to be created. These constraints largely concern *continuity*, and are determined by the real world knowledge of the director and editor. The illusion of a contiguous space and time is created by shared features of the shots in the film.

Kuleshov (see Pudovkin, 1968) demonstrated that even neutral material can be attributed with various meanings according to context. The same shot of an actor's expressionless face was juxtaposed with differing second shots. Audiences of the different sequences stated that the actor's face suggested either hunger, sadness or affection.

The above discussion serves to highlight the following key points:

*   When a film fragment is combined with others in a sequence, its meaning is likely to change. The meaning of a film sequence is more than a simple sum of the meanings of its component parts.
*   Though Cinema Theory is often regarded as an art, it serves to identify rules and patterns relevant to film editing that can be implemented in computational form, and used as a basis for automatically editing video.

3.0   Important systems

A small number of existing systems apply strategies or rules based on cinema theory to a database of annotated film in order to re-order or assemble video output. The most important of these are now briefly discussed.

3.1   Bloch's system

Bloch (1988) describes a system for generating film sequences from annotated shots. The annotation formalism used features shot descriptions consisting of the semantic slots: action, setting, actors, direction of looks of actors, position of actors within the frame, and motion of the main actors and objects.

Bloch's system draws inferences concerning the "meaning" of a shot, based on the content of the semantic slots, by applying rules of filmic knowledge adapted from film editing manuals. Bloch points out, however, that techniques in editing manuals usually lack the precision required for computational implementation. Bloch's rules maintain continuity in the direction of a character's look, the position of actors, and motion, in successive shots. Bloch's system is limited by the small range of semantic slots implemented, which, in turn, limits the amount of filmic knowledge that can be applied to the shots in the form of rules. Moreover, the user has to specify the number of shots required. More recent systems, especially AUTEUR (Nack and Parkes, 1995) have surpassed Bloch's achievements. AUTEUR is briefly discussed later.

3.2   IDIC

IDIC generates trailers for "Star Trek The Next Generation" (Sack and Davis, 1994). The narrative complexity of trailers is, as Sack and Davis correctly point out, limited. Trailers do not have to feature narrative continuity, as represented in conventional cinema and TV, as viewers appreciate a trailer as a disjoint summary. In addition, by limiting the system to footage where characters usually wear the same outfits and featuring similar locations, the researchers avoid the requirements of continuity editing.

3.3   The stratification system

Aguierre-Smith and Davenport (1992) describe a system, Strata, which is a design environment for random access video. Their work highlights the importance of context for the interpretation of a given annotation, a basic premise also adopted in our work. Their annotations are keywords associated with portions of film.

Strata features multiple *partially overlapping* annotations. Combinations of multiple keywords produce the layered data structure. The system's visual representation occurs as a histogram, with the frame numbers of the video along the x axis, and the keywords along the y axis. The result is a series of horizontal bars representing the span of relevance for each keyword.

3.4   Media streams

Media Streams (Davis, 1995), is a "retrieval and repurposing" system for video.

The examples in Davis (1995) indicate that the ordering of the segmentation in the resulting film is specified in the query. However, it is often useful to reorder the query in order to satisfy it by film. Such facilities appear not to be available in Davis' scheme. For example, it appears that parallel action sequences cannot be generated (we return to this later).

3.4   Video retrieval and sequencing system

Chua and Ruan (1995) describe a Video Retrieval and Sequencing System (VRSS) which supports segmenting, indexing, retrieving, and sequencing of video. They adopt a shot based partitioning methodology, justifying this in terms of the excessive work involved in annotating using the stratification methodology, and the familiarity with the shot as a unit on the part of traditional video operators.

The user of VRSS selects an editing rule, along with the concepts required in the sequence to be produced. Enabling the user to select a rule and apply it to the film content and required concepts has produced a unique tool for assisting human editors. Chua and Ruan are clearly aware that retrieval and editing must occur together, due to the change in meaning of fragments when juxtaposed with others.

3.5   Splicer

Splicer (Sack and Don, 1993), like Bloch's system, AUTEUR (briefly described below), and LIVE (described later), features film editing rules. However, the user must specify the editing rule to be applied, and the associated shots. The assembled sequences are presented to the user on a random access "video wall".

3.6   AUTEUR

Nack and Parkes (1996) describe AUTEUR, a system for the "automated generation of humorous video sequences from arbitrary video material." AUTEUR embodies strategies for film sequence generation and presentation of humorous concepts. The annotation approach used in AUTEUR, although based upon multiple overlapping intervals, makes no effort to be compact. Such an approach allows the implementation of complex and subtle editing rules, but limits the applicability of the strategies. The strategies that determine the joke structure are dependent upon filmic knowledge. For example, to create *anticipation* in a joke, one part of the system may request a *highlight* from the other. AUTEUR successfully generates humorous sequences only because its video database and knowledge representations are kept to a manageable level.

3.7   Struct

Butler and Parkes (1996) describe the Struct system, which visually displays the relationships between fragments of video during editing by a human operator. This is done via a directly manipulatable spacetime diagram. Types of cut such as flashback and parallelism have obvious visual shapes in the system. Figure 1 shows the interface to Struct. The system supports the editor by enabling the drawing of the structure of the film under construction. However, Struct neither contains film editing rules, nor provides automatic editing facilities.

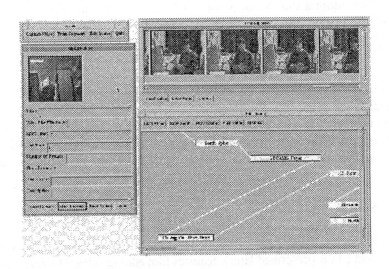

Figure 1: The struct interface presenting a flashback

4.0   The Lancaster intelligent video environment (LIVE)

We now discuss our own research, which has resulted in the Lancaster Intelligent Video Editor (LIVE). LIVE is a system that edits film in response to an external request. It is implemented in Prolog and C on a Sparc 5, using the Sun Video Technologies XIL.

4.1   Overview of system

There are four main components of the system:

Database Of Video - A set of compressed MPEG1 video files stored on hard disk.
Video Annotations - A database of manually applied annotations. These will

be discussed later.

Rule Base Of Cinematic Primitives - Film fragment construction rules. They operate on the entered query and the annotations to edit parts of the Database and create fragments matching input concepts

Scene Creation Strategies - A set of rules to analyse a sequence of the outputs from the cinematic primitives, and attempt to discern a possible scene structure. This is not discussed further in this paper.

A query is entered, and is compared with the contents of the database. If there is no directly applicable clip of video, the query is fed to the rule base of cinematic primitives. These rules attempt to reformulate the original query as a set of new queries, which will yield a portion of film from the database. If this process is successful, and appropriate fragments of video are found, these are fed, in turn, into the Scene Creation Strategies. These strategies attempt to mould the sequence given into a scene or set of scenes, by inserting additional footage. Each of the sections of LIVE continually accesses the database of video annotations in order to maintain continuity as fragments are retrieved and assembled. This process is summarised in Figure 2.

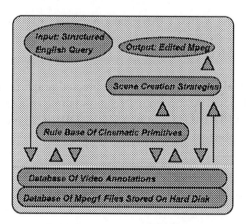

Figure. 2: Overview of the structure of LIVE

4.2   Video Annotation

In this section, we describe the video annotation methodology of LIVE, and focusing particularly on its inference mechanism. We provide examples of the flexibility that our approach offers compared to other schemes.

4.3   Multiple overlapping state descriptions

Our video annotations use conceptual graphs (Sowa, 1984), a complete scheme

570

for concept description, established as applicable to the description of film by the CLORIS system (Parkes, 1989a; Parkes, 1989b). We combine the CLORIS hierarchical approach to representation with stratification layers (discussed above).

Overlapping descriptions can be combined to create richer descriptions. For example, in Figure 3, at frame 100 we know it is raining, that Fred is driving the bus, that he is driving it fast, and that the bus is skidding.

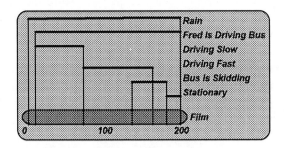

Figure 3: Overlapping interval descriptions

4.4   Conceptual Structures

In LIVE, a conceptual graph is a connected directed graph formed from concepts and conceptual relations. A conceptual relation is one of a finite set of relations such as AGENT, ATTRIBUTE, LOCATION, OBJECT, etc., and a concept is an instantiation of a concept type.

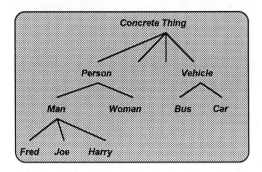

Figure 4: conceptual hierarchy

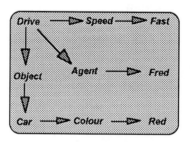

Figure no. 5 - Conceptual graph

A *concept type* is a member of a hierarchy (or lattice) of classes of entities, attributes, states and events, etc. (see Figure 4). The hierarchy facilitates simple reasoning about a conceptual graph (See Figure 5). This reasoning is primarily based upon inheritance within the hierarchy, and, in some circumstances, the distance between concepts in the hierarchy. Example descriptions will reveal more about the approach than further discussion. Let us create an example conceptual graph and say it is true for a specific interval of a film.

[alan, agent, drive], [car, object, drive]   frames 100 to 200

Below we define additions to this concept. The first holds over a sub interval of that immediately above, and thus is implicitly dependent on it.

[fast, manner, drive]   frames 100 to 140

The second addition holds over an interval that overlaps with that associated with the first graph.

[veryfast, manner, drive]   frames 160 to 200

Thus, we have now specified three intervals:

[alan, agent, drive], [car, object, drive], [fast, manner, drive]   frames 100 to 140
[alan, agent, drive], [car, object, drive], [veryfast, manner, drive]   frames 160 to 200
[alan, agent, drive], [car, object, drive]   frames 141 to 159

Note that, while similar to the stratification method discussed earlier, our scheme is more powerful in that our interval annotations are non atomic, and can be used to support reasoning, in ways discussed later.

The above approach supports our stated aim of a cost-effective annotation method by facilitating reuse of state descriptions. Mise-en-scene descriptions may also be represented in this way, and we now present a selection of such descriptions to highlight the advantages of our approach over more structured frame-based approaches.

4.5   Shot Type Description

It is usually the case that video annotation schemes constrain the specification of shot type parameters such as *long, medium,* and so on, to apply to the whole of a shot , as for example, does AUTEUR (see above). It is actually more useful if such parameters can be defined for objects *within* the shot. LIVE permits this. For example, a shot may be a long shot of Alan, but could feature a close up of a lamp post in the foreground. This information can simply be attached to the interval descriptions from above, thus:

> [[alan, agent, drive], [car, object, drive], [longshot, shottype, alan], [mediumshot, shottype, car], [alan, agent, look], [lamppost, object, look], [closeup, shottype, lamppost]]

The effect of this type of annotation is to allow further re-use of footage. The above interval is suitable if a close up of a *lamppost* is required, or if a long shot of *alan* was requested. Traditional annotation approaches concentrate on the main action of the interval and ignore the alternative framing.

4.6   Ilumination

Suppose *alan* is walking into, and out from, the light cast by the lamp in our lamp post. The following two conceptual graphs specify this:

> [alan, agent, walk], [street, location, alan], [dark, illumination, alan]   frames 100 to 150
> [alan, agent, walk], [street, location, alan], [light, illumination, alan]   frames 151 to 200

Of course, the inheritance mechanism outlined in section 4.3.2.1 can apply to any aspect of a description. So the lighting section could be specified like this:

> [alan, agent, walk], [street, location, alan]   frames 100 to 200
> [dark, illumination, alan]   frames 100 to 150
> [light, illumination, alan]   frames 151 to 200

4.7   Effects

For each of the concepts, we may wish to state the special effects involved. e.g. monochromatic, iris etc.

> [[sophia, agent, sunbathe], [beach, location, sophia], [iris, effect, sophia]]

Thus, the annotator can apply characteristics usually applied only to the image as a whole, e.g. illumination and effects, to individual items. This is a further feature that distinguishes our annotation scheme from others.

5.0   Fragment construction rules

As noted earlier, when film units are juxtaposed new meanings are created. The different ways of juxtaposing units of film can be regarded as rule based. However, it is difficult to define an actual grammar for film (Monaco, 1981). Thus, while we have implemented a set of film editing "rules", it must be appreciated that such rules do not work in all circumstances. As such they might better be termed strategies, or heuristics.

5.1   Creative geography

Creative Geography, as discussed earlier in this paper, is manifested in the sense of coherent location that we usually experience when we watch a scene of a film. To achieve it, we juxtapose events that feature common agents, or take place in common locations, or that feature other common attributes. If we show someone walk along a corridor, down some stairs and then outside, the actual locations may well be different, but as long as the shots used do not *conflict* in geographical terms, the viewer would assume the events to be taking place with respect to the same building.

The element common to separate fragments of film may be different parts of the same action. As we see from the gunfight during The Naked Gun 2 1/2: The Smell Of Fear (Zucker, 1991, US), the audience's expectations of the information missing from the portrayed action defines the space in which the fictional action occurs. In the gunfight, we see two characters shooting at each other, both portrayed in separate shots. Then we see them together in the same shot and they are only 1 metre apart.

The person, or some other common element, is the detail to which the viewers devote their attention, and thus creates the link between the locations. Consider the following query, which requests a "leaving the building" episode, such as that discussed above, for the character "Dave":

[[[dave, agent, walk], [lab, location, dave]], [[dave, agent, walk], [corridor, location, dave]],
[[dave, agent, walk], [carpark, location, dave]]]

The above query might be partitioned into separate queries based on the parentheses (which are used to indicate episode ordering). This yields a first query of:

[dave, agent, walk], [lab, location, dave]

Upon being issued to the database, the query immediately above may yield the following description:

[dave, agent, walk], [lab, location, dave], [dave, agent, wear], [jacket, object, wear], [paul, agent, work], [lab, location, paul]

A second query is then generated from this result, after removing the original query, by extracting all the attributes from the elements common to both the first and the second of the short queries derived from the original user query. In the above case *dave* and *walk* are the common element, so we extract those attributes of the description pertaining to them (note that in this case, walk has no associated attributes):

[dave, agent, wear], [jacket, object, wear]
[dave, agent, walk], [lab, location, dave], [dave, agent, wear], [jacket, object, wear]

However, when the immediately preceding query is issued to the database, a closest match, rather than an exact match, is requested. This yields a number of potential results, each of which is juxtaposed with a copy of the original result to create new alternatives. The same process is applied to the third, and any successive, queries, yielding a small set of final results. An suitable output for our example is depicted in Figure 6.

5.2   Parallelism, cross cutting, parallel action

Parallelism is used in many films, often to show two or more separate threads of plot occurring at the same time, though possibly in separate locations. A cliched example is the cavalry and the Indians both converging on the same wagon train. To achieve parallelism we interleave two or more events.

figure 6: Creative geography

Our annotation method has the side effect of creating segmentation points at state boundaries. State boundaries indicate places in the footage where units of action are complete, and so provide a convenient location at which to cross-cut. The following example requests two actions that occur at the same time.

[[frank, agent, type], [sparc, object, type], [sean, agent, read], [manual, object, read]]

This query is partitioned according to agent and event triples, yielding two new queries:

> [[frank, agent, type], [sparc, object, type]]
> [[sean, agent, read], [manual, object, read]]

These two queries are issued separately to the annotation database and the results interleaved at the segmentation points. If no segmentation points exist they can be arbitrarily generated (though this has not been implemented).

5.3   Subjective Shot, Point of View

Carroll (1980) points out that to show a two shot sequence of a person looking at something, we show a shot of the person looking out of the frame, then cut to a shot of the entity at which the person is assumed to be looking.
For example, consider the following query:

> [dave, agent, look], [sean, object, look], [up, direction, look]

If this query fails in the database, it is changed by the subjective shot rule into two new queries:

> [[dave, agent, look], [unknown, object, look], [up, direction, look]],
> [[sean, X, Y], [up, shotangle, sean]]

Example output from the above query is shown in Figure 7.

Figure 7: Subjective shot

The angle of the actor's look in the first shot must be similar to the camera angle of the second shot, and the actor must not feature in the second shot. It is possible to present   the viewer with more evidence that a subjective shot is occurring by making it appear as if the actions take place in the same location. Alternatively, less evidence is given if the direction of the look is violated. To this end, a hierarchy of subjective shot rules has been implemented which ranges from specific and effective, to general and less-effective.

576

5.4   Highlight

Pudovkin (1968) draws parallels between humans viewing their environment and the ways in which events are portrayed by film, in that we attend to an object within an observed scene at the expense of focusing either on other objects within the scene, or background details of the scene itself.

We can model this close-up examining of objects, and rely on the audience's ability to construct a whole from parts to create *false* impressions. To show that an entity possesses a particular attribute, when explicit footage is unavailable, we can show that object in a long or medium shot, then close up to a similar item portraying that attribute. However, if the attribute of the entity required is its location, we can show a close up of the entity in any location with an embedded longshot of the entity at the desired location.

Figure 8: Highlight

Consider this query:

[[frank, agent, walk], [path, location, frank], [frank, agent, smile]]

From this, two new queries are generated. However the resulting footage returned from the first of this pair (left) is partitioned, and used to bracket the result of the second query (on the right), as follows:

[[frank, agent, walk], [path, location, frank]] [[frank, agent, smile], [closeup, shottype, frank]]

If possible, the locations of the event must be similar and the other attributes of the object required must be the same. Figure 8 is an example output displaying such a highlight.

6.0   Conclusion

We have shown that with the LIVE system, a user can formulate a query, which LIVE decomposes so that it can be mapped onto the content of the footage available. Moreover, while the query is expressed non-filmically, the decisions as to how to express it filmically are made by the system itself.

There are a number of limitations to our prototype. Currently, no two rules can operate at the same time. For example, the system will not generate a sequence featuring cross-cutting, if one of the threads needs to have the subjective shot rule applied to be realised. This needs to be rectified in future versions. Future work also includes the implementation of *event-abbreviation*, described in Butler (1994), a form of linear deletion as described by Carroll (1980). Thus, we do not claim that LIVE embodies a *complete* film Grammar. A film grammar can never be complete, but must constantly evolve, as does any grammar that represents a "natural language".

REFERENCES:

1. Aguierre Smith, T. G. and Davenport, G. (1992) The Stratification System. A Design Environment for Random Access Video, MIT Media Lab Technical Report.
2. Andrew, J. D. (1976) The Major Film Theories - An Introduction, London, Oxford University Press.
3. Arnheim, R. (1958) Film as Art, London, Faber and Faber Ltd.
4. Balasz (1972) Theory Of The Film, New York, Arno Press and The New York Times.
5. Branigan, E. R. (1984) Point of View in the Cinema - A Theory of Narration and Subjectivity in Classical Film, Amsterdam, Mouton Publishers.
6. Butler, S. and Parkes, A. (1996) "Space Time Diagrams For Film Structure Visualisation", *Signal Processing: Image Communication*, 8(4), 269 - 280.
7. Carroll, J. M. (1980) Towards a Structural Psychology Of Cinema, The Hague, Mouton Publishers.
8. Chua, T. and Ruan, L.(1995) "A Video Retrieval and Sequencing System", *ACM Transactions On Information Systems*, 13(4), 373 - 407.
9. Davies, M. (1995) Media Streams: Representing Video for Retrieval and Repurposing. Ph.D Thesis, MIT.
10. Eisenstein, S. (1949) Film Form, New York, Harcourt Brace World.
11. Eisenstein, S. (1948) Film Sense, London, Faber and Faber Ltd.
12. Metz, C. (1974) Film Language: A Semiotic Of The Cinema, New York, Oxford University Press.
13. Monaco, J. (1981). How To Read A Film. New York, Oxford University Press.
14. Nack, F. and Parkes, A. (1995) AUTEUR: The Creation Of Humorous Scenes Using Automated Video Editing, Montreal, IJCAI-95 Workshop on Entertainment and AI/ALife.
15. Parkes, A. P. (1989a) An Artificial Intelligence Approach to the Conceptual Description of Videodisc Images, Ph.D. Thesis, Lancaster University.

16. Parkes, A. P. (1989b) "The Prototype CLORIS System: Describing, Retrieving and Discussing Videodisc Stills and Sequences", *Information Processing and Management*, 25(2), 171 - 186.
17. Pudovkin, V. I. (1968) Film Technique And Film Acting, London, Vision Press Ltd.
18. Sack, W. and Davis, M. (1994) "IDIC: Assembling Video Sequences from Story Plans and Content Annotations", *Proceedings of the IEEE International Conference on Multimedia Computing and Systems*, May 14-19, Boston, MA.
19. Sack, W. and Don, A. (1993) Splicer: An Intelligent Video Editor. Project4: Intelligent Interface Software Design Workshop. MIT Media Lab Technical Report.
20. Sowa, J. F. (1984) Conceptual Structures: Information Processing in Mind and Machine, Reading MA, Addison-Wesley Publishing Company.
21. Spottiswoode, R. J. (1955) A Grammar Of The Film - an analysis of film technique, London, Faber and Faber Ltd.
22. Tudor, A. (1974) Image And Influence, London, George Allen and Unwin Ltd.

9.11

THE POLITICS OF INTERNET TELEPHONY

V. Jeronimo,
The Claremont Graduate School, USA

The recent proliferation of software applications that make use of the Internet for telephony services has created debate among governments and regulatory bodies whether the Internet needs regulatory oversight. It appears petitions from players in the telecommunications industry to impose regulatory rules on the suppliers of Internet telephony and on Internet access and service providers appear to be nothing more than interest groups lobbying to avoid potential competitive threats. The proper role for government in regulating the Internet is to promote open competition.

1.0   Introduction

No other communications technology has spread across the globe as quickly as computer networks - especially the Internet. With the rapid growth of the Internet, one of the questions frequently asked is the impact the Internet will have on the telecommunications market. The Internet is considered to impact several areas of communications policy (Drake, 1993): infrastructure and communication services (Kahin et al., 1995), mass communications and online content (Rose, 1995), commercial law (Samuelson, 1996), Internet-mediated crime (Stoll, 1989), public relations and government party activity (Neumann, 1996), and international relations (Harasim, 1993; Nye and Owens 1996). The popularity of the Internet and the advent of Internet telephony suppliers as a less expensive voice alternative has led telephone companies in several countries to file petitions and formal complains with regulatory agencies or telecommunications ministries to ban companies from selling software that enable use of the Internet for voice communications or to subject them to regulatory conditions as applied to telephone companies. Policymakers now face new challenges as they try to keep abreast of new technological advances and decide whether regulatory oversight is needed for Internet telephony. In general, the formal complaints target Internet two-way voice communications but have implications for Internet video-conferencing and multicasting (broadcasting) applications as well. This paper reviews Internet telephony and recent policy debates for regulation in this area. The conclusions made in this paper suggests regulatory rules applied to telephone companies are not an appropriate policy response and should not be applied to Internet telephony. Regulation in this area will only hinder the development of real-time multimedia applications, obstruct the creation of national and global information infrastructures, and constrain the Internet from eventually becoming an alternative communications medium. These conclusions are drawn mainly from recent debates in the United States and provide policy direction to other countries facing similar policy discussions.

2.0 Internet telephony

Viewed in basic terms, the Internet -- the largest network of networks -- is merely a group of computers that route data packets to each other using whatever communications links are available (modems (analog), Integrated Services Digital Network (ISDN), T1, fiber optics, or wireless technologies). The Internet began as a loose association of cooperating international networks of government agencies and universities in the late 1960s established around a common protocol (TCP/IP). Today, the Internet is experiencing tremendous growth (Landweber, 1996) and forms the information and communications infrastructure for a number of activities in research, education, business, trade, government, advocacy, and entertainment. The Internet expands to 134 countries and includes roughly 95,000 networks, 9.5 million hosts, and 30,000 million estimated Internet users.

Table 1: A sample of Internet telephony applications

Product	Company	Platform	Web Address
CoolTalk	Netscape Comm.	Macintosh & Windows	http://www.netscape.com
CU-SeeMe	White Pine	Macintosh & Windows	http://cu-seeme.cornell.edu
DigiPhone	Third Planet Publishing	Windows	http://www.planeteers.com
FreeTel	FreeTel Comm.	Windows	http://www.freetel.inter.net
IBM-IC Phone	IBM	Windows	http://www.ibm.com
Intel Internet Phone	Intel	Windows	http://www.intel.com
Internet Phone (I-Phone)	VocalTec	Macintosh & Windows	http://www.vocaltec.com
NetMeeting	Microsoft	Windows	http://www.microsoft.com
Net Phone	Electric Magic	Macintosh	http://www.emagic.com
Quicktime Conferencing	Apple, Inc.	Macintosh	http:/qtc.quicktime.apple.com
Speak Freely	Autodesk	Windows	http://www.fourmilab.ch
TeleVox	VoxWare	Windows 95	http://www.voxware.com
TS Intercom	Telescape Comm.	Windows	http://www.telescape.com
WebPhone	NetSpeak	Windows 95	http://www.itelco.com
WebTalk	Quarterdeck	Windows	http://www.quarterdeck.com

*Note: Free demonstrations of most of these applications are available from their World Wide Web sites. For a review of these applications refer to http://rpcp.mit.edu/~itel/ .

2.1   Internet telephony applications

The computers connected to the Internet are capable of running software that support Internet TCP/IP protocol. Many of these computers can run sophisticated graphical applications designed to access, share, and exchange information across the network. Electronic mail has become the most common Internet application for exchanging messages. The character of network use, initially as a store-and-forward medium, and the kinds of applications carried over the Internet are changing accordingly. Text, in combination with graphics, audio, and video can now be exchanged over the network.   Interactive communications services now constitute the fastest-growing segment among Internet applications. The affordability of multimedia personal computers, the expanding usage of local and wide area networks, and the emergence of digital audio/video technologies that allow voice and images to be transmitted over networks are responsible for this growth (Jeronimo et al., 1996: p.2-6).

Since early 1995 when VocalTec first released its Internet Phone, a number of software applications have been introduced that allow users to make computer-to-computer, computer-to-phone (or phone-to-computer)   and phone-to-Internet-to-phone   real-time

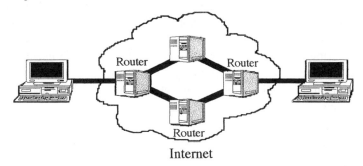

Figure 1.1: Computer to Computer

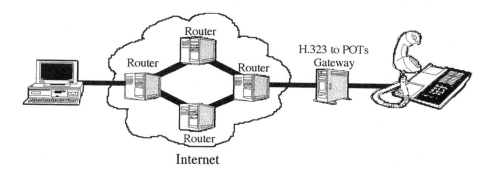

Figure 1.2: Computer to phone/phone to computer

582

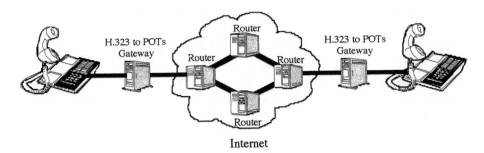

Figure 1.3: Phone- to- Internet- to- Phone

Figure I: The various forms of Internet telephony

voice calls over the Internet (see Table 1 & Figure 1). The computer-to-computer applications transform a caller's computer into a speaker phone. An extension to the computer-to-computer phone allows callers to use conventional phones to place calls that are routed across the Internet (via a gateway). Another example of a real-time voice system enhanced by the Internet is document sharing. This technology allows both (or all) parties on an Internet phone call to see and edit a document under discussion on their computer screens. The more exciting area in Internet technology is real-time collaborative work that integrates document sharing and audio, with video. Quicktime Conferencing and CU-SeeMe are two such video-conferencing systems that can even be used to broadcast events. The future development of broadband Internet communications applications lies in this area. These Internet telephony applications are targeted for individual use (personal communications, on-line shopping, games) and speculated to become as standard as the telephones and faxes are today. Outside of individual use, many companies are installing Internet telephony applications in branch offices enabling executives and employees to hook up with headquarters, other employees, or withoutside clients and customers. Educational facilities, non-profits, and governmental entities are also potential users of Internet telephony. Phone and video phone connections are now able to be built into corporate Web pages which can be useful for customer service and the announcement of new products. The potential uses of such applications that make use of the Internet are infinite and are only now being explored.

2.2   The economics of Internet telephony

Internet calling began as an amusing pastime in early 1995 and is starting to be used as less expensive medium to transmit voice and bypass high long-distance charges. The cost to a user using Internet telephony is basically the cost for the Internet connection. Unlike long-distance phone companies which charge according to time and distance (the longer you talk and further you call, the more you pay), Internet connections are usually sold at flat monthly

Table 2: Comparison between the Internet and PSTN

ATTRIBUTE	INTERNET	PSTN
Ubiquity	Almost Everywhere	Everywhere
Standards-based	Everywhere	Within Countries
Switching Mechanism	Packet	Circuit
Location	Transparent	Within Zones
Voice Capability	Emerging	Best Suited
Computer Capability	Optimized	Moderate
Ownership	Numerous	Small Number
Cost Mechanism	Bandwidth	Distance, Time, & Bandwidth
Cost Per User	Low, Fixed	Moderate, Variable
Usage and Content	Multifaceted	Simple, Spontaneous
User Interface	Numerous	Not applicable

Source: Hambrecht and Quist (cited in Krupinski, 1996).

rates, and the connection to an Internet Service Provider (ISP) is usually a local call. ISPs generally charge approximately US$10 for five hours of access plus US$3 for each additional hours or unlimited hours of 28.8 Kbps modem connections for as little as US$20-30 a month. An average US residential long distance call costs US$0.22 per minute ($13 per hour) in comparison to US$.033-.05 (US$1.98-3.00 per hour) for an Internet call. This is seven times less expensive than a regular phone call. Many countries bill originating long-distance calls at even higher rates, so expected savings can be even higher.

Internet telephony is cheaper than conventional telephony partly because of their different regulatory environments. Yet, a common misconception is that the majority of the price savings from Internet telephony are due to the unregulated nature of the Internet. In the US, the savings from regulation is US$.05 per minute, making an average phone call US$0.17, still much higher than an Internet call. Evidence tells us this is not the significant source of the savings.

Significant savings come from the fact that the Internet architecture is inherently more efficient (Hapgood, 1995: p.194; Sears, 1995). While the Internet shares some of the characteristics of other communications networks such as the public switched telephone network (PSTN) (see Table II), unlike the PSTN, the Internet is considered a more efficient form of communication. The Internet uses a technique called packet switching which allows communications between computers and permits many services to share the same network. This is a more efficient system than the standard telephone network built around voice calls connected by the plain old telephone service (POTS), known as circuit switching, in which a call gets a line to itself for its duration after which the circuit is switched to another call. While the packet switched architecture of the Internet is designed for all types of communications including audio and video, the PSTN was originally designed to only handle voice communications. As the Internet is a shared network (it allows for the same service to be delivered (i.e. voice) while leaving more bandwidth available for other uses) additional efficiency can be gained which also lowers costs. In understanding how Internet telephony produces a price savings:

> "to the end user...it becomes clear that Internet telephony is essentially the resell of long distance capacity. In fact, it probably...[is]...more efficient...than existing long distance resellers because of the savings from using packet switching and savings from the economies of scale of the Internet. Because of these efficiencies, if Internet telephony could produce reliable quality of service..., it could become the dominant technology in long-distance reselling..." (Sears, 1995: 4).

In summary, the combination of compression algorithms (a regular phone call is 64 Kbps while an Internet call is 8 Kbps), and the efficiencies of packet switching used by Internet, and the fact that the Internet exists on high capacity leased lines produce a significant cost savings to the end user. These price savings allows users of Internet telephony applications to make phone calls at substantially lower prices than if they were to use their long-distance provider.

3.0   Internet public policy

One of the most significant barriers to entry in the long-distance market is related to regulatory constraints, the other is related to size. Internet telephony reduces these barriers because it is not regulated and because it provides economies of scale by using the Internet as a common network. The overall affect Internet telephony has on the long-distance market is that it decreases barriers to entry and increases competition. The popularity of the Internet and the advent of suppliers of Internet telephony as a less expensive voice alternative along with these conclusions has led telephone companies in the US (and in other countries) to file petitions with regulatory agencies or telecommunications ministries to (i) ban companies from selling software that enable use of the Internet for voice communications or then subject these companies to pay access charges under the regulatory rules established for long-distance carriers and / or (ii) subject ISPs to pay access charges to the local exchange carriers to help bear the burden of Internet traffic over their networks caused by Internet telephony. In general, the formal complaints target Internet two-way voice communications, however, these complaints also have implications for multicasting and video-conferencing applications that make use of the Internet. The conclusion elaborated in more detail below suggests the regulatory means by which the telephone companies want Internet telephony regulated are not appropriate and represent nothing more than lobbying efforts by these companies to gain regulatory protection in the prospect of eventual competition from Internet telephony.

3.1 Policy developments in the United States

Currently, long-distance companies are regulated by the Federal Communications Commission (FCC) and state regulatory commissions. These companies are required to pay access fees, file tariffs in order to provide long-distance telephone services, and contribute to the Universal Service Fund to extend phone service to the general population. The access fee is paid by the interexchange carriers (IXCs or long-distance carriers) to the local exchange carriers (LECs) to connect to their local network and is currently US$.025 per minute to complete a call at each end. Under the public utility telecommunications paradigm this was established in order to compensate the LECs for the cost of using their network, and to promote universal service by subsidizing local access with long distance.

In March 1996, the America's Carriers Telecommunications Association (ACTA), a nonprofit trade association of approximately 170 resellers of long-distance services, filed a petition with the FCC maintaining that "the providers of this [Internet telephony] software [should be considered] telecommunications carriers and subject to FCC regulation like all telecommunications carriers" (refer to www.fcc.gov). The ACTA argues that "it is not in the public interest to permit long-distance services to be given away, depriving those who must maintain the telecoms infrastructure of the revenue to do so." The petition asks the FCC "to issue a declaratory ruling confirming its authority over interstate and international telecoms services using the Internet." Moreover, it asks the FCC to "grant special relief to maintain the status quo by immediately stopping the sale of Net telephones pending the imposition of regulations to govern the now completely unregulated field of Internet telephony." The petition names several suppliers of Internet telephony, including Third Planet Publishing, VocalTec, Quarterdeck, and "other providers of non-tariffed and uncertified interexchange telecoms services." The ACTA also argues that the traffic created by Internet telephony is causing congestion preventing residential and business calls from accessing the network.

In order to understand how Internet telephony may impact the market of ACTA members and the reason for the submission of the petition, we need to understand their market. ACTA members are non-facilities based IXCs, long-distance resellers that have no wires or switches of their own that represent one-third of the long-distance market. These companies buy long distance circuits at volume discount mainly from the three dominant long-distance facilities-based carriers (i.e. AT&T, MCI, Sprint) and resell them to individual or corporate customers at a regional level. As these resellers do not have any physical facilities of their own, the Internet telephony industry does have the potential for providing viable competition. On the other hand, long-distance facilities-based carriers which represent two-thirds of the long-distance market are not complaining about revenues being lost to Internet telephony These carriers are outspoken about letting the new technologies develop without government interference or regulation. This is in part due to the fact that these companies are wholesalers of capacity and the resell of long distance through Internet telephony is not a direct form of competition in their market. Also, facilities-based carriers stand to benefit from carrying all that Internet traffic as well as providing services.

3.2   Internet traffic jams - problems or opportunities?

Several of the LECs, providers of local service, are also lobbying the FCC to apply minute access fees, much like those already applied to long-distance calls, for calls to Internet services. Unlike the long-distance companies which lease capacity to carry Internet traffic, the LECs have little say over how their networks are used. MCI and AT&T have also begun to offer free Internet access by setting up a network of dial-in points located within a local call for most users, thereby exploiting the loopholes that allow them to use local networks for Internet service without paying the access charges MCI & AT&T would normally pay the Bells for long-distance calls. The LECs argue they (and their customers) bear a large part of the Internet's increasingly congestion problem and cost, while receive little or none of its revenues. While the Bells should be more eager to offer Internet services, the traditional regulatory system never imagined people would use their phones for long periods of time.

Internet congestion is a real problem. With the number of users and host computers connected to the Internet roughly doubling each year, and with traffic increasing at an even greater pace, the problem of congestion is increasingly rapidly. The Internet interconnects thousands of different networks, each of which only controls the traffic passing over its own portion of the network. There is no centralized mechanism to ensure that usage at one point on the network does not create congestion at another point. Because the Internet is a packet-switched network, additional usage, up to certain point, only adds additional delay for packets to reach their destination, rather than preventing a transmission circuit from being opened. This delay may not cause difficulty for e-mail, but could be fatal for real-time services such as Internet telephony, video-conferencing, and multicasting. Even when individual providers upgrade their networks to achieve sufficient capacity, end users may still experience congestion delays when traffic must traverse another provider's backbone. The increasing level of Internet use is beginning to a certain extent to affect the telephone network, as the lobbying by the LECs and the ACTA petition claim. The telephone network was designed on the assumption that the average voice call is about three minutes long, and the average telephone conversation lasts nine minutes or less during peak hours. Internet users typically engage in longer calls than voice users. Typical modem use starts at 15 minutes and moves upward. As a result, Internet usage is placing unexpected demand on local exchange carriers' switches, to the point that switch congestion may threaten the quality of voice service.

A cost study, recently conducted by an American local exchange carrier, addresses the impact of Internet usage on the telecommunications infrastructure (refer to www.fcc.gov). The study contains empirical evidence demonstrating the validity of the concerns expressed by the ACTA and the LECs. The study supports the realities of congestion created by Internet calls and the prevention of users from accessing the network. The study indicates the most serious aspect of the congestion due to surges in Internet traffic is service interruptions. Even a temporary length could affect public emergency services. The cost study also concludes the enormity of the cross subsidization of ISPs. ISPs pay 1/22 of the charges ACTA's members pay for the same service. The ACTA and LECs argues that the absence of usage charges means ISPs do not provide the revenue to cover the additional costs they impose on the network.

Congestion problems would not occur if digital telephone networks were in place, but few exist. Copper pipes have worked well for traditional needs, but Internet communications require more. Advances in high speed technologies that run over copper networks such as Asymmetric Digital Subscriber Line (ADSL) can carry up to 400 times as much data; and a cheaper technology known as ISDN can multiply transmission speed five-fold. Telephone companies are installing ISDN, but it is complicated to install, has never been widely promoted in the US, can run from US$20,000 - 40,000 to run the lines into the home, and is more costly for end users. Companies having billions invested in the old circuit-switched infrastructure, seem to be thinking more about recovering the investments that have already been made than promoting alternatives. The sooner the phone companies see the Internet as an opportunity than a threat, the sooner they will reap its financial benefits.

3.3   Reasons not To apply regulation to the Internet

A US policy decision was made in early 1980s that Internet access and services providers that are created by advances in the customer premises equipment (CPE) are not to be subject to interstate access charges that long-distance

588

carriers pay to local phone companies for originating and terminating calls. Instead, these companies are to be treated as enhanced service providers and end users able to purchase lines that have no per minute usage based charge for receiving calls from their customers. The question now is whether Internet access and services should continue to be exempt. One of the results from the ACTA petition would be to require telephony suppliers to pay the local access subsidy. However, this is not possible since Internet telephony is software and it represents an advance on CPE and makes it exempt from paying the fee. Moreover, severe problems emerge by requiring software companies to pay such fees, such as who should pay the local access fee when a range of applications all use the same connection? What about those applications that also allow video-conferencing and multicasting? Regulating software manufactures sets a precedent and may become a regulatory nightmare not only for Internet communications but also for other areas. For instance, what happens when a radio station decides to air its program via the Internet? Since broadcasters pay a fee for their licenses, would they also be susceptible to their own charges?

ISPs are another group targeted by the ACTA petition to pay the local access fee either by paying when Internet telephony applications are used or by paying the access fee for all Internet access. Paying the access fee for Internet telephony creates a problem since it is extremely difficult and costly for the ISP to distinguish voice from data. However difficult it may be to establish a differentiation monitoring mechanism, it would be possible but would bring up significant privacy issues and enforceability problems. In regards to paying for all Internet access, this brings up the issue that the FCC does not have the jurisdiction over ISPs. ISPs connect locally to the Internet through an ISP and thus transmissions of most ISPs never cross state lines. At first glance, the LECs may bear a real burden for Internet congestion, however, the primary effect of applying local access charges to ISPs would be a competitive advantage to the LECs. First, if an access fee were applied, as little as US$.025 per minute to the ISPs for each customer, this would increase the per minute charge from US$.033-.05 (US$1.98-3.00 per hour) to US$.058-.075 (US$3.48-4.50 per hour). This is a 150% increase per hour which would be a considerable disadvantage to ISPs. Second, if LECs decided to enter the Internet service business, they could use their own networks to deliver services without paying the access fees. This gives them a considerable competitive edge. Competitors would have an additional US$1.50 per hour which could affect the number of ISPs players in the market.

3.4   Other costs of regulation

The Internet is regarded as a good model for the future national information infrastructure (NII) (Miller, 1996). The goal is eventually to have a global information infrastructure (GII) in which a high performance digital network will facilitate high-speed data access and retrieval, and able to convey video in conjunction with data, image, text, and voice; and facilitate the exchange of information for a number of activities from research and education to business, trade, government, and entertainment. Regulating or banning Internet telephony has a significant effect on the innovation currently seen in the multimedia software industry and the Internet. Regulation also endangers the development of interoperability in the NII and the competitiveness of countries in the global market. Internet multimedia and other applications have been developed in large part due to countries that support a pro-competitive Internet environment. Some suggest Internet congestion isn't a problem, but an opportunity to create collaborative tools for many-to-many communications (McQuillan, 1996).

Moreover, Internet presents a powerful medium to provide competition in markets where it previously has not existed or Internet telephony can be used by governments as a force to introduce competition in local and long-distance markets. While the competitive paradigm is not perfect, worldwide, countries are increasingly relying on open entry and deregulation as the new structure for the telecommunications sector. In summary, it appears the only affect of not regulating Internet telephony would be to increase competition.

3.5   A US policy response

In June at the Internet Society's Annual Conference, Blair Levin on behalf of FCC Chairman Reed Hundt, stated that "the right answer at this time is not to place restrictions on software providers," or to "subject Internet telephony to the old rules that apply to conventional circuit-switched voice carriers." "The future of the Internet, and the ability of service providers to offer more bandwidth to their end users, will thus depend on how successful we [regulators] are at promoting competition in telecoms markets" (Hundt, 1996). These remarks support the decision in the 1980s that Internet access and service providers would not be subject to interstate access charges. The US answer, the one this paper also supports, is to continue to rely on competition and technology (i) to alleviate the congestion problem. This response corresponds to the US policy environment which supports competition as an important paradigm to further develop broadband multimedia applications which have proliferated already in large part due to a regulatory fee Internet environment. Real-time collaborative multimedia applications are also envisioned as a key element of NIIs and a GII which the US government considers to be a top priority.

590

3.6   Policy developments outside the United States

The economic and policy wars between phone companies and Internet telephony is international. In Britain, the company serving Hull, the only town with free local calls, recently banned a large ISP for transmission of data because its users would not get off the lines. Canadian regulators are trying to force an Internet company in Ontario to pay fees to Canadian telephone companies for the same reasons as stipulated under the US ACTA petition. An extreme case is that of the Pakistani government which has now banned Internet telephony. In fact, voice transmission of any sort is strictly prohibited and binds all ISPs operating in the country. Violation of this clause, according to the Pakistani government, will lead to prosecution according to the Telephone and Telegraph Act of 1885 (refer to www.von.org). This is in contrast to the US which opposes to apply old rules to new technologies. Complaints to Telecommunications Ministries and regulators over access fees and the threat of competition are also being heard in South Africa, Ireland, Switzerland, and Australia. Similar regulatory moves do not yet seem to have occurred in Asian countries.

4.0   Conclusion

It appears the lobbying efforts of ACTA are merely pleas for competition relief. The congestion problem is used to help build their case, but in reality, this is to avoid the competition threat caused by Internet telephony. On the other hand, congestion is a real concern, as voiced by the LECS, once again, regulation is not the answer as it does not directly solve the congestion problem. The question remains: who should support the upgrading of the network to support the explosion of Internet traffic? While this is an appropriate question, regulating ISPs and suppliers of telephony software does not directly solve the congestion problem. Instead regulation hinders the development of other Internet technologies as well as the further development of national and global information infrastructures. The effect of countries that have banned, as is the case of the Pakistani government, Internet telephony or regulated such applications is to find their societies and economies at a competitive disadvantage. For countries contemplating regulation, this paper suggests following the US lead by supporting competitive environments and enjoying the related socio-economic benefits, instead of regulation and its related costs.

5.0   Further research

Answers to several questions regarding Internet telephony are left open in this paper and merit further research: (i) How much of a threat is Internet telephony to the revenues of local and long-distance companies, and how soon before the telephone and computer networks merge? What technical barriers exist for Intenet telephony to become ubiquitous? (ii) What is the solution to Internet traffic jams? Should other countries follow the US lead in supporting the development of gigabit testbeds? The US goal for such testbeds is to support the growth of Internet traffic and services without degrading performance, and to help build pipes wide enough to deal with problems of real-time computing over high-speed networks. What about government collaborating on building regional Internet backbones? What is the right balance for collaboration between government and the business and scientific communities in this area? (iii) What is the impact of the Internet on the use of networking in social policy? How should policy and corporate communities proceed to address universal access to the Internet? What social and economic barriers exist for the evolution of an information society?

References:

1. Drake, W.J. (1993), "The Internet Religious War," Telecommunications Policy, Vol. 17(9), 643-649.
2. Hapgood, F. "I-Phone," Wired, Vol. 3(10): 140-142, 194-200.
3. Harasim, L. (1993, Global Networks: Computers and International Communications, Cambridge, MIT Press.
4. Hart, J.A., Reed, R.R., and Bar, F. (1992), "The Building of the Internet: Implications for the future of broadband networks, "Telecommunications Policy, Vol. 16(12), 666-689.
5. Hundt, R. (1996), "A+B=C (Access & Bandwidth equals Communications Revolution)," Speech delivered by B. Levin, INET'96, The 6th International Conference of the Internet Society, June 25 -28, Montreal.
6. Jeronimo, V. and Calvo, R. (1996), "The Internet: The Access Avenue for Video-Conferencing," INET'96 Paper and Proceedings, The 6th International Conference of the Internet Society, June 25 -28, Montreal.
7. Kahin, B. and Keller, J. (1995), Public Access to the Internet, Cambridge, MIT Press.
8. Krupinski, D. (1996), "Computer Telephony and the Internet," Cambridge, MA: Stylus Product Group, Artisoft,   Inc., http://www.stylus.com.
9. Landweber, L. (1996), "Entities with International Network Connectivity," OnTheNet, Vol. 2(4), 46-47.

592

10. Miller, S. (1996), Civilizing Cyberspace: Policy, Power, and the Information Superhighway, Reading, Addison-Wesley Publishing.
11. Mills, M. (1996), "Freebie Heebie-Jeebies: New Long Distance Calling Via the Internet Scare Small Phone Firms, Washington Post, March 8, F1.
12. Neumann, A.L. (1996), "The Resistance Network," Wired, Vol. 4(1), 108-114.
13. Nye, J. and Owens, W. (1996), "America's Information Edge," Foreign Affairs, Vol. 75(2), 20-54.
14. Rose, L. (1995), Netlaw: Your Rights in the Online World, Berkelely, Osborne MacGraw-Hill.
15. Sears, A. (1995), "The Effect of Internet Telephony on the Long-Distance Voice Market," Cambridge, The Internet Telephony Interoperability Consortium (ITIC), MIT, http://rpcp.mit.edu.
16. Stoll, C. (1989), The Cuckoo's Egg. New York, Doubleday Books.
17. Verity, J. W. (1996), "Try Beating These Long-Distance Rates," Business Week, February 27, 131.

L.-Brault

DATE DE RETOUR

0 8 OCT. 1999		
1 7 NOV. 1999		

ne 297B